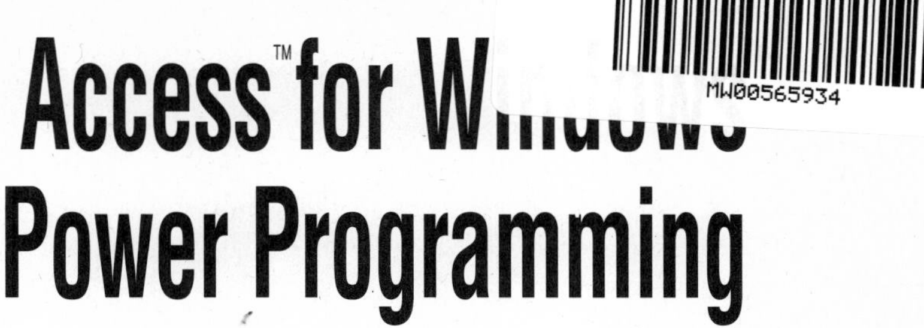

Access™ for Windows Power Programming

Susan Perschke

Michael Liczbanski

Access for Windows Power Programming

Library of Congress Catalog No.: 93-84421

ISBN: 1-56529-194-8

96 95 94 93 4 3 2 1

Interpretation of the printing code: the rightmost double-digit number is the year of the book's printing; the rightmost single-digit number, the number of the book's printing. For example, a printing code of 93-1 shows that the first printing of the book occurred in 1993.

Screen reproductions in this book were created with Collage Plus from Inner Media, Inc., Hollis, NH.

Publisher: *David P. Ewing*

Associate Publisher: *Rick Ranucci*

Managing Editor: *Corinne Walls*

Publishing Plan Manager: *Thomas H. Bennett*

Marketing Manager: *Ray Robinson*

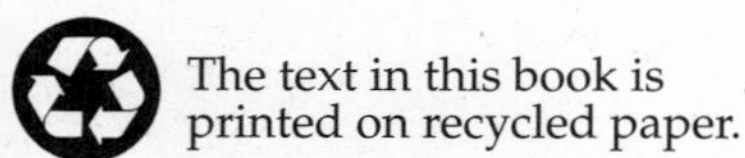

Dedication

This book is dedicated to my parents, for their selfless love and support throughout the years, and to Russell Freeland, who encouraged me to write my first magazine article.

Susan

To my mother, who somehow survived my youth.

Michael

Credits

Title Managers
Walter R. Bruce, III
Joseph Wikert

Acquisitions Editor
Sherri Morningstar

Product Directors
Robin Drake
Steven M. Schafer

Production Editor
Colleen Totz

Editors
Elsa M. Bell
Fran Blauw
Judy Brunetti
Lori Cates
Barb Colter
Lorna Gentry
Lori A. Lyons
Heather Northrup
Kathy Simpson

Technical Editors
Edward Jones
Rich Wolf
Rick Nelson

Book Designer
Amy Peppler-Adams

Production Team
Angela Bannan
Danielle Bird
Julie Brown
Paula Carroll
Charlotte Clapp
Michelle Greenwalt
Michael Hughes
Bob LaRoche
Joy Dean Lee
Jay Lesandrini
Sandra Shay
Amy L. Steed
Tina Trettin
Lillian Yates
Michelle Worthington

Composed in *ITC Century Light* and *MCPdigital* by Que Corporation

About the Authors

Susan Perschke

Susan Perschke has been enamored with the problem-solving potential of databases for over ten years. Holding a bachelor's degree in Business Administration, for the past six years she has operated her own consulting business, Spectrum Data Design, specializing in custom database design and programming. Susan has written numerous articles on database and client/server topics for publications such as the *Data Based Advisor*, *Access Advisor*, and *DBMS* magazines. Her experience also includes management consulting for a major software vendor. Currently she is developing two new projects in Microsoft Access.

Michael Liczbanski

As far as computers go, after programming on mainframes, he's interested only in systems light enough to be carried by a single person. An independent software consultant and database software developer, Michael is also a frequent contributor to the *Data Based Advisor* and *Access Advisor* magazines. He is known in PC computer trade circles for his unerring ability to track down elusive but deadly software bugs (no matter how long it takes). In a former life he was a psychologist, but doesn't regret changing professions.

Acknowledgments

Our heartfelt thanks to the following individuals without whom this book wouldn't be possible:

At Que Corporation:

Walt Bruce, who got involved in this book far beyond the call of duty.

Colleen Totz, Robin Drake, and Fran Blauw who waded through the manuscript trying to make sense out of murky passages.

Chris Katsaropoulos and Sherri Morningstar, who tried in vain to keep the project on schedule.

At Microsoft Corporation:

Ross Hunter, for having the unenviable distinction of being the only person at Microsoft whose telephone number we memorized. Thanx, Ross!

Mari-Ester Burnham, for painstakingly and thoroughly researching each and every inquiry.

Adam Bosworth, David Risher, Bill Bader, and the other architects of Access, for their vision.

Trademarks

Contents at a Glance

Table of Contents

Preface

Computer books fill a much-needed niche in today's dynamic information age. Our ability to process vast quantities of information can be greatly enhanced by a timely and helpful book on a particular subject. But the real challenge in a highly technical society where information can become obsolete overnight is to write books that convey not only a meaningful and useful message to the reader; but one that transcends the fleeting life of software and hardware products.

Access for Windows Power Programming embodies two symbiotic philosophies: one is that fundamental programming principles are the cornerstone of developing applications in any language. The other is that having a flexible and powerful application development environment can elevate the application of the first philosophy to an art. Microsoft Access is such a product. No longer must developers squander valuable time in the painstaking creation of user interface elements, or in writing custom routines to help users find and sort the data they've entered. Programmers can finally focus their attention on more productive tasks like adding functionality, transaction processing and bullet-proofing to their applications; areas that have been neglected for years because of the inherent weaknesses in other DBMS (notably MS-DOS) systems that require the endless tweaking of more superficial elements.

But this inspiration did not hit us overnight. After some time spent trying to figure out how to do simple things, it occurred to us that our linear programming methods and mindsets might be in need of some adjustment. We also theorized that if we, as reasonably seasoned developers, were experiencing such pains in transition to the Windows programming environment, surely we must keep good company.

This book is written primarily for developers and programmers who, like us, are migrating to Access from other systems. For this reason, we have packed the most useful information and examples into the Reference. In fact, we thought the Reference was a self-standing book, but the publisher asked us to provide some supplementary chapters to augment the reference materials. At about the same time we realized that many of the million or so copies of Access that Microsoft initially sold were probably still "shelfware," and that even experienced programmers might find some "how-to" material useful. So, this book contains a little bit on both ends of the spectrum. The majority of the text is suited to readers who have a general familiarity with databases, programming languages, multi-user environments, and operating systems, but not necessarily with Microsoft Access.

We'd like to acknowledge Paul Nielsen for his contributions to some of the tutorial sections of the book. But perhaps most significantly, we enjoyed a very productive working relationship with Microsoft while preparing the manuscript, especially in the area of undocumented features. Without the help of individuals at Microsoft such as Ross Hunter, the scope of materials presented in this book would not have been possible. Ross, quite naturally, probably never wants to hear from us again after our months of endless pestering, but to express our gratitude, we hope this book will answer some nagging questions and siphon off a few calls from Tech Support.

Please feel free to contact us on CompuServe with your comments.

Susan Perschke	72427,1651
Michael Liczbanski	71211,266

Introduction

Windows is unrivaled as the most popular graphical environment for the PC. And PC users have sent a clear message to software manufacturers: fail to develop for Windows at your peril. The resulting flurry of development activity for Windows has been unprecedented, except perhaps for the corresponding response to MS-DOS becoming the first true standard for the PC. Given the somewhat belated recognition of the consuming demand for Windows databases, many vendors have precipitously dumped their products—in various stages of readiness—to market.

In this respect, it is impressive that Microsoft had the vision, six years before the release of Access, to begin developing software that was years ahead of its time. Competitors who downplayed its importance have been caught off balance and are still reeling from the product's quick success. Having sold a half million copies in the USA and 800,000 copies worldwide at the time of the release of this manuscript, Access has managed to nearly double the apparent size of the entire database market. Rich in features, Access has defined new standards by which other products of its type will be judged.

What Is Access?

Developing a cogent definition of a product so rich in features was one of the marketing challenges faced by Microsoft when introducing Access. Is it an end-user query tool? Is it a DBMS? Is it an application development environment? The simple answer is: yes, yes, and yes. Although conceptually it seems paradoxical that one product could attempt to effectively satisfy a full range of requirements from end users to programmers, Access has tackled both ends of this spectrum remarkably well.

One of the ironies of Windows has been the lack of database applications software powerful enough to fully exploit its rich graphical environment. Products that claim to be user-friendly often accomplish their claims at the expense of needed functionality such as data manipulation and multi-table querying, and in many cases these products lack even rudimentary reporting capabilities. Stronger products with languages behind them have been criticized for skimping on the front-end tools needed by non-programmers.

Access provides both end users and developers with the capability to perform a wide range of functions necessary to manage data. In other words, Access has a full suite of front end tools, forms, query and report designers, together with a rich and full-featured programming language called Access Basic. To augment both of these, a macro facility enables you to create robust applications without, or with very little, programming.

Cross-Platform Capability

Access was designed to meet a growing need to access a variety of data formats across platforms. Access supports the following data formats.

For import/export:

- Btrieve
- dBASE III and IV
- Paradox
- SQL Server
- Spreadsheets
- ASCII text files
- FoxPro 2.x (new in version 1.1 of Access)

Table attachments:

- Btrieve
- dBASE III and IV
- Paradox
- FoxPro 2.x (new in version 1.1 of Access)
- SQL Server

One of the most powerful features of Access is its capability to work with data directly in its native format. Data can be accessed in one of two ways: by importing a table to an Access database, which converts it into an Access table, or by attaching the table to an Access database, which leaves the native format intact, allowing querying or even updating records without affecting the capability to use the table in its native format.

You can access different file formats simultaneously. For example, you can open a Paradox, a dBASE, and an Access table at the same time for querying, updating, reporting, or even creating a new table or logical view. For corporate users with disparate existing bases of applications, this capability provides all the benefits of using Access to work with existing databases without the prohibitive conversion costs usually associated with converting to a new system.

These feats of connectivity are accomplished through the use of either Microsoft ODBC (Open Database Connectivity) data access drivers or ISAM-level, Access-specific, native file format database drivers. For every file format supported by Access, there is a separate DLL that allows Access to decipher and perform database operations on that particular format. This open architecture approach also gives programmers the opportunity to write their own database drivers, which many third party developers are actively pursuing.

Flexible Querying and Reporting

One of the biggest productivity bottlenecks in many organizations is the lack of timely and accurate ad hoc querying and reporting capability. The data is there, but many times it is locked up inside a system that does not easily permit the creation of necessary queries and reports, especially when tables are in different formats. Access's powerful querying and reporting capabilities essentially eliminate these barriers by allowing users to easily design a query to filter and sort records in any fashion and to quickly produce the results in a printed format by designing a quick or custom report or even by just printing the table listings directly. This capability can mean a measurable boost in productivity without the necessity of expensive and time-consuming development efforts.

It is also possible to query data residing on servers such as Sybase SQL server or even on remote workstations with Windows for Workgroups or other peer-to-peer networks.

Data Security

As more companies turn to PCs for managing critical information, data security issues have become paramount. Once kept tightly guarded in the locked mainframe control room, data is now distributed about the organization, raising the specter of loss, destruction, or theft of crucial information. PC DBMSs have been criticized for their scant security systems, but Microsoft wisely anticipated these concerns and equipped Access with a system-level security system that allows assigning data access permissions to either individuals or groups, as low as the object level (forms, tables, queries, and reports).

Data Integrity

Another common complaint about PC database management systems is their lack of built-in data integrity controls. The data dictionary, which preserves definitions about how data is structured and used, has always been *de rigeur* in the mainframe world. Its notable absence in most PC databases has been a strike against the viability of desktop systems as enterprise-wide solutions to database management. Once again, Microsoft has at least partially compensated by building an extended set of field properties (one component of a true data dictionary) into the Access table design.

Who Should Read This Book?

This book is not intended to be a step-by-step tutorial of how to use Access. There are numerous other books which give insight into Access from the user's perspective. You should be familiar with the basic installation and configuration of Access, how to open and save a database, and the basics of Access surfaces (such as forms and queries). This book is primarily intended for developers and programmers who may be new to Access, but who probably have experience developing applications by using other DBMS packages. Some design basics are included mainly to aid programmers who are completely new to the product. Because design issues are paramount in achieving the best application, this book includes a complete chapter on database design.

The focus and primary purpose of this book is programming in Access. Notice that we did not say "programming in Access Basic." Although Access Basic programming issues are covered in depth, Access provides a complete retinue of features that are, by design, non-programmatic. If the reader gains only one insight from this book, we hope it will be an understanding that there is no clear distinction between programming and non-programming elements in Access, and that effective application development involves a combination of objects and code.

Procedural programmers who philosophically refuse to avail themselves of tools, such as the surface designers provided in Access, may struggle with the concepts presented in this book, which require a new mindset and approach to database design and programming. For even though it is possible to write an entire Access application in Access Basic, such an endeavor could be compared to cutting your lawn with a pair of scissors—it works but who would want to do it?

There are two emerging schools of thought concerning the Access development environment. One school advocates using Access as a non-programmatic development tool, emphasizing the use of forms and macros to build the application. The other school focuses on Access Basic as the fulcrum of the application, with forms, queries, reports, and macros used to supplement the language. The concepts in this book are based primarily on the latter approach because maximum control and design efficiency can be achieved only through the use of a flexible and powerful programming language.

This, however, should not discourage anyone who desires to reduce application development time through the liberal use of the tools provided in Access. The assumption throughout this book is that whenever a tool can do the job as well (or better) than Access Basic code, the tool will be used or suggested. For example, macros can and should be used to manipulate Access menus. In fact, there is no programmatic alternative.

The objective in developing applications in a product such as Access is to achieve the proper balance between code and objects. Defining that balance is ultimately the programmer's responsibility. The goal of this book is to provide the programmer with enough objective information to enable him or her to weigh the options and make an informed choice.

The Windows Programming Environment

The most problematic issue for traditional MS-DOS programmers is getting used to the Windows programming environment. Traditional programming is like driving on a closed course, where you start at one end, negotiate the course, and finish at the other end (*one entry, one exit*). On the driving course, there is no traffic to impact your negotiation of the course, and how well you get from start to finish is primarily dependent upon your driving skills.

Programming in Windows, on the other hand, is like driving in the city. Your driving skills are but one of many factors that can influence what happens from the time you leave until you arrive (or don't arrive) at your destination. Your child could unbuckle her seat belt and crawl into the back seat, forcing you to pull over to the side of the road. The light could turn red, causing you to stop. Another driver could pull in front of you, causing you to put on the brakes. These "intervening events" are similar to what can happen in the Windows operating environment.

In Access and other Windows applications, Windows is always checking for events. When an event occurs (such as a user clicking on a push button), Windows intercepts it and either processes it immediately or places it in the *events queue* for processing. Windows programmers must always be aware of the event-driven nature of the Windows environment and be prepared to bullet-proof their applications to protect data and critical operations. Access provides many *event trapping* features that allow you to do this, and they are explored in depth throughout this book and in the Reference.

Conventions Used in This Book

Access presents an entirely new paradigm for application development. Because Access Basic is so closely coupled with its graphical objects (such as forms, queries, and reports), some elements of Access Basic (such as operators, actions, methods, and properties) either act upon, modify, or are attributes of Access objects. As such, it is difficult to define a precise typographic convention for the syntax of these "pseudo-commands."

In general, the main part of the language element (statement, function, and so on) is provided in boldface, and arguments are presented in italics. Consider the following example:

FileAttr*(filenumber, attribute)*

FileAttr is the name of the Access Basic function, and *filenumber* and *attribute* are the arguments taken by the function.

Each word of multi-word names of Access functions, statements, methods, properties, and operators is capitalized according to the convention used by Microsoft in the Access documentation.

If a command has more than one verb, the main verb is specified in boldface, and the ancillary verb, which usually precedes the main verb, is provided in standard type. Square brackets ([]) means that the argument is optional. Consider the following example:

DoCmd **TransferText** [*transfer type*] [, *specification name*]
table name, *file name* [, has field names]

Please note that required arguments may appear in the middle of the expression, both preceded and followed by optional arguments. In some cases, information about whether an argument is required is provided in the usage notes. There are a few instances where an argument may or may not be required, depending upon the contextual use of the language element.

Literal strings in object syntax are enclosed in angle brackets, as shown in the following example:

Forms!<*formname*>

End [Function | If | Select | Sub | Type] indicates that only one of the arguments separated by vertical bars can be passed.

An ellipses (...) following an argument indicates that the argument (or group of arguments) can be repeated in the expression, as in the following example:

Global *variable* [(*subscript*)] [**As** *type*] [, *variable* [(*subscript*)] [**As** *type*]...]

Code examples are provided in monospace font and are clearly distinguishable from explanatory text, as shown in the following example:

```
Dim sString as String
sString = "Dec-30-1990"
Debug.Print VarType(sString)            ' 8 (string)
Result = DateValue(sString)
Debug.Print VarType(Result)             ' 7 (date)
```

Ellipses (...) found anywhere in the code examples indicate processing that is irrelevant to the example.

Lines of code that don't fit on one printed line are indicated with a code continuation character.

How This Book Is Organized

There are four main parts to this book:

- Part I, "Introduction to Access"
- Part II, "The Access Database"
- Part III, "Access Design Surfaces"
- Part IV, "Programming with Access Basic"
- Part V, "Reference"

Part II takes you through the preliminaries, explaining the structure and design of Access tables and indexes, the internal organization of an Access database, the types of data formats supported, and database administration issues such as security, maintenance, backup, and database repair and recovery. It also covers the basics of importing and attaching tables from other formats and the programming and design concerns associated with each method.

Part III discusses each of the Access Forms, Queries, Reports, and Macros designers from a developers and programmers perspective. The assumption is that the reader has some familiarity with the design surfaces, but may benefit from an explanation of how these objects interact with the entire application. The reader is also instructed on the methods of adding code to objects to increase their functionality.

Part IV explores programming issues in depth, including topics such as Access data types, declarations, functions, subroutines, variables and constants, performing operations, and working with recordsets, to name a few. Chapter 12, "OLE and DDE," presents the concepts of DDE and OLE and provides practical examples given for their use in Access and other Windows applications such as Microsoft Excel. Chapter 13, "Extending Microsoft Access and Access Basic," explains how to access the Windows API from within Access Basic by calling Windows or other DLLs (Dynamic Link Libraries), and discusses using and writing custom Wizards for Access. Chapter 14 covers error handling, and Chapter 15 covers the Access runtime environment including setup and operation in networking and server environments.

Part V is a complete language reference for Access versions 1.0 and 1.1, and includes an explanation of many undocumented features and "real life" examples showing how each part of the language is used in an actual application. The Reference contains numerous code examples and usage notes, as well as time-saving tips, cautions, and other helpful programming hints. Part V is cross-referenced and organized by language elements, as follows:

- Cross-reference of Access Basic language elements
- Actions
- Functions
- Methods
- Objects
- Operators
- Properties
- Statements

Finally, the appendixes provide useful information, such as a full listing of Access error messages, a listing of constants used in Access and Windows programming, an ANSI character set, and an introduction to InfoDesigner for Microsoft Access. (InfoDesigner/Q is supplied with the book.) Code listings from the book are also included on disk. To use the files on the disk, open the Que database in the ACCPP directory from Access version 1.1.

Part I

Introduction to Access

1

Modeling Data

The true function of a database system is to supply information in a form that enables people to make decisions or solve problems. For this reason, a well-designed database is much more than a collection of raw data; it needs to be dynamic and flexible to imitate what really takes place in the real world.

Information is refined, or usable, data. Raw data is often insufficient for most purposes; it must be compared with other data, or selected, sorted, and formatted, to be presented as meaningful information. A single data element (a part number, for example) provides little useful information for comparative analysis. A single record of related data (part sales history, safety records, cost analysis, or warranty return data) also provides little useful information. It is only when these individual data components are combined in a meaningful way that they become useful information on which to base business decisions.

Data is not only information in a computer. Data is real life. The computer database only *models* the data that exists in reality. For example, John Doe is a customer who placed an order for a new car. The order record in the database only represents the real transaction that took place.

Focusing on the computer application instead of the real object or action may lead you to limit the scope of your application. Concentrate instead on the people who will use your application and the events and processes that affect them. This will enable you to develop applications that better model the user's perception of the data. The more closely your application models real world activities, the more effective it will be.

This chapter provides a review of some fundamental issues and concepts concerning the design of databases:

- Representing data within a database
- Normalizing data
- Understanding the role of SQL
- Developing a relational schema

If you are new to designing databases, understanding these concepts will help you design and develop successful Windows database applications.

> **Note:** This chapter may be very basic for some experienced programmers. Feel free to skim.

Understanding the Difference between Flat-File and Relational Database Systems

This discussion compares two types of database organization models or *schema*: flat-file and relational. In a *flat-file* model, all the data is stored in one table. In a *relational* model, data is stored in several tables according to certain rules, often called *rules of normalization*.

Limitations of Flat-File Design

In a single-table (flat-file) database design, it is often the case that some of the data must be duplicated among several records. This duplication of data introduces several problems, including poor data integrity, data redundancy, wasted disk space, more difficult user entry, and problems with updating the data.

For example, in a flat-file design all information about a customer (such as name, address, and phone) would have to be duplicated in every order record for this customer. In other words, a lot of storage and processing power is wasted on redundant data. It also can lead to data corruption if some—but not all—customer records are edited. Data integrity is also compromised because the user must repeat the full customer record with every new order record.

But that's not the end of the potential problems; if any of the entries for a customer are spelled or capitalized differently, reports sorted and subtotaled by customer become virtually useless. If the customer's name changes, multiple records need to be updated, introducing the possibility of new data entry errors.

Because of data duplication, a large system flat-file database wastes considerable disk space. Depending on the data, a relational database often can store the same data as a flat-file database in a third of the space.

Comparing Record-Oriented and Set-Oriented Databases

Many flat-file databases, with the help of database languages, have evolved into systems that allow a number of flat-file tables to be linked together to emulate a relational model. But these systems are still not fully relational systems, partly because of the way they store data.

Record-oriented databases identify records by their record number (by their physical location in the table) and use *record pointers* to physically navigate the file and perform database operations. Record-oriented databases also specify a physical index to use when performing a search.

Consisting of nothing more than many flat files artificially connected by key fields, record-oriented models lack the data integrity and flexibility of a true relational database management system. Data in real world situations is more three-dimensional (one customer with many orders, for example) and by definition cannot be as well-represented in a flat file database. The fundamental problem is at the system level, not at the language or tools level. By using a database language, record-oriented systems can be made to look and act like real relational models, but the record-oriented database engine cannot handle data in a way consistent with the logic of the relational model.

By contrast, in *set-oriented* systems like Microsoft Access, the internal organization of data is relatively unimportant. Data is *logically represented* and queries to the database engine return data in *sets* instead of a collection of individual physical records. This architecture is more suited to modeling and processing data after real world activities. To use an oversimplification, if every customer only placed one order, you wouldn't need the relational model. But obviously this is not the case.

How Data Is Organized in a Relational Model

The field types in a relational data model fall into three categories:

- *Primary keys* uniquely identify the object or record. The primary key can consist of one or more fields or an artificially generated key to uniquely identify the record.
- *Foreign keys*, which identify records in a related table, are the same data as the primary key in the primary table; they are called foreign because they come from a different (secondary) table.
- *Description fields* are added to the record to complete the data required, but are never used to establish the relationships between tables.

To give an example, in the following tables the primary key (PK) is the first field (the Person field in the Person table and the ZIP Code field in the ZIP Code table). In the Person table, the ZIP Code field is the foreign key (FK) of the ZIP Code table. This enables the database modeler to perform a join between the Person table and the ZIP Code table. In the Person table, the Eyes field is not required to identify the person or join the table with another related table—so the Eyes field is merely a description field. It may be critical to the application, but it doesn't uniquely identify the record.

Person Table

(PK)Person	**(FK)ZIP Code**	**Eyes**
Paul	28602	Blue
Smitty	10000	Green
Joe	53511	Hazel
Mary Sue	90210	Brown

ZIP Code Table

(FK)ZIP Code	**(PK)City**	**State**
90210	Beverly Hills	CA
10000	New York	NY
53511	Beloit	WI
28602	Hickory	NC

To apply these concepts more generally, for each table ask (and answer) two questions:

- What is the primary key?
- What are the foreign keys and why?

If these two questions are answered correctly, the resulting design will be both functional and flexible.

Normalizing Data

The science of data normalization, first postulated by Dr. E. F. Codd in the early 1970s, provides guidelines for the design of a relational schema. The *database schema* is the term used to describe how data elements are arranged into relational tables. The purpose of data normalization is to make data tables better model the way the information is actually used. By logically defining the proper relational schema, data normalization prevents data duplication and preserves data integrity.

Because the relational database model was first proposed in the 1970s, many DBMS products have claimed to be relational. In the midst of the relational confusion, Codd offered 12 rules (plus rule 0 to make a baker's dozen) of an RDBMS. Because the rules are based on pure relational algebra (mathematical theory), however, no software product—not even Access—can meet all the rules all the time.

Codd's rules, therefore, should be used as guidelines—not absolutes. Their fundamental use is to provide a better understanding of the relational data model and as a guide to selecting and using RDBMS products. Codd's rules aren't listed in full here because each rule deserves a full discussion, which is beyond the scope of this text.

Data normalization, which Codd's rules seek to represent, is an equally technical subject which, if treated properly, would double the length of this book. While it is not our intention to trivialize its importance, out of respect for the scope and depth of the subject matter we can only summarize the "spirit" of data normalization and offer some practical guidelines that will help you implement a normalized schema. For more detailed information on the theory of normalization, please see the reference materials listed in the bibliography of this book.

Relational database tables can be thought of as made of columns and rows. Each column is a field in the record and each row is a record in the table. Fields and tables can have one-to-one, one-to-many, and many-to-many relationships. Many-to-many relationships are resolved through normalization.

The five most important data normalization rules:

Rule 1. Each entry in a table represents one data item (no repeating groups).

Rule 2. All items within each column are of the same kind.

Rule 3. Each column has a unique name.

Rule 4. All rows are unique (no duplicates).

Rule 5. The order of viewing the rows and columns does not affect the semantics of any function using the table.

Balancing Normalization with Performance

In a fully normalized database schema, each specific group of data is maintained in a separate table, although there may be instances when a separate table would be logically dictated but logistically impractical. If a normalized schema requires a separate table with only two fields, for example, and the data in the fields would be duplicated in only two percent of the records, you might consider including the repeated information in the original table instead of a separate related table.

The science of normalization provides a logically correct relational schema. As you create databases you will, over time, develop a sense of *practical*, logical design. This compromise, when artfully implemented, represents the best of the practical and theoretical models.

Practical Rules for Designing a Relational Schema

The following sections walk through the process of developing a relational database schema. Each section begins with a practical rule to describe the content of the entire section. While these sections don't read step by step as the five rules of data normalization, this method is tuned to working with Access and helps you define a well-designed relational database schema with good performance.

Rule #1: Precisely define the table columns as object identifiers and object descriptors, describing only one data item in each row.

Define the columns so that each row contains information about one and only one data object. All records should contain the same number of columns; each column should represent a different piece of data about the data object. At this point, the table would appear as a flat-file database.

Each record of every table should be uniquely identified by a primary key. The primary key should include the minimum number of fields to prove the data item is unique. There should be no repeating groups (duplicates) in the primary key. The primary key is a one-to-one relationship and must uniquely identify the record.

Rule #2: Remove any repeating groups into separate, related tables.

Within each table, there should be no repeating groups of data. For example, consider a sales table containing sales agent data and the agency's name, address, and phone number. If the same agent makes two sales, the agency information would be repeated needlessly. If the table is sorted by agent, the repeating data group would be clearly visible. To meet the first normalized rule, the repeated data group must be removed and placed in its own table.

Rule #3: Remove columns that depend on only part of the primary key.

The following example contains data tracking quotes from vendors. Each row is uniquely identified by the item number, vendor number, and the quote date. These three fields form the primary key. The item description, which is also found in the Item table, is based on only part of the primary key. It must be removed from this table for two reasons:

- If the item description is based on only part of the primary key, it must repeat somewhere. Otherwise, only part of the primary key is necessary to uniquely define the record.
- The partial primary-key descriptive data should already be in a separate table. Repeating the data here is redundant and risks data integrity.

The following example provides a quick view of the tables before and after normalizing:

Quote Table (before normalization)

Item No. (PK) - foreign key to Item table
Item Description
Item Cost
Vendor No. (PK) - foreign key to vendor table
Quote Date (PK)
Quote Amount

Quote Table (after normalization)

Item No. (PK) - foreign key to Item table
Vendor No. (PK) - foreign key to vendor table
Quote Date (PK)
Quote Amount

Item Table (after normalization)

Item No. (PK)
Item Description
Item Cost

Notice that in the normalized tables the item description and item cost are removed from the Quote table and included in the Item table.

Rule #4: Remove columns that depend on non-key values.

If the data in a column can be calculated from other data, don't include it in the table. Values that can be accurately determined from other stored values (known as *calculated fields*) generally shouldn't be stored in tables.

Understanding the Role of SQL

IBM developed *Structured Query Language* (SQL), in the mid-1970s for System R, a prototype relational database system. SQL is used with IBM's ISM, DB2, and SQL/DS databases. Several other software publishers—Oracle, Sybase, Novell, and Microsoft, to name a few—have developed high-performance database engines designed to process SQL statements and return data.

SQL (pronounced "sequel") is a language structure used to describe database objects and functions. SQL often is embedded within a *host language* (such as COBOL, C, BASIC, or Pascal) to extend the host language. SQL statements then are passed from the host language to a SQL database engine for processing. The SQL database engine could be a layer of a stand-alone database product, or a separate multiuser database engine.

Based on relational algebra (such as predicate logic), SQL works with sets of data. The SQL SELECT command returns a set of records as specified by the SELECT arguments or its qualifiers. Records are updated as a group. If a single record is updated, the primary key is used to identify the record.

SQL, at least theoretically, is data- and device-independent; thus the user doesn't need to be concerned with the physical organization of data and its location. The only spectacular failure of SQL was its end-user orientation; SQL has been touted as a simple (almost English-like) data access language for non-programmers but users almost always fail to master it in its native form. For this reason, the Access implementation of SQL is a true salvation for users; Access combines the functionality of SQL with an interactive front end (the Query Design surface) that shields the user from verbose and often puzzling SQL syntax.

Using the SQL SELECT Statement

The basic SQL statement is assembled from three clauses: SELECT, FROM, and WHERE. Consider the following example:

SELECT data item1, data item2, ..., data item *n*

FROM table1, table2, ..., table *n*

WHERE Boolean expression or SQL text comparison function

The SELECT clause identifies requested data items. A *data item* can be a field or expression that concatenates fields or performs a calculation.

The FROM clause identifies the tables (or other relational set) where the data items are located.

The WHERE expression is used to select certain records based on specified criteria.

The following example retrieves the LastName and FirstName fields from the Contacts table. It returns a set of records, including every record where the NextVisit field is within 30 days of today, and uses a Date function (which returns the system date) from the host language.

```
SELECT LastName, FirstName FROM Contacts WHERE NextVisit > Date()
   ➥and NextVisit < (date()+30)
```

Refining the SQL Statement

The SQL statement may be further qualified by adding one of the following optional clauses:

ORDER BY data item1, data item2, ..., data item *n*

GROUP BY data item1, data item2, ..., data item *n*

HAVING expression

The ORDER BY clause requests the sorting order (but not necessarily the one specified by any index); the SQL database engine—transparently to the requesting software—decides which index is the best, or sorts the data if a suitable index cannot be found. The data set also may be grouped by data value or by increments using the GROUP BY and HAVING clauses.

Other SQL commands include Insert, Update, and Delete, which handle database operations (such as data update), and Create Table, Create Index, and Drop Index, which perform database maintenance.

Chapter Summary

Sherlock Holmes used to say that when the impossible was eliminated, the result, however improbable, was the solution. In the same way, data problems, when carefully defined, often yield a solution. When developing with Access, the database definition is critical. You cannot program around a poor database schema. If the schema is well-designed, however, the Access application falls into place—almost by itself.

This chapter briefly summarized the differences between flat-file and relational databases and described the principles of relational database organization, mentioning SQL and its role in a relational database. Chapter 2 describes the Access database, its design and organization, and topics more specific to designing and working with Access databases.

Part II

The Access Database

2

Working with the Access Database

In Access the term *database* means the collection of all files associated with a particular project. An Access database is stored as one file, even though it contains all the tables, queries, forms, reports, and source code files associated with the database. The Access database therefore can be viewed as an integrated development environment, facilitating application development by providing all the necessary components in one place.

The database is in a sense a project folder, since it encompasses all files used for that database project. Organizationally, this is advantageous. You only need to worry about one file, instead of myriads of smaller files. There are some disadvantages for developers, however. Large databases are difficult to manage, and incremental changes can be harder to track. The Access database scheme makes version control virtually impossible without saving multiple copies of the entire database. Various methods to circumvent these and other database management problems are discussed throughout this book.

This chapter covers the following topics:

- Elements of the Access database and its internal organization
- Instructions for using the Database Analyzer and other tools
- Discussion of Access system tables
- Introduction to ODBC and JET
- Basics of database security and database administration
- Introduction to working with the database container and using a startup (AutoExec) macro

Understanding Access Database Organization

Unlike many other DBMSs, Microsoft Access databases are very tightly integrated. Although it is entirely possible to design an Access database that consists only of tables, queries, macros, and reports, without using a single form, the full power of Access is best achieved by linking form controls to Access queries, macros, and code. Access databases rely exclusively on *dynasets* produced by queries as the basis for data selection and filtering. From this perspective, the single file format for storing individual database components begins to make sense.

The components of an Access database are as follows:

- Tables
- Queries
- Forms
- Reports
- Macros
- Modules (Access Basic procedures and functions)

Access has its own database format, indicated by the default file extension MDB (although you can assign other file extensions). Access also has its own table format, which it uses by default when a new table is created from within Access. You can convert a non-Access table into Access format by *importing* it. You can maintain a table's native file format by *attaching* it rather than importing it.

The System (MSys) Tables

The internal structure of an Access database is actually a collection of tables called *MSys Tables*, which store information about individual database components (tables, fields in tables, queries, forms, and so on). These tables are currently undocumented by Microsoft but are accessible for viewing from the main database window. To view the MSys Tables, set Show System Objects to Yes from the View Options menu item (see fig. 2.1).

The most important of the system tables is *MSysObjects*, which stores information about all objects in the current database. Information stored in the MSysObjects table can be obtained by using properties (such as *DateCreated* and *LastUpdated*), but the MSysObjects table and other MSys Tables can also be directly searched. (For more information on properties, see Chapter 3, "Working with Access Tables.")

Table 2.1 shows some of the fields found in MSysObjects, which store basic information about the various components (*objects*) of an Access database. (More fields exist than are listed in this table.) For an example of how to use these fields to display available objects in the current database, see Chapter 5, "Using Access Basic with Forms."

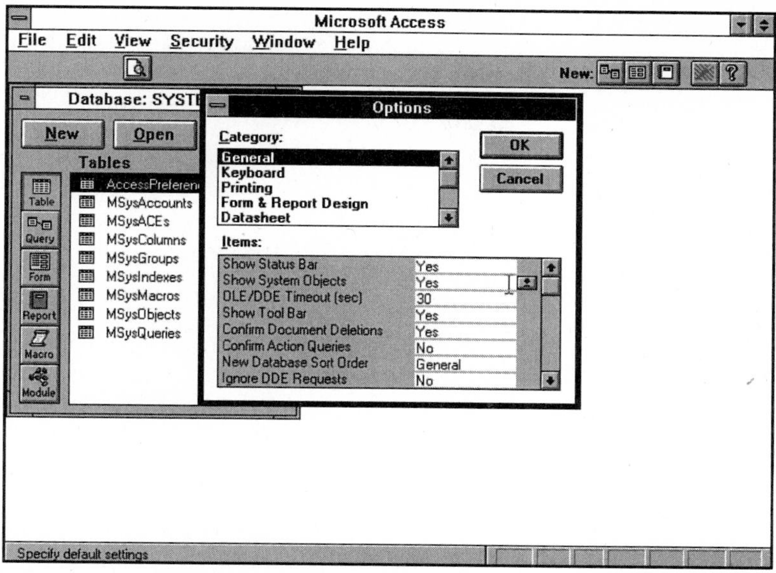

Figure 2.1. Configuring Access to display MSys Tables.

Table 2.1. Description of Relevant Fields in the MSysObjects Table

Field Name	*Description*	
Name	Name of the object	
ID	Object's unique ID number	
Type	Object type, as indicated below:	
	1	System and user tables
	5	Queries
	6	Attached tables
	32768	Forms
	32761	Modules
	32746	Reports
	32766	Macros
	32760	Form images of user tables
DateCreated	Date and time the object was created	
DateUpdated	Date and time the object was last updated	

The following system tables keep track of other components of the database:

- *MSysColumns*. Stores information about data columns in tables and their properties.
- *MSysQueries*. Stores information about fields and expressions in queries.
- *MSysIndexes*. Stores information about indexes.
- *MSysACEs*. Stores information about objects' security IDs.
- *MSysMacros*. Stores information about actions and arguments in macros.
- *MSysIMEXSpecs* and *MSysIMEXColumns*. Store user setups for data import-export.

Microsoft doesn't document the MSys Tables for Access versions 1.0 and 1.1, and discourages the publication of information about the MSys Tables by third parties. The structure of the tables probably will change in future versions of Access, breaking any code people write that depends on these tables.

This is unlikely to prevent the terminally curious from peering into the MSys Tables and drawing their own conclusions; however, given the likelihood that the next version of Access will use an entirely different database file structure, the returns on such an investment seem *de minimis*.

The next section describes how you can use tools supplied with Access to get information about the database.

The Database Analyzer and the Object Analyzer

To circumvent the lack of documentation of Access system objects, you can use the Database and Object Analyzers supplied with Access to get almost any kind of information about the individual objects and contents of a database, including the MSys Tables. The trick is in knowing how to use these tools.

The *Database Analyzer* is a utility supplied by Microsoft with every version of Access. Written by Don Madoni at Microsoft, the Analyzer is a tool that enables you to print basic structural information about tables, forms, and other objects in your databases. It installs in the Access startup directory (named ACCESS if you chose the default installation) and is called ANALYZER.MDA.

In order to use the Analyzer, you must first load it from inside the database you want to analyze. If you load the Analyzer by itself, you will not have access to any objects except those contained in the Analyzer. The PSSKB.TXT file included with Access contains a set of instructions for loading and running the Analyzer from a macro.

But there is actually a much simpler way to get the Analyzer up and running, and to make it easily available to all Access databases. You can add the Analyzer to the Access Help menu by making some quick changes in your MSACCESS.INI file. Just add the following text to the referenced sections of the MSACCESS.INI file, where <full path> is the name of the Access program files directory (the directory in which the ANALYZER.MDA file is located):

```
[Libraries]
<full path>\ANALYZER.MDA=ro

[Menu Add-ins]
&Database Analyzer==StartAnalyzer()
```

Notice that the ampersand in the "Database Analyzer" name makes the following character (the letter *D* in the preceding example) a shortcut key.

The next time you load Access, the Analyzer will appear as an option under the Help menu (see fig. 2.2). For more information about modifying menus, see Chapter 7, "Programming with Macros."

The Database Analyzer form is presented in an intuitive "Wizard" style. You can analyze more than one object at a time. To select an object, highlight it and click the right-arrow button, or double-click on the object. To select all objects of a single type, such as all queries, click on the double arrow. To analyze MSys Tables, check the box at the bottom of the form.

After you select the objects, the Database Analyzer prompts you for a destination database in which to write the results. Because all of the files produced by the Database Analyzer begin with an @, they are easy to identify. Table 2.2 summarizes the output tables produced by the Database Analyzer. Figure 2.3 shows the startup screen of the Database Analyzer.

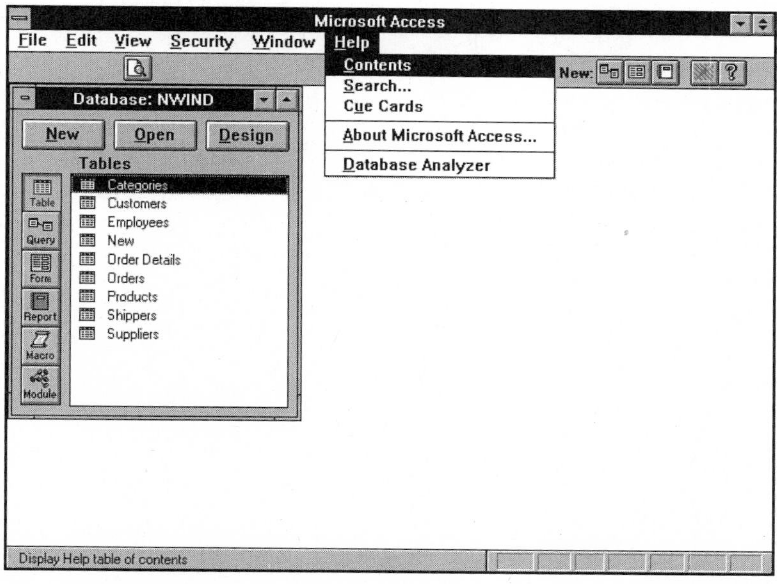

Figure 2.2. Database Analyzer option attached to Help menu.

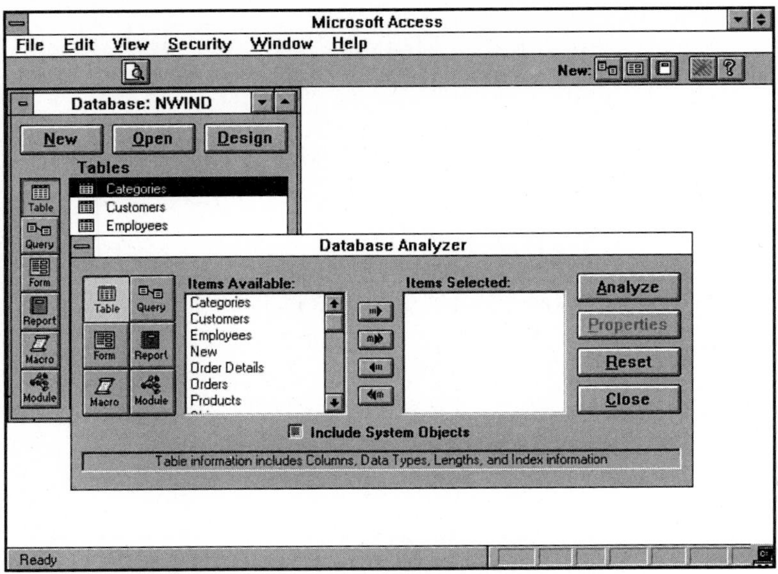

Figure 2.3. Database Analyzer invoked from within a database.

Table 2.2. Output Tables Created by the Database Analyzer

Object	*Output Table Name*	*Contents*
Table	@TableDetails	List of fields, data types, length, and indexes
Query	@QuerySQL	Query's SQL statement
	@QueryDetails	List of fields, data types, lengths, and source tables
Form	@FormProperties	Form properties
	@FormControls	Controls and selected control properties
Report	@ReportProperties	Report properties
	@ReportControls	Controls and selected control properties
Macro	@MacroDetails	Macro actions and arguments
Module	@ModuleProcedures	Module procedures and parameters
	@ModuleVariables	Variables declared with a Dim statement

The Database Analyzer is made up of three components: the Database Analyzer form, the Object Analyzer, and the Object Analyzer utilities.

- The *Database Analyzer* is the form you see when you start the Analyzer.

- The *Object Analyzer* is the "engine" that creates the object tables, performs the analysis, and writes the resulting information to the object tables.
- *Object Analyzer Utilities* are global Access Basic procedures and functions that support some of the commands in the Object Analyzer.

In addition to using the built-in form (Database Analyzer), you can access commands in the Object Analyzer utilities from Access Basic. Because these commands and functions can be called from Access Basic, you can use them outside the Database Analyzer—to document design work in progress, for example—without loading the Database Analyzer, as shown in table 2.3. (The ANALYZER.MDA database must be loaded as a library database if you want to access these functions.)

Table 2.3. Functions Available in the Object Analyzer Utilities Module

Function Name and Syntax	*Parameter and its Data Type*	*Definition*
DumpTableInfo<TargetDB>	TargetDB$	Name of the database to receive the table
<DetailsTable>	DetailsTable$	Name of the table to receive the information
<ObjectName>	ObjectName$	Name of the table to analyze
<IsAttached>	IsAttached%	True if the table being analyzed is an attached table; otherwise False
DumpQueryInfo<TargetDB>	TargetDB$	Name of the database to receive the table
<SQLTable>	SQLTable$	Name of the table to receive the SQL representation of the query
<DetailsTable>	DetailsTable$	Name of the table to receive detail information about the query
<ObjectName>	ObjectName$	Name of the query to analyze
DumpFormOrReport<TargetDB>	TargetDB$	Name of the database to receive the table
<PropsTable>	PropsTable$	Name of the table to receive information about the form's/report's properties
<DetailsTable>	DetailsTable$	Name of the table to receive detail information about the form or report

continues

Table 2.3. Continued

Function Name and Syntax	*Parameter and its Data Type*	*Definition*
<ObjectName>	ObjectName$	Name of the form or report
<IsForm>	IsForm%	True if analyzing a form; False if analyzing a report
DumpMacroInfo<TargetDB>	TargetDB$	Name of the database to receive the table
<DetailsTable>	DetailsTable$	Name of the table to receive detail information about the macro
<ObjectName>	ObjectName$	Name of the macro to analyze
DumpModuleInfo<TargetDB>	TargetDB$	Name of the database to receive the table
<ProcsTable>	ProcsTable$	Name of the table to receive the listing of procedures
<VarsTable>	VarsTable$	Name of the table to receive the listing of variables
<ObjectName>	ObjectName$	Name of the module to analyze

You will learn more techniques for calling and using functions and procedures such as these in subsequent chapters.

ODBC and JET

The Microsoft *Open Database Connectivity interface* (ODBC) is an interface for database connectivity, using SQL as a standard for accessing data. ODBC allows a single application such as Microsoft Access to access different file formats through the use of database drivers—*dynamic link libraries* (DLLs) that use specific communications methods to access particular data formats. In other words, there is a separate database driver for every type of file format.

Using ODBC, developers can write their own data drivers for different data sources. Microsoft and other commercial developers are writing ODBC database drivers for a variety of data formats, such as DB2, Progress, and Oracle.

ODBC has four components:

- *Application* performs processing and calls ODBC functions to submit SQL statements and retrieve results.

- *Driver Manager* loads a driver on behalf of an application.
- *Driver* is a DLL that processes ODBC function calls, submits SQL requests to a specific data source, and returns the results to the application.
- *Data Source* consists of the data the user wants to access and its associated operating system, DBMS, and network platform (if any) used to access the DBMS.

The Driver Manager and driver appear to the application as one unit that processes ODBC function calls. Figure 2.4 shows the relationship among the four components.

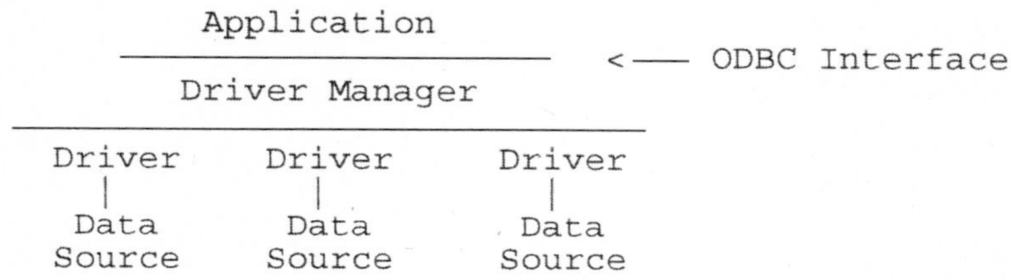

Figure 2.4. Four components of the data access scheme via ODBC.

Access uses ODBC for connecting to some database formats such as SQL Server, Oracle, and Rdb. It uses a built-in *joint engine technology* (JET) with an architecture similar to ODBC (including a driver manager and drivers) to connect to its own (Access), dBASE, Paradox, and Btrieve files. These are *ISAM-level* (Indexed Sequential Access Method) *drivers*, as opposed to the ODBC-level drivers.

Ensuring Database Security

With the migration of applications from centralized data repositories to a more distributed environment, concerns about data security have become paramount. Some networks have upwards of 200 users, and each workstation poses a potential threat to data stored on a network file or database server.

Only by implementing appropriate security measures can data be adequately protected in such an environment. Fortunately, Access has a built-in security mechanism to assist database administrators in the task of maintaining data security. You can implement database security on four levels:

- Users
- Groups
- Password protection
- Permissions

All Access security options are available from the Security menu displayed with the database container (see fig. 2.5).

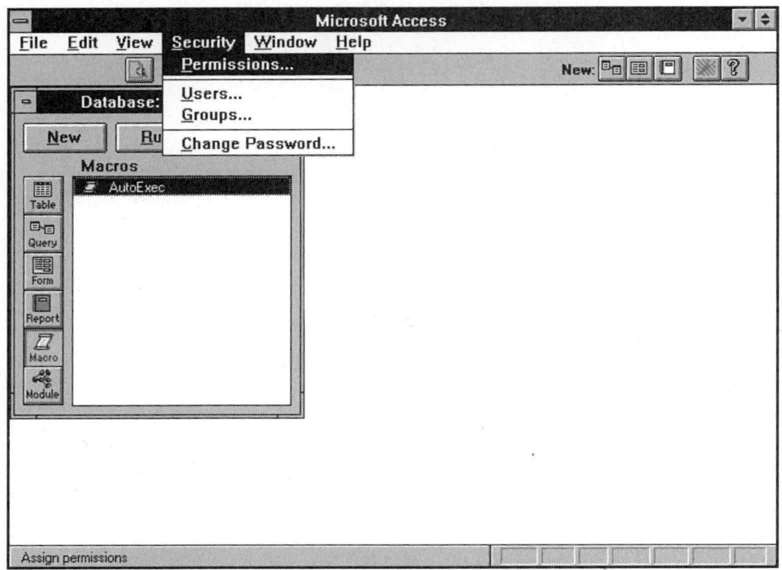

Figure 2.5. Access database security options.

All user and group account information, encrypted password information, and permissions are stored in an Access database named SYSTEM.MDA. This database is created by Access when it is first installed. A unique version of SYSTEM.MDA is created for each installation of Access, including distribution sites if you are running the Access Distribution Kit (ADK). For more information about the ADK, see Chapter 15, "Using Access in Network, SQL Server, and Runtime Environments."

Users, Groups, and Passwords

Access creates two user accounts upon installation: Admin and Guest. Only users can log on to Access. The default usr account is Admin (with a blank password). The first step in implementing security is to activate the logon procedure by changing the password of the Admin user. Next, create a new user account for the system administrator and assign a password to it. Add the system administrator account to the Admin group. Finally, delete the Admin account. (The Admin account cannot be deleted until there is at least one more user in the Admin group.)

The system administrator can then add individual users and groups, and assign users to appropriate groups. After you change the Admin user's password, all users are prompted for user name and password upon entering Access. Changes to security are maintained in the SYSTEM.MDA database.

> **Note:** It is important to restrict user access to the SYSTEM.MDA and MSys Tables.

Groups are used to designate logical or physical categories of users having access to specific Access databases or objects. For example, there may be a group called "Accounting" to which all users in the company's accounting department will be assigned.

Note: In organizations where system administration and database administration fall under the same umbrella, group-level security may be better managed from the network operating system level. Assigning application-specific groups inflates the system administrator's responsibilities by adding yet another area to administer, coordinate, and maintain. Exceptions to this are applications running under the Microsoft ADK, which should have security implemented at the group level. For more information, see Chapter 15, "Using Access in Network, SQL Server, and Runtime Environments."

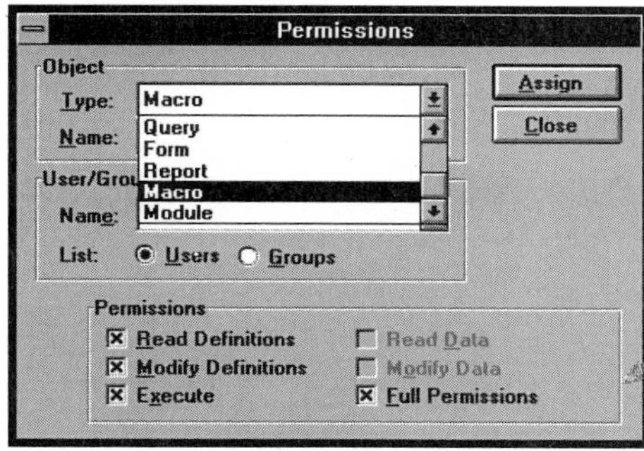

Figure 2.6. Object-level permissions.

Permissions

Permissions can be prescribed for both users and groups as low as the object level, which means down to a block of Access Basic code, if necessary. Figure 2.6 shows how permissions can be specified by object. Read, write, execute, and full permissions can all be prescribed by checking the appropriate boxes in the Permissions dialog box.

Limiting permissions can create difficulties in running an application. Some processes require full permissions to operate correctly. Also remember that permissions can be restricted at the network operating system level. If the user doesn't have the right to create files in a directory, for example, Access cannot create temporary or other necessary files.

If you are experiencing user-specific difficulties, such as inexplicable error messages, check to see whether the user's rights and permissions are causing the problem.

Encrypting Databases

Another tack in the line of data security defense strategies is to *encrypt* the database. Encrypting the database makes its tables indecipherable to other (non-Access) applications such as word processors or utility programs.

Never encrypt a database until you have verified the following conditions:

- You have adequate space on the drive to store both the encrypted file and the unencrypted version. (Access keeps the unencrypted version so you can reverse the encryption if desired.)
- All copies of the database are closed. (Encryption fails in a multiuser environment when another user has the database open.)
- You have a separate backup of the unencrypted database. (For maximum security, back up to tape or a removable disk and store the backup copy in a secure place.)

Maintaining Access Databases

Access, as a full-fledged multiuser database system, includes many tools to administer the database and keep it optimized and running smoothly. Database maintenance involves periodic tasks such as compacting (compressing) databases and performing regular backups. These tasks should be performed at daily, weekly, and monthly intervals by the database administrator. The best rule of thumb is to use the same backup schedule as is used for the local area network.

Compacting the Database

Because text fields are compressed (stored as variable length), editing text fields can cause the data to become fragmented because Access has to write the field's data in two or more locations. So even if no objects or records have been deleted, compacting reduces the size of the database by compressing the text fields to the space actually used by the entries.

Databases should be regularly compacted. Compacting a database frees space used by the following:

- Temporary files
- Deleted records
- Null values and blanks in records
- Deleted objects

A database should be compacted before putting it in production. Since objects are constantly changed during the development stage, the database can become bloated with temporary files and may not perform optimally. Compacting the database also improves performance by optimizing fragmented data. The Compact Database... selection is available from the Access main File menu (see fig. 2.7).

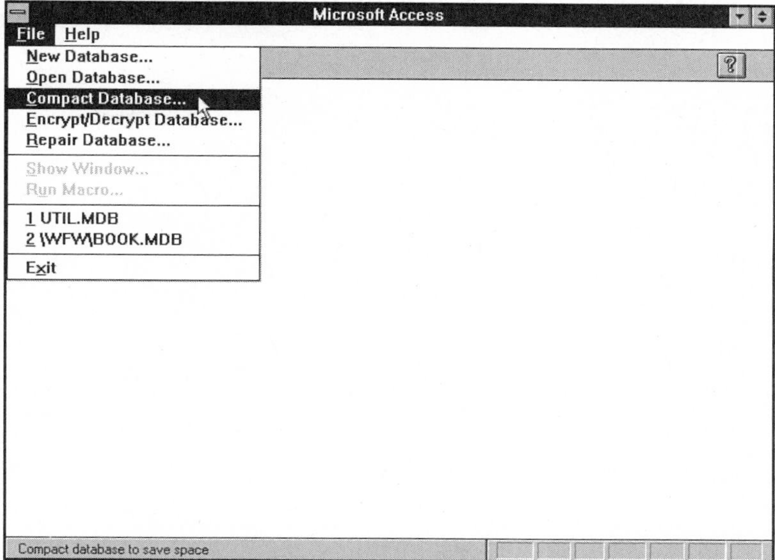

Figure 2.7. Compacting a database.

To compact a database, use the Compact Database... menu command. Like the Encrypt command, this command is available only from outside a database, and you must have enough free space on your hard disk to write the compressed database. When you choose the Compact Database... menu command, Access creates a compacted version of the database. With very large databases, this process can be quite time-consuming.

You can use the DoMenuItem Macro Action to compress a database programmatically, but you must be careful not to encrypt, compress, or repair the open database running the macro.

> **Tip:** Database administrators should figure database compaction into their list of periodic maintenance duties. It is also a good practice to back up the database before compacting it.

Repairing the Database

Access databases can become corrupted under certain conditions, such as power failures or the abnormal termination of Windows. If the database becomes corrupted, the Access Repair Database utility attempts to rebuild records and indexes.

Access usually detects a corrupted database when it first tries to open the database, and prompts you to repair it. However, this is not always the case. If you are getting strange results, such as records missing or indexes not operating properly, the database may be corrupted and in need of repair.

Caution: The repair utility provided with Access has its own internal algorithm for repairing the database. There is no information available from Microsoft about how this utility works. What this means to developers is simple: back up Access databases frequently! If you lose an Access database, you lose everything—all your forms, reports, tables, and code.

Some developers, unwilling to commit all their resources to one file, have started setting up separate databases for tables, objects, and libraries. To manage a multiple-database operation such as this, you need to use Access Basic code rather extensively. The technique is not for novices, but in the hands of a competent programmer, it can significantly reduce the risks of storing everything in one file.

Backing Up the Database

Because everything is stored in one file, incremental backup simply doesn't work with Access databases. Unless you store data in one database and objects in another (requiring the use of Access Basic code to manage the opening and closing of the various databases), or regularly use the **Transfer Table** action to move data to a different database, the whole database must be backed up if one record is edited. The following is the minimum recommended backup schedule.

Files to back up weekly:

The entire Access directory

All databases regardless of changes

SYSTEM.MDA

Files to back up every day:

All databases with changes

SYSTEM.MDA

Your backup software will most likely require that the file be closed before backing up the database.

Using the Access Database Window

Upon starting Access, the first window that appears is the database window. This window presents the entire collection of files found in the database including tables, forms, queries, reports, macros and modules. The first view presented is the table view, which lists the tables found in the database (see fig. 2.8).

Double-clicking on any object opens that object. To open an object in Design mode, for example, highlight the desired object and click on Design. Different design options are presented, depending on the type of object selected. These options are discussed in greater detail in Part III, "Access Design Surfaces."

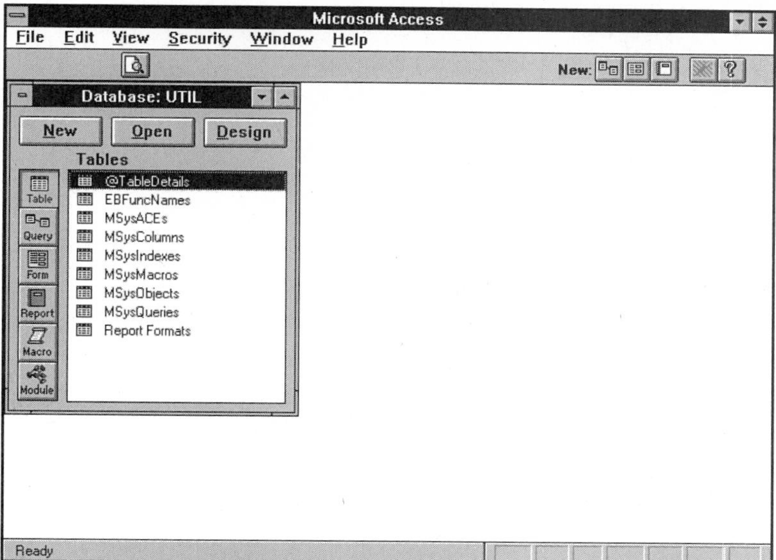

Figure 2.8. The Access Database Window.

> **Tip:** With the user interface Access menus, you can open only one database at a time. You can open additional databases (limited only by the amount of available memory) by using the Access Basic OpenDatabase function. You also can attach to as many tables (including Access tables located in different Access databases) as memory allows by choosing File|Attach Table.

> **Tip:** Use the Ctrl+M key combination to open any highlighted object in the database window in Design mode.

One of the first questions asked by developers is how to suppress the display of files in the Design window. If you want to bypass the database window and open a form, display a different menu, or start some other process upon opening a database, create a macro with the name AutoExec; that macro will run automatically when the database is opened. For more information about creating and using AutoExec macros, see Chapter 7, "Programming with Macros."

Unfortunately, if you choose to display the database window, you cannot suppress the display of certain files while showing others. Microsoft says it is planning this capability for a future release of Access.

Using the Toolbar

As with most Windows applications, Access includes a toolbar whose characteristics (or attributes) change, depending on the active operation. Learning to use the toolbars is time well spent; clicking on the toolbar icon launches the process behind it and eliminates the multiple keystrokes needed to launch the same operation with menu selections.

The toolbar is displayed by default. However, some applications, including the sample applications included with Access, turn off the toolbar display. To turn it back on, select Options from the View item on the main menu. Change the Show Toolbar item to Yes. The toolbar is then displayed.

The following table describes the icons and their associated actions from the database window. All actions operate on the currently highlighted object.

Icon	*Description*
	Shows a WYSIWYG (what-you-see-is-what-you-get) preview of the screen before printing
	Activates the design mode for a new query
	Activates the design mode for a new form
	Activates the design mode for a new report
	Activates Microsoft Access help

The toolbar, like many other Access objects, is really just an Access form located in the UTILITY.MDA database. It can be modified with Access Basic. For an example of a modified toolbar, see Chapter 13, "Extending Microsoft Access and Access Basic."

Chapter Summary

Although this is a book about programming, it is essential to understand how Access stores data and objects. This chapter provided an overview of the Access database, including its unique components and the various mechanisms for maintaining and securing it. The following chapters expand on the basics by providing detailed descriptions of individual database objects, including specific design and programming techniques for each type of object.

3

Working with Access Tables

The key to Access productivity is to ensure the proper design of tables and their interrelationships. This is especially true with Access because the table fields contain properties which, if properly used, can speed form development and reduce coding.

This chapter covers the following topics:

- Designing tables
- Defining table properties
- Creating fields
- Using field descriptions
- Reordering fields
- Defining a relational schema
- Understanding primary and secondary tables and their relationships
- Using validation criteria in tables
- Optimizing for performance
- Editing field properties

Designing Tables

The ability to properly define a relationship between two or more tables is one of the most critical elements of effective database design. Some beginning database developers may have difficulty understanding the relationship between primary and secondary tables. If you are new to this process, be sure to read Chapter 1, "Modeling Data."

The following sections describe how to use built-in Access features such as table definition properties and default relationships to create and maintain the proper relationships between tables.

Using the Table Design Window

The Access Table Design view provides an interactive method of creating and editing tables. In keeping with the Windows design concept of recognition instead of memorization, the Design view is filled with features to make building tables easier.

An Access database can include up to 32,768 tables, but you can have only 254 tables open at once. Each table can be as large as the database (128MB in version 1.0, and up to 1 gigabyte in version 1.1). A table can include up to 255 fields and 32 indexes.

Whether you want to create a new table or redesign an existing table, you use the *table design window*. The table design window is divided into two sections (see fig. 3.1). The top section lists the fields with their field type and description. The lower section is used for field properties that vary depending on the data type of the field. To the right of the lower section is a help box that displays context-sensitive help.

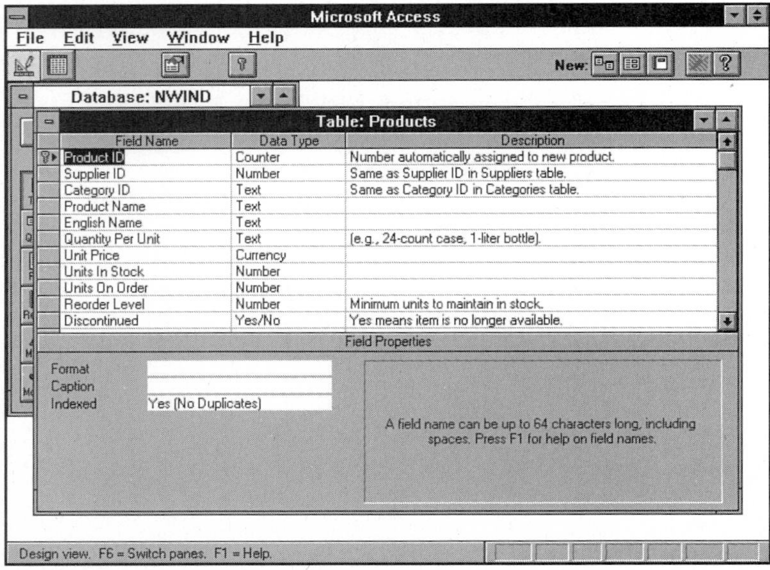

Figure 3.1. Using the Table Design view.

> **Tip:** Press the F6 key to toggle between the two sections.

To create a new table, begin at the database window. Select the Table icon and click on the New Command button, or select the File|New|Table menu command. The new table appears in Design view, ready for field definitions.

The structure of existing tables may be modified by opening the table in Design mode. Select the table in the database window and use any of these methods:

- Click on the Design button.
- Double right-click on the table in the list.
- Press Ctrl+Enter.
- Hold down Ctrl and double-click.

> **Tip:** From the Table Datasheet view, the toolbar Design icon switches to Design view.

Tables are named as they are saved. A table name can be up to 64 characters long.

> **Note:** The table design may not be edited if any current dynasets such as a form or an action query are using the table. If any dynasets are running, Access limits the table design to read-only mode. Also, when you are editing a table design, the table must be opened in exclusive mode. No one else can use any dynasets that reference the table while its design is being modified.

Defining Table Properties

Tables have properties apart from field properties. Clicking the Properties button on the toolbar or choosing the View|Properties menu command brings up the Table Properties window.

Use the Description property to document the table and its relationship to other tables in the database. The description is limited to 255 characters.

The primary key (PK) is the index used to uniquely identify records in the primary table of a default relationship. The fields used to build the primary key are listed in the primary key property in the Table Properties window. Primary keys are covered later in this chapter.

Multifield index fields are listed in the Table Properties window. Unlike single field indexes or primary key indexes, multifield indexes must be created or edited in the Properties window. For more information on multifield indexes, see the "Indexing for Performance" section.

Creating Fields

An Access table can contain up to 255 fields. To create a field, you first must enter the field name, which can be up to 64 characters long. The field name is used to identify the field when you build queries, design forms and reports, and program in Access macros or Access Basic.

Try to seek a balance with descriptive names; users remember short names better. Many Access settings are selected with pull-down menus, but field names must be typed when used in expressions. Spaces should be avoided. Access automatically encloses single-word names with the required brackets, but you must remember to add the brackets around names that include spaces. Also, long field or control names may make expressions too long. If you export tables to another format (such as the DBF format), names with spaces will not convert properly. Therefore, CustomerID is a better name than Customer ID.

> **Tip:** Use identical field names in related tables to help identify related fields.

Fields are further defined by their properties, as described later in this chapter. You can save a significant amount of work by using field properties. For further reference, see Chapter 10, "Understanding Access Data Types."

> **Note:** If you modify field names or field properties, the changes will not be reflected automatically in other Access objects that reference the changed fields. You must manually correct every reference to the field or update field properties in forms or reports based on the modified table.

Using Field Descriptions

Field descriptions, which may be up to 255 characters long, appear as a status bar message to the user in forms and datasheets when the cursor is positioned on the field. Some developers use descriptions to document the use and purpose of each field. Unfortunately, Access does not provide a way to print these descriptions.

Setting Field Properties

Fields employ several properties, depending on their data type. You can set many of these properties in a form or report, but defining them in the table causes the entire application to follow the same set of properties. Data validation, for example, becomes consistent throughout the application because every time a field is attached to a control in a form or report its properties are applied to that object.

> **Caution:** Field properties and field descriptions are transferred to form control properties when the field is dragged onto the form and the bound control is first created. Subsequent changes to the field description and properties in the table are not propagated throughout the application and have no effect on existing form controls.

The field properties (listed in the order they appear in the Properties window) are as follows:

- *Field Size*. Specifies the length of text fields and type of number fields.
- *Format*. Specifies the formatting of data according to standard or custom formats (applies to every type of data except OLE objects).
- *Decimal Places*. Used by number and currency fields to specify the number of places to the right of the decimal.
- *Caption*. The Caption property is used to label fields in datasheets, forms, and reports. It appears instead of the field name. Captions should be brief (one or two words). For a field named LNAM, for example, the caption might be Last Name, which is more readable.
- *Default Value*. This value or expression is used as a default when a new record is created. Unless otherwise specified, it may be overwritten by the user.
- *Validation Rule*. Simple to complex, the Validation Rule property checks entries against an expression or list of possible entries supplied by the developer. Complex validation rules requiring more than a single expression can be attached to the action properties of forms by calling Access Basic functions or macros.
- *Validation Text*. Text of message to display when a validation rule fails.
- *Indexed*. Specifies indexing for individual fields. The choices are no index, index allowing duplicates, and index with no duplicates allowed. It is not possible to index OLE objects, Memo, and logical (Yes/No) fields.

Reordering Fields

You can change the order of fields by highlighting one or more fields and dragging them to the new location. You can insert new fields by selecting the insert location and pressing the Insert key or choosing the Edit|Insert command.

You may want to reorder fields for several reasons:

- Primary keys based on multiple fields are easier to define when the field order is the same as the primary key order. (The order of the primary key and multifield indexes depend on the order of the fields in the Table Properties window, not the order in the table.)

- FormWizards and ReportWizards can quickly lay out forms and reports in the order used in the table, saving the time of manually selecting the field order.
- Fields of a similar nature, when grouped together, are easier to find and use.

Establishing Relationships between Tables

In a relational database, commonly there is a primary table (sometimes called the *parent table*) and one or more secondary tables (sometimes called *child tables*). The parent table must have a unique field that identifies a record or records in each secondary table. In Access, this unique field is referred to as the *primary key* (PK).

The secondary table must have a field whose data matches the data in the matching field in the primary table. The matching data is referred to as the *foreign key* in the secondary table.

> **Tip:** It is advisable to use a Counter data type for the primary key field, because Counter fields are not editable. Using a Counter data type protects the primary key in the parent table from being changed, which might destroy relationships with secondary tables.

Using One-to-One Relationships

A one-to-one relationship matches a single record in a primary table to a single record in a secondary table. For each primary record there is only one matching secondary record. Both the primary and secondary tables must base the relationship on primary keys.

> **Tip:** You can use a one-to-one relationship (with referential integrity turned off) to extend a table by adding what appear to be additional fields to the record. For example, a Contacts table could use a one-to-one relationship to a Vendor Data table. Each contact that was a vendor would have a record in the Vendor Data table, adding vendor information to the Contacts record. Another table called Customer Data could extend the database further. This keeps the overall size of each table manageable.

Using One-to-Many Relationships

The most common type of relationship is the one-to-many relationship. This relationship is the database designer's workhorse. The number of secondary records associated with each individual primary record can range from zero to the upper limits of an Access table size.

In the classic example of an Order Entry system, the relationship between Customers and Orders is a one-to-many relationship. Each record in the Customer table can have multiple "child" records in the Order table. Figure 3.2 shows how this type of relationship may be specified in the Relationships dialog box.

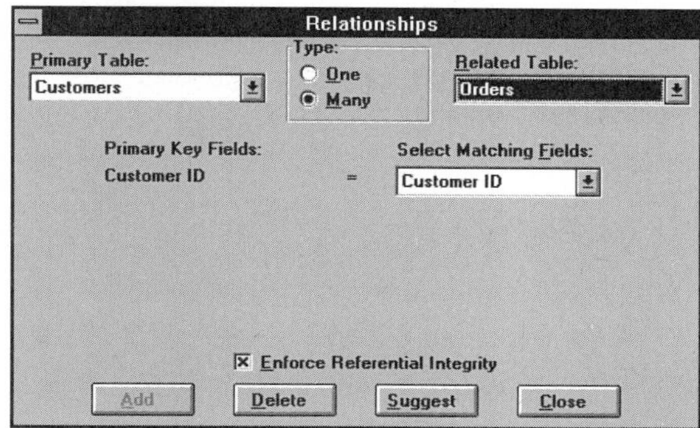

Figure 3.2. Using the Relationships window to specify a one-to-many relationship.

Using Many-to-Many Relationships

A many-to-many relationship is one constructed from two one-to-many relationships connected with a junction or *connection* table. The classic many-to-many relationship is the Orders and Products tables in the Order Entry sample database included with Access. Each order can contain many products and each product can be purchased on many orders. The solution is the Order Detail junction table that relates to both Orders and Products. Both relationships are many-to-one, as applied to the junction table.

To build a many-to-many relationship, create a junction table that relates to both primary tables involved in the many-to-many relationship. You may want to add other data, such as sales quantity in the above example, to the junction table to define the relationship between the two main tables.

Defining Default Relationships

First, a word about the mechanics of setting a relationship. The Relationships dialog box, shown in figure 3.2, is a little clumsy and does not present a list of current relationships. However, using this dialog box is the only way to define default relationships in Access versions 1.0 and 1.1.

To open the Relationships dialog box, choose the Edit|Relationships menu command, which is available when the database window is active. Then follow these steps to set the relationship:

1. Select the primary table. The fields used to create the primary table's primary key appear below the primary table name.
2. Select the secondary table.
3. Click on the Suggest command button. For each primary table PK field, Access tries to find a secondary table field that matches in data type and closely matches in name.
4. If the suggested secondary table fields are not correct, change the field to the correct field. Each field in the primary table's primary key must have a match in the secondary table.
5. Select the Enforce Referential Integrity check box.
6. Select either One or Many to define the relationship as one-to-one or one-to-many.
7. Click on the Add button to establish the default relationship.

To remove a relationship, choose the primary and secondary tables and use the Remove Button.

Viewing Current Relationships

You can view the default relationships in at least four ways:

- The easiest way to view the default relationship is to add all the tables to a query. It is recommended that every Access database have one query, called Relationship Map or Database Schema, that is used for this sole purpose (see fig. 3.3). Note that the query is not updated to reflect changes made in the Relationships dialog box.
- Use the Database Analyzer utility that ships with Access. The Analyzer creates tables and stores information about your database design. You can then query and report your database objects. See Chapter 2, "Working with the Access Database," for more information about the Analyzer.
- The best alternative is to use the InfoDesigner/Q program provided on the disk in the back of this book. InfoDesigner provides a complete method for documenting Access databases, and will greatly simplify your organizational and design tasks.
- The relationship information is stored in MSysObjects, the system table that maintains the database objects. The relationships can be reported directly from these objects with queries and reports.

Setting Referential Integrity

Referential integrity is one of Access' most powerful features. Simply put, *referential integrity* means the following:

- Prohibiting the deletion of a primary record which has associated secondary records
- Prohibiting the creation of a secondary record without relating it to a primary record

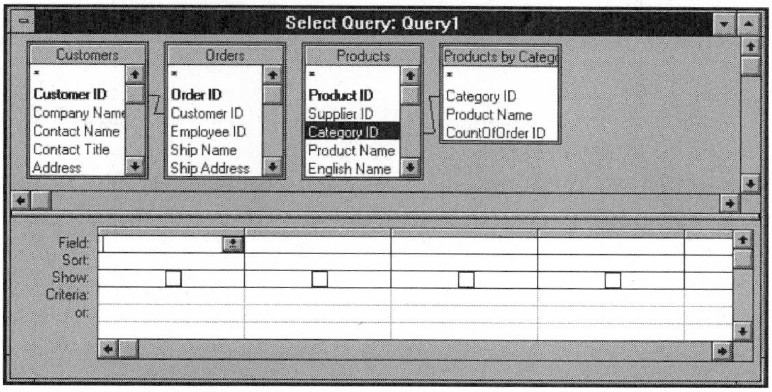

Figure 3.3. Relationships—Query view.

When you turn on referential integrity, Access performs relational checks before saved or deleted records are written to the disk. If the operation does not conform to the relational model, a warning box appears on-screen and prevents the user from completing the operation. Referential integrity can only be applied to native Access tables within the same database.

Thankfully, referential integrity requires no programming. The database integrity validation checks are handled internally.

> **Caution:** Referential integrity only applies to default relationships. Relationships and joins created at the query level do not enforce referential integrity.

Finding Duplicates

Relationships require a primary key index on the parent table. Remember that primary key fields are not editable in Access. The problem is adding this unique index to existing data. Often you will find duplicates or null values that halt the Access re-indexing process when you create a primary key.

Finding duplicates can get a little tricky, but it's possible by using a query (Chapter 6 explains how to use queries). To find duplicates, use a query and follow these steps:

1. If the table doesn't already have a Counter field, add a Counter field and save the table. Access automatically numbers each record.
2. Create a query to join two copies of the table that's giving you problems. Open a new query and add the table twice. Access names the second iteration of the same table *tablename_1*.
3. Join the two tables by dragging the field containing duplicate data from the first table to the identical field in the second table. If the primary key will include multiple fields, repeat the drag-and-drop operation for each field (see fig. 3.4).

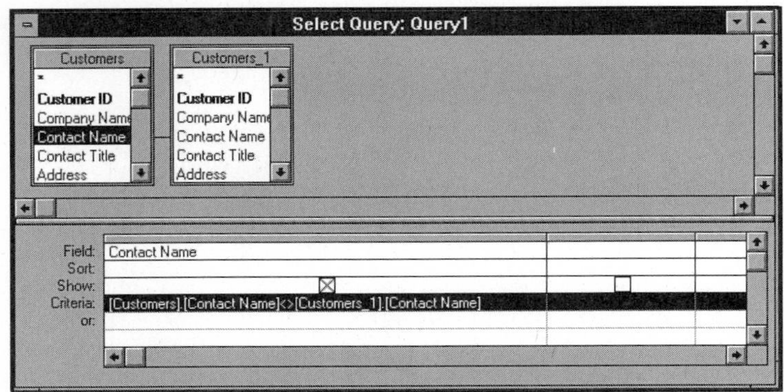

Figure 3.4. Finding duplicates with a query.

4. Adding a query's criteria of [Table].[Counter] <> [Table_1].[Counter] eliminates matching data from the same record and leaves only the duplicate records from the join. Running the query lists the duplicate records and enables you to print them. Because of the query's multiple-record join from one table, you cannot delete records from a duplicate query. Use another query sorted on the Counter field to quickly edit and delete the duplicate records.

Using Validation Criteria

You can validate data entry in many ways, but one of the simplest ways is to specify validation criteria in the Properties section of the table design window. When specified at the table design level, validation checks are automatically transferred to forms when the field is dragged from the field list box onto the form.

Remember the old GIGO (garbage-in, garbage-out) admonition? This is the time to resolve to keep the data in your system clean and error-free! Robust validation routines are the best way of ensuring that only accurate data gets entered into your application. To perform more complex validation routines, you can attach Access Basic code or macros to form action properties such as BeforeUpdate.

Validating with an Expression

A validation expression may be any valid Access Basic expression, including a reference to a user-defined function. For example, mixed Boolean expressions using And, Or, and Not operators are valid. The following expressions are all valid usages:

```
= "Access"

Like "Acc*"

Between "Lincoln" and "Roosevelt"
```

```
Between .02 and 2.6
Between "ARock" and "AHardPlace"
(>200 and <250) or (=75)
```

> **Note:** Table level validation expressions are evaluated after the user enters data. But if the user doesn't change the data in a particular field, that field's validation criteria will not be evaluated.

Validating from a List

You can check an entry against a list in two ways. The first method enters the list directly into the validation expression:

```
in("AAA","BBB","CCC")
```

> **Tip:** When editing long expressions, use the Shift+F2 key to display the Zoom window. This window displays the expression text in a larger window.

The second method uses the DLookup function to test the entry against the contents of a table. In the following code example, the DLookup function is used to return the value of the field Category Name from the database Categories where Prod Category = Category Name. If the lookup fails to find a match, a Null value is returned.

```
DLookup("[Category Name]","[Categories]","[Prod Category]=[Category Name]") Is Not
Null
```

or

```
DLookUp("[Job]","[Jobs]","[Two]=[Job]") Is Not Null
```

The DLookup method provides a dynamic checklist for validation, but tends to be slow. The DLookup method would be appropriate where the validation list is a table that contains data that gets modified from time to time.

Displaying a Validation Message

The Validation Text property is any text you want to display when the validation expression fails. The validation message can be up to 255 characters in length. The text is presented in a warning dialog box. The user cannot turn off these warnings.

Indexing for Performance

Under average conditions, Access performs quite acceptably without indexes. If your tables are very large, however, you can achieve even better performance by selectively indexing your tables. This enables Access to optimize SQL operations before they are carried out, resulting in improved speed for overall database operations, especially when running queries.

Access tables are limited to 32 indexes per table, although you probably would never need that many indexes on a single table.

Indexing a Field

To index a single field, use the Indexed Field property. The property may be set to the following:

- *No (default)*. The field is not indexed.
- *Yes (duplicates OK)*. The field is indexed allowing duplicates.
- *Yes (no duplicates)*. This unique index is the fastest indexing method. This index also forces entries to be unique.

> **Tip:** Yes/No (logical) fields cannot be indexed. If you require indexing in a Boolean field, use the -1 and 0 values in a Number—Integer field. Alternately, a Yes/No field can be indexed with another field in a multi-field index.

When you save the table definition, Access automatically creates or removes indexes to reflect your changes.

Indexing on Multiple Fields

Indexes that sort on more than one field are created by entering the fields in the table's Properties window. Access allows five multifield indexes in addition to the primary key. Each index can include up to 10 fields. One drawback to using multiple field indexes is that they are non-unique and slower than the primary key index or single field no-duplicates indexes.

> **Tip:** Access doesn't include an option to specify multifield indexes as unique, but as a workaround—if you can specify one multifield unique index as the primary key, you can force a unique multikey index.

Access automatically uses partial-key searches when working with multiple-field indexes. For example, if a multiple-field index includes Region, State, City and you want to sort by Region, Access uses the first field from the multiple-field index.

Creating a Primary Key

As described earlier, the primary key (PK) is a unique key used to define relationships. If a table is to be used as the parent or primary table in a relationship, the table must have a PK—one suitable for relationships. Part of the Codd definition of a proper relational database is that every table should have one primary key that uniquely identifies each record and is used for establishing relationships. (See Chapter 1 for more details on the Codd rules of database design.)

> **Tip:** If a counter is used as the PK in a primary table in the relationship, the secondary table must use a Long Integer data type to relate it to the primary table's counter PK.

PKs are also used to optimize searches in Access Basic. Datasheets and forms based directly on a table are by default sorted by the PK.

> **Tip:** Add a Counter field to a non-unique field or group of fields to force the index to be unique and a legal candidate for the PK.

Optimizing Index Performance

The key question of Access table and index optimization is data entry time (more indexes mean longer updates) versus query execution time (more indexes mean better performance when a query executes). Microsoft's Help documentation suggests using a minimum of indexes to make updating records faster. However, Access is usually fast even when updating multiple indexes with large tables. Where Access is notably slow is when a query is run to produce a dynaset when a form loads or a report is prepared. Whether you optimize to improve data entry or query execution speed depends upon the individual requirements of each application. With larger databases, the best approach is probably to optimize for faster query execution (use more indexes).

> **Optimization Tips**
>
> - Use Counter fields for primary keys. The short, single-field index is the fastest way to find related records.
> - Index any field used in a relationship or a join.
> - Study your queries to ensure that underlying tables have the indexes required to speed query execution.
> - Remove redundant indexes. For example, the first field in a multiple-field index should not also be indexed as a single-field index.
> - Remember—unique indexes are faster. Wherever possible, make your indexes unique.

Editing Table Designs

Editing the database definition of some early PC databases sometimes involved programming a routine to export and import the data. For Xbase systems, only one operation could be carried out at a time. For example, in dBASE or FoxPro you cannot change both the field name and its length at the same time without losing data! If you've ever gone through this experience, you'll appreciate how Access handles editing a table definition.

Deleting Fields

You can delete fields by pressing the Delete key or by choosing Edit|Delete. If deleting a field will delete data, Microsoft Access provides a warning.

> **Caution:** Access does not currently support cascading deletes. If a query uses the field you just deleted from the table, the field is converted to an expression in the query. The next time the query is executed (or the form or report based on that query), the query treats the expression as a parameter and prompts the user for the value of the expression. To solve the problem, delete the field in the query after you delete it from the table.

Changing Data Types

When field types are changed in the table design mode, Access automatically converts data from one type to another without programming. However, you still can lose data, depending on the data types and field sizes involved. If you change a Double data type to a Single data type, for example, precision to the right of the decimal (the decimal places) of the number will be lost. Fields may not be converted to a Counter data type field. Date/Time fields are converted to text in general date format. See Chapter 10, "Understanding Access Data Types," for a full discussion of data type conversions.

Editing Field Properties

You can edit a field's properties, but remember that the changes are not automatically applied to existing forms or data. Some properties (such as descriptions, validation information, and defaults) must be manually entered into forms if the changes are made after the bound control is created on the form or report.

Indexes added or deleted during the editing are created or removed when the table definition is saved.

Importing/Exporting Tables

Between Access databases, you can transfer any object (tables, queries, forms, reports, macros, modules) from one database to another by importing or exporting the object. With other database formats, Access imports or exports data. Access can even transfer data with spreadsheet ranges.

The process of importing or exporting data involves selecting the type of database format and the file to be transferred. If a table already exists with the same name as the data being imported, Access appends a number to the name to make it unique.

> **Tip:** When importing related tables, import them from the top down (meaning parent table first) so that child records relate to parent records. Turn off relational integrity when importing if you intend to fix the related data in Access. Turn on referential integrity if the related data is okay in the external file, and Access will check the data for referential integrity as the data is imported. Note that counters can be imported or they can be added after the import.

Between the numerous Import/Export formats available and the flexible Text Import/Export, you should have no difficulty moving data to Access from any current database. You can take advantage of this feature when converting clients to your Access application. In several industries, data is generated daily by automation machines, shipping scales, or time clocks. Using a defined text import, you should be able to integrate your Access application with any real world set of data.

Transferring Access Objects

You can pass any Access object (including tables) from one database to another in the following ways:

- Copying and pasting the object via the Clipboard
- Exporting the object to the receiving database
- Importing the object from the original database
- Using the TransferDatabase macro action

The straightforward process of transferring objects between Access databases involves specifying the following from the File|Import/Export menu:

- Transfer type: import or export
- Type of database: Microsoft Access
- Source or destination database
- Object type: table, query, form, report, macro, module
- Source name of object
- Destination name of object
- Structure only: Yes/No

The TransferDatabase macro uses the same parameters as the Import/Export command (see fig. 3.5).

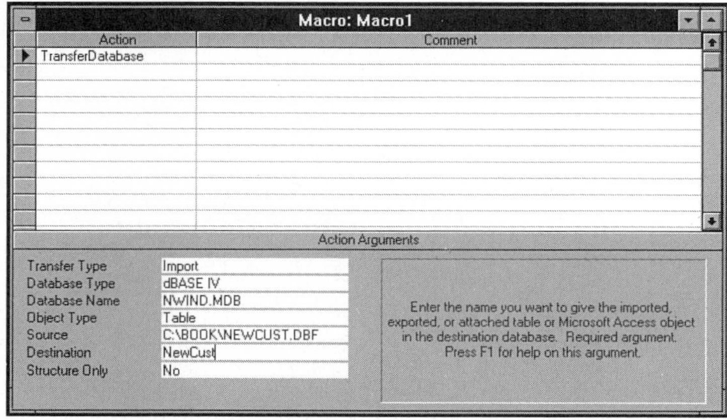

Figure 3.5. The TransferDatabase macro.

Transferring Data with Other DBMS Formats

Access supports the following import/export formats (see fig. 3.6):

- Microsoft Access
- Paradox 3.x
- dBASE III
- dBASE IV

- Novell Btrieve
- SQL databases (Microsoft SQL Server, Sybase SQL Server, and Oracle)
- FoxPro 2.0
- FoxPro 2.5
- Text (delimited and fixed width)
- Microsoft Excel
- Lotus (WKS, WK1, WK3 files)

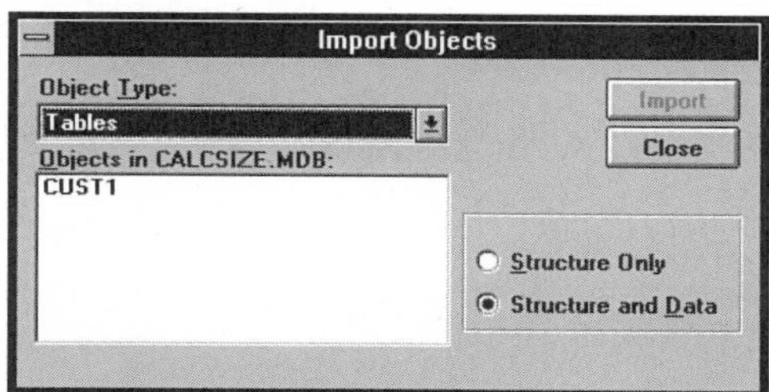

Figure 3.6. Import dialog box.

Transferring Text

Text files (often called ASCII or flat ASCII files) can be divided into two types—fixed and delimited. Access will work with either type, and its capability to work with fixed length types has been greatly improved in version 1.1.

A delimited file uses a specific character to separate fields and to surround, or *delimit*, text. The field separator is usually a comma. Text is usually delimited by a quotation mark. If the text file uses these de facto standards, Access will import or export without any setup changes. If your file uses different delimiters, however, Access can accommodate the file by setting the Text Import options. After you define the options, you can save them so that they can be reused by macros or users.

In a fixed-file-length text file, each field occupies a specific portion of each record. The 20-character-length field, for example, can run from character position 8 to character position 27. The position is the same in every record, and any unused positions are filled with spaces.

To work with a fixed-length file, you must create a file definition with the Imp/Exp Setup menu command. The Import/Export Setup grid is used to define each field and its position in the record (see fig. 3.7). As with delimited setups, the fixed-length setup can be saved for future use.

You can also specify the date, time, and number formats used when importing or exporting either delimited or fixed-length text files.

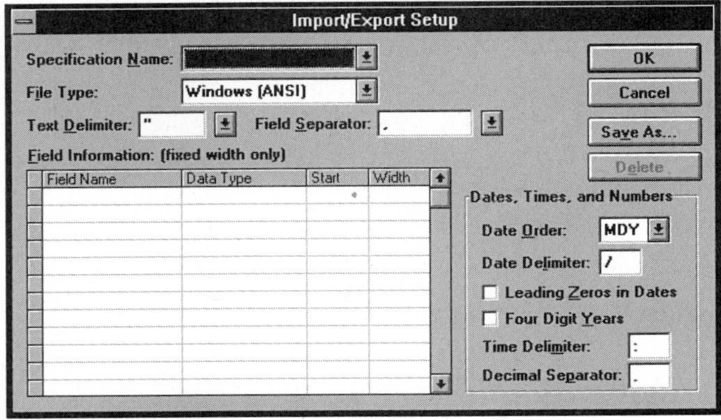

Figure 3.7. Text Import/Export Setup dialog box.

Transferring Spreadsheet Data

Many small business-application databases are still stored in spreadsheets. This approach works well for a single-table database. Sorting data or calculating totals from a data range is easy in Excel. As Access becomes more popular as both an end-user database and corporate database solution, these small spreadsheet "databases" can easily be combined with larger databases and transferred to Access.

Access supports Import and Export to the following popular spreadsheet formats:

- Microsoft Excel
- Lotus 1-2-3 (WKS, WK1, or WK3 format)
- Lotus 1-2-3 for Windows

Access will import the entire spreadsheet or a selected range. You can enter a named range (SALESDATA) or use the cell locations (C5:K150 or C5..K150). Note that only data is imported. Any calculations or formulas are lost, and only the current result is imported.

> **Note:** Access version 1.0 cannot import the Excel version 3 or version 4 named-range database called DATABASE. As a workaround, name the database range something other than DATABASE or save the spreadsheet as an Excel version 2 spreadsheet. This problem has been corrected in version 1.1.

Working with Attached Tables

Access can use tables (Access or other formats) that are outside the active database. This is one of the most flexible features of the product. The ability to work with data in different formats from foreign (non-Access) databases is increasingly important in today's distributed environments.

One design for managing large projects with Access is to separate the database into two databases—one for code and the other for data. The code database, containing all the queries, forms, reports, macros, and Access Basic modules, would attach the tables from the second database. The scheme solves the Access database size limit. It is also possible to load your code database as a library database, and therefore avoid attaching tables at all (see "CodeDB" in the functions section of the Reference).

After external tables are attached, they are displayed with a modified table icon (see fig. 3.8).

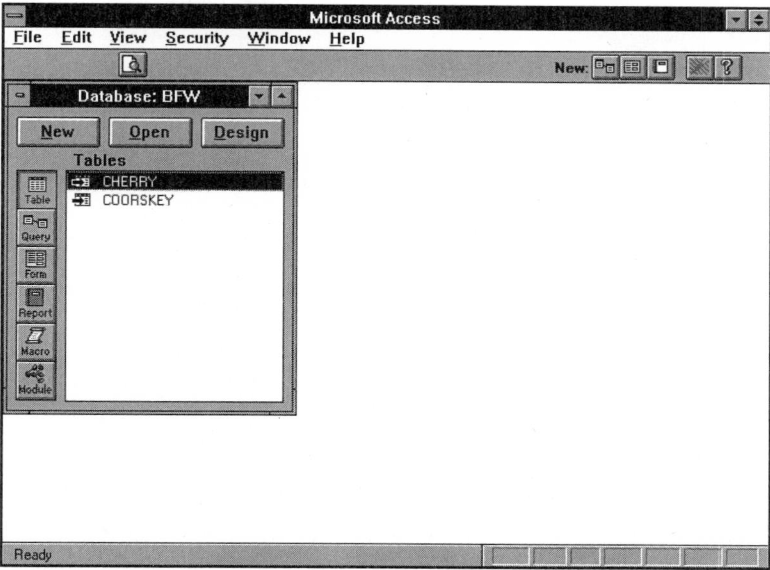

Figure 3.8. Attaching external tables.

When attaching tables from other databases, Access supports the multiuser rules established for the external database. For example, Access respects the external table's file and record locking.

Attaching and Removing External Tables

Attaching a table is very simple. Define the type of database and file location, and Access does the rest. For SQL databases, Access requires a user name and/or password to access the external data.

To remove an attached table, select the table in the database window and press Del or choose Delete from the File menu. This action doesn't affect the external table in any way; it merely removes the link between Access and the external table.

> **Caution:** The Access Basic OpenTable method does not allow opening attached tables. If you use attached tables or plan to move your tables from the local database to an external database before shipping your application, you must use the CreateDynaset or CreateSnapShot methods in Access Basic to access the attached tables. Also, the path for the attached table is hard coded in the Access database; therefore, if the location of the attached table changes, it must be reattached or Access will not be able to locate it.

Editing Attached Tables

Not all the properties of attached tables may be edited. The following editing actions are not allowed on attached tables:

- Adding or deleting fields
- Changing field names and lengths
- Adding or deleting indexes
- Adding default relationships

Chapter Summary

The foundation of every database is in its data structures and relational design. The key to Access productivity is to ensure the proper design of tables and their interrelationships. Let Access do as much of this work as possible! Making liberal use of Access built-in features, such as table definition properties and default relationships, eliminates many pages of coding that you would otherwise have to do to create and maintain the proper relationships between tables.

Strive for a system that is driven by the data, not by hard coding rules and relationships. That way, when your data definitions change, the system can change to accommodate your modifications. You maintain both your database and your sanity!

Part III

Access Design Surfaces

4

Designing Forms

The Windows graphical user interface (GUI), in addition to its intrinsic appeal to end users, has introduced significant advantages for software developers. By using the Access design surfaces, a developer can design forms quickly and visually, and create reports and queries without worrying about programming. Because the user interface can comprise up to 60 or 70 percent of a finished application, these WYSIWYG (what-you-see-is-what-you-get) design tools, such as the form and report design surfaces, can save many hours of coding.

Eliminating the tedium of coding the user interface enables the programmer to allocate more resources to the "working" parts of the application that demand more attention in programming. In contrast, many (if not most) text-based systems can involve endless tweaking of code to position and move objects around on-screen.

Although an Access application can exist without using a form, Access provides utility by way of its forms. Forms provide not only a convenient way to enter and edit data, but also can be used for tasks like launching another part of the application, or automatically performing actions specified in the form's event properties. All this functionality for the user is usually just a mouse click away.

Access forms can be used to perform any of the following tasks:

- Find and view a specific record
- Edit a record
- Scroll through records by user-defined sort or selection method
- Delete records
- Enter new records
- Print records
- Launch operations
- Call macros or Access Basic functions

A properly designed form appeals to users and expedites data entry. As you master working with Access forms, you will come to appreciate the integration between forms and tables, and the flexibility of form properties.

This chapter briefly discusses the Windows user interface and then concentrates on designing Access forms, understanding form properties and events, customizing forms, and using built-in Wizards to create forms.

Windows User Interface Standards

One of Windows' chief benefits is the functional and visual similarity between application programs—all Windows programs adhere to the same user interface (UI) standards. Developers new to Windows who are accustomed to working in text-based systems, however, may find the transition to programming in Windows difficult. Text-based systems lack UI standardization and have few interface building blocks; these limitations often result in user interface designs that may seem creative to the programmer but are not directly translatable into Windows designs.

Many developers of DOS-based systems are not used to the concept of rigid design standards. They may have difficulty, therefore, adhering to the explicitly stated and commonly accepted standards of the Windows user interface design. These standards govern items such as the placement and look of menus, keyboard shortcuts, and visual considerations such as screen design and the judicious use of color. In Windows, unlike the DOS environment, the use of too much creativity in these areas only confuses the user and unravels the benefits of the Windows user interface standards and conventions.

To complicate things, Access offers virtually unlimited flexibility in forms design. For this reason, adhering to some form of standards is even more important. In a graphical environment, users can be distracted if there are too many elements on-screen, elements that are poorly organized, or elements that are aesthetically displeasing. This is why it is important to follow Windows UI conventions. If you are unfamiliar with Windows interface design standards, you should pick up and read one of the good reference materials on the subject (see Appendix D, "Bibliography").

Note: The subject of Windows UI design is covered in detail in the *The Windows Interface, An Application Design Guide*, available from Microsoft.

You also can learn much by simply studying the screen and menu designs of finished commercial applications. The next section offers some general guidelines.

Form Design Tips

A well-designed data entry form presents data in a logical sequence and uses fonts that are easy to read. When creating forms, try to think like a desktop publisher or graphic designer. Consider the following ideas:

- Avoid crowding too much information on one screen. If necessary, break the data into two or three separate forms, with connectors (such as buttons) that enable the user to move back and forth easily between forms.
- Use color sparingly, if at all. As a rule, use no more than two contrasting colors on any page.
- Leave white space around the form.
- Group related data sparsely, using lines and 3D rectangles to subtly suggest the groupings.
- Make data entry as logical as possible. If some fields are required to calculate other fields, place them in the most logical sequential order.
- Avoid design elements, such as logos and pictures, that are of purely ornamental value; these objects are generally too resource-intensive to have much practical value.

In order to apply these guidelines, you need to become familiar with the Access design environment.

The Design Environment

The Access design environment benefits from Microsoft's previous experience with Visual Basic. The Properties window, Toolbox, and Toolbar are examples of how Microsoft has worked on making Access productive for developers as well as end users.

Access forms are usually designed in Design view, as shown in figure 4.1. Use the Design view to accomplish the following tasks:

- Place and position controls of forms
- Link controls with the underlying table/query
- Manipulate form and control properties
- Assign macros or Access Basic functions to event properties
- Polish the appearance of the form

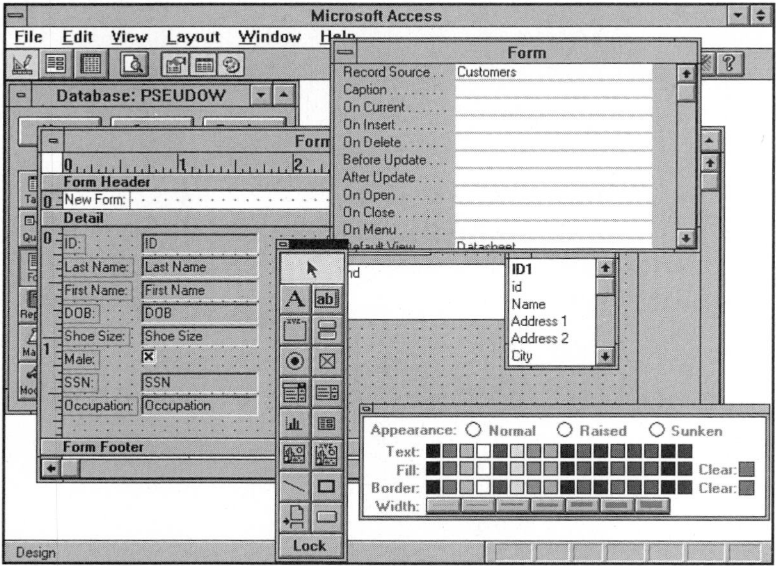

Figure 4.1. A form in Design view.

You call up a form in Design view by selecting the form in the database window and then doing any of the following:

- Clicking the Database Window Design button.
- Double right-clicking on the form name in the database window list.
- Ctrl+double-clicking on the form name or pressing Ctrl+Enter with the form name selected.

If the form is open and the Design view is allowed, you can switch to the Design view by clicking on the Toolbar's Design icon and executing the View|Form Design menu command.

> **Note:** The Design view may be disabled by various settings of the form property *ViewsAllowed*, or you may have no Permissions to modify objects (which has the same effect).

Every object placed on the form is referred to as a *control*. Controls are available from the Toolbox, and can range from text boxes and labels to embedded OLE objects and lines. Controls are divided into two types: bound and unbound. *Bound* controls link to the underlying dynaset (a table or a query). *Unbound* controls are independent of the dynaset and operate more like standard Windows controls such as push buttons, check boxes, and so on.

> **Note:** Unlike Visual Basic, Access versions 1.0 and 1.1 do not have the capability to create or attach custom controls.

You also can enter the Design view and create a form programmatically using Access Basic code, as discussed in Chapter 13, "Extending Microsoft Access and Access Basic."

The Toolbox Window

Visual Basic developers are familiar with the Toolbox, which is used to place controls on a form. The Toolbox in Access floats on top of other windows and is not bound to Access's borders. The Toolbox contains the pointer, 16 types of controls, and the Lock option. You also can use the Toolbox to set the control type's default properties, by clicking the Toolbox control while the Properties window is visible. Figure 4.2 shows the Toolbox, Palette, and Field List.

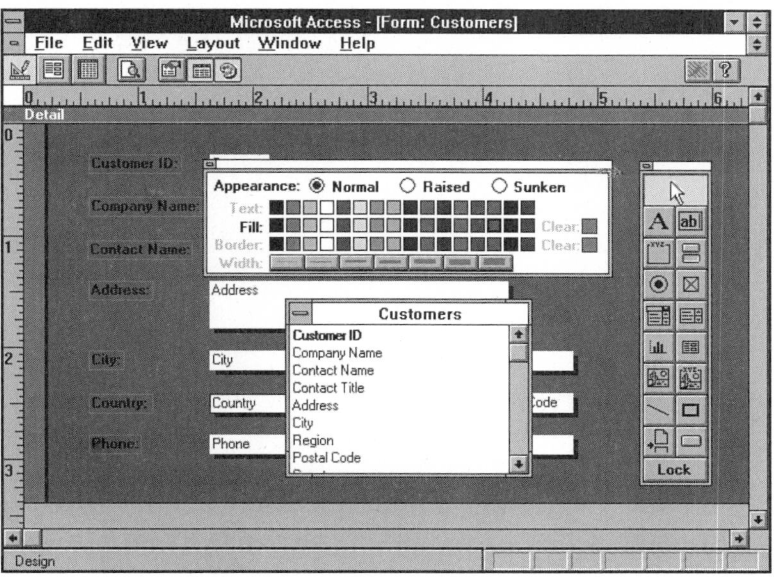

Figure 4.2. The Access Toolbox, Palette, and Field List.

When the Lock option is on, you can place multiple controls of the same type repeatedly without reselecting the control type from the Toolbox.

The Properties Window

The Properties window displays all the appropriate properties for the selected control. It floats on top of other windows and, as a Multiple Document Interface (MDI) child window, is not restricted to the Access border . The full Properties window—in which many properties can be viewed simultaneously—is a welcome feature and a development time-saver.

You access the Properties window by doing any of the following:

- Double-clicking on a control to view the properties of that control.
- Using the Properties button on the Toolbar.
- Selecting the View|Properties menu command.

> **Tip:** When using VGA and Super-VGA systems with low resolution (less than 1024x768), the "always on top" nature of the Properties window can make it difficult to work inside your form, so you may need to display and then hide it frequently. Use the Properties Window button on the Toolbar to quickly toggle the Properties window on and off.

> **Tip:** When setting properties, the expressions can sometimes be longer than the Properties window's display area. You can resize the Properties window or, if screen space is at a premium, use the Zoom window (which you open by pressing Shift+F2) to view and edit long expressions.

The Palette

The palette window applies colors to text, fill, and borders of controls and forms. You also can set special effects (such as a sunken or raised 3-D effect and border width) with the palette window. Settings on the palette change the corresponding property for the control or form. The following table cross-references the elements on the palette with the property settings they affect.

Palette Setting	*Form or Control Property Affected*
Appearance	Special Effect
Text	Fore Color
Fill	Back Color

Palette Setting	*Form or Control Property Affected*
Border	Border Color
Width	Border Width
Clear (Fill)	Back Style
Clear (Border)	Border Style

Although all of the above properties can be accessed from the Properties window, setting them with the Palette is much quicker.

You enable the Palette from the Toolbar or the menu by clicking the Palette button on the Toolbar or by choosing View|Palette.

Note: In Access versions 1.0 and 1.1, the Palette is implemented as an Access form; if you are interested in "how did they do it," the form can be found in the UTILITY.MDA database included with Access.

The Field List

The Field List presents a list of all the fields from the recordset declared in the form's *RecordSource* property. Dragging a field from the Field List and dropping it on the form creates a bound control and transfers default properties for the particular control (such as a validation rule specified for this particular field) to the form.

Tip: Because there may be only one record source for a form, the Field List displays all fields available to this form. If you need to use multiple tables, queries, or any combination of the two as the basis for your form, first create a query that includes the desired fields from all required sources to use as the basis of the form.

Note: Access automatically updates the Field List for a form when you change any of the fields in the underlying table. However, it automatically updates the Field List for queries only if you have updated the query field columns to reflect new or changed field names.

Using the Forms Ruler

You use the ruler to visually align controls. The ruler measurements apply to the control properties *Left*, *Top*, *Width*, and *Height*. The View|Ruler menu command enables and disables the ruler. What you see on the rulers in Access (and any other Windows program) depends on the international settings of the Windows Control Panel (governed by your Windows WIN.INI file). If you shut down Access, go into the Windows Control Panel, and change Measurement from English to Metric, then restart Access, the rulers will be in centimeters, not inches.

> **Tip:** Turn off the ruler to work with the form in a size that's closer to the size the user will see.

The Toolbar

In any stage of form development, the Toolbar's Design View and Form View buttons enable you to toggle to Form view and test the form's operation. Note that the toolbar changes according to the selected control; therefore, some toolbar options are not available to some controls (see fig. 4.3). The following table describes the major buttons on the Toolbar.

Button	*Description*
	Switch views from Design view to Form view to Datasheet view
	Display a print preview in Form mode or Datasheet mode
	Toggle the Properties window
	Toggle the Field List window
	Toggle the Palette window
	Undo changes
	Help

If a certain control type (such as a label or a text box) is selected, the buttons described in the following table are added to the Toolbar.

Button	*Description*
B	Bold
I	Italic
U	Underline
	Left-align
	Center-align
	Right-align
ABC 789	General alignment (default, text right-aligned, numbers left aligned)

> **Tip:** You can create a macro that toggles the Toolbar on and off by using the macro action DoMenuItem, Form Design, View, Toolbar. You then can use the AutoKeys macro to assign the macro to a key.

The Grid

The grid lines superimposed on the form design are very effective for aligning controls. The default grid display is toggled by the View Grid setting in the Form & Report Design, which you can access by choosing View|Options. You also can choose View|Grid to toggle the display of the grid for an individual form.

Objects (controls) can be either automatically left-aligned and top-aligned to the nearest grid lines (when the Snap to Grid option is on) or resized to fit the Grid when the Size to Grid option is selected. The Snap...and Size... settings are accessible from the Layout menu.

You set the grid size (vertical—GridY property, and horizontal—GridX property) in the Properties window for the form. The setting represents the number of grid locations (dots) per inch. A setting of 15, for example, results in a tighter grid than does a setting of 8. No single perfect grid spacing exists; the best grid size is one that enables the controls to fit the font size.

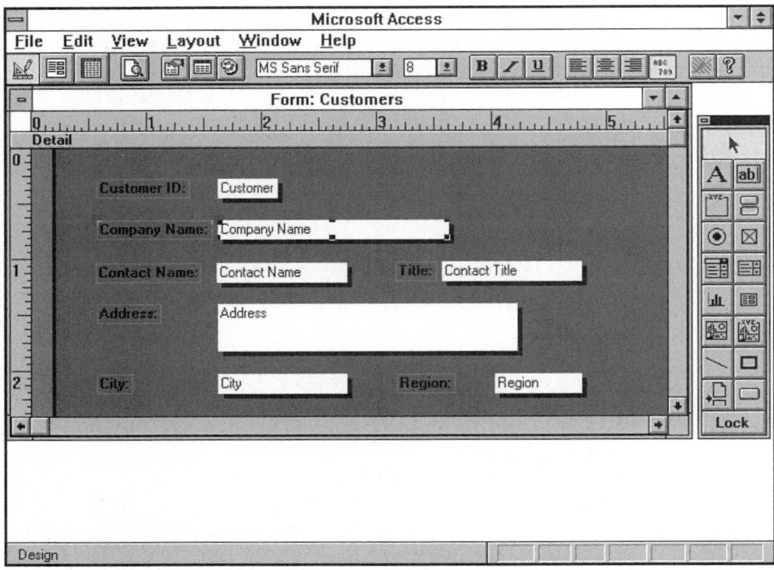

Figure 4.3. The Form Design Toolbar.

> **Note:** If the any of the grid properties is set to more than 16 dots per inch, it becomes invisible.

> **Tip:** Microsoft Access Wizards effectively disable the grid by shrinking the form's *GridX* and *GridY* properties from the default of 10 per inch to 64 per inch. To use a grid with forms initiated by a Wizard, edit the form's *GridX* and *GridY* properties back to 10 and select Grid from the View menu to enable displaying the grid for this form.

Understanding Form Sections

A form is divided into five sections, as shown in figure 4.4. Each of these form sections has specific purposes:

- *Form header*. The form header section is best used for record identifiers, status indicators, form identifiers, and application form toolbars.
- *Detail section*. Use the detail section for displaying data from the dynaset.
- *Form footer*. The form footer section is ideal for record totals, balances, record audit trail, and embedded OLE objects such as voice messages. Custom record navigation buttons and bookmark buttons are also candidates for the form footer.
- *Page header/footer*. The page header and page footer sections are visible only when the form is printed (or in Print Preview mode) and are generally used to provide more general information, such as form title, icons, or totals.

Page and form header and footer sections are optional, but the detail section is always present on the form.

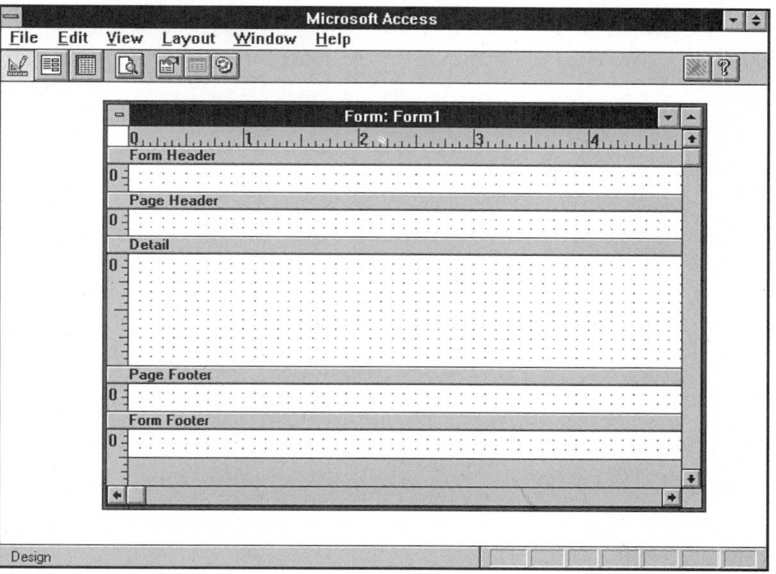

Figure 4.4. Sections on a form.

> **Tip:** When working with lots of data on a form, use a header and a detail section. Identify the record in the header, and use page breaks to ensure that the detail section scrolls nicely.

The detail section of a form is used to present the data (or other controls). The detail section can be formatted as a single form (to display a single detail section per page), or as a continuous form (to display multiple detail sections on a single page, space permitting). If any of the sections doesn't fit in the form window, it can be scrolled using the standard Windows scroll bars. The appearance of the form and other properties can be set on the form level and on the section level. Some properties, such as Help File, must be set manually (by making an entry in the Properties window). Others, such as Back Color, can be set using the palette, and some, such as Width and Height, are set automatically when the form is resized or otherwise changed. Figure 4.5 shows the properties available on the form level and figure 4.6 displays properties available on the section level.

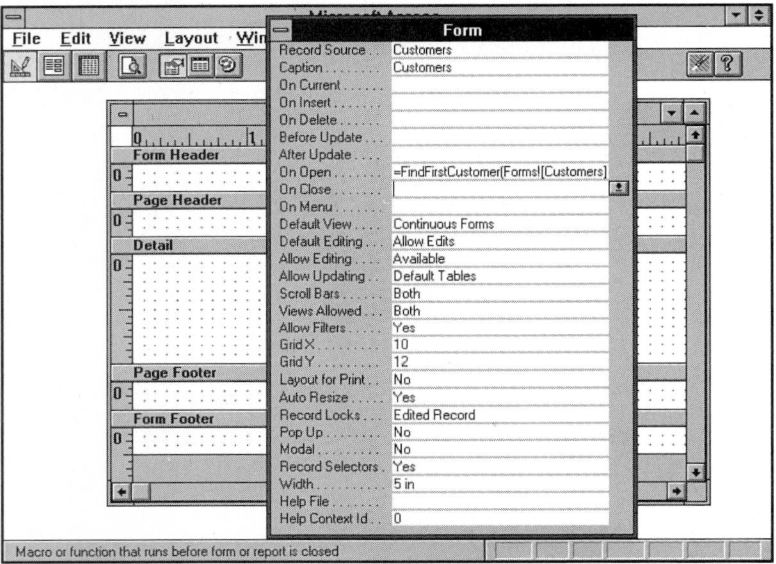

Figure 4.5. Properties available to a form.

Creating Modal and Pop-Up Forms

Access combines several standard form attributes to enable you to create modal or pop-up forms by setting just two properties: *PopUp* and *Modal*. For example, to define a pop-up form (a non-resizable form, without Minimize and Maximize buttons, that floats always on the top of other forms), all you have to do is to set the form's PopUp property to True; Access takes care of the other settings.

Because it uses a standard MDI child window, a *normal* form has Minimize and Maximize buttons. It cooperates with Windows multitasking and enables other forms or applications to gain focus. A *modal* form, on the other hand, forces the user to close the form before another Access task can gain focus. Because they maintain focus until they are closed, you can use modal forms to be certain that a question or message is dealt with by the user before proceeding.

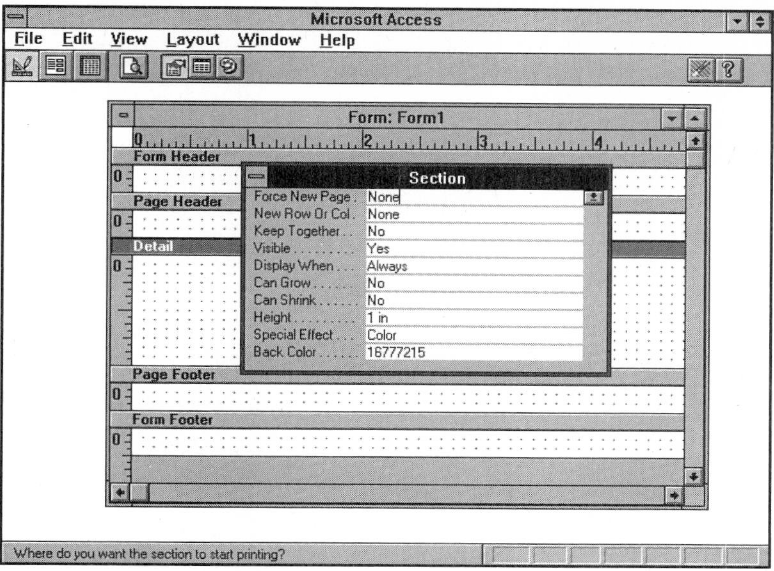

Figure 4.6. Properties available to a form section.

> **Note:** Modal windows (forms) in Access can be only application-modal. To create a system-modal window, you must call Windows API functions. Calling Windows API functions from Access is discussed in Chapter 13, "Extending Microsoft Access and Access Basic."

A *pop-up* form has a special appearance. A pop-up form has no border by which you can resize the form, nor does it have Minimize and Maximize buttons. Pop-up forms retain the Control menu, so you can still close or move the form. The pop-up form also floats above other Access forms or windows. As a floating window, the pop-up form is not an MDI child window and is not restricted to the Access borders.

A pop-up form also can be defined as modal; in such a case, it not only cannot be resized, but also needs to be closed before other windows can gain focus. For example, an Access error dialog box is a modal pop-up form. You may want to use this kind of form for critical data-entry functions that must be performed before the user can proceed.

> **Note:** Removing the Control menu from an Access window requires calling Windows API functions. This procedure is described in Chapter 13, "Extending Microsoft Access and Access Basic."

Choosing the Presentation Style of a Form

Access forms are very flexible; you can create forms with any "look and feel" you want. The following list describes some standard forms (also used by the Form Wizard):

- *Single forms.* A single detail section to a page—by far most common look for an Access form.
- *Tabular forms.* Forms that display data in columns.
- *Continuous forms.* Many detail sections to a page.
- *Datasheet forms.* Forms that display data in gridded rows, like tables.

Use the single-record form view for data that is normally used one record at a time. Forms that require certain fields are also best displayed in a single-record form view.

Tabular forms (available from the Forms Wizard), which present data from multiple records in a "column style" format, are best suited for listings and directories (such as a phone directory or a price list).

The continuous form shows as many detail sections as will fit on the screen; the smaller the form, the more detail sections that will be displayed from the continuous form view. This type of form is well suited for applications such as Rolodex-type listings with relatively few controls, where it would be beneficial to view more than one entry at a time.

You can also present a form as a datasheet. Although running a query or opening a table produces a Datasheet view, and may seem easier than designing a form, forms presented in the Datasheet view offer more flexibility with field placement, attaching controls (such as list boxes), and displaying—or hiding—certain fields from the underlying dynaset.

The form's *DefaultView* property determines whether the single form, continuous form, or datasheet view is initially presented to the user. After the user is in the form, the *ViewsAvailable* property, set to *Form*, *Datasheet*, or *Both*, determines whether the user can view only the form, only the datasheet, or toggle between the datasheet and form views, respectively. See the Properties Reference section of this book for more information about form properties.

Sizing the Form

Some forms that look great on your super computer system don't look as good or don't fit on the target computer's "plain Jane VGA." The ideal solution to this problem would be if everybody had the same display system, of course. But until then, you can use the recommended ruler measurements described in the following table to make forms fit on a screen displayed with any Windows resolution.

Resolution	*Vertical Size*	*Horizontal Size*	*Available Area*
VGA 640x480	3.5 in.	6.25 in.	21.88 sq. in.
SuperVGA 800x600	4.75 in.	7.75 in.	36.81 sq. in.
1024x768	4.88 in.	8.25 in.	40.26 sq. in.

> **Tip:** If you are using a high-resolution video system for development work, be sure to switch back to the user's video mode when you check the form and controls for sizing. For a polished look after the form is fully designed, switch from the Design view to the Form view, resize the form, then switch back to the Design view and save the form.

Printing Forms

You can print forms; in fact, the form Toolbar includes a Print Preview button for this purpose, and forms you print in Access may look better than any report you've ever seen. One caution about printing forms—if the current view is a continuous form, the printed result may not fit correctly on the printed page. To make the print job easier, Access includes page header and page footer sections similar to the page headers and footers in reports; these sections may contain information normally included in the page header/footer or a report, such as report title, column headings, or logo.

Understanding Form Events

Various events on a form or control can trigger actions attached to the event properties associated with these events; for instance, when the form is opened, the *OnOpen* property of this form is inspected and any action (macro, Access Basic or user-defined function) attached to this property is executed. The event properties described in the following table apply at the form level.

Property	*When Activated*
OnMenu	An event attached to this property occurs first; if a custom menu is attached to a form, it is activated.
OnOpen	The form is drawn on the screen, but no record or control is made *current* (accessible) yet. The form also is not considered current. Therefore any expressions that refer to a current form or current control will trigger an error.

continues

Property	*When Activated*
OnCurrent	Inspected after the focus moves to a different record; useful to conditionally skip a record.
OnInsert	Inspected when a new record is added to the underlying dynaset.
OnDelete	Inspected if a record is deleted from the underlying dynaset; any action attached to this property is triggered after the user chooses to delete a record, but before the record is actually deleted, making the deletion reversible.
BeforeUpdate	Inspected after changes are made to a record but before the record is saved; if a *CancelEvent* action is used in an action attached to this property, the changes to the record are reversed.
AfterUpdate	Inspected after changes are made to a record and the record is saved.
OnClose	Any action attached to this property is triggered when the form is closed.

Form sections don't have any event properties.

Understanding Control Events

Control events are triggered by an event occurring within a control on a form. For example, when the control gains focus (in other words, the control "is entered"), an action attached to the *OnEnter* property of a control is triggered. Control events may be used to check for validation at the field level; to reverse certain actions, such as an update, to trigger Access Basic code, macros, or queries; to open other forms; or even to launch other applications.

The event properties described in the following table are available for controls in Access. Not all events are available for all controls, however; for more detailed information, see the entries for a particular event property in the Properties Reference section of this book.

Property	*When Activated*
OnEnter	Triggered when the control gains focus. Often used to skip a control, based on the value of another control.
BeforeUpdate	Occurs only if the data in the control is updated, before the control loses focus and before the updated data is saved (thus making the update reversible with the *CancelEvent* action).

Property	*When Activated*
AfterUpdate	Occurs only if the data in the control is updated, before the control loses focus, and after the updated data is saved (thus making the update irreversible).
OnDblCLick	Occurs when the control is double-clicked with a mouse.
OnExit	Occurs before the control loses focus. The user can be prevented from exiting a control (for instance, when no valid data is entered) by including a *CancelEvent* action in the action triggered by an *OnExit* event.
ValidationRule	Triggered after changing data in the control but before exiting from the control; prevents exiting the control if an expression attached to this property evaluates to False.
OnPush	Occurs when a command button (push button) is clicked.

Customizing the Form with Controls

There are two basic types of controls: *bound* (a control that is attached, or bound, to a field in an underlying dynaset), and *unbound* (a control that is not directly tied to any data source). A form requires controls to accomplish anything; most forms are used to display and edit data, and usually have many controls bound to data fields. On the other hand, some forms don't use bound controls at all, such as when a form is used as a menu (a *switchboard* in Access lingo) and its only control is to offer the user a choice of push buttons. But the majority of Access forms use a mix of bound and unbound controls. Knowing which control best meets the given task is an important part of mastering controls and their properties.

Controls available in Access are described in the following sections.

Labels 

The simplest of controls, labels are used to identify associated controls with text, to provide instructions, and to identify the form. This control cannot be bound to any data source.

Text Boxes 

Text boxes are the mainstay of forms in most database applications and can be bound to many table field data types (text, numbers, dates, and Boolean types). Text boxes are also very versatile—they can even operate as mini word processors with word wrap and scroll bars!

Option Groups and Logical Controls 

Option groups contain mutually exclusive logical (Yes/No) controls, grouped by function. In other words, one and only one control in an option group can be true at any given time; for example, a person can belong to one and only one age group. Access offers three types of logical controls that indicate a Yes or a No (or True or False) state, as shown in the following table. Any of the three types of logical controls can be bound to a Yes/No field or used as a stand—alone Boolean (Off/On) control.

Control	*Description*
	Toggle buttons—similar to command buttons, but stay pressed when selected.
	Option buttons—often called *radio buttons*.
	Check boxes—Windows traditional check boxes.

List Boxes and Combo Boxes  

A common Windows control, the list box displays the following items:

- Single- or multiple-field data items from an underlying dynaset (although the user can select only one from the list presented)
- Values from a value list
- Field names from a table or query

The kind of data displayed in a list box is based on the setting of its *RowSourceType* property.

A combo box can be viewed as a combination of a text box and a list box. Combo boxes are powerful because they enable the user not only to select from a list, but also to enter new values.

Lines and Rectangles  

Access enables you to use lines and rectangles to improve the appearance and readability of forms. For example, a sunken three-dimensional option group is usually more readable than an option group enclosed in a flat frame. Using sunken and elevated lines and rectangles, together with varying shades of gray, helps to create a chiseled look in your applications and can help group related types of data in a way that is visually easier for the user.

On the other hand, too many lines and rectangles are worse than no visual aids. Publishers use a lot of white space to give the page a clean look, then add lines and rectangles to supply subtle suggestions. The same principles apply to the presentation of information in a form.

Object Frames

You can use the object frame controls to include Windows objects, sound, pictures, and so on in your application.

The *bound object frame* stores the object in the database, where it is editable by the user. *Unbound object frames* embed the object into the form itself. An unbound object frame can be linked to the form, but draws its data from a different query, in a manner similar to subforms and list boxes.

Page Breaks

Page breaks, which do exactly what their name implies, force a new page at a specified point. This simplifies the process of working with long forms. Access scrolls the data in a much more pleasing manner if you control the scroll bar with a page break.

Be sure the page break does not overlap any controls; otherwise, the control can become difficult to read.

Command Buttons

The command button (push button) is one of the most common Windows controls. When a command button is *pushed* (clicked with the mouse), the OnPush event property can trigger a macro or a function to perform almost any task.

Setting the Access AutoRepeat property causes the command button to repeat the action specified in the OnPush property as long as the button is pressed, just as if you press a key on the keyboard and hold it down.

Creating Controls

Access provides numerous methods of creating forms and their controls. You can start from scratch, and place all required fields and controls on a form manually. Or you can begin the form with a Wizard. The Wizard can place desired fields from the underlying dynaset (and their default properties) on the form for you, so you need only polish the result. With complex forms, however, you may need to add and move controls manually, even if you started with a Wizard. For more information on using Wizards, see the section "Jump-Starting Forms with Wizards," later in this chapter.

Creating Controls from the Toolbox

To create controls from the Toolbox, select the type of control to be placed on the form. Clicking on the form while the control is selected creates a new control. Click and hold the mouse button to size the control as it's placed on the form. Use the Lock option to repeatedly place controls of the same type.

> **Tip:** After you decide on a pleasing design, you can easily apply your design standards to all your forms. Simply click on the form portion of the Toolbox (the white space at the top) and then click on each Toolbox element individually, changing color, shading, and border attributes as desired. The next time you select an element from the Toolbox, Access automatically applies the new attributes.

Creating Controls from the Field List

To create controls from the Field List, drag the field from the Field List to the form. As the field is dropped on the form, Access creates a control along with a linked label. The label caption, control status bar, default, validation, and validation text are transferred from the field properties of the underlying table.

To select multiple contiguous fields, press the Shift key and click the mouse. To select noncontiguous fields, Ctrl+click the fields you want. To select the entire list, double-click on the title bar of the Field List; you then can drag multiple fields to the form simultaneously by clicking and dragging any of the selected fields.

Creating Automatic Controls from the Database Window

The Windows *drag-and-drop* technique (selecting an object and dragging it with the mouse to another object) is well implemented in Access. For example, you can use drag-and-drop from the database window to create certain types of controls, such as subforms and command buttons.

By dragging a form from the database window and dropping it on a form that is open in Design view, you automatically create a subform control (without setting the applicable properties!). Dragging a macro from the database window to the form being designed creates a command button control and automatically sets the *OnPush* event property to run this macro. (Alas, for macros in macro groups, you must edit the *OnPush* event to add the name of the macro from the group you want to actually execute.)

Creating Controls from the Clipboard

You can copy controls from one form to another (or even to a different Access database) by using the Windows Clipboard. The controls retain their property settings when copied.

> **Tip:** To paste objects from other Windows applications, use Paste|Special to determine how the pasted data will behave. For example, you can paste text from Word for Windows as text to create a label; or you can paste the text as a link to create an object frame control. The link can be updated automatically from Word, or it can be an OLE link that launches Word to edit the text.

Using a Template to Speed Control Creation

Even if you don't create your forms with a Wizard, you still can speed up the development process by using a form template. The template—a form with preset form, section, and control defaults—can be an existing form or a new form with desired default settings. Just insert the template name in the Form Template setting of the Form & Report Design dialog box, available from the View|Options menu (only the settings, not the form, are transferred to the new form from the template).

> **Note:** If you don't use any specific template, the setting of the Form Template should be Normal (the default); this specifies that newly created forms inherit Access default settings.

Recordset Properties

Every form is based on an underlying dynaset (a table, a query, or a combination of both). The dynaset properties described in the following table manage the way the form works with the dynaset.

Property	*Description*
RecordSource	Specifies the underlying table or query.
AllowUpdating	Determines whether the underlying tables can be updated.
DefaultTables	Specifies whether only bound tables on the many side of a one-to-many relationship can be updated.
AllowEditing	Determines whether the Records|Allow Editing menu command is available; if the form is read-only from the *AllowUpdating* property, the *AllowEditing* property has no effect.
DefaultEditing	Determines the editing mode of the form when opened (edit, update, or insert).

continues

Property	*Description*
AllowFilters	Determines whether the user is able to apply a filter to the form. If set to No, the filter buttons and menu commands are disabled.
RecordLocks	Determines how records are locked in a multiuser setting—can be very restrictive (All Records), very permissive (No Locks) or in-between (Edited Record).

Window Properties

Access forms are displayed in a window, and certain properties determine what the window looks like and how it fits into the rest of the Access database. The following table lists these properties (which also are discussed in depth in the Properties Reference section of this book).

Property	*Description*
Caption	The window title (name at the top of the window).
ScrollBars	Determines whether the form includes scroll bars (horizontal, vertical, or neither).
RecordSelectors	Determines whether the form includes the record selectors at the left side of the form.
ViewsAllowed	Sets the view options available to the user: (Form, Datasheet, or Both).
DefaultView	Determines both the initial view of the form and whether the form is a single form or continuous form when viewed in Form view.
Modal	Determines whether the form retains focus until it is closed.
PopUp	Determines whether the form appears as a pop-up form.

Database Function Properties

This set of properties affects how the control interacts with the underlying dynaset and determines which controls are accessible to the user. The following table describes these properties.

Property	*Description*
ControlName	Specifies the name of the control as used in expressions, macros, and Access Basic. For example Field65.
ControlSource	Specifies the field that the control is bound to, or the expression that is the source of the control.
Enabled	Determines whether the control can have focus. A control with Enabled set to No does not respond to the user clicking on it, nor can the user tab to the control. A disabled control is also dimmed.
Locked	A locked control does not accept any changes. Keystrokes inside the control are ignored.

The Enabled and Locked properties limit or enable user interaction with the control. Combining these two properties gives you considerable control over the actions of an user. (These combinations, and their implications, are discussed at length in the Properties Reference section of this book.)

Lists and combo boxes add the properties described in the following table.

Property	*Description*
BoundColumn	Binds a combo box or list box column to a field specified in the ControlSource property.
ColumnCount	Specifies the number of columns displayed in a combo box or list box, or sent to an OLE object in a graph or object frame.
RowSource	Specifies the source of the data (field, expression).
RowSourceType	Specifies the type of the object's data (table/query, value list, field list).

Note: For more detailed information about the properties listed in the above sections, or other properties not mentioned here, please see the Properties Reference section of this book.

Jump-Starting Forms with Wizards

When you first create a form, Access gives you the choice of beginning with a blank form or using a Wizard to create the form (see fig. 4.7). Developers have a tendency to avoid software that appears to be intended for unsophisticated end-users—but don't let the Wizards fool you. The Wizards can save development time by (at least) placing all the controls on the form quickly. Further, if you have customized the Toolbox, you don't need to fiddle with the appearance of every control. Think of the Wizards as application generators rather than as a Microsoft end-user feature. Wizards are work-horses and should be used as such.

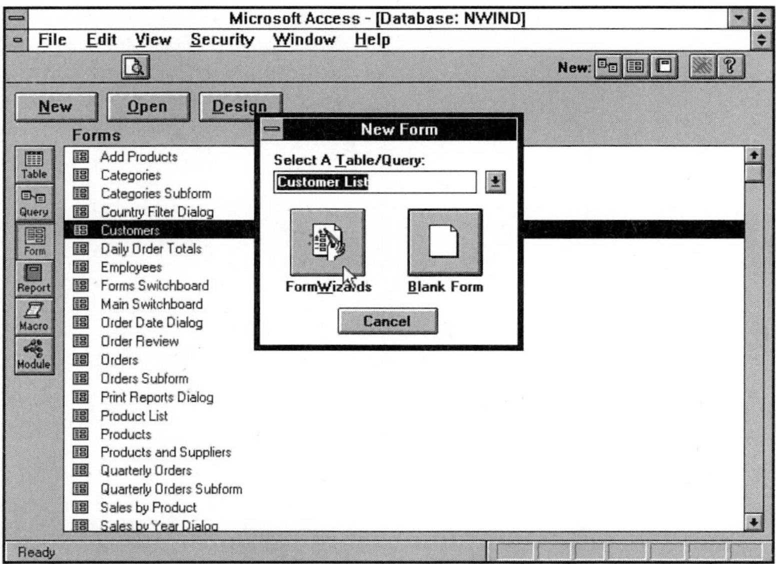

Figure 4.7. Selecting a Wizard.

The Form Wizard also enables you to choose a style for the form. The style incorporates the color scheme and special effects used to polish the controls. Each Wizard style is detailed later in this section.

For more information on writing Wizards, see Chapter 13, "Extending Access and Access Basic."

> **Note:** The Wizards are actually Access Basic programs. The Wizards are packaged in the WIZARD.MDA database and are loaded as a special case of the Access library using the following entry in the MSACCESS.INI file:
>
> ```
> [Libraries]
> C:\ACCESS\wizard.mda=ro
> ```

Access offers four Form Wizards as described in the following paragraphs.

The Single Column Wizard creates standard forms that display one record from the *RecordSource* per detail section. The controls are constructed in one vertical column (see fig. 4.8).

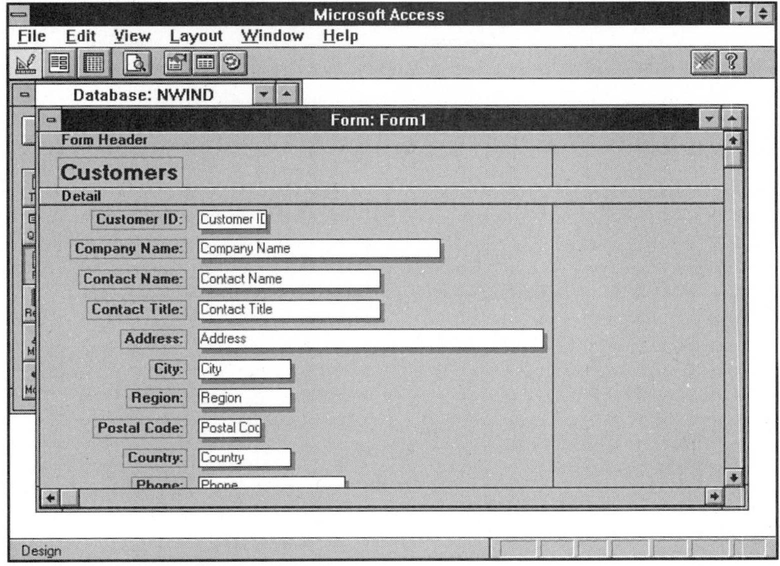

Figure 4.8. A single-column form.

The Tabular Wizard asks the same questions as the Single Column Wizard, but the results are very different. The Tabular Wizard creates horizontally oriented forms consisting of multiple records in a columnar form, similar to that of a telephone directory or a spreadsheet, as shown in figure 4.9.

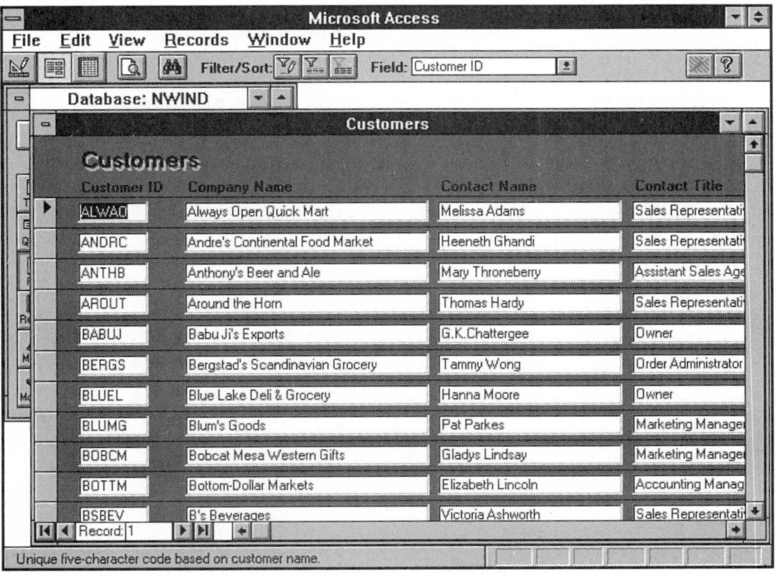

Figure 4.9. A tabular form.

The Graph Wizard sets up an OLE link between Access and the mini-application Microsoft Graph included with Access. The resulting form is one large unbound object frame control. The Wizard uses your field definitions to create a SQL statement for its *RowSource.* The Graph Wizard enables you to select from one of five basic graph types, plus a hi-lo graph (see fig. 4.10). Each basic graph type is available in 2-D or 3-D. The graph can present either totals or averages from the database.

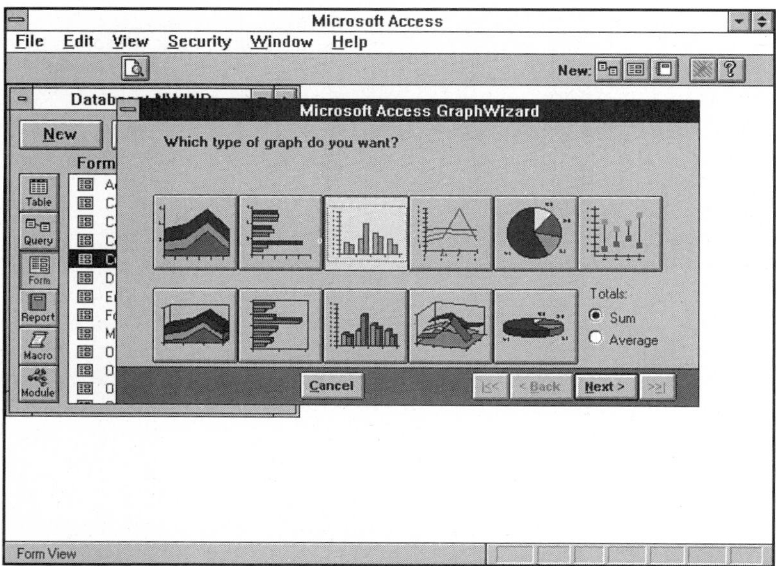

Figure 4.10. Specifying the graph type.

The Main/Subform Wizard is similar to the Single Column Wizard, but includes an embedded subform of related data. Subforms are saved as individual forms that then are embedded in the main form. The Wizard needs to know the name of the subform, so it can include it in the main form. Figure 4.11 shows the form Orders with a superimposed form created by the Main/Subform Wizard.

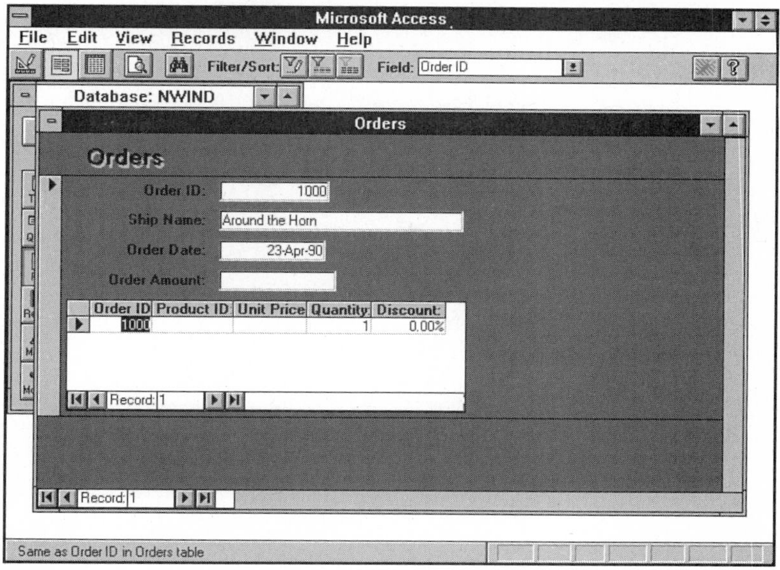

Figure 4.11. The subform created by the Main/SubForm Wizard.

Chapter Summary

Forms are a powerful part of the Access application-development environment. Even if you are an expert programmer, learning to use forms and their robust event properties is crucial to putting together a usable and flexible application. Applying this knowledge with what you learn in the next chapter, "Using Access Basic with Forms," will give you an arsenal of tools that will help shave time off the development cycle.

5

Using Access Basic with Forms

As discussed in Chapter 4, Access Basic forms are flexible and powerful tools that can eliminate a large percentage of the time spent coding the user interface. By combining forms, reports, and macros, you can create some applications without writing a single line of code.

So why use Access Basic code with forms? The answer is simple: some things can be done only with code. If you need to validate a data entry item with more than a single expression, for example, calling a block of Access Basic code is the only sensible solution. You might think of a way to string macros together to do this, but debugging such an operation would be a nightmare.

Or perhaps you want to automatically fill in a list box from data in a table, instead of typing everything manually. Access Basic can automate the job for you.

If you're interested in establishing a dynamic data exchange (DDE) with another application, no macro can do it; once again you need a routine in Access Basic. Instead of just wishing you could create at runtime a form with no scroll bars, no Minimize and Maximize buttons, no system menu, and a custom caption, Access Basic allows you to call Windows API functions to perform this task and many others. No macro has this capability.

Essentially you should consider Access Basic as a means to enhance, but not replace, the built-in design tools provided with Access. Use code to extend the functionality of forms and macros so that you can exercise maximum control over the application environment. Access Basic functions can be attached to the action properties of a form or directly to a control.

This chapter provides an overview of the ways in which Access Basic can be used as a powerful extension of forms, such as the following:

- Calling code from the action properties of a form
- Using forms as menus
- Using code to set the value of fields
- Changing the name of forms at runtime

- Updating values depending on user input

Many of these techniques are undocumented but essential for building the most robust applications.

Calling Code from the Action Properties of a Form

Calling code from any of the action properties (such as *OnPush*, *BeforeUpdate*, or *OnExit*) is useful for performing data lookups and validation, setting the value of other properties based on the value of the current property, activating other objects based on the user's input, and more. One application for this technique is to use forms as menus (as described in the next section). You also can use this technique in less-obvious programming situations, as described later in this section.

> **Note:** Only Access Basic function procedures (not Sub procedures) can be called directly from forms. If you need to call a Sub procedure from within a form, create a function that will in turn call the Sub procedure.

The following list shows the action properties you can use to execute a macro or Access Basic code from various controls on forms. The available control properties vary, depending on the type of control. These properties and controls are fully explained in the properties section of the Reference. Also see Chapter 13, "Extending Microsoft Access and Access Basic," for examples of Access Basic functions that are used to extend Access forms.

Form Properties	**Control Properties**
OnCurrent	BeforeUpdate
OnInsert	AfterUpdate
OnDelete	OnEnter
BeforeUpdate	OnExit
AfterUpdate	OnDblClick
OnOpen	OnPush
OnClose	

Using Forms as Menus

A simple technique for designing a form to be used as a menu is to assemble a collection of command buttons (push buttons) with Access Basic code attached to their *OnPush* properties. This method is less complicated than building a custom menu bar, but just as effective. An example of such a form is the main menu of the sample application provided with this book (see fig. 5.1). The code is attached to all command buttons on this form.

For example, the **SwapMouseButton** Windows API function that toggles the left and right mouse buttons can be directly attached to the *OnPush* property of a command button (see fig. 5.2).

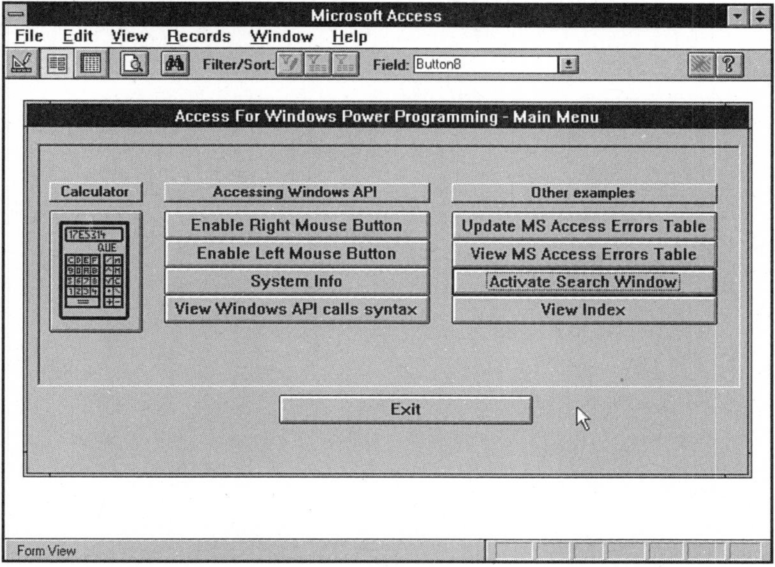

Figure 5.1. Form used as a menu by attaching Access Basic code to push buttons.

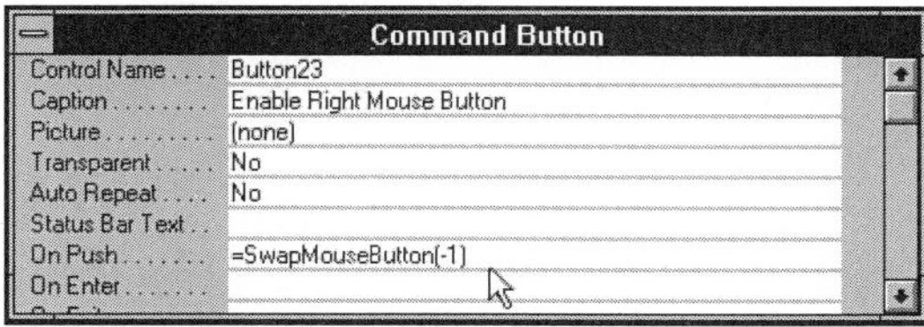

Figure 5.2. Calling a Windows API function from the *OnPush* property of a command button.

> **Note:** The external Windows API function must be declared in the declarations section prior to its use, as shown in the following example:
>
> ```
> Declare Function SwapMouseButton Lib "User" (ByVal i As Integer) As
> Integer
> ```

See Chapter 13, "Extending Microsoft Access and Access Basic," for more information about calling Windows API functions.

Using Code to Set the Value of Fields

In the next example, the values of two fields (City and State), on the form from which the function is called, are set based on the value of the ZIP code field on the same form. The data is obtained from the file State Codes related on the field ZIP:

```
Function LookupCityAndState (cForm As Form, cZip As String)
    Dim cDb As Database, cTb As Table
    Set cDb = CurrentDB()
    Set cTb = cDb.OpenTable("State Codes")
    cTb.index = "Zip"
    cTb.Seek "=", cZip
    If Not cTb.noMatch Then
        cForm.City = cTb.City
        cForm.State = cTb.State
    End If
    cTb.Close
End Function
```

To call this function from a form, simply attach it to the *OnExit* property, as illustrated in figure 5.3. As you can see, the function is mostly generic; only the names of the two fields being updated are hard coded, so it can be called from within any form that contains these two fields, and can be easily modified to use with other fields.

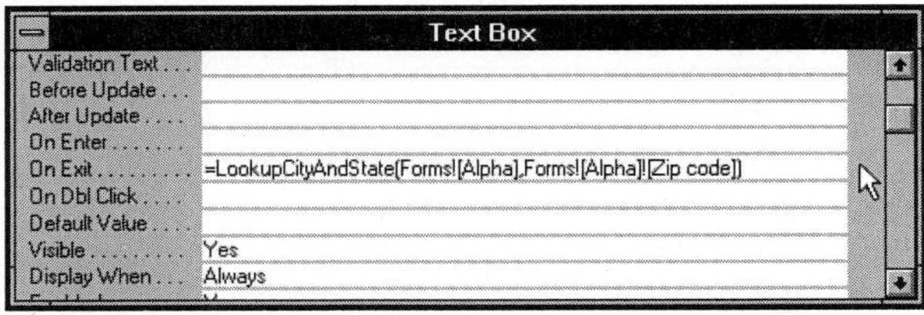

Figure 5.3. Function LookupCityAndState attached to *OnExit* property.

> **Note:** You don't need to return a value from this function because Access ignores the return value of functions attached to the action properties of forms.

Changing the Name of a Form at Runtime

Some uses for code are less obvious. The next example shows how to change the name of a form based on some other event. The function Ranking( ) sets the value of the control named Verbal Ranking on the form Customers based on the contents of the field AppsUsed (evaluated by the Eval function). In the following example, the caption of the form reflects user input:

```
Function Ranking()
    If Eval("Forms!Customers!AppsUsed Between 6 And 9") Then
        Forms!Customers![Verbal Ranking] = "Average Computer User"
    End If
End Function
```

The purpose of this function is to demonstrate that Access Basic, combined with form controls and properties, provides a flexible means with which to exercise control over the runtime environment. It cannot be done with every type of property, but put this capability to use wherever you can. (Even more control over runtime properties should be available in the next release of Access.)

Updating Values Depending on User Input

Perhaps the most common use for functions attached to action properties is to update certain values in Access objects (mainly tables and forms) based on user input, as shown in figure 5.4. In the next example, two forms are open: MainForm and OtherForm. Depending on the value entered in the Customer Name control on MainForm, the form OtherForm will be updated with some data about the customer: spouse's name, income, and phone number.

```
Function OtherFormUpdate (SourceForm As Form, TargetForm As Form)
    TargetForm.Name = SourceForm.Name
    TargetForm.Spouse = SourceForm.Spouse
    TargetForm.Pant = SourceForm.Pant
    TargetForm.Phone = SourceForm.Phone
    TargetForm.Income = SourceForm.Income
End Function
```

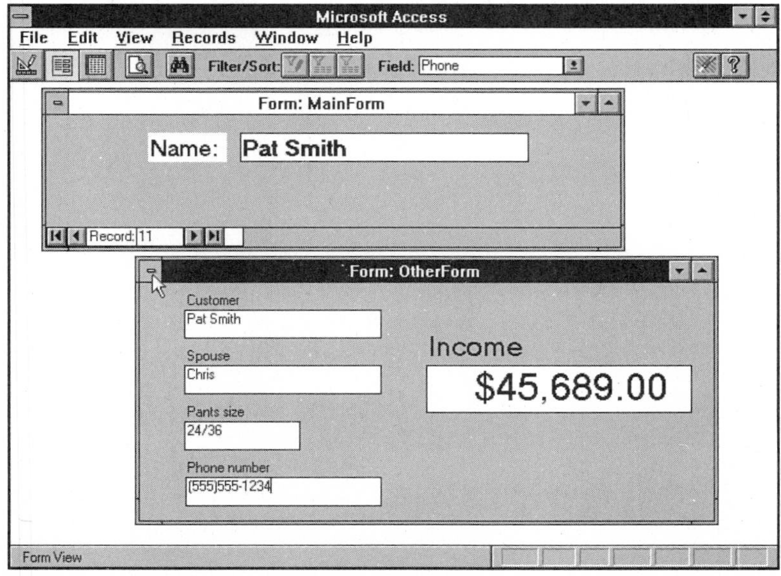

Figure 5.4. Updating OtherForm values based on data entered in MainForm.

The function is attached to the *OnEnter* property of the Customer Name control of the MainForm using the following syntax:

```
= OtherFormUpdate(Forms![MainForm], Forms![OtherForm]
```

The primary benefit of this coding method is that the fields don't have to appear on MainForm to be displayed on OtherForm.

Using Code to Add New Features

Yet another use for attaching code is to furnish capabilities that Access lacks, such as serial communications. The following function—DialPhone—provides very basic phone dialing capabilities. The function accepts two parameters (both String data type) and calls three Windows API functions that must be declared in the declarations section of a module. Without getting any deeper into the complex subject of Windows serial communications, the following example shows the declarations of the three required Windows API serial communication functions (OpenComm, WriteComm, and CloseComm) and the function DialPhone that dials a voice line from within Access. This function, although fully operational, is intended only as a demonstration of Access capabilities, and lacks meaningful error trapping.

First, declare required windows API functions in the declarations section of a module:

```
Declare Function OpenComm Lib "User" (ByVal lpComName As String,
➥ByVal wInQueue As Integer, ByVal wOutQueue As Integer) As Integer
Declare Function WriteComm Lib "User" (ByVal nCid As Integer,
➥ByVal lpBuf As String, ByVal nSize As Integer) As Integer
Declare Function CloseComm Lib "User" (ByVal nCid As Integer) As Integer
```

And here's the function:

```
Function DialPhone (szPhone$, szPort$)
Dim wPort%, wClosePort%
szPort = "COM" & szPort
wPort = OpenComm(szPort, 1024, 128)
If wPort < 0 Then
    MsgBox "Couldn't open specified comm port", , "Dialer"
Else
    ' Initialize modem
    If WriteComm(wPort, "ATE1Q0V1X4S0=0" + Chr$(13), 15) Then
        ' Introduce some delay (give the modem time to respond)
        dwTimer = Timer
        Do
        Loop Until Timer > dwTimer + 5

        ' Dialing successful?
        If WriteComm(wPort, "ATDT" & szPhone & Chr$(13),
        ➥Len(szPhone) + 5) > 0 Then
            ' Give the modem time to dial
            dwTimer = Timer
            Do
```

```
            Loop Until Timer > dwTimer + 5
            MsgBox "Success! Pickup the receiver and
            ➥press OK", , "Dialer"
         Else
            MsgBox "Dialing failed", , "Dialer"
         End If
     End If
     wClosePort= WriteComm(wPort,"ATH", 3)
     wClosePort = CloseComm(wPort)
 End If
 End Function
```

To attach the function DialPhone to the Dial Phone command button (named Button0) on the form Dialer, use the following syntax (see fig. 5.5):

```
=DialPhone(Forms!Dialer.[Phone Number], Forms!Dialer.[CommPort])
```

Figure 5.5. Form Dialer.

Using Functions Attached Directly to a Control

When a function is attached directly to the form's control (to its *RecordSource* property), the value returned by the function becomes the value of the control.

In the following example taken from the System Info form, the control will be updated by the word *Present* or the word *None*, depending on the evaluation of an **If...** construct in the function MathChip( ), which is attached to the control:

```
Function MathChip () As String
    If Flags& And WF_80x87 Then
        MathChip = "Present"
    Else
        MathChip = "None"
    End If
End Function
```

In fact, all controls on the System Info form are filled in by functions attached directly to their Control Source properties (see fig. 5.6).

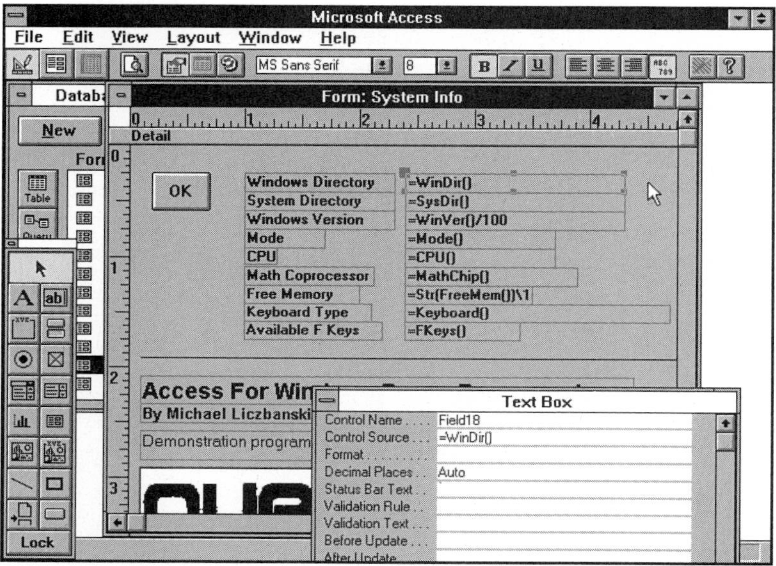

Figure 5.6. Function attached to Control Source property of System Info form.

In the preceding example, controls are not bound to any table field. If you want to store the values in a table, you also need to update the table fields with code, as shown in the following example:

```
(...)
cTable.AddNew
cTable.[Math Coprocessor] = MathChip()
(...)
cTable.Update
```

Writing Reusable Code That Works with Forms

As you can see in the previous examples in this chapter, Access allows a lot of flexibility in referring to its objects, making it possible to write *generic* (reusable) code that can be applied to more than one form, table, and so on. Without this capability, Access Wizards, which are written entirely in Access Basic, would not be possible.

The next section provides some guidelines to help you make your code more generic.

Referring to the Current Form

Use the Forms object to obtain the name of the open form. The following example returns the name of the first open form:

```
Result = Forms(0).FormName
```

You can define a Form control variable and use the value returned by the Forms object to make it refer to a specific form:

```
Dim cForm As Form
Set cForm = Forms(0)
```

You can also refer to the form with a name stored in a string variable. The following example returns the number of controls on the form specified in the *szFormName* string:

```
szFormName = "This form"
Result = Forms(szFormName).Count
```

For more information about the Forms object and other Access objects, see the objects section of the Reference.

You can use the Screen object to obtain the name of the active form or to set the Form variable to refer to a specific form:

```
Result = Screen.ActiveForm.FormName
```

or

```
Dim cForm As Form
Set cForm = Screen.Active Form
```

Many of the preceding methods can also be used to refer to specific controls without knowing the control name:

```
Dim cCtrl As Control
Set cCtrl = Screen.ActiveControl
```

or

```
szControlName = Screen.ActiveControl.ControlName
```

or

```
szFormName = "Form1"
szControlName = "Button49"
Forms(szFormName)(szControlName).Enabled = True
```

In any case, referring to a form and its controls requires either creating a Form control variable or using one of the Access objects—Forms or Screen.

Let's apply the above methods to a more robust piece of code. The function in the following example opens any form specified in the *szFormName* variable as an icon in Design mode and changes its title (depending on the value returned by the User function) and the width of the control that displays the title.

For simplicity, the user's input has already been assigned to memory variables. The title is displayed by the Label specified in the *szControlName* variable. The width is expressed in twips. For security we'll check to see if the control type of the control specified in *szControlName* variable is Label and whether it is located in the form header section (section number 1):

```
Dim szFormName$, szControlName$, szCaption, cCtrl As Control

szFormName = "Computer Time"
szControlName = "FormTitle"
szCaption = "Computer time used by user " & User()

DoCmd OpenForm szFormName, A_DESIGN, , , , A_ICON
Set cCtrl = Forms(szFormName)(szControlName)
If TypeOf cCtrl Is Label Then
   If Forms(szFormName)(szControlName).Section = 1 Then
      Forms(szFormName)(szControlName).Caption = szCaption
      Forms(szFormName)(szControlName).Width = 4000
   End If
End If
DoCmd Close A_FORM, szFormName
```

This example demonstrates yet another way to use Access Basic with forms to exercise more control over their behavior and properties.

Some Caveats about Generic Code

The type of coding demonstrated in the preceding examples is particularly useful in writing Wizards and library code. Unfortunately, the more generic the code gets, the more overhead it incurs (notice that there is no error checking and very little exception handling in the preceding code). This can slow performance and increase memory requirements.

Also, the development effort to develop fully generic applications and libraries is enormous! Compare the unstable performance of the ORDENTRY sample application provided with Access with the polished and smooth appearance of Access Wizards. Underneath every Access Wizard, however, lies very complex and optimized Access Basic code that takes a lot of time to write and test.

Chapter Summary

We hope that the examples in this chapter have encouraged you to try out some Access Basic routines to extend and enhance the functionality of Access forms. But remember the basic rule: custom code should be used only when necessary—when there is no Access built-in tool to do the job. Still, it is reassuring to have a powerful language to keep you from "hitting the wall" when you need to do something that only some old-fashioned programming can handle.

6

Mastering Queries

If any one object embodies the philosophy and power of Access, it is the query. Access queries provide recordsets for forms, reports, and other queries. Attached tables are treated by Access as queries as well. The omnipresence of queries makes a full understanding of queries and dynasets one of the most important factors in mastering Access.

Queries create *dynasets*, which serve as the link between tables and the front-end objects that the user sees—forms, graphs, and reports. The query-generated dynaset ties Access together. A form or report can be no more powerful than its underlying query. Whenever you create a form, Access creates a dynaset based on the underlying table or query and links it to the form.

Although other databases include a query tool, developers often view the tool as a simple end-user feature; and often, it is. Not so with Access. True, Access's "query by example" is user friendly; but in the mind of a developer, the query object becomes Access's power tool. A clever query solves problems that otherwise can consume days or weeks of code in a traditional database language. In addition, queries execute much faster than Access Basic code (such as *Do...Loop*) that traverses a recordset. To add even more flexibility, queries can be defined programmatically in Access Basic.

This chapter discusses Access query types and constructing and using various types of queries. You learn how to use queries with Access Basic and how to construct queries programmatically. This chapter also introduces several Access Basic programming methods for using queries in Access Basic, such as filling a list box on a form with selections using Access Basic code.

Introduction to Queries

Access uses a query-by-example (QBE) grid as a graphical method of assembling a query. Except for expressions, you can build an entire query with mouse actions. The *query design view* is split in halves (see fig. 6.1). The upper half holds the field lists of the data sources being combined by the query. The lower portion is used to assemble the query. Each column is used for a field, and each row sets one property.

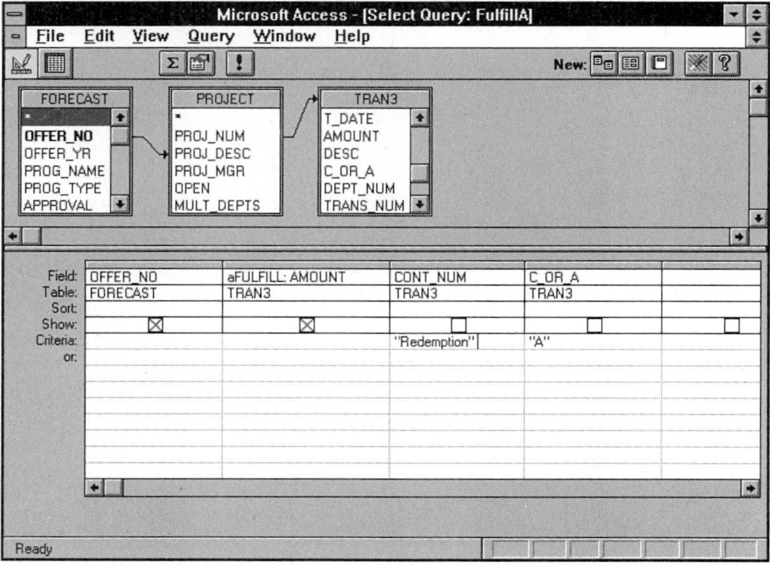

Figure 6.1. A Select query in QBE view.

Results of Select queries are presented in a *datasheet view*. The datasheet view, which presents many records in a table format, provides an easy way to navigate the often large dynasets that result from queries. Switching to the datasheet view or running the query brings up the datasheet.

Access assembles the query design from the QBE into a SQL statement (see fig. 6.2). SQL is the core of the query object. You call up an editable SQL statement by choosing View|SQL. The *SQL view* is the true representation of the query. When you save a query to disk, it is the SQL statement that is recorded.

Understanding Query Types

Access uses two basic categories of queries: Select and Action. *Select* queries extract information and perform analyses without making any changes to the data source. *Action* queries also extract information, but they edit or append data back to the data source or create new data tables. Action queries can be Make Table, Update, Append, and Delete.

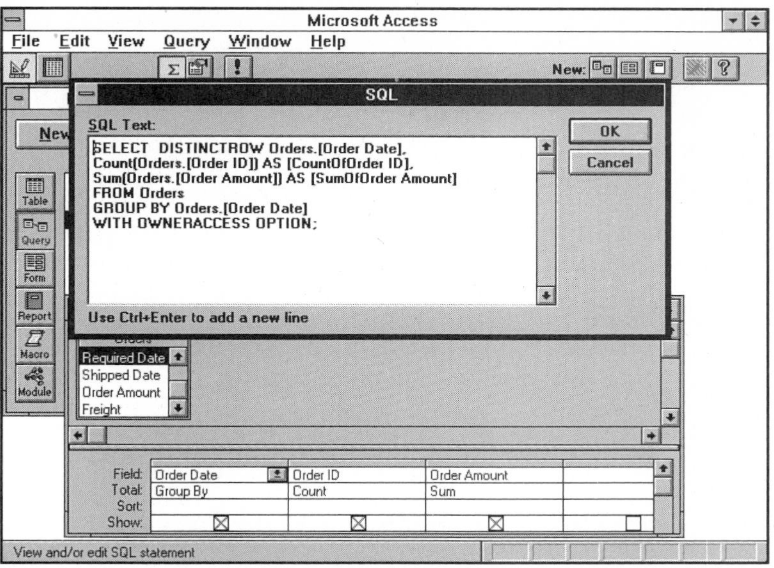

Figure 6.2. A query in SQL view.

One special set of Action queries is sometimes considered a separate type of query. These Aggregate (or Total) queries perform summary operations on recordsets. Aggregate queries are available only to *Select*, *Make Table*, and *Append* queries and cannot be used with *Crosstab*, *Delete*, or *Update* queries.

Select Queries

The most common query type in Access is the *Select* query. You use Select queries to extract information as the basis for most forms and reports.

The Select query includes all the components for a SQL select statement: tables and fields, sort order, expressions and calculations, and a means for setting the record selection criteria.

Crosstab Queries

Another version of the Select query is the *Crosstab* query. This useful analysis tool creates a dynaset for comparing the values of two fields. The Crosstab query lists the value of one field across as column headings, and the values of a second field as row identifiers (see fig. 6.3). A third field or expression is calculated for each value intersection to provide a clear picture of relationships and trends. You also can use the Crosstab query as the basis for reports (which can add totals and groups) and Graph forms. The results of this query are presented in a spreadsheet style, as shown in figure 6.4.

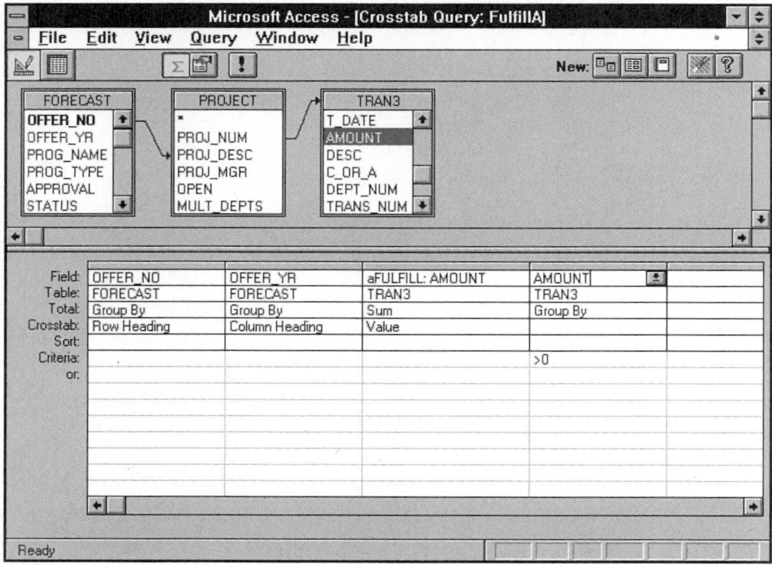

Figure 6.3. Design view of a Crosstab query.

Microsoft Access - [Crosstab Query: FulfillA]

File Edit View Records Layout Window Help

Field: OFFER_NO New:

OFFER_NO	1990	1991	1992	1993
1042				
1043				
1044				10
1044				31
1044				62
1044				69
1044				135
1044				175
1044				204
1044				219
1045				13
1045				38
1045				250
1045				264
1046				5
1046				14
1046				96
1046				103
1046				188
1047				
1048				8
1048				25
1048				100
1048				167
1048				180
1049				8

Record: 53

Datasheet View

Figure 6.4. Results of a Crosstab query.

Action Queries

Action queries enable the user to create new tables or make calculated changes to several selected records in one or more tables in one pass. After the records are selected and the action is defined, Access performs a global update on the records in the dynaset. Action queries come in several types, as described in the following sections.

Action queries are defined using the same basic principles as Select queries. Rather than reporting the selected data, Action queries perform a database operation on the selected records.

You can convert a Select query to an Action query by choosing the query type you want—Make Table, Update, Append, or Delete—from the Query menu. Action queries are indicated in the database window with an exclamation point beside the Query icon.

Creating Tables with Make Table Queries

Make Table queries extract information from the current table(s) and create an entirely new table in the current database or a different database. A Make Table query creates a dynaset in the same manner as a Select query. But when you execute the query, a table is created from the dynaset. This fact is particularly useful when you must export data, because dynasets (the results of executing a query) cannot be exported—only tables may be exported.

The Make Table query is useful for creating a subset of data—for example, as part of automated export routines or for purging old records. If you want to perform a series of analyses on a month's data, for example, you can export just that month's data to a new table and then perform the analysis from the new table.

Creating Records with Append Queries

The *Append query* is a variation of the Make Table query. Both queries select records, but the Append query adds records to an existing table in the current or another database.

The Append query offers the option of appending all fields (by dragging the asterisk onto the field column) or individual fields. You also can specify the name of the field to which the data should be appended in the receiving table.

Performing Updates with Update Queries

Update queries add an update row to the QBE grid. The query performs the calculation in the update row and writes the results back to the database. Combined with the parameters from a control on a form, these queries can save time and are faster than writing Access Basic code to accomplish the same thing.

This type of action query is particularly useful for posting calculation results and performing selective transactional processing. (For more information, see this chapter's section on creating queries with Access Basic.) Because you can make global changes to many records with just a few clicks of the mouse, use update queries judiciously, and—just to be safe—you may want to make a copy of the table to be updated before you execute the query.

Deleting Data with Delete Queries

Delete queries, as the name implies, delete selected records. A Delete query selects records in a manner similar to a Select query, and then deletes them. As a precaution, create the Delete query as a Select query first, run the Select query to ensure that the correct records are selected, and print a copy for safekeeping (or even create a table with the records to be deleted and store it somewhere for safekeeping). Then convert the query to a Delete query.

Aggregate (Total) Queries

The Totals option on the Views menu adds aggregate capabilities to Select, Make Table, and Append queries to create an *Aggregate query*. The Total row of the query design window is used to perform calculations on the selected data to produce aggregate totals including Group By, Sum, Avg, Min, Max, Count, SdDev, Var, First, Last, Expression, and Where.

> **Note:** Every column of the Aggregate query must use one of the **Totals** functions. The default function is Group By.

An example of an Aggregate query is shown in figure 6.5. This query counts the number of orders and sums order amounts for a particular employee. The resulting dynaset has one record for each employee, consisting of employee name, employee ID, number of orders, and total of orders.

Creating Simple Access Queries

You create a new query from the database window. Select the Query icon and click the New button. Access generates a new query grid and displays a list of available record sources (tables and queries).

A faster way to initiate a new query is to highlight, in the database window, the existing table or query on which the new query is to be based. Then choose File|New Query. Access creates a new query and places the selected table or query in the new query's QBE window. As the next section demonstrates, you easily can add tables to the query, so don't worry about getting it perfect.

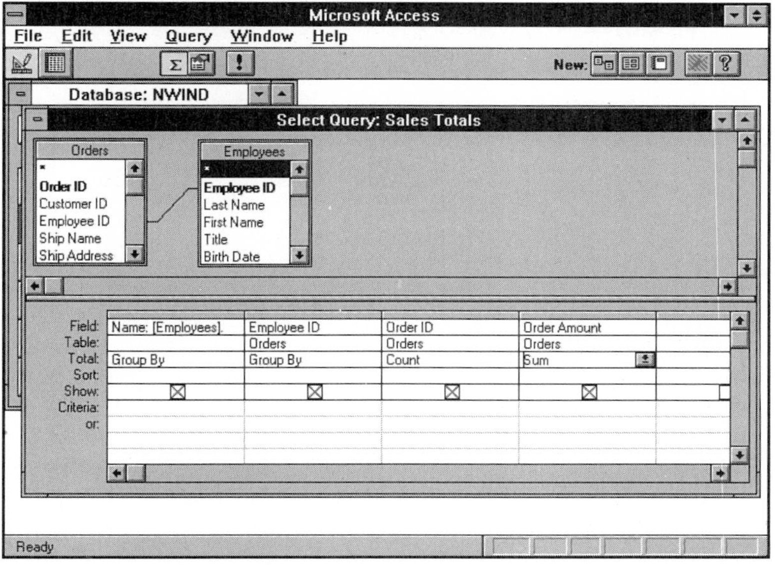

Figure 6.5. An Aggregate query.

Selecting Fields

You must specify which fields to add to the query dynaset. You can add fields to the query by taking one of the following actions:

- Typing the field name directly into the Field row.
- Dragging the field from the Field list to a column in the QBE grid. You also can select multiple contiguous fields from the Field list by holding down the Shift key and clicking on the desired fields with the mouse (or use the down or up arrow); or use the Ctrl key with the mouse (or the up or down arrow) to select individual fields and move them in a group to the query grid. Double-clicking the title of the Field list selects all the fields. You then can drag the multiple fields to the QBE grid.
- Dragging the asterisk (*) from the Field list to the QBE grid. In SQL, the asterisk represents all the fields in a table. The benefit of using the asterisk is that if your underlying table expands, the query automatically reflects any new fields that are added to the table.
- Selecting the field name from the pull-down list, which you access through the Field row in the QBE grid.

You can reorder fields by highlighting the column and dragging the column to a new position—the same way you reorder columns in the datasheet.

Specifying the Sort Method

Access enables you to sort by most fields (with the exceptions of Memo, Yes/No, or OLE fields) regardless of whether the field is indexed.

If the Sort row in the QBE grid is left empty, the query is not sorted on this field. Select ascending or descending sort order from a pull-down combo box to enable the sort. The left-to-right order of the fields in the QBE determines the sort order. You can sort by up to 10 columns.

> **Tip:** To speed query execution, make sure that key fields are indexed.

Adding Fields to the Query Dynaset

Use the Show option (toggled by a checkbox in the QBE window) to make the field a part of the output dynaset. Removing the check from the checkbox enables a field to be present for specifying criteria or building an expression, but does not include the field in the resulting dynaset.

You may want to display all records for a particular city may, for example. You would include the field containing the city in the query, and specify the city name in the Criteria row, but toggle its display off (by removing the check in the checkbox). The query runs based on the criteria you specified but does not clutter your dynaset with the name of the city repeated over and over for each record.

> **Note:** A field that is not shown is not a part of the resulting dynaset, and therefore is unavailable to forms or reports based on the query.

Using Queries to Solve Complex Problems

Access queries provide the muscle with which you can accomplish even highly complex data manipulation operations. By using queries imaginatively, you can eliminate hours of writing Access Basic code. The following sections introduce the ways in which queries can be customized to perform almost any task.

Filtering Data with Criteria

Record selection from underlying query recordsets is based on the expressions entered in the Criteria rows beneath field names. Criteria entered in the same row are considered to be "AND-ed" together.

Criteria on separate rows are "OR-ed" together. The criteria may use any valid Boolean (True/False) or SQL expression.

Figures 6.6 and 6.7 demonstrate the difference between the "Or" and "And" criteria. Figure 6.6 displays the QBE grid for a query that will select Customers from London whose income exceeds 50,000 (in other words, the criteria for record selection will be "[City] = "London" And [Income] > 50000").

The query shown in figure 6.7 uses the same table (Customers) to select customers from London whose income exceeds 50,000, or customers from Paris whose income exceeds 80,000. The criteria now reads "([City] = "London" And [Income] > 50000) Or ([City] = "Paris"] And [Income] > 80000)"

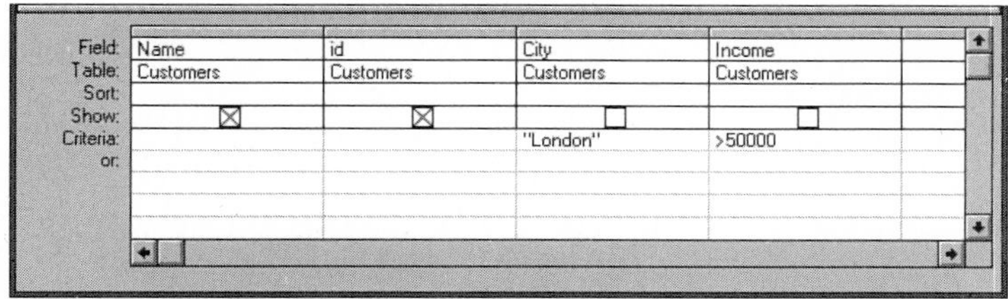

Field:	Name	id	City	Income
Table:	Customers	Customers	Customers	Customers
Sort:				
Show:	☒	☒	☐	☐
Criteria:			"London"	>50000
or:				

Figure 6.6. A Select query using "And" record selection criteria.

Field:	Name	id	City	Income
Table:	Customers	Customers	Customers	Customers
Sort:				
Show:	☒	☒	☐	☐
Criteria:			"London"	>50000
or:			"Paris"	>80000

Figure 6.7. A Select query with the "Or" and "And" record selection criteria.

> **Note:** And and Or also can be used to explicitly specify criteria, such as "London" or "Paris" or "Istanbul" in the criteria row.

The Criteria row becomes the part of the WHERE clause of the resulting SQL statement. Figure 6.8 shows the SQL statement that this query generates.

To specify criteria other than "equal to", in which the **=** operator is assumed, you need to use criteria operators. The following table displays valid criteria operators.

Operator	*Explanation*
=	equal to (often assumed)
<	less than
>	greater than
<>	not equal
=>	equal to or greater than
=<	equal to or less than
between	between...and...
like	like <pattern>

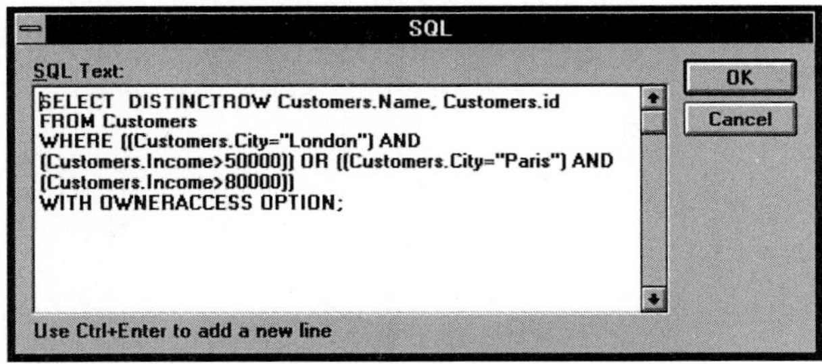

Figure 6.8. The WHERE part of the SQL string.

The query example shown in figure 6.9 selects customers named "Smith" living in a state with an abbreviation code that starts with the letter *C* (California, Colorado), with income between $100,000 and $200,000.

> **Note:** The equals sign in the Criteria row in the Name column can be omitted (it is assumed).

One of the important issues when specifying sorting criteria is precedence (the order in which the criteria will be applied to selected fields). The rule of thumb is to select first the most general criteria, and then narrow the search to more specific criteria. In the query shown in figure 6.9, all customers named Smith will be selected first. Then, only those Smiths with incomes between $100,000 and $200,000 will be selected. Finally, only those Smiths with incomes between $100,000 and $200,000 who live in a state whose code starts with the letter *C* will be selected.

Field:	Name	id	Income	State
Table:	Customers	Customers	Customers	Customers
Sort:				
Show:	☒	☒	☒	☒
Criteria:	="Smith"		Between 100000 And 200000	Like "C*"
or:				

Figure 6.9. A Query using various criteria operators.

> **Tip:** Because the order of criteria precedence can significantly influence the speed of executing a query, experiment with various orders of criteria and select the one that executes fastest, while still producing the desired output—especially when dealing with large datasets. To determine the criteria precedence, check the SQL statement generated by the query by selecting the View SQL command from the Query menu.

Setting Query Properties

You can set query properties to customize Select queries. The properties are available from the View menu in query Design view or by clicking the Toolbar Properties button. Figure 6.10 shows the Query Properties dialog box.

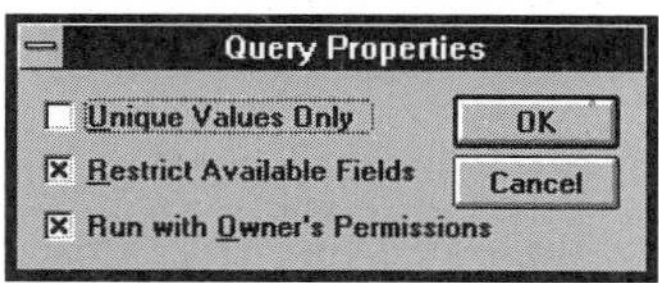

Figure 6.10. The Query Properties dialog box.

The following list describes the query properties:

- *Unique Values Only*. The query retrieves unique data values. This property is similar to performing a Group By calculation on every field in the query. Use this option when you don't want to see duplicates of the same information. If this option is enabled, it is translated in the SQL string as SELECT DISTINCT.
- *Restrict Available Fields*. This property determines whether all the fields in the underlying tables are available to the dynaset. If the fields are restricted, then only those added to the QBE grid with the Show property enabled are in the dynaset. With *Restrict Available Fields* off, every field is included, regardless of the field's Show setting. This powerful

feature enables you to build queries that include many fields from multiple record sources, and then to add to the grid only the fields used for sorting and selecting. Without this property, some query grids would be extremely large and difficult to navigate. If this option is enabled, an asterisk is inserted after the last field in the SELECT clause of the SQL statement. For example:

```
SELECT Customers.Name, Customers.id, Customers.Income,
  Customers.State, Customers.m_date, *
```

- *Run with Owner's Permissions*. This property enables users to use the results of a query when they normally would not be allowed to because of the lack of permission for this particular object. This property enables you to freely create queries and use them in forms or reports, without worrying, from a security standpoint, about which query is used for which form or report. The table and form or report's security permissions are used to determine whether the user can run the form or report without problems from the query. See Chapter 2, "Working with the Access Database," for detailed information on securing systems. If this option is enabled, it is translated in the SQL string as WITH OWNERACCESS OPTION.

Using Expressions in Queries

You can use expressions to combine fields, to perform calculations, or to make a decision. For example, if a Phone Contacts table stores customer data for a person's last name, first name, and salutation in separate fields (as it should), it can be very helpful to display this data as "Mrs. Pamela Brown" on a form used to actually contact the customer. This requires concatenating (adding together) the fields necessary to create the output string.

You can speed up a form's record selection by performing calculations or string concatenations in the query instead of in an unbound control in the form. The only drawback to this approach is that calculated fields in the dynaset produced by the query cannot be updated.

To create an expression in the QBE grid, you can enter the expression, beginning with an equal sign (=) in the Field row. Alternatively, if you want to name the expression, use a name followed by a colon. The expression can be any valid expression, including Access Basic functions, user-defined functions, constants, or literal strings. Mathematical operators are allowed, and the concatenation operator (&) can combine text. (See the Access Operators section in the Reference for more information about creating expressions with operators.)

Access names expression columns with the word `Expr`*n*`:` (where *n* is the sequential number assigned to the expression). You can rename the column by editing the text before the colon. Changing the name is especially useful if the query is going to be used as a record source. While designing a form, working with a Total field is much easier than working with an Expr1 field. For example:

Expr1:[Amount][Tax]*

can be changed to:

TotalDue:[Amount][Tax]*

> **Caution:** The name that identifies the expression is used to refer to the column when the query is used as a record source in a form, report, or other query. If you change the name, forms or reports that used the previous name as a record source will produce an error.

Grouping Records with Aggregate Functions

A dynaset produced by an Aggregate query dynaset does not include individual records. Instead, the query reports totals, averages, and other summary data. Adding aggregate totals to queries enables you to extract summary information from tables and dynasets. The aggregate function is set from the pull-down combo box in the QBE grid's Totals column. The column is turned on with the View Totals menu command or by choosing the Totals button on the query design view toolbar.

As indicated earlier, Aggregate queries can be built from Select, Append, or Make Table queries. The Append and Make Table queries write the aggregate result to the disk, and the Select Aggregate query creates a dynaset which can be used for reports and graphs.

An Aggregate query accomplishes a task similar to those accomplished with the Access Basic domain aggregate functions (such as DSum, DCount, and associated functions) or with Access Basic SQL aggregate functions, such as Avg or Min. The Aggregate query has the benefit, however, of its capability to be combined with other queries and used as the basis for reports and graphs. The Aggregate query also is speedier than the equivalent Access Basic code.

The following sections discuss the aggregate operators available in the query design view.

Grouping Data

Group By is the most commonly used Aggregate function. The **Group By** function is used to group records for summary analysis. An Aggregate Select query from a sales table, for example, can group by salesperson to produce averages and total sales.

The **First** and **Last** functions pull specific records from the underlying table or tables. These functions can be used to include nonaggregate data in the query; however, a nested query (discussed later in this chapter) may be a cleaner alternative.

Using Mathematical and Statistical Functions

Mathematical and statistical Aggregate functions provide the basis for mathematical/statistical calculations in queries. These functions are **Sum**, **Avg**, **Min**, **Max**, and **Count**.

Standard Deviation and Variance are statistical methods of determining the bell curve or consistency of the number group. These functions are named in Access Basic **StDev** and **Var**.

Creating Flexible Queries by Defining Parameters

Adding parameters to queries is a quick and simple way to make any query flexible. Parameters enable you to ask specific questions whenever the query is run. These parameters can be used in expressions to specify the criteria or as factors in performing calculations. A parameter query can be useful for printing reports for a range of dates, for example, because the query can prompt the user for the dates to use.

> **Note:** Other methods of setting the value of parameters at runtime are discussed in the section "Using Access Basic with Parameter Queries," later in this chapter.

Basing any form or report on a parameter query can benefit users. When the form or report is loaded and Access runs the query to create the dynaset for the form or report, the parameter questions are displayed for the user.

You declare a parameter within an expression by enclosing it with brackets. "[Please enter the Month]" is an example of a valid parameter. When the query is run, a dialog box with the message `Please enter the Month` appears on the user's screen.

If you choose to declare the parameter and its data type, use the Parameter option from the Query menu. The Query Parameters dialog box lists all the parameters for the current query (see fig. 6.11).

Query parameters don't need to be explicitly declared, but doing so improves the performance of the query. The data types of parameters (declared at the beginning of the SQL statement that executes the query) are known to the query engine and can be incorporated into its optimization process, as shown in figure 6.12.

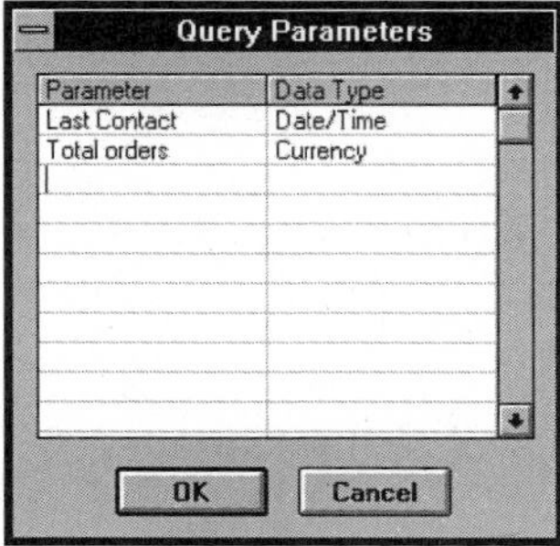

Figure 6.11. The Query Parameters dialog box for specifying parameters.

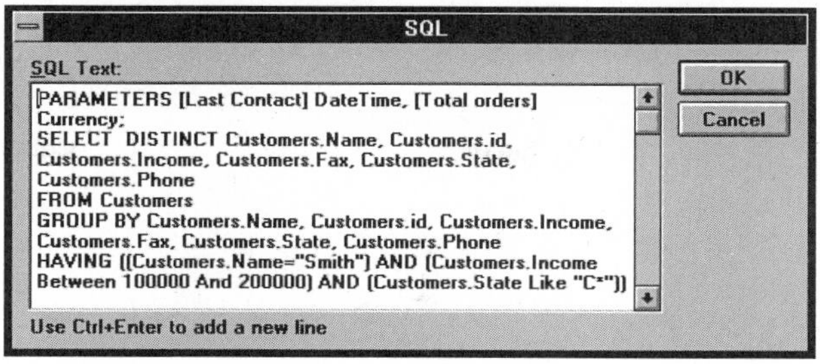

SQL

SQL Text:

```
PARAMETERS [Last Contact] DateTime, [Total orders]
Currency;
SELECT  DISTINCT Customers.Name, Customers.id,
Customers.Income, Customers.Fax, Customers.State,
Customers.Phone
FROM Customers
GROUP BY Customers.Name, Customers.id, Customers.Income,
Customers.Fax, Customers.State, Customers.Phone
HAVING ((Customers.Name="Smith") AND (Customers.Income
Between 100000 And 200000) AND (Customers.State Like "C*"))
```

OK

Cancel

Use Ctrl+Enter to add a new line

Figure 6.12. A sample SQL statement with predefined parameters.

Working with Fields from Multiple Sources

Queries can combine data from many sources. You can add tables to an existing query by dragging the new table from the database window to the query or by using the Add Table menu command. Any default relationship between the two tables is displayed as a line connecting the related fields. If the primary key involves multiple fields, each field is connected. (Primary keys are discussed in Chapter 1, "Modeling Data," and in Chapter 3, "Working with Access Tables.")

Note: Because related tables often use the same field name (such as Customer ID in both Customers and Orders tables), a query with multiple data sources can be confusing in the QBE grid and can generate an `Ambiguous Field Reference` error. You can avoid this error by specifying the name of the field's source table, and by adding a label in front of the field name (such as CustID:ID). To add a Table row, which displays the name of the column source (table or query) to the QBE grid, use the View|Table Names menu choice.

Tip: Although an Access query doesn't indicate the primary or secondary tables in default relationships, it does bold the primary key (PK) of any table. Because a table defined in a relationship as a primary table must have a primary key, the bold highlighting is an easy way to identify the primary table of the relationship while in the Query view.

To remove a table from the query, select a field in the table's Field list and press Delete, or choose Delete from the Edit menu.

> **Caution:** When you remove a table, you also remove all columns using that table's fields. If you are removing a table so that you can reintroduce a newer version of the same table, add the new table first, before removing the old table. If any field names have changed, the query columns containing the old names will be converted to expressions!

Some queries produce read-only dynasets. You cannot edit the data within a dynaset produced by Crosstab queries and Aggregate queries, for example. Also, if the Unique Values Only property is set, the dynaset becomes read-only. Further, you cannot edit columns that are based on expressions. Some joins also produce read-only queries. This is because Access will always attempt to prevent illogical updates to underlying tables; or in more technical terms, it will always seek to ensure the referential integrity of two or more joined tables.

So, when creating a query for a form from related tables, you must be careful to include the correct fields. If you don't include the correct fields in the query, the form becomes read-only.

A classic example of this situation occurs when you are creating a form that includes data from the secondary table (many records) that also include fields from the related primary table (one record). These queries have a limitation: If any fields from a one-to-many secondary table are included in the query, the primary table becomes read-only.

This is logical, because updating any fields in the primary table (such as the Customer ID field that links customers with orders in the Orders table) could "orphan" the related item records for a particular customer. Therefore, fields from the primary table become read-only on the form. In Access terminology, this is called a *Consistent* dynaset (as opposed to an *Inconsistent* dynaset in which records from both the primary and secondary tables can be updated). For more information on this topic, see "CreateDynaset" in the methods section of the Reference.

For more information on designing relational forms, see Chapter 4, "Designing Forms."

Nesting Queries

One of Access's most powerful and flexible capabilities is that of the nested query or cascading query. Instead of building a dynaset from one or many tables, a nested query can include other queries, often mixed with tables. To add a query to the query design window, you drag it from the database window in the same manner as you drag a table, or select the query from the Add Table dialog box. The SQL statements that Access somehow generates from complex nested queries will give you an even greater appreciation of this capability.

An example of a nested query is combining an Aggregate query (which cannot include fields not used to perform the aggregate function) with a table containing the fields you want to display. The resulting dynaset can include Aggregate functions, meaning that the records from the table can be selected using the result of the Aggregate query.

Queries can be nested 50 levels deep, although this is seldom necessary or advisable. The practical limit of nesting also is dictated by memory. Because Query compilation is limited to a 64K memory segment, large complex queries—or those nested too deep—may abort with an `Out of memory` error. The only way to run such a query is to simplify it by deleting columns from any of the chained queries or decreasing the nesting depth.

> **Note:** If *any* query in the chain of nested queries is read-only, the final query becomes read-only. This usually doesn't pose a problem for reports, where data is read-only anyway, but it can shut down a form in a hurry (forms, no matter how elegant, cannot enable the user to enter data into a read-only dynaset). For this reason, if you need an updatable, nested query, you must test it every time you add an object or field column to make sure that it is still updatable.

Understanding Complex Joins

In Access, you are not limited to combining tables with the default relationships. You can create ad-hoc joins within the query object by using operators. The Join operation enables Access to produce a dynaset, and thereby to use data from two tables as if the tables were merged into one. This capability unleashes a powerful feature—the capability to use different joins with different queries and dynasets.

The type of join determines how the tables are merged, as described in the following sections.

Using Inner Joins

A default relationship is an *inner join*. Inner joins (also called *equi-joins*) include only those records from each table with associated data identical to that in the other table, and therefore constitute a one-to-one relationship. Records in either table without a match in the other table are not added to the resulting dynaset.

If only the values "CCC" and "DDD" appear in both table A and table B, for example, an inner join of table A and table B results in a set with only the values "CCC" and "DDD". Consider the following example in which table A (describing countries and their capitals) is joined with table B, which contains data on countries and the continents on which they lie.

Table A (Left table)

Joined Field A	**Other Field A**
USA	Washington D.C.
England	London
Russia	Moscow
Libya	Benghazi
Canada	Ottawa
Eritrea	Asmara

Table B (Right table)

Joined Field B	**Other Field B**
USA	North America
England	Europe
Iraq	Asia
Eritrea	Africa
Brazil	South America
Poland	Europe

Inner joined dynaset

Joined Field	**Other Field A**	**Other Field B**
USA	Washington D.C.	North America
England	London	Europe
Eritrea	Asmara	Africa

An inner join is not limited to a one-to-one relationship between associated records, as in the preceding example. If table B had numerous records with values equal to values in table A, many records in table B would be associated with a single record in table A. The inner join would have formed a one-to-many relationship.

> **Note:** In a one-to-many relationship, data elements in the "one" table, called a *primary table*, must be unique. The relational database model uses a unique primary key in the primary table to uniquely identify each data element in the child table—for example, a unique customer ID to identify all orders for a particular customer. (Primary keys are discussed in Chapter 1 "Modeling Data" and in Chapter 3, "Working with Access Tables.")

The next example, using a classic customer table and order table relationship, demonstrates a one-to-many inner join.

Customer Table

Name	Address
ABC Corp	LA, CA
Smith Bros.	NY, NY
Prentice Hall	Carmel, IN

Order Table

Name	Order #
ABC Corp	930001
ABC Corp	930002
Smith Bros.	930003
Prentice Hall	930004
Prentice Hall	930005

The inner join produces a set of data as shown in the following example.

Name	Address	Order #
ABC Corp	LA, CA	930001
ABC Corp	LA, CA	930002
Smith Bros.	NY, NY	930003
Prentice Hall	Carmel, IN	930004
Prentice Hall	Carmel, IN	930005

As you can see, the join in the preceding example presents all orders for all customers; this type of join is used most frequently to produce invoices, orders, and so on. This use of an inner join with one unique key is similar in function to the parent-child database model found in other hierarchical databases, such as DataFLEX.

Using Outer Joins

Outer joins are similar in function to inner joins, but include unassociated records from one or the other table. These joins include all the records from one table and limit the records from the related table to those with matches. Another way to picture an outer join is as an inner join that includes the outsiders from one of the source tables. Outer joins are described as *left* or *right*, depending on which table is fully included in the join. The first table is considered to be the left table.

Outer joins are indicated in the query by an arrow pointing from the Include All table to the related table.

In the following example, table A (countries and their capitals) is joined with table B (countries and continents). As you can see, all records from the table designated as the "left" (fully included) table are included in the resulting dynaset, but only the matching records from the "right" table are included.

Table A (Left table)

Joined Field A	Other Field A
USA	Washington D.C.
England	London
Vietnam	Saigon
Russia	Moscow
Libya	Benghazi
Canada	Ottawa
Eritrea	Asmara

Table B (Right table)

Joined Field B	Other Field B
USA	North America
England	Europe
Iraq	Asia
Eritrea	Africa
Brazil	South America
Poland	Europe

Table C (Left outer-join dynaset)

Joined Field	Other Field A	Other Field B
USA	Washington D.C.	North America
England	London	Europe
Vietnam	Saigon	
Russia	Moscow	
Libya	Benghazi	
Canada	Ottawa	
Eritrea	Asmara	Africa

Table D (Right outer-join dynaset)

Joined Field B	Other Field B	Other Field A
USA	North America	Washington D.C.
England	Europe	London
Iraq	Asia	
Eritrea	Africa	Asmara
Brazil	South America	
Poland	Europe	

Joining Field Lists

Double-clicking on the join connecting line brings up the Join Properties dialog box, which specifies the default inner join and the two outer-join options (see fig. 6.13).

To perform the join, follow these steps:

1. Identify the fields between the two tables that contain similar data. More than one field may be required to build the connection.

2. Drag the field(s) from one table to the other table. Drop the field onto the field with which it is to be joined. Access displays a line connecting the two fields.

To break a join, select the connecting join line and press Delete.

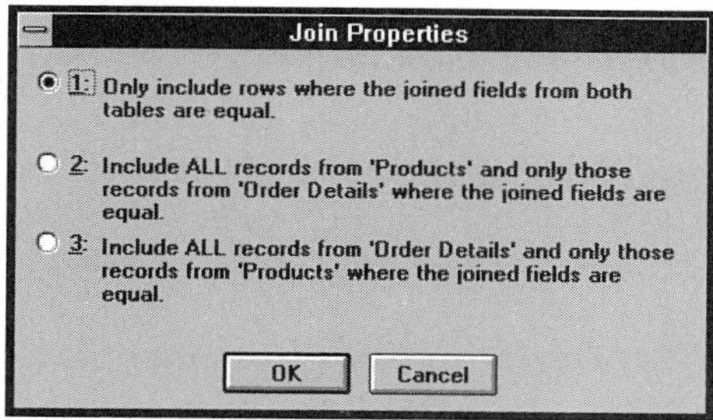

Figure 6.13. The Join Properties dialog box.

Using Self-Joins

A table can be related to itself. More specifically, one field of a table can be joined with another field (or fields) from the same table. Examples of self joins are genealogy trees or employee charts that have a natural one-to-many relationship within the data.

To create a self join, you first place multiple copies of the same table in the query design window. As copies are placed, Access uniquely identifies each copy by adding an incrementing number to the table name (see fig. 6.14). After you place multiple copies of the table in the query design window, drag the fields to create the join as you do with any other table. In the example shown in figure 6.14, the Employees table is self-joined to show which employees are assigned to which managers and vice versa.

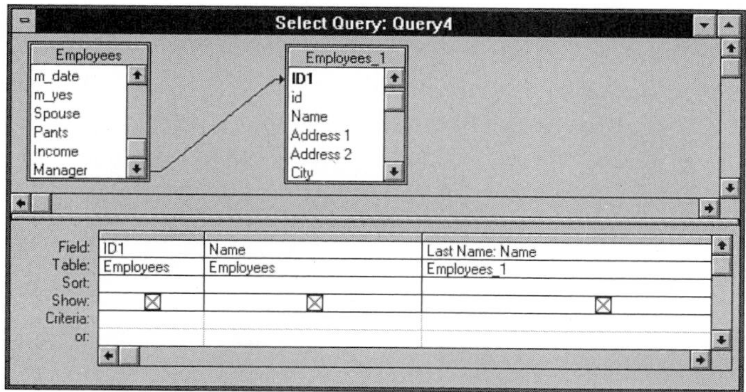

Figure 6.14. Creating a self join.

Analyzing Data with Crosstab Queries

Crosstab queries, which analyze the relationship between two fields in a spreadsheet fashion, are rare and may appear to be daunting in their complexity. When understood and properly applied, however, Crosstab queries are very useful. Think of Crosstab queries as an X-Y coordinate table. An example of a Crosstab query is the performance of a sales analysis of salespersons and counties. Rather than producing two queries from the sales database, one sorted by salesperson and the other sorted by county, the Crosstab query produces a single spreadsheet with every county across the top, and every salesperson listed down the side.

The value in the spreadsheet cell can be a count of sales by salesperson X in county Y, or it can be a sales dollar amount. The Crosstab query even can calculate the average sales, commission earned, or new customer sales.

To begin creating a Crosstab query, create a new query and set the query type to Crosstab in the Query menu. In the QBE grid, Access adds a new row, Crosstab, to specify the Row Heading, Column Heading, and Value fields.

Setting the Row Heading and Column Categories

The Crosstab query lists every unique value in a given field. Each value becomes a row. In the salesperson/county example, the salespersons are the row headings (see fig. 6.15). Set the Salesperson column to Row Heading with the pull-down menu in the Crosstab row of the QBE. Set the column headings the same way. The counties are the column headings for this example. You must keep the Total row set to Group By for the Crosstab to group the heading records. To improve the readability of the Crosstab datasheet, use the field with the most items as the row heading (see fig. 6.16).

Calculating the Resulting Value

The value in each cell is an aggregate function comparing the combination of column heading value and row heading value. For the salesperson example, the value can be the total sales for each salesperson in each county. Or, the value can report the largest sale for each salesperson in each county, the average sale, or the cumulative sales.

Change the Total row to reflect the type of aggregate function you want to use to compare the column and row items.

Creating Graphs from Crosstab Queries

Because Crosstab queries provide highly readable information, such as sales by salesperson by county, the results of such Crosstab queries are perfectly suited to be displayed in a graphical form, which is suited for Microsoft Graph, a miniapplication (or *applet*) included with Access and many other Microsoft software packages. The Crosstab's two-dimensional grid of data, just like a spreadsheet, converts well to a three-dimensional bar chart or line graph (see fig. 6.17). The best (or at least quickest) way to make a graph from a Crosstab query is to design a new form using the Graph Wizard.

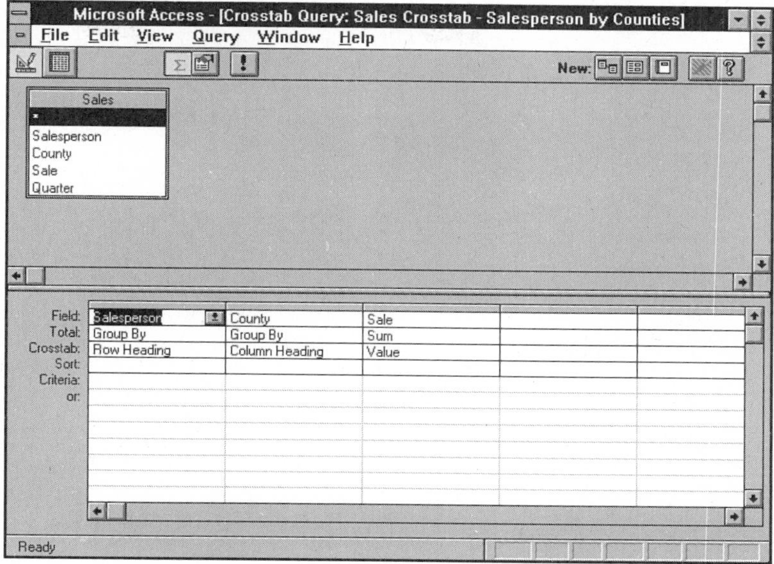

Figure 6.15. Defining the Salesperson/County Crosstab query.

Crosstab Query: Sales Crosstab - Salesperson by Counties

Salesperson	Dade	Orange	Palm Beach	Palm Beach Fla
Judy Ann Johnson				123
Candy	2961	746	1455	
Danny	2469	1788	1844	
David	3651	4515	2775	
DJ	2925	1270	1119	
Judy	1110	910	1477	
Sean	2529	3615	1578	

Record: 1

Figure 6.16. The Salesperson/County Crosstab datasheet.

The resulting form includes a large bound-object frame linked to the Microsoft Graph mini-application, as shown in figure 6.17.

Until now, we discussed how to create and use various types of queries by using Access's QBE query design surface. The next section describes how to use queries in Access Basic and how to create queries programmatically.

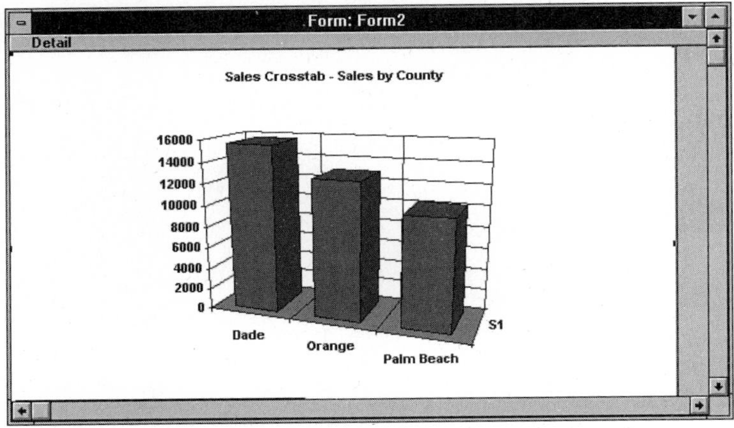

Figure 6.17. A Crosstab-generated graph.

Creating and Using Queries with Access Basic

From both users' and programmers' perspectives, the Access query mechanism is one of Access's strongest points. Not only does Access offer many kinds of queries, but the query optimization mechanism makes queries fast and efficient—more efficient, in fact, than programmatically traversing recordsets to search for (or update) a set of records.

End-users can find designing complex queries to be a confusing process, however, even when aided by the robust Access query design surface. Moreover, from a design perspective, anticipating the kinds of queries needed in turnkey applications is virtually impossible. As powerful as the query mechanism is, you still need to rely on Access Basic code at times to get the job done, especially in a runtime environment.

Fortunately, Access Basic offers quite a variety of methods for creating and executing queries, from the straightforward **CreateQueryDef** method to various methods and actions that enable you to construct and execute SQL statements. (All Access queries are eventually mapped to SQL.) Access Basic actions and methods form the program's backbone for creating and using queries. A list of the Access Basic query methods and actions follows:

Methods	**Actions**
CreateQueryDef	OpenQuery
OpenQueryDef	RunSQL
Execute	
CreateDynaset	
CreateSnapshot	

These actions and methods are described in the following sections, which demonstrate some techniques for using Access Basic to create and manipulate queries.

Creating a Make Table Query

You start by using Access Basic and SQL to construct a simple Make Table query. The user supplies the following input: source table, destination, and fields. For simplicity, the user's input is already assigned to memory variables. You use these variables to construct the appropriate SQL statement to create the table, and you assign this statement to a string named *sSQLstring*. Finally, you execute the SQL statement with the Access Basic **RunSQL** action.

```
Dim sSource$, sDestination$, sField1$, sField2$, sField3$, sSQLstring$

sSource = "Customers"
sDestination = "NewCustomers"
sField1 = sSource & "." & "Id" & ","
sField2 = sSource & ".Name,"
sField3 = sSource & ".City"

sSQLstring = "SELECT DISTINCTROW " & sField1 & sField2 & sField3 & " INTO " &
  ➥sDestination & " FROM " & sSource & ";"

DoCmd SetWarnings False
DoCmd RunSQL (sSQLstring)
```

The result of the query is a new table called NewCustomers that consists of some of the fields from the Customers table. The new table is not opened automatically, but can be selected from the database window.

Executing SQL Statements from Access Basic

As you can see from the example, in the preceding section any SQL string can be created in Access Basic using the concatenation operator. The next example uses a single line of code to perform a join of a few fields from two related tables (a one-to-many relationship)—Customers and Phone numbers—to form a new table, New Customers:

```
DoCmd RunSQL("SELECT DISTINCTROW Customers.Id, Customers.Name,
 ➥Customers.[Address 1], [Phone numbers].[Phone number] INTO [New Customers]
 ➥FROM Customers, [Phone numbers], [Phone Numbers] INNER JOIN Customers ON
 ➥[Phone numbers].Owner =
 Customers.Id;")
```

Notice that this time you didn't assign the SQL statement to a variable, but executed it directly using the RunSQL action. Be aware, however, that executing SQL statements with the Access Basic **RunSQL** action has three disadvantages:

- You can execute only action queries (Append, Update, Delete, or Make Table).
- The length of the SQL statement is limited to 256 characters.

- Queries are not reusable; in other words, they cannot be saved.

To create a reusable query, you must use the **CreateQueryDef** method, which can execute the same SQL string as the **RunSQL** action and also can save the query for later reuse or modification. You can hardcode the SQL string or construct it from user input.

Creating Modifiable Queries

A query definition can be modified by updating its SQL property. The next example creates an empty query (named New Query) and then updates its SQL property with a SQL string. Note that you also can open an existing query and modify its SQL property:

```
Dim cDB As databse, cQy As QueryDef, szSQLstring$, szQname$
Set cDB = CurrentDB()
szQname = "New Query"

' Assign a SQL string to a variable
szSQLstring = "SELECT DISTINCTROW MSysObjects.Id,
➥MSysObjects.Name, MSysObjects.Type, MSysObjects.DateCreate,
➥MSysObjects.DateUpdate
➥FROM MSysObjects
➥ORDER BY MSysObjects.Type, MSysObjects.DateCreate;"

'Create the query, update its SQL property and close it.
Set cQy = cDB.CreateQueryDef(szQname)
cQy.SQL = szSQLstring
cQy.Close
```

To modify this query, you first must open it (using the **OpenQueryDef** method) and then update its SQL property (the SQL string).

> **Note:** One potential drawback to this method is that modifications to the SQL property of a query tend to be code-intensive, because they involve a great deal of string parsing (searching and replacement). It is sometimes much easier to rebuild the SQL property from scratch rather than to try to modify it.

Comparing SQL and Access Basic Query Methods

Access Basic code can be used not only to define new queries or to modify existing queries, but also in lieu of queries. The next example shows two ways to query a single table, using SQL or the Access Basic **CreateDynaset** method and Filter and Index properties. The results produced by each method are identical—a subset (from the Phone Calls table) of all phone calls made in September, sorted by their cost.

SQL Example:

```
SELECT DISTINCTROW [Phone Calls].[Call date], [Phone Calls].[Call charge],
➥[Phone Calls].[Phone number] FROM [Phone Calls] WHERE ((Month([Call date])=9))
➥ORDER BY [Phone Calls].[Call charge]
```

Access Basic Example:

```
Dim cDB As Database, cTable As Table, cDy As Dynaset, cDy1 As Dynaset

sIndex = "Call charge"
sFilter = "Month([Call date]) = 9"
Set cDB = CurrentDB()
Set cTable = cDB.OpenTable("Phone calls")
Set cDy = cTable.CreateDynaset()
cDy.Filter = sFilter            'Apply previously defined filter
Set cDy1 = cDy.CreateDynaset()

(...)
```

The final dynaset, pointed to by the `cDy1` object variable, contains only calls made in September.

As you can see, this Access Basic example isn't really a query at all, because it simply uses a filter to perform the same operation as the SQL statement.

> **Note:** Note to Xbase programmers: The Access Basic method shown in the preceding example may be comfortingly familiar. Note, however, that even this Access Basic code is internally mapped to SQL before the results are produced. *In Access, using SQL is always the most direct and efficient method.*

Using Access Basic with Parameter Queries

Access queries can accept parameters at runtime, which increases their flexibility. Unfortunately, when a query is defined as a parameter query, an ungainly dialog box appears on-screen, demanding the parameter's value (this box appears whether or not the query is executed from within Access Basic). Access and Access Basic offer at least three easy techniques to circumvent the dialog box:

- Access the parameters directly
- Use a user-defined function to supply the value of the parameters
- Use a value from a control on a form to supply the value of a parameter

The following sections describe these three methods.

Accessing Parameters Directly

If the query is designed as a parameter query, its parameters are accessible directly from Access Basic by using the **!** operator.

Consider a Make Table query, named Customers by City, which picks three fields from the Customers table and uses them to create a New Customers table, with the scope of records limited to the city of Hatfield. First, you use the standard Access query designer to design a query named Customers by City. The query generates the following SQL statement:

```
SELECT  DISTINCTROW Customers.id, Customers.Name, Customers.City INTO [New Customers]
➥FROM Customers
➥WHERE ((Customers.City=[cName]))
```

The WHERE clause uses a parameter `cName`. You set this parameter at runtime using the following syntax:

*<object>***!***<parameter name> = value*

The following example uses Access Basic to get the same results by opening a Customers by City query definition, setting the value of the parameter `cName` to "Hatfield", and then executing and closing the query:

```
Dim cDB As Database, cQy As QueryDef
Set cDB = CurrentDB()
Set cQy = cDB.OpenQueryDef("Customers by City")
cQy!cName = "Hatfield"
cQy.Execute
cQy.Close
```

> **Note:** You can apply the **Execute** method only to action queries; any attempt to execute a Select query generates an error. To execute a Select query from Access Basic, use the **CreateDynaset** method. In the preceding example, replace the next-to-last line (cQy. Execute) with
>
> cDynaset.cQy.CreateDynaset()
>
> Alternatively, you can design a Select query as a Make Table query to save the recordset returned by the query to a table and process the table.

As you can see, these methods supply parameters transparently to the query as long as the query is executed from Access Basic. If the user decides to run the query directly from the query design surface (or from within a macro), the value of the parameter must be entered again, manually.

Using the User-Defined Function

User-defined functions often are used to supply parameters to queries at runtime. This method has one big advantage over accessing the query parameters directly as described in the preceding section; it transparently supplies the parameter, whether or not the query is executed from Access Basic.

The following query-design-generated SQL statement illustrates the basic idea:

```
SELECT [Call date], [Call charge], [Call bill to]
➥FROM [Phone Calls]
➥WHERE (([Phone Calls].[Call date]=SupplyDate()) AND ([Phone Calls].[Call bill
➥to]=SupplyBillTo()));
```

The above SQL statement was generated by a Select query that selects three fields from the Phone Calls table, based on the value of Call Date and Call Bill To fields, supplied by the **SupplyDate()** and **SupplyBillTo()** functions, respectively:

In order for the above query to execute properly, you need to include the following two functions in any module of the database:

```
Function SupplyDate () As Variant
    SupplyDate = #8/15/93#
End Function

Function SupplyBillTo () As String
    SupplyBillTo = "IRS"
End Function
```

> **Caution:** The values returned by these functions must be of the same data types as applicable fields in the query. Otherwise, a `Type mismatch` error occurs, and the query returns an empty recordset.

Both the **SupplyDate()** and **SupplyBillTo()** functions include hard-coded values for simplicity. The return values can be obtained, however, from the user's input; or they can be the result of calculations, data searches in another table, or a result returned by another query, to name a few of the almost unlimited possibilities.

The principle of supplying the value of parameters to queries with a user-defined function works equally well whether the query is executed from within Access Basic, from a macro, or run directly from the query container.

Using Values from a Control on a Form to Supply Parameters

You also can use the values of certain controls on forms to supply parameters to queries at runtime. Because Access is essentially a form-based system, it lends itself naturally to this technique. To use this method, you first must open the form and supply the required value to the applicable control; the query then can be executed using this value as the parameter.

A value from a control can be used to supply parameters in two ways:

- By using the ActiveControl property of the Screen object (this way the same query can be attached to many forms)
- By using the Forms object to specify the form and control name that is to supply the value of the parameter

The first method necessitates executing the query when the control in question is in focus. The second method enables the query to be executed from other controls (such as a button) or even from the outside of the form, as long as the form remains active. These two methods are illustrated by figures 6.18 and 6.19.

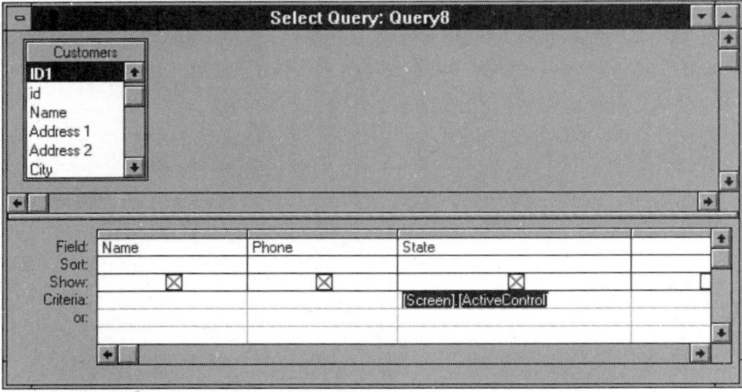

Figure 6.18. Using the *ActiveControl* property to supply parameters.

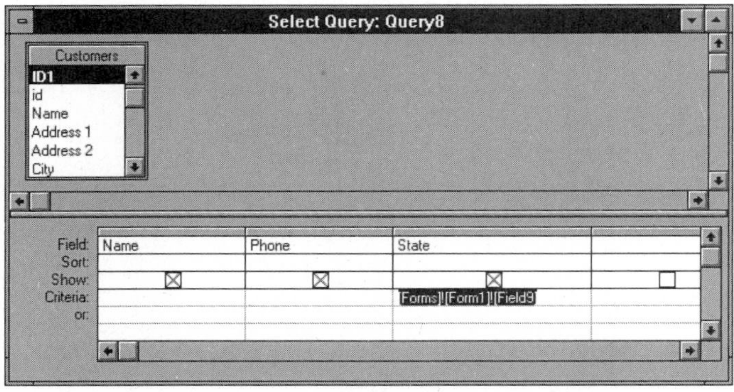

Figure 6.19. Using external controls to supply parameters.

The following is the SQL code generated by the query in question:

```
SELECT  DISTINCTROW Customers.Name, Customers.Phone, Customers.State
➥FROM Customers
➥WHERE ((Customers.State=[Screen].[ActiveControl]))
➥WITH OWNERACCESS OPTION;
```

You can execute the query from any action property that executes after the value is entered in the control (the AfterUpdate and OnExit properties are the most likely candidates), as shown in figure 6.20.

Figure 6.20. The macro RunQuery6 attached to the *OnExit* property.

Creating an Interactive Query in Access Basic

In a runtime environment, you may find it necessary to go through an interactive process with the user to produce a query. Although you can accomplish this task in several ways, for demonstration purposes, you can use a method that involves the following steps:

1. Allowing the user to select the type of query to create.
2. Showing a list of available tables to the user.
3. Linking the tables.
4. Allowing the user to specify the fields to be contained in the query.
5. Constructing the SQL statements necessary to create the query.

The following sections describe these steps in detail.

Allowing the User to Specify the Query Type

First, let the user select the type of query to be created; different types of Access queries use different elements of SQL. The query type also has some effect on the type of processing necessary to construct and execute a query. For this example, a simple list box with hard-coded query types suffices. Create a listbox control on the form, set its RowSourceType property to Value List, and set its RowSource property to a list of available query types (see fig. 6.21).

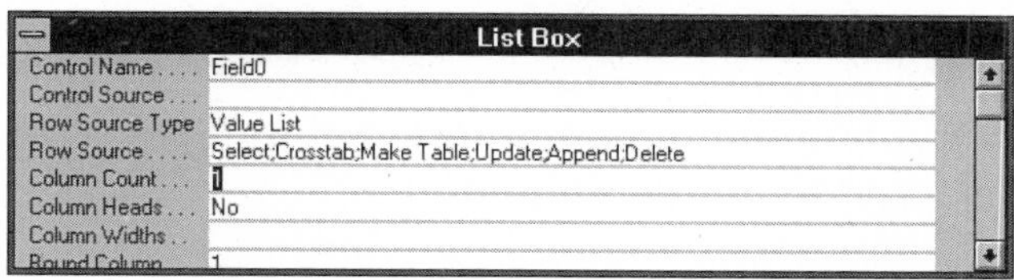

Figure 6.21 Relevant properties of a list box displaying available query types.

Presenting the User with a List of Available Tables

Creating an Access Basic query is exactly like designing a query in the query Design view, in that the process starts with the selection of the underlying table(s). You can present the list of tables and queries in the database to the user by querying the MSysObjects table for the names of available tables, or by using the **ListTables** method to fill in a list programmatically (with Access Basic code).

To query the MSysObjects table for available tables, attach the following SQL statement to the RowSource property of a list box on a form (see fig. 6.22):

```
SELECT Name FROM MSysObjects WHERE (Type = -32760) ORDER BY Name
```

> **Note:** Type -32760 is the form image of an Access table. (For more information about MSysTables, see Chapter 2, "The Access Database.") To access the MSysObject table, you need at least Read Data permissions to this table.

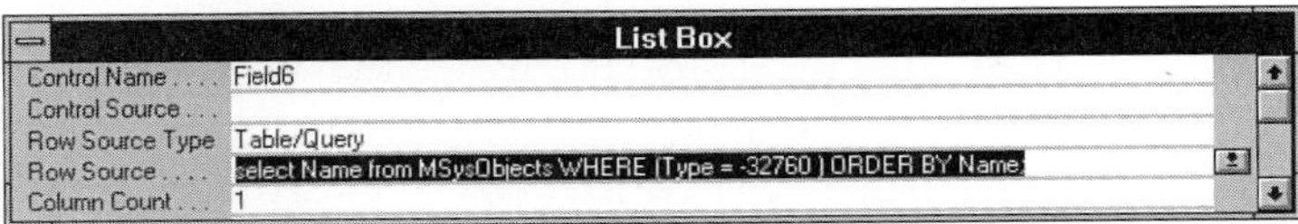

Figure 6.22. Attaching a SQL statement to the *RowSource* property of a list box on a form.

The second option for presenting the list of tables and queries in the database to the user is to write a function to programmatically fill a list to be displayed in a list box (or a combo box) on a form. The **TablesAndQueries** function fills a list box with the listing of tables available in the current database. This function uses the **ListTables** method to create a snapshot of all tables and queries in the current database. The program then transfers this snapshot to a static array which is used to fill the list. The actual data is transferred to the list in the block of statements in the Case 6 option of the Select Case code block. The framework for this function is documented by Microsoft in the "Introduction to Programming" manual supplied with Access.

The **TablesAndQueries** function accepts the following parameters:

- *fld*. A Control variable referring to the calling list or combo box.
- *id*. A unique identifier of the control (if the same function is used to fill multiple controls).
- *row*. The row being filled (starts with 0).
- *col*. The column being filled (starts with 1).

- *code*. A value that specifies the kind of information being requested, from the following choices:

0	Initialize list (returns any nonzero value if successful; False or Null if the list cannot be initialized)
1	Open (returns a nonzero value on success; False or Null on failure)
2	(reserved)
3	Number of rows (use -1 if unknown)
4	Number of columns (greater than zero; must match the Column Count property)
5	Column width (expressed in twips—there are 1440 twips to an inch, use -1 for default width)
6	Entry to be displayed
7	Format string used to format the list (returns Null if none)
8	(reserved)
9	End list (no return value)

Because the basic framework for this function is known to Access, Access automatically passes all of these parameters (if this function is attached to the RowSourceType property of a list box or a combo box on a form). The following function, TablesAndQueries, fills a list box on a form with available tables and queries:

```
Function TablesAndQueries (fld As Control, id, row, col, code)

Static RecCount, aTables()
RetVal = Null

Select Case code

Case 0                              ' Initialize
    Dim cDb As Database, cDy As Snapshot
    Set cDb = CurrentDB()
      'Create Snapshot using the ListFields method
    Set cDy = cDb.ListTables()
    RecCount = 0
    Do Until cDy.EOF
       ' Filter out system objects and queries
        If ((cDy.Attributes And DB_SYSTEMOBJECT) = 0) Then
            ReDim Preserve aTables(0 To RecCount)
            aTables(RecCount) = cDy.name
            RecCount = RecCount + 1
        End If
```

continues

```
            cDy.MoveNext
        Loop
        RetVal = RecCount

    ' Explanation of the code argument in the paragraph above describes the values of
    ' the Case values
    Case 1                          'return a random value
        RetVal = Timer
    ' *** Note *** No Case 2 (this value is reserved by Access)
    Case 3                          'Number of rows in the list
        RetVal = RecCount
    Case 4                          'Number of columns in the list
        RetVal = 1
    Case 5                          'Column width (default)
        RetVal = -1
    Case 6                          'Transfer the data item
        RetVal = aTables(row)

    End Select
    TablesAndQueries = RetVal
    End Function
```

Note: The TablesAndQueries function can be found in the sample database (QUE.MDB) included with this book.

Attach the **TablesAndQueries** function to the RowSourceType property of the desired control (a list or combo box) without including parentheses or arguments.

When you use either of the methods described in this section for presenting the list of tables and queries in the database to the user, the user sees the list box showing the available tables.

Linking the Tables

If the user selects more than one table, you must link the tables before proceeding. On the query design surface, this process is straightforward and involves drawing lines between the desired fields.

In Access Basic, you also can accomplish the same task with ease, because links between tables are converted into SQL "JOIN" syntax. You can define the relationships with user input or by hard coding the relationships. To create the code to link two tables—Phone Numbers and Customers—using the Owner field from the Phone Numbers table and the Id field from the Customers table, for example, the relevant part of the SQL string would be as follows:

```
INNER JOIN Customers ON [Phone numbers].Owner = Customers.Id
```

Allowing the User to Specify the Fields to be Used in the Query

After selecting and linking the table(s), the user is presented with a list of fields from all selected tables to include in the query. You can accomplish this in three ways:

- By using the **ListFields** method (which also provides other information such as field type and length)
- By running another Select query to return all fields for the selected table from the MSysColumns table (which stores information about fields in tables)
- By setting the RowSourceType property of a combo box (or a list box) to Field List, and the Row Source property to the desired table name (which displays the list of available fields)

If you want to use the ListFields method, pattern your function after the **TablesAndQueries** function used to display the listing of available tables and queries; the only significant change in this process is replacing the ListTables method with the ListFields method.

> **Tip:** To retrieve only the field names that belong to the selected table, use the ID field of the Snapshot created with the ListFields method. (This field provides the link between the file names in the table MSysObjects and field names in the MSysColumns table.)

Constructing a SQL Statement to Perform the Query

This part of the process is the most challenging, due to the syntactical complexities of SQL. The programmer is responsible for ensuring that all syntactical elements are put in the proper place in the string to be executed, for example, for trapping runtime errors and providing a method for graceful error recovery.

If you intend to perform much programmatic query building, establishing syntactical templates of various types of queries may be helpful.

For example, the Select query consists of the following elements:

Keywords: PARAMETERS...

database SELECT (required)

Field names (required)

Source table (required)

WHERE clause

ORDER BY clause (sort options)

Other options

The general format of the Select query is Keywords, Field names, Source table, WHERE clause, ORDER BY clause, and Other options.

Your final query must have at least the required elements or an error occurs.

> **Note:** The best way to dissect Access query SQL syntax (which is slightly different from the ANSI standard) is to generate sample queries from the query designer and view the resulting SQL code in the SQL window. You can copy the code to the clipboard by blocking it and pressing Ctrl+C (the Copy choice on the Edit menu does not work, because the SQL window is defined as modal).

You may have noticed that you're precariously close to writing our own replacement for the Access query creation surface. The moral of the story is that, from a purely practical standpoint, queries created programmatically are best limited to simple operations, such as creating ad-hoc subsets of recordsets. For constructing full interactive queries, use Access Basic *only if you have a compelling reason for not using the query designer*. After all, saving you time is why Access has such design tools in the first place!

Chapter Summary

The query is the heart of Access. Every other Access object depends on the query, either explicitly, such as when a query is specified as the Record Source for an object, or implicitly, when Access creates an underlying dynaset for an object.

In this chapter you explored how queries enable you to perform many data-manipulation tasks without programming. You learned how Crosstab queries simplify jobs like complex trend analysis, and how Action queries perform global updates without code. You also learned how multiple queries support a complex relational form with multiple related look-ups and subforms. Finally, you learned how to create and manipulate queries directly with Access Basic code, but, as the examples here demonstrate, except for the simplest operations, this exercise is generally not for the beginning programmer. To program queries, you must have a very thorough working knowledge of two languages: Access Basic and SQL. In the next chapter, you will explore another of Access's powerful automation tools—the macro.

7

Programming with Macros

Macros automate tasks and add actions to the events in forms and reports. Because macros perform actions that might otherwise require many lines of code, they often speed the program development process significantly.

An Access macro is not like a macro in other types of application software. Typically you think of a macro as a stored series of keystrokes to be played back when the macro is run. But Access macros are much more like internal functions. They are truly built-in features of the product. Because of their design and internal storage, macros actually may perform better than the same task written in Access Basic.

Access has 42 macro actions, ranging from a simple beep to a complex database transfer, as shown in the following listing:

AddMenu	Maximize	RunApp
ApplyFilter	Minimize	RunCode
Beep	MoveSize	RunMacro
CancelEvent	MsgBox	RunSQL
Close	OpenForm	SelectObject
CopyObject	OpenQuery	SendKeys
DoMenuItem	OpenReport	SetValue
Echo	OpenTable	SetWarnings
FindNext	Print	ShowAllRecords
FindRecord	Quit	StopMacro
GoToControl	Rename	StopAllMacros
GoToPage	RepaintObject	TransferDatabase
GoToRecord	Requery	TransferSpreadsheet
Hourglass	Restore	TransferText

For detailed information about each of these macros and their uses, see the actions section in the Reference.

This chapter covers the following topics:

- Creating and running macros
- Working with macro groups
- Using conditional macros
- Branching with macros
- Debugging macros
- Polishing macros for use in your applications
- Examining MsysMacros

Creating a Macro

You create macros by clicking on the Database window New button when the Macro object is pressed. The Macro Design window shown in figure 7.1 then is used to select a macro and fill in its properties.

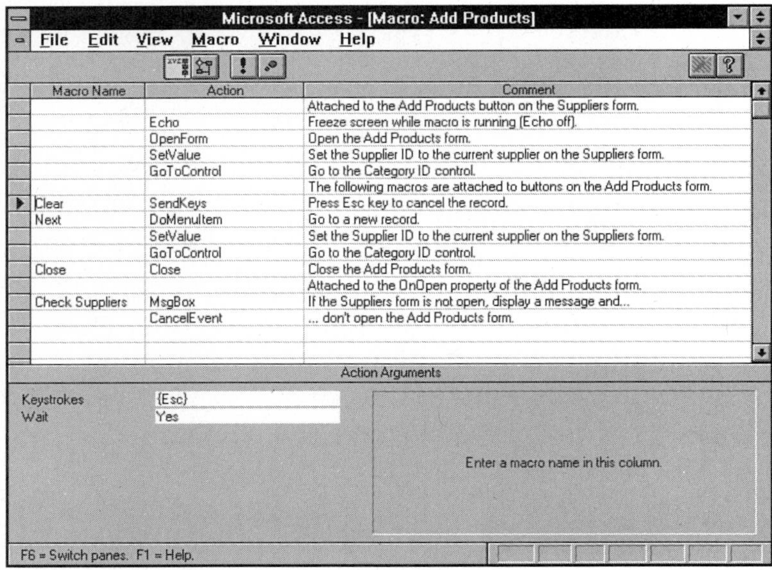

Figure 7.1. The Macro Design window.

Most macro actions have a set of properties. The properties are similar to a procedure's parameters. By setting the properties, you define how the macro action will behave or perform. When possible, Access uses combo boxes with pull-down lists to offer the choices for a property.

The Macro Design window uses the bottom left panel for the properties. This configuration is consistent with the Table Design and Report Sorting and Grouping Windows. To switch between panels (also called *panes*), press F6.

Note: Unlike a Table Design view field description column, macro descriptions are used only to comment the macro actions. The descriptions do not appear to the user on the status bar in forms or other objects as do table descriptions.

Some Macro actions may be created by dragging an object from the Database window to the Macro Design window. Dragging a form, for example, creates a macro line with the OpenForm action. The properties are set automatically with the form's name.

Running a Macro

Access provides numerous methods for executing a macro. When the macro object in the database window is selected, you can execute any macro by selecting it from the database window and clicking the Run button.

If a different object type is selected within the database window, macros still are available by choosing the Run Macro command from the File Menu, which presents a pull-down list of macros to select from.

Tip: If a macro requires a specific form to be the current window, but you don't yet want to add the macro to an event, you can run the macro from the File menu to select the form and then test the macro.

Form, Report, Section, or Control events can run a macro. The pull-down list in the Event Properties combo box includes every macro in the current database. If you are using macro groups (several related macros are put into one functional group) to add a group action to a form or report, you can specify the macro group and add the individual macro separated with a period (see the following section on macro groups).

Using an AutoExec Macro to Start Your Application

An AutoExec macro executes when the database is opened. The AutoExec macro is commonly used to hide the database window and open a user's menu or, in the case of the NorthWind Traders sample database that comes with Access, the AutoExec macro opens a form called the Switchboard.

> **Tip:** To circumvent an AutoExec macro, when selecting the database in the Open Database dialog box, press Shift+Enter to open the database without running the AutoExec macro. Holding down the Shift key while opening a database has the same effect. Bypassing the AutoExec macro is often necessary in the development and debugging stages, when you need to directly inspect an Access database object. This back door also works when you open a database using the list of up to four last opened databases provided at the bottom of the File menu. Note that this trick doesn't bypass an AutoExec macro when an application is run under the Access Distribution Kit (ADK).

Any macro can be used to start an application; the key is to name it AutoExec so that Access recognizes it as the macro to run before opening the database.

Defining a Macro Group

A macro object may contain from one to several macros. Macro groups hold several macro scripts in one macro object. Macro groups make it easier to work with macros by bringing together several macros into one design window. It's good planning to use one macro group for each form. Other macros that will be reused in several events throughout your Access application can be gathered into one global macro group. Without this planning, the database window quickly becomes cluttered with numerous macros, making it difficult to attach macros to events and debug macros.

> **Note:** End-users may prefer to use single *macros*, keeping only one macro script per macro object. In form design, the event properties combo box presents a pull-down list of all the macros in the database. Calling a single macro is as simple as selecting the macro in the event property.

To create a group, click on the Names toolbar button or the View|Names menu command to display the Names column. Figure 7.2 shows the macro Design view with the Macro Name and Condition columns enabled.

The individual macros are created within the macro group by specifying a name in the name column.

> **Tip:** You can make the Name column appear as part of the default macro environment in the Macro Design dialog box that appears after you choose Option from the View menu.

Individual macros control the execution of the macro by starting and ending a macro script. Macro execution ends if the next macro line includes a macro name.

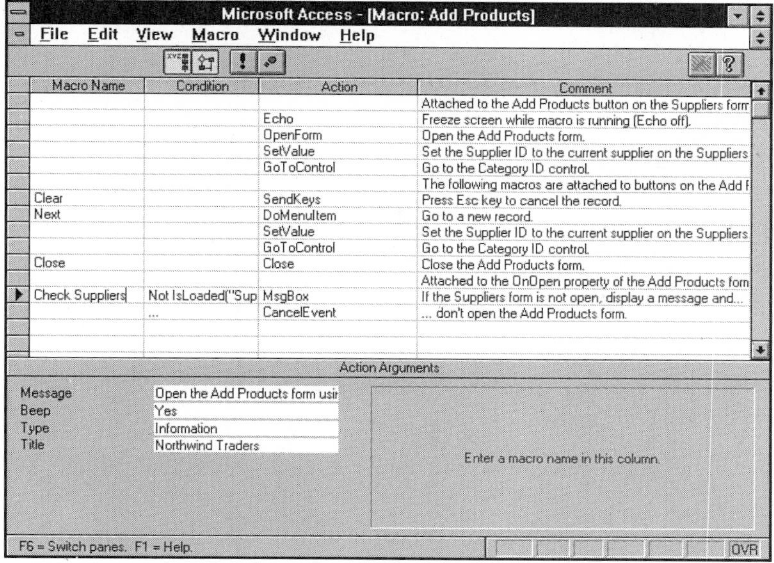

Figure 7.2. The Macro Design window with the Macro Name and Condition columns enabled.

Macro groups typically are used to execute a series of macros that are logically related to one operation. You may want to turn off error messages, turn on the hourglass, run a query, and then restore the environment, for example. These macro actions can be made part of a group so that you just need to reference only one name to run all the macros necessary to complete the operation.

Using Conditional Macros

Macro actions also may be executed conditionally. The condition affects only the macro action associated with the condition. The condition, even if False, has no effect on the next macro action. The logical condition in a macro is similar to the expression used in an Access Basic **If** statement (without the If).

> **Note:** A condition is repeated to the following line(s) with an ellipsis (...). This saves the trouble of repeating a condition and editing several conditions, and also prevents typing errors.

If the branch directs logical control to a previous macro (For-Next), Do While loops or other Access Basic control structures such as If...Then may be simulated, as illustrated in the example displayed in figure 7.3. This macro group opens a form, loops through all records in the underlying dynaset, and updates the daily and weekly total controls on the form. When the end of the dynaset is reached, the macro closes the form and stops running. Note the conditional expressions simulating the Do Until... and If...Then control structures.

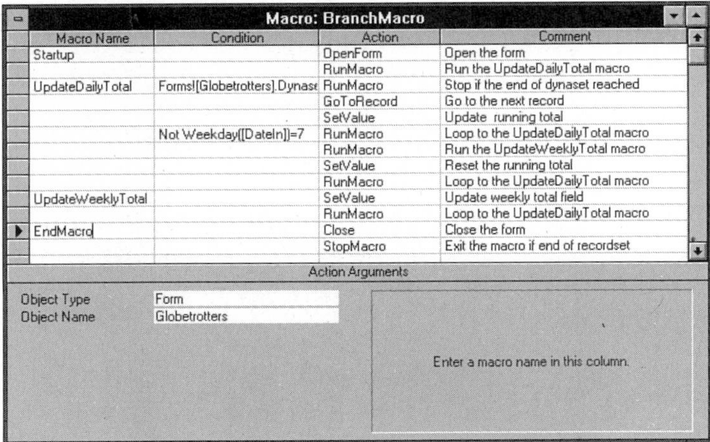

Macro Name	Condition	Action	Comment
Startup		OpenForm	Open the form
		RunMacro	Run the UpdateDailyTotal macro
UpdateDailyTotal	Forms![Globetrotters].Dynase	RunMacro	Stop if the end of dynaset reached
		GoToRecord	Go to the next record
		SetValue	Update running total
	Not Weekday([DateIn])=7	RunMacro	Loop to the UpdateDailyTotal macro
		RunMacro	Run the UpdateWeeklyTotal macro
		SetValue	Reset the running total
		RunMacro	Loop to the UpdateDailyTotal macro
UpdateWeeklyTotal		SetValue	Update weekly total field
		RunMacro	Loop to the UpdateDailyTotal macro
EndMacro		Close	Close the form
		StopMacro	Exit the macro if end of recordset

Figure 7.3. The BranchMacro macro.

Testing a Control for a Value

You can use conditional macros to respond to form control values by referencing the control in the condition property of the Macro Design window with the following syntax:

Forms!formname!controlname

The exclamation point separates the object names. If the Object name (form or control) includes spaces, enclose the object name in brackets so that Access treats the words as one object. Consider the following example:

Forms![Order Entry]![Invoice Printed]

> **Note:** You do not need to include *Forms!formname* if you are referencing a control in the form that launched the macro.

Suppose that you want to test a control to see if it has a value by using the IsNull function. To test the Customer field for an entry, use the following condition:

IsNull(Forms![Order Entry]![Customer])

Calling Access Basic to Return a Logical Value

An Access Basic function, either native to Access Basic or one you have created, can be called from the Condition column. Valid functions must return a logical value. This provides information that the macro then can act on, as in the following example. The macro DOB, shown in figure 7.4, checks whether the birth year is a leap year by using a user-defined function IsLeapYear, and also checks whether the birthday falls on a Sunday by using the Access intrinsic function **Weekday()**. It displays a message box congratulating the lucky person if he or she was born in a leap year or on a Sunday.

```
Function IsLeapYear (wYear%)
    IsLeapYear = False
    If Month(DateSerial(wYear, 2, 29)) = 2 Then IsLeapYear = True
End Function
```

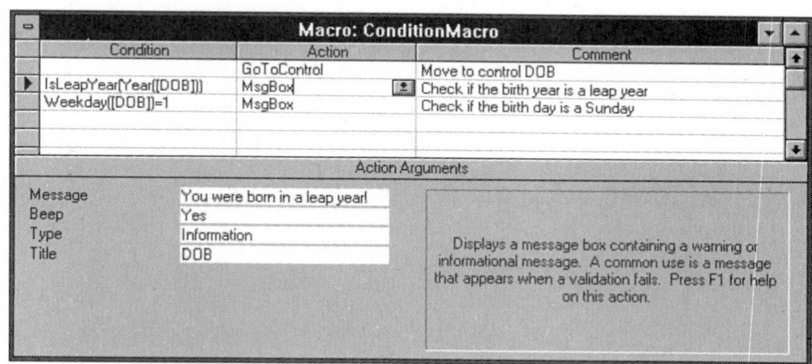

Figure 7.4. The macro DOB.

Branching within a Macro

You can branch to a different macro within the same macro group, or to a different macro, by using the **RunMacro** action. After the called macro is executed, control returns to the line following the calling RunMacro action. This process enables you to execute macros in any sequence that is logical for the operation. Figure 7.5 shows an example of a branching macro.

The branch can be performed conditionally by adding a logical expression in the Condition column. If the branch occurs within a macro group, you still must specify the macro group name and macro individual name.

> **Note:** You do not need to use the macro group name when branching within a group, but in fact it *is* necessary to use the group name.

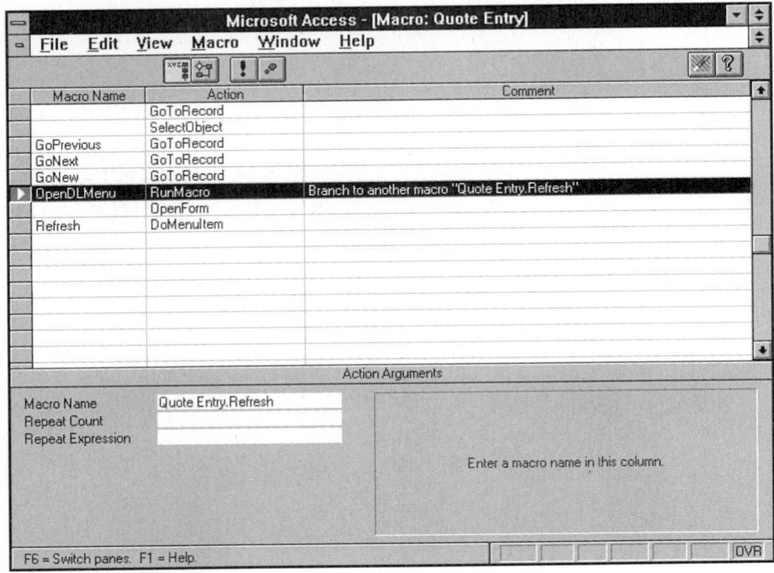

Figure 7.5. A branching macro.

Be sure to document the macro branching structure in the Description column. The lack of indenting and traditional branching structure (begin, end) can make branching macros difficult to follow.

> **Tip:** To temporarily comment out a macro action while debugging, enter a 0 in the Condition column. Zero is the logical equivalent of False. The macro action will be skipped.

Debugging Macros

The best way to debug a macro group is to watch its performance one step at a time. Turn on Single Step mode with the toolbar icon of a single footprint. As long as the Single Step icon is selected, each macro action pauses and displays its properties (see fig. 7.6). In other words, the macro performs normally but pauses before each macro action.

The Single Step dialog box shows the command to be performed. Your options are to perform this one step and then pause again, to stop the macro, or to continue without the single step.

If you choose Continue, Access continues the macro without single stepping and disables single stepping.

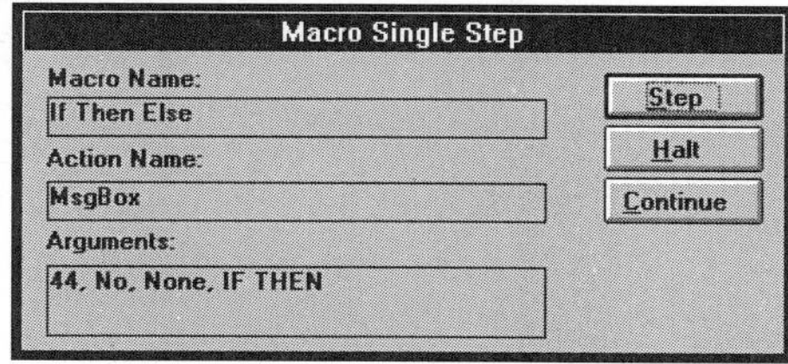

Figure 7.6. The Macro Single Step dialog box.

If an error occurs while a macro is running, the macro stops and an error dialog box displays the failed macro action and its properties. This box enables you to cancel the macro but doesn't restore the application to it's pre-error state. If a macro fails after you have turned on the hourglass, for example, the hourglass remains even after you cancel the macro from the error dialog box. Unfortunately, there is no good way to trap errors in a macro.

To exercise a greater degree of control, use individual macros. Better yet, execute actions from Access Basic code, where errors can be trapped and handled before they cause problems.

Assigning Macros to Keys

A macro group can have its individual macros assigned to keys by naming the macro AutoKeys. The Macro Name column is used to specify the key used to execute the macro (see fig. 7.7). The AutoKeys macro loads with the database and stays in effect as long as the database is open.

You can change the name of the group that contains the macros from the View Options dialog box.

Polishing Macros for Use in Applications

Access includes a few macro actions that clean up macro execution, such as turning on the hourglass and suppressing screen updates and warnings. These actions keep your application from looking like a recorded keystroke script while the macro is executing.

Using the Hourglass

The hourglass lends a finished look to your application. Note that the hourglass changes back to a pointer over any pop-up message boxes you create during the macro.

Turn on the hourglass before you begin an operation (such as running a query or report) to let the user know that something else is going to happen. Remember to turn off the hourglass after your operation is finished!

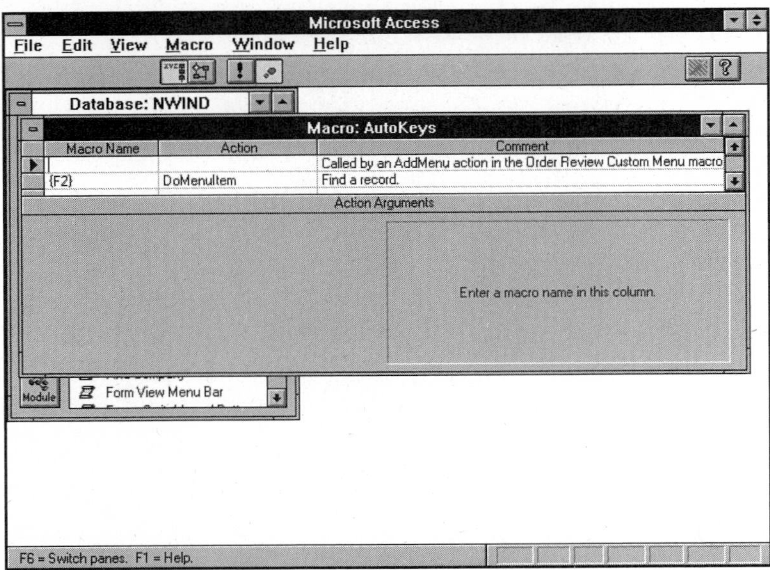

Figure 7.7. The AutoKeys macro.

Turning Off the Echo

This macro action prevents screen updates while the macro is running. This action also sets the status bar text while the macro is running. Access automatically repaints the screen and turns the echo back on when the macro is complete. Include the Echo action at the beginning of a macro. You also can specify the text, such as `Operation in progress...Please wait`, that will be displayed on the status bar while the macro is running to prevent Access from displaying potentially distracting and puzzling messages.

Note that setting the Echo action doesn't affect error messages and other modal dialog boxes. Often the SetWarnings action is used with the Echo action to turn off not only screen updates but the warning messages as well.

Turning Off Warnings

Setting SetWarning to No turns off all system warnings, except actual error messages and modal boxes such as msgboxes. When running an update query, for example, a dialog box with the message `<number> of records will be appended...` interrupts processing, but it can be turned off with the SetWarnings action. Be sure to fully test the macro before setting SetWarning to No.

Preventing Users from Running Macros

Macros within a macro group are executed from their individual names. Take advantage of this rule to prevent the user from running the macro outside of its intended event. Begin the macro group with a CancelEvent action. This macro action immediately aborts any attempt to run the macro without specifying an individual macro. Because an individual macro within a macro group cannot be specified from the database window, this action prevents users from erroneously executing the macro.

> **Note:** Beginning the macro with a blank line before the first individual macro has the same effect as using the CancelEvent action. Using the CancelEvent action draws attention to the macro abort process however, and may help someone understand the macro later.

Examining MsysMacros

All the macro actions for the entire database are stored within one system table—MSysMacros. You can view the MSysMacros table by setting View System Objects to Yes in the options dialog box (see fig. 7.8). The following table describes the MSysObjects fields.

MSysMacros Field	*Description*
ActionID	The macro's action is identified as a number. The 42 actions are numbered from 1 to 49. Macro ActionID 2, 10, 16, 18, 28, 39, and 42 are not used.
ActionNo	The sequential number indicating the location of the macro line within the macro.
Argument 1-10	The macro line's arguments or properties.
Comments	Comment column.
Expression	Condition column.
Label	Individual macro name from Name column in Macro Design view.
ScriptID	Used internally by Access.
ScriptName	The name of the macro (or macro group).

Armed with this understanding of how macros are stored within Access, it is not difficult to query MSysMacros and to document macros. Because the macro actions are stored as numbers, a table that contains the macro actions by name must be added. Other tables are required to store the macro parameters, parameter options, and the menu structure for DoMenuItem.

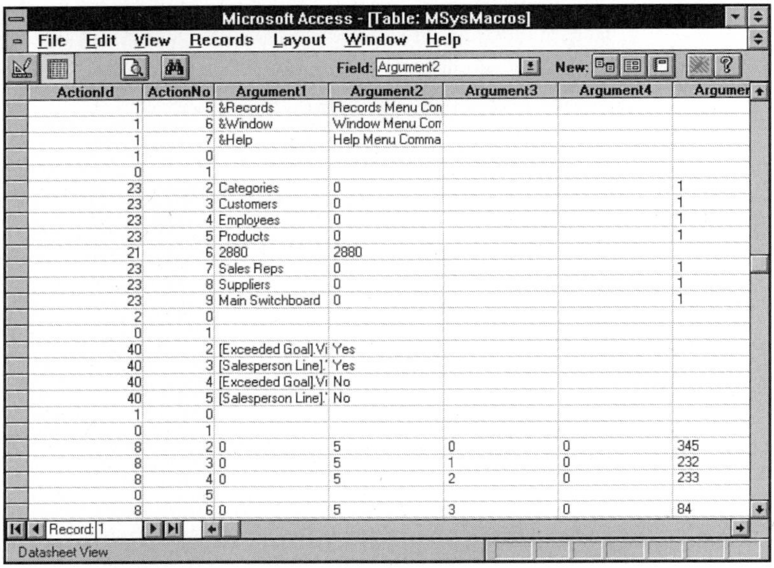

Microsoft Access - [Table: MSysMacros]

File Edit View Records Layout Window Help

Field: Argument2 New:

ActionId	ActionNo	Argument1	Argument2	Argument3	Argument4	Argumer
1	5	&Records	Records Menu Con			
1	6	&Window	Window Menu Com			
1	7	&Help	Help Menu Comma			
1	0					
0	1					
23	2	Categories	0			1
23	3	Customers	0			1
23	4	Employees	0			1
23	5	Products	0			1
21	6	2880	2880			
23	7	Sales Reps	0			1
23	8	Suppliers	0			1
23	9	Main Switchboard	0			1
2	0					
0	1					
40	2	[Exceeded Goal].Vi	Yes			
40	3	[Salesperson Line].'	Yes			
40	4	[Exceeded Goal].Vi	No			
40	5	[Salesperson Line].'	No			
1	0					
0	1					
8	2	0	5	0	0	345
8	3	0	5	1	0	232
8	4	0	5	2	0	233
0	5					
8	6	0	5	3	0	84

Record: 1

Datasheet View

Figure 7.8. Viewing MSysMacros.

Chapter Summary

Access macros provide a quick way to add actions to events and to automate your application. If you're a programmer who hates the mere thought of using something called a *macro*, at least try one or two of them before you write it off as an exercise in futility. Macros can be useful in prototyping and getting a system up and running quickly (you can convert macros to code anytime). Combined with conditions and the capability to perform expressions in conditions, macros become a powerful tool for both programmers and nonprogrammers.

8

Mastering Reports

The Report generator is another of Access's many strengths. From a developer's viewpoint, the report generator has the following benefits:

- The report object uses the same design interface as forms.
- The report generator uses bands for convenient grouping and subtotaling.
- The report generator produces desktop publishing quality reports with TrueType fonts, embedded pictures, art, graphs, and logos.
- You can summarize data with multiple grouping levels and optional headers and footers.
- The report object uses an accurate two-pass report data generation method, so you can place totals or percentages anywhere.
- Designing a report is easy enough that with Wizards end-users can create their own reports.
- Reports are based on dynasets in the same way that forms are based on dynasets. Each time the user runs the report, the underlying query generates a dynaset, making it easy to create reports with parameters and variable selections.

The report Design view is very similar to the form Design view. Rather than rehash the similarities, this chapter builds on the previous chapters by explaining what is new and different about the Access report object.

Designing Effective and Attractive Reports

Before you begin creating a report in Access, take time to define the scope of the report. Begin by answering the following questions:

- Who is the reader? Direct the report toward the reader by using the reader's terms and reference points.
- What question will the report answer? Keep the report concise. Make it answer a pointed question and delete everything from the report that doesn't directly answer the question at hand.
- Is there some way the selection criteria can help the reader find trends or unusual data faster and more accurately? Work with the query's section criteria to focus the data.
- How can the summary information help the reader apply the data in the report? Plan the report's objective and data on paper with the reader before building the report.
- What level of detail interests the reader? Make sure that the report satisfies the reader without becoming overwhelming.
- Would a graph enhance the readability of the report? Use the MS-Graph miniapplication to embed a graph.

As you design the report layout, keep in mind the following desktop publishing guidelines suitable for reports.

Planning the Pages

- Use white space to make the page less intimidating. A report should not look like a spreadsheet.
- Design the report right to the edges of the screen and let the page setup handle the margins.
- Print the report title, date, and page number on every page.
- Keep the report to the best size of paper—8 1/2 by 11.
- Always try to use as few pages as necessary to help save paper costs and the environment.
- Use as few fonts as possible.

Enhancing Group Sections

- Use group headers with bold text and line drawings to help identify data faster.
- Use horizontal lines to highlight groups.
- When using multiple groupings, use shading and line drawings to highlight higher levels of groups instead of indenting each successive group level.
- Indent the detail section to help highlight groups.

Uncluttering the Detail Section

- Offer a summary and detailed version of the report by hiding the detail in a second summary report.
- Use parentheses to identify negative numbers.

- Use bold and italic fonts sparingly in the detail section.
- Avoid underlining.
- Use multiple lines of data for the detail section if needed.
- Keep your report readable—no smaller than 10- to 12-point type.
- Limit the variety of type styles to two: one for headers and titles and the other for the detail section. Preferably, use a sans serif font for groups and titles and a serif font for details. Fonts have personality; it's good to combine two fonts that fit well together. One suggested pair of TrueType fonts is Arial for groups and titles, and Lucida Bright for the detail section.
- When using graphs, avoid three-axis graphs—they may be confusing in black and white.

Connecting the Report with Access

Reports, like just about everything else in Access, are based on dynasets. If you use a parameter query as the basis for a report, the query invokes the parameter request when the report runs.

Reports only use the Design view and the Print Preview view. There is no Datasheet view. To test the data selected from the query being used to build the report, use the report's Print Preview or Datasheet view of the underlying dynaset.

The report Design view functions essentially in the same manner as the form Design view, meaning that you can create controls by dragging them from the field list window, you set properties in the Properties window, and so on. You save the default settings of report controls in a report template.

> **Caution:** Reports re-sort the dynaset according to the report's sorting and grouping window settings.

> **Tip:** You may want to set different defaults for your reports and save them in a template. Assign the name of the report template to the report template section after choosing Form & Report Design from the Options menu.

To ensure that the data in the underlying recordset does not change while the report is being generated, you can set the report *Record Locks* property to All Records. This setting prohibits any changes to the recordset until the report generation is complete.

You can execute reports from the database window by using the Preview button. Alternatively, you can use the **OpenReport** macro action to print the report, preview the report, or open the report in Design view. You also can use the same action to start a report from within Access Basic.

Creating Reports from Forms

Not only is report design similar to form design, but a form may be converted conveniently into a report. When in form Design view, you can use the Save as Report menu command to save the form object as a report object.

The File menu in the Form view includes a command to print the current form, and the print set-up has an option to print data only. When printing with data only, only bound controls print. No other controls, including labels, are printed. When printing with the Data Only option off, the form's background color often darkens the page, making it unreadable. To solve this problem, use a white background for forms that will be printed.

The solution is to convert the form into a report and optimize the special effects, colors, and graphics for the printed page. You can launch the report from the form by using a macro and command button.

> **Tip:** When designing reports for preprinted forms, you can use the Data Only option to test the form with labels, and then run the form without labels.

You also can use the Screen Only setting of the *DisplayWhen* form property to make certain controls on the form visible only in Form view and hidden when the form is printed.

Creating Reports with Wizards

The ReportWizards operate similarly to the FormWizards. The ReportWizards create three types of reports with three styles. As with the form Wizards, Access offers the Wizards option whenever you begin to design a new report.

> **Tip:** Wizards, by default, add fields to the bottom of the report/field list. You can insert a field into the report/field list by selecting a position in the middle of the list and then clicking the Move Field button [>]. The new field is inserted beneath the selected field.

Using the Single-Column Wizard

The single-column Wizard produces lengthy reports suitable for single-record presentations. The single page vertical listing type of report is useful for creating reports that will be distributed to several persons, where each person needs to see only one record. Insurance estimates, invoices, and performance statistics are examples of data that may be generated in bulk and then distributed individually. Because Access uses a two-pass data report generator, the report can compare individual records with other records in the reporting group.

The single-column Wizard enables you to sort the records but does not create reports with groupings. Of course, you can add groupings later. Figure 8.1 shows how a report designed with the single-column Wizard appears when generated.

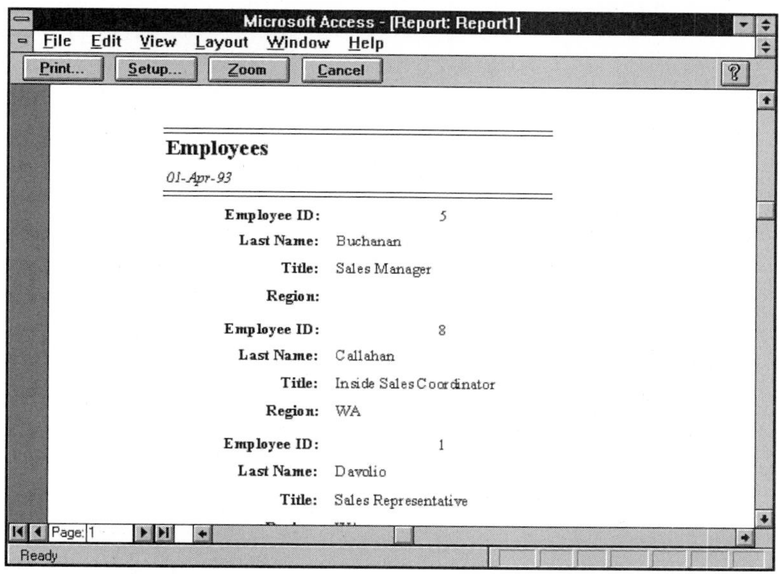

Figure 8.1. The result of a single-column Wizard.

Due to this Wizard's vertical line of controls, you should clean up the report layout to make it more readable. Many of the guidelines for cleaning up a form also work to clean up a single-column report. For more information, refer to Chapter 4, "Designing Forms."

> **Tip:** The single-column Wizard does not include page headers because the fields are identified by labels. You may want to choose to add page headers to help identify the report.

> **Tip:** Instead of using the single-column Wizard, you may want to transfer a form into a report to save time and produce a report that is more consistent with its related form view.

Using the Groups/Totals Wizard

The Groups/Totals Wizard is a powerhouse report Wizard that supports multiple groupings with subtotals and headers, and it polishes the groups with line art.

Defining the report with the Groups/Totals Wizard is similar to using the single-column Wizard. The Groups/Totals Wizard, however, enables you to group data and subtotals, and provides three grouping levels. You can use the report design view to add up to the report maximum of 10 grouping levels.

Sorting options are prompted in the Wizard sorting dialog box, as shown in figure 8.2.

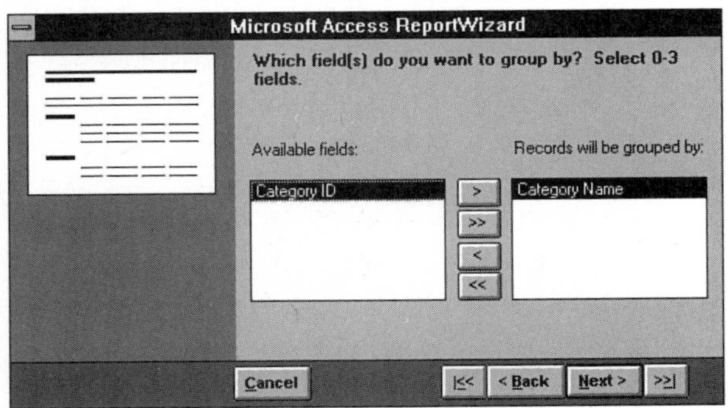

Figure 8.2. The Groups/Totals Wizard sorting dialog box.

Selecting Wizard Report Styles

The single-column and Groups/Totals Wizards enable you to choose from three styles for the report's appearance. Each style is suitable for a different application or reader.

The *executive* style is the beginning of a boardroom-quality report. This style uses double lines to highlight the page headers. You can polish this report style by highlighting the group information and adding a corporate logo (see fig. 8.3).

The *presentation* style uses single clean lines instead of the more traditional executive-style double lines, as shown in figure 8.4. The presentation style also bolds the group information, which makes the report easier to read. Presentation style is the recommended style for most reports.

The *ledger* style, as the name implies, appears to represent a spreadsheet or ledger. This style is suitable for large sets of numbers—particularly when designed for a wide-carriage printer.

The ledger style simulates group headers by placing the group header fields in the detail and enabling the Hide Duplicates property (see fig. 8.5).

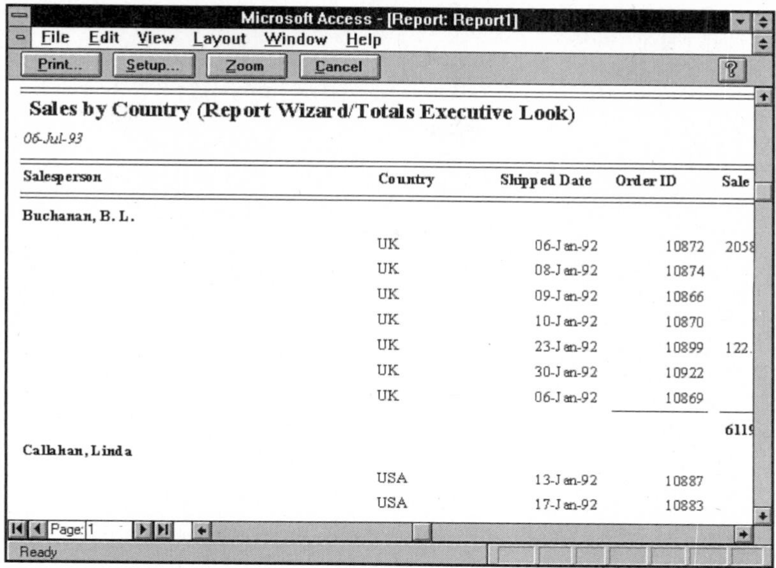

Figure 8.3. An executive style Groups/Totals report.

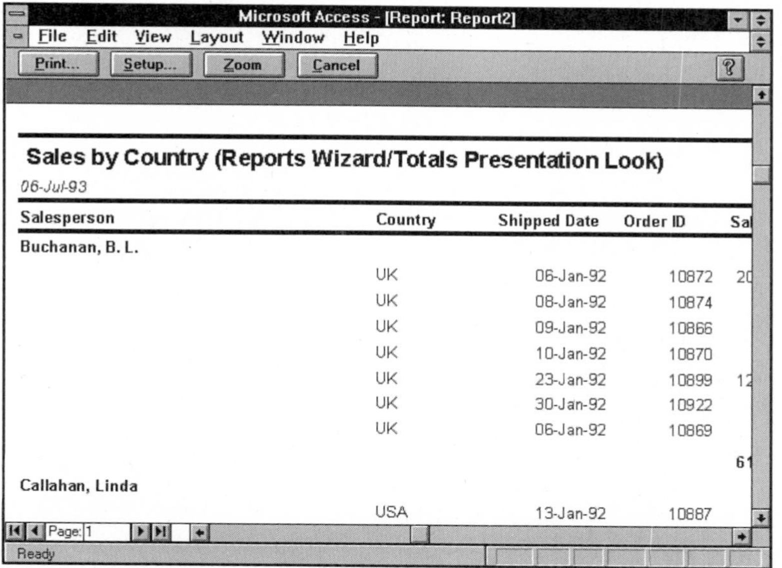

Figure 8.4. A presentation style Groups/Totals report.

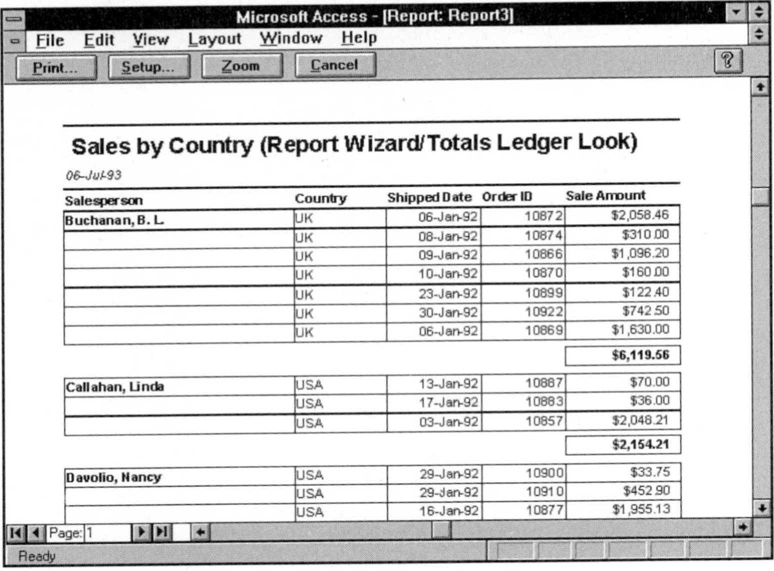

Figure 8.5. A ledger style Groups/Totals report.

Using the Mailing Label Wizard

The Mailing Label Wizard supports all standard Avery-brand labels. Instead of defining the label size and layout on the page, you simply select the Avery stock number for the mailing label and press Enter (see fig. 8.6).

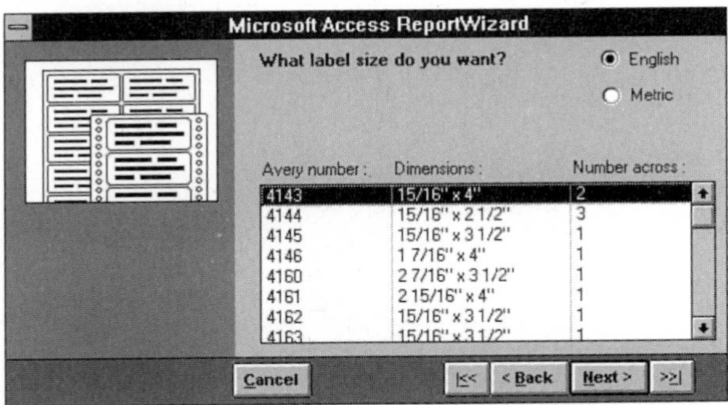

Figure 8.6. Selecting a label size from the Labels Wizard.

You assemble the mailing label by adding fields, text, and punctuation symbols to the label. You add fields by selecting the field and clicking the [>] button. Clicking any of the punctuation buttons inserts the punctuation symbols. You can add literal text by entering the text in the text box and clicking the Text button. You can add new lines to the mailing label by pressing Enter.

To remove an item from the label, select the mailing label and click the [<] button. The items are peeled off the mailing label line from right to left (see fig. 8.7).

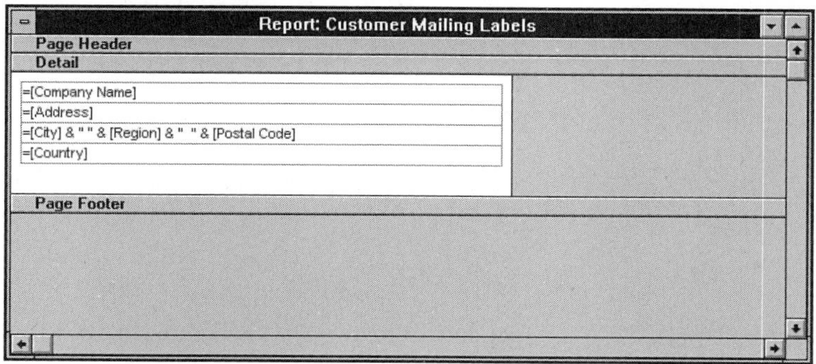

Figure 8.7. Removing an item from the label.

The Mailing Label Wizard includes 107 predefined mailing label sizes, which you can select according to their Avery label numbers. Of course, after the Wizard creates the report, you can enter Design view and adjust the size to any setting.

> **Tip:** To add new labels or edit label designs, go into the WIZARD.MDA database and open the Mailing Label table. For more information on accessing the WIZARD.MDA database, see Chapter 13, "Extending Microsoft Access and Access Basic."

Sorting and Grouping the Report

You can group records with similar values in the Group field. In the Yellow Pages, for example, the first grouping is the letter of the business category. The second grouping is the first business category. Each time the business category changes, a group header with the new business category is printed. Within the detail section, records are sorted by business name.

You can access the Sorting and Grouping window by clicking the Sorting and Grouping button on the toolbar. You can define the groups by choosing the Group field in the Field/Expression column of the Grouping/Sorting window. Use the pull-down list to display all the fields and expressions in the underlying dynaset.

The Group properties appear in the panel below the field list. You can press the F6 key to toggle between the two panes.

Multiple group headers are nested as follows:

Group-level 1 Header

Group-level 2 Header

Group-level 3 Header

Group-level 4 Header

.

.

.

Group-level 10 Header

Detail Section - Records

Group-level 10 Footer

.

.

.

Group-level 4 Footer

Group-level 3 Footer

Group-level 2 Footer

Group-level 1 Footer

Defining the Group

The Group On property determines the amount of change in the group field's value required to trigger a new group. A new group can be triggered by every new value in the field, or alternatively, by a greater change in the field's value. You can group date fields by year, quarter, month, week, day, hour, minute, or even second.

Text fields may change groups by the first character or any other number of characters. If the text field changes by a character prefix, the *Group Interval* property specifies the number of characters used in the group prefix. This property can be useful when you are sorting by ZIP codes or a product code, for example, where only the first three or four numbers comprise the relevant sorting category. Group Interval can also be very useful when you are sorting on dates, such as by week or month intervals.

Using Group Headers and Footers

If the next record to be printed has a new value in the group field, a group header is issued before the record with the new value prints. The group header can include any number of controls or no controls. You may want simply to print a blank line to provide a break in the report every time the first letter of the last name changes. Often, the group header includes lines and bold fonts to make the report easier to scan quickly.

You can turn on or off the group header for each group in the Sorting and Grouping windows.

> **Caution:** Turning off the group header causes you to lose any controls and formatting present in the group header.

You can force a group header always to begin at the top of a page by using the *Force New Page* property. You can choose to start a new page at different points in the report by selecting from the *Before Section*, *After Section*, and *Before & After* options.

You can use the *Keep Together* property to try to keep the section from being split by a page break. This property does not force a new page unless necessary. Using this property keeps information grouped together on the same page and, with smaller sections, can save paper (compared to the behavior of the Force New Page property).

The group footer, a counterpart of the group header, is enabled by the *Group Footer* property. Group footers usually contain subtotals or counts of the group.

To use subtotals in a footer (or header), edit the control source to add the function you want to subtotal. Of course, you can use any valid expression to calculate the footer subtotals. Following are some possibilities:

=Avg(field)

=Count(field)

=First(field)

=Last(field)

=Max(field)

=Min(field)

=StDev(field) or StDevP(field)

=Sum(field)

=Var(field) or VarP(field)

Figure 8.8 shows groups in report Design view.

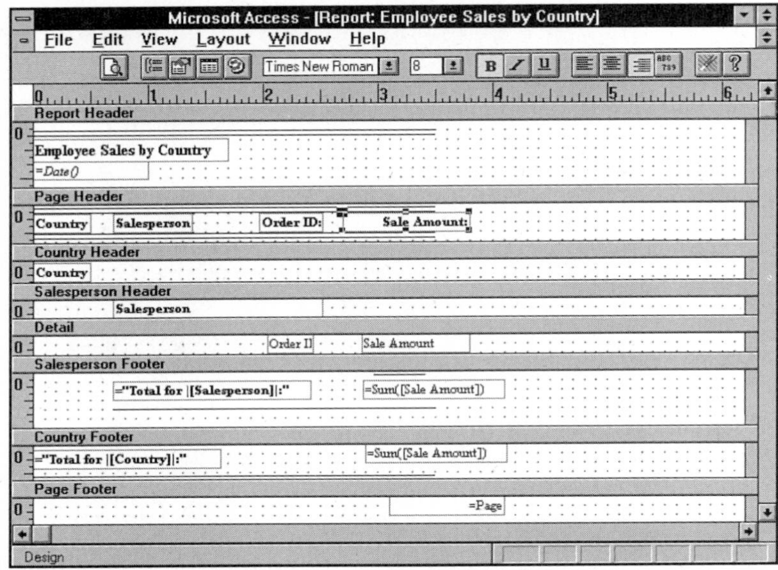

Figure 8.8. Using the report Design view to show groups.

Using Domain Functions

You also can attach any of the following domain financial functions directly to report controls.

The following are domain functions:

DAvg	DStDev
DCount	DStDevP
DFirst	DSum
DLast	DVar
DMax	DVarP
DMin	

Domain functions perform aggregate financial operations on a current or different dynaset. Domain functions are particularly useful when the value of a control is based on a calculated value or an aggregate operation in another recordset (table or query).

Building Report Header and Footer Sections

The report header prints at the beginning of the report and typically is used for the report title or title page.

The report footer is the final section to be printed. Grand totals, final calculations, and the bottom line belong in the report footer section. As an alternative example, the NorthWind Traders Catalog report imaginatively uses the report footer to print a complete order form (see fig. 8.9).

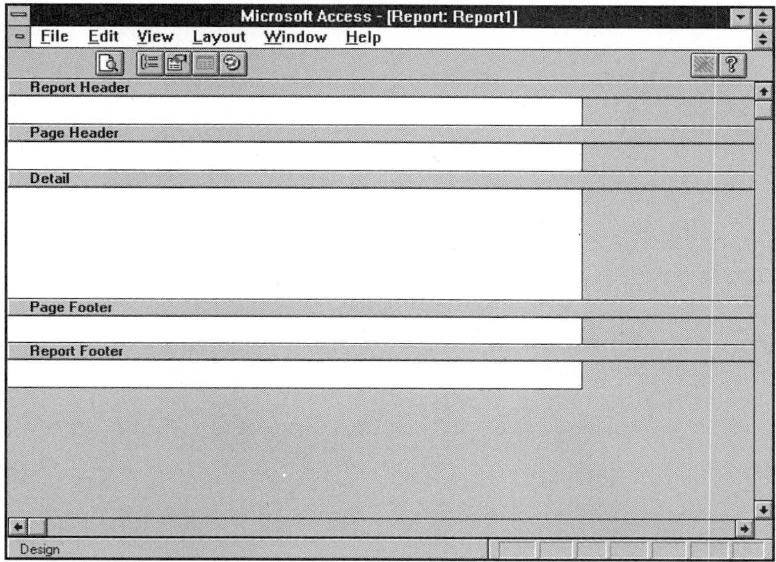

Figure 8.9. The default Report Header and Footer, Page Header and Footer, and the Detail sections.

You can turn the report header on and off by selecting or deselecting the Layout - Report Hdr/Ftr menu command.

Building Page Header and Footer Sections

The page header and footer print at the top and bottom of every page, similar to the header and footer of a word processing document. The page number, date, time, report title, column headers, copyrights, and confidential statements often appear in page headers and footers.

You can disable the page header or footer section on pages with report headers or footers by using the *Page Header* and *Page Footer* properties. You also can take advantage of this section to include a custom page header or page footer on the first or last page of data.

You can turn on and off the page header and footer by selecting or deselecting the Layout - Report Hdr/Ftr menu command.

> **Note:** The page number is available in the Access Page variable. For example, =Page, and, ="page no. " & Page, in an unbound text box, both print the page number. The first example, =Page, prints the page number not preceded by any heading. The second example, ="page no. " & Page, prints the text, "Page no.", followed by the page number.
>
> The date() function returns the current date. Using "=Date()" as the control source for a text box prints the date on the report. You can use text box's Format property to set the date format.

Handling Report Events

Report events differ from form events. Form events handle the creation, editing, and updating of records; reports are concerned only with opening the report and formatting the report. You assign actions to report events in the Reports Properties window (see fig. 8.10).

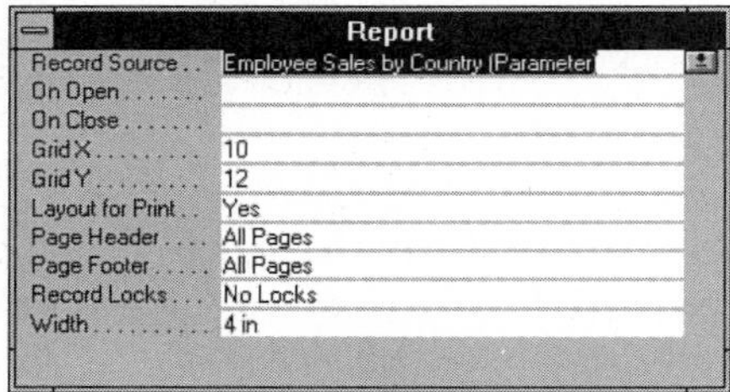

Figure 8.10. The Reports Properties window.

The section events are invoked each time the section is triggered. In a long report, these events may execute several hundred times.

Opening and Closing the Report

The **OnOpen** event occurs as the report is opened, and before the report requests a dynaset from the underlying query. This event is useful for calling a form to collect report-format options and record-selection criteria.

A *CancelEvent* macro action, during an **OnOpen** event, cancels the report.

The **OnClose** event is a counterpart to the OnOpen event. Several of the OnOpen actions may require opening pop-up forms. You can use the **OnClose** event to close any pop-up forms and clean up after the report.

Formatting the Section or Record

The OnFormat event occurs after the data is known, but before the records are formatted for printing for each section and each record in the detail section. This event is useful for changing the format on a record-by-record or group-by-group basis.

You can hide or show controls to optionally print record- or group-specific messages. When printing catalogs or other visual impact reports, the event may trigger an Access Basic macro to select randomly from four or five control layouts in order to vary the appearance as needed.

> **Note:** A CancelEvent during an OnFormat event prevents the section or record from printing and does not leave a blank space.

Printing the Section or Record

An event specified in the *OnPrint* property occurs after the controls are formatted but before they are printed. This seldom-used event may be useful for checking the page number and adjusting the layout of the page. You cannot, however, use *OnPrint* to alter data controls; you can do this only in the event specified in the *OnFormat* property.

> **Note:** A CancelEvent during an OnPrint event prevents the section or record from printing and leaves a blank space.

Enhancing the Report with Special Control Properties

Reports add several control properties not found in forms, which enable you to further refine the display, as listed below:

- *Hiding duplicate values.* You can enable the *Hide Duplicates* property to cause a value to print only once. All recurrences will be blank.

> **Tip:** Hiding duplicate values is a great way to save space in a report. Instead of using a separate line for the group header, place the group header field in the detail section with the *Hide Duplicates* property set to Yes, as shown in figure 8.11.

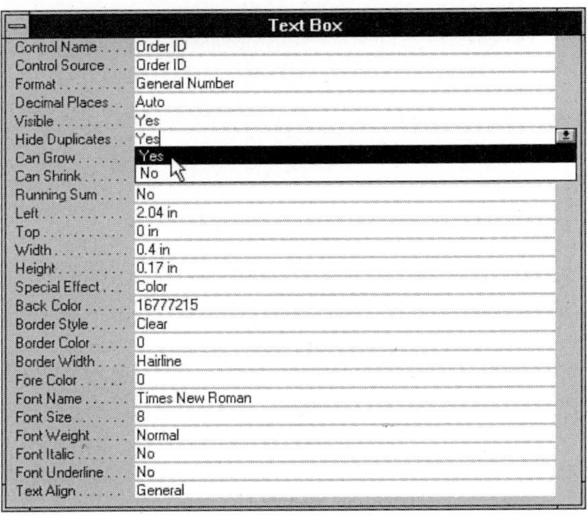

Figure 8.11. Using *Hide Duplicates* to save space in a report.

- *Using flexible text controls.* You can set the *Can Shrink* and *Can Grow* properties to Yes in order to enable text fields to resize automatically according to their lengths. The result is a nicely flowing report that appears to have been created with a word processor rather than a database report generator.

> **Tip:** Because the page lengths will be variable, some reports may require page breaks to improve the appearance. You can force a page break by setting the *Force New Page* property to Yes.

- *Keeping a running sum.* You can set the *Running Sum* property to Yes to enable the control to calculate cumulative sums for the control's bound field. The running sum value is reset with every increment of a group value. A running sum in the detail section, for example, resets with each new group. A running sum in a group resets with each new group value—one level higher than the running sum.

  If you set the *Running Sum* property to *Over Group*, a control with running sums enabled can reset the running sum with each higher group change. If you set *Running Sum* to *Over All*, the control continues to maintain the running sum throughout the report.

> **Tip:** Display the record's data next to a running sum by placing the field on the report twice—creating two bound controls linked to the same field. Set *Running Sums* to Yes on the right-hand field.

- *Referring to the section by number.* You may identify sections by their section number. To refer to the detail section's visible property, for example, use the following syntax:

```
Reports![ReportName].Section(0)
```

Other section numbers are as follows:

Number	*Section*
0	Detail
1	Report Header
2	Report Footer
3	Page Header
4	Page Footer
5	Group-level 1 Header
6	Group-level 1 Footer
7	Group-level 2 Header
8	Group-level 2 Footer
9	Group-level 3 Header
10	Group-level 3 Footer
11	Group-level 4 Header
12	Group-level 4 Footer

The section numbers continue to Section number 23 and 24 for group-level 10 header and footer. (For more information, see "Section" in the properties section of the Reference.)

Including Subreports

Reports can draw from multiple levels of record detail in much the same way relational forms use multiple dynasets with subforms and list boxes.

You can add subreports to a report by dragging a report from the database window and dropping it on a report open in Design view. If the report dynasets are linked in the default relationships, the Link Child fields and the Link Master fields will be filled automatically.

Figure 8.12 shows a subreport added to a report in the Report Design view.

Subreports are linked to the main report in the same manner that subforms are linked to the main form. The same caveats also apply; be sure to update the main report after editing the subreport.

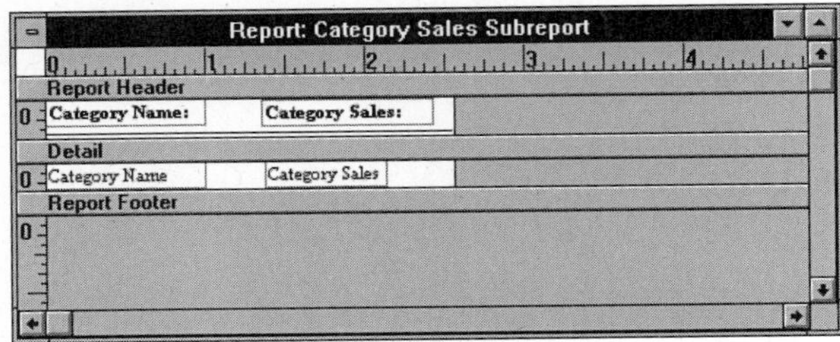

Figure 8.12. A subreport in Design view.

Combining Reports

Another technique for building complex reports is to combine two or more reports as one report. Add the reports as subreports to be combined to the blank report. If management always asks for the sales summary, region summary, and productivity analysis every Tuesday, for example, you can place all three reports into the Tuesday report. Running the Tuesday report creates a small book including all the data requested.

This method benefits from consecutive page numbers and an overall report header page. The drawback is that combining the report uses one level of subreport nesting. If the original reports use two levels of subreport nesting, the bottom level is lost. If subreport nesting is a problem, you can sequence the reports together in a macro.

Including Forms

You also can use forms as subreports. Set the subform control's source object to Forms.NameofForm. The subform's three-deep nesting limit still applies when you mix forms and reports. The capability to mix forms and reports is a one-way street (you cannot use reports within forms).

Printing to a Text File

As shipped, Access Versions 1.0 and 1.1 print only to a printer or a file containing Access print codes. There is no built-in option to print to an ASCII text file, or other file formats such as Microsoft Word. With OUTPUT.MDA, however, an Access add-on library, you can print to an ASCII file or a rich text format file. You must add OUTPUT.MDA to your Access MSACCESS.INI file. OUTPUT.MDA, with instructions for installation, is available in the Reports section of the MSAccess Forum on CompuServe (Go MSAccess).

Chapter Summary

The report engine offers a great deal of publishing horsepower. For the developer, the integration between the forms and reports is a true time-saver. Even if you prefer to build forms from scratch, chances are good that you may use the Wizards or Save Form as Report options to speed your report designs.

Remember to think about the reader while designing a report. Key decision makers may judge your whole application on the merits of the reports alone. You will make the best impression with a clean, well-designed report that answers a specific question.

Part IV

Programming with Access Basic

9

Introduction to Programming in Access Basic

In comparison with most MS-DOS-based systems, Access introduces an entirely different concept in programming and application development. Unlike its MS-DOS database counterparts, Access is designed to fully exploit the rich graphical environment offered by Microsoft Windows. This architecture has two significant implications:

- It blurs the distinction between design tools, objects, and code.
- It places more emphasis on a data-driven, event-driven model.

Many traditional programmers will be tempted to learn just the Access Basic language, without any particular regard for the Access tools such as forms, reports, queries, and macros. Just learning the language may be a serviceable methodology in a text-based, linear environment like DOS, but it simply will not work with a product like Access!

Of course, the practical result of this challenge is that the overall learning curve for Access is expanded significantly. This difficulty can be aggravating to some programmers who, for years, may have been rather effortlessly cranking out line after line of procedural code. Developing a new attitude is essential, however, so before launching headfirst into an attempt to master the language, you should consider the whole scope and philosophy of the product.

Preparing to Learn Access Basic

The task of learning everything necessary to become really proficient in Access can be quite formidable. You may want to use these tips to optimize your learning effort:

- Before attempting to learn Access Basic, resign yourself to learning, or at least becoming familiar with, Access tools and objects.
- Don't make the presumption that code is always the most efficient method for handling tasks. Macros or queries may be a better choice in terms of both design efficiency and performance.
- If you have never used a data dictionary, take time to explore Access's table properties and the Relationships design surface. Using these tools properly will save you hours of programming time. Seeing them put to use may also change your fundamental thinking about application design in favor of a more data-driven approach.
- Forget about the elaborate coding schemes (such as random-number generators) you once needed to produce unique values for maintaining relational integrity. The Access Counter data type handles the job quite nicely, and relationships are enforced internally.
- Each time you are about to do something the way it's always been done before, ask yourself if Access provides an easier way—chances are it does! Keep in mind that Access Basic has a plethora of direct object-manipulation capabilities.
- If you're new to the Windows programming environment, take some time to familiarize yourself with Windows conventions such as menu design, the look and feel of the standard Windows interface, and the internal settings of MS Windows and Access. This will avoid the disappointment of discovering that your application doesn't work properly because of some obscure INI setting.

If you internalize these points, you will be well on your way to developing the proper mindset for applications programming in Access.

Understanding the Role of Access Basic

Access Basic is derived from predecessor versions of the Basic programming language, but it is significantly enhanced with Windows-specific features and database-handling capabilities. For programmers familiar with Visual Basic, learning Access Basic is a relatively straightforward proposition. Access Basic has much of the same structure as Visual Basic in the way of statements and functions.

However, Access objects are tightly integrated with the language, so Access Basic has an expanded repertoire of controls to directly manipulate Access-specific *objects* (such as tables, forms, queries, and so on). Because the capability to directly manipulate data and to perform operations on data are the cornerstones of a database application, these unique features of Access Basic make it truly database-oriented.

So how does Access Basic fit into the picture? Simply put, you should rely on Access Basic to perform tasks that cannot be performed with Access objects. Or, you can use Access Basic to perform the same tasks as objects, but under a controlled run-time environment where you want to shield the user from the inner workings of the application. Here are some examples of tasks to which Access Basic is particularly suited:

- Transaction processing
- Graceful error trapping
- Robust program flow-control structures
- Performing DDE (dynamic data exchange) and calling Windows API functions
- Creation of reusable modules (code libraries)

Enough of theory—it's time to start learning Access Basic! First, you need an overview of the language and the tools needed to help you write Access Basic modules. The next sections guide you through the module Design environment and present the steps necessary to write an Access Basic module.

Working with Modules

Modules are Access Basic objects which store the procedures (code) you write in Access Basic. *Modules* and *procedures* give Access Basic a flexible method for organizing code into compact, reusable parts. Modules can also perform as a contained set of procedures when some or all of the procedures in a module are declared as private. This has useful implications such as allowing procedures in different modules to have the same name while making only procedures contained in the same module visible to other procedures in the same module. These two structural components of Access Basic, procedures and modules, facilitate the implementation of structured programming.

Structured Programming with Modules

Structured programming implies at least two things: dividing a program into procedures that perform just one task, and organizing the program in such a way that allows a programmer to easily follow the program flow. In Access, the former is accomplished with Sub and Function procedures, and the latter by organizing code into modules.

You create a new module from the database window. As with other Access objects, module names can contain up to 64 characters and can contain spaces. The default name of a newly created module is Module1..., but you can change the default name of a module during the Save operation or rename a module by choosing the Rename option from the File menu.

> **Tip:** Be careful with your naming conventions. Because Access database cannot have two procedures with the same name (except for procedures declared as private in different modules), consider using an application-specific prefix for the names of modules and procedures if you anticipate transferring modules between databases.

When you develop Access Basic modules, you probably will begin by placing all procedures for a single database in the same module. There's nothing wrong with this strategy while you're learning, but after you develop several applications, you probably will want to take advantage of using different modules to organize your code. Besides, searching for a specific procedure in a thousand-procedure module can be rather tedious! As you write more code and develop more applications, you will find some procedures that you rely on continuously. You may consider then organizing these procedures into separate library modules so that you can easily transfer them to new database projects.

A good approach for organizing modules with a view toward building a procedures library is to divide your code into separate functional modules. These could include global declarations, procedures related to the user interface, procedures related to calculations, and so on. Name these modules in a self-documenting way (for example, MyApp Global Declarations). Also, name your procedures within modules in the same self-documenting manner.

There are at least four important reasons to divide your code into distinct modules:

- To group functionally similar procedures (such as global declarations in one module, user interface procedures in another, etc.), as mentioned above
- To segregate in one module a set of task-specific procedures declared as Private and visible only to other procedures in the same module
- To be able to use a specific setting of **Option Compare** or **Option Explicit** for a particular module that differs from other modules in the same application.
- To be able to quickly transfer an entire module from one database to another (using the TransferDatabase action)—an important consideration when the same code (such as global declarations) is used in more than one application.

But first, you need to know some basics about working in the Access Basic module design environment.

Using the Development Environment

Access offers a rich set of Access Basic development tools. Just as forms and queries are integrated closely with data, the modules Design view is integrated closely with Access and its procedures. Borrowing heavily from the success of Visual Basic, the Access development environment includes several Visual Basic programmers' favorites, such as the Immediate window and the word-sensitive on-line Help feature. Access also provides a Procedure View dialog box—a useful, database-wide, procedure-selection method.

The module-development environment, also called module Design view, makes it easier for you to work with modules. You use controls on the toolbar to select module procedures and to navigate the module. The primary module development tool is the module editor, which is nearly identical to the Visual Basic code editor (but unfortunately it doesn't use color coding of keywords, comments, etc., like the editor in Visual Basic 3.0 does). The Immediate window also provides a powerful method for testing variables and commands in an interactive, immediate mode.

Using the Module Design Toolbar

As with other parts of the Access development environment, the module Design toolbar can save a lot of effort while you write and debug Access Basic modules, and learning it is time well spent. The module toolbar offers several module-oriented buttons, as described in the following table.

Icon	*Button*	*Function*
Procedure: IsLeapYear	Procedure Box	Lists the module's procedures and selects the procedure to be displayed.
	Previous Procedure and Next Procedure	Sequences through the module's procedure
	Run	Resumes execution of a stopped or paused procedure.
	Single Step	Executes one line of Access Basic code and then stops.
	Procedure Step	Executes one Access Basic procedure and then stops.
	Reinitialize	Stops execution and clears all variables, including the current line variable (Access Basic P Register). Prepares Access to attempt to rerun the module.
	Breakpoint	Sets a breakpoint at the current line.

Using the View Procedures Window

Although the toolbar enables you to switch to other procedures within the same module, there is another, even faster method, that is not on the toolbar. The View Procedures dialog box (which you can access from the View menu or by pressing F2 while in the module Design view) presents a list of the procedures in the current module as well as all modules and their procedures in the current database. You use the View Procedures dialog box, shown in fig. 9.1, to open modules so that you can work with the code.

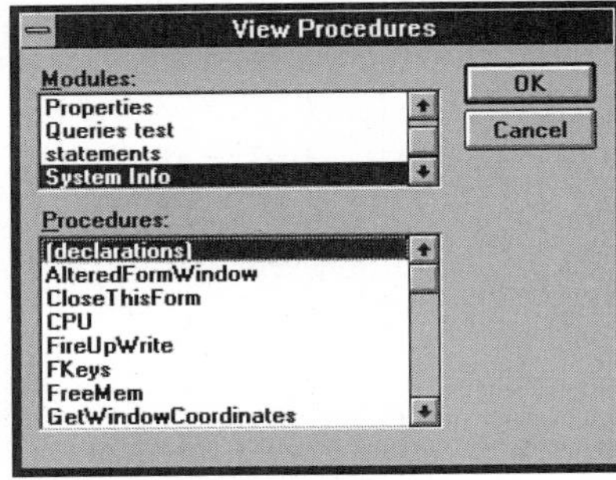

Figure 9.1. The View Procedures dialog box.

> **Tip:** You may want to modify your toolbar to make the View Procedures dialog box more accessible. The module Design toolbar is the METB form in UTILITY.MDA. See Chapter 13 "Extending Microsoft Access and Access Basic" for more information on this subject.

You can also navigate within a module in the following ways:

- Choosing another procedure from the Procedure pull-down list.
- Using the Next Procedure and Previous Procedure buttons on the toolbar and scrolling through the procedures until you arrive at the procedure you want.
- Pressing PgUp or PgDn to move to the next page of the editor. A new procedure always starts on a new page.

Using Module Shortcut Keys

The keyboard shortcuts described in the following table help you navigate between and within procedures and perform many operations while in the module window.

Shortcut	*Function*
Ctrl+Break	Halts execution of code
F2	Views Procedures list
Shift+F2	Selects GoTo procedure in the Module window
F5	Runs the current procedure
F8	Single Step through a procedure (one instruction at a time)
Shift+F8	Executes one procedure at a time

Using the Module Editor

The Access Basic module editor behaves like a monospaced superset of the basic Windows Notepad with a few powerful exceptions. Notably, you can use the module editor to call the Access Basic word-sensitive Help feature, to set execution breakpoints, and to follow execution during single-step mode.

As a programming convenience, the editor includes a semi-smart indentation method. It continues the current level of indentation with any new line. Also, you can indent or unindent several lines by selecting the lines and pressing Tab or Shift+Tab. You can set the number of spaces used for indentation in the Access Options dialog box.

The editor also adjusts the line's spacing and automatically capitalizes most of Access Basic's keywords (statements, methods, functions, actions, operators, and properties); not all keywords are automatically capitalized because some methods are not capitalized properly. Although the editor usually improves the readability of the code, there are times, particularly with long lists of similar code, when it would be nice to turn off the autospacing feature. However, this is not an option.

The editor also can check each line for syntax as the line loses focus. This capability makes cutting and pasting extremely frustrating, however, and should be turned off in the Access Options dialog box.

While using the editor, you may find several of the shortcuts described in the following table useful.

Shortcut	*Function*
F1	Presents Help information on the command under the insertion point
F2	Views procedures
F3	Finds next occurrence
Shift+F3	Finds previous occurrence
F6	Switches panes in split window
F7	Activates the Find dialog box
Shift+F7	Opens the Replace dialog box
F9	Toggles a breakpoint
Tab	Indents multiple selected lines
Shift+Tab	Unindents selected lines
Ctrl+N	Inserts line above current line
Ctrl+Y	Cuts current line to the clipboard
Ctrl+↑	Displays preceding procedure
Ctrl+↓	Displays next procedure
Double-clicking a word	Selects a word

Splitting the Module Window

You can split the editor window to view two procedures simultaneously, as shown in figure 9.2. This window functions much like a split window in Excel or Word for Windows. Note that you don't have to view different procedures in the split halves; you can choose to view two portions of the same procedure. You can split the module editing window by using either of these two methods:

- Toggling the split on and off by using the View Split menu command
- Dragging the split bar down from the unsplit position above the vertical scroll bar

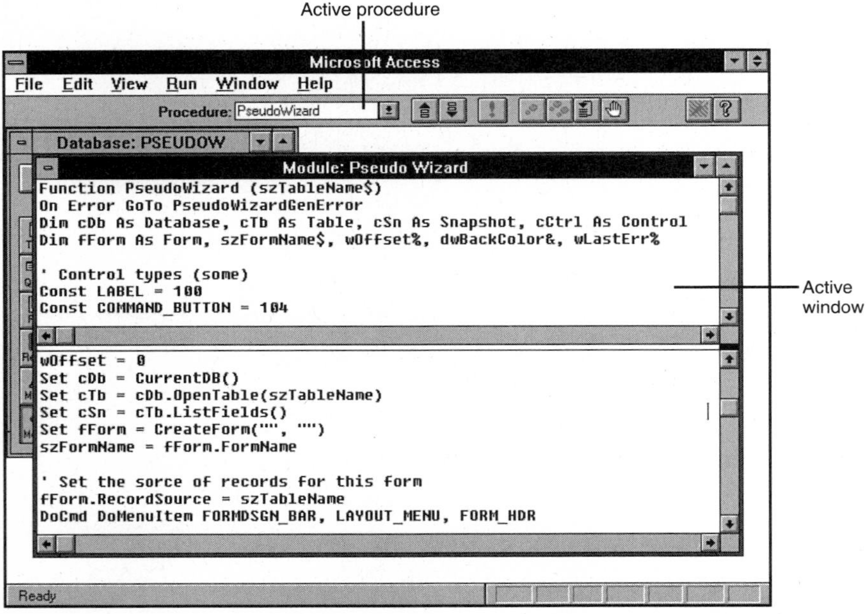

Figure 9.2. The split module edit window.

After you split the editor window, you can select the current half by clicking that half or by pressing the F6 key.

> **Tip:** The procedure box in the toolbar identifies the current procedure. This is the quickest way to see the procedure name, and is especially useful when the module editor window is split.

Reusing Modules

Since modules are treated as objects; you can copy and paste them from database to database, or you can save them to or load them from text files. You can use the Export and Import commands from the

File menu, or the Transfer Database macro, to copy a module to another database. You also create a module in any text editor as a standard ASCII text file and load it into an Access module.

Sharing Modules among Applications

Although it is not mentioned in the Access documentation, you can create library modules which become available to all databases instead of just the current database. These modules, consisting of code, forms, and queries (but not macros), are standard Access databases loaded by Access at startup. By declaring such a database in the [Libraries] section of MSACCESS.INI (as shown below), its code becomes available to all other Access databases:

```
[Libraries]

C:\ACCESS\MyLib.mdb=rw
```

See Chapter 13, "Extending Microsoft Access and Access Basic," for more information on designing and attaching code libraries.

Compiling a Module

Although Access Basic doesn't produce an EXE file during compilation, it does speed the execution of code by performing certain variable and code syntax checks and saving the code in an executable form. Access checks uncompiled code and converts it to an executable form when the procedure is executed.

> **Tip:** Compile your code (by choosing Compile All from the Run menu) before executing it—especially if the code is attached to controls or reports. Otherwise, you may experience unexpected (and preventable) runtime errors.

Printing a Module

A module is printed with the Declarations section first, followed alphabetically by every procedure. If you want to print just one procedure, highlight your selection, choose File | Print, and use the Print Section option.

The module editor is a powerful and convenient method of working with Access Basic code; its capability to check syntax on the fly, proper capitalization of most Access keywords, and tight debugging integration between the module editor and Access enables you to write code more quickly and efficiently. But if you prefer, you can use a different programmer's editor (such as Qedit or Brief) to work with Access Basic code, and then load the text for compilation and execution (using the Load Text selection of the File menu).

Now that you've learned how to use the design environment, you're ready to gain an understanding of the Access Basic language and start writing Access Basic modules.

Understanding Access Basic Language Elements

The best way to get an overview of the Access Basic language is to think of it in terms of seven basic language categories. The following list presents these categories according to the purpose of each type of Access Basic language *element*:

- *Actions.* Actions are intrinsic commands used to build Access macros. You can execute actions directly from Access Basic with the **DoCmd** statement.
- *Functions.* Functions are intrinsic language elements that return a value you can use in an expression. Functions may accept or require arguments. Some functions, like **DDESend**, can be attached only to certain controls and are not available from Access Basic. Return values from such functions are sent directly to the control to which they are attached. Do not confuse intrinsic Access functions with user-defined functions and user-defined Sub procedures, which are not part of the language.
- *Methods.* Methods are intrinsic Access directives that act on a specified Access object. Methods may accept or require arguments.
- *Objects.* Objects are predefined Access elements. Each has certain *properties* (attributes) and applicable *methods*. Access has 10 predefined objects:

  Control
  Database
  Debug
  Dynaset
  Form
  QueryDef
  Report
  Screen
  Snapshot
  Table

- *Operators.* Operators are language elements used to build expressions: string operators ("Adam **&** "Eve"), arithmetic operators (**+**, **-**, *****, for example), and logical operators (such as **And** and **Or**).
- *Properties.* Properties define the attributes of an Access object such as its appearance (the Font Size property, for example), behavior (the *PopUp* property, for example), or how the object reacts to an action (such as the *OnPush* property, for example). You can set or change most Access properties in Design view only.
- *Statements.* Statements include language commands and control structures.

See also the Reference, which contains in-depth documentation of all the language elements listed above.

As discussed at the beginning of the section, Access Basic is organized into modules and procedures. Modules contain or store procedures. Many development tasks—compiling, creating, and saving—are performed on the module level rather than the procedure level.

Access Basic offers two type of procedures: Sub procedures and functions.

Sub procedures do not return a value and can be called only from within Access Basic. Access form and report events properties (such as *OnOpen*, *OnExit*) and Access Basic expressions cannot call or refer to Sub procedures. Sub procedures can accept *parameters* (a variable that passes a value, or the address of a value, from the calling procedure).

Procedures that return a value are called function procedures or just *functions*. Because functions return a value, you can use them in Access expressions and have them called by the event properties of Access forms and reports. A function can accept multiple parameters, but returns only one value.

Access Basic code is executed only as a called procedure. A specific event (such as a *RunCode* macro or an Access Basic function attached to an action property of a control) must start the Access Basic program. Unlike other languages such as the C programming language, no main program routine is executed each time the program starts. For debugging and development purposes, you also can execute Access Basic procedures from the Immediate window.

Developing Coding Conventions

Access Basic is a very new language and has not yet established common coding and naming conventions. The proposed naming conventions in this book are a combination of Hungarian notation and common sense. These are only recommendations and not a rigid standard.

Standard Hungarian notation in the C language is called *Hungarian* not only because it was created by a Hungarian (Charles Simonyi at Microsoft), but because, like the Hungarian language, it is difficult for most people to understand.

The following two tables present the naming conventions that this book uses for Access Basic variables and objects. Declared variables are preceded by a prefix depending on their data type. The following table enumerates the prefixes.

Data type	*Prefix*	*Example*	*Note*
Byte	byt	bytAge	For identification only Declared as Integer
Counter	cnt	cntPrimaryKey	For identification only Declared as Long
Currency	cur	curSalary	
Date/Time	dat	datToday	For identification only; Declared as Variant

continues

Data Type	*Prefix*	*Example*	*Note*
Double	dbl	dblWeight	
Integer	w	wYear	
Long	dw	dwDistance	
Memo	mem	memNotes	For identification only; Declared as String
Ole	ole	oleMugShot	For identification only; Declared as String
String	sz	szLastName	
Variant	v	vWhoKnowsWhat	
Yes/No	f	fOn	For identification only Declared as Integer

Object variables (for example, Table) are identified by the universal prefix *c* followed by a two-letter type identifier, as described in the next table:

Object Variable Type	*Prefix*	*Example*	*Note*
Control	cct	cctCurrentControl	
Database	cdb	cdbCurrentDatabase	
Dynaset	cdy	cdySortedTable	
Form	cf	cfForm1	Often abbreviated as f
QueryDef	cq	cqSalesByMonth	
Report	cr	crReport1	Often abbreviated as r
Snapshot	cs	csFieldsList	
Table	ctb	ctbTable1	

Please note that we do not recommend using special prefixes (or suffixes) to denote the scope (such as Global) or the lifetime (for instance Static) of variables declared in Access Basic.

Keep in mind that this is not a rigid naming convention and that names of many Access objects are better served by using descriptive names (such as FirstQuarterSalesReport) than by a convoluted combination of prefixes and suffixes. Use the preceding scheme or create your own, as long as you are consistent and the naming convention you choose is documented somewhere in your code.

Working with Functions, Procedures, and Sub Procedures

The basic element of Access Basic code is the procedure. You can add a new procedure to a module by choosing New Procedure from the Edit menu. You can use the dialog box to create Sub procedures or functions.

Alternatively, the editor creates a new viewing page if you simply enter a new procedure name in the editor, such as:

```
Function Test()
```

With the Enter keystroke, the module editor adds the End Function statement and displays the new procedure in the new page.

Understanding Declarations

When you open a module (by creating a new module or by selecting an existing module), you first see the Declarations section, shown in figure 9.3. You use this section of the module for the following tasks:

- Declaring modules options for the lower bound of array subscripts, the type of text comparison, and forcing explicit variable declarations: **Base**, **Compare**, and **Explicit**, respectively. (See entries for: Option Base, Option Compare, Option Explicit statements in the Reference, and Chapter 11 for more information on these settings.)
- Defining user-defined data types (data structures; see Chapter 13, "Working with Data")
- Declaring module level and Global constants
- Declaring module level and Global variables and arrays
- Defining **DefInt** statements, which cause variables to default to a certain data type according to the first characters of the variables' names
- Declaring external procedures (such as those from the Windows API) called by an application

> **Tip:** Because the Declarations section is the first page displayed with every module, this is the best place for identifying the module, its programmer, the purpose of the code, and all changes made to the code. Be as descriptive as possible. Access Basic is a self-documenting language, but be sure to briefly describe at least the function of each module and procedure and which objects (forms, reports, and controls) call the procedure. Otherwise, you must open every form (or report) and control to determine the calling objects.

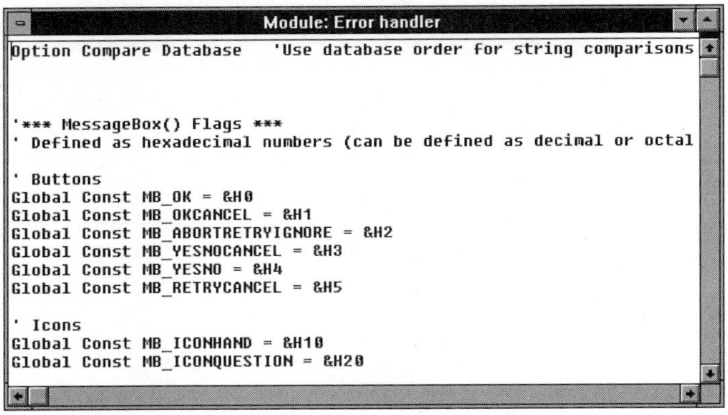

```
Module: Error handler
Option Compare Database   'Use database order for string comparisons


'*** MessageBox() Flags ***
' Defined as hexadecimal numbers (can be defined as decimal or octal

' Buttons
Global Const MB_OK = &H0
Global Const MB_OKCANCEL = &H1
Global Const MB_ABORTRETRYIGNORE = &H2
Global Const MB_YESNOCANCEL = &H3
Global Const MB_YESNO = &H4
Global Const MB_RETRYCANCEL = &H5

' Icons
Global Const MB_ICONHAND = &H10
Global Const MB_ICONQUESTION = &H20
```

Figure 9.3. The Declarations section.

Defining Sub and Function Procedures

Sub procedures are declared with the keyword Sub, as in the following:

```
Sub MyProcedure (szLastName As String)
```

Functions use the keyword Function, as in the following:

```
Function MyFunction (wFileNumber)
```

Because Function procedures in Access can return a value, you also can declare functions with a variable type to explicitly declare the type of data returned. Consider the following example:

```
Function Test (A as String,) As String
```

This examples causes the test function to receive a string parameter and return a string parameter.

Both Sub and Function procedures can accept parameters, but none are required, therefore Sub and Function procedure declarations can also look like this:

```
Function MyFunction()
     (...)
End Function
```

or

```
Sub MyProcedure
     (...)
End Sub
```

Note that Access Basic does not have the equivalent of the C language Void function (a function that doesn't return a value). If you don't want to return a value from the function, declare such functions as Sub procedures or do not assign any value to the function name inside the function. See the Function and Sub procedure statements in the reference part of this book for more information on declaring and executing procedures in Access Basic.

> **Tip:** Access Basic does not force you to program with a modular and organized structure. For example, nothing prevents you from using the GoSub... statement to unconditionally branch (transfer) the execution of a program to a certain line or label. However, such unconditional branching clouds the logic of your code and makes the program more difficult to debug. It is better to use calls to functions or sub procedures (which, after executing, returns control to the line of code immediately following the calling line of code) to execute logically separate blocks of code.

Defining Procedure Parameters

A procedure can include parameters or values passed to the procedure when the procedure is called. Parameters enable you to create flexible procedures that can be controlled by the calling statement. The following function, BeepMeUp, for example, uses a parameter to determine the number of beeps:

```
Function BeepMeUp (wCount as Integer)
     For i = 1 To wCount
          Beep
     Next
     MsgBox "There were " & Str(wCount) & " beeps"
End Function
```

Each parameter is declared within parentheses following the procedure name. Multiple parameters are separated with commas. As you can see in this example, the value received by the procedure is available to the code within the procedure by the parameter name in the procedure definition line.

Passing Parameters by Value

By default, parameters to Access Basic functions and Sub procedures are passed *by reference*; the *address* of the parameter (its physical location in memory) is passed to the function or Sub procedure. This method has one disadvantage. Because the address of the parameter is known to the called function or Sub procedure, its value may be modified. This result usually is not desirable.

Alternatively, parameters may be passed *by value*; the value of a variable is made available to the procedure instead of actually referencing the variable. This method keeps the procedure from changing the value of the variable from the calling code. Use the keyword **ByVal** to pass parameters to functions and Sub procedures by their values. Note that almost all Windows API procedures require that parameters be passed by value. Consider the following two examples:

- *Passing values by value*. The changes to the variable *i* in the function TestByValue are not reflected in the variable *w* in the calling routine. Only the value of *w* is passed to the TestByValue function:

```
w% = 100
Result = TestByValue(w%)        ' The result = 1100; w = 100


Function TestByValue(ByVal i%)
      TestByVal = i + 1000
      i = i + 1
End Function
```

- *Passing values by reference*. Note that the change to the variable *i* made inside the function TestByReference is reflected in the calling routine in variable *w,* whose address was passed to the function TestByReference:

```
w% = 100
Result = TestByReference(w%)       ' Result = 10000; w = 678

Function TestByReference(i%)
      TestByReference = i * i
      i = 678
End Function
```

Using Private and Static Procedures

All functions and Sub procedures declared in Access Basic are *global* by default; that is, they are accessible to all modules in the database. You can use the keyword *Private*, however, to limit the visibility of the procedure to the module in which it is placed. You can call a private procedure only from within the same module.

When using the private procedure option, you can have two or more functions or Sub procedures with the exact same name in different modules in the same database (although this is not a recommended programming practice). From the module with the private procedure, only the private procedure is called. Outside the module, the other procedure with the same name is called.

> **Tip:** To avoid possible conflicts between database code and library code, declare all procedures within libraries and Wizards as private except the function or procedure that provides the entry point.

The keyword *Static* determines the lifetime of the values stored in the procedure. Usually, after a procedure terminates, the values of local variables are discarded. If you want to keep the variable's value available for the next time the procedure runs, such as in the case of counters, running totals, and so on, declare the procedure as static. Variables in a static procedure are local to the procedure.

Another method is to use a module-wide variable (declared in the Declarations section of a module) to maintain its value. The variable would not be local to the procedure, however, and its value could be changed by other procedures.

You can mix procedure types; for example, you can declare a private procedure as static.

Calling a Procedure

There are two ways to call procedures in Access Basic. You can execute a procedure in Access Basic code with the Call statement, but this statement almost always is implied. You can also just use the name of the procedure by itself. For example, both statements that follow execute the Procedure1 sub procedure and pass two parameters:

```
Call Procedure1(1,2)

Procedure1 1,2
```

If you use the Call statement, you must enclose the list of arguments, if any, within parentheses.

> **Tip:** For testing, you can execute procedures directly within the Immediate window. To execute the Procedure1 sub procedure, simply open the Immediate window, type **Procedure1**, and press Enter.

Passing Parameters to a Sub Procedure

Parameters pass a value (or its address) to a procedure. Sub procedures, like functions, can receive parameters. If the Sub procedure is defined with parameters, you must include the parameters when the procedure is called. The following MySub sub procedure, for example, includes a single parameter defined as an integer. When this procedure is called, one integer value must be passed. Optionally, you can enclose a Sub procedure's parameters within parentheses:

```
MySub 2
```

or

```
MySub (2)
```

You also can use a variable or function in the calling statement as the parameter, as in the following example:

```
MySub Date()
MySub FreeFile
MySub szLastName
```

Parameters are an efficient way to pass information between procedures and functions without having to declare these variables separately module-wide or Global. You can also use them to pass values from Access objects such as forms and reports.

Calling a Function

Functions are executed within expressions, and return a value that the expression then uses in its calculation. Because functions are called by expressions, they may be called from nearly anywhere within Access—unlike Sub procedures, which may be called only from within Access Basic. *Assignment expressions*, in which the return value of a function is assigned to a variable, usually call functions in Access Basic.

Note that Access doesn't discard unneeded values returned by functions (even if a particular function doesn't really return any value). Therefore, the value returned by a function must be assigned to a variable or an expression. You can use the following function to set the value to be returned by a function and assign it to the name of the function:

```
Result = MyFunction (a,b,c)
```

To demonstrate calling functions and passing parameters, use the sample function below, MyFunction(). This function receives three parameters: *a*, *b*, and *c*. It then returns the result of multiplying these three parameters. The returned value is assigned to the variable *Result*. Because the function is declared as an integer, it returns an Integer data type. Note that the parameters also are declared as an integer data type (with the % type specifier). If a function,or a parameter passed to a function, has no explicit data type declaration, Access assumes the appropriate Variant data type.

The following code initializes three values passed as parameters to the function MyFunction and calls the function:

```
Dim a%, b%, c%
a = 10 : b = 20 : c= 1
Result = MyFunction(a,b,c)
```

An here is the the function MyFunction:

```
Function MyFunction(Wint1%,wInt2%,wInt3%) As Integer

     MyFunction = (wInt1 * wInt2 * wInt3)          ' Return the value

End Function
```

Procedure Nesting

Procedures can call other procedures, which can in turn call other procedures. Procedure A can call procedure B, which then can call procedure C, and so on. Although sometimes there may be a legitimate need for such a deep nesting of procedures, this should be the exception and not the rule.

Try to keep the nesting of procedures reasonable so that your code is as readable and maintainable as possible.

Another important consideration when deciding on the depth of nesting procedures is error trapping. Because an error can be repeated through all nested procedures, error recovery is more difficult to code and less reliable.

Exiting a Procedure

A procedure—a function or Sub procedure—terminates when it encounters an **End Sub** or **End Function** statement. You can force a procedure to terminate earlier by including an **Exit Sub** or **Exit Function** statement anywhere in the code. If you want to return a value from within a function procedure, you must make the assignment before the **Exit Function** statement in the code. When a procedure terminates, local variables are released and their values no longer are accessible to other procedures.

Understanding Access Basic Program Flow Control Structures

Program flow control structures help you to write clear and understandable code, and also to equip your program with flexible decision-making capabilities. Access Basic has three categories of flow-control structures: decision structures, loop-control structures, and branching structures.

Decision Structures

Access Basic provides two structures to test conditions and to take appropriate actions based on the result of the test of a condition: **If...Then...Else** and **Select Case**. The condition must evaluate to True or False.

If...Then...Else enables you to execute two or more groups of statements based on the evaluation of the condition specified in the If (or **ElseIf**) part of the statement. The If..Then...Else structure stops evaluating and executes the statement following the **End If** statement after encountering a True condition in any of the If (or ElseIf) statements, or after evaluating all If (or ElseIf) statements. The Else part executes if no condition in If (or EndIf) statements evaluates to True:

```
If dwSavings > 100000 Then
     Debug.Print "Lots of dough..."
ElseIf dwSavings > 50000 Then
     Debug.Print "You should save more"
ElseIf dwSavings > 20000 Then
     Debug.Print "Ho-Humm..."
Else
     Debug.Print "Savings? What savings?!"
End If
```

Tip: For simple binary (true/false) evaluation, use the **IIf** function instead of the **If...Then...**structure, as shown in the following example:

```
Able2Drive = IIf(Age > 16, "Can drive!", "Must wait...")
```

The **Select Case** statement evaluates different values of the same expression (condition) specified in the **Select Case** statement. This statement breaks out to the statement following the **End Select** statement after executing the code that follows the value of the appropriate Case statement. If no condition evaluates to True, the code following the optional **Case Else** executes. The following function takes a different action based on the value of the parameter dwSelector:

```
Function TestCase (dwSelector#)
     Select Case dwSelector
     Case 123
          TestCase = Func123()
     Case 255
          TestCase = "The value is 255"
     Case 1024
          TestCase = "Kilobyte"
     Case Else
          TestCase = "No match...."
     End Select
End Function
```

The major difference between the **If...Then** and **Select Case** constructs is that the former can evaluate a set of different statements in every **If** (or **ElseIf**) part, while the latter needs to have just one condition to test. The **If...Then...Else** statement can digest painlessly the following illogical combination:

```
If Date = #01/01/93# Then
     MsgBox "New Year!"
ElseIf szLastName = "Smith" Then
     Debug.Print "This is Mr. or Ms. Smith"
ElseIf City = "Istanbul" Then
     City = "Constantinople"
Else
     Debug.Print "Apples are not Compaqs"
Endif
```

The Select Case construct acts on only the *first* condition that evaluates to True, however. If subsequent statements also are True, they are ignored.

Loop Structures

To execute a specified block of code more than one time, Access provides five loop-control structures: **Do Until...Loop**, **Do While...Loop**, **Do...Loop Until**, **Do....Loop While**, and **For...Next**. **Do Until...**, **Do While**, **Do...Loop Until**, and **Do...Loop While** (collectively called *Do loops*) are variations on the same theme. These Do loops all enable you to execute a block of code while (or until) a condition is True. The **For...Next** construct executes a block of code until the counter does not reach a certain value.

DoUntil and Do While evaluate the condition at the top of the loop. You therefore have no guarantee that the code inside the loop will execute at all. Do...Loop Until and Do...Loop While structures check the condition at the bottom of the loop. The loop therefore is guaranteed to execute at least once. Both variations of the Do Until Loop are in essence equal to the Do While Not... loop. The following example demonstrates the use and the results of these four Do loops:

```
Function TestDoLoops ()
    i = 1
    Do While i < 3
        i = i + 1
    Loop
    Debug.Print i                       ' i = 3

    Do Until i >= 3
        i = i + 1
    Loop
    Debug.Print i                       ' i = 3

    Do
    i = i + 1
        Loop While i < 3
    Debug.Print i                       ' i = 4

    Do
        i = i + 1
    Loop Until i > 3
    Debug.Print i                       ' i = 5

End Function
```

To exit a Do loop, use the Exit Do statement placed anywhere inside the Do loop structure:

```
Do Until cTable.EOF
     If cTable.LastName = "Szczebrzeszynski" Then
          Exit Do
     End If
     cTable.MoveNext
Loop
```

Do loops work best in situations where the number of iterations of the loop depends on a condition that changes inside the loop, or the number is caused by some sort of external event (such as time, a change in data values, and so on).

If you know the number of iterations of a loop, use the For...Next structure. The For...Next structure executes a specific number of times, as long as the counter does not reach the specified value. The counter is incremented automatically at the bottom of the loop by the Next statement. Note that, because the counter is treated by Access as any other variable, incrementing the counter inside the For...Next loop can cause unexpected results. To execute a loop for each day of the year (of any year, including leap years), for example, set up the counter as follows:

```
'Calculate the upper limit for the counter (leap years has 29 days in February
 wNoOfDays = IIf(Month(DateSerial(wYear, 2, 29)) = 2, 366, 365)

  For i = 1 To wNoOfDays
        (...)
  Next
```

You can increment or decrement the counter (as in For i = 400 To 1) by any value, specified in the Step option . For example,

```
For i = 1 to 8000 Step 1000
     (...)
Next
```

increments the counter i by 1,000 after every iteration of the loop. To prematurely exit a For...Next loop (before the counter reaches the predefined value, for example) use the **Exit For** statement anywhere inside the loop.

Branching

Even in the most structured approach to programming, you occasionally may need to unconditionally branch or "jump" to a specified part of code. Usually, there is a better means of branching (such as executing a separate function or Sub procedure), and "jumps" should be kept to an absolute minimum. Access Basic provides two control structures that simply branch to the specified place in the current procedure: **GoTo** and GoSub...Return.

The **GoTo** statement branches to a specified line number or label within the same procedure. For example:

```
Function VeryBadHabit(wCounter%)
     If wCounter = 100 Then Goto OneHundred
     (...)
Exit Function

TwoHundred:
     Exit Function

OneHundred:
     (...)
     GoTo TwoHundred
End Function
```

GoTo is a fossil from the era of unstructured programming and, as illustrated by the preceding example, introduces unnecessary complexity and produces difficult to follow *spaghetti code*. Moreover, because the **GoTo** statement doesn't provide an orderly way to return to the calling line (except by using another **GoTo** statement that makes the code even murkier), using it is like setting off a time bomb in your code. It surely will blow up, and debugging such code is a nightmare. To keep branching orderly, use a function or Sub procedure to execute statements that otherwise would follow a label in a procedure executed with a **GoTo** statement. For example, **GoSub....Return** branches to a label (or a line number) within the same function or Sub procedure and returns to the statement following the most recent GoSub statement, as in the following example:

```
Function BetterButStillNoCigar()
     GoSub Mess1
     (...)

     Exit Function
Mess1:
     Debug.Print "I've entered this subroutine at " & Time()
     Return
End Function
```

Although **GoSub...Return** is more usable than the **GoTo** statement, it still is an outdated control structure and therefore is not recommended for use in Access Basic. You easily can replace the **GoTo** statement with a function or Sub procedure performing an equal function.

A special case of **GoTo** and **GoSub...Return** statements is the **On ...** statement that branches to a label depending on the value of the expression, such as in the following example:

```
wWhereTo = 2
On wHereTo GoSub Label1, Label2
```

or

```
On wWhere GoSub Sub1, Sub2
```

The best rule of thumb is to let data and events, not code, determine branching.

Nesting Control Structures

All control structures in Access Basic can be nested (or placed) within one another, as in the following example:

```
Do Until cTable.EOF
     If cTable.Type = "Sales" Then
          For i = 1 To 31
               Debug.Print Sales(i)
          Next
     Endif
     cTable.MoveNext
Loop
```

Nested control structures cannot overlap (cross boundaries). The following construct is illegal:

```
Select Case wCounter
     Case 10
     Case 20
     If Date = #01/01/93# Then
          Case 1
     Endif
     Case Else
End Select
```

The level of nesting has no practical limit, but should be kept to a minimum because every level of nesting decreases the readability of your code.

Commenting Your Code

You add comments to your Access Basic code with the ' symbol. You can place comments anywhere—for example, at the beginning of the line or after the line of code. Comments placed after code document the line in a manner visually consistent with the macro description column.

You also should plan to document each procedure's operation at the beginning of the procedure. Document modules in the Declarations section.

Using the Database Analyzer to Document Your Code

The Database Analyzer can provide two sets of module documentation. First, the Database Analyzer can write to the **@ModuleProcedures** table all the procedure names in a module, including their parameters. Second, the Database Analyzer can report to the **@ProcedureVariables** table a listing of all the variables used in the module (see fig. 9.4.).

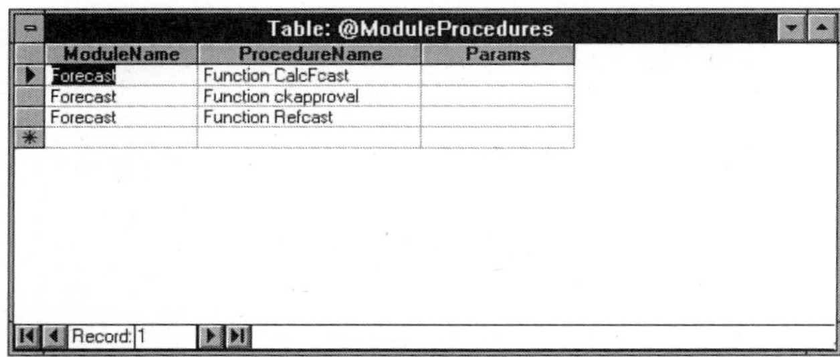

Figure 9.4. Listing procedures generated from Database Analyzer data.

For more information about the Database Analyzer see Chapter 2, "Working with the Access Database."

Debugging Access Basic Modules

To completely debug your application, you need to fully understand the entire application—from tables and queries to form properties to Access Basic modules. Although Access Basic offers a strong suite of debugging tools, it will not help solve an ill-defined query, misapplied property settings, or logic errors. The point is that you need a holistic approach to the debugging process. With that understanding, the following sections will help you use debugging tools to find errors in your Access Basic code.

Setting Breakpoints

A breakpoint allows you to establish a place in your code that the code stops executing so you can test the run time environment at that moment. Each breakpoint operates as if there were a Stop command just prior to the breakpoint line.

To set or clear a breakpoint, move to the Access Basic line. You then can toggle on or off the breakpoint by using one of these three methods:

- Click the Breakpoint button on the toolbar.
- Press F9.
- Choose the Toggle Breakpoint command from the Run menu.

When execution reaches the breakpoint line, Access halts the procedure. You can continue with the option of stopping again at the next line or the end of the procedure, by using the Run, Single Step, or Procedure Step command.

A breakpoint line is in boldface. You can set as many breakpoints as you want. Although you could place a Stop command in your code instead of a breakpoint, the Stop command remains until you remove it. Breakpoints last only until you clear the breakpoint or close the database.

Access does not provide variable or data breakpoints. These breakpoints, as used in other languages, enable you to set a breakpoint if variable XYZ meets a certain condition or if data element ABC is changed. Often, these debugging devices display the values of selected variables during execution.

Using Access, you must create your own variable breakpoints. By strategically placing Message box statements inside your code, you can report the value of a variable whenever you want.

Stepping through Access Basic Code

When execution is stopped by a breakpoint, you can continue the execution by using one of the options described in the following table.

Command	*Toolbar Button*	*Keyboard*	*Description*
Procedure Step		Shift+F8	Continue through end of procedure and stop again
Run	!	F5	Continue running at full speed
Single Step		F8	Single-step execution of the next Access Basic line of code

The procedure step is best used when execution drops down to another procedure known to be working. The procedure step then completes the procedure and stops execution when control returns to the procedure being debugged.

Access highlights the line about to be executed with a dim gray border. You can press F8 or click the Single Step button to process the code one line at a time.

> **Tip:** While you are single stepping, you can change which line is executed next by using the Set Next Statement command.

Using the Immediate Window

One of the powerful features from Visual Basic, the Immediate window, enables you to test variables or execute Access Basic commands. The Immediate window can be compared to the Xbase (dBASE, FoxPro) dot prompt; however, the Immediate window is better suited to debugging rather than primary program control.

To enable the Immediate window, choose the Immediate Window command from the View menu. This command acts as a toggle, so you also can choose it to remove the Immediate window. This window is a pop-up window, so it appears on top of other windows and remains until you remove it.

The Immediate window can be used to perform the following tasks:

- Execute Access Basic code
- Execute Access Basic intrinsic functions, statements and actions
- Inspect the value of controls on active forms
- Display the properties of active objects
- To test short "code snippets" before using them in the code

To query the value of a property or variable, or to execute a function, use the ? command followed by the desired expression. For instance, to inspect the value of the *RecordSource* property of the form MyForm, type:

```
? Forms![MyForm].RecordSource
```

You can also type code sequences in the Immediate window, such as the following three lines below:

```
s1$ = "Joan"
s2$ = "d'Arc"
? s1$ & " " &  s2$
```

> **Note:** Pressing Enter executes the current line; it does not insert an Enter character. To enter a new line in the Immediate window, press Ctrl+Enter.

Another advantage to using the Immediate window is that you can print to the Immediate window during execution by using the debug.print object and method. This method is not foolproof; it works only when the module retains the focus. If the code selects other objects, the Immediate window no longer is visible.

Chapter Summary

This chapter introduced you to Access Basic and the Access Basic programming environment. There are many tasks for which Access Basic is particularly suited; but keep one caution in mind: No amount of Access Basic code can overcome the failure to master and use Access objects and tools. If you learn these objects and tools, you will significantly reduce the amount of programming needed for your applications; and the code you do write will perform more efficiently.

10

Understanding Access Data Types

Selecting the proper data type in which to store information is an important consideration when designing a database application. Good table design is one of the key components of application development, particularly in a data-driven model. It is best to specify the proper data type at the table level, even though you may use a variety of formatting options in your forms and reports. Skimping on this process in the haste to design a "working" application inevitably results in disappointment.

For example, a common beginner's mistake is to use a numeric data type for items such as phone numbers and social security numbers. Although this may seem logical because the data is in the form of numbers, from a database design perspective it is inefficient to allocate space for a numeric data type if the data will not be used in numeric operations.

This chapter guides you through the different data types available in Access, helps you choose the proper data type, explains how to specify data types in tables and from Access Basic code, and provides numerous practical examples showing how to use and convert data types.

Choosing the Right Data Type

In determining which data type to use, there are a number of factors to consider, including the following:

- *The nature and amount of information to be stored.* You have the most flexibility in controlling this element when you are designing a new table from scratch. Look carefully at each data element and try to match it as closely as possible with the appropriate data type.

- *For numeric data, the number and type of operations to be performed, and the range of values and accuracy expected from the results of such operations.* Numeric operations in scientific applications, for example, must meet a higher degree of precision than do those in most business applications.
- *Whether the data is being converted from a non-native file format.* Because Access offers more data types than most corresponding MS-DOS database management systems, converting (importing) data from non-native formats can require a two-step process. The first step is to import the data and allow Access to automatically convert data types according to its prescribed internal formula. You then can convert some data types manually, to take advantage of the additional data types offered by Access. Paradox 3.5, for example, does not support memo fields; but an Import operation automatically converts character data into Access as Text, and you can manually convert the text field into a memo field.
- *Size of the table, expected size of the application, and Access storage requirements.* Many design errors result from paying insufficient attention to the ultimate amount of data to be stored. You may use a Long Integer (four bytes of storage), for example, when an Integer type (two bytes of storage) actually suffices. Initially, this point seems relatively insignificant, but as the database grows, and new tables, forms, reports, and other objects are added, design inefficiencies such as wasted space become evident. Try to anticipate and plan for the overall size of the application.

The following table shows how Access data types are referred to in the Table Design view, the equivalent of each data type in Access Basic, and the internal storage requirements for each type.

Table Design	*Access Basic*	*Storage Size*
Text	String	1 byte per character
Numbers	Integer	2 bytes
	Long (integer)	4 bytes
	Single	4 bytes
	Double	8 bytes
Currency	Currency	8 bytes
Date/Time	Double	8 bytes
Boolean	Integer	2 bytes
Counter	Long (integer)	4 bytes
Memo (free-form text)	String	1 byte per character
OLE objects and other binary data (BLOBs)	No equivalent	Varies with size of object

Table Design	*Access Basic*	*Storage Size*
Variant	Varies according to data type	Varies according to data type

Using the Variant Data Type

Variant is the most flexible data type in Access because it can accept, store, and process any type of data. Although Variant is the least economical (and slowest) data type, it has one important application; unlike other Access data types, Variant can store both Empty and Null values. Further, the Variant data type doesn't have a type declaration character (suffix); its contents and its usage determine the internal storage class of the variant. To test for the internal storage class, use the **VarType** function. The following table shows the values the **VarType** function returns for Variant internal storage classes.

Value Returned	*What the Variant Contains*
0	Empty (no data, variable not initialized)
1	Null (no valid data)
2	Integer
3	Long integer
4	Single
5	Double
6	Currency
7	Date/Time
8	String

The following list shows the largest values stored by Variant:

- For all numeric data types, including date and time (the internal storage class depends on the actual value):

  From -1.79769313486231E308 to -4.94066E-324 for negative numbers and from 4.94066E-324 to 1.797693134862315E308 for positive numbers.

- For strings in a Variant of VarType 8:

  Approximately 64K (the maximum string length allowed in Access).

Example:

If a Variant string variable (VarType 8) is converted to a number, it can be used in numeric expressions just like any other numeric data type.

```
Dim v1 As Variant, v2 As Variant
v1 = "100"
v2 = 6
Result = v1 * v2          'Returns 600 (integer type)
```

When used in arithmetic operations, numeric variant data types behave exactly as "real" numeric data. If the result of an operation overflows the original data type, it is pushed up to the next more precise (longer) internal storage class.

Using the Access Basic VarType Function

The VarType function returns a value that indicates how Access Basic internally stores a Variant. Access Basic uses this value to distinguish, for example, between subtypes of the Integer data type such as Currency, Counter, Single, and Double. (See later sections in this chapter on numeric data types.)

The syntax of this function is as follows:

VarType(*variant*)

variant is a variable of the Variant data type.

The following table shows the values that are returned by the VarType function, depending on the type of data contained by the Variant.

Value Returned	*What the Variant Contains*
0	Empty
1	Null
2	Integer
3	Long
4	Single
5	Double
6	Currency
7	Date
8	String

Handling Text with the Text Data Type

Text or Memo character data is stored internally by Access as String data type. If no data type is specified in the Table Design view, Access uses Text as a default.

Text is the most widely used data type. Text fields can include alphanumeric characters, which means any printable ASCII character, including numbers. As mentioned in the introduction, text fields should be used even for numeric data when there will be no numeric operations performed. Typical examples are ZIP codes, phone numbers, and product ID codes.

The following table shows the formatting options for text that are available from the Table Design view.

Text Formatting Option	*Formatting Character*
Uppercase	>
Lowercase	<
Text character required	@
Text character not required	&
Display a digit or nothing	#

You often may want to validate data that is entered into a text field. The next two sections describe methods of improving on the limited selection of text formatting options available from the Table Design view.

Entering Numeric Data into a Text Field

One popular formatting option in dBASE or Xbase systems that is unavailable from the Access Table Design view is forcing the entry of numeric data into a Text field. In most Xbase systems this option is indicated with the picture formatting symbol '9'. This option is used primarily for data validation with numeric data that is not going to be used for numeric calculations, such as Social Security numbers and phone numbers.

You can encounter problems using the # formatting symbol in Access. When you use the # symbol format, Access accepts the entry of non-numeric data into the form, but displays nothing. For example, in a five-character text field formatted with # for customer number, Access accepts an entry of ASDFG, but when you move to the next field, the display appears blank. If you inspect the datasheet view of the table, however, you see that the value ASDFG appears in the customer number field. For this reason, it is not a good idea to use the # symbol to validate such data.

The challenge then becomes to find another way to validate this type of numeric data at the point of data entry. You may consider, for example, changing the field type to numeric. The problem with using the numeric field type is that it provides no way to display non-numeric characters, such as a hyphen (-) to separate the numbers for easier reading. Further, numbers require more storage overhead (two bytes for Integers, as opposed to one byte per character for character data).

A preferable solution is to use an Access Basic validation function to evaluate the entry and return an error message if an incorrect value is entered. You can attach the function to the form.

The following function evaluates an entry into the SSN field and returns an error message if the data entered is non-numeric or less than nine characters in length (see fig. 10.1):

```
Function CheckSSN (szSSN As Control)
Dim wLen%
wLen = Len(cSSN)
 If wLen < 9 Then                  'First check the length
    CheckSSN = False
   Exit Function                   'If less than 9 exit with an error
 End If

 For x = 1 To wLen                'Loop to check all 9 characters

   If Not IsNumeric(Mid(szSSN,x,1)) Then
    CheckSSN = False           'If any values are non-numeric,
    Exit Function              'Exit the function and return an error
   End If

 Next

CheckSSN = True
End Function
```

Mixing Uppercase and Lowercase Text

Another common example of text formatting is that used to display data in uppercase, lowercase, or mixed case. Many times data is "inherited" from an older database. Some applications (particularly those in a mainframe environment where video display terminals have limited display capabilities) accept character data only in uppercase. Further, when very large amounts of data need to be entered, enabling data entry only in uppercase reduces the number of keystrokes and improves overall accuracy. Regardless of how the data is stored, you may want to display the data in a mixed-case format for reporting or other purposes.

The LASTNAME and FIRSTNAME fields in the table shown in figure 10.2 contain data in all uppercase. The objective for purposes of this example is to format the data in mixed case; for example, John Smith instead of JOHN SMITH. You cannot create the proper display from the Table Design view, because that view offers no formatting symbol to indicate mixed case. Combining upper- and lowercase formatting symbols doesn't work, because the last symbol takes precedence. You can use the following short routine in Access Basic, however, to handle the job quite well:

```
Function MixCase ()
  Dim cLastname As Control, cFirstname As Control
  Set cLastname = Forms![names]![lastname]
  Set cFirstname = Forms![names]![firstname]

'Translate to mixed case
cLastname  = UCase(Left(cLastname, 1)) +  LCase(Right(cLastname,
➥Len(cLastname)  - 1))
cFirstname = UCase(Left(cFirstname, 1)) + LCase(Right(cFirstname,
➥Len(cFirstname) - 1))

End Function
```

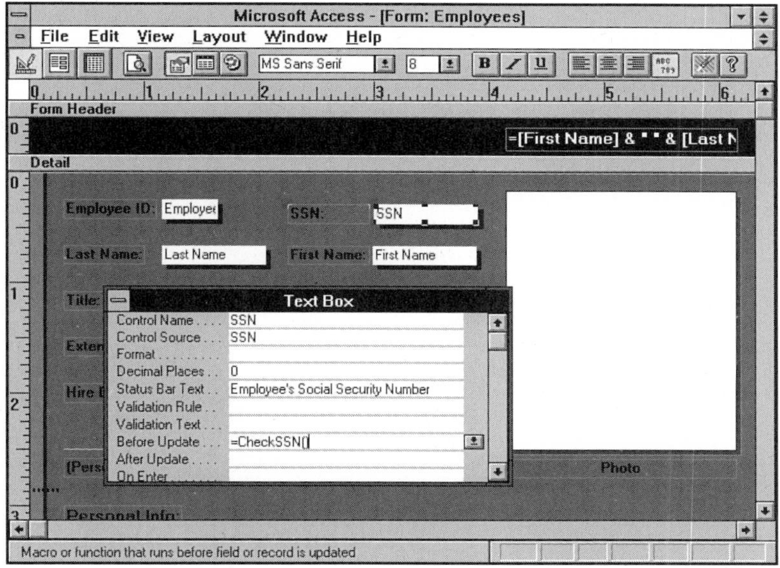

Figure 10.1. Form using the function Check SSN( ) as a validation rule.

Microsoft Access - [Table: NAMES]

File Edit View Records Layout Window Help

Field: FIRSTNAME New:

LASTNAME	FIRSTNAME
SMITH	JOHN
WILLIAMS	MARY
WILSON	ROBERT
JONES	SHARON
KELLY	JACK
JAMISON	ROBERTA

Record: 6

Datasheet View

Figure 10.2. Table showing data in uppercase.

It might seem logical to use this function as a validation rule in the form. Because the function changes data, however, attaching it as a validation rule produces the error message shown in figure 10.3. To avoid this error, assign the function to another property in the form, such as *Before Update*.

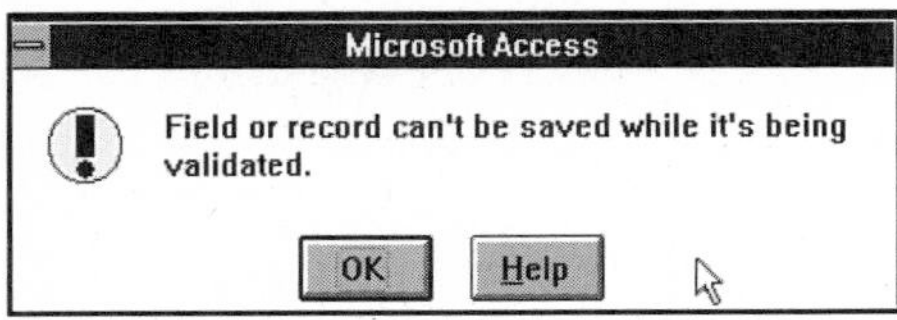

Figure 10.3. Message box indicating error in attempting to save while data is being validated.

If you decide to globally convert all instances of the data to mixed case, you can use an Update query, as shown in figure 10.4. Executing the Update query produces the results shown in figure 10.5.

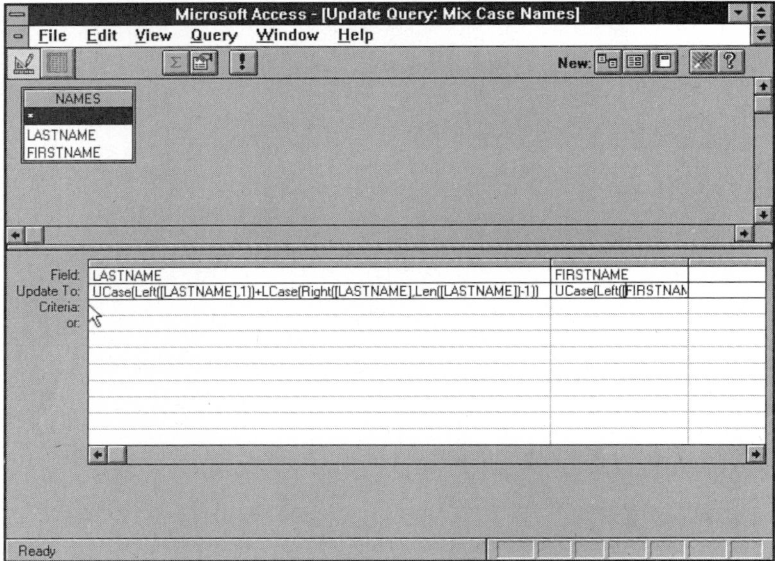

Figure 10.4. Update query to convert text data to mixed case.

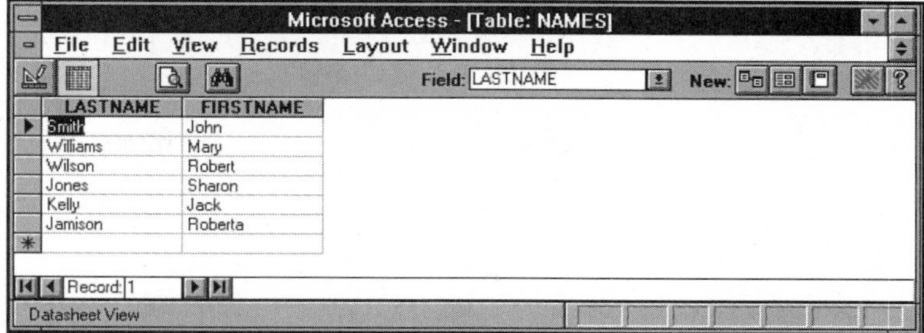

Figure 10.5. Table showing conversion to mixed case.

Using the Memo Data Type

Access uses the Memo data type to store blocks of character information. Although the internal storage is still one byte per character, unlike text fields, whose maximum size is determined by the length of the field assigned in the Table Design view, Access memo fields can dynamically increase the amount of storage needed as data is added to the field.

Memo fields are best used for narrative information such as notes, where allocating a fixed length for each record is impractical. But keep in mind that formatting options are unavailable for Memo data.

Storing Binary Objects with the Binary Data Type

Access can also store and manipulate various forms of binary data, such as OLE objects, graphics, sound, formatted text, and so on. The length of OLE or other binary data that can be stored is up to 128M (in version 1.0) or 1G (in version 1.1).

An OLE file doesn't have a counterpart in Access Basic (because of its length, the OLE file cannot be assigned to a variable anyway). The chief application for this data type is for storing various binary objects such as Paintbrush pictures in Access tables.

> **Tip:** Because data in OLE fields can be longer than the 64K limit for strings, to manipulate (copy, append) this type of data, use the Access Basic **AppendChunk** and **GetChunk** methods to break the OLE field into smaller parts.

Using the Numeric Data Type

In the Access Table Design view, the term *numbers* refers to all numeric data types. If no data type is specified in the *Field Size* property, Access assigns Double as a default. Selecting the appropriate numeric data type depends upon one or more of the following factors:

- Range of values
- Precision required
- Number and type of operations to be performed
- Data storage requirements

A good rule of thumb is to select a data type that requires the minimum amount of precision and storage space necessary to accomplish the objectives of the application without compromising accuracy. Following this rule saves both memory and processing time. For example, the Currency data type is an appropriate choice to handle a field named Salary, because that data type enables quick and accurate arithmetic operations with a minimum of rounding errors.

Table 10.1 lists the various numeric data types and sizes and their equivalent names from the Table Design view Properties dialog box.

Table 10.1. Numeric Data Types

Field Size Property	*Access Basic Data Type*	*Range of Values*	*Type Declaration Suffix*	*Decimals*	*Size*
Double	Double (double-precision floating point)	-1.797 * 10^308 to +1.797 * 10^308	# (ANSI char. 35)	15	8 bytes
Single	Single (single-precision floating point)	-3.4 * 10^38 to +3.4 * 10^38	! (ANSI char. 33)	7	4 bytes
Long Integer	Long	-2,147,483,648 to +2,147,438,647	& (ANSI char. 38)	None	4 bytes
Integer	Integer	-32,768 to +32,767	% (ANSI char. 37)	None	2 bytes
Byte	Integer	0 to 255	% (ANSI char. 37)	None	1 byte
Currency	Currency	-922337203685477.5808 to +922337203685477.5808	@ (ANSI char. 64)	4	4 bytes

Using Integers

An Access integer is a whole number; it never has a fractional part and contains no decimal places. In Access Basic, integers also can represent Boolean values (-1 for True, 0 for False). In general, integers require less storage space than floating point numbers and less processing time in arithmetic operations. Access automatically increments integers in the Counter data type every time a new record is added. The Counter data type is used primarily to establish and maintain referential integrity between two tables.

Using Floating-Point Numbers

An Access floating-point number corresponds more or less with what mathematicians call a *real number*. Real numbers include all values between integers (fractional values), and thus represent a much larger range of values than integers. You must make a trade-off, however, if you want to take advantage of the greater ranges of values and precision available with floating-point numbers. The internal scheme Access uses to store a floating-point number is more complex than the one it uses to store an integer. Floating-point representation involves breaking a number into three parts: the sign, the exponent, and the mantissa, as shown in the following table.

Numbers	*Sign*	*Exponent*	*Mantissa*
Single 32-bit (4 bytes)	1 bit	8 bits	23 bits (plus an additional implied bit)
Double 64-bit (8 bytes)	1 bit	11 bits	52 bits (plus an additional implied bit)

The practical result of this more complex storage scheme is that operations on floating-point numbers require more processing time than operations on integers.

Formatting Numbers from the Table Design View

A number of default formatting options for numbers are available in the Access Table Design view. You can also customize the display with Access Basic by using a special set of characters to create a "picture" of the desired display. Although most formatting options are available from Access Basic, you save time by using the table design options whenever possible.

The following table shows the numeric formatting options available from the Table Design view, and the table property to which they are attached.

Format Choice or Symbol	*Table Design Property or Formatting String*	*Unformatted Value*	*Will Display As*
General Number	Field size	1234.5	1234.5
Currency	Field size	1234.5	$ 1,234.50
Fixed	Field size	12345	12345
Standard	Field size	1234.5	1,234.50
Percent	Field size	1234.5	0.1234
Scientific	Field size	1234.5	1.23E + 03
null string	Format	12345	12345 (unformatted)
0	00000.00	1234.5	01234.50
#	#####.##	1234.5	1234.5
$	$*#####,###.00	1234.5	$1,234.50
	##.###	1234.5	1234.5
%	#0.00%	0.12345	12.35%
,	###,###,###.00	1234.5	1,234.50
E- e-	#.###E00	1234.5	1.234.50
E+ e+	#.###E-00	1234.5	1.2345E+03

Working with Date and Time Values

Access provides a variety of date and time formats. From the Table Design view, you can specify a Date/Time field type. Any time you enter a date value, the time (according to the system time on the computer) is automatically stored with the date. Numerous formatting options for displaying the date and time should give you enough flexibility for almost any formatting need.

In addition to display (formatting) options, Access Basic also has a number of date and time manipulation functions, which are presented and discussed in later sections. These functions enable you to convert numbers to dates and dates to strings, to obtain a day of the week or month, and so on.

It is always advisable to use the Access Date data type for tracking dates; otherwise you must write lengthy custom routines to handle date-specific arithmetic operations.

Using the Date/Time Data Type

Date and time values are stored internally by Access as eight-byte double-precision numbers. Time is internally stored as a fractional portion of this double-precision number, ranging from 0 (which expresses midnight as `00:00:00`) and .99999 (`11:59:59 P.M.`). Time is automatically "attached" to the date at the time of creation of the entry. Displaying the time along with the date is optional, and can be specified with formatting options.

Access can store and process dates from January 1, 100 through December 30, 9999. Access interprets dates earlier than January 1, 100 AD, as falling into the current century. Suppose that you try to calculate the number of days between 01-01-0010 (meaning 10 AD) and today by using the following code:

```
= DateDiff("yyyy",", Date(), "01/01/0010")
```

Access assumes the year in the entered date to be 1910. January 1, 1900 equals 2, and negative numbers represent dates prior to December 30, 1899. Access date and time functions accept a double-precision number in addition to any other legal date and time formats and, if the number can be interpreted as a valid date and/or time, return the correct result. Adding an hour, for example, to a fractional number .1234 (as in `DateAdd("h", 1, .1234)`) produces 3:57:42 AM.

When designing tables, select the date/time format that best suits your needs because all date and time values take up eight bytes of storage, no matter how they appear to be formatted on-screen. A date/time format specified in the table design is applied automatically to forms and reports as a default (if an applicable control is bound to a particular field). You can override the table format, however, by respecifying the date/time format inside the Form Design view or Report Design view.

To override the default date/time format for a particular bound control, simply specify a different format in the Properties window for the control. You can accomplish this task by attaching an Access Basic intrinsic function to the control, or by using a user-defined function if the desired format is unavailable in Access.

The following table shows the date and time formatting options available from the table design Format property.

Format Option or Symbol	*Description*	*Example*
General Date	Default setting—if the value is date only, no time is displayed; if the value is time only, no date is displayed	Defaults to MS Windows date settings
Long Date	Same as the Long Date setting in the MS Windows International section	Tuesday, March 8, 1993
Medium Date	Uses character abbreviation for month	08-Mar-93

continues

Format Option or Symbol	*Description*	*Example*
Short Date	Same as the Short Date setting in MS Windows	3/8/93
c	Same as the General Date format	Defaults to MS Windows date settings
/	Date separator	**mm/dd/yy** displays 03/08/93
m	Picture symbol for months	**m** displays 3 **mm** displays 03 **mmm** displays Mar **mmmm** displays March
d	Picture symbol for days	**d** displays 3 **dd** displays 08 **ddd** displays Tue **dddd** displays Tuesday
y	Picture symbol for years	**yy** displays 93 **yyyy** displays 1993
d	Day of the month in one or two numerical digits, as needed	8
Long Time	Same as the Time setting in MS Windows (usually includes the display of seconds)	8:10:27 AM
Medium Time	Suppresses the display of seconds	8:10 AM
Short Time	Suppresses the display of AM/PM	8:10
:(colon)	Time separator, set in the International Section of the WIN.INI file	8:10 AM
h	Picture symbol for hours	**h** displays 8 **hh** displays 08 If the AM/PM picture symbol is used, **hh** displays 8AM for 0800 hours.
m	Picture symbol for minutes—Access determines whether **m** is used to format a date or time by its context	**m** displays 8 **mm** displays 10

Format Option or Symbol	*Description*	*Example*
s	Picture symbol for seconds	**s** displays 2 **ss** displays 27
AM/PM	Adds AM or PM to the time display	03-08-93 AM

Formatting Date and Time Values in Access Basic

Access Basic has over 20 date- and time-related functions and commands. Because Access date and time functions are **ss** displays closely interrelated, you can use many Access date functions to calculate time as well as date. The function **Now( )**, for example, returns both the date and time.

These functions can be divided roughly into four groups:

- Functions that return a specified component of the date or time:

Day	**Month**
DatePart	**Second**
DateSerial	**Timer**
DateValue	**Weekday**
Hour	**Year**
Minute	

- Functions that perform date arithmetic:

  DateAdd

  DateDiff

- Functions that set or return date and time values based on the system clock:

  Date and **Date$**

  Now

  Time and **Time$**

- Conversion functions:

  CVDate converts an expression into the Date data type Variant of VarType 7

Many Access Basic date and time functions accept formatting parameters and therefore can return different values (intervals) based on the contents of the formatting string. The formatting parameters are shown in the next table and enclosed in quotes in the examples that follow.

To Return	*Formatting Character to Use*
Year	yyyy
Quarter	q
Month	m
Day of year	y
Day	d
Weekday	w
Week	ww
Hour	h
Minute	m
Second	s

Examples:

```
DatePart("yyyy", Date())      'Returns the current year
DatePart("m", Now())          'Returns the current month
DatePart("s", Now())          'Returns the 'current' second
```

Another way to change the formatted display of date and time values is to use the **Format[$]** function. The Access incarnation of this traditional BASIC language workhorse accepts almost 30 different formatting strings.

```
Format("c",#12/01/92#)   'Displays: Wednesday, December 1, 1992
```

Changing Windows' Date and Time Settings

If the format of your Access date and time functions output doesn't meet your expectations, some Windows internal settings may be contending with your format. The following entries in the WIN.INI file influence date and time formatting:

```
[intl]
s1159=AM
s2359=PM
sDate=/
sTime=:
sShortDate=M/d/yy
sLongDate=dddd,MMMM dd,yyyy
```

Understanding How Data Types Are Used in Access Basic

In Access Basic, both variables and functions can have types. Access functions return values by assigning a return value to the name of the function. The following example returns the number 124 as a Variant:

```
Function MyFunction
     MyFunction = 124
End Function
```

You declare the data type of the returned value by using either the As... clause in the function name, or by using the Access data type suffixes. The following declarations, for example, are equivalent:

```
Function MyFunction& ()
Function MyFunction() As Long
```

Both functions return a long data type.

If you declare a function without specifying its return value, the data type returned is Variant—even if the value being returned is explicitly declared as a different data type inside the function. Consider the following example:

```
Function MyTest()
     Dim i As Integer
     i = 100
     MyTest = i
End Function
```

This function returns a Variant Type 2 data type.

If the function type is declared and no explicit assignment of the returned value is made inside the function, the function returns 0 (zero) for numeric types and (if the function is declared as a String) a zero-length string ("").

If the function is declared without specifying its type, and no explicit assignment of the returned value is made within the function, the returned value is a zero-length string ("") of the Variant 0 (Empty) type.

> **Tip:** Always declare the function type if the function returns a value; declaring the function type not only increases the speed of processing the function, but also enables Access to manage memory more efficiently.

Access Basic includes seven data type conversion functions, as shown in the following table. These functions can convert data from one type to another, or control the results of arithmetic operations.

Function	*Converts From*	*To*	*Syntax*
CCur	Any valid expression	Currency	CCur*(expression)*
CDbl	Any valid expression	Double	CDbl*(expression)*
CInt	Any valid expression	Integer	CInt*(expression)*
CLng	Any valid expression	Long	CLng*(expression)*
CSng	Any valid expression	Single	CSng*(expression)*
CStr	Any valid expression	String	CStr*(expression)*
CVar	Any valid expression	Variant	CVar*(expression)*

Tip: Exploring the results of numeric conversions is worthwhile, especially in the design phase of application development, because the conversions can give unexpected results. In particular, rounding results may differ from what you expect. Avoid unpleasant surprises by running test functions to determine whether the results of the actual calculations to be performed meet your application requirements.

The following examples show how Access Basic converts values based on their type.

Example 1:

With all data conversion functions (except CStr), passing a character string that cannot be converted to a number results in a `Type mismatch` error:

```
Dim s As String
s = "567"
Result = CCur(s)              ' 567
s = "Mary had a little lamb"
Result = CCur(s)              ' Error #13 (Type mismatch)
```

Example 2:

Passing a Null to any of the data conversion functions triggers an `Invalid use of Null` error:

```
Dim v As Variant
v = Null
Result = CLng(v)              ' Error #94 (Invalid use of Null)
```

Example 3:

Data conversion functions can convert valid numerical expressions of numbers of any base. The following example of this conversion uses function **CDbl** and a hexadecimal number; the **CDbl** function converts the hexadecimal number expressed as Variant 8 (String) to a double decimal number:

```
Dim v As Variant
v = "&H100"                    ' 100 hexadecimal
Result = CDbl(v)               ' 256
```

Example 4:

Avoid confusing assignments and conversions like this one (used here with the CInt function):

```
Dim i As Integer          'The variable i is supposed to be an integer
i = 123.67                'But it is assigned a value that is a non-integer
Result = CInt(i)          'Returns an integer (124)
```

Example 5:

Because Access Basic stores date and time values internally as numbers (Double), data type conversion functions also treat these arguments as numbers:

```
Result = CDbl(Date())          '34038 (which equals March 10, 1993)
```

Using the data conversion functions, you can explicitly convert values of one type into values of another type. But Access Basic also can implicitly convert numeric values in expressions. The results of such a conversion take the form of the most precise data type used in the expression (with the Integer data type being the least precise, and the Double data type being the most precise). Access Basic performs implicit conversion with all arithmetic operations. If the value of the result exceeds the range of the most precise data type in the expression, an "Overflow" error occurs.

Consider the following examples.

Example 1:

This example illustrates how the data type of the result of an expression can vary according to the data types of the elements:

```
Dim i As Integer
i = 100
v = 23                    ' data type of v is VarType 2 (Integer)
c = i * v                 ' data type of c is Integer
```

Example 2:

Two variant variables are involved in an expression:

```
v1 = 45.87                ' data type of v1 is VarType 2 (Integer)
v2 = 500                  ' data type of v2 is VarType 5 (Double)
c = v1 + v2               ' data type of c is VarType 5 (Double)
```

Example 3:

If one of the elements in the expression is a Variant of VarType 8 (String) that can be converted to a number, the result is converted to its data type after the conversion:

```
Dim i As Integer, v As Variant
i = 100
v = "23.45"          ' data type of v is 8 (string), Double after conversion
c = i + v            ' data type of c is Double
```

Example 4:

If a Variant variable in an expression is a Null (VarType 1) or Empty (VarType 0), no error occurs (except as an operand in division, where it triggers a "Division by zero" error):

```
Dim i As Integer, v1 As Variant, v2 As Variant
i = 100
v1 = Null

c = i * v1                    ' data type of c is Null
c = i * v2                    ' data type of c is Integer
```

Chapter Summary

Learning to distinguish between data types and their uses is time well spent. Using the proper data type will save you many headaches as your application grows and you discover more ways to use the data it contains.

11

Working with Data

This chapter continues the discussion of data types and their uses from Chapter 10. You learn how to use the intrinsic Access Basic data types to create user-defined data types, improving the logic and readability of your code. The chapter discusses options for checking data types, including the use of the VarType function and the Option Explicit statement. This chapter also teaches you how to use strings to manipulate data—by converting, parsing, concatenating, changing the alignment, and so on.

Understanding User-Defined Data Types

To briefly review, the Access Basic intrinsic data types are as follows: String, Integer, Long, Single, Double, Currency, and Date/Time. Additionally, a variable in Access Basic can be declared as a Variant data type; Variant is also the default data type for undeclared variables (variables declared implicitly). A Variant can store any type of data (numbers, strings, binary, and so on). Special characteristics of the Variant data type, such as its capability to store Null values and to automatically assume the appropriate data type, render it indispensable in Access Basic.

User-defined data types can be a combination of Access Basic intrinsic data types (such as Integer, String, or Date/Time) used to build data structures that can be referred to by one variable name. You can create user-defined data types in Access Basic by using the **Type...End Type** statements. For more information on the Type...End Type statement, see the statements section of the Reference.

User-defined data types are introduced in this chapter instead of Chapter 10 because the term *user-defined data type* is something of a misnomer. The user doesn't really create a new data type; the user creates a new data structure that may contain many elements of different data types.

Why define an entirely new data type when Access Basic data types are so flexible? One non-essential but useful reason is that using user-defined data types can vastly improve the logic and readability of your code, which in turn improves your efficiency as a programmer.

There are many instances when it is much easier to refer to logically related data by using a user-defined data type than by using separate variables. For example, the following code block uses the logical category Employee as a user-defined data type and assigns related data *elements* to it:

```
Employee.LastName
Employee.Salary
Employee.DOB
```

An essential reason to use user-defined data types is that some calls to Windows API functions return values into predefined data structures that must be referred to by a common name (see also Chapter 13, "Extending Microsoft Access and Access Basic").

> **Note:** Access user-defined data types are the equivalent of the C language *struct* and *records* in Pascal.

A user-defined data type is defined in the declarations section of a module, and then becomes application-wide (global). The data type of every element of the new type must be explicitly declared as Integer, Long, Single, Double, String (variable or fixed-length), Variant, or a previously declared user-defined type.

To create a user-defined data type, you first must define it in the declarations section as follows:

```
Type <name>
   item As <data type>
   item As <data type>
   (...)
End Type
```

Here's a specific example:

```
Type Beast
     Name As String
     NumberOfHeads As Integer
     LengthOfTail As Integer
End Type
```

To refer to a user-defined data type, you first must create a variable (or an array) of the specified data type such as the following:

```
Dim Monster As Beast
```

You then must refer to individual elements of the data type with this variable, as follows:

```
Beast.Name
Beast.LengthOfTail
```

To summarize: create the desired data structure and then declare the variable of the new data type either in the declarations section (which makes it accessible to all procedures in the module) or inside a procedure (which makes the data type variable local to the procedure). You then can use the variable to refer to the elements of the new data type, as shown in the following example:

```
Function DescribeMonster()
     Monster.Name = "Hydra"
     Monster.NumberOfHeads = 7
     Monster.LengthOfTail = 20
End Function
```

You can also use the Global keyword to make the data type variable accessible to all modules in the application.

User-defined data types can also simplify the process of working with copies of table records. Because the data type prefix identifies elements within the record that refer to a specific entity (an employee, in the following example), the possibility of coding errors is greatly diminished. Each element is clearly and consistently identified by its data type prefix.

In the following example, first declare the user-defined data type Employee in the declaration section. This data type matches the structure and field data types of the Employees table.

```
Type Employee
    Id As Long           'counter field in the table
    SSN As String * 9
    FirstName As String * 10
    LastName As String * 20
    Phone As String * 15
End Type
```

You can now populate an array of the new user-defined data type with the information about the first ten employees in the Employees table (ten is an arbitrary figure). To do so, you need to declare an array (Emp) of the data type Employee, some object (database and table) variables, and an array subscript (i). Next, traverse the first ten records in the Employees table and copy their contents into the array (Emp):

```
ReDim Emp(0 To 10) As Employee
Dim cDB As Database, cTable As Table, i%
i = 1
Set cDB = CurrentDB()
Set cTable = cDB.OpenTable("Employees")
Do Until cTable.EOF Or i > 10
    Emp(i).Id = cTable.Id
    Emp(i).SSN = cTable.SSN
    Emp(i).FirstName = cTable.FirstName
    Emp(i).LastName = cTable.LastName
    Emp(i).Phone = cTable.Phone
    cTable.MoveNext
    i = i + 1
Loop
cTable.Close
```

As mentioned earlier in this chapter, user-defined data types are also useful for creating data structures for use with external functions that place data into predefined structures (such as Windows API functions). The Windows API function **GetCursorPos**, for example, returns the X and Y coordinates of the cursor and places them in the following data structure:

```
Type POINT
    x As Integer
    y As Integer
End Type
```

Because this Windows API function doesn't return a value, you can declare it as a Sub procedure:

```
Declare Sub GetCursorPos Lib "User" (lpPoint As POINT)
```

Finally, write the Access function that utilizes the **GetCursorPos** function to obtain the current coordinates of the cursor:

```
Function AbcGetCursorPos ()
    Dim Pnt As POINT
    GetCursorPos Pnt
    Debug.Print Pnt.x, Pnt.y            ' Display it in the Immediate window
End Function
```

As these examples demonstrate, user-defined data types are not only practical, but often indispensable (in the case of certain Windows API functions). In addition to their usefulness with external functions, because they are more readable, user-defined data types provide self-documenting code when referring to entities such as table records.

Checking Data Types

Determining data types is important because many Access functions expect arguments of a certain type. The **Hex** function, for example, expects either a number or a string that can be converted to a number. Passing a Null, a zero-length string, or a string that cannot be converted to a number triggers an error.

Null values can create other problems as well. For example, the MsgBox function, which is often used extensively in debugging operations, will not work with Null values and triggers an aggravating `Invalid use of Null` error. For this reason, checking for Nulls and converting them before they blow up your code is an important programming imperative in Access Basic.

Using the Option Explicit Statement

Access Basic is not a strongly typed language (one that requires you to declare the names and types of variables before you use them). As a rule, however, forcing declarations is advisable; Access works faster with declared and explicitly typed variables. Also, using such variables reduces the likelihood of making spelling mistakes and using confusing data types. By including the **Option Explicit** statement in the declarations section of a module, you can force Access Basic to require explicit declarations of variables.

> **Note:** Because **Option Explicit** is enforced only in the current module, in order to enforce application-wide Option Explicit declarations, you must include them in every code module the application contains.

Access Basic offers several functions to check the data type of the variable. These functions work with both Table fields and variables.

Using the VarType Function

The most obvious method of type checking is to use the **VarType** function, which checks the data type of a variable or an expression. The **VarType** function returns a number that indicates either the internal storage class of the Variant data type or the explicitly declared type of the variable. In the following example, the **VarType** function tests some variables; typed variables are declared explicitly, and variant variables are initialized implicitly with various data types:

```
Dim v As Variant, c As Currency, d As Double

v = #1/1/93#             'Variant
Result = VarType(v)      '7 (date)

v = 1                    'Variant
Result = VarType(v)      '2 (Integer)

c = 123.5                'Currency
v = 123.5                'Variant
d = 123.5                'Double

Result = VarType(c)      '6 (Currency)
Result = VarType(v)      '5 (Double)
Result = VarType(d)      '5 (Double)
```

The **VarType** function returns the following values when applied to Table fields that contain data of various types (note that the values may be different if the field contains no valid data). For consistency, the names of the variables representing the table field data types use the same names as those shown in the Table Design view (after the "t_" prefix).

```
Dim cDB As Database, cTable As Table
Set cDB = CurrentDB()
Set cTable = cDB.OpenTable("Data Types")

Result = VarType(cTable.t_counter)      '3 (Long Integer)
Result = VarType(cTable.t_text)         '8 (String)
Result = VarType(cTable.t_memo)         '8 (String)
Result = VarType(cTable.t_currency)     '6 (Currency)
Result = VarType(cTable.t_date)         '7 (Date)
Result = VarType(cTable.t_yes)          '2 (Integer)
Result = VarType(cTable.t_ole)          '8 (String)

' Numeric data types
Result = VarType(cTable.t_byte)         '2 (Integer)
Result = VarType(cTable.t_integer)      '2 (Integer)
Result = VarType(cTable.t_long)         '3 (Long Integer)
Result = VarType(cTable.t_double)       '5 (Double)
Result = VarType(cTable.t_single)       '4 (Single)
cTable.Close
```

Chapter 10, "Understanding Access Data Types," discusses Access data types in detail.

Finding Empty or Null Values with IsEmpty and IsNull

Access Basic offers two functions, **IsEmpty** and **IsNull**, that explicitly check for a Null and Empty Variant data type. If either of these functions returns True (-1), the data in question is not only Null or Empty but a Variant type as well (only a Variant can store Null and Empty values).

The IsNull function is the only method in Access Basic of specifically checking for a Null. Because of Null *propagation* (the Null value copies or *propagates* itself from one side of an expression to another; a Null on one side of an expression makes the entire expression Null), the following expression doesn't work:

```
If a = Null...
```

The following example shows the differences in the operation of the Access Basic functions IsNull and IsEmpty:

```
Dim v As Variant, i As Integer
```

Test an uninitialized integer (or any other explicitly declared data type) with these functions:

```
Result = IsNull(i)                  'False
Result = IsEmpty(i)                 'False
Result = i                          ' 0 (zero)
```

Test an uninitialized variant variable:

```
Result = IsNull(v)                  'False
Result = IsEmpty(v)                 'True
Result = VarType(v)                 '0 (Empty)
```

Test a variant variable explicitly initialized to Null:

```
v = Null
Result = IsNull(v)                  'True
Result = IsEmpty(v)                 'False
Result = VarType(v)                 '1 (Null)
```

Tip: You can indirectly detect the data type by using the **On Error** statement to trap invalid assignments of Null values and assign a valid value (such as zero) instead of a Null. This technique is demon-strated in the following example, in which the `Invalid use of Null` error (trappable error #94) is trapped and the value of the numeric variable reset to zero:

```
Dim i As Integer
On Error Resume Next
i = Null
If Err = 94 Then
     If IsNumeric(i) Then i = 0
End If
```

Because many Access Basic functions and statements trigger an error when one or more of their arguments is Null, the **IsNull** function is one of the most used functions in Access Basic. To avoid runtime errors, it is important to test every Variant variable for Null before making it part of a calculation or passing it as an argument to a function or statement. If the value is Null, reinitialize the variable to 0 (for numeric data types) or to a zero-length string (for string data types). For explicitly declared data types other than Variant, you should trap error #94 if there is even a slight possibility that the value may be a Null, such as when assigning a value from a table field (which can be Null if no data is present in the field) to a variable with an explicit data type.

Using IsDate and IsNumeric

Two more Access Basic functions that enable implicit data type checking are **IsDate** and **IsNumeric**. To determine whether a Variant can be converted to a date or a number, knowing whether the data can be *treated* as either a date or a number usually suffices. In the following example, date arithmetic is performed only after the input data type is checked:

```
If IsDate(d) Then
     Result = DateAdd("d", 7, d)
End If
```

The next example uses the **IsNumber** function to confirm that the argument is (or can be converted to) a valid number:

```
If IsNumeric(wKounter) Than wKounter = wKounter + 1
```

Working with Strings

Strings in Access Basic can be up to 64K long; the actual length is somewhat less, because every string incurs a small overhead. String variables can store all ANSI characters, including binary data, such as data stored in OLE fields. Because Access Basic lacks a dedicated "binary" data type, the data type of objects stored in OLE fields evaluates to VarType 8 (String) when evaluated with the **VarType** function.

Access strings can be declared either as fixed-length or as variable-length (zero-terminated):

```
Dim s1 As String * 30
Dim s2 As String
```

The first line above declares a fixed-length string; the second declares a variable-length string.

> **Caution:** Memory overhead is an important factor to consider when working with large strings. Access strings are stored in a single data segment of 64K. Therefore, initializing two near-limit strings can lead to an `Out of string space` error (trappable error #14).

Detecting String Variables

Strings in Access are one of two types: String variables declared explicitly as such; and Variant of VarType 8 variables, declared either explicitly or implicitly. If valid data is stored in both variables, the **VarType** function, which returns the data internal storage class, returns 8 (String) for either type. Consider the following example:

```
Dim v As Variant, s As String
v = "Mary"
s = "Joan"
Result = VarType(v)      '8 (String)
Result = VarType(s)      '8 (String)
```

Database Text and Memo fields can be assigned to either String or Variant variables. The **VarType** function returns 8 (String) for both Text and Memo data types.

The next example involves the table called Customers. Two of the table's fields, Note (declared as Memo in the table), and Name (declared as Text in the table), are assigned to two different variable types.

```
Dim v As Variant, s As String, d As Database, t As Table
Set d = CurrentDB()
Set t = d.OpenTable("Customers")
s = t.Name
v = t.Note
Result = VarType(t.Name) '8 (string)
Result = VarType(t.Note) '8 (string)
Result = VarType(s)      '8 (string)
Result = VarType(v)      '8 (string)
t.Close
```

If you attempt to assign a field with any of the numeric data types to a variable declared explicitly as a String data type, you receive a `Type mismatch` error (trappable error #5).

Note: When deciding between the Variant and String (or any other for that matter) data types, keep in mind that Variant variables can store Empty (no valid data) and Null (no data) values, whereas String variables cannot. The following example shows the difference in behavior:

```
Dim v As Variant, s As String
Result = VarType(v)      '0 (Empty)
Result = VarType(s)      '8 (String)

v = Null
Result = VarType(v)                '1 (Null)

s = ""
Result = VarType(s)                '8 (String)

s = Null                           'Run-time error #94
```

This difference aside, these two data types operate very similarly from the user's perspective. Keep in mind, however, that operations performed on *explicitly typed* variables (variables declared with the Dim statement using one of the Access Basic intrinsic data types) are faster and take up less internal storage—an important consideration for large systems.

Comparing Strings in Access Basic

String comparison operations such as the following are performed very frequently on text data:

```
s1 = "Joseph"
s2 = "Frank"
If s1 > s2 Then Debug.Print s1 & " is greater than " & s2
```

All Access Basic comparison operators can be used with strings. These operators are as follows:

<	Less than...
<=	Less than or equal to...
>	Greater than...
>=	Greater than or equal to...
=	Equal to...
<>	Not equal to...
Like	The Like operator is a pattern-matching operator that compares strings for the occurrence of any given pattern or character. It returns an integer True (-1) if the patterns match, or False (0), otherwise. The Like operator returns a Null if either of the arguments is a Null. Wild-card characters (such as ?, *, #) can be used as patterns to match with the Like operator.

> **Note:** Some languages, such as dBASE, enable the equal sign (**=**) to be placed on either side of a greater-than or less-than (**>** or **<**) comparison operator. In Access Basic, the editor automatically positions the equal sign to the right of the comparison operator.

The result of an Access Basic comparison operation is an integer or a Null: 0 if the comparison is negative, or -1 if the comparison is positive. (You also can use the Access constants False and True, respectively.) The Null is returned if either or both operands is Null.

> **Caution:** To avoid runtime errors, make sure that the data type of the variable that stores the result of a comparison is a Variant—only a Variant can store Nulls.

The following examples show the results of different string comparison operations:

```
Dim s1 As String, s2 As String
s1 = "123"
s2 = "250"
Result s1 <= s2                    'True
```

You also can use comparison operations if one of the operands is a Variant data type and the other is a String:

```
Dim v As Variant, s As String
v = "Earth" : s = "Sun"
Result = v > s                        ' False
```

The keyword **Not** also can be used to negate the result of the comparison, as follows:

```
Dim s1 As String, s2 As String
s1 = "Blue"
s2 = "Red"
Result = Not( s1 > s2 )               'True
```

The Empty value of either operand doesn't affect the result of the comparison, as shown in the following example:

```
Dim v As Variant, s As String
s = "Florida"
Result = IsEmpty(v)                   'True
Result = v > s                        'False
```

The following are examples of comparisons made with the *Like* operator:

```
Result = "Jones" Like "J????"        ' True (-1)
Result = "Alert!" Like "????![!]"    ' True
```

Understanding the Option Compare Settings

For the purpose of comparisons, Access Basic converts individual characters in a string to ANSI characters; it then compares the individual characters based on the setting of the **Option Compare** statement in the declarations section of the module in which the code comparison occurs. The **Option Compare** statement setting is specific to the module in which it is included, not to the entire application; in other words, every module can have its own setting of Option Compare.

The possible settings of Option Compare are *Database*, *Binary,* or *Text*. Using the Database setting causes the comparison to be performed according to the sort order specified for the database. If there is no setting of the Option Compare statement in a module, the Binary setting is assumed, causing case-sensitive comparisons on characters as they appear in the ANSI character set. (The Option Compare setting is accessible from the Options selection of the View menu.) The Text setting of the Option Compare statement causes case-sensitive comparisons based on the country code entry in the [International] section of the Windows WIN.INI file. When a new module is created, Access places the "Option Compare Database" statement in its declarations section.

Figure 11.1 displays the Access 1.1 dialog box for setting the new default database sort order; this order is also used for any module that contains the Option Compare Database statement.

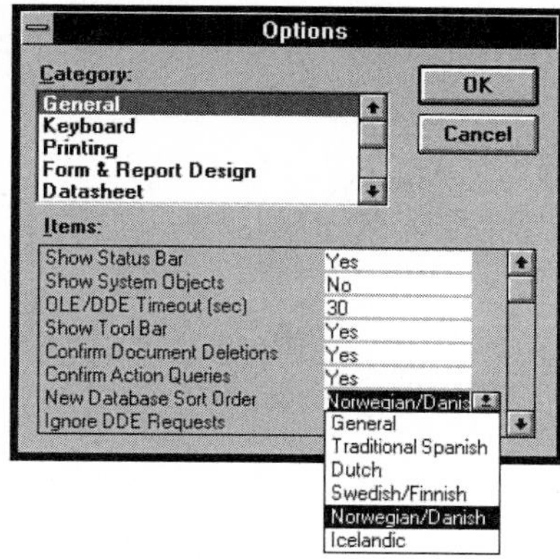

Figure 11.1. Specifying the default database sort order.

The following examples demonstrate how different **Option Compare** settings influence the results of string comparisons:

```
Dim s1 As String, s2 As String
s1 = "Earth"
s2 = "EARTH"
```

Option Compare Binary (or no setting at all):

```
Result = s1 = s2                   'False
Result = s1 > s2                   'True
```

Option Compare Database:

```
Result = s1 = s2                   'True
Result = s1 > s2                   'False
```

Option Compare Text (US and Canadian versions):

```
Result = s1 = s2                   'True
Result = s1 > s2                   'False
```

Caution: If neither of the operands is a Variant or a String, a runtime `Type mismatch` error occurs (trappable error #13).

Comparing Strings with the StrComp Function

The Access Basic function **StrComp** explicitly compares two strings. In the following example, two strings are compared using the Greater Than comparison operator. For more information on this function, see "StrComp" in the functions section of the Reference.

```
Dim s1 As String, s2 As String
s1 = "BIGGIE"
s2 = "small"
Result = StrComp(s1, s2)                '-1 (True)
Result =  s1 < s2                       '-1 (True)
```

The **StrComp** function also has an option to override the setting of the **Option Compare** statement. You use this option by adding a third argument: 0 (zero) for case-sensitive comparison, 1 for case-insensitive comparison, and 2 for the Database method of comparisons.

See "Comparison Operators" in the operators section of the Reference for more general information on the comparison operators.

Concatenating and Adding Strings

Strings in Access can be concatenated using either of the "and" operators (**&** or **+**), as in the following example:

```
s1 = "Adam"
s2 = "Eve"
Result = s1 + " and " + s2    'Adam and Eve
```

When using the **&** operator, any numeric operands in the expression are converted to a Variant VarType 8 (String) data type, and Null and Empty values are treated as zero-length strings. The result of the concatenation is as follows: a String, if both operands are Strings; a Variant of VarType 8, if one or both operands are Variant; or a Null, if both operands are Null. Because the result may be a Null, assign the Variant data type to the variable that is to receive the result.

When using the **+** operator, concatenation occurs in any of the following scenarios:

- Either or both operands are String data type.
- One operand is String and the other operand is Variant data type.
- Both operands are Variant of VarType 8 (String) data type.

Empty values are treated as zero-length strings. The result of the concatenation is as follows: a String (if both operands are strings); a Variant of VarType 8 (if one or both operands are Variant); or a Null (if either operand is Null). Because the result may be a Null, assign the Variant data type to the variable that is to receive the result.

If both operands contain valid data, the result of using the **+** and **&** operators is the same, as shown in the following example:

```
Dim v As Variant, s As String
v = Date            'Assume 01/01/93
s = "Today is "

Result = s & v      'Today is 01/01/93
Result = s + v      'Today is 01/01/93
```

If one operand is Null, using the **+** operator produces a Null result:

```
Dim s As String, v As Variant
s = "Mary had "
v = Null
Result = s1 + v      '#NULL#
Result = s1 & v      'Mary had
```

Caution: When Access attempts to concatenate large strings, the result may overflow the single segment reserved for string storage and trigger an `Out of string space` error (error #14), as in the following example:

```
Dim s1 As String, s2 As String
s1 = Space(20000)
s2 = Space(60000)
Result = s1 & s2                    ' Error #14
```

Note: Unlike Xbase, Access doesn't support the minus operator applied to strings.

Converting, Formatting, and Aligning Strings

Data conversions and formatting operations are an important part of working with Strings. You can convert Strings to a different data type or a different case. You can format Strings for display and printing, without affecting their storage. The conversion process can work both ways (for example, a String can be converted to a number and vice versa).

Converting String Data to a Different Data Type

In rare instances, a String must be converted into another data type, such as one of the numeric types for use in arithmetic operations. Access data conversion functions provide an excellent method of converting any valid type of data into another type.

You can use the following functions to convert any string data that can be converted to a number into another data type:

- **CCur** converts to Currency
- **cDbl** converts to Double
- **CInt** converts to Integer
- **CLng** converts to Long Integer
- **CSng** converts to Single
- **CVar** converts to Variant

See also the examples of data conversion functions in Chapter 10, "Understanding Access Data Types."

Consider the following example of converting string data:

```
Dim s As String
s = "123.45"
Result = CLng(s)              '123.45
Result = CInt(s)              '123

s = "&H1234"                  '1234 hex
Result = CInt(s)              '4660 decimal
```

The conversion may be unnecessary if string data is declared as Variant of VarType 8, and if the variable can be used directly in numeric expressions, as in the following example:

```
Dim v As Variant, i As Integer
v = "123"
i = 40
Result = v + i                '163
Result = VarType(v + i)       '5 (Double)
```

Variant of VarType 8 (String) data that can be converted to a number also can be used as an argument to the **Int**, **Fix**, **Hex**, and **Oct** functions. Attempting the same feat with data explicitly declared as Strings triggers a `Type mismatch` error. Consider the following example:

```
Dim v As Variant, s As String
v = "123"
s = v
Result = Int(v)           '123 (decimal)
Result = Fix(v)           '123 (decimal)
Result = Hex(v)           '7B  (hexadecimal)
Result = Oct(v)           '173 (octal)

Result = Int(s)           'Error #13 (Type mismatch)
```

Converting Partial Strings

Sometimes you may need to convert to a number only the leading numeric portion of the string (such as a number in front of a street address). Access Basic provides the **Val** function, which converts the leading numeric portion of a string into a numeric data type (always Double). Consider the following example:

```
Dim s As String
s = "12345 Main Street Apt. 77"
Result = Val(s)           '12345
```

Two related functions, **Chr** and **Asc**, convert only individual characters. The **Chr** function converts ANSI character code to the character; **Asc** converts a single character (or the first character of a string expression) to its ANSI value. Consider this example:

```
Dim s1 As String, i As Integer
s1 = "Andromeda"
i = 100
Result = Asc(s1)          '65 (A)
Result = Chr(i)           'd
```

Converting a Number to a String

The need to convert a number to a string occurs frequently. Access Basic provides two functions for that conversion. The **Str** function and the **Format** function both convert any type of numeric data to String (or Variant of VarType 8) data. The **Str** function is very straightforward; converting numbers to strings is its only function. On the other hand, the **Format** function is very robust and accepts many formatting patterns. **Str** holds the leading space for the sign of the positive number, but **Format** does not. Consider the following example:

```
Dim s As String, dw As Double
dw = 1234.765                          ' Double
s = Str$(dw)                           ' 1234.765 (String)
s = Format$(dw, "#####.##")            '1234.77 (String)
```

> **Note:** Be careful when formatting the number of decimal places to display with the **Format** function. If you specify insufficient decimal places, Access rounds the number off.

Formatting Strings for Output

Format, and its related function **Format$**, are two of the most versatile functions in Access; they accept a plethora of formatting symbols for character strings, as described in the following table.

Formatting Symbol	*Action*
@	Displays a character or a space
&	Displays a character or nothing
<	Displays all characters in lowercase
>	Displays all characters in uppercase
!	Forces placeholders to fill from left to right rather than from right to left

You can use up to two different formatting strings for character strings. You separate the sections with a semicolon. The first section applies to valid string data; the second section applies to Nulls and zero-length strings.

The following examples show the **Format[$]** function in use:

```
Dim s1 As String, f1 As SString
s1 = "123456789"
f1 = "@@@-@@-@@@@;Unknown"
Result = Format$(s1, f1)      '123-45-6789
s1 = ""                       ' Empty string
Result = Format$(s1, f1)      'Unknown
```

```
s1 = "usa"
f1 = ">"
Result = Format$(s1, f1) 'USA
```

Trimming and Aligning Data within a String

Sometimes formatting means aligning data in a string. Access Basic makes this task easier by supplying two statements, **LSet** and **RSet**, that (among other things) align one string within another. The following example demonstrates their usage. In the example, the zero-terminated string `s1` (initialized as "Here I am") is copied to the fixed-length string `s2`, and left-and-right aligned within that string.

```
Dim s1 As String, s2 As String * 20
s1 = "Here I am"
LSet s2 = s1          ' "Here I am           "
RSet s2 = s1          ' "           Here I am"
```

LSet and **RSet** statements are useful for generating dynamic runtime-aligned titles and messages on reports and other printed output. Because Access doesn't have a centering statement to center one string within another, we write our own.

Our **CenterString** function accepts two parameters:

wLen (Integer)—the width (length) of the string within which to align

szString (which is passed as a zero-terminated string)

CenterString returns a string data type (which is specified by the type identifier in the function name):

```
Function CenterString$ (wLen%, szString$)

Dim wNoSpaces%       ' number of spaces
wNoSpaces = (wLen - Len(szString)) / 2
If wNoSpaces > 0 Then
   CenterString = Space$(wNoSpaces) + szString + Space$(wNoSpaces)
Else
   CenterString = Space$(wLen)
End If

End Function
```

To improve this function you may want to add data conversion part, error trapping, and so on.

The family of trim functions (**LTrim$**, **RTrim$**, and **Trim$**) removes blanks, or spaces, from the specified area of the string: **LTrim** removes blanks from the left side of the string; **RTrim** removes blanks from the right side of the string; and **Trim** removes both leading and trailing spaces (unlike in Xbase, where the Trim function removes only right trailing spaces).

```
Dim s1 As String
s1 = "      Trim me     "
Result = LTrim$(s1) ' "Trim me     "
Result = RTrim$(s1) ' "      Trim me"
Result = Trim$(s1)  ' "Trim me"
```

Converting Case

Access Basic offers two functions, **LCase$** and **UCase$**, that convert character data to lower- and uppercase respectively, as shown in the following example:

```
Dim s1 As String
s1 = "tHiS iS A WeirD StrING"

Result = LCase$(s1)              ' "this is a weird string"
Result = UCase$(s1)              ' "THIS IS A WEIRD STRING"
```

Chapter 10, "Understanding Access Data Types," contains more detailed explanations and examples of these functions.

Parsing Strings

Parsing operations involve searching strings for certain values, replacing parts of a string with another string, and isolating portions, or substrings, of a string.

The functions **Left$**, **Right$,** and **Mid$** return a part of the string. **Left$** returns a specified number of characters from the left of the string; **Right$** returns a specified number of rightmost characters from the string; **Mid$** returns the specified number of characters, starting with a specified character. **InStr** returns the starting point of one string within another. Consider the following examples:

```
Dim s As String
s = "Mary had a little lamb"
Debug.Print Left$(s, 5)                 'Mary
Debug.Print Right$(s, 4)                'lamb
Debug.Print Mid$(s, 6, 12)              'had a little
Debug.Print Mid$(s, InStr(s, "little")) 'little lamb
```

The **InStr** function has one more interesting property: it can override the string comparison method specified in the **Option Compare** statement if you include its fourth (optional) parameter, as in the following example:

```
Dim s1 As String, s2 As String
s1 = "ABCDabcd"
s2 = "c"
Result = InStr(1, s1, s2, 0)  '7th character
Result = InStr(1, s1, s2, 1)  '3rd character
Result = InStr(1, s1, s2, 2)  '3rd character

'No Option Compare setting exists (defaults to Binary)
Result = InStr(s1, s2)        '7th character
```

The value of the fourth parameter can be 0 (case-sensitive comparison), 1 (case-insensitive comparison), or 2 (Database method). If the parameter is omitted, Access Basic uses the comparisons method specified in the **Option Compare** setting (or the Binary method, if no **Option Compare** setting exists in the given module).

In the following examples, we put some string functions to use and build a user-defined function that checks for palindromes (expressions that read the same from the beginning and from the end), such as *Madam I'm Adam* or *A man, a plan, a canal—Panama!* (without punctuation and spacing), in a case-insensitive manner. Because we want to deal only with alphanumeric characters (numbers and letters), we can employ the Windows API function **IsCharAlphanumeric**, declared in the declaration section as:

```
Declare Function IsCharAlphanumeric Lib "User" (ByVal wCharacter As Integer) As
➥Integer.
```

The **IsCharAlphanumeric** function accepts one parameter, the Integer ANSI code representing the character. **IsCharAlphanumeric** returns zero if the character is not alphanumeric, and a non-zero value, otherwise:

```
Function IsPalindrome% (szString$)

Dim n%, m%
n = Len(szString)   ' length of the input string

' Note that the following line uses the integer division operator
m = n \ 2           ' we need to check just a half of the string
szString = LCase$(szString)

'Traverse the string and compare the current leftmost and rightmost character
For i = 1 To m + 1
   If IsCharAlphanumeric(Asc(Mid$(szString, i, 1))) And
➥IsCharAlphanumeric(Asc(Mid$(szString, n - (i - 1), 1))) Then
      If Not (Mid$(szString, i, 1) = Mid$(szString, n - (i - 1), 1)) Then
         Exit For                  'Quit comparing after the first no match is found
      End If
    End If
Next

'Return the value from the function
If i > m Then
    IsPalindrome = True
Else
    IsPalindrome = False
End If
End Function
```

String operations are important in every modern programming language, and Access Basic is no exception. Fortunately Access Basic provides a robust arsenal of string manipulation functions. If you want to broaden your repertoire of string manipulation functions beyond those provided by Access Basic, you may want to investigate Windows string functions, such as **IsCharLower**, **IsCharAlphanumeric**, and **IsCharUpper**. See the Windows API documentation included on the sample code disk.

Chapter Summary

In this chapter you learned about user-defined data types, methods for determining data types, and methods for working with and converting various types of data. The primary emphasis was on string data because string manipulations are usually the most prevalent in database applications. The next chapter covers another important subject in the world of Windows programming: manipulating OLE objects and performing DDE (dynamic data exchange).

12
OLE and DDE

Access uses two Windows programming methods—OLE (object linking and embedding) and DDE (dynamic data exchange)—to store binary and other forms of data and to communicate seamlessly with other Windows applications such as spreadsheets and word processors.

No book on programming in a Windows environment would be complete without a discussion of OLE and DDE methods and their uses. Both subjects are complex, however, and both have been the subject of entire books, so it is quite beyond the scope of this book to cover every aspect of OLE and DDE.

Our more modest objective is to present some basic concepts about OLE and DDE for those who may be new to the Windows programming environment. Another goal is to give some concrete examples of how OLE and DDE can be used in Access. For programmers interested in expanding their knowledge of OLE and DDE, see the bibliography for further reading. Also, the reference section includes more examples and discussion of OLE and DDE under the pertinent Access Basic language elements.

OLE Basic Concepts

Object linking and embedding (OLE) is actually two Windows programming methods: object linking and object embedding. For OLE, an object is anything a user can manipulate with a Windows application. Common examples of such objects are bitmap images and sound.

In Windows programming, it is common to refer to *client applications* and *server applications*. Without belaboring the technicalities, for the purposes of this discussion the client application is Access, and the server application is any other Windows application used to create an object or with which you use DDE to communicate.

Note: Access versions 1.0 and 1.1 cannot act as an OLE server.

Linking Objects versus Embedding Objects

In *object embedding*, the object becomes a physical part of the client application. If an object is *linked*, it remains separate from the client application. To edit a linked object, the client application must invoke the server application. To edit a Paintbrush picture (which is a bitmap object) linked to Access, for example, Access must first activate Paintbrush.

The obvious advantage of linking is that you extend the capabilities of the client application by enabling it to integrate other Windows applications at runtime (subject to available resources, such as memory).

Embedded objects are *static* (non-editable), unless the client application has the tools with which to edit them. Access is unable to edit bitmap, sound, or other binary objects.

Linked objects update in the client application whenever you edit them with the server application that created them.

How Access Uses OLE

Access allows objects to be linked or embedded. Determining which method to use depends largely upon how you plan to use the object in the application. If you want to use an object merely for reference and you will not need to update it, you should embed it. If the application must be made aware of changes that its server application made, or if the object needs to be edited by invoking the server application, you should link the object.

You can use OLE with Access in the following ways:

- Embed OLE objects
- Link OLE objects
- Paste non-OLE objects from the Clipboard
- Create OLE objects from objects in non-OLE applications

Embedding OLE Objects

Access uses the OLE Object field data type to store graphic images and other types of binary data, such as sound. The OLE Object field in Access is a BLOB (binary large object) data type with values limited to OLE objects and pictures. You can embed external BMP files or objects from Access tables, where the data type is an OLE object field.

To display an OLE object, Access requires the object to be contained in a bound object control, called an *object frame*. An embedded object is merely displayed and cannot be edited.

The object frame has specific properties relating to the OLE object. (See the properties section of the Reference.) Figure 12.1 shows one of the embedded bitmap images used by the opening form in the Northwind Traders database.

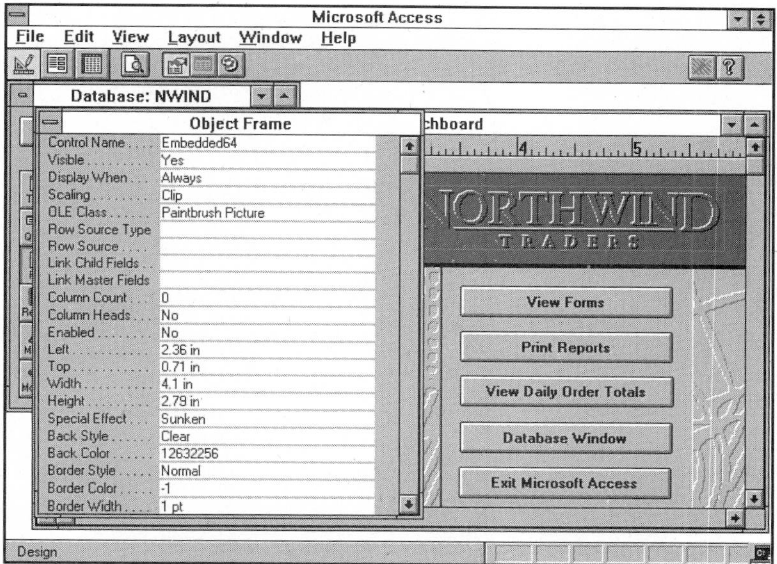

Figure 12.1. Embedded graphics image in Northwind Traders form.

Notice the property *OLE Class*, which indicates that the contents of the frame were created in Microsoft Windows Paintbrush. The *Control Name* property indicates that the contents are embedded rather than linked (that is, the picture is non-editable).

Linking OLE Objects

The sample Northwind Traders database stores Paintbrush pictures of employees in an OLE object field named "Photo" in the "Employees" table. These images can be linked to an Access form by dragging the field from the field list onto the unbound control (see fig. 12.2).

When an object is linked, double-clicking on the control frame invokes the application that created the object—in the example illustrated in figure 12.2, double-clicking on the control frame activates Paintbrush (see fig. 12.3). The [Extensions] section of the WIN.INI file specifies the selection of Windows applications invoked by double-clicking on different image types.

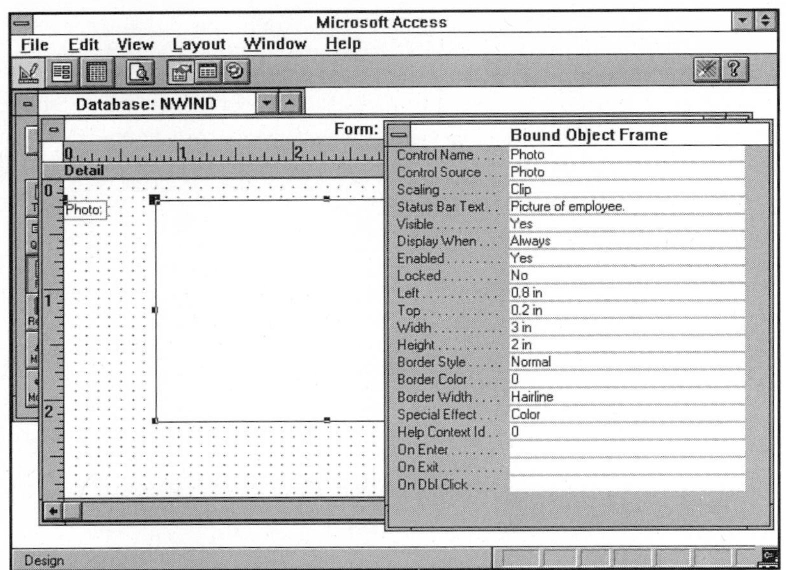

Figure 12.2. Embedding a Paintbrush object (bitmap image) stored in an Access table.

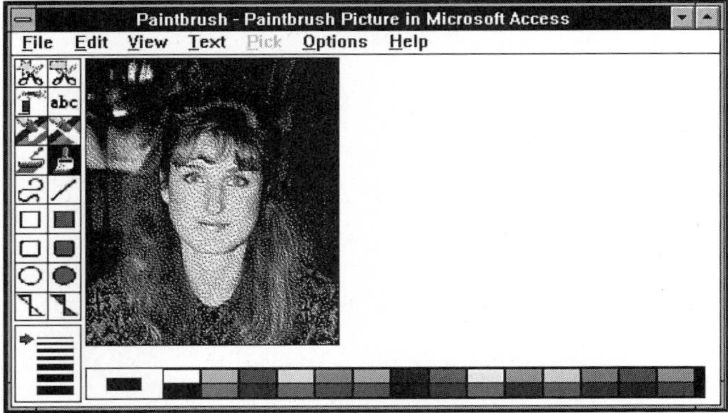

Figure 12.3. Invoking the OLE server application.

Pasting Non-OLE Objects from the Clipboard

Access can display non-OLE images in an Access OLE object field. You can copy images created by a non-OLE server application to the Windows Clipboard and then paste (use Edit|PasteSpecial). Four import options are available:

- Picture
- Device
- Independent bitmap
- Bitmap

> **Note:** If the image was created by a non-OLE server application, the Paste Link button is disabled because you cannot link to an OLE object that is not created by an OLE server.

Creating OLE Objects from External Applications

If you need an image you can edit, one option is to convert the image from a non-OLE to an OLE object. You can convert the image in Paintbrush, for example, by pasting the non-OLE image from the Clipboard and saving it in Paintbrush as a BMP or PCX file. The object then becomes an OLE object and you can link it by using any of the above methods.

Using Access Basic with OLE

In addition to linking and embedding in forms, there are two Access Basic methods you can use to manipulate OLE objects: GetChunk and AppendChunk. By transferring data in "chunks," OLE object and memo data types circumvent the 65535 bytes (64K) size limit of strings in Access. GetChunk applies to Table, Dynaset, and Snapshot objects, and AppendChunk applies to Table and Dynaset objects.

For example, to copy a larger-than-64K graphics image stored in an OLE object field to another table using Access Basic, you must use the GetChunk/AppendChunk methods.

Start by opening the table Employees in the Northwind Traders database, and finding out how big the first image is in the Photo field.

```
Function HowBigIsBLOB ()
  Dim cdb As Database, ctb As Table, obj As Variant
  Set cdb = CurrentDB()
  Set ctb = cdb.OpenTable("Employees")
  nObjSize = ctb![photo].FieldSize()
  MsgBox "This record is" & Str(nObjSize) & " bytes long"
End Function
```

Notice that the Access Basic **FieldSize** function returns the size of the Photo field from the first record. Executing this function returns the message shown in figure 12.4.

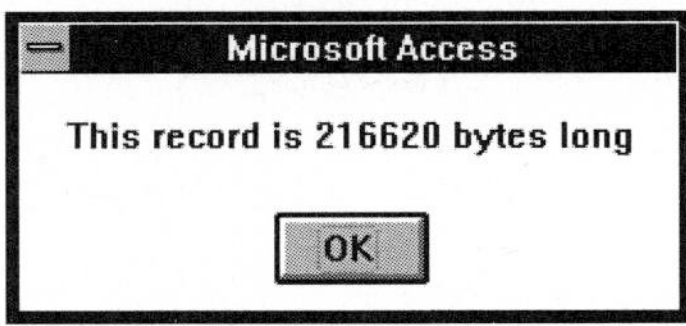

Figure 12.4. A FieldSize message.

Next, create another function to break the BLOB into chunks and move the image to the field Big BLOB in the table ("New") in the same database.

```
Function ChunkAndMoveIt ()
  Dim dwObjSize As Long, nChunkSize As Integer, ntotchunks As Integer
  Dim cTarget As Table, cSource As Table
  Dim cDb As Database

  dwObjSize = HowBigIsBLOB()    'Get the size from the previous function
  nChunkSize = 1024             'Use 1K bytes for the chunk size
  nTotChunks = (dwObjSize \ nChunkSize) 'Determine the # of total "chunks"

  'Specify Source and Target tables
  Set cDb = CurrentDB()
  Set cTarget = cDb.OpenTable("New")
  Set cSource = cDb.OpenTable("Employees")
  cTarget.AddNew                    'Add a new record to the Target table
  DoCmd Hourglass True

  'Loop while appending
  For i = 0 To nTotChunks
    cTarget.[Big BLOB].AppendChunk(cSource.[Photo].GetChunk(i*ChunkSize,
    ➥nChunkSize))
  Next i

  'Housekeeping
  cTarget.Update                    'Remember to update the Target table
  cTarget.Close
  cSource.Close
  DoCmd Hourglass False
End Function
```

Note: If you put this function to a real test, you'll see that we fudged a bit with the size of the image returned by the first function. The actual size of the image is only 21662 bytes, but because the idea is to use the GetChunk and AppendChunk methods for BLOBs larger than 64K, we reported a larger size for illustration purposes.

The hourglass is on at the beginning of the actual data transfer to discourage the user from interrupting the transfer before it completes. Performing this process behind a modal form (a form that stays in focus until the process is completed) would be an even better idea.

DDE Basic Concepts

Dynamic Data Exchange (DDE) is a method of communicating between Windows applications. The actual process is called *interprocess communication* (IPC), which consists of a protocol for synchronizing the data exchange and an internal method for exchanging the information.

DDE applications fall into four categories:

- *Client application.* A DDE conversation occurs between a client application and a server application. A client application requests data or services from a server application.
- *Server application.* A server responds to a client application's request for data or services.
- *Client/server application.* A client/server application is both a client application and a server application, thus requesting and providing information.
- *Monitor application.* A monitor application can intercept DDE messages from all other DDE applications but cannot act on them. Monitor applications are useful for debugging.

The DDE protocol is a set of rules that all DDE applications should follow. A DDE conversation begins when a client application initiates a conversation by sending an initiate message with an application and a topic name. For a conversation to begin, there also must be a server application to respond to the initiate message. The client application provides some information about itself, such as its window handle and which server it wants.

After establishing a DDE conversation, the client and server applications begin their real work: exchanging data and performing services. Data exchanging can occur in three ways:

- A client application can request data on a one-time basis from a server application.
- A client application can send data to a server application.
- The server application advises the client application that an item has changed value.

> **Note:** Access can act as both a DDE client and server application.

The methods for exchanging data are often associated with the term *link*. A link denotes how data is exchanged. If a client application requests data and the server application immediately sends the data to the client application, that is a *cold link*. A *warm link* occurs when a server application advises a client application that a data item has changed values, but does not send the value to the client application. A *hot link* occurs when the server application sends the new value for a data item to the client application every time the value changes. Either a client or a server application can terminate a DDE conversation.

How Access Uses DDE

DDE is one area where Access clearly outdistances other Windows databases. Access Basic has a full suite of DDE-handling tools. Most of these can be called from Access Basic routines or attached directly to certain controls on Access forms. The following table lists the Access Basic language elements used to initiate, execute, and terminate DDE conversations.

Access Basic language element	*Element type*	*Purpose*	*Available from*
DDE()	Function	Initiates a DDE process with another application and returns the requested information	Record Source property of certain controls only
DDEInitiate()	Function	Initiates a DDE and conversation with another application	Access Basic form controls
DDERequest()	Function	Requests an item from a DDE server application	Access Basic form controls
DDESend()	Function	Initiates a DDE process with another application and sends data to the specified item in that application	Record Source property of certain controls only
DDEExecute	Statement	Sends a command to another application over an established DDE channel	Access Basic and form controls
DDEPoke	Statement	Sends data to another application over an established DDE channel	Access Basic and form controls
DDETerminate	Statement	Closes a specified DDE conversation channel	Access Basic and form controls
DDETerminateAll	Statement	Closes all open DDE conversation channels	Access Basic and form controls

> **Note:** No Access macros have DDE capabilities, but if you're still determined to use a macro, try RunCode, which will call the specified Access Basic DDE-handling routine.

Because Access can act as both a DDE client and DDE server application, the flexibility for establishing DDE links with other Windows applications is virtually unlimited (subject, as always, to available system resources such as memory). Access can even establish DDE conversations with itself.

> **Tip:** The capability of Access to initiate DDE conversations with itself is useful for overcoming the limitation of having only two databases open.

Access supports the following five topics as a DDE server:

- System
- <database>
- <table name>
- <query name>
- SQL <expr>

System is a standard topic for all Windows applications; it returns information about topics supported by Access. The following table lists the valid items for the System topic.

Item	*Returns*
SysItems	A list of items supported by the topic System
Format	A list of the formats Access can copy to the Clipboard
Status	`Busy` or `Ready`
Topics	A list of all open databases
<macro name>	Runs a macro in the current database

The <database> topic refers to the file name of an existing database. After a DDE link to a database is established, you can request a listing of the objects in the database, as shown in the following table.

Item	*Returns*
TableList	A list of tables
QueryList	A list of queries
MacroList	A list of macros
ReportList	A list of reports
FormList	A list of forms
ModuleList	A list of modules

> **Note:** You cannot use DDE to query the SYSTEM.MDA.

Both <table name> and <query name> topics support the same items. The syntax for requesting the contents of a table or the results of a query is as follows:

<database>;TABLE <table name>

or

<database>;QUERY <query name>

<database> is the name of the database in which the table or query is found, followed by a semicolon and the keyword TABLE or QUERY, and then the name of an existing table or query.

For example, to request the contents of the Customers table in the Northwind database, type just the name of the database or its full path and file extension, as shown in the following:

```
NWIND;TABLE Customers
```

or

```
C:\ACCESS\NWIND.MDB;TABLE Customers
```

The following table lists the items that are valid with the <table name> and <query name> topics.

Item	*Returns*
All	All the data in the table, including field names.
Data	All rows of data without field names.
FieldNames	A list of field names.
NextRow	The next row in the table or query. When the channel is first opened, NextRow returns the first row. If the current row is the last record, executing a NextRow request fails.
PrevRow	The previous row in the table or query. If PrevRow is the first request over a new channel, the last row of the table or query is returned. If the current row is the first request, the request for PrevRow fails.

Item	*Returns*
FirstRow	The data in the first row of the table or query.
LastRow	The data in the last row of the table or query.
FieldCount	The number of fields in the table or query.

The SQL <expr> topic returns the results of the specified SQL expression. The syntax for this topic is as follows:

```
<database>;SQL <expr>
```

For example, to select all fields from the Customers table in the Northwind database, type the following:

```
NWIND;SQL Select * from Customers;
```

> **Note:** Be sure to end each SQL statement with a semicolon (;).

To select only the values in the CustomerID and Company Name fields:

```
NWIND;SQL Select [CustomerID],[Company Name] from Customers;
```

The SQL <expr> topic supports the same items as the <table name> and <query name> topics.

Using Access as a DDE Client

DDE can enhance an Access application in several ways. For example, because Access has such a powerful query tool, it may be useful to import some spreadsheet data to take advantage of the almost limitless querying possibilities. Importing spreadsheet data by using DDE allows more flexibility in the table design than merely using the default Import or Attach functions.

Or perhaps you want to use Access math or statistical functions to process numeric data from a spreadsheet, and then send the results back to the spreadsheet. The following example (kept simple for clarity) performs the following DDE tasks:

- Opens a DDE channel and initiates a conversation with Microsoft Excel
- Obtains a list of available DDE topics
- Returns the name of an Excel worksheet
- Terminates the topic channel and opens a new channel for sending data
- Loads the Excel spreadsheet cell A1 with the value 1.234

The following example demonstrates most of Access Basic's DDE-handling capabilities:

```
1: Dim nChannel, cTopic, cWorksheet
2: nChannel = DDEInitiate("Excel", "System")
3: DDEExecute nChannel, "[New(1)]"
4: cTopic = DDERequest(nChannel, "Selection")
5: cWorksheet = Left(cTopic, InStr(1, cTopic, "!")-1)
6: DDETerminate nChannel
7: nChannel = DDEInitiate("Excel", cWorksheet)
8: DDEPoke nChannel, "A1", "1.234"
9: DDETerminate
```

> **Caution:** This example assumes that Excel is already running. Always make sure that the application with which you are trying to establish a DDE conversation is active, or trap the error. If the requested application is not active, the system may hang (especially with Access version 1.0).

Analyzing the code in the preceding example clarifies the manner in which Access Basic DDE functions and statements work together from start to finish.

Line 1—Declares variables to store the channel number, topic name, and Excel worksheet name.

Line 2—Uses the DDEInitiate function to start a DDE conversation. The DDEInitiate function accepts two arguments: *application* (the name of the Windows application to function as the DDE server) and *topic* (a string expression that evaluates to a topic recognized by the server application).

> **Note:** Topic identifies the subject of the DDE conversation. It may be a file name or a System topic, which may be a list of all files open in the server application or a list of non-file-based application strings.

Line 3—Uses the DDEExecute statement to select a topic (which in the preceding example opens a new spreadsheet). The DDEExecute statement accepts two arguments: *channel* (the value returned by the DDEInitiate function) and *command* (any valid command recognized by the server application in the topic context of the current DDE conversation).

Line 4—Uses the DDERequest function to request an item (or *topic*) from the server application, which in the preceding example is Excel. The DDERequest function accepts two arguments: *channel* (the value returned by the DDERequest function) and *item* (the name of the Excel worksheet).

Line 5—Uses Access Basic string-handling functions to trim the exclamation point from the name of the spreadsheet. The name of the spreadsheet will be necessary later when you establish a new DDE conversation to send data to it.

Line 6—Uses the DDETerminate function to terminate the topic channel to conserve system resources—DDE conversations are very resource-intensive. Also, you cannot use the same DDE channel to do two different things simultaneously (such as both sending and receiving information).

Line 7—Uses the DDEInitiate function to open a new DDE conversation channel with Excel, and opens the new spreadsheet created in the first DDE conversation.

Line 8—Uses the DDEPoke statement to send the value 1.234 to cell A1 of the specified spreadsheet. The DDEPoke statement accepts three arguments: channel (the DDE channel number returned by the DDEInitiate function), item (the name of the data item recognized by the server application, in this case Excel spreadsheet cell A1), and data (a literal string or expression representing the data to be sent to the server application—in this case, data is a literal value: 1.234).

> **Caution:** In Access, DDE data is always exchanged as Windows plain text (a null-terminated string). The server application converts it according to its own numeric format. Be aware that this creates the potential for inaccuracies in precision and rounding due to numeric data type inconsistencies between Access and the DDE server application.

Chapter Summary

In this chapter, you saw how Access uses OLE and DDE to manipulate objects and communicate with other Windows applications. Using Access Basic with these Windows methods expands the limitations of traditional databases and opens up an entirely new set of possibilities for sharing data transparently between applications and incorporating multimedia features such as sound and pictures.

13

Extending Microsoft Access and Access Basic

Although Access is a robust DBMS with a powerful language, Access Basic, you may need to extend it at times by accessing external routines. The following list describes some of these situations:

- *Lack of built-in features.* Access lacks some features that may be necessary to develop high level applications. Access or Access Basic provides no way to obtain the MS-DOS date and time stamp of a file, for example. You can place a simple function in a DLL, however, to quickly return the results.

- *Limited functionality.* Sometimes the features offered by Access or Access Basic may lack the functionality or flexibility necessary to achieve the programmer's goals. Access Basic has a MsgBox function, for example, that displays a Windows dialog box with a specified icon, message, title, and buttons. This message box display in Access, however, always defaults to application-modal (you cannot access any other part of Access while the message box is displayed). By calling the MS Windows API, you can make the message box system-modal and deny access to all parts of Windows while the message box is displayed.

- *Performance considerations.* Performance may be another valid reason to try to go beyond the features offered in Access. Some operations, such as those involving searches or parsing of long character strings, may be unacceptably slow if coded with Access Basic. A fast routine written in C and placed in a dynamic link library may improve performance significantly.

- *System-wide access to function libraries.* Finally, you may want to write a system-specific set of functions and make it accessible to many applications executing from within different Access databases. A possible solution is to place these functions in a DLL.

This chapter discusses some simple but effective techniques for extending Access and Access Basic, including the following:

- Calling MS Windows API functions from Access
- Calling functions in dynamic link libraries (DLLs) from Access
- Facilitating various user-oriented design tasks in Access by using Access Wizards

Extending Access with Windows API Functions

The file WIN31API.WRI (located on the disk included with this book) contains the syntax and declarations required to call Windows version 3.1 API functions from within Access Basic code. Never mind that this file refers to Visual Basic rather than to Access; the calling conventions are identical. This text is included with the permission of Microsoft Corporation.

> Please note that neither the authors, Publisher, nor Microsoft Corporation can be held responsible for any errors, omissions, or inaccuracies in the WIN31API.WRI file.

Declaring External Functions

Because many examples in this chapter require declaring external functions (most of which are part of the Windows Application Programming Interface or API), this section begins with a short discussion of Windows API functions.

Because the bulk of Windows programming was done until very recently in the C language, C calling conventions were adopted for general use with MS Windows. By convention, functions that do not return a value are declared *void* in C. Because this function type is not available in Access, external functions that don't return a value can be declared as functions or subprocedures in Access. This is largely a matter of personal preference, but in this book, the authors have tried to use functions exclusively, even if a function procedure doesn't return a value. All examples therefore are declared as functions—not as subprocedures.

To differentiate between functions that return a value and functions that do not return a value, those that do not return a value are declared without specifying the type of the returned value. Because Access loads only its own DLLs at startup, you must declare explicitly any external functions in the Declarations section of an Access Basic module. The declaration must include the following elements:

- Name of the function or procedure
- Name of the library (DLL) that contains the declared procedure

- Optionally, the procedure alias (the name of the procedure in the library if called by another name in Access)
- A list of arguments (parameters) passed to the procedure
- Type of value returned by the procedure

The MS Windows function **IsCharUpper**, for example, which resides in the USER.EXE dynamic link library (DLL), can be declared in Access Basic as **Abc_IsCharUpper**. (Note about the EXE extension of the library: A DLL library doesn't need to have a DLL extension.) This function accepts one parameter: an integer representing the ANSI code for the character being tested. It returns an integer (nonzero for True, zero for False). The following code line provides the full declaration of the function IsChrUpper:

```
Declare Function Abc_IsCharUpper Lib "User" Alias "IsCharUpper" (ByVal wChr As
➥Integer) As Integer
```

> **Note:** External functions should be given a different name (an alias) than the function name to avoid potential errors, if the same functions are declared in other modules. In the example in this section, the IsCharUpper function is called in Access Abc_IsCharUpper.

After declaring the function, you need to determine what parameters to pass, if any, and in what form.

Passing Parameters to External Functions

Many of the external procedures you will be calling require parameters. Parameters usually are passed to external procedures from Access *by value* (which is indicated in Access Basic with the keyword **ByVal**)—not *by reference*. (If an argument is passed by reference, its address actually is passed. The called procedure therefore can make changes to the argument itself.)

Passing parameters by value simply sends a copy of the variable to the calling procedure. The exceptions to this rule are user-defined data types, which are passed by reference. Numeric parameters are converted into the data type specified in the **As...** clause of the parameter type. String data type arguments are passed as the address of the null-terminated string.

> **Caution:** Some external functions don't require certain data types in the argument(s). To override the type-checking of arguments, you can pass an argument with the data type *Any*, as in the following code line:
>
> ```
> Declare Function Catch Lib "Kernel (Buff As Any) As Integer
> ```
>
> This however, may trigger an error if an external function expects a parameter of a particular data type.

To avoid the potential traps and pitfalls of making calls to the Windows API or other external procedures, keep the following tips in mind:

- Arguments passed to external procedures must be of the type required by the procedure. Otherwise, a `Bad DLL calling convention` error (untrappable error #49) may occur. In some cases, no error is triggered and the function being called returns unexpected results, the system crashes, or simply nothing happens.
- Sometimes it takes only a minuscule error in a call to an external procedure to crash the system. Save your work often! Above all, don't complicate your life; use calls to the MS Windows API only if you have a compelling reason to do so.

The following sections briefly analyze several short examples of useful calls to Windows API functions from Access.

Obtaining System Information

MS Windows is a very complex system with hundreds of internal settings. It also tends to be somewhat miserly in voluntarily dispensing information about itself to application programs. The following example coaxes Windows for some information about itself and the computer system on which it is running. By using this example, you can get quite a bit of information that isn't available from within Access. Some of the items returned by this example are purely informational (such as the number of available F keys), but others, like free disk space and the windows start-up directory, are crucial to performing everyday programming tasks such as managing files. Figure 13.1 displays the information obtained with calls to Windows API.

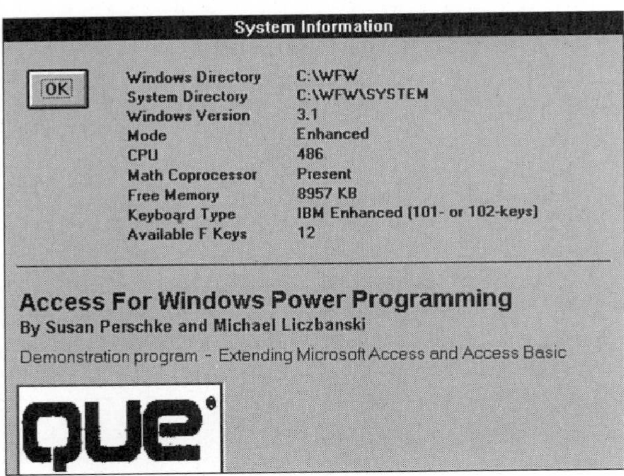

Figure 13.1. An Access form displaying results of calls to the Windows API.

It will be helpful to analyze one of the calls made from within this form to test for the presence of a math coprocessor. The MathChip( ) function relies on the MS Windows API **GetWinFlags** function that resides in the KERNEL DLL (KRNL386.EXE or KRNL286.EXE) and the Windows constant **WF_80x87** defined as &H400 (400 HEX).

You know from referring to the WIN31API.TXT file (or Windows SDK documentation) that the **GetWinFlags** function returns a 32-bit (double) number, which represents the memory configuration of the system on which Windows is running. Because of the 32-bit number, the function is declared as a Long (Access Basic) data type in the Declarations section.

By performing a simple bitwise **And** operation on this number and some predefined constants, it is easy to verify not only the presence or absence of the math coprocessor, but also the type of CPU and the mode in which Windows is running.

Here are the elements needed to implement the **MathChip** function, which is attached directly to the applicable control (text box) on the System Information form:

```
' In the Declarations Section
Declare Function GetWinFlags Lib "Kernel" () As Long

' And the function itself
Function MathChip() As String

     Flags& = GetWinFlags()

     If Flags& And WF_80x87 Then
          MathChip = "Present"
     Else
          MathChip = "None"
     End If

End Function
```

The MathChip function returns `Present` for every Intel-compatible math coprocessor, including the unit integrated in the 80486 CPU.

Now you can use the Windows API to perform some other useful tasks in Access such as removing the Minimize and Maximize buttons from a window, changing the caption of a window on the fly, or obtaining useful information about the Windows runtime environment.

Removing the Minimize and Maximize Buttons from a Window

Each time a window is displayed in Access, it has all the default elements of a standard window (the System menu, caption, and Maximize and Minimize buttons), as shown in figure 13.2. You may have a functional or aesthetic reason to change the attributes of a default window, however. If you remove the window's System menu and its Maximize and Minimize buttons, for example, the user cannot obscure other elements of the application with a maximized window or iconize it.

Access Basic does not have the built-in means to remove the Maximize and Minimize buttons (other than to define the form as a pop-up form or to enable you to open a form as a dialog box using the OpenForm action) and to remove the System menu from a window. You must call the Windows API function.

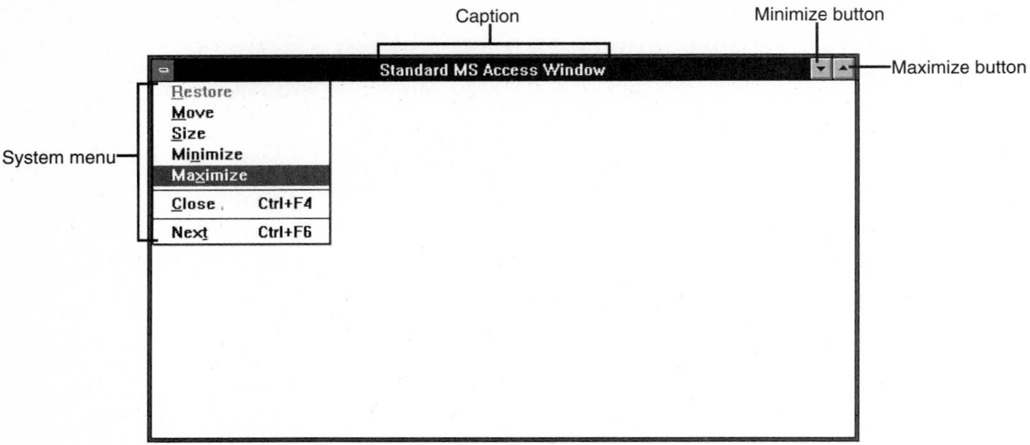

Figure 13.2. A default window displayed by Access.

While you are modifying this window, you also may want to change its caption when it is active. Although Access has a *Caption* property that defines the active window caption, this property can be changed only while in form Design view. For exercising more control at runtime, it is better to use the Windows API function because it changes the window caption on the fly, such as in response to some event triggered in the runtime environment. Note also that even though many windows may be active, you can change only the window that has focus from within Access Basic. You therefore must call the function that performs the change after you create the window.

You perform three steps to change the default window attributes:

1. Declaring constants and external functions
2. Obtaining the handle to the current window and getting its style
3. Performing a set of bitwise operations to set the bits of the desired window style

As step 1 states, you first must declare the constants and external functions in the Declarations section:

```
Declare Function SetWindowLong Lib "User" (ByVal hWnd%, ByVal wOffset%, ByVal
➥dwStyle&) As Long
```

To change the style of a window, you need two Windows functions: **GetWindowLong** and **SetWindowLong**. Start by declaring both functions in the Declarations section of the module:

```
Declare Function GetWindowLong Lib "User" (ByVal hWnd%, ByVal wOffset%) As Long
```

Because both functions return a long integer, they are declared as Long. The Windows API **GetWindowLong** function, used to obtain the style of a window, accepts two (integer) parameters: the handle to the current window (hWnd) and the byte offset of the attribute to return (wOffset). The Windows API **SetWindowLong** function, which actually sets a window attribute to a specified value, accepts three parameters: the handle to the window (*hWnd*, an integer), the byte offset of the attribute to set (*wOffset*, an integer), and *dwStyle* (the new value of the attribute—a long integer).

The **SetWindowLong** function returns the preceding value of the specified attribute or 0 if the setting was unsuccessful. The value returned by the function **GetWindowLong** depends on the variable **wOffset**, which specifies the byte offset of the attribute to return. In this case, you are interested in only the window style attribute, defined as MS Windows constant **GWL_STYLE.**

```
'Declare the constants needed to set the desired window style

Global Const GWL_STYLE = -16
Global Const WS_SYSMENU = &H80000
Global Const WS_MINIMIZEBOX = &H20000
Global Const WS_MAXIMIZEBOX = &H10000
```

Now you are ready to create the function AlteredFormWindow (the line numbers are used for subsequent reference):

```
1: Function AlteredFormWindow(fForm As Form)

2: Dim dwOldWinStyle As Long, dwNewWinStyle As Long, hWnd As Integer

3: hWnd = fForm.hWnd

4: dwOldWinStyle = GetWindowLong(hWnd, GWL_STYLE)

5: dwNewWinStyle = dwOldWinStyle And Not WS_SYSMENU And Not WS_MINIMIZEBOX And Not
   ➥WS_MAXIMIZEBOX

6: dwOldWinStyle = SetWindowLong(hWnd, GWL_STYLE, dwNewWinStyle)

7: End Function
```

As you can see, the function uses a mixture of Windows functions and Access intrinsic features (such as the *hWnd* property). Now take a closer look at the operations involved. The parameter *fForm* (the name of the open form that Access also uses to reference its window) is passed as a reference to a form object (see the open Form properties list in figure 13.3).

The variables used by the function are declared in line 2: *dwOldWinStyle* and *dwNewWinStyle* are declared as long integers to be consistent with the data types required by the Windows API **GetWindowLong** and **SetWindowLong** functions. The handle to the window (*hWnd*) is declared as an integer.

The code in line 3 uses the Access *hWnd* property to obtain the handle to the current window. The call to the **GetWindowLong** function in line 4 is used to obtain the current style of the window and to store it in the *dwOldWinStyle* variable. The code in line 5 sets the bits of the *dwNewWinStyle* (using the bitwise **And** and **Not** operations). Finally, the code in line 6 calls the **SetWinLong** function and sets the new window style for the active window. Activate this function from the *OnOpen* property of a form and watch the window change.

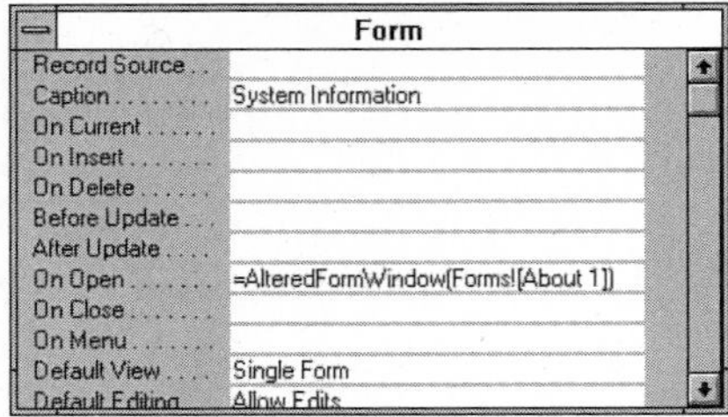

Figure 13.3. The Form property list with the function AlteredFormWindow attached to the OnOpen property.

To change the caption of the current window, use the **SetWindowText** function. Add the following statement to the Declarations section:

```
Declare Sub SetWindowText Lib "User" (ByVal hWnd%, ByVal szCaption$)
```

This Windows function doesn't return a value, so it is declared a subprocedure. This function accepts two parameters: the handle to the window (an integer) and the new caption (a zero-terminated string).

> **Note:** If you declare **SetWindowText** as a function in Access, you must use a dummy variable for the nonexisting returned value. Access does not discard the value returned by a function if there is no storage allocated for it.

To actually change the caption, insert the following line into the **AlteredFormWindow** function after line 3 (after obtaining the handle to the window):

```
SetWindowText(hWnd, "This is the new caption")
```

Finally, after calling the **AlteredFormWindow** function, the System Information window looks like figure 13.4.

> **Warning:** Do not use Access Maximize and Minimize actions with a window that has its Maximize and Minimize buttons removed. Attempting this procedure usually freezes Access or causes the entire system to crash.

Swapping the Function of the Right and Left Mouse Buttons

So far, all the examples in this chapter have shown you how to call Windows functions from Access Basic code. You also can attach these functions directly to Access controls. In the following example, you use the Windows function **SwapMouseButton** (found in the DLL library USER.EXE) to swap the roles of the right and left mouse buttons. This function accepts one integer-type parameter, fSwap, and returns an integer. (Access discards the return value when a function is attached to an action property, such as *OnPush*, *OnOpen*, and so on.)

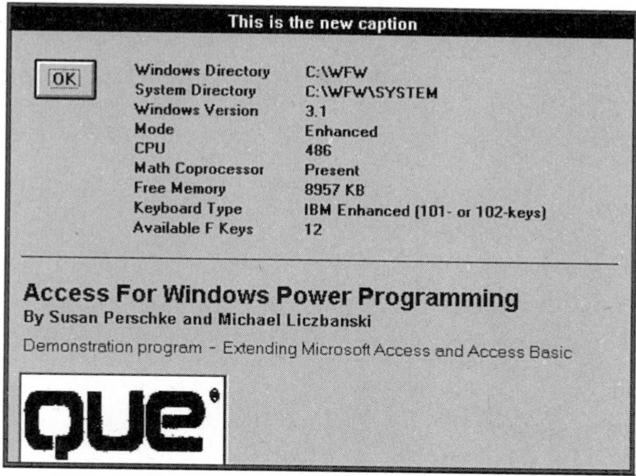

Figure 13.4. The final system information window after making your changes.

After you declare the function in the Declarations section of a module, attach it to one of the *On...* properties (with *OnPush* being the most logical choice) of a form, as shown in figure 13.5:

```
Declare Function SwapMouseButton Lib "User" (ByVal fSwap As Integer) As Integer
```

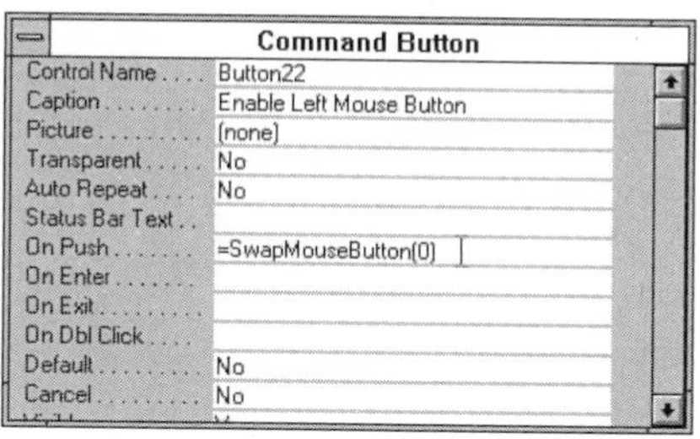

Figure 13.5. Attaching the SwapMouseButton function directly to the *OnPush* property.

Using User-Defined Data Types with External Procedures

You should remember a few more things about calling Windows API functions. Some functions require you to create a predefined data structure to store the value(s) returned by the function. One example is the **GetWindowRect** function, which returns the coordinates of the specified window. This function (declared in the following example as a subprocedure) doesn't explicitly return a value, but instead puts the return values into a predefined data structure. When using such a function, declare the required data structure using the **Type...End Type** statements.

First, declare the required data structure for storing the coordinates of the top left and bottom right corners of the window in question—a simple user-defined type called RECT, consisting of four integer variables:

```
'Declare structure for storing return values from GetWindowRect function
Type RECT
    aleft As Integer
    atop As Integer
    aright As Integer
    abottom As Integer
End Type
```

Then declare the function itself:

```
Declare Sub GetWindowRect Lib "User" (ByVal hWnd As Integer, Coord As RECT)
```

> **Note:** When referring to values returned by this function, be sure to follow the standard Access Basic convention of referring to user-defined data types—putting the name of the user-defined type first and using the dot operator to indicate its elements (for example, RECT.aleft, RECT.abottom, and so on).

As you can see, there is little mystery in calling Windows API functions from Access Basic if you know the exact syntax of the call and can re-create the exact sequence of calls to produce the results you want. If you are interested in pursuing this topic further, here are some potential steps that can point you in the right direction:

- Examine the file WIN31API.TXT on the disk included with this book for the exact syntax of calls made to Windows API functions from Access Basic and values for Windows constants.
- Explore the Windows API Routines module in the ORDENTRY sample database provided with Access.
- Think in MS Windows terms. Often, you need to perform more than one step in order to accomplish the final task. Study MS Windows sample code (written mostly in the C language), even if you are not a C programmer. The organization of Windows programs and the general flow of logic may be the source of programming inspiration and may help you construct the appropriate Access Basic routines.

Extending Access Basic with Dynamic Link Libraries

Access is a feature-laden DBMS with a powerful programming language, but it still may lack the functionality or flexibility to accomplish certain application-specific programming tasks—even when augmented by Windows API functions or commercial libraries. If you feel really brave and creative, you may want to consider writing a custom procedures library (DLL) that can be dynamically linked to your application.

You may want to consider the benefits of a customized DLL, for example, if your application is meant to run in different countries. By using DLLs, you easily can localize your application to a particular country without affecting the actual code base (by providing messages, units of measurement, and so on in the local language according to local traditions and conventions). This technique is popular among commercial vendors of Windows, including Microsoft. The C language is most commonly used to write Windows DLLs, but languages like Pascal can be used as well.

The concept of dynamically linking procedures at runtime is one of the strongest architectural points of Windows; it provides flexibility (Windows applications can share libraries) and immense savings in storage space. It is impractical, to say the least, to link some of these huge Windows libraries to every application that uses them. Although a comprehensive discussion of writing Windows dynamic link libraries is beyond the scope of this book, you explore some of the general concepts in the following sections. For more specific information, refer to the MS Windows SDK documentation or one of the many books on programming for Windows 3.x, such as *Programming in Windows 3.1* (Que, 1992).

Writing procedures to include in a dynamic link library is very similar to writing standard C language Windows code, with some twists: DLLs do not have their own stacks, the Main( ) function is replaced by the LibMain( ) function, a DLL must have defined entry and exit points, and so on. Almost every Windows-compatible C compiler facilitates this task by providing a ready framework for a DLL or options to generate DLLs from C source code, however. In effect, even a rudimentary knowledge of the C language can be enough to write a useful Windows DLL.

Some limitations to using DLLs in Access Versions 1.0 and 1.1 exist, primarily because one or more of the DLL features in question are not allowed or are undocumented. For example, DLLs are an excellent place to put custom controls for an application (such as those allowed in Visual Basic), but because custom controls are not permitted in Access, you cannot use this feature. Similarly, some applications can use custom device drivers, but this area of Access is not yet documented, which effectively prevents developers from writing custom device drivers for Access.

Keeping these limitations in mind, you still can use some DLLs with Access to provide a library of unified and consistent routines to perform various tasks.

Declaring Procedures in DLLs

Declaring procedures in external libraries (DLLs) is the same as declaring Windows API functions. As long as Access can find the DLL and its functions follow MS Windows requirements, the DLL executes as if it were a native Access function. The following entry in the Declarations section of an Access module declares a hypothetical GetFileDate function residing in the X_SAMPLE.DLL:

```
Declare Function GetFileDate Lib "X_SAMPLE.DLL" (ByVal szFileName as String) As Double
```

After you declare the function, you can call it by using standard Access calling conventions, such as the following code:

```
Dim dWFileDate&
dwFileDate = GetFileDate("COMMAND.COM")
```

If the referenced DLL does not exist in the current directory, Access uses default Windows methods to find the library and searches directories in the following order:

Current directory

Windows directory

Windows system directory

Directories included in DOS search path

Mapped network directories (if any)

Writing Libraries in Access Basic

There is yet another way to make routines available to Access applications that does not involve fiddling with C compilers and linkers: by building a dedicated library database (or augmenting an existing one with desired features) and accessing these features from another Access database. Some developers use this method as a security measure by storing data in a separate database or out of necessity, because this is the only way to bypass the allowed size of an Access database.

The simplest way to make custom functions and features available to all Access applications is to add them to the UTILITY.MDA that comes with Access. Even though it has an unfamiliar file extension, MDA, UTILITY.MDA is just like any Access database. It is interesting to explore UTILITY.MDA, because it contains all the familiar elements of the Access user interface: the toolbar, ribbon, form and report design surfaces, icons used throughout Access, and so on. UTILITY.MDA also contains the underlying Access Basic code for these objects.

In addition to adding your own customized procedures, you can modify the native objects in the UTILITY.MDA database, as long as their basic functionality remains intact. (Don't delete critical controls from the forms in UTILITY.MDA, for example.)

The following entry in the MS Windows MSACCES.INI file designates UTILITY.MDA as the utility library for Access (in Version 1.0 only; Version 1.1 loads the UTILITY.MDA as the utility database automatically):

```
[Options]

UtilityDB=C:\ACCESS\UTILITY.MDA
```

The Database container in the UTILITY.MDA utility database shows the names of Access default forms included in this database (see fig. 13.6).

Figure 13.7 shows the Access color palette which is implemented as an Access form in the UTILITY.MDA database.

> **Tip:** Most Access user-interface elements are defined as standard Access forms in the UTILITY.MDA database. You can edit any or all of these elements to customize the look and feel of Access.

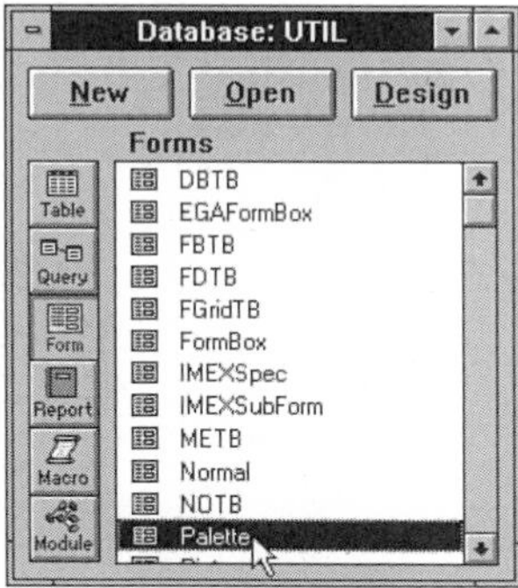

Figure 13.6. The Database container in the UTILITY.MDA utility database.

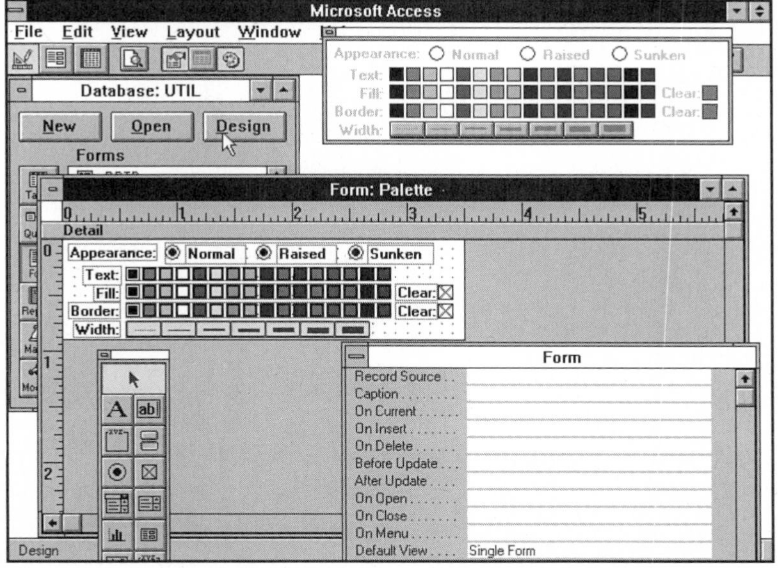

Figure 13.7. The Access default color palette form.

Customizing the UTILITY.MDA Database

If you want to include a new feature in the UTILITY.MDA database, simply make a copy of it under a different name and open it as an ordinary database. (Disregard any error messages on startup caused by duplicate Access Basic code modules, because the original UTILITY.MDA database already is loaded by default.) You now can add Access Basic code, forms, reports, and so on to this database. Or, you can modify existing features, taking care not to affect basic functionality. To make your changes available to the system, exit Access and copy the modified database to UTILITY.MDA (after thorough testing). Or, better yet, modify the UTILITY.DB entry in the MSACCESS.INI file to reflect the new name.

> **Note:** Version 1.1 loads UTILITY.MDA automatically without an entry in the MSACCESS.INI file. To load UTILITY.MDA as a user database, rename the original UTILITY.MDA database to something else—for example, UTIL.MDA—and create a dummy (empty) database named UTILITY.MDA. Then load the renamed database as a user database and—after making desired changes—rename it back to UTILITY.MDA. *Remember to backup the original UTILITY.MDA file just in case.*

One of the most frequent modifications made to UTILITY.MDA is deleting certain controls (such as the Design button from the toolbar) in order to permanently disable certain features from end-user systems. You may want to simply rearrange buttons and other controls (see fig. 13.8). You also can change text and its attributes (font or color, for example) on forms, add your company logo or other text and pictures, or otherwise customize the standard Access look.

> **Warning:** This convenient method of extending and modifying Access objects, although undocumented, should not cause problems in Versions 1.0 and 1.1 as long as you don't make structural changes to any of the objects (such as forms, code, and so on) used by Access.

Extending Access with Wizards

More and more software embraces the beneficial concept of guiding a user through repetitive operations—especially those involving multiple steps and many decisions. In Access, such operations can include form and report design. If a custom report (or form) was the default, the user would be left staring at an empty design surface with few menus and no clue of what to do next (see fig. 13.9).

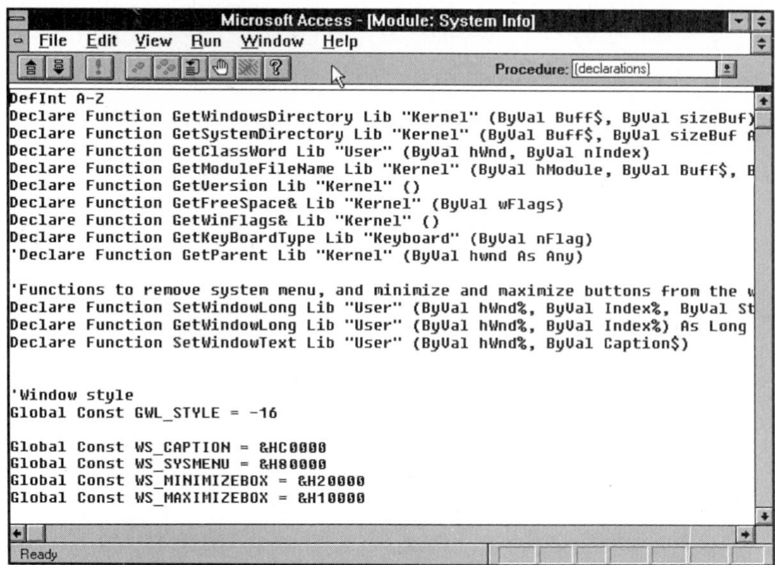

Figure 13.8. The Access Basic editor with a modified toolbar.

Access provides a useful feature, Cue Cards, however, to guide users while they design forms and other objects. *Cue Cards* are a set of minihelp topics grouped into functional sets that guide the user step by step by using descriptions and examples for a particular operation. One important distinction between Cue Cards and the regular Help system is that Cue Cards remain on-screen no matter what the user is doing. As helpful as Cue Cards are for the user, custom user-defined Cue Cards cannot be added to Access (Versions 1.0 and 1.1).

Access *Wizards*, the second way of making the user's life easier, are, on the other hand, easy to add to Access. Wizards are applications written in Access Basic—using Access modules, forms, tables, and so on—that enable the user to perform a task by making guided choices. In essence, a Wizard is an Access program, coupled with a predefined set of rules and forms, that can automatically accomplish what usually is done by the user "by hand" (manually placing and moving controls on the design surface). Wizards simplify the design process by presenting a predefined set of design choices, which eliminates the confusion of selecting from the entire gamut of design possibilities. Even if the result falls somewhat short of the user's needs (or expectations), the bulk of the work is done already.

From the user's perspective, the results of something like the Report Wizard are just shy of miraculous. After answering a few questions, Access presents the user with a ready (not only finished, but most of the time, very polished) report.

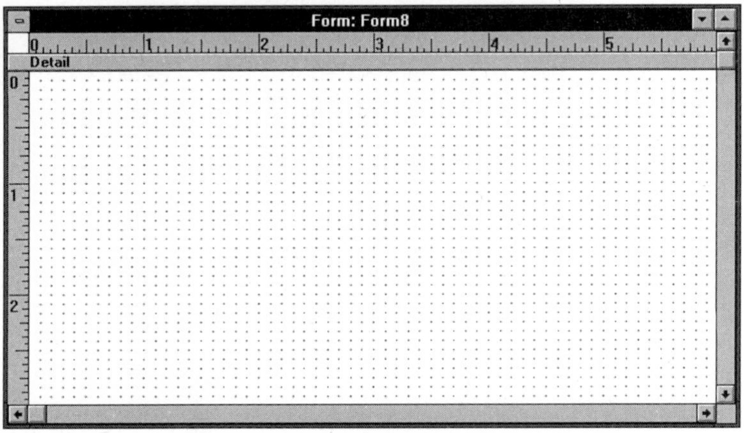

Figure 13.9. An empty and uninviting Access custom form design surface.

Wizards reside in library databases attached to Access with the following entry in the MSACCESS.INI file:

```
[Libraries]
C:\ACCESS\wizard.mda=ro
C:\ACCESS\MyWizard.mdb=rw
```

The first entry installs the standard wizard database included with Access; the second is a custom one that has been added by the programmer.

All library databases specified in the [Libraries] section of the MSACCESS.INI file, including Wizard libraries, are loaded when Access starts. There are at least two consequences of this fact: the library databases must be well-tested, because compilation errors prevent their loading, and code contained in these databases is loaded into memory, thus imposing a potentially huge memory penalty on the system. (Forms contained in the library databases are called on an as-needed basis.) One major limitation of library databases is that they cannot contain macros. You must use Access Basic code to perform all operations (however, you can execute Access actions with the DoCmd statement).

Loading the library database is just the first step in making it usable to Access. You also must enter the name of the new Wizard and the name of the function that activates it in the WIZARDS table contained in the WIZARD.MDA database. The functions that activate the Wizard must accept two parameters: the table name (type String), and the Wizard ID (type Integer), as in the following example:

```
Function StartMyWizard(szTable As String, wWizID As Integer)
     (...)
End Function
```

Figure 13.10 shows the entries in the WIZARDS table for all seven Wizards supplied with Access. It also shows an extra entry for the custom report, Snake Report, activated by the function StartSnakeReportWizard.

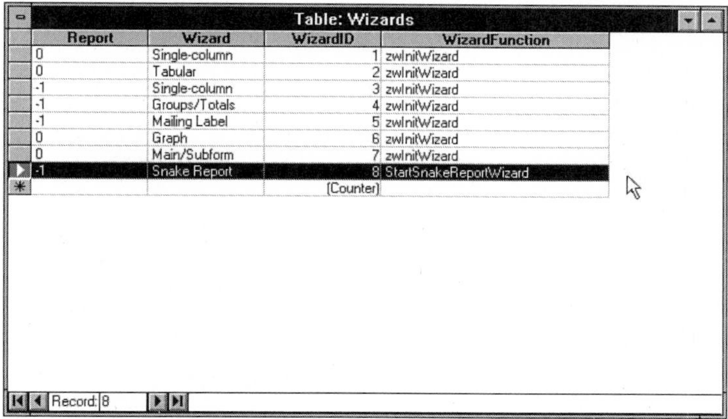

Table: Wizards

Report	Wizard	WizardID	WizardFunction
0	Single-column	1	zwInitWizard
0	Tabular	2	zwInitWizard
-1	Single-column	3	zwInitWizard
-1	Groups/Totals	4	zwInitWizard
-1	Mailing Label	5	zwInitWizard
0	Graph	6	zwInitWizard
0	Main/Subform	7	zwInitWizard
-1	Snake Report	8	StartSnakeReportWizard
		(Counter)	

Record: 8

Figure 13.10. A view of the Wizards table in the WIZARD.MDA database.

Using Standard Access Wizards

The Wizards included with Access—Report Wizard, Form Wizard, Graph Wizard, and Crosstab Wizard (in Version 1.1 only)—can be found in the WIZARD.MDA database loaded by Access as a read-only library database. You can learn a great deal by studying the code in this database. In fact, if you are thinking of writing Wizards, it is a good idea to start by printing out the Access Basic code found in the WIZARD.MDA database and analyzing it thoroughly. This is no minor task, but because Microsoft does not document the process, this is the only way to get started.

Because databases loaded as library databases cannot also be loaded as user databases, to view such a database you first must exit Access and comment out the appropriate entry in the [Libraries] section of the MSACCESS.INI file (using a semicolon), restart Access, and then open the database in the usual way.

Creating Custom Wizards

Writing wizards is in essence a three-phase process of creating empty objects (forms or reports), populating them with desired controls (most often table and query fields), and setting their properties to desired values. Unfortunately, this simple description hides many of the complexities of writing and implementing Wizards, such as keeping track of "what is where" on a form or a report, calculating the proper placement of controls on the design surface, error trapping, and optimizing performance. To make matters even more complex, Microsoft elected not to document certain features of Access Basic in versions 1.0 and 1.1 (although ADK documentation covers this omission) that are necessary and used extensively to write the Wizards supplied with Access. Because all of these undocumented features are explained and documented in the Reference, here is just a short list:

Undocumented Functions

CodeDB( )

CreateControl, CreateReportControl

CreateForm, CreateReport

CreateGroupLevel

DeleteControl, DeleteReportControl

SysCmd

Undocumented Properties

GroupInterval

GroupLevel

GroupOn

Painting

PrtDevMode

PrtMip

You need to use almost all these items to create (by programming in Access Basic) a form or a report, to define and position its controls, and to specify its properties.

A Sample Wizard

To bring the concept of creating Wizards closer to home, analyze the following code example, which is a simplistic Form Wizard. It creates a single column form from all fields in the specified table (or query). This example is far from being a polished, "production quality" Wizard, but it is used here to demonstrate most of the elements necessary to write Wizards. It also relies heavily on the undocumented features mentioned earlier in the preceding section. The code is liberally commented, with comments separating distinct (logically related) sections of the code.

First, you need to pass the name of the desired table (or query) as the argument to this function:

```
Function PseudoWizard (szTableName$)
```

Then declare needed variables:

```
Dim cDb As Database, cTb As Table, cSn As Snapshot, cCtrl As Control
Dim fForm As Form, szFormName$, wOffset%, dwBackColor&
```

Define constants for some types of controls:

```
Const LABEL = 100
Const CHECK_BOX = 106
Const TEXT_BOX = 109
```

Define bar and pull-down menu constants:

```
Const FORMDSGN_BAR = 3
Const LAYOUT_MENU = 3
Const FORM_HDR_FOOTER = 9
```

Define constants for form sections:

```
Const FORM_DETAIL = 0
Const FORM_HDR = 1
Const FORM_FOOTER = 2
```

Define the background color (light gray) for the form's sections and controls and initialize the variable used to position controls on the form:

```
dwBackColor = RGB(192, 192, 192)
wOffset = 0
```

Set the current database object, open the desired table, and create a snapshot of all fields in the opened table and their attributes:

```
Set cDb = CurrentDB()
Set cTb = cDb.OpenTable(szTableName)
Set cSn = cTb.ListFields()
```

Create the form and save its name to a variable:

```
Set fForm = CreateForm("","")
szFormName = fForm.FormName
```

Add the form header and footer to the form:

```
DoCmd DoMenuItem FORMDSGN_BAR, LAYOUT_MENU, FORM_HDR_FOOTER
```

Set the source of records for this form:

```
fForm.RecordSource = szTableName
```

Set the background color for the Detail section:

```
fForm.Section(FORM_DETAIL).BackColor = dwBackColor
```

Set the DefaultView property (single form):

```
fForm.DefaultView = 2
```

Include only the horizontal scroll bar:

```
fForm.ScrollBars = 1
```

Allow the form header to be auto-sized and put a New Form label on the Form Header section:

```
fForm.Section(FORM_HEADER).Height = 0
Set cCtrl = CreateControl(szFormName, LABEL, FORM_HEADER, "", "New Form")', 0, 100 +
➥wOffset)
```

Traverse the snapshot containing all fields in the desired table or query:

```
Do Until cSn.Eof
```

Create a default label (consisting of the name of the field) and set its background color to light gray:

```
Set cCtrl = CreateControl(szFormName, LABEL, 0, "", cSn.Name, 0, 100 + wOffset)
cCtrl.BackColor = dwBackColor
```

If the field data type is Yes/No, create a check box. Otherwise, create a text box and set its background color to light gray (note that a check box doesn't have the background color property):

```
If cSn.Type = 1 Then
      Set cCtrl = CreateControl(szFormName, CHECK_BOX, FORM_DETAIL, "",cSn.Name,
      ➥1000, 100 + wOffset)
Else
      Set cCtrl = CreateControl(szFormName, TEXT_BOX, FORM_DETAIL, "", cSn.Name,
      ➥1000, 100 + wOffset)
      cCtrl.BackColor = dwBackColor
End If
```

Make the control appear "sunken" on the form:

```
cCtrl.SpecialEffect = 2
```

If the control is not updatable, disable (gray) it by setting its enabled property to False:

```
If cSn.Attributes = 49 Then cCtrl.Enabled = False
```

Move to the next record in the snapshot and update the variable used to position controls on the form:

```
    cSn.MoveNext
    wOffset = wOffset + 300

Loop
```

Add some white space at the bottom of the Detail section of the form:

```
fForm.Section(FORM_DETAIL).Height = fForm.Section(FORM_DETAIL).Height + 300
```

Allow the form footer to be auto-sized and add text ("New Form ends here") on the form footer:

```
fForm.Section(FORM_FOOTER).Height = 0

Set cCtrl = CreateControl(szFormName, LABEL, FORM_FOOTER, "", "New Form ends
➥here")', 0, 100 + wOffset)
```

Close opened objects:

```
cSn.Close
cTb.Close
```

Finally, open the form in Design view:

```
DoCmd Restore

End Function
```

This code, found in the Pseudo Wizard module in the sample database included with this book, can be executed from the Immediate window using the **?PseudoWizard(<table/query name>)** command. Figure 13.11 shows a form produced by the code in this section.

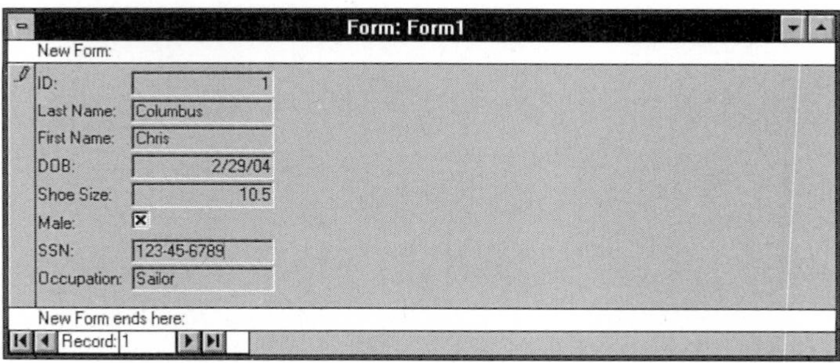

Figure 13.11. Form produced by the function PseudoWizard.

As you can see from the preceding example, writing even the simplest Wizard requires quite a few lines of code, most of which handle the setup and housekeeping chores. More sophisticated Wizards must contain a lot of error-trapping and exception-processing code; the latter is used mostly to position controls on forms or reports and to establish sort and grouping levels. Here are a few pointers to follow while designing and implementing custom Wizards:

- A Wizard should do just one thing (such as helping the user to export data to MS Excel) but should do it thoroughly.
- A Wizard should expertly and effortlessly guide the user through the desired process, so you as the programmer must gain a thorough understanding of the process and all required steps before you design your Wizard.
- Avoid creating new user interface standards. Try to reuse as many elements (list boxes and forms, for example) from the WIZARD.MDA and UTILITY.MDA as possible.
- Because Access Basic is not the fastest language on Earth and because Wizards must do many things, optimize the code for speed.

Chapter Summary

In this chapter, you covered quite a bit of ground. You learned the basics of calling and using external procedures from within Access Basic and of declaring and using external procedures. You learned about the limitations and potential pitfalls of calling Windows API procedures, and how to use MS Windows API functions to obtain information about the system. This chapter showed you how to manipulate the attributes of a window, how to build a library of functions written in Access Basic, and how to extend the capabilities of Access by writing custom Wizards. Armed with this knowledge, you should be able to customize your applications to fit almost any need.

14

Error Handling

One of the most overlooked aspects of application development is error handling. Many factors can cause errors, and sometimes even the most aggressive testing fails to create the conditions in which an error is triggered. Error trapping therefore should be a fundamental component of all serious applications.

Error trapping in the Windows development environment offers such an improvement over DOS that you may be tempted to become lax in applying application-level error trapping. After all, Windows traps most errors and usually provides at least a graceful exit from an error condition, even if it means closing the focused application. Although Windows 3.1 has *greatly* tamed the dreaded unrecoverable application error (from which there was sometimes no return), you should not entirely trust your database applications to the vague and sometimes unpredictable nature of Windows error handling.

Adding error-trapping routines to your applications is not particularly glamorous or exciting; it is usually one of those low-visibility steps in the development cycle, expected but not rewarded by the client, and may even occur as an afterthought. Moreover, because Access is a new product, you cannot plug in a garden variety of published libraries to supplement your code.

The good news is that Access Basic has the fundamentals for enabling you to write some pretty serviceable error-trapping routines. If you are careful enough to make the procedures modular and generic, you even may be able to apply yourself only once to the task.

This chapter covers the following topics:

- Detection of errors in Access
- Phases of error trapping and recovery in Access
- Trapping Windows errors

Handling Errors in Access Basic

Table 14.1 provides an overview of the built-in Access Basic language elements used for error handling.

Table 14.1. Error-Handling Features of Access Basic

Element Name	*Element Type*	*Purpose and Use*	*Value Returned*	*Arguments*
Err, Erl	Function	Returns the error status.	Integer identifying the error message.	None
Err	Statement	Sets Err to a specific value. Enables you to create user-defined errors and to communicate application-specific error information between procedures.	N/A	*n* is an integer to specify an error. Or, 0 specifies no error.
Error[$] [(*errorcode*)]	Function	Returns the error message that corresponds to the error code.	**Error** returns a variant. **Error$** returns a string.	*errorcode* must be an integer between 1 and 32,767.
Error	Statement	Simulates the occurrence of an error. May be used to generate a user-defined error.	N/A	*errorcode* must be an integer between 1 and 32,767.
On Error [GoTo *line*| Resume Next | GoTo 0]	Statement	Calls or disables an error-handling routine.	N/A	*line* specifies next line to execute within the procedure.

Establishing an Access Error-Handling Methodology

Trapping errors is a multifaceted operation that can be summarized as a three-phase process consisting of *detection*, *damage control*, and *recovery*.

Each phase typically involves the following steps, to greater or lesser degrees of refinement:

Detection phase:

1. Setting up an error-handling loop or *trigger*
2. Branching to an error-handling procedure after an error occurs

Damage control phase:

1. Analyzing the error and determining the extent of the problem
2. Logging the error for later analysis (optional)
3. Presenting an error message and options to the user
4. Capturing run-time information from the application for reconstruction (optional)

Recovery phase:

1. Implementing repair/reconstruction procedures
2. Restoring the environment to its pre-error status

The following sections describe each phase of the error-handling process.

Phase One: Detection

Some programming languages offer a variety of means to detect errors, but in Access Basic there is only one way: by using the *On Error* statement. (This does not apply to user-defined errors, which you may force by using the *Error* statement.)

The *On Error* statement sets up a module-wide loop or event handler. The event that triggers the loop or handler is, of course, an error. When an error is detected, control of the process is handed back to the *On Error* statement, and one of three things may happen:

- If you use the *Go To line* option, the program branches to the specified line label or line number, and processing continues from that point.
- If you use the ***Resume Next*** option, control is handed to the line of code immediately following the line at which the error occurred.
- If you use the *Go To* 0 option, any event handler in the current procedure is disabled.

> **Note:** Unlike in Xbase, the Access Basic **On Error** statement requires you to use one of these three options.

Trapping Errors

The capability of Access Basic to handle errors depends on whether the error is trappable. Of a total of 718 Access Basic returnable errors, only 41 are documented. (See Appendix B for a full listing of all Access error messages.) But fortunately, only one Access Basic error is not trappable: `Error in loading DLL` (error #48).

If the error is trappable, it is intercepted by the **On Error** statement.

Handling System (Windows) Errors

Access Basic can trap only its own errors; system-wide (Windows) errors are not trappable with Access Basic.

This next simple error-handling routine does nothing more than trap the error and display its corresponding **Error** message:

```
Sub ErrTrap

  On Error GoTo DispErr

DispErr:

  MsgBox Error
  Resume Next

End Sub
```

This example achieves the same results that Access would by itself. We're using this example to build something a little more robust, however. Using the same procedure, we can add some conditional display options (you need to substitute a real case statement for the bracketed<> statements below):

```
Sub ErrTrap

  On Error GoTo DispErr

DispErr:

Select Case Err           'Display a different message depending on the error
  Case <#1> : MsgBox "The following error has occurred: " & Error
  Case <#2> : MsgBox "The following error has occurred: " & Error
  Case <#3> : MsgBox "The following error has occurred: " & Error
End Select

Resume Next               'Start processing again at point of interruption

End Sub
```

In this example you really aren't "handling" the error in the sense of doing something about it, and you have not allowed for errors other than the three listed. If a different error occurs, it is intercepted but not displayed because the event handler takes control from Access and gives it to the error-handling procedure, and processing continues as if the error had not occurred.

On the other hand, this result may be exactly what you intended. If only certain errors require intervention on the part of the application or the user, only those errors need to be trapped; all other trappable errors become transparent to the application.

Using this approach is a little like playing Russian roulette, however, unless you have tested the application against *each and every* possible error. Because most application development budgets would be stretched too thin by this scenario, you need to come up with a more economical approach.

Without adding too many layers of complexity, it is usually sufficient to trap certain *kinds* of errors, depending on the process that is executing at the time of the error. If a process is performing arithmetic operations, for example, errors that are most likely to affect the results (such as division by 0) should be specifically trapped and corrected with in-line code:

```
Function Error2 ()
    On Error Resume Next
    Dim a%, b%
    a = 100: b = 0
    c = a / b
    If Err = 11 Then          'If division by zero
        c = 0                 'Assign a value to c
    End If
End Function
```

Trapping specific kinds of errors sets up the next phase, which involves taking some kind of action to correct the error condition.

Phase Two: Damage Control

Now that we have trapped the error, the next question becomes what to do with it. Because Access sometimes automatically resets the value of an error to 0 when an error-handling routine is called, the first step after trapping the error is to store the corresponding value of the error in a memory variable, as follows:

```
Sub ErrTrap

  On Err Go To DispErr

DispErr:

  Dim wErr as Integer
  wErr = Err        'First capture the error #!

....
  Resume Next

End Sub
```

After the error is trapped and logged to a memory variable, you can proceed with the following steps to handle the error:

- Analyze the error and determine the extent and severity of the problem.
- Log the error for later analysis (optional).

- Present a custom error message and options to the user.

The example in the following section demonstrates all three of these options.

Creating Special Error-Handling Routines

The function in the following example demonstrates some possible methods for trapping, logging, reporting, and handling errors. You probably will want to develop specific routines of your own—perhaps even a different error handler for every process.

```
Function error1 ()
Const PROC_NAME = "Error1" 'Declare the procedure name for later reference
On Error GoTo err1

Error 7                        'Force an error

err1:
   Dim wErr%, wId%, nFile%
   wErr% = Err

    nFile = FreeFile
    Open "ERROR.LOG" For Append Shared As nFile     'Open a file to
    Write #nFile, Now, Err, Error, PROC_NAME        'log errors
    Close nFile

    Select Case wErr
    Case 7  ' Out of memory
        wId = MsgBox(Error & ".  Program will terminate", MB_OK + MB_ICONSTOP)
        wId = IDABORT
    Case 17 ' Can't continue
        wId = MsgBox(Error, MB_RETRYCANCEL + MB_ICONSTOP + MB_DEFBUTTON2)
    Case 58 ' File already exists
        wId = MsgBox(Error & ".  Overwrite?", MB_YESNOCANCEL + MB_ICONQUESTION +
        ➥MB_DEFBUTTON2)
    End Select

    If wId = IDABORT Then
        End
    ElseIf wId = IDCANCEL Or wId = IDNO Then
        Exit Function
    ElseIf wId = IDRETRY Then
        Resume 0
    ElseIf wId = IDIGNORE Or wId = IDYES Or wId = IDOK Then
        Resume Next
    End If
 End FunctionNormal error.
```

> **Note:** Constants like MB_OK and MB_ICONSTOP are predefined Windows constants. For more information, see the **MsgBox** function in the reference section.

The following paragraphs are an analysis of the function in the preceding example (unreferenced lines are commented in the code or are self-explanatory):

It's important to declare the procedure name; there is no intrinsic function in Access Basic for indicating the current procedure (line 2).

Line 7 forces a critical error: `Out of Memory` (for the purpose of testing the function; you can change the error as indicated in the Select statements starting on line 17 to test for different errors).

Lines 8 and 9 set up memory variables to store the error number, the error ID, and a file number.

Line 11 returns the value of the next available file number, and line 12 opens the file with the name ERROR.LOG (in Append mode so that you don't write over previously stored information). Line 13 writes the error information to the error log file, and Line 14 closes the file.

Next, in line 16, a **Select Case** construct is used to test for the error number. Depending on the number, a different message box and options are presented to the user (lines 18 through 23).

Lines 26 through 34 determine the next action to take based on the user's response to the error message.

Capturing Information for Reconstruction

In sophisticated applications containing critical functions, you may need to implement a high level of fault tolerance (the capability of the application to shield itself and recover gracefully from error conditions without damage to the data, for example). In most systems, ensuring this high level of fault tolerance requires transaction processing, such as provided by the Access Basic **Begin ... End Transaction** statements (see the statements section in the Reference).

One aspect of fault tolerance is the system's capability to be restored to a preprocessing state (see the next section, "Phase Three: Recovery"). There is no specific recommendation for capturing system-wide information, because the appropriate amount of information to keep track of varies from application to application. With error-handling procedures, however, the best time to determine the status of the system is at the time of the error, before you perform any repair or restoration procedures or otherwise alter the system status.

> **Note:** Access Basic offers no facility for capturing system-wide information at any given moment (such as the Xbase command *Save To <mvar> All Like ...*). You must code these procedures individually for each application.

Phase Three: Recovery

You have trapped the error and preserved whatever important information you may need to reconstruct the environment. Now you have another set of possibilities: implementing repair/reconstruction procedures or restoring the environment to its pre-error status.

Repairing or reconstructing may not be practical, or even possible. Certain errors make recovery impossible, especially if they are nontrappable errors such as `Failure to Load DLL` or errors generated by Microsoft Windows. Assuming that you have built some fault tolerance into your application, however, you may be able to, at best, repair the damage and continue processing, or at least stabilize the situation and return it to its preprocessing state. (See the example in "Creating Special Error-Handling Routines," earlier in this chapter.)

Restoring the environment to pre-error state assumes that you know what the pre-error status was, which is largely an application-specific determination. Restoring to a pre-error condition may mean reinitializing some or all values: clearing memory or even starting over. If you use transaction processing, the simplest recovery technique is to undo or roll back the last transaction to its pre-processing state. Even though some work may be lost (typically the transaction in process at the time the error occurs), the overall integrity of the system is maintained.

Chaining Error-Handling Procedures

It is quite possible that one error-handling procedure will call another, which will call another, and so on. Chaining or cascading these procedures is entirely possible in Access Basic, but it can have very unpredictable consequences. If one of the nested or chained error-handling procedures triggers a new error, for example, the current procedure is unable to process the error. Control is passed to preceding calling procedures until an inactive error routine is found, at which time the error is processed by that procedure. This process can circumvent your error-handling logic, assuming that different procedures have different methods for handling errors. This process also can pass control inadvertently to somewhere you least expect.

To prevent this, after trapping the error and saving it to a memory variable, you should disable error handling within each individual error routine by using the On Error GoTo 0 statement at the beginning of each routine. This prevents a subsequent (recoverable) error from blowing up your routine. Then, at the end of each routine, remember to enable the error handler again, as in the following example:

```
Sub AlohaError()
     On Error GoTo Rorre                         'Enable the error handler
     Dim wError%
     (...)
     Exit Sub

Rorre:
     wError = Err          'Save the last error
     On Error GoTo 0       'Disable the error handler for the duration
     (...)                 'Process errors
     On Error GoTo Rorre   'Enable the error handler again
     (...)

End Sub
```

This method will prevent many of the problems you may encounter when chaining error-handling routines.

Chapter Summary

This chapter covered the basic concepts of error handling: detection, damage control, and recovery. You learned how to trap errors, how to determine what method to use in handling errors, and traps to avoid in your error-handling procedures.

15

Using Access in Network, SQL Server, and Runtime Environments

Access was introduced into a very dynamic computing environment. "Downsizing," "rightsizing," client/server, peer-to-peer, and local area networks are now the norm rather than the exception. The old days where there was a clear distinction between mainframes and desktop PCs are gone forever. This environment means that Access must meet a variety of interoperability challenges.

Fortunately, at least some of these challenges have been met quite successfully. For example, every copy of Access is *network-ready*. The only difference between the Access single user and multiuser versions is that each network workstation needs to have a license—either a full retail package or a Microsoft License Pack. Access is relatively easy to configure for network operation; the few difficulties are covered in the following sections.

For client/server installations, Access comes with an ODBC driver that allows it to be used as a front-end query tool for Microsoft and Sybase SQL server products.

Finally, for developers who need to distribute their applications royalty-free, the ADK does the job.

This chapter provides an overview of these important topics, including the following:

- Using Access on a network
- Using workgroups in Access
- Ensuring network database security

- Backing up data
- Locking records
- Using Access with SQL Server
- Installing the ODBC driver
- Hints for troubleshooting SQL Server connections
- Using Access databases and tables in a Windows for Workgroups network
- Using Access with Novell, WFW, and SQL Server
- Using the Access ADK

Note: The battle of the operating systems continues. Microsoft Windows NT, IBM OS/2 2.x, and various versions of the UNIX operating systems are duking it out for supremacy in the desktop market. Access versions 1.0 and 1.1 can run under either Windows NT or OS/2, but Access doesn't take advantage of any of the advanced features of these operating environments. Access is not yet available for any version of UNIX.

Using Access on a Network

In a multiuser environment, you can install Access in two ways:

- Install a complete copy of Access on every workstation.
- Store a complete installation of Access on the file server with individual workstations each storing only configuration files.

The full installation of Access takes about 15M of hard disk storage or approximately 1M for workstations if you decide to store only the configuration files. On busy networks, performance improves (sometimes dramatically) if the complete Access system is installed on individual workstations. This installation method reduces network traffic by eliminating calls to the file server for file access.

Caution: Choose only one method of installation! Because the Windows directory can have only one copy of the MSACCESS.INI file, full server and local installations don't coexist peacefully. With two concurrent installations, the most recent installation overwrites previous entries to the MSACCESS.INI file.

Using Workgroups in Access

Part of the Access installation and setup process in a multiuser environment consists of allowing users to join workgroups. A *workgroup* is a group of users needing access to the same data, which is usually located in a shared directory on the network file server or peer workstation. The most important distinction concerning workgroups is that each workgroup has its own SYSTEM.MDA database in which Access stores security information about users and their rights. Well-designed workgroups can increase data security by making certain databases or even tables available only to selected users.

Users are not limited to one workgroup, but they may participate in only one workgroup at a time. During installation, Access creates a *Change Workgroup* item in the Access group that allows users to switch workgroups (log on to different SYSTEM.MDA databases) by using the Access Setup utility.

To create a workgroup on the network file server, you first create a directory for the workgroups and then assign all members of the workgroup appropriate rights to this directory. On a peer-to-peer network, such as Windows For Workgroups, you need to create a shared directory on the designated WFW computer and assign all members of the workgroup read and write rights to this directory.

The current workgroup is saved in the [Options] section of the MSACCESS.INI file with the following command line:

SystemDB=*drive:\path*\SYSTEM.MDA

Using workgroups reduces data redundancy and dispersion because users are able to cross workgroup boundaries and attach or import tables from other workgroups' databases. By pushing the concept of workgroups even further, you can create essentially a poor man's version of a distributed database; individual databases can reside in different physical locations and still be accessible to all connected workstations.

Ensuring Network Database Security

Each network needs to have security precautions in place. Access implements security on both group and individual user levels. A user must be a member of a group before she/he can be assigned rights in the Access security system. After creating groups and assigning users to one or more groups (everybody becomes a member of the Users group by default), you can proceed to assign rights to groups and to individual members. In network environments, you should assign rights at the group level to avoid the confusion of having a multitude of individual accounts with different rights and to make adding and deleting users easy.

When security precautions are in place, each user must log on and specify a password to start Access. Keep in mind that Access doesn't exist in a vacuum and network-level and Access-level security measures are interdependent. For example, lack of read and write rights to certain directories enforced at the network level may prevent a user from accessing data in a database to which she or he has full rights in Access. Multilayer security, taken to the extreme, may force a user who runs Access from Windows For Workgroups on a Novell network using data from SQL Server, for example, to pass four levels of security and supply four passwords. Although this process may be effective for security purposes, you are likely to hear grumbling from users.

For more information about activating security, see Chapter 2, "The Access Database."

Backing Up Data

If databases are stored on the network file server, the server backup procedure should back up these databases as often as necessary for adequate data security on the particular network installation. You also can back up Access database objects from within Access by using the TransferDatabase action. This action allows you to export specified objects from the current database to another Access database (or other file format). In a production environment (when the application is actually used), static Access database objects such as forms, reports, macros, and modules do not need to be backed up as frequently as tables and queries.

Locking Records

Simultaneous editing of data records (concurrency) is of paramount importance in every multiuser installation. The vital part of this issue is the locking strategy implemented by the database manager.

Unless you issue explicit locks on the entire database or recordset, Access uses two types of default record locking:

- *Pessimistic locking* (default). Locks the entire page as soon as you apply the **Edit** method to the recordset, and sustains the lock until either the **Update** method is applied or the changes are reversed with the **Rollback** statement.
- *Optimistic locking*. Doesn't lock the page containing the record until the record is updated.

When Access creates a new record that doesn't fit on the current memory page, Access uses pessimistic locking (even if optimistic locking is specified) for the new page Access makes for the record. This page is locked until the new record is updated.

Record locking strategy is also important when using transaction processing. Depending on the number of updates involved in the transaction, Access may need to lock many records, which may not be possible. Obviously, **CommitTransaction** does not succeed if another user has locked any of the records involved in the transaction. If these types of problems occur frequently, use pessimistic locking to ensure that all records involved in a transaction are available for commit or rollback.

The next three sections discuss the various types of record locking available in Access and explain the network implications of each type.

Default Record Locking

Unless the locking strategy is explicitly overridden, Access locks items according to the *Default Record Locking* setting in the Multiuser section from the View-Options menu. The following table itemizes the Default Record Locking options.

Choice	*Operation*
No Locks	Does not lock records
All Records	Locks all records upon use
Edited Record	Locks only the record being edited

If the *No Locks* setting is used, Access doesn't prevent simultaneous editing of the record by two or more users but attempts to arbitrate saving changes by displaying the message shown in figure 15.1 and attempts to alleviate the situation in the next dialog box, shown in figure 15.2. If you use the *Edited Record* setting, Access doesn't save any changes made by another user.

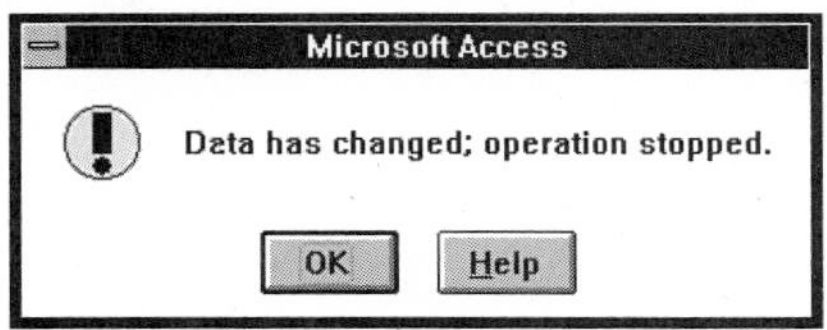

Figure 15.1. Warning message displayed by Access when there are conflicting edits to the same record.

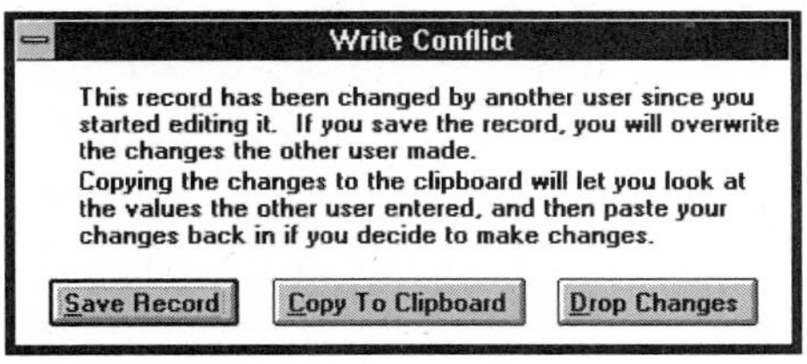

Figure 15.2. Dialog box attempting to alleviate potentially destructive simultaneous edit to the same record by two different users.

Editing options are specified in the RecordLocks property dialog box, explained in the next section.

> **Note:** Record Locking settings in Access have no effect on data tables stored on SQL Server.

The RecordLocks Property

To determine the current locking type, you can inspect the setting of the *RecordLocks* property for forms and reports. A setting of 0 indicates No Locks, 1 indicates All Records, and 2 indicates Edited Records.

> **Tip:** Because the *RecordLocks* property is read-only at runtime, examine it *before* opening a form (or a report) and if the setting is too restrictive (for example, *All Records*) notify the user to change it to a less restrictive setting and restart the operation. Note that forms and reports inherit the setting of the Default Record Locks when created (this can be overridden in the design view).

The LockEdits Property

You can use the *LockEdits* property at runtime to specify the type of locking in effect during recordsets editing while using the Edit and update methods. The type can be either optimistic or pessimistic. If you force optimistic locking (Access locks the page when the **Update** method is applied to the recordset) an error occurs if another user has already locked the record. If you specify pessimistic locking (Access locks the page as soon as the **Edit** method is applied to the recordset), other users cannot make any changes until the page is unlocked using the Update method and instead see something like the message shown in figure 15.3.

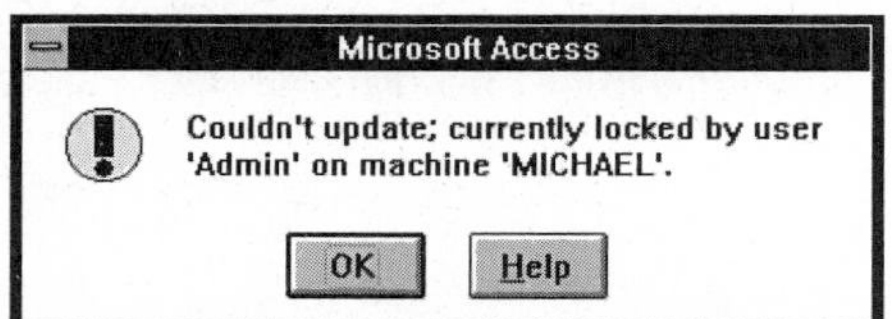

Figure 15.3. Access notifies the user that it cannot perform the update because of conflicting record locking.

Novell Netware Locking Precautions

The Access locking scheme also has repercussions for Novell Netware. The maximum number of record locks on NetWare 3.11 is 200,000, but the system defaults to 20,000 during installation. Because Access locks 2K pages at a time (with potentially many records), the number of record locks on the network server must be increased or the server may run out of locks during database operations and crash, causing the loss of data. Use the NetWare Monitor utility to view how many record locks are actually used when running Access and adjust the number accordingly.

Using Access with SQL Server

With client-server network computing rising in popularity, the ability to seamlessly access data on a SQL server is one of the interconnectivity goals Microsoft seeks to achieve with Access. Microsoft's Open Database Connectivity scheme (ODBC) introduces a bidirectional format "translation" level between the source of data (such as dBASE or DB2 database) and the application that actually uses the data (such as Access). The ODBC driver for SQL Server was the first ODBC driver supplied by Microsoft for Access.

Understanding ISAM and ODBC Data Access

Access can use many different data formats, including Paradox, dBASE, FoxPro, SQL databases, and Btrieve. Communicating with different data formats requires data drivers that operate either on the native level of the particular file format (such as dBASE, FoxPro, or Paradox) or that connect to data through the ODBC layer. Data drivers that operate on the native level are called ISAM-level drivers because file formats such as dBASE or Paradox are Indexed Sequential Access Method (ISAM) files. ISAM drivers must be written individually for each supported file format and must operate on the same principle as the data drivers in the file format's native application.

ODBC-level drivers use Microsoft's Open Database Connectivity protocol to translate data between the native format, such as a SQL database, and the format supported by the application using the data. This approach is more flexible because it uses a predefined set of calls, but it is also slower because ODBC is essentially a translation layer between two data formats and access methods. With the proper ODBC drivers, Access can use many different data formats. ODBC drivers are currently available for SQL Server, Rdb, and Oracle. Other drivers (such as DB2) may soon be made available by Microsoft or third-party vendors.

Installing ODBC Drivers

To access data stored on SQL Server, you first install the ODBC driver for connecting to SQL data. The ODBC disk included with Access has its own Setup program to install the ODBC drivers. As with the Access installation in a multiuser environment, you can install the ODBC files on each workstation that will use SQL databases or install the files in a shared directory on the network drive.

After you install the ODBC files, use the ISQL (Interactive SQL) facility of SQL server to run the INSTCAT.SQL script (included on the ODBC disk) to properly configure the server's stored procedures.

Troubleshooting SQL Server Connections

If you have problems accessing SQL server data after installing the ODBC files and configuring the server (assuming that the server is available and not overloaded), try the items on the following troubleshooting list:

1. Check the [SQLSERVER] section in the WIN.INI file for correct entries (especially the name of the server).
2. Check the dates of the following files in the WINDOWS\SYSTEM directory for outdated versions:

File Name	*Valid Dates*
ODBC.DLL	10-16-92 or later
DBNMP3.DLL	9-15-92 or later
SQLSRVR.DLL	10-16-92 or later
COMMDLG.DLL	10-25-92 or later

3. Increase the TIMEOUT setting in the MSACCESS.INI [ODBC] section.

If you still have problems attaching to the server, use another application to attach to the same server; if you still can't attach, the cause of the problem may be the network itself, not ODBC or Access.

> **Note:** If you are running under Windows For Workgroups and are having difficulties attaching to SQL server, see the notes on SQL server in the Windows For Workgroups section later in this chapter.

Using SQL Tables

An Access application can use SQL tables after you import or attach them to an Access database. If you frequently bring data from SQL server to local files for processing (batch update, reporting, etc), you can use the **TransferDatabase** action to automate this process. Instead of supplying the database name, insert the SQL connect string into the Database Name argument of the **TransferDatabase** action in the following format:

```
ODBC;DSN=<server name>;DBQ=<name of the SQL server database>;
➥WSID=<workstation id>;USID=<user login id>;PWD=<password>
```

> **Tip:** If you attach SQL tables to a database, make sure that the SQL server data will be available every time the table is used, or an error will occur. To prevent this error, use and process the file locally, if practical.

Ensuring Sufficient SQL Connections

Because performing an operation on a single dataset may require more than one connection to the SQL server, you can easily run out of connections when performing many data access operations from within Access. For example, using an update query as a basis for a form and attaching validation and search routines to the form that use different tables probably requires more than one connection to the server. Use the following coding techniques to help prevent premature exhausting of available SQL connections and improve the performance of the network:

- Keep the number of open forms, data sheets, and reports to a minimum (each form, subform, data sheet, report, and list box requires a query).
- Bring server data to a local database where practical, especially when using it for validation, lists, reports, and so on.
- Use snapshots instead of dynasets when making changes if updating the data is not required. This action helps you avoid using the connections needed to support dynasets.
- Design a separate form for adding data to an external table and set its *DefaultEditing* property to Data Entry; Access does not request or display any current records from the foreign table.
- Limit the use of aggregate functions while querying an external table; aggregate functions cause Access to retrieve all records from all tables involved in the query, which causes a lot of network traffic and uses up server connections.

Accessing Data on SQL Server

As it does with other external (foreign) data formats, Access introduces a few limitations on accessing data on a SQL server:

- Access ignores a SQL Server table index if the index has a DOUBLE data type. (Access uses the value of the index to find the row in the SQL table to update, but because Access introduces rounding errors during the conversion between SQL binary numbers and Access decimal numbers that can violate the index uniqueness, Access cannot identify the row to be updated in this kind of SQL table.)
- Access can update only SQL tables that have a unique index.
- Access does not directly support the use of pass-through SQL (the ability to pass SQL commands directly to a server to execute stored procedures and other SQL commands). To use this feature in Access, you must use an application that provides such support as a middleman. Write Access Basic code to perform dynamic data exchange (DDE) with the middleman application and pass the SQL statement as the expression in the DDEexecute statement.
- A record sent to be inserted into a SQL Server table for which a unique key is created by a trigger on that table, is treated by Access as deleted because the unique key stored in Access is different from the key that the trigger just generated.
- If you are using SQL Server 4.2, you cannot use TINYINT values between 128 and 255. Also, exporting or inserting a date value of 1/1/1900 causes an incorrect time portion to be sent to the server. These problems are not Access problems; they are SQL Server 4.2 problems.

Using Access with Windows For Workgroups

Microsoft Windows For Workgroups (WFW) is a Windows 3.1 based peer-to-peer networking system. Aimed at local, departmental, groups of users, WFW delivers a cost-effective networking solution even to computers not previously networked. Some WFW kits even include the networking hardware to connect computers into a peer-to-peer network, including a screwdriver!

WFW allows the sharing of resources between connected computers (a *workgroup*) and use of the electronic mail and scheduling system included with the product. Users can designate which resources (drives, directories, printers) to share with other users and to what extent.

Access versions 1.0 and 1.1 support WFW resource and storage sharing, but do not support mail capabilities (you cannot directly send mail from within Access). As far as resource sharing is concerned, Access can use remote databases, attach remote tables, print and plot to remote devices, and send files to remote storage.

A WFW installation can coexist peacefully with server-based networks, such as Novell Netware or Microsoft LAN Manager. This kind of setup gives the best of both worlds; you can share resources on local workstations and have access to resources on the file server. However, running what is tantamount to two networks in parallel increases the complexity of the installation and may require more fine-tuning to achieve satisfactory performance for peer-to-peer operations and connections to the server (or servers). Because maintaining both peer-to-peer and network connections is memory- and resource-intensive, such installations require at least 386 DX class workstations with a minimum of 8M of RAM.

Using Access Databases and Tables on a Windows For Workgroups Network

With WFW you are not limited to local databases, or even shared databases on network drives. If WFW runs on top of a network, you can transparently connect to shared databases stored on peer workstations as well.

WFW substitutes a drive letter for the shared directory, so there is no difference between referring to files on local drives and referring to files on remote shared drives as long as the remote drive is available (WFW must be connected to the computer and directory in question).

If you open databases with Access Basic code (such as the **OpenDatabase** function), all you need to do is supply the full path to the database, including the remote drive letter. To be able to edit data in a database on the remote drive, you must have read and write privileges to the directory in question or WFW generates a `Database '<name>' is read only...` error and opens the database in the read-only mode.

To ensure that all tables residing on remote drives are always available, make sure that the machine running the Access application is always connected to the peer machines that supply data. You may have to leave the power on to the machines in the workgroup and not exit Windows.

Combining Access with Novell, WFW, and SQL Server

If you need to log on to SQL server from Access running under WFW and Novell, you need Microsoft's Network Integration Kit (supplied separately by Microsoft at no charge); Access needs Novell's NETAPI.DLL to communicate with SQL Server through named pipes (SQL Server communication protocol). However, WFW uses its own NETAPI.DLL, which doesn't support named pipes. The Network Integration Kit provides an alternative to using Novell named pipes for communicating with a SQL server over a Novell network.

Using the Access Distribution Kit (ADK)

The Access Distribution Kit is a runtime version of Access. As such, most of the Access development and design capabilities are disabled, which allows developers to distribute end-user applications. The ADK is not a separate "back-end" engine to run Access databases and execute Access programs; it is simply a full Access engine with some features disabled.

The following list describes the features that are missing from the ADK:

- Design views are disabled (forms, reports, macros, queries, tables, and Access Basic modules).
- The toolbar is hidden by default.
- The Database window (container) is hidden.
- The following menu selections are unavailable (either disabled or hidden) according to Microsoft documentation:

Menu	*Disabled Selection*
File	New Save As Load From Query Print Preview and Report
Save	Save As Print Preview Run Macro
Print Preview, Form	Save Form Save Form As Save Record Print Preview Run Macro
Window	Hide

continues

Menu	*Disabled Selection*
Help	Show Cue Cards About

- The following keystrokes are disabled:

  Ctrl+Break

  Shift

  F11

  F12

  Shift+F12

Be sure not to use these keystrokes in any SendKey actions or statements in applications intended for ADK.

Because all objects of an Access database (tables, queries, forms, reports, macros, and Access Basic code) are stored in one physical file, the Access ADK doesn't produce a self-standing executable file but instead uses a *runtime* engine to support its operations. The heart of the ADK is the file MSARN110.EXE, which provides the runtime engine. The ADK includes also many runtime support files and DLLs (for accessing various data formats, using fonts, and so on).

Installing the ADK

The ADK requires approximately 3M of hard drive space to install. Otherwise, its hardware and software requirements are exactly the same as Access version 1.1. By default, the ADK installs itself in a subdirectory of the same name (ADK) off the ACCESS directory. The first disk is "branded" with the registered owner's name and company name during the initial installation.

Executing the Runtime System

Microsoft provides a customizable Setup program with the ADK that installs the runtime application on the target machine. The hardware and software requirements of the target machine are the same as for the full Access system.

To execute the ADK runtime system, you use the MSARN110.EXE file with command line arguments that specify the database to open and the INI file to use. For example

MSARN110.EXE MYDATA.MDB \INI MYDATA. INI

opens the database named MYDATA.MDB using options specified in the MYDATA.INI file.

You must specify the database name to open as the first argument on the command line; if you don't include any arguments on the command line, the ADK aborts with a `Can't run application -- Missing command line arguments` error.

You can also use command line options, including the /X command line option, which forces the ADK to execute a specified macro when the database is opened. Similar to the full Access system, the macro specified with the /X option executes after an AutoExec macro (if there is one).

Programming for the ADK

Follow these guidelines when you develop applications for distribution with the ADK:

- *Plan for ADK from the outset.* Because the location of files is important in the Access runtime environment, you may want to duplicate the target environment on the development machine down to the specific directory structure. Most importantly, make sure that any attached tables are installed in the correct directory because the entire path established when attaching the table is required at runtime!
- *Remove all operations that refer to unsupported features.* An example of this type of operation is using the SendKey action to execute a nonexistent (in ADK) menu choice.
- *Remove all debugging code.* This one is easy to miss, but it will cause users endless consternation if your cryptic debugging messages start to appear out of the blue.
- *Watch for anomalies and inconsistencies of the ADK.* Although the database container is hidden, many menu options, such as Run Macro, are still available (although disabled under certain conditions) and can be potentially confusing to the user. Also, selecting some menu choices produces unexpected results (such as taking the user to a blank and unusable table design surface).
- *Start the application with an AutoExec macro.* To develop turn-key applications, use an AutoExec macro to start the application's main menu, constructed either as a form or a custom menu bar attached to a form, which effectively hides unnecessary menu choices.
- *Design a graceful way to exit the application.* Avoid making the user select the Exit choice from the default file menu. You should either remove the system menu from the form that serves as a main menu or execute an "Exit Access" macro attached to the form's *OnClose* property so that the user never ends up at the ADK menu.

Trapping Errors

The ADK runtime is unforgiving; untrapped runtime errors usually result in an abrupt termination of the application and an unceremonious return to the Program Manager. Good error trapping routines are a must for ADK applications. Thorough testing is also very important; code and macros must be thoroughly debugged, and exception handling must be well implemented. Even trivial errors, such as an unexpected value entered by the user, can result in a crash of the ADK application. Keep in mind that any abnormal termination can corrupt the database.

All Access error trapping methods (discussed in Chapter 14, "Error Handling") are valid in applications destined for the ADK. Code more defensively than you would normally code for the full Access system. This defensive code may inflate the development cycle, but it will certainly avoid runtime problems later. Keep in mind that one bug will be propagated across every runtime application; the effect is geometric. You don't want scores of users calling to complain about one bug that you could have avoided with a few lines of error-handling code.

Ensuring Database Security with the ADK

Because applications distributed with the ADK are used by users other than the original creator of the database objects, the developer resolves all security considerations during the development stage of the application. Because the ADK supports all Access security features, you can simply follow the normal Access security considerations, with one exception. Implement security at the group level, not on the user level, so you can add additional users without modifying (and redistributing) the application.

Because rights to created objects are assigned to their creator, when developing applications meant for the ADK, you may want to use a special account (such as Developer) with all permissions to all objects. Alternatively, you can change the rights to objects after completing the development process. The latter method is more flexible but also more tedious because you must change permissions for each object individually.

Refer to Chapter 2, "The Access Database," for a more detailed discussion of implementing database security.

> **Caution:** Changing the ownership of tables deletes table relationships!

> **Tip:** To avoid any chance of unauthorized users changing preassigned permissions, remove all privileges to the system tables (especially the MSysObjects table) for all users except the application developer.

Separating Application and Data into Two Databases

Access Basic can execute two or more databases at one time. This feature may be put to good use in applications running under the ADK runtime because you can separate the user's data from the application (forms, code, reports, and so on).

In addition to improving data integrity and back up procedures, one of the chief benefits of separating data from the other objects in the application when using the ADK is to simplify the upgrade process—only the upgraded application itself is redistributed; the user's data is not disturbed.

There are at least three ways to separate the code and data into two databases. One is to create all data tables in a "data" database and attach them to a "code" database. Then use these attached tables as the basis for forms, reports, and queries. This method is the most convenient, even though Access imposes some limitations on attached tables (see the **OpenTable** function in the reference section for more information).

Another method of separating data and code into two databases is to load the code database as a library database. The drawback is that you will not be able to use macros in the code database because macros cannot execute from the library database.

You may also use the **OpenDatabase** function to open other Access databases; in this case, data stored in such a "remote" database can be seamlessly blended with the data from the current database. This is arguably the most convenient method of separating the data from the application itself.

Customizing Help Files

The ADK includes the Microsoft Help Compiler and supporting files that enable you to create standard Windows help files. To perform this procedure, you need a text editor capable of producing rich text format (RTF) files (such as Microsoft Word). The documentation accompanying the Microsoft Help Compiler explains this procedure. Note that you are not limited to Microsoft products in this respect; various Windows help creation and authoring tools are included with the majority of Windows language products from vendors such as Borland and Symantec. There are also commercial Windows help authoring products that include all components needed to create help for Windows applications (including the required RTF-compatible editor).

You must copy the custom Help file onto the distribution disks (either manually or by using the Setup Wizard) after the development of the help system for your application is finished.

Attaching the Help File to an Application

With Access, you can attach a custom help file to an application in two ways:

- Use the specified help file as a default help file for the entire system (its name must be entered in the [Run-Time Options] section of the INI file included with the runtime application).
- Specify the name of the Help file in the *HelpFile* property and the help ID number in the *HelpContextId* property.

The *HelpFile* property is available in forms and reports. You can specify the *HelpContextID* property for the following controls on forms and reports: bound object frame, check box, combo box, command button, list box, [linked] object frame, option button, option group, text box, and toggle button. Using the *HelpFile* property, you can specify different help files for different parts of the application (forms and reports) or even specify different help files for different controls.

By providing the *HelpContextID* property, Access makes it possible to easily implement context-sensitive help on the individual control level by assigning a numeric value to the specified help topic.

> **Note:** You must assign a value greater than zero to the *HelpContextID* property either on the form (or reports) level or on the controls level for each control, or the help file specified in the HelpFile property will not be loaded.

Designing a Help System

A help system must be well designed to be of any use. The following guidelines may be useful in designing and executing a reliable help system:

- Know your audience; users with various levels of computer expertise require different help. Also, the user's needs change after she/he gains expertise with the application. Some developers use a three-tiered approach, providing different levels of help for novice, advanced, and expert users.
- Use Windows default colors and icons to specify keywords, cross-referenced terms, and so on.
- Plan and structure the help system logically; provide definitions for terms and explanations of keywords. Provide a help menu and search mechanism to quickly move from topic to topic.
- Provide as many cross-referenced examples as possible.
- Supply context-sensitive help whenever possible. For example, if a user often calls the help system from within a certain form, make the help for that particular form the default text topic.

Creating a Custom Startup Screen

A database opened by the ADK behaves exactly as any other Access database with one significant difference; because the database container is hidden, it doesn't initially provide any built-in means to open a form, report, table, query, or run a macro or Access Basic code. This difference is the reason you should use an AutoExec macro to launch the ADK application by using the **OpenForm** action in the AutoExec macro or code executed from this macro.

Before starting the application, you may want to display a custom startup screen, containing information such as the application's title, owner, and copyright notice. This can be accomplished in Access by designing a form with the appropriate messages.

Creating Distribution Disks with the Setup Wizard

Microsoft provides a Setup program to install the runtime portion of ADK and the required database(s). It should be on distribution disk number 1 and able to be executed like any other Windows setup program (by using the Run selection from the Program Manger File menu). The Setup program also creates the SYSTEM.MDA database (which stores security information about Access and ADK databases).

Leave the creation of distribution disks for your application to the Setup Wizard rather than doing it manually. The Access distribution setup requires that certain files be placed on certain disks or the Setup program does not work. Also, because not all required files are included with ADK but some need to be copied from the Access or Windows directory, creating the distribution disks yourself increases the possibility for error.

Before using the Setup Wizard, make sure that there is enough space on your hard drive. The Setup Wizard effectively duplicates all files needed for distribution of your application and the application itself. You also need to create a custom setup file for your application. Copy the MSACCESS.INI file (found in the WINDOWS directory) to a new file and modify it to suit your needs. For example, you can delete all unused options (especially in the Wizards section) and libraries not included with your distribution disks.

The Setup Wizard resides in the database SETUPWIZ.MDB in the ADK directory. To use it, open it the same way you open any other Access database. The wizard starts automatically from an AutoExec macro and guides you through the process. Using the Setup Wizard, you specify the distribution disk(s) size, the name of the databases (up to 3) to include, the name of a custom INI file, icon, and help files, the names of ISAM drivers to install, the default target directory for the application, and other options.

The Setup Wizard creates a subdirectory for every disk included in the installation set and creates the SETUP.RPT text file with the listing of contents of every disk included in the distribution set. Note that even the tiniest installation requires at least 4 high-capacity disks to hold all the required run-time files plus the application.

The Setup Wizard also creates a STFSETUP.IN_ file, which contains installation directives for the ADK runtime and databases. This INI file contains numerous user-configurable options such as the following:

- Where to find the application files
- Where to install the application files
- Which parts of ADK to install
- What messages are displayed during installation

The following example shows just one section with entries for the application name (displayed as the caption of the main Access window), graph installation (no graph), change workgroup option (no), default directory to install the ADK and databases, and the title for the program group in the Program Manager.

```
[Custom]
NameOfApp="Access For Windows Power Programming - Sample Database"
InstallGraph="NO"
InstallChangeWorkGroup="NO"
DefaultPath=":\\QUE_MSA\\"
ProgGroupDesc="QUE Database"
```

An important section of the custom INI file is [Program Manager], which tells the setup program what program group and program group items to create. For example, you may want to provide an option to compress and/or repair the database. The following example displays the [Program Manager] of the STFSETUP.IN_ file, which creates a program group and two items in this program group:

```
[Program Manager]
CreateProgManGroup $(ProgGroupDesc), "QUE Sample Database"
CreateProgManItem $(ProgGroupDesc), "QUE Database", $(AppPath)"MSARN110.EXE
➥QUE.MDB /Ini QUE.INI"
CreateProgManItem $(ProgGroupDesc), "Compact and Repair QUE Database",
➥$(AppPath)"MSARN110.EXE QUE.MDB /repair /compact"
Exit
```

If you still insist on creating your own distribution disks, the following table lists all required files, their sources, and the disk they have to be placed onto. Use the SUFILES option created during the installation of ADK to move all required files to their designated directories and compress them (using the supplied COMPRESS utility).

File	*Source*
Disk 1:	
COMMDLG.DL_	ADK
COMMDLG.DL$	Access
DDEML.DL$	Access
DETCMD.DL_	ADK
OLECLI.DL$	Access
OLESVR.DL$	Access
SETUP.EXE	ADK
SETUP.INI	ADK (copied from SETUPNEW.INI)
SHELL.DL$	Access
SMALLB.FO$	ADK
SMALLE.FO$	ADK
STFSETUP.EX_	ADK
STFSETUP.IN_	developer (application specific)
VER.DL_	ADK
VER.DL$	Access
WORKGRP.IN_	Access

File	*Source*
Disk 2:	
GRAPH.EX$	ADK (runtime version of MS Graph)
MSACCESS.RE$	Access
SHARE.EX$	Access
WINHELP.EX$	Access (installed in the Windows directory)
WINHELP.HL$	Access (installed in the Windows directory)

The files described in the following table are also required but may be distributed on any floppy disk.

File	*Source*
<application>.INI	developer (use MSACCESS.INI as a guide)
MSARN110.EXE	ADK
CTL3D.DLL	Access (installed in the \WINDOWS\SYSTEM directory)
MSABC110.DLL	Access
MSAES110.DLL	Access (installed in the \WINDOWS\SYSTEM directory)
MSAIN110.DLL	Access
MSAJT110.DLL	Access (installed in the \WINDOWS\SYSTEM directory)
MSAJU110.DLL	Access
UTILITY.MDA	Access (utility database)

In addition, you must install the following files on the machine that will execute your application using ADK if your application uses any of the ISAM-level drivers described in the following table.

File	*Source*
BTRV110.DLL (Btrieve)	Access (installed in the \WINDOWS\SYSTEM directory)
PDX110.DLL (Paradox)	Access (installed in the \WINDOWS\SYSTEM directory)
XBS110.DLL (dBase)	Access (installed in the \WINDOWS\SYSTEM directory)

If your application uses standard Access Wizards, you must include the two files listed in the following table.

File	*Source*
WIZARD.MDA	Access
MSAFIN.DLL	Access (installed in the \WINDOWS directory)

Also, all files included on the ODBC disk must be included with your application if it uses ODBC level drivers (such as SQL server). The ODBC disk has its own Setup program. Be sure to make a copy of this disk and include it with your runtime application.

Chapter Summary

This chapter discussed using Access on various types of networks, both server-based and peer-to-peer, and accessing data in such distributed processing environments as SQL Server and Windows For Workgroups. It also covered designing an application for distribution and dealing with the Access Distribution Kit runtime environment, including instructions on providing customized help and distributing a finished application with the ADK.

Part V
Reference

Reference

The following Reference provides a comprehensive summary of all Access language elements. The Reference is divided into sections by language category, as follows:

- Actions
- Functions
- Methods
- Objects
- Operators
- Properties
- Statements

Each reference section provides the following information for every language element:

- Syntax
- Application
- Usage notes
- Exceptions and error conditions
- Cautions and tips
- Code examples

The "Access Basic Reference Locator" lists all Access Basic language elements in alphabetical order and provides a listing of language elements by subject matter.

The Reference provides valuable information—such as known anomalies and workarounds and quirky behavior, as well as describing how to perform related operations and avoid problems that are not always obvious.

The Reference includes hundreds of undocumented features, or features which are documented only in the ADK (Access Distribution Kit). We also have documented the usage of Access and Windows constants with Access Basic code and provided cross-references to related language elements and appropriate chapters in the book.

Where the information in the Reference differs from Microsoft's documentation, we have thoroughly tested to confirm the accuracy of the information provided. If you have any questions about the following reference sections, please feel free to contact us on CompuServe (see the Preface for CIS IDs), or write to us in care of the publisher.

Access Basic Reference Locator

One of the most challenging aspects of mastering Access is learning to distinguish the types and usages of individual language elements. Because there are seven language categories (Actions, Functions, Methods, Operators, Properties, Statements, and Objects), it is easy to confuse which language element belongs to which category.

This chapter attempts to demystify the process of finding individual language elements by providing a variety of cross-referencing tables. Table 16.1 is simply an alphabetical listing of all Access Basic language elements for determining to which language category a particular language element belongs.

The Access Basic language elements in table 16.2 are organized by their function; for example, Date and Time-related elements are grouped together in one table, regardless of their language category.

Table 16.3 is a listing of Access Basic methods and the objects to which they apply.

These tables are provided as a supplement to the reference section to give you several different cross-referencing methods for locating a specific Access Basic language element. You do not need prior knowledge of Access Basic commands to use these tables.

Table 16.1. Alphabetical Listing of All Access Basic Language Elements

Language Element Name	*Language Category*	*Language Element Name*	*Language Category*
Language elements marked with the asterisk are either undocumented or are documented only in the Access Distribution Kit.			
& (concatenation)	Operator	BackStyle	Property
* (multiplication)	Operator	Beep	Action
+ (addition)	Operator	Beep	Statement
– (subtraction)	Operator	BeforeUpdate	Property
/ (division)	Operator	BeginTrans	Statement
\ (integer division)	Operator	Between...And	Operator
^ (exponentiation)	Operator	BOF	Property
Abs	Function	Bookmark	Property
ActiveControl	Property	Bookmarkable	Property
ActiveForm	Property	BorderColor	Property
ActiveReport	Property	BorderStyle	Property
AddColon	Property	BorderWidth	Property
AddMenu	Action	BoundColumn	Property
AddNew	Method	Call	Statement
AfterUpdate	Property	Cancel	Property
AllowEditing	Property	CancelEvent	Action
AllowFilters	Property	CanGrow	Property
AllowUpdating	Property	CanShrink	Property
And (logical and bitwise)	Operator	Caption	Property
AppActivate	Statement	CCur	Function
AppendChunk	Method	CDbl	Function
ApplyFilter	Action	ChDir	Statement
Asc	Function	ChDrive	Statement
Atn	Function	Choose	Function
AutoLabel	Property	Chr	Function
AutoRepeat	Property	Chr$	Function
AutoResize	Property	CInt	Function
Avg	Function	CLng	Function
BackColor	Property	Clone	Method

Language Element Name	*Language Category*	*Language Element Name*	*Language Category*
Close	Action	CurrentX	Property
Close	Method	CurrentY	Property
CodeDB*	Function	CVar	Function
Column	Property	CVDate	Function
ColumnCount	Property	DataType	Property
ColumnHeads	Property	Date	Function
ColumnWidth*	Property	Date	Statement
ColumnWidths	Property	Date$	Function
Command	Function	Date$	Statement
Command$	Function	DateAdd	Function
CommitTrans	Statement	DateCreated	Property
Comparison	Operator	DateDiff	Function
Const	Statement	DatePart	Function
ControlName	Property	DateSerial	Function
ControlSource	Property	DateValue	Function
CopyObject	Action	DAvg	Function
Cos	Function	Day	Function
Count	Function	DCount	Function
Count	Property	DDB	Function
CreateControl*	Function	DDE	Function
CreateDynaset	Method	DDEExecute	Statement
CreateForm*	Function	DDEInitiate	Function
CreateGroupLevel*	Function	DDEPoke	Statement
CreateQueryDef	Method	DDERequest	Function
CreateReport*	Function	DDESend	Function
CreateReportControl*	Function	DDETerminate	Statement
CreateSnapshot	Method	DDETerminateAll	Statement
CSng	Function	DecimalPlaces	Property
Cstr	Function	Declare	Statement
CurDir	Function	Default	Property
CurDir$	Function	DefaultEditing	Property
CurrentDB	Function	DefaultValue	Property

continues

Table 16.1. Continued

Language Element Name	*Language Category*	*Language Element Name*	*Language Category*
DefaultView	Property	End	Statement
Deftype	Statement	Environ	Function
Delete	Method	Environ$	Function
DeleteControl*	Statement	EOF	Function
DeleteReportControl*	Function	EOF	Property
Description	Property	Eqv (logical and bitwise)	Operator
DFirst	Function	Erase	Statement
Dim	Statement	Erl	Function
Dir	Function	Err	Function
Dir$	Function	Err	Statement
DisplayWhen	Property	Error	Function
DLast	Function	Error	Statement
DLookup	Function	Error$	Function
DMax	Function	Eval	Function
DMin	Function	Execute	Method
Do...Loop	Statement	Exit	Statement
DoCmd	Statement	Exp	Function
DoEvents	Statement	FieldName	Property
DoMenuItem	Action	FieldSize	Method
DrawMode	Property	FieldSize	Property
DrawStyle	Property	FileAttr	Function
DrawWidth	Property	FillColor	Property
DStDev	Function	FillStyle	Property
DStDevP	Function	Filter	Property
DSum	Function	FindFirst	Method
DVar	Function	FindLast	Method
DVarP	Function	FindNext	Action
Dynaset	Property	FindNext	Method
Echo	Action	FindPrevious	Method
Edit	Method	FindRecord	Action
Enabled	Property	First	Function

Language Element Name	*Language Category*	*Language Element Name*	*Language Category*
Fix	Function	GroupOn*	Property
FontBold	Property	Height	Property
FontItalic	Property	HelpContextID	Property
FontName	Property	HelpFile	Property
FontSize	Property	HelpFile	Property
FontUnderline	Property	Hex	Function
FontUnderline	Property	Hex$	Function
For...Next	Statement	HideDuplicates	Property
ForceNewPage	Property	Hour	Function
ForeColor	Property	hWnd	Property
Form	Property	If...Then...Else	Statement
Format	Function	IIf	Function
Format	Property	Imp (logical and bitwise)	Operator
Format$	Function	In	Operator
FormatCount	Property	Index	Property
FormName	Property	Index1...Index5	Property
FreeFile	Function	Indexed	Property
FreeLocks*	Statement	Input	Function
Function	Statement	Input #	Statement
FV	Function	Input$	Function
Get	Statement	InputBox	Function
GetChunk	Method	InputBox$	Function
Global	Statement	InStr	Function
GoSub...Return	Statement	Int	Function
GoTo	Statement	IPmt	Function
GoToControl	Action	IRR	Function
GoToPage	Action	Is	Operator
GoToRecord	Action	IsDate	Function
GridX	Property	IsEmpty	Function
GridY	Property	IsNull	Function
GroupInterval*	Property	IsNumeric	Function
GroupLevel*	Property	Item	Property

continues

Table 16.1. Continued

Language Element Name	*Language Category*	*Language Element Name*	*Language Category*
KeepTogether	Property	LockEdits	Property
Kill	Statement	LOF	Function
LabelAlign	Property	Log	Function
LabelX	Property	LSet	Statement
LabelY	Property	LTrim	Function
Last	Function	LTrim$	Function
LastUpdated	Property	Max	Function
LayoutForPrint	Property	Max	Function
LBound	Function	Maximize	Action
LCase	Function	Mid	Function
LCase$	Function	Mid	Statement
Left	Function	Mid$	Function
Left	Property	Mid$	Statement
Left$	Function	Min	Function
Len	Function	Minimize	Action
Let	Statement (anachronism)	Minute	Function
Like	Operator	MIRR	Function
LimitToList	Property	MkDir	Statement
Line	Method	Mod	Operator
LineInput #	Statement	Modal	Property
LineSlant	Property	Month	Function
LinkChildFields	Property	MoveLayout	Property
LinkMasterFields	Property	MoveSize	Action
ListFields	Method	MsgBox	Action
ListParameters	Method	MsgBox	Function
ListRows	Property	MsgBox	Statement
ListTables	Method	Name	Statement
ListWidth	Property	NewRowOrCol	Property
Loc	Function	NextRecord	Property
Lock	Statement	NoMatch	Property
Locked	Property	Not (logical and bitwise)	Operator

Language Element Name	*Language Category*	*Language Element Name*	*Language Category*
Now	Function	Or (logical and bitwise)	Operator
NPer	Function	Page	Property
NPV	Function	PageFooter	Property
Oct	Function	PageHeader	Property
Oct$	Function	Painting*	Property
OldValue	Property	Parent	Property
OLEClass	Property	Partition	Function
On...GoSub	Statement	Picture	Property
On...GoTo	Statement	Pmt	Function
OnClose	Property	PopUp	Property
OnCurrent	Property	PPmt	Functio
OnDblClick	Property	PrimaryKey	Property
OnDelete	Property	Print	Action
OnEnter	Property	Print	Method
OnExit	Property	Print #	Statemen
OnFormat	Property	PrintCount	Property
OnInsert	Property	PrintSection	Property
OnMenu	Property	PrtDevMode*	Property
OnOpen	Property	PrtMip*	Property
OnPrint	Property	Put	Statement
OnPush	Property	PV	Function
Open	Statement	QBColor	Function
OpenDatabase	Function	Quit	Action
OpenForm	Action	Randomize	Statement
OpenQuery	Action	Rate	Function
OpenQueryDef	Method	RecordCount	Property
OpenReport	Action	RecordLocks	Property
OpenTable	Action	RecordSelectors	Property
Option Base	Statement	RecordSource	Property
Option Compare	Statement	ReDim	Statement
Option Explicit	Statement	Rem	Statement
OptionValue	Property	Rename	Action

continues

Table 16.1. Continued

Language Element Name	*Language Category*	*Language Element Name*	*Language Category*
RepaintObject	Action	Seek	Function
Report	Property	Seek	Statement
Requery	Action	Select Case	Statement
Reset	Statement	SelectObject	Action
Restore	Action	SendKeys	Action
Resume	Statement	SendKeys	Statement
RGB	Function	Set	Statement
Right	Function	SetValue	Action
Right$	Function	SetWarnings	Action
Rnd	Function	Sgn	Function
RollBack	Statement	Shell	Function
RowSource	Property	ShowAllRecords	Action
RowSourceType	Property	ShowGrid	Property
RSet	Statement	Sin	Function
Rtrim	Function	SLN	Function
RTrim	Function	Sort	Property
RTrim$	Function	SortOrder	Property
RunApp	Action	SourceObject	Property
RunCode	Action	Space	Function
RunMacro	Action	Space$	Function
RunningSum	Property	Spc	Function
RunSQL	Action	SpecialEffect	Property
Scale	Method	SQL	Property
ScaleHeight	Property	Sqr	Function
ScaleLeft	Property	Static	Statement
ScaleMode	Property	StatusBarText	Property
ScaleTop	Property	StDev	Function
ScaleWidth	Property	StDevP	Function
Scaling	Property	Stop	Statement
Second	Function	StopAllMacros	Action
Section*	Property	StopMacro	Action

Language Element Name	*Language Category*	*Language Element Name*	*Language Category*
Str	Function	Trim	Function
Str$	Function	Trim$	Function
StrComp	Function	Type	Statement
String	Function	TypeOf...Is...	Statement
String$	Function	UBound	Function
Sub	Statement	UCase	Function
Sum	Function	UCase$	Function
Switch	Function	Unlock	Statement
SYD	Function	Updatable	Property
SysCmd*	Function	UpdateMethod	Property
Tab	Function	Val	Function
Tan	Function	ValidationRule	Property
TextAlign	Property	ValidationText	Property
TextHeight	Method	Var	Function
Time	Function	VarP	Function
Time$	Function	VarType	Function
Timer	Function	ViewsAllowed	Property
TimeSerial	Function	Visible	Property
TimeValue	Function	Weekday	Function
Top	Property	Width	Property
Transactions	Property	Width #	Statement
TransferDatabase	Action	Write #	Statement
TransferSpreadsheet	Action	Xor	Operator
TransferText	Action	Year	Function
Transparent	Property		

Table 16.2. Access Basic Language Elements Grouped by Their Function

Name	*Language Category*	*Name*	*Language Category*
Access Object Manipulation		CreateControl	Function
Close	Action	CreateForm	Function
CopyObject	Action	CreateGroupLe	Function

continues

Table 16.2. Continued

Language Name	*Category*
DeleteControl	Statement
InputBox	Function
InputBox$	Function
Maximize	Action
Minimize	Action
MoveSize	Action
OpenForm	Action
OpenQuery	Action
OpenReport	Action
OpenTable	Action
Print	Action
Rename	Action
RepaintObject	Action
Requery	Action
Restore	Action
SelectObject	Action
SetValue	Action
ShowAllRecord	Action
TypeOf...Is...	Statement
Array Manipulation	
Erase	Statement
LBound	Function
Option Base	Statement
ReDim	Statement
UBound	Function
Conversion	
Asc	Function
CCur	Function
CDbl	Function
Chr	Function
Chr$	Function
CInt	Function
CLng	Function
CSng	Function
Cstr	Function
CVar	Function
CVDate	Function
DateSerial	Function
DateValue	Function
Day	Function
Hex	Function
Hex$	Function
Oct	Function
Oct$	Function
Str	Function
Str$	Function
TimeSerial	Function
TimeValue	Function
Val	Function
Weekday	Function
Year	Function
Data in Forms and Reports	
ApplyFilter	Action
FindNext	Action
FindRecord	Action
GoToControl	Action
GoToPage	Action
GoToRecord	Action

Language Name	*Category*	*Language Name*	*Category*
Database Manipulation		*Domain*	
CodeDB	Function	DAvg	Function
CurrentDB	Function	DCount	Function
OpenDatabase	Function	DFirst	Function
		DLast	Function
Date and Time		DLookup	Function
Date	Function	DMax	Function
Date	Statement	DMin	Function
Date$	Function	DStDev	Function
Date$	Statement	DStDevP	Function
DateAdd	Function	DSum	Function
DateDiff	Function	DVar	Function
DatePart	Function	DVarP	Function
Hour	Function		
Minute	Function	*Error Handling*	
Month	Function	Erl	Function
Now	Function	Err	Function
Second	Function	Err	Statement
Time	Function	Error	Function
Time$	Function	Error	Statement
Timer	Function	Error$	Function
		On Error	Statement
DDE		Resume	Statement
DDE	Function		
DDEExecute	Statement	*Execution*	
DDEInitiate	Function	CancelEvent	Action
DDEPoke	Statement	DoMenuItem	Action
DDERequest	Function	Quit	Action
DDESend	Function	RunApp	Action
DDETerminate	Statement	RunCode	Action
DDETerminate	Statement	RunMacro	Action

continues

Table 16.2. Continued

Language Name	*Category*
RunSQL	Action
StopAllMacros	Action
StopMacro	Action
File I/O	
ChDir	Statement
ChDrive	Statement
CurDir	Function
CurDir$	Function
Dir	Function
Dir$	Function
EOF	Function
FileAttr	Function
FreeFile	Function
Get	Statement
Input	Function
Input #	Statement
Input$	Function
Kill	Statement
LineInput #	Statement
Loc	Function
Lock	Statement
LOF	Function
MkDir	Statement
Name	Statement
Open	Statement
Print #	Statement
Put	Statement
Reset	Statement
Seek	Function
Seek	Statement
Spc	Function
Tab	Function
Unlock	Statement
Width #	Statement
Write #	Statement
Financial	
DDB	Function
FV	Function
IPmt	Function
IRR	Function
MIRR	Function
NPer	Function
NPV	Function
Partition	Function
Pmt	Function
PPmt	Function
PV	Function
Rate	Function
SLN	Function
SYD	Function
Functions and Procedures	
Call	Statement
Declare	Statement
Function	Statement
Sub	Statement

Language Name	*Category*	*Language Name*	*Category*
Graphics		*Miscellaneous*	
QBColor	Function	AddMenu	Action
RGB	Function	AppActivate	Statement
		Beep	Action
Import/Export		Beep	Statement
TransferDataba	Action	Command	Function
TransferSpreads	Action	Command$	Function
TransferText	Action	Echo	Action
		Environ	Function
Inspection of Variables		Environ$	Function
IsDate	Function	Eval	Function
IsEmpty	Function	MsgBox	Action
IsNull	Function	MsgBox	Statement
IsNumeric	Function	Rem	Statement
VarType	Function	SendKeys	Action
		SendKeys	Statement
Math		SetWarnings	Action
Abs	Function	Shell	Function
Atn	Function	SysCmd	Function
Cos	Function		
Exp	Function	*Program Flow Control*	
Fix	Function	Choose	Function
Int	Function	Do...Loop	Statement
Log	Function	DoCmd	Statement
Randomize	Statement	DoEvents	Statement
Rnd	Function	End	Statement
Sgn	Function	Exit	Statement
Sin	Function	For...Next	Statement
Sqr	Function	GoSub...Return	Statement
Tan	Function	GoTo	Statement

continues

Table 16.2. Continued

Language Name	*Category*
If...Then...Else	Statement
IIf	Function
On...GoSub	Statement
On...GoTo	Statement
Select Case	Statement
Stop	Statement
Sub	Statement
Switch	Function
SQL	
Avg	Function
Count	Function
First	Function
Last	Function
Max	Function
Min	Function
StDev	Function
StDevP	Function
Sum	Function
Var	Function
VarP	Function
Strings	
Format	Function
Format$	Function
InStr	Function
LCase	Function
LCase$	Function
Left	Function
Left$	Function
Len	Function
LSet	Statement
LTrim	Function
LTrim$	Function
Mid	Statement
Mid	Function
Mid$	Function
Mid$	Statement
Option Compare	Statement
Right	Function
Right$	Function
RSet	Statement
RTrim	Function
RTrim$	Function
Space	Function
Space$	Function
StrComp	Function
String	Function
String$	Function
Trim	Function
Trim$	Function
UCase	Function
UCase$	Function
Transaction Processing	
BeginTrans	Statement
CommitTrans	Statement
RollBack	Statement

Language Name	*Category*	*Language Name*	*Category*
Deftype	Statement	Option Explicit	Statement
Dim	Statement	Set	Statement
Global	Statement	Static	Statement
Let	Statement (anachronism)	Type	Statement

Table 16.3. Methods and Objects to which the Methods Apply

Method	*Applicable object(s)*
AddNew	Table and Dynaset objects
AppendChunk	Table and Dynaset objects
Clone	Table, Dynaset, and Snapshot object
Close	Table, Dynaset, Snapshot, and QueryDef objects
CreateDynaset	Table and QueryDef objects
CreateQueryDef	QueryDef objects
CreateSnapshot	Table, Dynaset, and QueryDef objects
Delete	Table and Dynaset objects
Edit	Table and Dynaset objects
Execute	QueryDef objects
FieldSize	Memo fields and OLE objects
FindFirst	Dynaset and Snapshot objects
FindLast	Dynaset and Snapshot objects
FindNext	Dynaset and Snapshot objects
FindPrevious	Dynaset and Snapshot objects
GetChunk	Recordset objects
Line	Report objects
ListFields	Table, Dynaset, and Snapshot objects
ListParameters	QueryDef objects
ListTables	Table and QueryDef objects
OpenQueryDef	QueryDef objects

continues

Table 16.3. Continued

Method	*Applicable object(s)*
Print	Debug and Report objects
Scale	Report objects
TextHeight	Report objects

Actions

AddMenu

Miscellaneous

Adds a drop-down menu to a menu bar.

Applies to

Forms; not available from Access Basic.

Arguments

Menu Name is the name of the drop-down menu to add to the menu bar. This argument is required.

Menu Macro Name is the name of the macro group that contains the macros with menu commands. This argument is required.

Status Bar Text is the text to display on the status bar. This argument is optional.

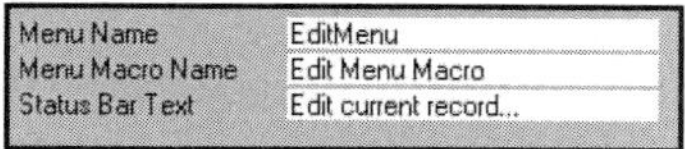

Usage Notes

You can attach this macro only to a form's *OnMenu* property; attaching it to any other property generates an error. Note that if you attach this macro to the OnMenu property and to another property (*OnOpen*, for example), the menu is duplicated and no error occurs.

The bar menu with custom items added with the AddMenu action replaces the default Access bar menu; to simulate the default Access bar menu, use the DoMenuItem action to place the desired Access commands in the macro groups for the specified menus.

Each drop-down menu requires a separate AddMenu action.

See Also

Actions: DoMenuItem and RunMacro

ApplyFilter

Data in Forms and Reports

Applies various forms of filters to recordsets on which forms or reports are based.

Applies to

Forms and reports

Arguments

Filter Name is the name of an existing query that restricts or orders records in the recordset.

WHERE Condition is a valid SQL WHERE clause or expression without the word WHERE.

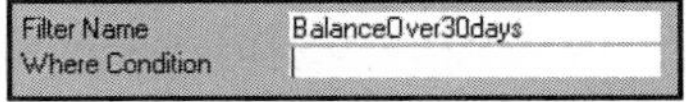

Usage Notes

This action applies a filter, a query, or a SQL WHERE clause to the underlaying recordset.

If both arguments are used, the WHERE condition takes precedence over *filter name*.

If applied to reports, this action can be used only in a macro attached to the *OnOpen* property.

To remove the filter specified with ApplyFilter, use the **ShowAllRecords** action.

Access Basic Syntax

DoCmd **ApplyFilter** [filter name] [, WHERE condition]

At least one argument must be used with this action or an `Action requires at least 1 argument(s)` error (trappable error #2504) occurs.

If both arguments are entered, *WHERE condition* takes precedence over *filter name.*

If only the second argument is used, the separating comma must be entered as well.

Access Basic Example

To display only records for the United Kingdom in the Fossils form:

```
DoCmd OpenForm "Fossils"
DoCmd ApplyFilter, "[Country] = 'UK'"
(...)
```

See Also

Actions: OpenQuery and ShowAllRecords

Methods: CreateDynaset, CreateQueryDef, and CreateSnapshot

Properties: Filter, Index, and Sort

Beep

Miscellaneous

Sounds a beep through the computer speaker.

Arguments

None

Usage Notes

Use the Beep action in error -handling routines or to signal the end of a crucial step of the operation.

The frequency and duration of the sound are system (hardware) dependent and may vary greatly from system to system.

Tip

If you want greater control over the generated sound, you can use the Windows MessageBeep function instead of the Beep action.

Access Basic Syntax

DoCmd **Beep**

See Also

Action: MsgBox

Statement: Beep

Chapter 13, "Extending Microsoft Access and Access Basic"

CancelEvent

Execution

CancelEvent cancels the event that caused the macro containing this action to run.

Applies to

Forms and reports

Arguments

None

Usage Notes

The macro containing the CancelEvent action should be attached to one of the "event" properties, such as BeforeUpdate, OnOpen, OnClose, or OnPrint.

Tables 17.1 and 17.2 furnish a list of forms and reports properties to which a macro containing the **CancelEvent** action can be attached plus a list of potential pitfalls and problems caused by side effects of the **CancelEvent** action attached to specified properties.

Table 17.1. Forms and Controls on Forms

Property	*Side Effect*
BeforeUpdate	No capability to save changes to the record and/or exit the form without generating error messages.
OnDelete	No capability to delete the record.
OnInsert	No capability to add records to the underlying recordset.
OnClose	No capability to close the form without generating error messages. If the form is a modal form, you cannot edit the macro containing this action either!
OnDblClick	Cancels the double-click action (note that the effect of a double-click varies from property to property).
OnExit	No capability to exit the control to which the macro containing CancelEvent is attached.
OnOpen	No capability to open the form.

Table 17.2. Reports and Report Sections

Property	*Side Effect*
OnOpen	No capability to open the report.
OnClose	No effect.
OnFormat	Depending on the section in which the macro containing the CancelEvent is used, header, footer, or detail sections will not be generated.
OnPrint	Depending on the section in which the macro containing the CancelEvent is used, header, footer, or detail sections will not be printed.

If you attach this macro to properties other than those listed in the preceding tables, the **CancelEvent** action has no effect.

Access Basic Syntax

DoCmd **CancelEvent**

The CancelEvent action is meaningful in Access Basic only if it is included in a function attached to the event property on a form or a report.

See Also

Actions: MsgBox and StopMacro

Close

Access Object Manipulation

Closes a specified Access database object.

Applies to

Tables, queries, forms, reports, macros, modules, and windows

Arguments

Object Type is the type of the object to close and must be one of the following: Table, Query, Form, Report, Macro, Module. Leave the argument blank to close the active window.

Object Name is the name of the valid object of the specified type.

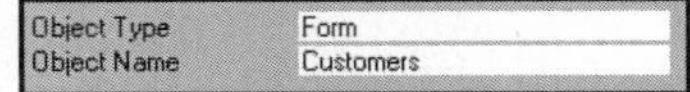

Usage Notes

You must leave *object name* blank if you left *object type* blank.

If no arguments are used, **Close action** closes the current window.

The Close action with no arguments (that is, an argument that would close the current report window) attached to report properties triggers a `Can't run this action while processing a report event` error (trappable error #2585).

Access Basic Syntax

DoCmd **Close** [*object type, object name*]

Object Type must be one of the following:

Value	*Constant*
0	A_TABLE
1	A_QUERY
2	A_FORM
3	A_REPORT
4	A_MACRO
5	A_MODULE

You must specify *object type* if *object name* is used. If no arguments are used, **Close** action closes the current window.

If a nonexistent *object name* is specifed, this action has no effect and no error occurs. Passing an invalid object type generates an `Invalid object type` error (trappable error #2487).

See Also

Action: Quit

CopyObject

Access Object Manipulation

Copies the selected object to a different database or to the same database with a new name.

Applies to

All Access database objects

Arguments

Destination Database is a valid path and file name for the destination database.

New Name is a new name for the object.

Usage Notes

Any database object (Table, Form, Report, Query, and Module) can be copied with this action.

At least one argument must be included with this action; if you omit *destination database*, the object is copied to the current database under its *new name*.

Access Basic Syntax

DoCmd **CopyObject** [destination database] [, new name]

If you attempt to duplicate the object in the current database under the same name, a `Can't copy '<name>' to itself` error (trappable error #2548) occurs. Attempting to use an existing name for *new name* brings up a dialog box with the `Replace '<name>' with '<name>'` question, and an `Action CopyObject was cancelled` error (trappable error #2501) occurs if the user chooses not to proceed with the replacement.

Caution

CopyObject in Access version 1.0 exhibits the following quirks while used to copy modules (Access Basic code):

- *destination database* must be included even if the current database is the destination.
- If the *new name* module already exists, an Illegal function call error (trappable error #5) is generated at the end of the procedure and no copy is made.

See Also

Actions: Rename, SelectObject, and TransferDatabase

DoMenuItem

Execution

Executes an Access menu command.

Arguments

Menu Bar is the name of the menu bar that contains the command to execute.

Menu Name is the name of the menu that contains the command to execute.

Command is the command to execute.

Subcommand is the subcomand (assuming that command has a submenu) to execute.

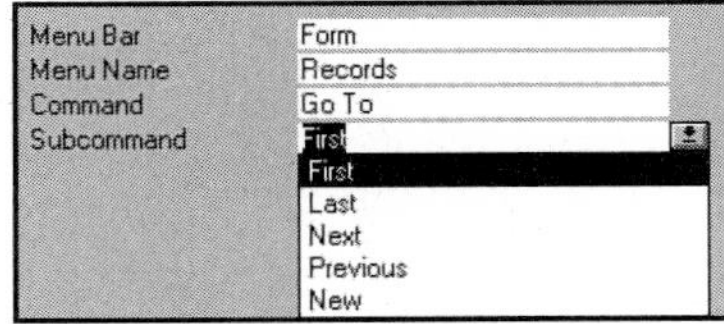

Usage Notes

The **DoMenuItem** action can run any Access command and therefore executes operations without keyboard input. When used with the **SendKeys** action, it also becomes a useful testing technique.

Choices for all options are available from the drop-down menus after selecting the **DoMenuItem** action in the Macro design window.

Note that selections for *menu name*, *command*, and *subcommand* are context-sensitive and depend on one another.

To run an Access operation "automatically," use the **SendKeys** action if necessary to fill in information for dialog boxes activated by some menu selections.

Access Basic Syntax

DoCmd **DoMenuItem** *menu bar*, *menu name*, *command* [, *subcommand*]

You can obtain the sequential number of the *menu bar*, *name*, *command*, and *subcommand* to execute from the listing under the Menu Bar, Menu Name, Command, and Subcommand choices, respectively, for the **DoMenuItem** action on the Macro design surface. It is a zero-based list: the first element equals 0, the second equals 1, and so on.

You also may use the folowing Access constants for some choices:

- For *menu bar*, you can use A_FORMBAR.
- For *menu name*, you can use A_FILE, A_EDITMENU, and A_RECORDSMENU.

- For *command*, you can use A_NEW, A_SAVEFORM, A_SAVEFORMAS, A_SAVERECORD, A_UNDO, A_UNDOFIELD, A_CUT, A_COPY, A_PASTE, A_DELETE, A_SELECTRECORD, A_SELECTALLRECORDS, A_OBJECT, and A_REFRESH.
- For *subcommand*, you can use A_OBJECTVERB (the first command on the submenu as determined by the parent menu and the object type) and A_OBJECTUPDATE (which is often available from the Edit menu of OLE objects).

Access Basic Examples

The following code puts the active form in Form Design view. Form Design is the first (i.e., No. 0) selection on the View menu (which is the third menu and therefore has the number 2). It must be called from a property on a form:

```
DoCmd DoMenuItem 0,2,0
```

The next code example switches the focus to the next record on the current form (runs the third choice of the **GoTo** submenu from the Records drop-down menu of the Forms bar menu). It must be called from a property on the form. It also may be used in lieu of the default record selectors on the form:

```
DoCmd DoMenuItem 0, 3, 1, 2
```

or

```
DoCmd DoMenuItem A_FORM, A_RECORDSMENU, 1, 2
```

Caution

Access constants are not implemented consistently. The numeric value of the A_DELETE constant (which specifies the Delete menu choice) is 6, for example. Using this constant to specify a Delete Table operation triggers a `Not a valid name for a menu bar, menu, command or subcommand` error (trappable error #2065) because only 5 selections (numbered 0 through 5) are on the Edit menu in the table bar menu. In a situation like this, use the numeric value instead.

See Also

Actions: AddMenu and SendKeys

Echo

Miscellaneous

Suppresses or enables screen updates during execution of a macro.

Applies to

Macros

Arguments

If *Echo On* is False (0), the display is supressed; if *echo on* is True (-1), the display is enabled.

Status Bar Text is text to display on the status bar.

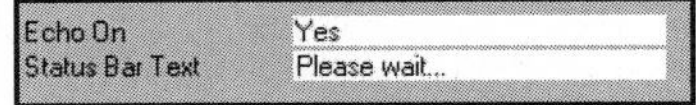

Usage Notes

There is no need to explicitly turn Echo on at the end of the macro; Access does it automatically and also restores the previous status bar message.

Turning Echo off doesn't supress the display of dialog or input boxes; use the SetWarnings False action to entirely supress the display (except error messages) during macro execution. Note that Access status bar messages (such as `Run Query`) may not be suppressed.

Tip

Because the status text display is rather diminutive, you also may want to use the Hourglass action to visually confirm that a macro is running.

Access Basic Syntax

DoCmd **Echo** *echo on* [, *status bar text*]

Don't include the separating comma if *status bar text* is not used.

Access Basic Example

The following code turns off the display while running a macro; the display is restored automatically when the macro terminates:

```
DoCmd Echo False, "Please wait..."
DoCmd (...)                               ' run a macro
```

See Also

Actions: Hourglass and SetWarnings

FindNext

Data in Forms and Reports

Finds a record using the criteria specified in the most recent FindRecord action.

Applies to

Tables, forms, and queries

Arguments

None

Usage Notes

This action is used to repeatedly locate all records that meet a particular condition.

FindNext uses exactly the same criteria as the most recent FindRecord action. **FindNext** also can use the criteria set in the Find dialog box.

If there is no open recordset, a `Command not available` error (trappable error #2046) occurs.

Example

See the **FindRecord** action.

Access Basic Syntax

DoCmd **FindNext**

See Also

Actions: FindRecord and GoToControl

Methods: FindFirst, FindLast, FindNext, and FindPrevious

FindRecord

Data in Forms and Reports

Finds a record using the specified criteria.

Applies to

Tables, forms, and queries

Arguments

Find What is the data to search for; it may be a literal or an expression (required argument).

Where matches *Find What*—either the **Whole Field** (default), **Any Part of Field**, or **Start of Field**.

If *Match Case* is No (default), the search is not case-sensitive; it becomes case-sensitive if *Match Case* is set to Yes.

If *Direction* is Down (default), the search continues from the current record to the end of the recordset; if *Direction* is Up, the search continues from the current record to the beginning of the recordset. The *Find First* argument can override this setting.

Search As Formatted indicates whether Access will search for data as stored in the recordset (if set to No), or as the data is displayed (formatted) if set to Yes. For this option to take effect, the current field is a bound field, the *Where* argument must be set to **Match Whole Field**, the *Search In* must be set to **Current Field**, and the *Match Case* argument must be set to No.

Search In searches either the current field or all fields.

If *Find First* is Yes (default), the action starts from the first record; if *find first* is No, it starts from the current record.

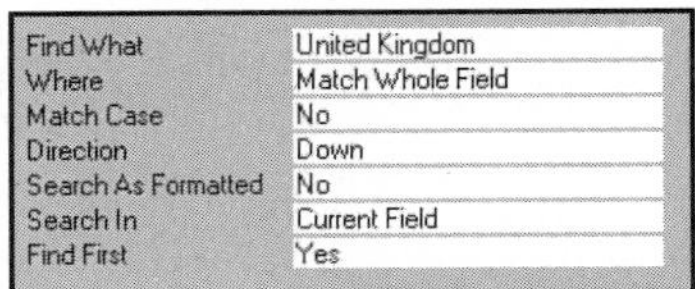

Usage Notes

The options used by the most recent FindRecord action also can be viewed in the Find window.

If an argument of the **FindRecord** action is left blank, Access uses the most recent setting of the argument (either set from the Find window or the most recent FindRecord action).

If there is no open recordset, a `Command not available` error (trappable error #2046) occurs.

You may use a *search as formatted* argument to limit the searches to certain formatting of the same data only, which may be useful for editing erroneously formatted entries.

Access Basic Syntax

DoCmd **FindRecord** *find what* [, *where*] [, *match case*] [, *direction*] [, *search as formatted*] [, *search in*] [, *find first*]

Use True (-1) or False (0) (instead of Yes or No) for the *match case*, *search as formatted*, and *find first* arguments.

Use the following Access constants: A_ANYWHERE, A_ENTIRE (default), A_START for *where*, A_UP, A_DOWN (default) for *direction*, and A_CURRENT (default) or A_ALL for *search in*. If an optional argument is left blank, the default is assumed; the separating commas must be used to delimit the position of the argument.

A syntax error (such as a misplaced comma) may become apparent only at runtime and will trigger a `Can't search data using current FindRecord action arguments` error (trappable error #2162).

Access Basic Example

The following code demonstrates options of the FindRecord action by finding the first occurence of the string "ALOHA" anywhere in a field, searching all fields of the current recordset, and searching data as stored, starting from the first record, without performing a case-sensitive search:

```
DoCmd FindRecord "ALOHA", A_ANYWHERE, , , , A_ALL
(...)
DoCmd FindNext
```

See Also

Action: FindNext

Methods: FindFirst, FindLast, FindNext, and FindPrevious

GoToControl

Data in Forms and Reports

Moves focus to the specified control.

Applies to

Forms, reports, queries, and tables

Arguments

Control Name is the name of the control to which Access moves the focus.

Usage Notes

Use this action to switch focus to a different control either explicitly, or conditionally (based on data entered by the user).

The **GoToControl** action also may be used to move to a subform.

Referring to a nonexistent control triggers a `There is no control named '<name>'` error (trappable error #2109).

Access Basic Syntax

DoCmd **GoToControl** *control name*

You can use a *Control* data type variable to refer to the control name.

ACTIONS

Access Basic Example

Both constructs move the focus to the Current Balance field. The first syntax may be preferable, because it refers just to the control name on any current object (the second example uses the form name):

```
DoCmd GoToControl "Current balance"
```

or

```
Dim cControl As Control
Set cControl = Forms![Checking Accounts].[Current balance]
DoCmd GoToControl cControl.ControlName
```

Caution

This action doesn't work if a form (or report) is opened in Design view.

See Also

Actions: GoToPage, GoToRecord, and SelectObject

GoToPage

Data in Forms and Reports

Moves the focus to the first field on the specified page of a form.

Applies to

Forms

Arguments

Page Number is the number of the page to move to (first page = 1).

Right is the horizontal position of the pages' upper left corner.

Down is the vertical position of the pages' upper left corner.

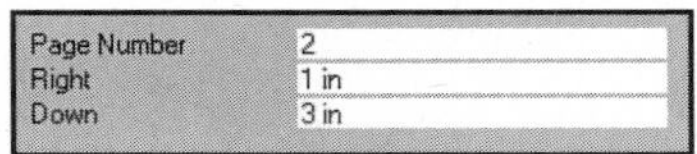

Usage Notes

This action can be used only with multipage forms (created with page breaks).

Right and *down* are used to display a specified region of a form that is larger than its window.

Right and *down* measurements are relative to the borders of the window that contains the form. Their units of measurement (inches, centimeters) depend on the setting in the International section of the WIN.INI file.

If *page number* is greater than the actual number of pages in the form, a `Page number given as an argument for the GoToPage action is out of range` error (trappable error #2163) occurs.

Access Basic Syntax

DoCmd **GoToPage** *page number* [, *right*] [, *down*]

In Access Basic, both *right* and *down* are measured in twips.

See Also

Actions: GoToControl, GoToRecord, and SelectObject

GoToRecord

Data in Forms and Reports

Moves to a specified record in the current recordset.

Applies to

Forms, tables, and queries

Arguments

Object Type is the type of object (Form, Table, Query) that contains the record to move to (leave blank to assume the current object).

Object Name is the name of the object of selected *object type* (leave blank if *object type* is blank).

Record is the record to move to (Previous, Next [default], First, Last, GoTo or New).

Offset is an expression that evaluates to an integer specifying the number of records to skip if *record* is Previous or Next; GoTo requires a valid record number to move to.

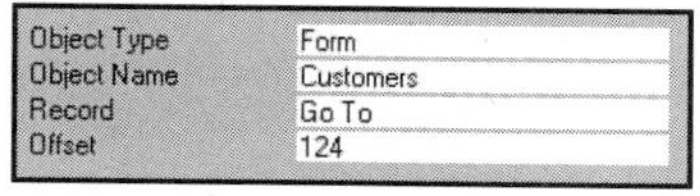

Object Type	Form
Object Name	Customers
Record	Go To
Offset	124

Usage Notes

GoToRecord moves focus to the specifed record and makes it active (current).

If First, Last, or New is specified for *record*, any specified *offset* is ignored.

The focus on the particular field is preserved in the new record.

An invalid record number specified in *offset*, or an attempt to skip beyond the end or beginning of the record results in a `Can't go to specified record` error (trappable record #2105).

A negative value specified as *offset* triggers a `Not a valid value for argument '<argument number>'` error (trappable error #2505).

Access Basic Syntax

DoCmd **GoToRecord** [*object type*, *object name*] [, *record*] [, *offset*]

If *object type* and *object name* are left blank, the current object is assumed but two commas must precede *record* and *offset*.

The following constants are allowed as arguments in this action:

Argument	*Applicable Constant*	*Numeric Value*
object type	A_FORM	2
	A_QUERY	1
	A_TABLE	0
record	A_PREVIOUS	0
	A_NEXT (default)	1
	A_FIRST	2
	A_LAST	3
	A_GOTO	4
	A_NEWREC	5

The number of records to skip in *offset* must be specified if *record* is A_PREVIOUS or A_NEXT; A_GOTO requires a valid record number to move to.

Access Basic Example

You can use the following example to move to the next record in the current recordset (form, dynaset, or table):

```
DoCmd GoToRecord
```

You can use this example to skip 20 records backwards in the current object:

```
DoCmd GoToRecord , , A_PREVIOUS, 20
```

See Also

Actions: GoToControl, GoToPage, and SelectObject

Hourglass

Miscellaneous

Changes the shape of the mouse pointer to an hourglass.

Arguments

Hourglass On displays the hourglass if set to Yes (default); the original mouse pointer is displayed if set to No.

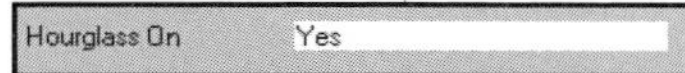

Usage Notes

Changing the shape of the mouse pointer to the image of an hourglass is a standard Windows practice to signal that an operation (sometimes without visible screen output) is in progress.

The hourglass turned on with the **Hourglass** action takes effect only inside Access; switching to any other application restores the mouse pointer to its original shape.

Access by default turns the hourglass off at the end of a macro.

Tip

Avoid confusing users, always remember to turn off the hourglass when an action (a batch operation, for example) that triggered the hourglass display is concluded.

Example

See the **Echo** action.

Access Basic Syntax

DoCmd **Hourglass** *hourglass On*

Hourglass On displays the hourglass if True (-1) and changes the cursor back to its original shape if False (0).

Access Basic Example

Use the following example to turn on the hourglass:

```
DoCmd Hourglass True
```

See Also

Actions: Echo and SetWarnings

Maximize

Access Object Manipulation

Expands the active window to fill the entire Access window.

Applies to

Windows

Arguments

None

Usage Notes

This action is equal to clicking the Maximize button on the active window.

The proper window may have to be selected (using the SelectObject action) before maximizing it.

Please note that there is no practical method of removing the Maximize and Minimize buttons from a window by using Access Basic, but you can remove them by using Windows API functions. See Chapter 13 for more information and an example.

Caution

An attempt to use the Maximize action on a window with the Maximize button removed may crash Access!

Access Basic Syntax

DoCmd **Maximize**

See Also

Actions: Minimize, MoveSize, Restore, and SelectObject

Minimize

Access Object Manipulation

Reduces the active window to an icon displayed at the bottom of the screen.

Applies to

Windows

Arguments

None

Usage Notes

You can use this action to iconize an object while leaving it open or to open an object in the minimized (iconized) state. Use the **Restore** action to restore the minimized object to its previous size, or the **Maximize** action to restore it to the full size of the Access window.

You also can remove an object from the screen by setting its *Visible* property to False (to restore it, set its *Visible* property to True).

Another way of removing an object from the screen is to use the **Hide** and **Show** commands from the Window menu to hide and unhide the active window; you also can accomplish these operations by using the **DoMenuItem** action or **SendKeys** statement (or action).

The **Minimize** action is analogous to clicking the Minimize button on the active window.

The proper window may have to be selected (using the SelectObject action) before minimizing it.

Please note that there is no practical method of removing the Maximize and Minimize buttons from a window by using Access Basic, but you can remove them by using Windows API functions.

Caution

An attempt to use the Minimize action on a window with the Minimize button removed may crash Access!

Access Basic Syntax

DoCmd **Minimize**

See Also

Actions: DoMenuItem, Maximize, MoveSize, OpenForm, Restore, SelectObject, and SendKeys

Property: Visible

Statement: SendKeys

MoveSize

Access Object Manipulation

Moves and/or resizes the active window.

Applies to

Windows containing objects in Design, Form, and Datasheet view

Arguments

Right is the new horizontal position of the window's upper left corner.

Down is the new vertical position of the window's upper left corner.

Width is the desired window's width.

Height is the desired window's height.

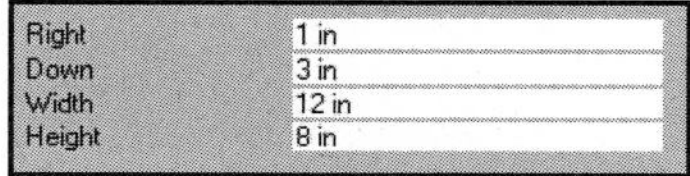

Usage Notes

This action moves, resizes, or moves and resizes the active window; leave unnecessary argument(s) blank.

Right and *left* are measured from the upper left edge of the parent window.

To obtain a visible result of this action, you must use at least one argument; a blank argument will be interpreted as the current setting.

Caution:

Exercise caution when you use this action because the active window can be moved beyond the visible portion of the screen.

Access Basic Syntax

DoCmd **MoveSize** [, *right*] [, *left]* [, *width*] [, *height*]

All arguments must evaluate to valid integers or an `Argument type mismatch` error (trappable error #2498) occurs.

The default unit of measurement for arguments is twips.

Access Basic Example

Use the following example to select a form, move, and resize it:

```
DoCmd SelectObject A_FORM, "Customers"
```

Move the form first:

```
DoCmd MoveSize 400, 300
```

Then resize it (change its width and height):

```
DoCmd MoveSize , , 5000, 10000
```

Tip

There is no direct way in Access Basic to obtain the coordinates of the active window; to do so, it is necessary to call a Windows API function, such as **GetWindowRect**. Because this function doesn't return a value, it can be declared as a subprocedure in Access. Because the **GetWindowRect** function requires a data structure to place the coordinates into, define it first in the Declaration section and name it RECT, as follows:

```
Type RECT
    aleft As Integer
    atop As Integer
    aright As Integer
    abottom As Integer
End Type
```

Declare a global variable of the type RECT (this also can be done inside a function):

```
Global WinXY As RECT
```

Declare the function by typing the following:

```
Declare Sub GetWindowRect Lib "User" (ByVal hWnd As Integer, Coord As RECT)
```

Note that the argument Coord is of the user-defined data type RECT.

Finally, the sample function that follows makes use of these declarations and obtains the coordinates of the active window. It first obtains the handle to the current window, calls the GetWindowRect functions and displays the data in the Immediate window. Activate this particular function from any of the Action properties of a form (excluding OnOpen) by typing the following:

```
Function GetFormWindowCoordinates ()
     Dim hWnd As Integer
     hWnd = Screen.ActiveForm.hWnd
     GetWindowRect ahWnd, WinXY
     MsgBox (Str(WinXY.aleft) & Str(WinXY.atop) & Str(WinXY.aright)   &
Str(WinXY.abottom))
End Function
```

See Also

Actions: Restore and SelectObject

Properties: hWnd, ActiveForm, and ActiveReport

MsgBox

Miscellaneous

Displays the Windows message box.

Applies to

Not available from Access Basic.

Arguments

Message is the message to display.

Beep sounds the bell when the message is displayed; the default is Yes.

Type is type of icon to display.

Title is the title (caption) of the message box; the default is “Microsoft Access.”

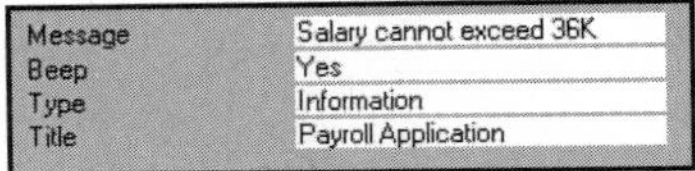

Usage Notes

Message can be up to 255 characters; if the expression is entered, it must be preceded by the equal sign.

Icon type can be as follows:

None

Critical

Warning?

Warning!

Information

The **MsgBox** action is used most commonly in data -validation macros (such as to inform the user that the entered data is invalid).

Access Basic Syntax

Not available from Access Basic; use the **MsgBox** function/statement instead.

See Also

Action: CancelEvent

Function: MsgBox

Statement: MsgBox

OpenForm

Access Object Manipulation

Opens an Access form.

Applies to

Forms

Arguments

Form Name is the name of the form to open.

View is the desired view of the form (Form, Design, Print preview, Datasheet).

Filter Name is a name of the valid query (or a filter that was saved as a query) used to restrict or sort records on which the form is based.

Where Condition is a valid SQL WHERE clause (or expression) used to select records from the underlying table or query.

Data Mode is the data-entry mode, as described in the following table:

Mode	*Description*
add	New records can be added, but existing records cannot be edited.
edit	Both append and edit are enabled, read-only. Applicable only to forms opened in Form and Datasheet views. This setting is the default.

Window Mode is the window mode in which the form opens, as described in the following table:

ACTIONS

Mode	*Description*
normal	The (default) window is opened according to settings of its properties.
hidden	The form is open but not visible.
icon	The form is opened as an icon.
dialog	The form is opened as a modal pop-up form.

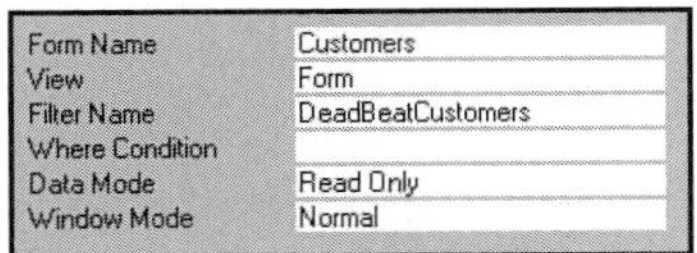

Form Name	Customers
View	Form
Filter Name	DeadBeatCustomers
Where Condition	
Data Mode	Read Only
Window Mode	Normal

Usage Notes

If you specify *dialog* for the window mode, the form's Popup and Modal properties are set to Yes; this setting doesn't become permanent—and it is valid only for this instance of the form.

If the form was opened as *dialog* and activated from within a macro, the macro execution is suspended until the form is closed.

Some view options are not available with some settings of *window mode*; for example, a form can be opened in Design mode only if *window mode* is *normal*.

A form opened as *icon* or *hidden* returns to its former properties setting when restored.

Tip

If you need to open a form from within a macro, the simplest way to create the **OpenForm** action is to drag the form from the database container onto the Action column on the macro design surface; Access will open the form in Form view, Edit Data mode, and Normal Window mode.

Access Basic Syntax

DoCmd **OpenForm** *form name* [,*view*] [,*filter name*] [, *where condition*] [, *data mode*] [, *window mode*]

You can use one or more of the Access constants for these arguments, as described in the following table:

Argument	*Numeric Value*	*Constant*
view	0	A_NORMAL (Form view, default)
	1	A_DESIGN
	2	A_PREVIEW
	3	A_FORMDS (datasheet)
data mode	0	A_ADD
	1	A_EDIT (default)
	2	A_READONLY
window mode	0	A_NORMAL (default)
	1	A_HIDDEN
	2	A_ICON
	3	A_DIALOG

Access Basic Example

Use the following example to open the Customers form as an icon:

```
DoCmd OpenForm "Customers",,,,,2
```

Usage Notes

Passing an invalid form name causes a `There is no form named '<name>'` error (trappable error #2102).

An invalid value for view, data, and window mode triggers a `Not a valid value for argument '<number>'` error (trappable error #2505).

See Also

Actions: Close, SelectObject, and SetValue

OpenQuery

Access Object Manipulation

Opens or runs the specified query.

Applies to

Queries

Arguments

Query Name is the name of the query to open.

View is the desired view of the query (Design, Print Preview, or Datasheet).

Data Mode specifies the data entry mode, as follows:

Mode	*Description*
add	New records can be added but existing records cannot be edited.
edit	(default) Both append and edit are enabled, read-only. Applicable only to queries opened in Form and Datasheet views.

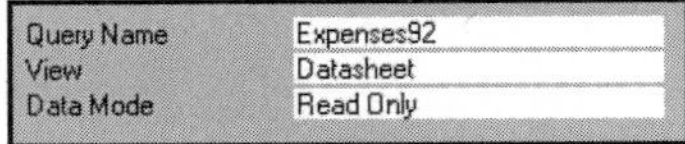

Usage Notes

The OpenQuery action opens a Select or Crosstab query in Datasheet, Design, or Print Preview view. Or, it runs an action query.

Switching to query design while in query nullifies the *data mode* argument.

Tip

If you need to open or run a query from within a macro, the simplest way to create the OpenQuery action is to drag the query from the database container onto the Action column on the macro design surface. Access opens a Select or Crosstab query in the Datasheet mode or executes an action query.

Access Basic Syntax

DoCmd **OpenQuery** *query name* [, *view*] [, *data mode*]

You can use one or more of the Access constants for these arguments, as described in the following table:

Argument	*Numeric Value*	*Constant*
view	0	A_NORMAL (default)
	1	A_DESIGN
	2	A_PREVIEW

Argument	*Numeric Value*	*Constant*
data mode	0	A_ADD
	1	A_EDIT (default)
	2	A_READONLY

Choosing A_NORMAL runs an Action query or opens a Select query.

Specifying the name of a nonexisting query triggers a `Couldn't find object '<name>'` error (trappable error #3011).

An invalid value for View or Data mode triggers a `Not a valid value for argument '<number>'` error (trappable error #2505).

Access Basic Example

The following example opens a Select query, "Expenses 1992," in Edit mode:

```
DoCmd OpenQuery "Expenses 1992", , A_EDIT
```

See Also

Actions: SelectObject and SetWarnings

OpenReport

Access Object Manipulation

Opens a specified report in the specifed mode.

Applies to

Reports

Arguments

Report Name is the name of the report to open.

View is the desired view of the report (Print, Design, or Print Preview).

Filter Name is a name of a valid query (or a filter that was saved as a query) to restrict or sort the records on whch the report is based.

Where Condition is a valid SQL WHERE clause (or expression) used to select records from the underlying table or query.

ACTIONS

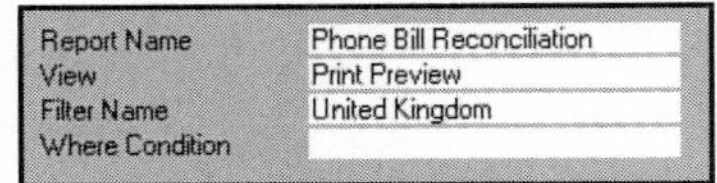

Usage Notes

Reports opened in Print view are printed immediately (no Print dialog box opens). Reports opened in other modes can be printed using the standard Access print facilities.

Tip

If you need to run a report from within a macro, the simplest way to create the OpenReport action is to drag the report from the database container onto the Action column on the macro design surface. Access will open the report in Print Preview mode.

Access Basic Syntax

DoCmd **OpenReport report** *name* [,*view*] [,*filter name*] [, *where condition*]

You may use one or more of the following Access constants for the *view* argument:

0	A_NORMAL
1	A_DESIGN
2	A_PREVIEW (default)

Passing the name of a nonexisting report triggers a `There is no report named '<name>'` error (trappable error #2103).

Access Basic Example

The following example opens the Expenses 1993 report in Print Preview view, and limits the records according to the *Where Condition*:

```
DoCmd OpenReport "Expenses 1993", A_PREVIEW, , "Category = 'M'"
```

See Also

Actions: Close, OpenForm, OpenQuery, and Open Table

OpenTable

Access Object Manipulation

Opens a specified table in the specified mode.

Applies to

Tables

Arguments

Table Name is the name of the table to open.

View is the desired view of the table: Design, Print Preview, or Datasheet (default).

Data Mode specifies the data-entry mode, as follows:

add	New records can be added but existing records cannot be edited.
edit	Both append and edit are enabled, read-only. This is the default setting.

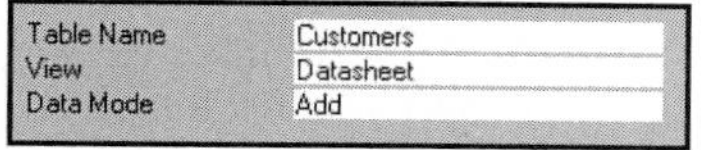

Usage Notes

The OpenTable action opens a specified table in Datasheet, Design, or Print Preview view and allows you to select the data-entry mode.

Caution

Switching to Design mode nullifies the data-mode setting. The Read Only setting no longer applies when you return to Datasheet view, for example!

Tip

If you need to open a table from within a macro, the simplest way to create the OpenTable action is to drag the table from the database container onto the Action column on the macro design surface. Access will open the table in Datasheet view.

Access Basic Syntax

Docmd **OpenTable** *table name* [, *view*] [, *data mode*]

You may use one or more of the following Access constants for the *view* argument:

0	A_NORMAL (Datasheet view, default)
1	A_DESIGN
2	A_PREVIEW

You may use one or more of the following Access constants for the *data mode* argument:

0	A_ADD
1	A_EDIT (default)
2	A_READONLY

Passing an invalid table name triggers a `Couldn't find object '<name>'` error (trappable error #3011).

Access Basic Example

Open the Customers table in Datasheet view in read-only mode:

```
DoCmd OpenTable "Customers", , A_READONLY
```

See Also

Action: Close

Print

Access Object Manipulation

Prints the active Access database object.

Applies to

Datasheets, reports, and forms

Arguments

Print Range specifies the range to print, as follows:

All	[default] Prints the entire object.
Selection	Prints the selected part of the object.
Pages	Prints the range of pages (specified in *page from...page to...*).

Page From is the starting page. Page from is valid only if Pages is specified as *print range*. The default is the first page of the object.

Page To is the ending page. Page to is valid only if Pages is specified as *print range*. The default is the last page of the object.

Print Quality is the print quality offered by the printer. You can choose from High (default), Medium, Low, and Draft.

Copies is the number of copies to print. The default is 1.

If *Collate Copies* is Yes (default), the printer collates the copies.

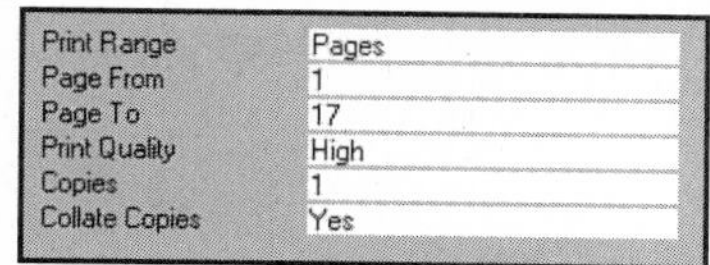

Usage Notes

The Print action without any arguments prints the current object in its entirety.

If there is no active object and the Print action is activated from within a macro, a `Can't print macros` error is most likely to occur.

The arguments of this macro are the same as in the Print dialog box, but there is no communication between the Print dialog box and settings of the Print action arguments.

If this action is attached to **OnOpen** or **OnClose**, **OnFormat** or **OnPrint** properties of a form or report, a `Can't run this action while processing a report event` error (trappable error #2585) occurs. You can attach this action to other event properties, such as **OnPush**, or use it with the **Open...** and **SelectObject** actions to make an object current and then apply the print action.

Tip

You may use this action (without any arguments) from within a module to print this module; in the Immediate window, type the following:

```
DoCmd Print
```

Access Basic Syntax

DoCmd **Print** [*print range*] [, *page from*] [, *page to*] [, *print quality*] [, *copies*] [, *collate copies*]

You may use the following Access constants for the *print range* argument:

0	A_PRINTALL (default)
1	A_SELECTION
2	A_PAGES

You may use the following Access constants for the *print quality* argument:

0	A_HIGH (default)
1	A_MEDIUM
2	A_LOW
3	A_DRAFT

You may use True (-1), or False (0) for the *collate copies* argument. The default is True.

Access Basic Example

Use the following example to print five copies of the current object without collating copies:

```
DoCmd Print ,,,, 5, False
```

See Also

Actions: OpenForm, OpenQuery, OpenReport, OpenTable, and SelectObject

Quit

Execution

Exit Access by using one of the specified options.

Arguments

Options specifies whether unsaved objects are saved automatically (Save All is the default), saved after a prompt (Prompt), or not saved at all (Exit).

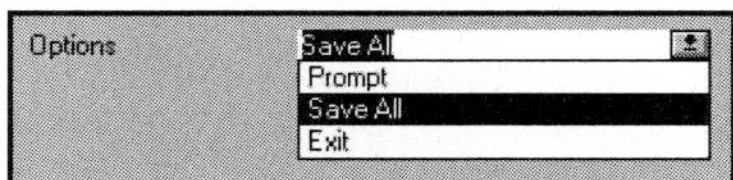

Usage Notes

This action exits Microsoft Access.

Access Basic Syntax

DoCmd **Quit** [options]

You may use the following Access constants for the *options* argument:

0	A_PROMPT
1	A_SAVE (default)
2	A_EXIT

Access Basic Example

Use the following example to quit Microsoft Access and automatically (without prompting) save all unsaved objects:

```
DoCmd Quit
```

See Also

Actions: StopAllMacros and StopMacro

Rename

Access Object Manipulation

Applicable to all Access database objects.

Description

Renames a selected Access database object.

Arguments

New Name is a new name for the given object; you must follow Access's naming conventions.

Usage Notes

The object to be renamed must be selected in the database window (container) or an `Object '<name>' isn't open` error (trappable error #2489) occurs.

An open object cannot be renamed; attempting to do so triggers a `Command not available: Rename` error (trappable error #2046).

Access Basic Syntax

DoCmd **Rename** *new name*

Access Basic Example

Use the following example to select the "Old And Tired Form" form in the database container and give it a more respectable name. Note that the third parameter ("Select object in database window" - True) must be passed to the SelectObject action or an error (#2489) will occur.

```
DoCmd SelectObject A_FORM, "Old And Tired Form", True
DoCmd Rename "HaHaHeeHo"
```

See Also

Actions: CopyObject and SelectObject

RepaintObject

Access Object Manipulation

Completes any pending screen updates for an Access database object.

Applies to

All Access database objects

Arguments

Object Type is the type of the object to repaint (Table, Query, Form, Report, Macro, or Module).

Object Name is the name of the object to repaint.

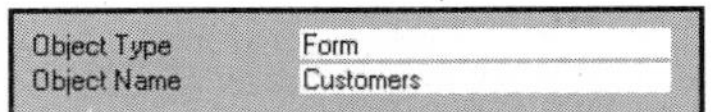

Usage Notes

This action forces an immediate screen update. Use **Requery** or **ShowAllRecords** actions to cause the requery of the database or display changed/added/deleted records from the underlying table(s). Use the **Refresh** option from the Records menu to display the most recent changes to the database made by other users.

This action is most likely to be attached to properties (such as **Validation Rule** or **OnExit**) of the controls that supply values to other calculated fields or expressions, or used in the Access Basic code after the **SetValue** action. Because Access doesn't always display changed data immediately, the **RepaintObject** action "forces" the changes to be displayed at once.

If no object is specified, the action operates on the active object (window)—sometimes without any apparent result (for example, if the data hasn't changed).

The specified object must be open or an Object '<name>' isn't open error (trappable error #2489) occurs.

The same error occurs if *object type* is specified and *object name* is not.

Access Basic Syntax

DoCmd **RepaintObject** [*object name*, *object type*]

You may use one or more of the following Access constants for the *object type* argument:

0	A_TABLE
1	A_QUERY
2	A_FORM

3	A_REPORT
4	A_MACRO
5	A_MODULE

Access Basic Example

Use the following example to repaint the current object:

```
DoCmd RepaintObject
```

See Also

Actions: Requery, SetValue, and ShowAllRecords

Requery

Access Object Manipulation

Requeries the source of the specified control on the active object.

Applies to

Controls

Arguments

Control Name is the name of the control in which you want to update the data.

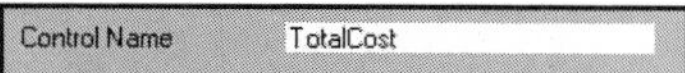

Usage Notes

The Requery action reruns the underlying query or displays updated records from the underlying dataset. This action operates on controls whose record source is a table or a query, such as list boxes, combo boxes, and subform controls. It also acts on OLE objects and controls containing aggregate functions (such as DSum or DCount).

Leave *control name* blank to update the active control and if the active object is a datasheet or a query dynaset.

Use only the name of the active control (such as "Last name"), note the full syntax (such as Forms!<name>.<control name>).

If no object is active, a `Command not available: Requery` error (trappable error #2046) occurs.

Access Basic Syntax

DoCmd **Requery** [*control name*]

Access Basic Example

Use the following example to requery a control named "Salary" on the current form:

```
DoCmd Requery "Salary"
```

You also may use a variable declared as a Control:

```
Dim a As Control
Set a = Forms!Employees.Salary
DoCmd Requery a.ControlName
```

See Also

Actions: RepaintObject and ShowAllrecords

Restore

Access Object Manipulation

Applies to windows.

Description

Restores a window to its previous size.

Arguments

None

Usage Notes

The Restore action restores a minimized or maximized window to its previous size. It does not reestablish the former dimensions of the window when its size was changed with the **MoveSize** action.

This action applies only to the current window. Use the **SelectObject** action to select the window (Form, Report, or Table) to restore.

Access Basic Syntax

DoCmd **Restore**

Access Basic Example

Use the following example to open and select the Abc form, maximize it, and then restore its size to the premaximized state:

```
DoCmd OpenForm "Abc"
DoCmd SelectObject A_FORM, "Abc"
DoCmd Maximize
DoCmd Restore
```

See Also

Actions: Maximize, Minimize, MoveSize, and SelectObject

RunApp

Execution

ACTIONS

Runs an application program; not available in Access Basic.

Arguments

Command Line is the command line used to start the application. It must include the name of the application to execute. It also can include the drive, path, command line parameters, or switches.

Usage Notes

The **RunApp** action can run both DOS and MS Windows-based applications.

The desired application runs in the foreground while the remaining actions in the macro that contains this action (if any) execute in the background.

Data can be transferred between applications using DDE or the Clipboard. Use the **SendKey** action (in a macro) or the **SendKey** statement (in Access Basic code) to send keystrokes to other applications from within Access.

Access Basic Syntax

Not available in Access Basic; use the Shell function instead.

See Also

Function: Shell

Statement: SendKeys

RunCode

Execution

Executes an Access Basic Function procedure; not available in Access Basic.

Arguments

Function Name is the name of the Access Basic function to execute. It may include arguments (in parentheses).

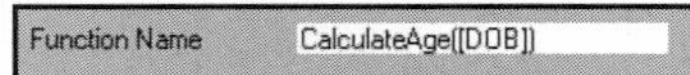

Usage Notes

Only procedures declared as functions can be executed using this action. To execute a subprocedure, create a function that calls the desired subprocedure and use the RunCode action to execute the function.

The RunCode action can execute Access Basic Function procedures and external functions (declared with Declare Function... in the Declarations section).

The value returned by a function executed with the RunCode action is discarded by Access.

Access Basic Syntax

Not available in Access Basic; call function or subprocedures directly.

See Also

Function: Eval

RunMacro

Execution

Executes a macro.

Applies to

Macros

Arguments

Macro Name is the name of the macro to execute.

Repeat Count is the maximum number of times the macro will run. The default is one time; the maximum is 32,767 times.

Repeat Expression is a condition (expression) that indicates the number of times the macro executes. The macro will run again up to the number of times specified in *repeat count* while the repeat expression evaluates to True.

Usage Notes

This action runs a specified macro from within another macro or from Access Basic code. You also may use it to execute a macro attached to a custom menu (using the **AddMenu** action).

If a macro group name is specified as *macro name*, only the first macro in this group is executed. Use *macrogroupname.macroname* notation to identify the particular macro within the group to run.

The macro runs as many times as specified in *repeat count* (or one time if *repeat count* is blank), or until *repeat expression*—if any—evaluates to False (whichever comes first).

Specifying a RepeatCount greater than 32,767 triggers a `RepeatCount argument in RunMacro action cannot be less than 0` error (apparently due to overflow).

Tip

If you need to run a macro from within a form, the simplest way to place a macro on a form is to drag the macro from the database container onto the form. Access creates a pushbutton and updates its OnPush property to execute the macro.

Access Basic Syntax

DoCmd **RunMacro** *macro name* [, *repeat count*] [, *repeat expression*]

Passing the name of a nonexisting macro triggers a `Macro '<name>' not found` error (trappable error #2485).

Specifying a repeat count greater than 32,767 causes an `Argument type mismatch` error (trappable error #2498).

Access Basic Example

Execute the macro named Test from Access Basic:

```
DoCmd RunMacro "Test"
```

See Also

Action: AddMenu

RunSQL

Execution

Runs Access SQL statement.

Applies to

SQL statements

Arguments

SQL Statement is the SQL code you want to run.

Usage Notes

Only SQL statements that relate to action queries can be executed using the RunSQL action. Attempting to run a SQL statement depicting a select query, such as the following, triggers a `RunSQL action can only run action query SQL statements` error (trappable in Access Basic code as error #2342).

```
DoCmd RunSQL "SELECT *FROM Employees;"
```

To run a select query from within a macro, use the View argument of the OpenQuery action.

The Access SQL operands described in the following table can be used in various types of action queries:

Query type	*Operand in the SQL statement*
Append query	INSERT INTO...
Delete query	DELETE
Make table query	SELECT...INTO
Update query	UPDATE

Although this action is convenient to run ad-hoc queries without actually designing and storing the query, a parameter query may be better suited to perform repetitious queries.

Tip

Access queries are mapped to SQL statements that can be viewed by selecting the **SQL...** option from the View menu on the query design surface.

Access Basic Syntax

DoCmd **RunSQL** *SQL statement*

Access Basic Example

Use the following example to make a copy of the Employees table (make-table query):

```
DoCmd RunSQL "SELECT DISTICTROW Employees.* INTO [Backup Employees] FROM Employees;"
```

Use the following example to increase the salaries of all employees by 46 percent in the Employee table (update query):

```
DoCmd RunSQL "UPDATE Employees SET Employees.Salary = Employees.Salary * 1.46;"
```

See Also

Actions: OpenQuery and SetWarnings

ACTIONS

SelectObject

Access Object Manipulation

Selects the specified database object.

Applies to

All Access database objects

Arguments

Object Type is the type of the database object you want to select: Table, Query, Form, Report, Macro, or Module.

Object Name is the name of the object you want to select.

In Database Window determines whether the object is selected in the database window (container).

The default is No.

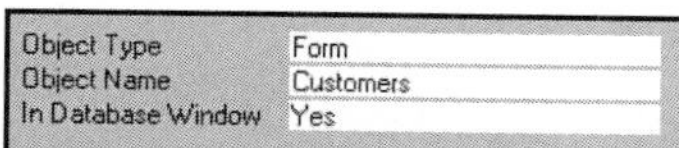

Object Type	Form
Object Name	Customers
In Database Window	Yes

Usage Notes

The **SelectObject** action moves the focus to the specified Access database object. It also displays the object if it is hidden.

If the *object name* is left blank, and *in database window* is Yes, the focus moves to the database window (container) specified by *object type*.

Note that some other Access actions (such as **CopyObject** and **Rename**) require that the object be selected in the database window. Other actions (such as **Maximize** and **Restore**) require that the object must be in focus; otherwise, an error occurs.

Unless *in database window* is set to Yes, an attempt to select an object that is not open results in an `Object '<name>' isn't open` error (trappable in Access Basic as error #2489).

Access Basic Syntax

DoCmd **SelectObject** *object type*, *object name* [, *in database window*]

You may use one or more of the following Access constants for the *object type* argument:

0	A_TABLE
1	A_QUERY
2	A_FORM
3	A_REPORT
4	A_MACRO
5	A_MODULE

Use True (-1) or False (0) for the *in database window* argument. The default is False.

Access Basic Example

Use the following example to open a Customers form in Design mode, select it, and maximize its window:

```
DoCmd OpenForm "Customers, A_DESIGN
DoCmd SelectObject A_FORM, "Customers"
DoCmd Maximize
```

See Also

Actions: CopyObject, OpenForm, OpenQuery, OpenReport, OpenTable, Rename, Restore, and SetValue

SendKeys

Miscellaneous

Sends keystrokes simulating keyboard input.

Arguments

Keystrokes is the keystrokes to send.

Wait specifies whether the macro pauses until all keystrokes are processed. The default is No.

Usage Notes

The **SendKeys** action can send up to 255 keystrokes to Access or another Windows application. Keystrokes appear to the application exactly as if they were typed from the keyboard.

To send more than 255 keystrokes, you may use this action as many times as necessary in succession.

To send a printable character, use the character itself enclosed in double quotation marks. To send the letter *A*, for example, use SendKeys "A"; to send a sequence *<ABCDEF???>*, use SendKeys "<ABCDEF???>". A single keypress character can be sent many times using the {keytext number}—for example, {A 12}.

The key codes described in the following table are used for nonprintable characters and other special keys:

Key	*Code(s)*
Backspace	{BACKSPACE}, {BS}, {BKSP}
Break	{BREAK}
Caps Lock	{CAPSLOCK}
Clear	{CLEAR}
Del	{DELETE}, {DEL}
Down Arrow	{DOWN}
End	{END}
Enter	{ENTER}, ~
Esc	{ESCAPE}, {ESC}
Help	{HELP}
Home	{HOME}

continues

Key	*Code(s)*
Ins	{INSERT}
Left Arrow	{LEFT}
Num Lock	{NUMLOCK}
Page Down	{PGDN}
Page Up	{PGUP}
Print Screen	{PRTSC}
Right Arrow	{RIGHT}
Scroll Lock	{SCROLLLOCK}
Tab	{TAB}
Up Arrow	{UP}
F1 - F16	{F1} - {F16}
Ctrl	^
Shift	+
Alt	%

Because some characters have a special meaning to the **SendKeys** statement, they must be enclosed in curly braces if sent as literal characters, as shown in the following table:

Character	*How to send it*
{, }	{{}, {}}
+	{+}
^	{^}
%	{%}
~	{~}
(,)	{(}, {)}
[,]	{[}, {]}

Access Basic Syntax

Not available in Access Basic; use the **SendKeys** statement.

See Also

Actions: GoToControl, SelectObject, and SetValue

Statement: SendKeys

SetValue

Access Object Manipulation

Sets the value of the specified item (field, control, or property).

Applies to

Fields, controls, and properties on forms, datasheets, and reports. Not available in Access Basic.

Arguments

Item is the name of the item (field, control, or property) to set.

Expression is the expression used to set the value of the specified item.

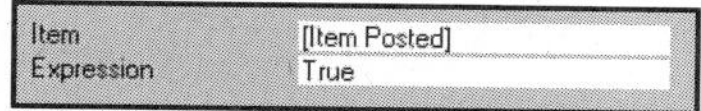

Usage Notes

Use this action to set values of fields and controls on a form, report, or datasheet and the value of properties in Form or Design view.

The **SetValue** action cannot be used to set the value of calculated controls on forms and bound and calculated controls on reports. It also cannot be used with certain properties. For the information on which properties can be set using this action, see the Properties section in the Reference.

The **SetValue** action cannot be attached to the **BeforeUpdate** action property but can be attached to the AfterUpdate property.

Both arguments are mandatory and require the full syntax. Consider the following example:

> **Forms**!*<form name>.<field/control/property name>*

This action also can be used to set the value of a field in the underlying recordset that is not on the current form or report. Use the fully qualified field name as the item, as in the following example:

> Forms!<Formname>.<field name>

Note that using the SetValue action doesn't cause the validation rule (specified in the applicable property of a field) but will trigger recalculation.

Caution

Be careful when using the equal sign preceding *expression*; if a part of the expression is string, Access may interpret it as the name of a control, field, or property on the form or report and display an error message if an item with such name doesn't exist.

Access Basic Syntax

Not available in Access Basic; set values directly from Access Basic code.

See Also

Actions: RepaintObject and SendKeys

SetWarnings Miscellaneous

Turns on or off Access messages.

Arguments

Warning On displays the system messages if set to Yes. The default is No.

Usage Notes

The **SetWarnings** action suppresses only warnings and modal-system messages in a macro; it doesn't suppress error messages.

If the warning messages are turned off in the macro, Access resets warning messages after the macro executes.

Tip

Debug a macro throughly before turning off the warning messages.

Access Basic Syntax

DoCmd **SetWarnings** *warnings on*

Access Basic Example

Turn on warning messages before executing a macro:

```
DoCmd SetWarnings True
```

See Also

Action: Echo

ShowAllRecords

Access Object Manipulation

Removes active filters and conditions from the underlying recordset of a form.

Applies to

Forms

Arguments

None

Usage Notes

The **ShowAllRecords** action removes any existing filters and conditions from the underlying recordset and requeries it, causing Access to display all records (including those changed or added) on a form.

Access Basic Syntax

DoCmd **ShowAllRecords**

See Also

Actions: ApplyFilter, OpenForm, RepaintObject, Requery, and SetValue

StopAllMacros

Execution

Stops all running macros.

Applies to

Macros

Arguments

None

Usage Notes

If echo is turned off, the StopAllMacros action turns it back on.

Access Basic Syntax

Not available in Access Basic.

See Also

Actions: Echo and StopMacro

StopMacro — Execution

Stops the running macro.

Applies to

Macros

Arguments

None

Usage Notes

If echo is turned off, the StopMacro action turns it back on.

Example

See StopAllMacros action.

Access Basic Syntax

Not available in Access Basic.

See Also

Actions: Echo and StopAllMacros

TransferDatabase

Import/Export

Imports or exports data between an Access database and other databases or attaches a native table from another database system to the Access database.

Applies to

Databases

Arguments

Transfer Type is the type of transfer to perform: Import (default), Export, Attach Table.

Database Type is the database type to import from: in Access version 1.0, Microsoft Access (default), Paradox 3.x, FoxPro 2.0, dBASE III, dBASE IV, Btrieve, and SQL Database; in Access version 1.1, and FoxPro 2.5. *Database Name* is the name of the database to perform the import from, export to, or attach to. Enter the Access database name for Access database. For file-oriented database systems (such as dBASE or Paradox) enter the file name with the applicable extension. For Btrieve databases, enter the file name of the DDF file. For SQL databases, enter the entire ODBC connect string.

Object Type is the type of the object to import or export. Select Table (default), Query, Form, Report, Macro, or Module. This selection is applicable only if the specified *database type* is Microsoft Access. If any other type is selected, or *transfer type* is Attach Table, this argument is ignored (it defaults to Table).

Source is the name of the table or Access object to import, export, or attach.

Destination is the name of the imported, exported, or attached table or Access object in the destination database.

Structure Only imports or exports the structure of the Access table only if Yes (or True in Access Basic). Applicable only to Microsoft Access tables being transferred between Access databases. The default is No.

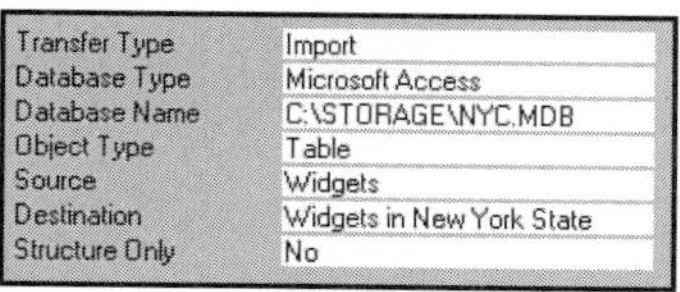

Transfer Type	Import
Database Type	Microsoft Access
Database Name	C:\STORAGE\NYC.MDB
Object Type	Table
Source	Widgets
Destination	Widgets in New York State
Structure Only	No

Usage Notes

Tables ("files" in some database systems) can be imported and exported between Access and other database systems. Other Access database objects can be imported and exported only between two Access databases.

Currently there is no means in Access Basic to directly attach a table (file) from another database system with its index(es). Such an operation must be performed manually using the Import/Export dialog box.

Caution

If the table (or an Access object) being exported to another database already exists, it is replaced without a warning!

Access Basic Syntax

DoCmd **TransferDatabase** [*transfer type*] [, *database type*, *database name*] [, *object type*], *source*, *destination* [, *structure only*]

You may use the following Access intrinsic constants for the *transfer type* argument:

0	A_IMPORT (default)
1	A_EXPORT
2	A_ATTACH

You may use the following Access intrinsic constants for the *object type* argument:

0	A_TABLE (default)
1	A_QUERY
2	A_FORM
3	A_REPORT
4	A_MACRO
5	A_MODULE

Use True (-1) or False (0) for the *structure only* argument. The default is False.

Access Basic Example

Use this example to import a dBASE IV WATER.DBF file to a new Access table called Water Contamination:

```
DoCmd TransferDatabase ,"dBASE IV", "C:\DB415\DEV\WATER.DBF",,
➥"C:\DB415\DEV\WATER.DBF", "Water Contamination"
```

See Also

Actions: TransferSpreadsheeet and TransferText

TransferSpreadsheet

Import/Export

Imports or exports data between an Acces database and a spreadsheet file.

Applies to

Tables

Arguments

Transfer Type is the type of transfer to perform: Import (default) or Export.

Spreadsheet Type is the type of spreadsheet to import from or export to—in Access version 1.0; Microsoft Excel (default); and Lotus 1-2-3 WKS, WK1, and WK3 files.

Table Name is the name of the Access table to import data to or to export from. If Import is selected, and the table doesn't exist, Access will create one.

File Name is the name of the file to import from or export to. It must include the file name (with extension if applicable). It also may include a drive designation and/or path.

If *Has Field Names* is set to Yes (or True in Access Basic), Access uses the field names as field names in a table when importing data from a spreadsheet, or inserts names of the Access table fields into the first row of the created spreadsheet when exporting data.

Range is the range of the spreadsheet cells to import. If omitted, the entire spreadsheet is imported. This is not applicable to exporting data from Access (but does not generate an error when used with Export).

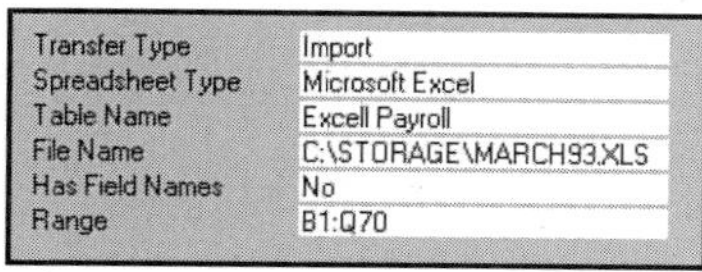

Transfer Type	Import
Spreadsheet Type	Microsoft Excel
Table Name	Excell Payroll
File Name	C:\STORAGE\MARCH93.XLS
Has Field Names	No
Range	B1:Q70

Usage Notes

Spreadsheet data being appended to an existing Access table must match (both order and type) the structure of this table. If *has field names* is set to Yes (or True in Access Basic), the field names (and data types) must match the Access table field names as well.

Access version 1.0 cannot export data to Microsoft Excel versions 3.0 and 4.0, and Lotus 1-2-3, or WK3 files (although data can be imported from these formats). Access generates a `Not a valid value for Spreadsheet Type argument` error (trappable error #2508) if "3" (WK3 file) is specified as *spreadsheet type*. Access version 1.1 has these restrictions removed.

Access Basic Syntax

DoCmd **TransferSpreadsheet** [*transfer type*] [, *spreadsheet type*] *table name*, *file name* [, *has field names*] [, *range*]

You may use one or more of the following Access constants for the *transfer type* argument:

0	A_IMPORT (default)
1	A_EXPORT

For *spreadsheet type,* use the following numbers only:

0	Microsoft Excel (default)
1	Lotus 1-2-3 (WKS files)
2	Lotus 1-2-3 (WK1 files)
3	Lotus 1-2-3 (WK3 files)

Access Basic Example

Import a range of cells from the Lotus 1-2-3 WK1 file (version 2.01) spreadsheet named Exp92 into Access table Expenses 1992

```
DoCmd TransferSpreadsheet, , 2, "Expenses 1992", "C:\123\1992\EXP92.WK1", ,"B1:F30"
```

See Also

Actions: TransferDatabase and TransferText

TransferText

Import/Export

Imports or exports data between an Access table and a text file.

Applies to

Tables

Arguments

Transfer Type is the type of transfer to perform: Import Delimited (default), Import Fixed Width, Export Delimited, or Export Fixed Width.

Specification Name is the name of the previously defined (using the **Import/Export Setup** selection from the File menu) import/export specification. This argument may be omitted for delimited import/export. Access then uses the Import/Export Setup defaults. This argument is required for import/export of fixed-width data.

Table Name is the name of the Access table to import from or export to. If the Import operation is selected as *transfer type* and the specified table doesn't exist, Access creates one.

File Name is the name of the text file to import from or export to. It must contain the file name. This argument may contain drive designation and/or path.

If *Has Field Names* is Yes, Access treats the first row of data as containing field names. If an export operation is selected as *transfer type*, Access puts field names in the first row. If *has field names* is No, the first row is treated as regular data. The default is No.

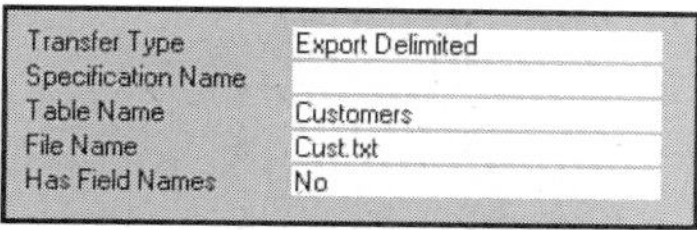

Transfer Type	Export Delimited
Specification Name	
Table Name	Customers
File Name	Cust.txt
Has Field Names	No

Usage Notes

If *has field names* is set to Yes (or True in Access Basic), and an Import operation is selected as *transfer type*, the field names in the text file and in the Access table must match, or a `None of the import field names match fields in the appended table` error (trappable error #3243) occurs.

If you specify **Export Fixed** or **Import Fixed** (or A_EXPORTFIXED or A_IMPORTFIXED in Access Basic), you must use the existing *specification name* or a `A Specification Name is required for fixed-width import/export` error (trappable in error #2511) occurs.

Currently Access Basic has no means of creating *specification name* programatically. You must use an existing *specification name* if one is required.

Caution:

Access version 1.0 exports mutliword table field names with all spaces between the words removed. A field named **Four Word Field Name** will be exported as **FourWordFieldName**, for example, and is therefore not suitable for reimporting into the same Access table.

Access Basic Syntax

DoCmd **TransferText** [*transfer type*] [, *specification name*][,*table name*][,*file name*] [, *has field names*]

You may use one or more of the following Access constants for the *transfer type* argument:

0	A_IMPORTDELIM (default)
1	A_IMPORTFIXED
2	A_EXPORTDELIM
3	A_EXPORTFIXED

Use True (-1) or False (0) for the *has field names* argument. The default is False.

Example

Export the contents of the MSA Errors table to a comma-delimited text file named A_ERR.TXT. The first row of the MSA_ERR.TXT will contain the field names.

```
DoCmd TransferText A_EXPORTDELIM, , "MSA Errors", "MSA_ERR.TXT", True
```

See Also

Actions: TransferDatabase and TransferSpreadsheet

Functions

Abs

Math

Returns the absolute value of a number.

Syntax

Abs(*number*)

number is any number or an expression that evaluates to a number.

Usage Notes

number can be used to find the range of two numbers.

If the argument is Null, Abs returns Null.

The data type of the result is the same as the arguments.

If a string expression (Variant VarType 8) can be converted to a number, Abs returns the result as Double (Variant VarType 5). For further explanation of this behavior, see Chapter 10, "Understanding Access Data Types."

An empty string results in a `Type mismatch` error (trappable error #13).

You also can use the Abs function to convert hexadecimal (base 16) and octal (base 8) numbers to positive decimal numbers.

Examples

The following examples show the results of the Abs function with different data types:

```
Result = Abs(-1.34)          ' 1.34
Result = Abs(1)              ' 1
Result = Abs(#01-01-92#)     ' 1/1/92
Result = Abs(20-(-90))       ' 110(range of two numbers)
Result = Abs(&HA)            ' 10 (hexadecimal A)
Result = Abs(&O12)           ' 10 (octal 12)
```

Note

The following expression returns a Type mismatch error when executed from the immediate window.

```
? Abs("1")                        ' Error #13
```

The same example works fine if called from within a program, however:

```
Result = Abs("1")                 ' 1
```

See Also

Functions: Atn, Cos, Exp, Fix, Int, Log, Rnd, Sgn, Sin, Sqr, and Tan

Asc

Conversion

Returns the ANSI code for the first character of a string argument.

Syntax

Asc(*expression*)

expression is any Variant data type, except Null.

Usage Notes

All types of the Variant data type, except Variant 0 (Null), are converted to String. Null, a zero-length string and a non-variant data type generates a `Type mismatch` error (trappable error #13). Passing an explicit number (such as *Result = Asc(1)*) generates a compile-time error.

Example

The following example illustrates using the Asc function with various arguments:

```
nNumber = 1
Result = Asc(nNumber)             ' 49 (number 1)
Result = Asc("a")                 ' 97 (lowercase a)
Result = Asc("Aloha")             ' 65 (uppercase A)
```

Caution

Always test for Null and zero-length strings before using the Asc( ) function to avoid a Type mismatch error. Convert non-variant data to Variant before using the Asc function.

See Also

Functions: Chr, Chr$, and CVar (in Data Type Conversion section)

Atn

Math

Returns the arctangent of a number.

Syntax

Atn(*number*)

number is any valid numeric expression representing the ratio of two sides of a right triangle.

Usage Notes

Atn returns the angle corresponding to the ratio (the length of the side opposite to the angle divided by the length of the side adjacent to the angle) of two sides of a right triangle.

Atn returns the result in radians, in the range -Π/2 to Π/2.

To express the result in degrees, multiply it by 180/Π.

See Also

Functions: Cos, Sin, and Tan

Avg

SQL

Returns the average (arithmetic mean) of values in a specified field.

Syntax

Avg(*expression*)

expression is a field name containing values to average; the name of a control in the form, query, or report; or an expression that uses values in that field or control to perform calculations.

Usage Notes

Avg can be used only in queries, reports, and forms; use the DAvg function in Access Basic code.

The Avg function returns the sum of all the values divided by the number of values. Null values are discarded.

expression cannot contain other aggregate SQL or domain functions (such as Count or Sum).

Avg can be a part of the SQL SELECT statement.

Examples

The following examples show two usages of the Avg function.

Usage in a control in a form or report:

```
= Avg( [Employee age] )
= Avg( Year(Now()) - Year([Employee Dob] )
```

Usage as a part of an expression:

```
SELECT Avg([Item price]) FROM Sales WHERE [Item Name] = "Widget1"
```

See Also

Functions: DAvg, Count, First, Last, Min, Max, StDev, StDevP, Sum, Var, and VarP

Choose

Program Flow Control

Returns a choice (value) from a list of arguments based on the value of the *indexnum*.

Syntax

Choose(*indexnum, varexpr1 [, varexpr2]...[, varexpr13]*)

indexnum is the ordinal position of the desired choice from the list of choices contained in varexpr1...varexpr13. It must evaluate to a number between 1 and the number of *varexpr* choices (but no more than 13).

varexpr can be any Variant expression that evaluates to a number, date, or string. A maximum of 13 *varexpr* expressions are allowed.

Usage Notes

Choose returns Null if *indexnum* evaluates to less than 1 or more than the actual number of choices. A `Type mismatch` error (trappable error # 13) occurs when *indexnum* cannot be evaluated as a number.

All fractional values of *indexnum* are rounded to the next whole number.

Examples

The *varexpr* argument of the Choose function can be an expression, as shown in the following example:

```
Dim a As Variant, b As Variant
a = "DOS"
b = "MS Windows"
Result = Choose(2, "DOS", a & " and " & b, "Solaris", "Unix")
' in this case Result equals "DOS and MS Windows"
```

Different data types such as numbers, strings, and date/time may be mixed in one call to Choose. The following example is just for the record (it has a very limited practical use):

```
Result = Choose(1, Now(), 12 /4, "DOS", "Now is " & Time() )
```

Caution

Because all varexpr choices are evaluated by the Choose function, avoid using screen I/O functions (such as MsgBox, InputBox); these appear on-screen every time the Choose function is called.

See Also

Functions: DLookup, Fix, IIf, and Switch

Chr, Chr$

Conversion

Return a character represented by a number. Chr returns a variant data type; Chr$ returns a string.

Syntax

Chr[$](*number*)

number is an integer or a string (Variant 8) that can be converted into a number between 0 and 255.

Usage Notes

An out-of-range argument results in an `Illegal function call` error (trappable error #5).

A null value or an empty string generates a `Type mismatch` error (trappable error #13).

Examples

The following examples illustrate sample calls to the Chr( ) function:

```
Result = Chr(65)                ' Uppercase A
Result = Chr("97")              ' Lowercase a
Result = Chr(256)               ' Error #5
```

See Also

Functions: Asc, Str, and Str$

Appendix C, "ANSI Character Set"

FUNCTIONS

CodeDB

Database Manipulation

Returns a reference to the database object containing the currently executing code. This function is documented only in the ADK (Access Distribution Kit).

Syntax

CodeDB( )

Usage Notes

If the code executes from the same database, the CodeDB and CurrentDB( ) functions behave identically.

The value returned by the CodeDB function is most often used to identify the database containing executable code. This value is particularly useful to run code from a library database (such as Wizards) but can also be used to manipulate two databases simultaneously.

Example

Use the CodeDB function to refer to objects in the database containing code, forms, queries, and so on to manipulate data in a database opened with the OpenDatabase function:

```
Dim  c As Database, d As Database, t As Table
Set c = CodeDB()
Set d = OpenDatabase("Sales")
Set t = d.OpenTable("April 1992")
(...)
```

See Also

Function: CurrentDB

Code in WIZARD.MDA (included with MS Access)

Chapter 13, "Extending Microsoft Access and Access Basic"

Command, Command$

Miscellaneous

Return command line arguments used to start Access. Command returns a Variant; Command$ returns a String.

Syntax

Command[**$**]*[()]*

Usage Notes

The empty parentheses must be included only if Command is used outside Access Basic, such as in an expression placed directly in a form or report property.

You can use the Command function in conjunction with the Autoexec macro to launch specific applications depending, for example, on the name of the user or options included on the command line.

Example

Start Access with the /cmd command line option (from the Program Manager):

C:\ACCESS\ACCESS.EXE /cmd "Greetings from the Program Manager"

If you enter the following line in the Immediate window, the message box displays `The command line is Greetings from the Program Manager`:

```
? MsgBox("The command line is " & Command)
```

See Also

Action: Autoexec

Cos

Math

Returns the cosine of an angle in radians.

Syntax

Cos(*angle*)

angle can be any valid number or expression measured in radians.

Usage Notes

Cos returns the ratio of two sides of a right triangle in the range -1 to 1.

To convert radians to degrees, multiply radians by 180 divided by the constant Π. To convert degrees to radians multiply degrees by the constant Π divided by 180.

See Also

Functions: Atn, Sin, and Tan

Count

SQL

Returns the number of selected records in a query, form, or report.

Syntax

Count(*expression*)

expression can be a field name containing values to count, the name of a control in a form, query, or report, or an expression that uses values in that field or control to perform calculations.

Usage Notes

Count can be used only in queries, reports, and forms. Use the DCount function in Access Basic code.

The Count function returns the sum of all the values. Null values are not counted unless Count is used to count all records and *expression* is a wild card (*).

expression cannot contain other aggregate SQL or domain functions (such as Count or Sum).

If *expression* includes more than one field name, the record is counted only if at least one of the fields is not Null.

Count can be a part of the SQL SELECT statement.

Examples

The following examples demonstrate various usages of the Count function.

To count all records in the Employee table:

```
SELECT Count (*) FROM [Employees]
```

To count all employees named "Smith"

```
SELECT Count [Employee SSN] FROM [Employees] WHERE [Employee name] = "Smith"
```

Usage in the control of a form or report with control names as arguments:

```
= Count([Employee name] & [Employee DOB] )
```

See Also

Functions: Avg, DAvg, DCount, First and Last, Min and Max, StDev, StDevP, Sum, Var, and VarP

Property: RecordCount

CreateControl CreateReportControl

Object Manipulation

Creates a control on a specified open form or report and returns the control object. These functions are documented only in the ADK (Access Distribution Kit).

Syntax

CreateControl(form_name, control_type [, section_number [, parent [,field_name[, posX,
➥posY]]]])

or

CreateReportControl(report_name, control_type [, section_number [,
➥parent [,field_name[, posX, posY]]]])

form_name, report_name identifies an open form or report on which to create the control.

control_type is a number identifying the type of control.

section_number is a number identifying the section which will contain the control.

parent is the name of the parent control; if any, use the zero-length string ("").

field_name is the name of the field to which the control is bound.

posX, posY is the vertical and horizontal coordinates of the control relative to the upper left corner of the form/report expressed in twips.

Usage Notes

CreateControl/CreateReportControl allows programmatic change to a form or report; both functions are primarily used to write Wizards.

control_type can be any of the values described in the following table.

Value	*Control Type*
100	label
101	box
102	line
103	picture
104	pushbutton
105	radiobutton
106	checkbox

continues

FUNCTIONS

Value	*Control Type*
107	option group
108	OLE object
109	text box
110	list box
111	combo box
112	subform/subreport

section_number can possess any of the values described in the following table.

Section Number	*Description*
0	Detail section (Default)
1	Form or report header
2	Form or report footer
3	Form or report page header
4	Form or report page footer
5	Reports group level 1 header
6	Reports group level 1 footer
7	Reports group level 2 header
8	Reports group header 2 footer

If a report has more than two group levels, additional pairs of header/footer sections are numbered consecutively starting with 9.

If *section_number* is omitted, 0 is assumed.

Setting *field_name* bounds the control to the field; defaults from the underlying table (such as validation rule, default value) are set for this control.

If *posX* and *posY* are omitted, the control is created starting with the upper left corner of the form or report.

Example

Create a new form, assign the record source property, create a pushbutton control labeled Exit in the detail section of the form, and assign a close form action to its *OnPush* property:

```
Dim f As Form, s As String, c As Control
Const CT_PUSHBUTTON = 104
Set f = CreateForm("","")
s = f.formname
f.RecordSource = "MyTable"

' Create a pushbutton
Set c = CreateControl(s, CT_PUSHBUTTON, ,"",1000, 1000)
c.Caption = "Exit"
c.OnPush = "=ExitForm()"                ' or whatever...
(...)
```

See Also

Functions: CreateGroupLevel, CreateReportControl, CreateReport, DeleteControl, and DeleteReportControl

Property: ControlSource

CreateForm
CreateReport

Object Manipulation

Creates a new form or report. This function is documented only in the ADK (Access Distribution Kit).

Syntax

CreateForm*([database[, template]])*

or

CreateReport*([database[, template]])*

database identifies the database that stores the report or form template.

template identifies the name of the form or report template.

The alternate syntax is:

CreateForm( )

or

CreateReport( )

Usage Notes

If database is omitted (or a zero-length string are used), the current database is assumed.

If template is omitted (or a literal Normal or a zero-length string is used), the standard template set with the Options command from the View menu is assumed.

This function is necessary to create a blank form or report from within Access Basic and is roughly equivalent to selecting New Form/Report from the File menu. After creating the new form/report you can modify its properties, create controls, and access them from within ABC.

Example

Using the CreateForm function to create a new form:

```
Dim cForm as Form, szName as String
Set cForm = CreateForm("","")
szName = cForm.formname
(...)
DoCmd Close A_FORM, szName
```

See Also

Functions: CreateControl, CreateGroupLevel, CreateReportControl, CreateReport, DeleteControl, and DeleteReportControl

Code in WIZARD.MDA library

Chapter 13, "Extending Microsoft Access and Access Basic"

CreateGroupLevel

Object Manipulation

Creates a new group level on a specified report and returns its ID. This function is documented only in the ADK (Access Distribution Kit).

Syntax

CreateGroupLevel(report, expression, header, footer)

report is the report name (string).

expression is the group level name (string).

header, footer indicates the presence of a header and/or footer in the group (boolean).

Usage Notes

Use this function to create a new group level on a report, and—optionally—group header and/or footer for this group.

This function works only with report objects; attempting to use it with other objects, such as forms, triggers an `Invalid reference to report <name>` error (trappable error #2451).

This function is particularly useful in writing Access libraries such as wizards.

Caution

If the Sorting and Grouping dialog box on the report design surface is open while using the CreateGroupLevel function, a `Can't execute this function with the Sorting and Grouping box open` error (trappable error #3041) occurs.

Example

Create a new report with two group levels (one with the footer and header, the other without footer and header).

```
Dim orRpt As Report, szName As String, id1 As Variant, id2 As Variant
Set orRpt = CreateReport("","")
szName = orRpt.FormName
' Create two group levels
id1 = CreateGroupLevel(szName, "Test Group 1", True, True)
id2 = CreateGroupLevel(szName, "Test Group 2", False, False)
(...)
```

See Also

Functions: CreateControl, CreateForm, CreateReportControl, CreateReport, DeleteControl, and DeleteReportControl

Property: GroupLevel

CreateReport

Object Manipulation

See the "CreateForm" function.

CreateReportControl

Object Manipulation

See the "CreateControl" function.

CurDir, CurDir$

File I/O

Returns the current (logged) directory for the specified drive. CurDir returns a Variant; CurDir$ returns a String.

Syntax

CurDir[*$*][(*drive letter*)]

drive letter must be in the range from A to Z, in either lower- or uppercase, (or the last available drive specified in the CONFIG.SYS file with the LASTDRIVE statement).

Usage Notes

If no drive is specified, or the argument is an empty string, the function returns the current directory on the current drive.

The empty parentheses must be included only if CurDir is used outside Access Basic, such as in an expression placed directly in a form or report property, and no drive is specified.

Passing a letter for a nonexistent drive triggers a `Device unavailable` error (trappable error #68).

Passing a non-alphabetic argument triggers an `Illegal function call` error (trappable error #5).

Trying to access a removable disk drive without a disk in it results in a `Disk not ready` error (trappable error #71).

Example

Assuming that the start-up directory for Access is (C:\ACCESS), all three of the following usages of the CurDir function return the same answer:

```
Result = CurDir("C")          ' C:\ACCESS

Result = CurDir()             ' C:\ACCESS
Result = CurDir               ' C:\ACCESS
```

Caution

The literal drive letter must be enclosed in quotes. Passing a drive letter without quotes returns the current directory on the current drive, as in the following example:

```
Result = CurDir(A)            ' C:\ACCESS
Result = CurDir("A")          ' A:\
```

See Also

Statements: ChDir, ChDrive, MkDir, and RmDir

Functions: Dir and Dir$

DeleteControl DeleteReportControl

Object Manipulation

Delete a specified control from a form or report. These functions are documented only in the ADK (Access Distribution Kit).

Syntax

DeleteControl form_name, control_name

or

DeleteReportControl report_name, control_name

form_name and *report_name* identify the name of the form or report that contains the control.

control_name identifies the control to delete.

Usage Notes

Only controls on the active form or report can be deleted; if *form_name* or *report_name* refers to a form/report that is not active (open), `Invalid reference to form/report <name>` errors (trappable errors #2450 and #2451, respectively) occur.

If the form or report is not active, use SelectObject action to activate a form or report before using these statements.

If *control_name* refers to a nonexisting control an `Invalid reference to control` error (trappable error #2453) is triggered.

Tip

Use these functions to remove unwanted labels that are created automatically with some controls (such as text boxes).

Example

Create a new report, create a default text box control in the detail section, name it, and then delete it from the report:

```
Dim orRpt As Report, szName as String, c As Control
Set orRpt = CreateReport("","")
szName = orRpt.FormName
Set c = CreateReportControl(szName, 109, 0, "")
c.controlname = "MyTextBox"
DeleteReportControl szName, "MyTextBox"
(...)
```

See Also

Functions: CreateControl, CreateForm, CreateGroupLevel, CreateReportControl, and CreateReport

Action: SelectObject

DeleteReportControl

See the "DeleteControl" function.

CurrentDB

Database Manipulation

Returns the name of the current database object.

Syntax

CurrentDB( )

This function accepts no arguments.

Usage Notes

CurrentDB can be used only in Access Basic code; it cannot be attached directly to properties and controls.

The name of the current database object, supplied by CurrentDB, is a required argument in methods that perform data manipulation and navigation within a table in this database.

Failing to declare the receiving variable as a database object results in a compile-time `Invalid object reference` error message.

Example

Using the currentDB function to initialize an object variable that points to the current Access database:

```
Dim CurrDB as Database, CurrTable as Table
Set CurrDB = CurrentDB()
Set CurrTable = CurrDB.OpenTable("Test")
(...)
CurrTable.Close
CurrDB.Close
```

See Also

Functions: CodeDB and OpenDatabase

Methods: Close and OpenTable

Statement: Dim

CVDate

Conversion

Converts an expression to date data type (a Variant of VarType 7).

Syntax

CVdate(*expression*)

expression must be a string or a number that can be interpreted as a date.

Usage Notes

If *expression* evaluates to a number, it must be in the range of –657434 to 2958465 (representing January 1, 100 and December 31, 9999, respectively). Numbers outside this range generate a `Type mismatch` error (trappable error #13). The same error is generated if the string expression cannot be interpreted as a date.

CVDate converts any fractional part of a number to time, starting at 12:00:00 AM, with 0.00001 equal to 12:00:01 AM and 0.99999 equal to 11:59:59 PM.

If *expression* is a Null, CVDate returns Null. An invalid date passed as the argument (for example, February 31, 1992) is treated as a Null.

Examples

Results of the CVDate function with different arguments:

```
Result = CVDate(34000)              ' 1/31/1993
Result = CVDate(34000.00100)        ' 1/31/1993 12:01:26 AM
Result = CVDate("Jan 31, 1993")     ' 1/31/1993
Result = CVDate("USA")              ' Error #13
Result = CVDate("Feb 30, 1993")     ' #NULL#
Result = CVDate("0.1")              ' 12:01:00 AM
Result = CVDate(".1")               '  2:24:00 AM
Result = CVDate(.1)                 '  2:24:00 AM
```

See Also

Functions: DateSerial and IsDate

Data Type Conversion Functions

Conversion

These functions convert *expression* to the specified data type.

FUNCTIONS

Syntax

Syntax	*Converts to*
CCur(*expression*)	Currency
CDbl(*expression*)	Double
CInt(*expression*)	Integer
CLng(*expression*)	Long
CSng(*expression*)	Single
Cstr(*expression*)	String
CVar(*expression*)	Variant

expression can be any valid data type.

Usage Notes

Use these functions to change the type of the result of a calculation (to express a result of a multiplication of two Long numbers as the Currency data type, for example).

If the result of the conversion falls outside of the range of allowed values for CCur, CInt, Clng, and Csng, an `Illegal function call` runtime error (trappable error #5) occurs.

A null value (Variant of VarType 1) can be used only with the CVar function (which in such a case will return a Null). Passing a Null expression to any other data conversion function triggers an `Invalid use of Null` error (trappable error # 94).

These functions can also be used to convert hexadecimal (base 16) and octal (base 8) numbers to a specified data type.

Examples

The first example shows the possible difference between using the CCur function versus performing straight calculations:

```
Result = CCur(1234.56789 * .075)        '92.5926 (Currency data type)
Result = 1234.56789 * .075              '92.59259175 (Double data type)
```

The following example shows the difference in operation between CInt and Int and Fix functions:

```
Result = CInt(1.5)                      ' 2
Result = Int(1.5)                       ' 1
```

See Also

Functions: Int and Fix

Chapter 10, "Understanding Access Data Types"

Date, Date$

Date and Time

Returns the current system date.

Syntax

Date[$][()]

Usage Notes

Date returns a Date data type (Variant of VarType 7).

Dates$ returns a character string formatted as month-day-year. Its output is equivalent to the following:

Format$ (Now, "mm-dd-yyyy")

Example

Sample dates are returned by these functions:

```
Result = Date                          ' 1/1/93
Result = Date$                         ' 01-01-1993
```

See Also

Functions: CVDate, Format and Format$, and Now

Statements: Date and Date$

Chapter 10, "Understanding Access Data Types"

FUNCTIONS

DateAdd

Date and Time

Adds a number of specified intervals to a date.

Syntax

DateAdd(*interval, number, date*)

interval is a string expression that specifies the interval of time to add to the date. The following table describes the valid intervals. (The same intervals are also used by DateDiff, DatePart, and Format functions.)

interval	*Description*
yyyy	Year
q	Quarter
m	Month
y	Day of year
d	Day
w	Weekday
ww	Week
h	Hour
n	Minute
s	Second

number is a numeric expression that specifies the number of intervals to add to the date. If *number* is negative, it subtracts the interval from the date.

date is a date (Variant of VarType 7), or date/time expression to which to add (or subtract) the number of intervals.

Usage Notes

DateAdd performs date arithmetic, and always returns a valid date. Adding 1 month to January 31 1993, for example, returns 2/28/1993—not 2/31/1993.

If the year is omitted from the date and the date is enclosed in double quotation marks, the current year is inserted at runtime. If the date is delimited by number signs (#), the current year is inserted as a permanent part of the date.

If an invalid interval is passed as an argument to the DateDiff function an `Invalid argument used with DatePart, DateAdd or DateDiff function` error is triggered (trappable error #2468).

Note

Adding a number to a date has the same effect as using the "d" (day) interval; for example, the following two expressions return the same date:

```
Result = Date() + 100
Result = DateAdd("d", 1, Date)
```

Examples

The following examples use different intervals with the DateAdd function:

```
Result = DateAdd("m", 1, "Jan 31, 1993)              ' 2/28/1993
Result = DateAdd("w",12, #01/01/93#)                 ' 1/13/1993
```

```
Result = DateAdd("yyyy", 3, #02/29/92#)              ' 2/28/1995
Result = DateAdd("h", 3, #01/01/93 12:00:00 AM#)     ' 1/1/1993 3:00:00 AM
```

Caution

If the resulting date is greater than Dec 31, 9999, or smaller than Jan 1, 100 (year one hundred), the DateAdd function triggers an `Illegal function call` error (trappable error #5). When using day, day of year, and weekday intervals, the result must fall in the range between Jan 1, 100 and Dec 31, 9999. If the resulting date is earlier than Jan 1, 100, DateAdd may return garbage. Consider the following example:

```
Result = DateAdd("d", -691404, "01/01/1993")     ' 1/1/100
Result = DateAdd("d", -691405, "01/01/1993")     ' - 657435
Result = DateAdd("d", 400, "Jan 31 9999")        ' Error #5
```

See Also

Functions: Date and Date$, DateDiff, DatePart, and Now

Statements: Date and Date$

Chapter 10, "Understanding Access Data Types" (section "Working with Date and Time Values")

DateDiff

Date and Time

Returns the number of specified intervals between two dates.

Syntax

DateDiff(*interval, date1, date2*)

interval is a string expression that specifies the interval of time to add to the date. The following table describes valid intervals. (The same intervals are also used by DateAdd, DatePart, and Format functions.)

interval	*Description*
yyyy	Year
q	Quarter
m	Month
y	Day of year
d	Day
w	Weekday
ww	Week

continues

FUNCTIONS

interval	*Description*
h	Hour
n	Minute
s	Second

date1 and *date2* are expressions that evaluate to valid dates or date/time fields.

Usage Notes

If *date2* is smaller than *date1*, DateDiff returns a negative number.

DateDiff returns only whole intervals. It doesn't return, for example, "1 week 3 days 4 hours and 37 minutes."

If the year is omitted from the date and the date is enclosed in double quotation marks, the current year is inserted at runtime. If the date is delimited by number signs (#) the current year is inserted as a permanent part of the date.

If an invalid interval is passed as an argument to the DateDiff function an `Invalid argument used with DatePart, DateAdd or DateDiff function` error is triggered (trappable error #2468).

Examples

The following example calculates the number of weeks between two dates:

```
Result = DateDiff("ww", #1/3/93#, #1/16/93#)          ' 1
```

The following example calculates the number of minutes between two time values:

```
Result = DateDiff("n", #12:00:00 AM#, #11:59:59 AM#)   ' 719
```

See Also

Functions: Date and Date$, DateAdd, DatePart, DateSerial, and Now

DatePart

Date and Time

Returns a specified part of a date.

Syntax

DatePart*(interval, date)*

interval is a string expression that specifies the interval of time to add to the date. The following table describes valid intervals. (The same intervals are also used by DateAdd, DatePart, and Format functions.)

interval	*Description*
yyyy	Year
q	Quarter
m	Month
y	Day of year
d	Day
w	Weekday (Sunday = 1, Saturday = 7)
ww	Week
h	Hour
n	Minute
s	Second

date is a date or date/time expression, or a reference to a date/time field.

Usage Notes

If the year is omitted from the date and the date is enclosed in double quotation marks, the current year is inserted at runtime. If the date is delimited by number signs (#), the current year is inserted as a permanent part of the date.

If an invalid interval is passed as an argument to the DateDiff function an `Invalid argument used with DatePart, DateAdd or DateDiff function` error is triggered (trappable error #2468).

Example

The following example calculates the quarter in which a particular date falls:

```
Result = DatePart("q", Now)
```

See Also

Functions: Date, DateAdd, DatePart, Day, Format, Hour, Minute, Month, Now, Second, Weekday, and Year

FUNCTIONS

DateSerial

Conversion

Returns the date serial for a specified date component.

Syntax

DateSerial(*year, month, day*)

year is a number, or an expression that evaluates to a number. It must fall between 0 and 9999.

month is a number, or an expression that evaluates to a number. For meaningful results, *month* should fall between 1 and 12.

day is a number, or an expression that evaluates to a number. For meaningful results, day should fall between 1 and 31.

Usage Notes

DateSerial returns a date data type (Variant of VarType 7) in the range January 1, 100 through December 31, 9999.

The theoretical range for all arguments (year, month, and day) is the range of an integer (-32,768 to 32,767). Numbers outside of the range of an integer trigger an `Overflow` error message (trappable error #6).

If the year falls outside the 0 through 9999 range, an `Illegal function call` error message is returned.

Examples

Three integers (1993,12,3) will produce a valid date (Variant of VarType 7):

```
Dim a%, b%, c%
a = 1993: b = 12: c = 3
Result = DateSerial(a, b, c)          ' 12/3/1993
```

If either day or month fall outside of the practical range, the DateSerial function performs the date arithmetic and returns a valid date.

```
Result = DateSerial(1993, 97, 1)      ' 1/1/2001
```

See Also

Functions: DateValue, Day, Month, Now, Weekday, and Year

DateValue

Conversion

Returns the date represented by an expression.

Syntax

DateValue*(expression)*

expression is a string representing a valid date and/or time information.

Usage Notes

DateValue returns a date data type (Variant of VarType 7) in the range January 1, 100 through December 31, 9999.

DateValue recognizes date formats set in the international section of the WIN.INI file and other unambiguous date expressions, such as: *Jan 1 1993*, *30-Dec-87*, and so on.

If the year is omitted from the expression, DateValue uses the current year.

DateValue doesn't return time information if a valid time is included in the expression.

Example

The following example converts a string expression to a valid date:

```
Dim sString as String
sString = "Dec-30-1990"
Debug.Print VarType(sString)          ' 8 (string)
Result = DateValue(sString)
Debug.Print VarType(Result)           ' 7 (date)
```

See Also

Functions: Data Type Conversion Functions, DateSerial, Day, Month, Now, Weekday, and Year

FUNCTIONS

DAvg

Domain

Returns the average (arithmetic mean) of values in a specified domain.

Syntax

DAvg*(expression, domain [, criteria])*

expression can be a field name containing values to average, the name of a control in the form, query, or report, or an expression that uses values in that field or control to perform calculations. The expression cannot contain other aggregate SQL or domain functions (such as Avg or Sum).

domain identifies the record source; it may be a table or query name, or an SQL expression.

criteria identifies the range of data to average. If *criteria* is omitted, DAvg operates on the entire domain.

Usage Notes

The DAvg function returns the sum of all the values in the specified domain divided by the number of values. Null values are discarded.

When a non-numeric field is referenced in expression an `Illegal type in expression` error is generated (trappable error #3169). If expression refers to a Memo (or OLE) data type, a `Can't have Memo or OLE object in aggregate argument <name>` error (trappable error #3115) occurs.

DAvg can be used in ABC and directly attached to controls and properties.

Example

The following example uses the DAvg function in a control in a form or report:

```
= DAvg( [Employee age],"Employees","[Employee class] = 'Hourly'" )
```

Caution

Any changes to an edited record should be saved (by invoking the Save Record option of the File menu or by moving the focus to another record) before calling DAvg. In the multiuser environment results returned by DAvg may not contain the current values if data is being edited by another user.

See Also

Functions: Avg, Count, DLookup, First, Last, Min, Max, StDev, StDevP, Sum, Var, and VarP

Day — Conversion

Returns the day of the month.

Syntax

Day(*expression*)

expression can be either a date or a number that represents a date.

Usage Notes

Day returns an integer representing the day of the month for dates in the range January 1, 100 through December 31, 9999.

The year can be omitted from the expression.

If expression evaluates to a Null, Day returns Null.

Example

The following example returns the day of a valid date expression:

```
Result = Day(#01/01/1993#)          ' 1
```

See Also

Functions: Weekday DateAdd, DateDiff, DatePart, DateSerial, DateValue, Hour, Minute, Month, Second, YearDate, Now, and Time

DCount

Domain

Returns the number of selected records in a specified domain.

Syntax

DCount(*expression, domain [,criteria]*)

expression can be a field name containing values to count, the name of a control in the form, query, report, or an expression that uses values in that field or control to perform calculations. *expression* cannot contain other aggregate SQL or domain functions (such as Avg, Sum, etc.).

domain identifies the record source; it may be a table or query name, or an SQL expression.

criteria identifies the range of data to count. If *criteria* is omitted, DCount operates on the entire domain.

Usage Notes

DCount can be used in Access Basic and in queries, reports, and forms.

The DCount function returns the sum of all the values. Null values are not counted unless DCount is used to count all records and the expression is a wild card (*).

If the expression includes more than one field name, the record is counted only if at least one of the fields is not Null. Multiple field names can be separated with either an ampersand (&) or a plus sign (+).

If domain refers to a nonexistent table or query, a `Couldn't find input table or query <name>` error (trappable error #3078) is generated. If either expression or criteria refer to a nonexistent field name or control, an `Invalid reference to control <control name> in query` error (trappable error #2471) occurs.

Examples

The following example counts employees in Employee table with known date of birth:

```
Result = DCount( "[Employee name]", "Employees", "Not IsNull([Employee DOB])" )
```

The following code counts all record in the Employees table:

```
Result = DCount("*", "Employees")
```

Caution

Any changes to an edited record should be saved (by invoking the Save Record option of the File menu or by moving the focus to another record) before calling DCount. In a multiuser environment, results returned by DCount may not contain current values if data is being edited by another user.

See Also

Functions: Avg, DAvg, Count, First and Last, Min and Max, StDev, StDevP, Sum, DSum, Var, and VarP

Property: RecordCount

DDB

Financial

Returns the double-declining balance depreciation of an asset.

Syntax

DDB(*cost, salvage, life, period)*

cost is the initial cost of an asset.

salvage is the value of an asset at the end of its useful life.

life is the length of the useful life of an asset.

period is the period number for which asset depreciation is calculated.

Usage Notes

life and *period* must be expressed in the same units (for example, years or months); if the units are different (for example, *life* is expressed in years and *period* in months), and *period* is greater than *life*, an `Illegal function call` error message is triggered (trappable error #5), A Null or a negative value of any argument generates the same error.

All arguments can be Numeric (VarType 2, 3, 4, 5), Currency (VarType 7), or Variant VarType 8 (String) that can be converted to a number. The data types can be mixed.

An empty string, or a string that cannot be converted to a number, triggers a `Type mismatch` error (trappable error #13).

DDB can be used in ABC and directly attached to controls and properties in forms, reports, and queries.

The DDB function uses the following formula to calculate depreciation over a period:

depreciation = ((cost – total depreciation) * 2) /life

Caution

This function is implemented in the MSAFIN.DLL library, which is installed by Access in the Windows directory, and declared in the UTILITY.MDA database. To access this function from Access version 1.0, you need to load the UTILITY.MDA by placing the following entry in the Options section of the MSACCESS.INI file (found in your Windows program directory):

UtilityDB=<path>UTILITY.MDA

Access version 1.1 loads the UTILITY.MDA automatically.

Examples

The following examples calculate the double-declining balance depreciation of an asset when initial value equals 1000, salvage value equals 50, and the lifetime is 5 years. Depreciation is calculated for the first period.

```
Result = DDB(1000, 50, 5, 1)            '400.00
Result = DDB("1000", 50, 5, "1")        '400.00
```

See Also

Functions: SLN and SYD

DDE

Dynamic Data Exchange

Initiates a dynamic data exchange (DDE) process with another application and returns the requested information.

Syntax

DDE*(application, topic, item)*

application is a valid name of a Windows application used as a DDE server.

topic is a string expression that evaluates to a topic recognized by *application.*

item is a string expression that evaluates to a data item recognized by *application.*

Usage Notes

The Access application becomes a DDE client, and the application from which the data is requested becomes a DDE server. Because Microsoft Access can act as DDE server and client, the DDE function can also seek a DDE request from Access.

The DDE function can be attached only to the Control Source property of the following controls on a form: text box, option group, check box, and combo box. The behavior of the DDE function changes depending on the control to which it is attached:

- *Text box. item* can be either text or number. If *item* refers to a domain (such as a range of cells in a spreadsheet), the DDE function returns the first referenced entry.
- *Option group.* The expression returned by the DDE function determines which button in the option group to select. If the expression cannot be evaluated as a number, or the number doesn't match any buttons in the option group, no button is selected.

  If *item* refers to a domain (such as a range of cells in a spreadsheet), the DDE function returns the first referenced entry.
- *Check box.* If DDE returns 0, the box is cleared. Any non-zero number will select (check) the box.

  If *item* refers to a domain (such as a range of cells in a spreadsheet), or the returned value doesn't evaluate to a number, the box is unavailable.
- *Combo box.* The returned value (or values if *item* refers to a range of values) will be placed in the combo box.

If the request made by DDE fails for any reason (such as the requested application is configured to ignore DDE requests, doesn't recognize the topic or the item, or the maximum number of simultaneous DDE conversation has been exceeded), the function returns a Null. If the requested application isn't running, Access opens a dialog box asking for the user's permission to launch the application.

If the DDE request is successful, the function returns the requested data item as a string (Variant of VarType 8) data type.

Example

The following expression requests a value stored in cell A1 of the Quattro Pro for Windows spreadsheet titled TEST.WB1:

```
= DDE("QPW", "TEST.WB1","A1")
```

Caution

All controls with attached DDE function become read only to the Access application (any changes to data must be made in the server application).

The actual number of simultaneous DDE conversations is limited by the system's memory and resources utilization.

See Also

Functions: DDEInitiate, DDERequest, and DDESend

Chapter 12, "OLE and DDE"

DDEInitiate

Dynamic Data Exchange

Initiates a dynamic data exchange (DDE) conversation with another application.

Syntax

DDEInitiate(*application, topic*)

application is a valid name of a Windows application to be used as a DDE server.

topic is a string expression that evaluates to a topic recognized by *the application*.

Usage Notes

Upon success (when the DDE channel is established), the DDEInitiate function returns a channel number (as a Variant VarType 2) for use with other DDE functions and statements.

If the requested application isn't running, doesn't support DDE, or is configured to ignore DDE requests, or if the specified topic is not available, a `Can't open DDE channel; Microsoft Access couldn't find the specified application and topic` error message (trappable error #282) is triggered.

Caution

Because the actual number of simultaneous DDE conversations is limited by the system's memory and resources utilization, try not to keep unnecessary DDE links open.

See Also

Function: DDERequest

Statements: DDEExecute, DDEPoke, DDETerminate, and DDETerminateAll

Chapter 12, "OLE and DDE"

DDERequest

Dynamic Data Exchange

Requests an item from the DDE server application.

Syntax

DDERequest(*channel, item*)

channel is a number (integer) returned by the DDERequest function.

item is a string expression that evaluates to the name of a data item recognized by the application.

Usage Notes

Only plain text data can be transferred with this function.

If an invalid *channel* is passed to the DDERequest function, a `DDE conversation closed or changed` error (trappable error #292) is triggered.

If the request is successful, DDERequest returns the requested item as a string (Variant VarType 8).

See Also

Function: DDEInitiate

Statements: DDEExecute, DDEPoke, DDETerminate, and DDETerminateAll

Chapter 12, "OLE and DDE"

DDESend

Dynamic Data Exchange

Initiates a dynamic data exchange (DDE) process with another application and sends data to the specified item in that application.

Syntax

DDESend(*application, topic, item, data*)

application is a valid name of a Windows application to be a DDE server.

topic is a string expression that evaluates to a topic recognized by application.

item is a string expression that evaluates to a data item recognized by application.

data is a string to send to application. It can be a literal string or an expression.

Usage Notes

The Access application becomes a DDE server and the application to which the data is sent becomes a DDE client. Because Access can act as a DDE server and client, the DDESend function can also send information to Microsoft Access.

If *item* refers to a domain (such as a range of cells in a spreadsheet), DDESend places all data in the first location.

The DDESend function can be attached only to the Control Source property of the following controls on a form: text box, option group, check box, and combo box. If the DDESend function is attached to a text box or option group, data can refer to another control. Check box and combo box data must contain numeric data (or it won't be sent to the application).

If the requested application isn't running, Access opens a dialog box asking for the user's permission to launch the application.

If the request made by DDESend fails for any reason (the requested application is configured to ignore DDE requests, the requested application doesn't recognize the topic or the item, or the maximum number of simultaneous DDE conversations has been exceeded, for example), the function returns a Null.

Example

The following expression sends a value stored in cell the control [Salary] to cell A3 of the Quattro Pro for Windows spreadsheet titled "TEST.WB1":

```
= DDESend("QPW", "TEST.WB1", "A3", [Salary])
```

Caution

Because all controls with attached DDESend function appear as blank (or unselected), you may want to make them invisible by setting their Visible property to No. The actual number of simultaneous DDE conversations is limited by the system's memory and resources utilization.

See Also

Functions: DDE, DDEInitiate, and DDERequest

Chapter 12, "OLE and DDE"

DFirst, DLast

Domain

Returns a value from the first or last field in a specified domain.

Syntax

DFirst(*expression, domain [,criteria]*)

DLast(*expression, domain [,criteria]*)

expression can be a field name containing values to return, the name of a control in the form, query, report, or an expression that uses values in that field or control to perform calculations. *expression* cannot contain other aggregate SQL or domain functions (such as Avg or Sum).

domain identifies the record source; it may be a table or query name, or an SQL expression.

criteria identifies the range of data to process. If *criteria* is omitted, these functions operate on the entire domain.

If no record satisfies *criteria*, these functions return Null.

The current index is used if the domain is an indexed table.

Usage Notes

If *domain* refers to a nonexistent table or query, a `Couldn't find input table or query <name>` error (trappable error #3078) is generated. If *expression* or *criteria* refer to a nonexistent field name or control, an `Invalid reference to control <control name> in query` (trappable error #2471) occurs.

Examples

Both examples assume that the Employees file is indexed on "Employee hire date."

To display the name of the first employee hired in year 1993:

```
Result = DFirst( "[Employee name]", "Employees",
➥"Year( [Employee hire date] ) = 1993" )
```

To display the name of the last employee hired in 1993:

```
Result = DLast( "[Employee name]", "Employees",
➥"Year( [Employee hire date] ) = 1993" )
```

Caution

The results returned by DFirst and DLast functions may be meaningless unless the searched domain (table, query) is actually indexed on the field included in the expression.

See Also

Functions: DLookup, First, and Last

Methods: FindFirst, FindLast, FindNext, and FindPrevious

Dir, Dir$

File I/O

Return a specified file name from a specified directory. Dir returns a Variant; Dir$ returns a String.

Syntax

Dir[**$**][(*filespec*)]

filespec specifies a file name and/or drive and path to the file. Valid DOS wild cards are allowed.

Usage Notes

Because these functions fetch just one file at a time, the Dir[$] function must be placed in a loop to obtain a listing of all files matching *filespec*.

The first call to Dir must include a filespec; subsequent calls use the same *filespec* by default until there are no more matching files, in which case Dir[$] returns a zero-length string (Variant VarType 8).

The empty parentheses must be included only if Dir[$] is used outside Access Basic, such as in an expression placed directly in a form or report property, and no *filespec* is specified.

Example

The following code populates the dynamic array aDir with the names of all the TXT files in the current directory:

```
ReDim aDir(0) As String
Dim wIndex%, szFileSpec$

wIndex = 0
szFileSpec = "*.TXT"
aDir(wIndex) = Dir(szFileSpec)

Do Until Len(aDir(wIndex)) = 0
    wIndex = wIndex + 1
    ReDim Preserve aDir(0 To wIndex)
    aDir(wIndex) = Dir
Loop
(...)
```

See Also

Statement: ChDir

Functions: CurDir and CurDir$

DLookup

Domain

Returns a field value from the specified domain.

Syntax

DLookup(*expression, domain [, criteria]*)

expression can be a field name containing values to return by the DLookup function, the name of a control in a form, query, or report, or an expression that uses values in that field or control to perform calculations.

expression cannot contain other aggregate SQL or domain functions (such as Avg or Sum).

domain identifies the record source; it may be a table or query name, or a SQL expression.

criteria can either identify the range of data to process or explicitly provide the value to search for (see examples). If omitted, DLookup operates on the entire domain.

Usage Notes

DLookup returns the value from the requested field of the first record that satisfies criteria and therefore can be treated as a semantic equivalent of the DFirst function.

If no records satisfy *criteria*, or *domain* is empty, DLookup returns Null.

The current index is used if *domain* is an indexed table.

This function is used most frequently to search lookup tables for a desired value.

If *domain* refers to a nonexistent table or query, a `Couldn't find input table or query <name>` error (trappable error #3078) is generated. If either *expression* or *criteria* refer to a nonexistent field name or control, an `Invalid reference to control <control name> in query` (trappable error #2471) occurs.

Examples

To find the city name for a given ZIP code in the file "City":

```
Result = DLookup("[City name]", "City", "[Zip code] = '90278'"]
```

To return values from more than one field:

```
sEmpSSN = "123456789"
Result = DLookup("[First name] & [Last name]", "Employees", "[Employee SSN] =
➥sEmpSSN")
```

The name of a control (on a form or report) that's identical to the field name in the searched domain must be fully qualified with the form or report name. Consider the following example:

```
= DLookup("[Employee salary"], "Employees", "[Employee SSN] =
➥EmployeeForm.[Employee SSN]")
```

See Also

Functions: DFirst and DLast

DMin, DMax

Domain

Returns a minimum or maximum field value from the specified domain.

Syntax

DMin(*expression, domain [, criteria]*)

DMax(*expression, domain [, criteria]*)

expression can be a field name containing values to return by these functions, the name of a control in the form, query, or report, or an expression that uses values in that field or control to perform calculations.

The expression cannot contain other aggregate SQL or domain functions (such as Avg or Sum).

domain identifies the record source; it may be a table or query name, or an SQL expression.

criteria identifies the range of data to process. If *criteria* is omitted, DMin and DMax operate on the entire domain.

Usage Notes

If *expression* refers to numeric data, the highest (or lowest) number in *domain* is returned; for non-numeric data the first (or last) string is returned alphabetically.

DMin returns the lowest value from the requested field of *domain* that satisfies *criteria* and therefore can be treated as a semantic equivalent of the DFirst function if *domain* is sorted (or indexed) on the specified *expression* in ascending order.

DMax returns the highest value from the requested field of *domain* that satisfies *criteria*, and therefore can be treated as a semantic equivalent of the DLast function if *domain* is sorted (or indexed) on the specified expression in ascending order.

If no record satisfies *criteria*, or *domain* is empty, these functions return a Null.

If *expression* refers to a Memo (or OLE) data type, a `Can't have Memo or OLE object in aggregate argument <name>` error (trappable error #3115) occurs.

If *domain* refers to a nonexistent table or query, a `Couldn't find input table or query <name>` error (trappable error #3078) is generated. If either *expression* or *criteria* refer to a nonexistent field name or control, an `Invalid reference to control <control name> in query` (trappable error #2471) occurs.

FUNCTIONS

Examples

To find the smallest and highest ZIP code in the file "Zip Codes" for City = "Los Angeles":

```
Result = DMin("[ZIP Code]", "Zip Codes", "[City] = 'Los Angeles'") Result =
➥DMax("[ZIP Code]", "Zip Codes", "[City] = 'Los Angeles'")
```

The name of the control (on the form or report) identical to the field name in the searched domain, must be fully qualified with the form or report name.

```
= DMin("[Employee salary"], "Employees", "[Employee SSN] =
➥EmployeeForm.[Employee SSN]")
```

See Also

Functions: DFirst and DLast, and Min and Max

DStDev, DStDevP — Domain

Returns the standard deviation represented by values from a specified domain. DStDevP evaluates a population; DStDev evaluates a population sample.

Syntax

DStDev(*expression, domain [,criteria]*)

DStDevP(*expression, domain [,criteria]*)

expression can be a field name containing values to evaluate, the name of a control in the form, query, report, or an expression that uses values in that field or control to perform calculations. *expression* cannot contain other aggregate SQL or domain functions (such as Avg or Sum).

domain identifies the record source; it may be a table or query name, or a SQL expression.

criteria identifies the range of data to process. If *criteria* is omitted, these functions operate on the entire *domain*.

Usage Notes

DStDev and DStDevP operate on a domain with at least two records and return a Null when there are fewer than two records in the specified domain or less than two records satisfy the criteria.

If *domain* refers to a nonexistent table or query, a `Couldn't find input table or query <name>` (trappable error #3078) is generated. If *expression* refers to a Memo (or OLE) data type, a `Can't have Memo or OLE object in aggregate argument <name>` error (trappable error #3115) occurs.

If either *expression* or *criteria* refers to a nonexistent field name or control, an `Invalid reference to control <control name> in query` (trappable error #2471) occurs.

Example

Attached to a control in a form or a report, this example calculates the estimate of the standard deviation for a population for phone calls made to London:

```
= DStDev("[Phone charges]","Phone calls","[City] = 'London'")
```

See Also

Functions: StDev and StDevP

DSum

Domain

Returns the sum of a set of values in a specified domain.

Syntax

DSum(*expression, domain [,criteria]*)

expression can be a field name containing numeric values to sum, the name of a control in the form, query, or report, or an expression that uses values in that field or control to perform calculations. *expression* cannot contain other aggregate SQL or domain functions (such as Avg or Sum).

domain identifies the record source; it can be a table or query name, or a SQL expression.

criteria identifies the range of data to count. If *criteria* is omitted, DSum operates on the entire *domain*.

Usage Notes

If *domain* refers to a nonexistent table or query, a `Couldn't find input table or query <name>` error (trappable error #3078) is generated. If *expression* refers to a Memo (or OLE) data type, a `Can't have Memo or OLE object in aggregate argument <name>` error (trappable error #3115) occurs. If *expression* refers to a field containing nonnumeric data, an `Illegal type in expression` error (trappable error #3169) is generated.

If either *expression* or *criteria* refer to a nonexistent field name or control, an `Invalid reference to control <control name> in query` error (trappable error #2471) occurs.

Example

The following example sums salaries of all managerial employees in Employee table:

```
Result = DSum( "[Employee salary]", "Employees", "[Employee pos] = 'Manager'")
```

FUNCTIONS

Caution

Any changes to an edited record should be saved (by invoking the Save Record option of the File menu or by moving the focus to another record) before calling DSum. In a multiuser environment, results returned by DSum may not contain current values if another user is also editing the data.

See Also

Functions: DCount and Sum

DVar, DVarP

Domain

Returns estimates of the variance represented by values from a specified domain. DVarP evaluates a population; DVar evaluates a population sample.

Syntax

DVar*(expression, domain [,criteria])*

DVarP*(expression, domain [,criteria])*

expression can be a field name containing numeric values to evaluate, the name of a control in a form, query, or report, or an expression that uses values in that field or control to perform calculations. The *expression* cannot contain other aggregate SQL or domain functions (such as Avg or Sum).

domain identifies the record source; it can be a table or query name, or a SQL expression.

criteria can either explicitly identify the range of data to process, or *criteria* may consist of the WHERE clause of a SQL expression without the word WHERE. If *criteria* is omitted, these functions operate on the entire *domain*.

Usage Notes

DVar and DVarP operate on *domain* with at least two records and return a Null when there are fewer than two records in the specified *domain* or less than two records satisfy *criteria*.

If *domain* refers to a nonexistent table or query, a `Couldn't find input table or query <name>` error (trappable error #3078) is generated. If *expression* refers to a Memo (or OLE) data type, a `Can't have Memo or OLE object in aggregate argument <name>` error (trappable error #3115) occurs. If *expression* refers to a field containing nonnumeric data, an `Illegal type in expression` error (trappable error #3169) is generated.

If either *expression* or *criteria* refer to a nonexistent field name or control, an `Invalid reference to control <control name> in query` error (trappable error #2471) occurs.

Example

Attached to a control in a form or a report, this example calculates the estimate of the variance for a population for phone calls made to London:

```
= DVar("[Phone charges]","Phone calls","[City] = 'London'")
```

See Also

Functions: Var and VarP

Environ, Environ$

Miscellaneous

Returns the contents of the specified DOS environment variable. **Environ** returns a Variant; **Environ$** returns a String.

Syntax

Environ[**$**](*name*)

or

Environ[**$**](*number*)

name is a literal or an expression that evaluates to the name of the DOS environment variable.

number is a numeric expression specifying the position of the desired environment string in the environment table.

Usage Notes

When *name* is specified as the argument, Environ[$] returns the contents of the environment variable (the text to the right of the equal sign).

If *number* is used, Environ[$] returns the name of the environment variable and its contents, including the equal sign.

If an invalid *number* is specified, or a variable with the specified name doesn't exist, Environ[$] returns a zero-length string.

Examples

The following examples display the setting of COMSPEC:

```
Result = Environ("COMSPEC")        ' C:\COMMAND.COM
Result = Environ(1)                ' COMSPEC=C:\COMMAND.COM
```

FUNCTIONS

The following example displays the contents of the DOS environment in the immediate window:

```
n = 1
Do
     Debug.Print Environ(n)
     n = n + 1
Loop Until Len(Environ(n)) = 0


Display DOS path in the immediate window:

Debug.Print Environ("PATH")
```

Caution

Access doesn't have a built-in function to change the contents of the primary DOS environment.

EOF

File I/O

Returns a value indicating whether the end of the file has been reached.

Syntax

EOF(*filenumber*)

filenumber must evaluate to a valid open file number used in the Open statement.

Usage Notes

Using an invalid *filenumber* (one that doesn't refer to any open file) results in a `Bad file name or number` error (trappable error #52).

The EOF function can be used only with files opened with the Open statements and is not applicable to Access tables and recordsets.

Example

The following example reads data from an entire text file:

```
Dim vBuffer as Variant, wFileNo as Integer
wFileNo = FreeFile
Open "Test.txt" for Input as wFileNo
While Not EOF(wFileNo)
     Input #wFileNo, vBuffer
Wend
Close wFileNo
```

Caution

In text files, the EOF function returns true if an end-of-file character (ANSI 26) is encountered anywhere in the text, therefore processing may terminate before the entire file is processed.

See Also

Functions: Loc and LOF

Property: EOF

Statement: Open

Err, Erl

Error handling

Err returns error code; **Erl** returns the line number on which the error occurred.

Syntax

Err

Erl

Usage Notes

Both functions return an Integer.

Erl has no practical significance because Access Basic doesn't use line numbers. (Erl returns 0 if the program doesn't have line numbers.)

Err is reset to 0 ("no error" state) by Reset and On Error statements, and upon exit from an error handling routine.

Microsoft warns that since calling a function or a subroutine from within an error handler can also reset the value of Err to zero, it is advisable to capture its value into a memory variable before calling any functions or subroutines from within an error handler.

Example

The following example displays an error code:

```
Function MyDatePart()
On Error GoTo error
Result = DatePart("x", Now)        ' invalid expression
Exit Function

error:
     MsgBox Error & " Error #" & Str(Err)
     Exit Function
End Function
```

FUNCTIONS

Caution

Microsoft has documented 41 errors generated by Access. For the full listing of 718 errors generated by Access please see the Microsoft Access Errors table included on the sample disk. This table can be viewed from the main menu of the sample application in the Que database. Because error numbers may change in the next release, a routine to update the Microsoft Access Errors table is also provided.

See Also

Functions: Error and Error$

Statements: Error, On Error, and Resume

Error, Error$

Error Handling

Returns an error message. **Error** returns a Variant; **Error$** returns a String.

Syntax

Error[**$**][*(errorcode)*]

errorcode is an integer that corresponds to valid Microsoft Access error code.

Usage Notes

Error, when used without an argument, returns a message corresponding to the most recent runtime error (returned by the Err function). If there is no error, the error function returns a zero-length string.

These functions can be forced to return an error message by passing *errorcode* as an argument. In such a case, either the Access error message, or a string "User-defined error" or "Reserved error" are returned. If you pass *errorcode*, and the corresponding error message includes contextual information (such as a file name), no information is inserted in the message.

If *errorcode* is not a numeric expression, a `Type mismatch` error (trappable error #13) is returned. Passing a negative number as *errorcode* triggers an `Illegal function call` error (trappable error #5).

Caution

Microsoft has documented only 41 errors generated by Access. For the full listing of 718 errors generated by Access please see the MS Access Errors table included on the sample disk. This table can be viewed from the main menu of the sample application in the Que database. Because error numbers may change in the next release, a routine to update the MS Access Errors table is also provided.

Example

Display the error message corresponding to the Access error number 3048:

```
MsgBox(Error(3048))        ' "Can't open any more databases"
```

To force an error by attempting to pass an invalid argument to the Error function.

```
On Error GoTo ???error
Debug.Print Error(100000)      ' argument too big
Exit Function
error:
     MsgBox(Error & ". Error number " & Str(Err))
     Exit Function
```

The message box displays: `"Overflow.  Error number 6"`

See Also

Functions: Erl and Err

Statements: Err and Error

Eval

Miscellaneous

Returns the value of the evaluated expression.

Syntax

Eval(*expression*)

expression is a string to evaluate.

Usage Notes

Eval returns -1 (true) or 0 (false) depending on the result of the evaluation.

A `Type mismatch` error (trappable error # 13) occurs if *expression* is not a character string.

Most of the functionality of the Eval function is supplied by other Access Basic functions, such as IIf, but the Eval functions can also use operators not otherwise available in Access Basic, such as *In* and *Between...And.*

Examples

To use the In operator:

```
Result = Eval(" 'CA' In ('Hi', 'CO', 'ID', 'PR', 'CA')")      ' -1 (True)
```

Eval can be used also to evaluate expressions such as the following:

```
Result = Eval("135 + 12/4 < 43")          ' 0 (false)
```

See Also

Functions: Choose, IIf, and Switch

Exp

Math

Returns the base of natural algorithm raised to a power.

Syntax

Exp(*number*)

number is any valid number or an expression that evaluates to a number.

Usage Notes

The largest allowed *number* is 709.782712893. A larger *number* triggers an `Overflow` error (trappable error #6).

The Exp function complements Log and is often referred to as the antialgorithm.

Examples

The following examples show three usages of the Exp function:

```
Result = Exp(1)                   ' 2.718282 (= constant e)
Result = Exp(2)                   ' 7.389056
Exp(2) = ( Exp(1) )^2             ' 7.389056
```

See Also

Function: Log

Operator: ^

FileAttr

File I/O

Returns the mode in which the file was opened or the operating system file handle information.

Syntax

FileAttr(*filenumber, attribute)*

filenumber is the number of an open file, the same as used in the Open statement.

attribute indicates the type of information returned by FileAttr.

Usage Notes

If *attribute* equals 1, the following values are returned by FileAttr.

Return Value	*File Mode*
1	Input
2	Output
4	Random
8	Append
32	Binary

If *attribute* is 2, the operating system number (*file handle*) for this open file is returned. It can be used to pass to external programs (such as functions in other DLLs) to perform file I/O functions that require the operating system file handle.

If the value of attribute is other than 1 or 2, an `Illegal function call` error (trappable error #5) is triggered. Passing an invalid *filenumber* (one that doesn't refer to any open file) results in a `Bad file name or number` error (trappable error #52).

Example

The following example uses the FileAttr function to obtain various values for an open file:

```
nFileNum = FreeFile
Open "Test.txt" as nFileNum
Result = FileAttr(nFileNum,1)          ' 4 (Random access)
Result = FileAttr(nFileNum,2)          ' an integer
Close nFileNum
```

See Also

Statements: Open and Close

Function: FreeFile

FUNCTIONS

First, Last
Field Values (Not Available in Access Basic)

Return a value from the specified first or last record in a query, form, or report.

Syntax

First *(expression)*

Last *(expression)*

expression can be a field name containing values to return, the name of a control in the form, query, or report, or an expression that uses values in that field or control to perform calculations.

expression cannot contain other aggregate SQL or domain functions (such as Count or Sum).

Usage Notes

Both First and Last can be a part of the SQL SELECT statement.

First and Last can be used only in queries, reports, and forms; use DFirst and DLast functions in Access Basic code.

Neither function can be used in the page header or footer of a report or form.

Example

The following example shows the first record in the Employee table:

```
SELECT First([Employee name]) FROM [Employees]
```

The following example selects the first employee named Smith:

```
SELECT First([Employee SSN]) FROM [Employees] WHERE [Employee name] = "Smith"
```

Usage in a control of a form or report:

```
= Last([Employee name] & [Employee DOB] )
```

See Also

Functions: Avg, Count, dFirst and DLast, Min and Max, StDev and StDevP, Sum, and Var and VarP

Format, Format$
Strings

Returns an expression according to instructions in the format expression. **Format** returns a Variant; **Format$** returns a String

Syntax

Format[$] *(expression, format)*

expression is a string to be formatted.

format is the format expression.

Usage Notes

When *format* is omitted, Format[$] behaves like the CStr and Str[$] functions (unlike the Str[$] function Format[$] doesn't hold the placeholder for the sign when converting positive numbers).

The strings returned by the Format[$] function may vary depending on the setting in the International section of the WIN.INI file: all examples here assume the setting for United States. For example, changing the country to Germany switches placeholders for numbers (the decimal point in Germany is a comma and the thousand separator is a period, making the number "123456.78" formatted as "###,###.##" ("123,456.78") look like: "123.456,78").

Formatting numbers:

format for numeric expressions can be constructed from the formatting symbols described in the following table.

Formatting Symbol	*Action*
Zero-length string	No formatting.
#	Display a digit or nothing. Numbers longer than the formatting string are truncated; if the number is shorter than the formatting string nothing is displayed in lieu of "#" character.
.	Decimal placeholder.
%	Percentage placeholder. To ensure that the leading zero is always displayed for fractional numbers (as in: 0.17), use zero as a digit place holder at the position immediately preceding the decimal point.
,	Thousands separator.
E-E+e-e+	Display a number in scientific notation.
:	Time separator.
/	Date separator.
-+$( ) *space*	Display a literal character.

continues

FUNCTIONS

Formatting Symbol	*Action*
\	Display the next character as literal. To display a backslash, for example, use \\. Characters used in formatting strings (such as: a, c, d, h, n, p, q, s, t, w, y, / (forward slash), : (colon), #, 0, %, E, e, comma, period, @, &, <, >, !) cannot be displayed.
"ABC"	Display a string in quotes. You need to use Chr(34) to indicate quotes in ABC.
[color]	Display the string in a specified color. Valid are all basic colors (see the RGB function for the list of basic colors). The color of the control cannot be changed from within Access Basic, but can only be set in the property sheet for the particular control.
*	Don't display the next character.

Examples

The following examples illustrate using various formatting strings to format numeric expressions:

```
Result = Format(100,001.987, "")          ' 100,001.987
Result = Format(-32.5,"00,000.000)        ' -00,032.500
Result = Format(456.2,"##########")       ' 456
Result = Format(0.65,"###%")              ' 65%
Result = Format(12.5,"$###.00")           ' $12.50
Result = Format(111, "\\###\\")           ' \111\
Result = Format(1.5, "\*\*$###.00\*\*")   ' **$1.50**
Result = Format(345.67, "#*#*#*.#*#*")    ' 346
```

The Format function, when used to format numbers, can have up to four sections separated by a semicolon. If you use one section only, it applies to all data. If two sections are used, the first applies to positive values and zeros and the second to negative values. With three sections, the first applies to positive values, the second to negative values, and the third to zeros. When all four sections are used, the first applies to positive values, the second to negative values, the third to zeros, and the fourth to Nulls.

```
a = 123
b = -456
c = 0
d = Null
```

```
Result = Format(a, "####;0000-;Zip!;\(Nil\)       ' 123
Result = Format(b, "####;0000-;Zip!;\(Nil\)       ' 0456-
Result = Format(c, "####;0000-;Zip!;\(Nil\)       ' Zip!
Result = Format(d, "####;0000-;Zip!;\(Nil\)       ' (Nil)
```

Formatting character strings:

format for character strings can be constructed from the following formatting symbols:

Formatting Symbol	*Action*
@	Displays a character or a space.
&	Displays a character or nothing.
<	Displays all characters in lowercase.
>	Displays all characters in uppercase.
!	Forces placeholders to fill from left to right rather than from right to left.

Examples

Formatting character strings with various formatting options:

```
Result = Format("Los Angeles","@")                ' Los Angeles
Result = Format("123456", "!\-&&&&&")             '-123456
Result = Format("123456", "\-&&&&&")              '1-23456
Result = Format("123456789", "@@@\-@@\-@@@@")     '123-45-6789
Result = Format("Kawabunga!", ">")                'KAWABUNGA!
Result = Format("dBASE", "<")                     'dbase
```

Format for character strings can have up to two sections separated by a semicolon: the first section applies to string data; the second to Nulls and zero-length strings, as in the following example:

```
s = "Chicago"
Result = Format(s, "> ; Empty string")            ' CHICAGO
s = ""
Result = Format(s, "> ; Empty string")            ' Empty string
```

Formatting date and time:

The following formatting characters can be used to construct the date/time format. All examples in the following table assume Friday, January 8, 1993 8:01:01 a.m.

Formatting Symbol	*Display*	*Description*
c	ttttt	Time
	ddddd	Date
d	8	Day, no leading zero

continues

FUNCTIONS

Formatting Symbol	Display	Description
dd	08	Day with the leading zero
ddd	Fri	Abbreviated day name
dddd	Friday	Full day name
ddddd	1/8/93	Short Date
dddddd	Friday, January 08, 1993	Long Date
w	6	Day of the week
ww	2	Week number
m	1	Month, no leading zero
mm	01	Month with the leading zero
mmm	Jan	Abbreviated month
mmmm	January	Full month name
q	1	Quarter number
y	8	Day of year number
yy	9	Year as a two digit number
yyyy	1993	Year as a four digit number
h	8	Hour, no leading zeros
hh	08	Hour with the leading zeros
n	1	Minute, no leading zeros
nn	01	Minute with the leading zeros
s	1	Second, no leading zeros
ss	01	Second with the leading zeros
ttttt	8:01:01 AM	Complete time using the time separator defined in the international section of WIN.INI
AM/PM	8:01:01 AM	Time, 12 hour clock
am/pm	8:01:01 am	Time, 12 hour clock
A/P	8:01:01 A	Time, 12 hour clock
a/p	8:01:01 a	Time, 12 hour clock
AMPM	8:01:01 AM	Time, 12 hour clock depending on the WIN.INI am/pm setting

Examples

The following examples show various formats of date/time data:

```
Result = Format(Now,"")                    '1/8/93 8:01:01 AM
Result = Format(Now,"dddddd ttttt")        'Friday, January 08, 1993   08:01:01 AM
Result = Format(2.45, "dddddd ttttt")      'Monday, January 01, 1900   10:48:00 AM
Result = Format(Date, "yyyy")              '1993 (same as Year(Date))
```

See Also

Functions: Data Conversion Functions and Str and Str[$]

Property: Format

Chapter 10, "Understanding Access Data Types"

FreeFile

File I/O

Returns the next valid Access file number: a file handle, expressed as an Integer. The file handle—not its name—must be used by Access Basic file I/O functions when referring to an open file.

Syntax

FreeFile*[()]*

Usage Notes

FreeFile requires no arguments.

The empty parentheses must be included only if FreeFile is used outside Access Basic, such as in an expression placed directly in a form or report property.

If there are no more file numbers available, this function generates a `Too many files` error message (trappable error #67). Access allows a maximum of 255 file numbers but the actual number is limited by anomalies in different versions of Microsoft Windows. Under Windows 3.0, the limit will be close to 240 handles. Under Windows 3.1, the limit is lower (about 110 handles). In any case, the handle limit is just a theoretical obstacle; reaching the handle limit is rather unlikely.

Example

The following example uses the FreeFile function to obtain the next available file handle:

```
Dim FileNum as Integer
FileNum = FreeFile
Open "TEST.TXT" For Output as FileNum
Write FileNum "I fish therefore I lie"
Close FileNum
```

Caution

The FreeFile function returns the next available file handle, therefore the file handle returned must be used to open a file before obtaining another file handle.

This code doesn't work:

```
a = FreeFile                                    ' 1
b = FreeFile                                    ' 1
Open "File1" For Input As a
Open "File2" For Output As b                    ' File Already Open error
```

This code works fine:

```
a = FreeFile                                    ' 1
Open "File1" For Input As a
b = FreeFile                                    '
Open "File2" For Output As b
```

See Also

Statements: Open and Close

FV

Financial

Returns the future value of an annuity based on equal periodic payments and a fixed interest rate.

Syntax

FV(*rate, nper, pmt, pv, due*)

rate is the interest rate per period.

nper is the total number of installments (payments or deposits).

pmt is the payment made each period.

pv is the present value of the future payments.

due indicates when payments are due. If payments are due in the beginning of the period, its value is 1; if payments are due at the end of the payment period, its value is 0.

Usage Notes

All arguments must be numbers; passing a nonnumeric argument results in a `Type mismatch` error (trappable error #13).

rate and *nper* must be expressed in the same time units (monthly APR and number of monthly deposits, or yearly APR and number of yearly deposits, for example).

Negative numbers represent cash paid out (such as a deposit to a savings account); positive numbers represent cash received (a dividend, for example).

Caution

This function is implemented in the MSAFIN.DLL library, which is installed by Access in the Windows directory, and declared in the UTILITY.MDA database. To access this function from Access version 1.0, you need to load the UTILITY.MDA by placing the following entry in the Options section of the MSACCESS.INI file (found in your Windows program directory):

```
UtilityDB=<path>UTILITY.MDA
```

Access version 1.1 loads the UTILITY.MDA automatically.

Example

To calculate the future value of a new savings account with 3.5% APR, calculated monthly, with $100 deposited on the first of each month for a year:

```
= FV(.035/12, 12, -100, 0, 1)          ' $ 1222.99
```

The value of the annuity with a present value of $200,000, 7% APR and $3000 withdrawal per month at the beginning of each month, one year from now will be as follows:

```
= FV(.07/12, 12, 3000, -200000, 1)     ' $177,063.39
```

See Also

Functions: IPmt, NPer, Pmt, PPmt, PV, and Rate

Hex, Hex$

Conversion

Hex returns the hexadecimal (base 16) value of a decimal argument as a Variant. Hex$ returns a string.

Syntax

Hex[$](*number*)

number is any valid number or expression that evaluates to a valid number.

Usage Notes

These functions evaluate only whole numbers; any fractions are discarded.

If the argument is an Integer, the function returns up to 4 hexadecimal digits. For Long arguments, it returns up to 8 hexadecimal digits. If an argument (Date, String) can be converted to a number, the function returns a string.

Nonnumeric strings (such as "Santa"), Null arguments, and empty strings generate a `Type mismatch` error (trappable error #13).

The largest decimal number that can be converted to base 16 using these functions is 2,147,483,647 (the largest long integer). Larger numbers generate an `Overflow` error (trappable error #6).

Hexadecimal numbers can be represented directly by placing the &H prefix in front of a valid number. For example, &H20 equals decimal 32.

Examples

The following examples show results of the Hex function with various arguments:

```
Result = Hex(37)                          ' 25
Result = Hex("37")                        ' 25
Result = Hex(-37)                         ' FFDB
Result = Hex("Ringo Starr")               ' Error #13
```

See Also

Functions: Oct, Oct$, Fix, and Int

Chapter 10, "Understanding Access Data Types"

Hour

Date and Time

Returns the hour of the time represented in the expression.

Syntax

Hour(*expression*)

expression can be a number or an expression that evaluates to a valid time and/or date.

Usage Notes

Hour returns an integer between 0 and 23 ("military" hour).

Hour accepts expressions that evaluate to a date (and/or time) between January 1, 100 and December 31, 9999.

Dates are stored internally by Access as numbers, where Jan 1, 1900 equals 2 and negative numbers represent dates prior to Dec 30, 1899. Any fractions of this number are interpreted as time by the Hour function.

Examples

The following examples show values returned by the Hour function used with two different arguments:

```
Result = Hour("01/01/1993 12:00:00 AM")       ' 0
Result = Hour(2.35)                           ' 8
```

See Also

Functions: DatePart, Minute, and Second

Chapter 10, "Understanding Access Data Types"

IIf

Program Flow Control

Returns one of two arguments, depending on the evaluation of an expression.

Syntax

IIf(*expression, truepart, falsepart*)

expression is any expression that evaluates to true or false (-1 or zero).

truepart is the value to return if expression is true.

falsepart is the value to return if expression is false.

Usage Notes

The IIf function is very useful in converting Null values to empty strings.

Because IIf evaluates both *truepart* and *falsepart* when used in Access Basic, it may generate various runtime errors if one or both *expressions* are erroneous (such as division by zero, null variable value)—especially if *expressions* are based on the user's input or other values unknown to a programmer. When IIF is attached to a property in a form or report, only the appropriate part is evaluated.

Examples

To return an empty string if the Employee SSN field is Null:

```
Result = IIf(IsNull([Employee SSN]),"",[Employee SSN])
```

To return a verbal expression of the numerical value:

```
Result = IIf([Total sales] > 1000000, "Good!", "Bad!")
```

Caution

Avoid redundant coding with the IIf function, such as in the first of the following two examples:

```
Result = IIF( Date() = #01-01-93#, -1, 0 )    ' Redundant!
Result = ( Date() = #01-01-93# )              ' Better...
```

The simpler the expression, the more readable it is (the second expression automatically evaluates to true or false).

See Also

Functions: Choose, DLookup, and Switch

Statement: If...Then...Else

Operator: Between...And

Input, Input$ — File I/O

Reads *n* bytes from a sequential file. Input returns a Variant; Input$ returns a String.

Syntax

Input[**$**](*n, #filenumber)*

n is a number of bytes to read from the file.

filenumber is the Access Basic file handle used in the Open statement.

Usage Notes

These functions can be used only with files opened in Input or Binary mode. Using a different file open mode, or not specifying the mode at all in the Open statement, triggers a `Bad file mode` error (trappable error #52). The maximum number of bytes to read (*n*) is 65,534. Exceeding the value triggers an `Illegal function call` error (trappable error #5). Passing an invalid filenumber triggers a `Bad file name or number` error (trappable error #52).

Example

To open a text file and display the first 200 bytes in the Immediate window:

```
nFile = FreeFile
Open "TEST.TXT" For Input as nFile
Debug.Print Input(200, nFile)
Close nFile
```

Caution

Use the Input# statement rather than the Input function to read data from a delimited text file. The Input function returns all characters, including commas, quotation marks, spaces, linefeeds, and carriage returns, whereas the Input# statement discards them.

Use the Get statement to read from a random access file.

See Also

Function: FreeFile

Statements: Get, Open, and Input#

InputBox, InputBox$

Object Manipulation

Displays an edit box in a dialog box and returns its contents. InputBox returns a Variant; InputBox$ returns a String.

Syntax

InputBox[**$**](*prompt [,[title] [,[default] [, xpos, ypos]]]*)

prompt is a string expression displayed in the dialog box.

title appears on the title bar of the dialog box.

default is a default expression displayed in the edit box.

xpos specifies the distance between the left side of the input box and the left edge of the screen measured in twips.

ypos specifies the distance between the upper side of the input box and the upper edge of the screen measured in twips.

Usage Notes

These functions display a dialog box with two buttons (OK and Cancel) and an input box. When the OK button is pressed, these functions return the contents of the input box. When the Cancel button is pressed, a zero-length string is returned.

The only required argument is *prompt*; if you don't want a prompt to appear, pass a zero-length string as *prompt*. For multiline prompts, include a new line character (Chr$(13) + Chr$(10)) to break up the line.

The input box is modal. The user has to provide the input, or press a button, inside the box before proceeding with the application.

If optional positioning is used, both *xpos* and *ypos* must be specified. If both are omitted, the input box is centered at approximately one third the height of the screen.

The *twip* (the smallest unit of measure in MS Access) is expressed as a one-twentieth of a point. There are 1,440 twips to an inch and 567 twips to a centimeter. Access, like Microsoft Visual Basic, implements a twip as 1/1440 of the logical inch.

Examples

To display a simple input box with default positioning:

```
Result = InputBox("Enter your name","Login"]
```

To display an input box without a prompt or a title positioned in the upper left corner of the screen:

```
Result = InputBox("",,, 0, 0)
```

Caution

Paradoxically, the length of the input depends on the width of the entered characters, and on average is 32-33 characters; however, you can enter more lowercase than uppercase characters.

Use the optional input box positioning with caution; if the *xpos* or *ypos* values are too big, the input box is displayed outside the visible part of the screen.

See Also

Function: MsgBox

Statement: MsgBox

InStr

Strings

Returns the position of the first occurrence of one string within another.

InStr*([start], string1, string2)*

or

InStr*(start, string1, string2, compare)*

start specifies the starting position of the search in string1.

string1 identifies the expression being searched.

string2 identifies the expression being sought.

compare indicates the string comparison method.

Usage Notes

The following values are allowed in *compare*:

0	Case-sensitive comparison
1	Not case-sensitive comparison
2	Database method

See Option Compare statement and ListFields method for more information about comparison methods.

If *compare* is omitted InStr will use the string comparison method set in the Option Compare statement, or default to the Binary method.

Specifying an illegal *compare* method (other than 0, 1, or 2), a zero, a negative value, or a value greater than the 65,535 for start triggers an `Illegal function call` error (trappable error #5).

Examples

Results of string comparisons with different comparison methods:

```
Result = InStr("ABCabc", "a")              ' 1
Result = InStr(1, "ABCabc", "a" , 0)       ' 4
Result = InStr(1, "ABCabc", "a" , 1)       ' 1
Result = InStr(1, "ABCabc", "a" , 2)       ' 1
```

Caution

You cannot specify compare without indicating start as well. The following triggers a `Type mismatch` error (trappable error #13):

```
Result = InStr("ABCabc", "c", 1)           ' Error 13
```

Currently, there is no Access Basic facility to obtain the setting of the Option Compare.

See Also

Statement: Option Compare

Method: ListFields

Int, Fix

Math

Return the integer portion of a numeric expression.

Syntax

Int*(number)*

Fix*(number)*

number can be any valid numeric expression.

Usage Notes

Int and Fix functions truncate a fractional portion of *number* if *number* is positive. If *number* is negative, Fix returns the first integer greater than or equal to *number*. Int returns the first integer less than or equal to *number*.

These functions return the same data type as the argument type, except when *number* is Variant VarType 8 (string) and can be converted to a numeric value. In this case both functions return a Double (Variant VarType 5) data type.

If *number* is Null, Int and Fix return Null.

An argument that cannot be converted to a valid number triggers a `Type mismatch` error (trappable error #13).

Examples

For positive numbers, both functions behave identically:

```
Result = Int(1.9)                    ' 1
Result = Fix(1.9)                    ' 1
```

For negative numbers, the functions behave differently:

```
Result = Int(-.9)                    ' -1
Result = Fix(-.9)                    ' 0
```

You can use these functions to convert hexadecimal (base 16) and octal (base 8) numbers to decimal integers:

```
Result = Int(&H10A)                  'Hex 10A (decimal 266)
Result = Fix(&O25)                   'Oct 25 (decimal 21)
```

Both Int and Fix return only the date portion of the expression if the argument is a date data type (Variant VarType 7)

```
Result = Now()                       ' 12/31/1992 12:00:00 AM
Result = Int(Now)                    ' 12/31/1992
```

See Also

Functions: Abs, Exp, Hex and Hex$, Oct and Oct$, Rnd, Sgn, and Sqr

Function: Data conversion

Chapter 10, "Understanding Access Data Types"

IPmt

Financial

Returns the interest payment for a given period of an annuity based on equal periodic payments and a fixed interest rate.

Syntax

IPmt(*rate, per, nper, pv, fv, due*)

rate is the interest rate per period.

per is the specific payment period.

nper is the total number of installments (payments or deposits).

pv is the present value of the future payments.

fv is the future value (desired value after making the final payment).

due indicates when the payments are due: if payments are due in the beginning of the period, its value is 1; if payments are due at the end of the period, its value is 0.

Usage Notes

All arguments must be numbers; passing a nonnumeric argument results in a `Type mismatch` error (trappable error #13).

rate and *nper* must be expressed in the same time units (such as monthly APR and number of monthly deposits, or yearly APR and number of yearly deposits).

per must be in the range 1 through *nper*. If *per* is greater than *nper* an `Illegal function call` error (trappable error #5) occurs.

Negative numbers represent cash paid out (such as a deposit to a savings account); positive numbers represent cash received (a dividend, for example).

Caution

This function is implemented in the MSAFIN.DLL library, which is installed by Access in the Windows directory, and declared in the UTILITY.MDA database. To access this function from Access version 1.0, you need to load the UTILITY.MDA by placing the following entry in the Options section of the MSACCESS.INI file (found in your Windows program directory):

```
UtilityDB=<path>UTILITY.MDA
```

Access version 1.1 loads the UTILITY.MDA automatically.

Example

Calculate the total interest paid on a $14,000 car loan with 7.8% APR, payable in 48 monthly payments due at the beginning of the month:

```
nTot = 0                              ' running total
For i = 1 To 48
     nTot = nTot + IPmt(.078/12, i, 48, -14000, 0, 1)
Next
Debug.Print nTot                      ' $2236.93
```

See Also

Functions: FV, NPer, Pmt, PPmt, PV, and Rate

FUNCTIONS

IRR

Financial

Returns the internal rate of return for a periodic cash flow.

Syntax

IRR(*valuearray(), guess*)

valuearray is an array of transactions. It must contain at least one positive value (income) and one negative value (outlay).

guess is a value you guess the IRR function will return—usually 10% (.1).

Usage Notes

If the IRR function cannot calculate the internal rate of return in 20 iterations, it fails with an `Illegal function call` error (trappable error #5).

To obtain a meaningful value from the IRR function, enter outlays and income in the proper order. Because the IRR function requires an array, it can only be used in Access Basic.

Caution

This function is implemented in the MSAFIN.DLL library, which is installed by Access in the Windows directory, and declared in the UTILITY.MDA database. To access this function from Access version 1.0, you need to load the UTILITY.MDA by placing the following entry in the Options section of the MSACCESS.INI file (found in your Windows program directory):

```
UtilityDB=<path>UTILITY.MDA
```

Access version 1.1 loads the UTILITY.MDA automatically.

Example

The example below calculates the internal rate of return for a period with five transactions:

```
Dim Cash(5) as Double
Cash(0) = -2000 : Cash(1) = 1000
Cash(2) = 700 : Cash(3) = 3000 : Cash(4) = 2500
Result = IRR(Cash(), .1) * 100          '58.91
```

See Also

Functions: MIRR, NPV, and Rate

IsDate

Inspection of Variables

Syntax

IsDate(*variant*)

variant can be any Variant expression including a Null.

Usage Notes

IsDate returns 0 (false) if *variant* cannot be converted to a date, or -1 (true) otherwise.

The range of dates recognized by IsDate is January 1, 100 through December 31, 9999.

Examples

Results of the IsDate function with two different values:

```
Result = IsDate("Dec-14-1993")          ' -1 (True)
Result = IsDate("Sonny and Cher")       ' 0 (False)
```

Caution

The following usage returns true because the year will be interpreted as "1901" and may cause errors in calculations that are difficult to detect:

```
Result = IsDate("Dec-01-0001")                  ' True
Debug.Print Format(CVDate(Result), "yyyy")      ' 1901
```

See Also

Functions: IsEmpty, IsNull, IsNumeric, and VarType

Function: Data Conversion

IsEmpty

Inspection of Variables

Returns a value indicating whether a variable has been initialized.

Syntax

IsEmpty(*variant*)

variant can be any Variant expression, most often a single variable name.

Usage Notes

If *variant* is an expression that contains other expressions, the IsEmpty function returns -1 only if all expressions contain an Empty value.

Example

The following example shows the result of the IsEmpty function with two different expressions:

```
Dim v as Variant
Result = IsEmpty(v)                         ' -1 (true)
v = "Access"
Result = IsEmpty(v)                         ' 0 (false)
```

See Also

Functions: IsDate, IsNull, IsNumeric, and VarType

Function: Data Conversion

IsNull

Inspection of Variables

Checks whether a Variant variable has a Null value.

Syntax

IsNull(*variant*)

variant can be any Variant expression, most often a single variable name.

Usage Notes

The variable has a Null value if it doesn't contain any data.

Caution

The only way to determine whether a variable is Null from within Access Basic is to use the IsNull function. Direct comparisons (such as: var = Null or var <> Null) are always false because any expression containing a Null is itself a Null.

Example

The following example shows results of the evaluation of two variant variables by the IsNull function:

```
Dim v As Variant
v = Null
```

```
Result = IsNull(v)                     ' -1 (true)
v = "Access"
Result = IsNull(v)      FreeFile          ' 0 (false)
```

See Also

Functions: IsDate, IsEmpty, IsNumeric, and VarType

Function: Data Conversion

IsNumeric

Inspection of Variables

Checks whether a Variant variable is—or can be converted to—a number.

Syntax

IsNumeric(*variant*)

variant can be any Variant expression, including a Null.

Usage Notes

IsNumeric returns -1 (True) if *variant* can be converted to a number; 0 (False) otherwise. The IsNumeric function also recognizes legal octal and hexadecimal numbers.

Examples

The following examples show results of three different arguments evaluated by the IsNumeric function:

```
Result = IsNumeric("1")          ' -1 (true)
Result = IsNumeric("1A")         ' 0 (false)
Result = IsNumeric("&H1A")       ' -1 (true)
```

See Also

Functions: IsDate, IsEmpty, IsNull, VarType, and Data Conversion

Last

See **First** function.

LBound

Array Manipulation

Returns the smallest available subscript in a given dimension of an array.

Syntax

LBound(*array [, dimension]*)

array must be a declared and initialized array. .

dimension indicates for which array dimension the value is returned. If omitted, 1 is assumed.

Usage Notes

LBound can only be used in Access Basic; it cannot be attached to controls and properties in Microsoft Access objects.

In Access Basic, if an array is declared using the keyword To, its lower bound may start from any number smaller than the upper bound of the same dimension.

Attempting to apply this function to a nonexistent dimension triggers a `Subscript out of range` error (trappable error #9). The same error is returned when an array is declared (with the Dim statement) but not initialized.

Use this function with the UBound function to find out the actual number of available array elements for a given dimension.

Examples

To find the smallest subscript in the first dimension:

```
ReDim a(0 To 10,1 To 15)
Result = LBound(a)                  ' 0
```

To find the smallest subscript for a given dimension and the number of dimensions:

```
ReDim a(-3 To 5, 10 To 12)
Result = LBound(a,1)                ' -3
Result = LBound(a,2)                ' 10
Result = LBound(a,3)                ' Error #9
```

See Also

Function: UBound

Statements: Dim, Global, Option Base, ReDim, and Static

LCase, LCase$

Strings

Convert letters in a string to lowercase. LCase returns a variant; LCase$ returns a string.

Syntax

LCase[$]*(string)*

string is a literal string or any valid string expression.

Usage Notes

LCase can accept a Null value (in which case a Null is returned). LCase$ returns a `Type mismatch` error (trappable error #13) if the argument is not a valid string.

Only uppercase letters are converted to lowercase; other characters are not changed.

Example

The following example shows results of conversion by the LCase function:

```
Result = LCase("James Bond")          ' james bond
Result = LCase("JB - 007")            ' jb - 007
```

Caution

Access Basic doesn't have a built-in function to verify that a given character is lowercase, other than checking that the ANSI value of a character falls into the range of lowercase letters. One way around this limitation is to call the Microsoft Windows function IsCharLower (which resides in the USER.EXE DLL). Before calling IsCharLower, the function must be declared as external in the declarations section of an Access Basic module. To avoid library conflicts, use a prefix. For example, use "abc_" in the function name. See Chapter 13, "Extending Microsoft Access and Access Basic," for more information on accessing the Windows API.

```
' In the declarations section
Declare Function abc_IsCharLower Lib "User" Alias "IsCharLower" (ByVal CharCode As
Integer) As Integer
' In Access Basic code
Result = abc_IsCharLower( Asc("M") )         ' 0 (false)
'
Dim cChar As Variant
cChar = "h"
If abc_IsCharLower( Asc(cChar) ) Then
     Debug.Print cChar & " is lowercase."
End If
```

FUNCTIONS

See Also

Functions: UCase and UCase$

Left, Left$ — Strings

Returns the specified number of the leftmost characters. Left returns a Variant; Left$ returns a string.

Syntax

Left[$](*string, number*)

string must be a valid string (Variant VarType 8).

number specifies how many leftmost characters will be returned.

Usage Notes

Only Left can accept a Null value (Variant VarType 1) in which case it returns a Null value.

Number must be between 0 and 65,535. A negative number will trigger an `Illegal function call` error (trappable error #5). The entire string is returned when the *number* is equal to or greater than the length of the *string*. An empty string is returned if the number equals zero.

Example

The following example returns the four leftmost characters of the string "Mary had a little lamb":

```
Result = Left("Mary had a little lamb", 4)        ' Mary
```

See Also

Functions: InStr, Len, Mid, Mid$, Right, and Right$

Len — Strings

Returns the length (number of characters) of a string expression or the number of bytes required to store a variable with a particular data type.

Syntax

Len(*expression*)

or

Len(*variable*)

expression can be any valid Access expression.

variable can be any valid Access variable name.

Usage Notes

If the argument is Null, Len returns a Null.

If the *variable* is trailed by its type suffix, the Len function returns the number of bytes needed to store its contents, rather than the actual length of data. The type suffixes described in the following table are all valid in Access Basic.

Type Suffix	*Date Type*
%	Integer
&	Long
!	Single
#	Double
@	Currency

Tip

Using suffixes makes code look cluttered and difficult to read; use explicit declarations instead.

The Len function can also be used to determine the required storage size of a user-defined data type, and to determine the length of a record in a random-access file.

Examples

For an explicitly declared variable, Len returns the number of bytes needed to store its contents:

```
Dim i As Integer
i = 30000
Result = Len(i)                         ' 2 bytes
```

If you need to know the number of digits in a non-string variable, use the Len function in conjunction with the CStr data conversion function:

```
Dim d As Double
d = 123.56
Result = Len(d)                         ' 8 bytes
Result = Len(CStr(d))                   ' 6 digits
```

If the variable is a Variant data type, regardless of its VarType, Len always returns its length as if it were a string (Variant VarType 8):

FUNCTIONS

```
v = 30000
Result = Len(v)                          ' 5
```

See Also

Functions: InStr and Str

Chapter 10, "Access Data Types"

Loc

File I/O

Returns the current position within an open file (the location of the file pointer).

Syntax

Loc(*filenumber*)

filenumber must represent a valid open file number (the same as used in the Open statement).

Usage Notes

Passing an invalid *filenumber* triggers a `Bad file name or number` error (trappable error #52).

The returned value depends on the mode in which the file is opened.

- For sequential files, Loc returns the current byte position divided by 128.
- For random files, the number of the last variable read from or written to a file.
- For binary files, the position of last byte either read or written.

Examples

The following example uses the Loc function to return the position of two files opened in different modes:

```
Open "TEST.TXT" for Input As 1           ' sequential access
Temp = Input(50,1)
Result = Loc(1)                          ' 1
Close 1
Open "TEST.TXT" for Binary As 1
Temp = Input(50,1)
Result = Loc(1)                          ' 50
Close 1
```

See Also

Functions: EOF, LOF, and Open

LOF

File I/O

Returns the size of an open file (in bytes).

Syntax

LOF*(filenumber)*

filenumber must represent a valid open file number (the same used in the Open statement).

Usage Notes

Passing an invalid *filenumber* (one that doesn't refer to any open file) results in a `Bad file name or number` error (trappable error #52).

Example

The following example uses the LOF function to return the size of the specified file:

```
wFileNumber = FreeFile
Open "TEST.TXT" for Append as wFileNumber
Result = LOF(wFileNumber)          ' size of TEST.TXT in bytes
Close wFileNumber
```

Caution

Access Basic doesn't have built-in functions to obtain more information about disk files, such as date/time stamp or attributes. You must use Windows API functions to obtain this information.

See Also

Functions: EOF and Loc

Statements: Close and Open

FUNCTIONS

Log

Math

Returns the natural logarithm of a number.

Syntax

Log*(number)*

number is any valid number or an expression that evaluates to a valid number.

Usage Notes

Natural logarithm is a logarithm to base e (approximately 2.718282).

The *number* must be greater than zero.

Examples

The following example calculates the logarithm of 1:

```
Result = Log(1)                          ' 0
```

This example calculates a base-10 logarithm:

```
Result = Log(2) /Log(10)                 ' .30103
```

See Also

Function: Exp

Operator: ^

LTrim, LTrim$, RTrim, RTrim$, Trim, Trim$ — Strings

Returns a string with leading and/or trailing spaces removed. LTrim, RTrim, and Trim return a Variant; LTrim$, RTrim$, and Trim$ return a String.

Syntax

[L][R]Trim[$]*(stringexpression)*

stringexpression can be any valid expression or literal that evaluates to a String or Variant.

Usage Notes

LTrim and LTrim$ return *stringexpression* with leading spaces removed.

RTrim and RTrim$ return *stringexpression* with trailing spaces removed.

Trim and Trim$ remove both leading and trailing spaces.

Only LTrim, RTrim, and Trim functions accept a Null as a *stringexpression*, and return a Null; an attempt to pass a Null value as *stringexpression* to LTrim$, RTrim$, and Trim$ triggers an `Invalid use of Null` error (trappable error #94).

Examples

Three variations of the Trim function and their results:

```
s = "  Mary Jones  "
Result = LTrim(s)              ' "Mary Jones  "
Result = RTrim(s)              ' "  Mary Jones"
Result = Trim(s)               ' "Mary Jones"
```

See Also

Functions: Str and Data Conversion

Max

See the "Min" function.

Mid, Mid$

Strings

Returns a specified part of *stringexpression* (its *substring*).

Syntax

Mid[$](*stringexpression, start [,length]*)

stringexpression can be any valid expression or literal that evaluates to a String or Variant.

start is a starting position of the part to return.

length is a number of characters from *stringexpression* to return.

Usage Notes

Both *start* and *length* are Long integers, and must be in the range of 1 through 65,535: arguments outside this range trigger an `Illegal function call` error (trappable error #5). If *length* is greater than the total length of the *stringexpression*, the entire *stringexpression* starting with *start* is returned. If *start* is greater than the total length of *stringexpression*, or length equals 0, Mid[$] returns a zero-length string.

Example

The following example returns different parts of the same string using the Mid function:

```
s = "Microsoft Access Basic"
Result = Mid(s,1)              ' "Microsoft Access Basic"
Result = Mid(s,11)             ' "Access Basic"
Result = Mid(s,11,6)           ' "Access"
```

FUNCTIONS

See Also

Statements: Mid and Mid$

Functions: InStr and the Trim family of functions

Min, Max

Field Values (Not Available in Access Basic)

Returns a minimum or maximum value from a specified field on a query, form, or report.

Syntax

Min(*expression*)

Max(*expression*)

expression can be a field name containing values to return, the name of a control in a form, query, report, or an expression that uses values in the field or control to perform calculations.

expression cannot contain other aggregate SQL or domain functions (such as Avg or Sum).

Usage Notes

Max and Min can be used only in controls attached to forms and reports and in queries; use DMax and DMin in Access Basic.

If *expression* refers to numeric data, the highest (or lowest) number in the field is returned. For nonnumeric data the first (or last) string is returned alphabetically.

Min returns the lowest value from the requested field and therefore can be treated as a semantic equivalent of the First function if the underlying table or query is sorted (or indexed) on the specified *expression* in ascending order.

Max returns the highest value from the requested field and therefore can be treated as the semantic equivalent of the Last function if the underlying file or query is sorted (or indexed) on the specified *expression* in ascending order.

Examples

To find the lowest and highest salary in the current table:

```
Result = Min("[Salary]")
Result = Max("[Salary]")
```

See Also

Functions: Avg, DMin and DMax, Count, First and Last, StDev and StDevP, Sum, and Var and VarP

Minute

Date and Time

Returns the minute of the time represented in the expression.

Syntax

Minute(*expression*)

expression can be a number or an expression that evaluates to a valid time and/or date.

Usage Notes

Minute returns an integer between 0 and 59.

Minute accepts *expressions* that evaluate to a date (and/or time) between January 1, 100 through December 31, 9999.

Dates are stored internally by Access as numbers, where Jan 1, 1900 equals 2 and negative numbers represent dates prior to Dec 30, 1899. Any fractions of this number are interpreted as time by the Minute function.

Example

The following example shows results returned by the Minute function used with different arguments:

```
Result = Minute("01/01/1993 12:20:00 AM")    ' 20
Result = Minute(2.35)                        ' 24
```

See Also

Functions: DatePart, Hour, and Second

Chapter 10, "Understanding Access Data Types"

MIRR

Financial

Returns the modified internal rate of return for a periodic cash flow.

Syntax

MIRR(*valuearray(), financerate, reinvestrate*)

valuearray is an array of transactions. It must contain at least one positive value (income) and one negative value (outlay).

financerate is the interest rate paid on investment.

reinvestrate interest rate received on investment gain.

Usage Notes

To obtain a meaningful value from the MIRR function, enter outlays and income in the proper order. Since the MIRR function requires an array, it can only be used in Access Basic.

Caution

This function is implemented in the MSAFIN.DLL library, which is installed by Access in the Windows directory, and declared in the UTILITY.MDA database. To access this function from Access version 1.0, you need to load the UTILITY.MDA by placing the following entry in the Options section of the MSACCESS.INI file (found in your Windows program directory):

```
UtilityDB=<path>UTILITY.MDA
```

Access version 1.1 loads the UTILITY.MDA automatically.

Example

The following example calculates the modified internal rate of return for a period with five transactions; finance rate and reinvestrate are .1 (10%) and .12 (12%) respectively.

```
Dim Cash(5) as Double
Cash(0) = -2000 : Cash(1) = 1000
Cash(2) = 700 : Cash(3) = 3000 : Cash(4) = 2500
Result = MIRR(Cash(), .1, .12) * 100        ' 42.05
```

See Also

Functions: IRR, NPV, and Rate

Month

Date and Time

Returns the month number.

Syntax

Month(*expression*)

expression can be a date or a number that represents a valid date.

Usage Notes

Month returns an integer representing the month of the year for dates in the range January 1, 100 through December 31, 9999.

The year can be omitted from the *expression*.

If *expression* evaluates to a Null, Month returns a Null.

Because Access stores dates internally as Double (2 equals January 1, 1900 and negative numbers represent dates before December 30, 1899), this function accepts numbers as *expression*.

Examples

The following example shows the Month function used with date and numeric arguments:

```
Result = Month(#01/01/1993#)          '1
Result = Month(2)                     ' 1 (Jan. 1, 1900)
```

See Also

Functions: Weekday DateAdd, DateDiff, DatePart, DateSerial, DateValue, Day, Hour, Minute, Second, YearDate, Now, and Time

MsgBox Function, MsgBox Statement

Miscellaneous

Displays a message and specified buttons in a standard Windows dialog box. The **MsgBox** function also returns the value of the button pressed by the user.

Syntax

Function:

MsgBox(*msg [, type] [, title]*)

Statement:

MsgBox *msg [, type] [, title]*

msg is the message to display (a string literal or variable).

type describes the look of the dialog box: its icon, number and kind of buttons, and the default button (a sum of values from three groups—an integer).

title is the title of the dialog box (a string literal or variable).

Usage Notes

The maximum length of *msg* is 1,024 characters. A longer *msg* is truncated; continuous strings (with no spaces), are truncated after the 255th character. Messages that don't fit on one line are wrapped around; if you want to break your message at a certain point, insert line feed/carriage return characters (CHR(13) + CHR(10)).

If the **MsgBox** displays the Cancel button, pressing the ESC key is an equivalent to selecting this button.

Note

The MsgBox function creates an application-modal dialog box (no part of Access can be accessed when the dialog box is displayed). To create a system-modal dialog box (no parts of Access or Windows can be accessed when the box is displayed), use the Windows API **MessageBox** function.

type is the sum of the following values (no more than one from each group):

number of buttons + icon style + default button

The following table contains the values for various combinations of buttons used with MsgBox.

Value	*Button(s)*
0	OK
1	OK, Cancel
2	Abort, Retry, Ignore
3	Yes, No, Cancel
4	Yes, No
5	Retry, Cancel

The second table describes possible icons displayed by MsgBox.

Value		*Icon*
16	Critical Message	STOP
32	Warning Query	?
48	Warning Message	!
64	Information Message	i

Values for a default button (which button is enabled) are enumerated in the next table.

Value	*Enabled Button*
0	First
256	Second
512	Third

If the specified default button is greater than the number of buttons defined for this box, the default button is ignored and the first button becomes the default button.

Depending on which button is pressed, the following values are returned by the MsgBox function.

Value	*Button Pressed*
1	Yes
2	Cancel
3	Abort
4	Retry
5	Ignore
6	Yes
7	No

Caution

If you intend to use the value returned by MsgBox, use the function syntax rather than statement (statements don't return values).

If you plan to use many dialog boxes, you may want to replace explicit numeric dialog box arguments with standard Windows dialog box constants. You must define these constants in the declarations section of a module, most likely as global constants. These constants are defined here as hexadecimal numbers but can be defined as appropriate decimal numbers as well.

Following are the definitions of commonly used Windows dialog box constants.

Buttons displayed in the dialog box:

```
MB_OK = &H0
MB_OKCANCEL = &H1
MB_ABORTRETRYIGNORE = &H2
MB_YESNOCANCEL = &H3
MB_YESNO = &H4
MB_RETRYCANCEL = &H5
```

Icon displayed in the dialog box:

```
MB_ICONHAND = &H10
MB_ICONQUESTION = &H20
MB_ICONEXCLAMATION = &H30
MB_ICONASTERISK = &H40
```

Which button is enabled:

```
MB_DEFBUTTON1 = &H0
MB_DEFBUTTON2 = &H100
MB_DEFBUTTON3 = &H200
```

Values returned by buttons in a dialog box (defined as decimal numbers):

```
IDOK = 1
IDCANCEL = 2
IDABORT = 3
IDRETRY = 4
IDIGNORE = 5
IDYES = 6
IDNO = 7
```

Examples

To display an error message, the OK button only, and the critical error icon:

```
Dim wId%
wId = MsgBox("Program will terminate", 16)
```

To display Abort, Retry, Ignore buttons (shown in fig. 18.1), the warning query icon and the dialog box title, and make the second button (Retry) the default:

```
Dim wId%, sMsg$, sDlgStyle$, sBoxTitle$
sMsg = "Hard drive meltdown imminent!"
sBoxTitle = "Final warning"
sDlgStyle = MB_ABORTRETRYIGNORE + MB_ICONQUESTION + MB_DEFBUTTON2
wId = MsgBox(sMsg, sDlgStyle, sBoxTitle)
```

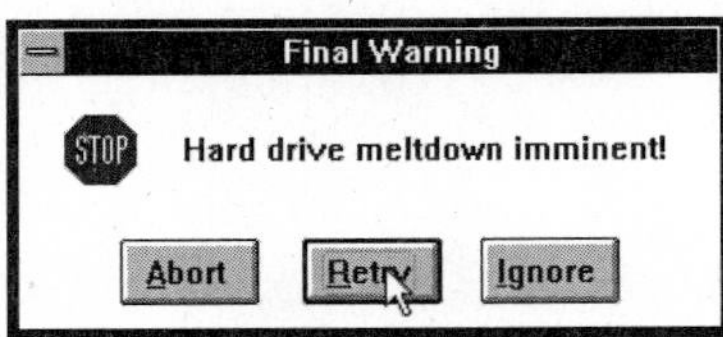

Figure 18.1. The Abort, Retry, Ignore buttons.

See Also

Functions: InputBox and InputBox$

Now

Date and Time

Returns the computer system date and time.

Syntax

Now[( )]

Usage Notes

The Now function requires no arguments.

The empty parentheses must be included only if Now is used outside Access Basic, such as in an expression placed directly in a form or report property.

The Now function returns the system date and time as date (Variant VarType 7) data type.

Access stores dates internally as Double (2 equals January 1, 1900, negative numbers represent dates before December 30, 1899, and the fractional part represents time). Use the Format function to transform the date/time returned by this function into other possible date and time formats.

Examples

The following example shows results of the Now function versus the Date function:

```
Result = Now                    ' 1/1/93 3:15:43 AM
Result = Date                   ' 1/1/93
```

See Also

Functions: Date, DateAdd, DateDiff, DatePart, DateSerial, DateValue, Day, Hour, Format, Minute, Second, Time, Weekday, and Year

FUNCTIONS

NPer

Financial

Returns a number of periods (payments) for an annuity based on equal periodic payments and a fixed interest rate.

Syntax

NPer(*rate, pmt, pv, fv, due*)

rate is the interest rate per period.

pmt is the payment made each period.

pv is the present value of the future payments.

fv is the future value (desired value after making the final payment).

due is 1 if payments are due in the beginning of the period, 0 if at the end.

Usage Notes

All arguments must be numbers; passing a nonnumeric argument results in a `Type mismatch` error (trappable error #13).

rate and *nper* must be expressed in the same time units. For example, monthly APR and number of monthly deposits, or yearly APR and number of yearly deposits.

Negative numbers represent cash paid out (such as a deposit to a savings account); positive numbers represent cash received (a dividend, for example).

Caution

This function is implemented in the MSAFIN.DLL library, which is installed by Access in the Windows directory, and declared in the UTILITY.MDA database. To access this function from Access version 1.0, you need to load the UTILITY.MDA by placing the following entry in the Options section of the MSACCESS.INI file (found in your Windows program directory):

```
UtilityDB=<path>UTILITY.MDA
```

(Access version 1.1 loads the UTILITY.MDA automatically.)

Example

Calculate the number of periods (payments) necessary to pay off a $100,000 8.5% APR mortgage with a $765 monthly payment due on the first of each month.

```
Result = NPer(.085/12, 765, -100000, 0, 1)        ' 357
```

See Also

Functions: FV, IPmt, Pmt, PPmt, PV, and Rate

NPV

Financial

Returns the net present value of an investment based on a series of payments and receipts (periodic cash flow) and a fixed interest rate.

Syntax

NPV(*rate, valuearray()*)

rate is a discount rate over the length period.

valuearray is an array of transactions. It must contain at least one positive value (income) and one negative value (outlay).

Usage Notes

All arguments must be numbers; passing a nonnumeric argument results in a `Type mismatch` error (trappable error #13).

The net present value is based on future cash flow, so if the first cash flow occurs at the beginning of the first period, it must be added to the result returned by the NPV function.

To obtain a meaningful value from the NPV function, enter outlays and income in the proper order. Because the NPV function requires an array, it can only be used in Access Basic.

Caution

This function is implemented in the MSAFIN.DLL library, which is installed by Access in the Windows directory, and declared in the UTILITY.MDA database. To access this function from Access version 1.0, you need to load the UTILITY.MDA by placing the following entry in the Options section of the MSACCESS.INI file (found in your Windows program directory):

```
UtilityDB=<path>UTILITY.MDA
```

Access version 1.1 loads the UTILITY.MDA automatically.

Example

The following example calculates the net present value rate of an investment for a period with five transactions with a discount rate of 10% (.1):

```
Dim Cash(5) as Double
Cash(0) = -2000
Cash(1) = 1000
Cash(2) = 700
Cash(3) = 3000
Cash(4) = 2500
Result = NPV(.1, Cash())                ' 3135.53
```

FUNCTIONS

See Also

Functions: FV, IPmt, NPer, Pmt, PPmt, PV, and Rate

Oct, Oct$

Conversion

Oct returns the octal (base 8) value of a decimal argument as a Variant. Oct$ returns a string.

Syntax

Oct[**$**]*(number)*

Usage Notes

These functions evaluate only whole numbers; any fractions are discarded.

If the argument is an Integer, the function returns up to 6 octal digits. For Long arguments it returns up to 11 octal digits. If an argument (Date, String) can be converted to a number, the function returns a string.

Nonnumeric strings (such as "Santa"), Null arguments, and empty strings generate a `Type mismatch` error (trappable error #13).

The largest decimal number that can be converted to base 8 by using these functions is 2,147,483,647 (the largest long integer). Larger numbers generate an `Overflow` error (trappable error #6).

Octal numbers can be represented directly by placing the &O prefix in front of a valid number. For example, &O20 equals decimal 16.

Examples

The following example shows the Oct function with different data types as arguments:

```
Result = Oct(10)                      ' 12
Result = Oct("10")                    ' 12
Result = Oct(-1)                      ' 177777
Result = Oct("Mike")                  ' Error #13
```

Caution

Access doesn't perform data conversion very well when using a string literal in the immediate window. Consider the following code:

```
? Oct("10")
```

When typed in the Immediate window, this code generates a `Type mismatch` error because the Oct functions expect a numeric argument and Access is unable to convert the literal string into a number. Note that a slight variation works quite well even in the immediate window:

```
a = "10"
? Oct(a)       '12
```

See Also

Functions: Hex, Hex$, Fix, and Int

Chapter 10, "Understanding Access Data Types"

OpenDatabase

Database Manipulation

Opens a specified database.

Syntax

OpenDatabase(*database, [, exclusive] [, readonly]*)

database is the name of the database to open, including the file extension (MDB in most cases).

exclusive is a Boolean expression; if 0 (false) database is opened for shared access; -1 (true) database is opened for non-shared (exclusive) access. The default is shared access.

read-only is a boolean expression; if 0 (false), the database is opened for read and write access; if -1 (true), database is opened for read-only access. The default is read-write access.

Usage Notes

If the *database* exists in another directory, drive, or computer (such as a server or a Windows For Workgroups peer), the path to the database must be fully qualified. Failure to specify the correct path triggers a `<path> isn't a valid path` error (trappable error #3044).

If no file extension is specified, or the *database* doesn't exist or is not in the current path, Access triggers a `Couldn't find file <filename>` error (trappable error #3024).

If the *database* is already opened in exclusive mode by another user in the network or Windows For Workgroups environment, a `Couldn't open file '<file name>'` error (trappable error #3051) occurs.

If the *database* refers to the currently open database, the OpenDatabse function behaves exactly as the CurrentDB function.

Since the maximum size of the Access database is 1 Gb (in version 1.1), it is sometimes necessary to separate the code and data. It is possible to house the code in one database and data in another. See the function CodeDB for more information.

The OpenDatabase function can be used only in Access Basic.

Tip

The OpenDatabase function helps circumvent the restrictions on manipulating attached tables from other Access databases. Certain properties and methods, such as OpenTable (and, as a consequence, other methods such as Seek, Update, Edit, and AddNew) cannot be applied to attached tables even if the attached table is from another Access database. In such a case, use the OpenDatabase function to open the Access database that contains the desired table. From this point on you can manipulate tables (and other objects) in this database as if they were in the current database. The two examples below explain the restrictions and the workaround (both examples assume that table "Gross Sales" is an attached table from another Access database named "Income.Mdb"):

```
Dim cDb as Database, cTb as Table
```

This code, on attempting to open an attached table, generates a `Can't perform operation`—illegal error #3219:

```
Set cDb = CurrentDB()
Set cTb = OpenTable("Gross Sales")   'Error #3219
(...)
cTb.Close
```

This code, using the OpenDatabase function, works fine:

```
Set cDb = OpenDatabase("INCOME.MDB")
Set cTb = cDb.OpenTable("Customers")
cTb.AddNew
(...)
cTB.Update
cTb.Close
```

(Note that yet another workaround exists—using the OpenTable action to open an attached table. The OpenTable action, however, has its own drawbacks because it doesn't return a table object.)

Example

The following example opens another database and a table in the current database:

```
Dim cDb As Database, cTb as Table
Set cDb = OpenDatabase("F:\ACCESS\DATA\NWIND.MDB")
set cTb = cDb.OpenTable("Customers")
(...)
cTb.Close
cDb.Close
```

See Also

Functions: CodeDB and CurrentDB

Methods: Close and OpenTable

Partition

Miscellaneous

Returns a string indicating where a number occurs within a specified range of numbers.

Syntax

Partition(*number, start, stop, interval*)

number is the number to evaluate (Long).

start is the lower bounds of the range of numbers (Long, not less than zero).

stop is the upper bounds of the range of numbers (Long; must be greater than *start*).

interval indicates the span of interval in the returned range.

Usage Notes

Because it allows calculating of various ranges easily, the Partition function is most useful in select queries for operations such as aging accounts receivable, where the number of events falls within a certain range (of dates, tolerances, weight, and so on).

By performing a series of tests on the same range using a different *number*, the data may be easily graphed.

The Partition function returns a range of numbers from the indicated group of numbers formatted as *lowervalue:uppervalue*, as shown in the following example:

```
Result = Partition(10, 1, 100, 3)       ' 10: 12
```

If only *uppervalue* is returned, *number* falls below the lower bounds of the specified range. For example:

```
Result = Partition(2, 20, 100, 1)       '  :19
```

If only *lowervalue* is returned, *number* falls above the specified range. For example:

```
Result = Partition(345, 1, 300, 20)         ' 301:
```

If *interval* equals 1, the returned range is *number:number*:

```
Result = Partition(76, 1, 100, 1)       ' 76: 76
```

If any of the arguments is Null, Partition returns Null.

The following examples illustrate the results returned by this function using various values:

```
Result = Partition(-1, 0, 99, 5)        '  :-1
Result = Partition(1, 0, 99 ,5)         ' 0: 4
Result = Partition(99, 0, 99, 5)        '95: 99
Result = Partition(1321, 0, 99, 5)      '100:
```

FUNCTIONS

The returned ranges represent four states:

- *number* falls below range.
- The first range is selected (*start* = *number*).
- The last range is selected (*stop* = *number*).
- *number* falls above range.

The returned range may not span the entire *interval* if the set of numbers defined by *start* and *stop* cannot be evenly divided by *interval* and the difference between *number* and *stop* is less than *interval*. For example:

```
Result = Partition(340, 0, 345, 10)      ' 340:345
```

Example

Create a dynaset that will hold the number of telephone calls that fall in the ranges of less than $1.00, $1.01-2.00, 2.01-3, and so on, by using the Partition function. Copy the dynaset to an array and process it:

```
Function TestPartition()
Dim cDB As Database, cDset As Dynaset
Set d = CurrentDB()
Set dy = cDB.CreateDynaset("SELECT DISTINCTROW Partition([Call charge],0,100,2) As
➥Range, COUNT([Phone calls].[Call charge]) As Count FROM [Phone calls] GROUP BY
➥Partition([Phone calls].[Call charge], 0, 100,2);")

'How many records are in the dynaset?
cDset.MoveLast
n = cDset.RecordCount
cDset.MoveFirst

' Declare an array large enough to store all records from the dynaset
ReDim aRanges(1 To n, 2)
i = 1

'Traverse the dynaset and copy data to the array
Do Until cDset.EOF
    aRanges(i, 1) = cDset.Range
    aRanges(i, 2) = cDset.Count
    cDset.MoveNext
    i = i + 1
Loop
cDset.Close

'Display the array in the Immediate window
For i = 1 To n
    Debug.Print aRanges(i, 1), aRanges(i, 2)
Next
End Function
```

The end result in the immediate window may look like the following:

```
Range ($)        Count
--------------------------------------
  0:  1           221
  2:  3            56
  4:  5            27
  6:  7             8
  8:  9             7
 10: 11            10
 12: 13             2
 14: 15             1
 16: 17             2
 24: 25             1
 26: 27             1
 32: 33             1
 44: 45             1
```

Pmt

Financial

Returns the payments for an annuity based on equal periodic payments and a fixed interest rate.

Syntax

Pmt(*rate, nper, pv, fv, due)*

rate is the interest rate per period.

nper is the total number of payments.

pv is the present value of the future payments.

fv is the future value (desired value after making the final payment).

due is 1 if payments are due in the beginning of the period, 0 if at the end.

Usage Notes

All arguments must be numbers; passing a nonnumeric argument results in a `Type mismatch` error (trappable error #13).

rate and *nper* must be expressed in the same time units. For example, monthly APR and number of monthly deposits, or yearly APR and number of yearly deposits.

Negative numbers represent cash paid out (such as a deposit to a savings account); positive numbers represent cash received (a dividend, for example).

Caution

This function is implemented in the MSAFIN.DLL library, which is installed by Access in the Windows directory, and declared in the UTILITY.MDA database. To access this function from Access version 1.0, you need to load the UTILITY.MDA by placing the following entry in the Options section of the MSACCESS.INI file (found in your Windows program directory):

```
UtilityDB=<path>UTILITY.MDA
```

Access version 1.1 loads the UTILITY.MDA automatically.

Example

To calculate the payments necessary to pay off a $100,000 8.5% APR mortgage in 360 monthly payments due on the first of each month:

```
= Pmt(.085/12, 360, -100000, 0, 1) ' $763.55
```

See Also

Functions: FV, IPmt, Pmt, PPmt, PV, and Rate

PPmt

Financial

Returns the principal payment for a given period of an annuity based on equal periodic payments and a fixed interest rate.

Syntax

PPmt(*rate, per, nper, pv, fv, due*)

rate is the interest rate per period.

per is the specific payment period.

nper is the total number of installments (payments or deposits).

pv is the present value of the future payments.

fv is the future value (desired value after making the final payment).

due is 1 if payments are due in the beginning of the period, 0 if they are due at the end of the period.

Usage Notes

All arguments must be numbers; passing a nonnumeric argument results in a `Type mismatch` error (trappable error #13).

rate and *nper* must be expressed in the same time units. For example, monthly APR and number of monthly deposits, or yearly APR and number of yearly deposits.

per must be in the range 1 through *nper*. If *per* is greater than *nper* an `Illegal function call` error (trappable error #5) occurs.

Negative numbers represent cash paid out (such as a deposit to a savings account); positive numbers represent cash received (a dividend, for example).

Caution

This function is implemented in the MSAFIN.DLL library, which is installed by Access in the Windows directory, and declared in the UTILITY.MDA database. To access this function from Access version 1.0, you need to load the UTILITY.MDA by placing the following entry in the Options section of the MSACCESS.INI file (found in your Windows program directory):

```
UtilityDB=<path>UTILITY.MDA
```

Access version 1.1 loads the UTILITY.MDA automatically.

Example

To calculate the total principal paid on a $14,000 car loan with 7.8% APR, payable in 48 monthly payments due at the beginning of the month:

```
nTot = 0                              ' running total
For i = 1 To 48
     nTot = nTot + PPmt(.078/12, i, 48, -14000, 0, 1)
Next
Debug.Print nTot                      ' $14000  (surprise!)
```

Pmt, PPmt, and IPmt functions can be used to construct an amortization table, in which the payment for each period is divided into the principal and interest portion.

See Also

Functions: FV, IPmt, NPer, Pmt, PV, and Rate

PV

Financial

Returns the present value of an annuity based on equal periodic payments to be paid in the future and a fixed interest rate.

Syntax

PV(*rate, nper, pmt, fv, due*)

rate is the interest rate per period.

nper is the total number of installments (payments or deposits).

pmt is the payment made each period.

fv is the future value (desired value after making the final payment).

due is 1 if payments are due in the beginning of the period, 0 if at the end.

FUNCTIONS

Usage Notes

All arguments must be numbers; passing a nonnumeric argument results in a `Type mismatch` error (trappable error #13).

rate and *nper* must be expressed in the same time units. For example, monthly APR and number of monthly deposits, or yearly APR and number of yearly deposits.

Negative numbers represent cash paid out (such as a deposit to a savings account); positive numbers represent cash received (a dividend, for example).

Caution

This function is implemented in the MSAFIN.DLL library, which is installed by Access in the Windows directory, and declared in the UTILITY.MDA database. To access this function from Access version 1.0, you need to load the UTILITY.MDA by placing the following entry in the Options section of the MSACCESS.INI file (found in your Windows program directory):

```
UtilityDB=<path>UTILITY.MDA
```

Access version 1.1 loads the UTILITY.MDA automatically.

Example

The present value of an annuity with a future value of $200,000, 7% APR, and $3000 withdrawal per month at the beginning of each month one year from now will be as follows:

```
= PV(.07/12, 12, -3000, -200000, 1)          ' $221,390.30
```

See Also

Functions: FV, IPmt, NPer, NPV, Pmt, PPmt, and Rate

QBColor

Graphics

Returns the Access Basic color RGB code for a QuckBasic-style color number.

Syntax

QBColor(*qbcolor*)

qbcolor is a color value used by Microsoft QuckBasic.

Usage Notes

qbcolor is an integer in the range from 0 through 15. A value outside this range triggers an `Illegal function call` error (trappable error #5).

qbcolor can be passed as either a decimal, octal, or hex number.

The value returned by QBColor is interpreted starting with the least significant bit for red, blue, and green color components.

qbcolor values are interpreted according to the following table.

qbclor	*Color*	*qbcolor*	*Color*
0	Black	8	Gray
1	Blue	9	Light Blue
2	Green	10	Light Green
3	Cyan	11	Light Cyan
4	Red	12	Light Red
5	Magenta	13	Light Magenta
6	Yellow	14	Light Yellow
7	White	15	Bright White

Examples

QBColor values can be converted to hex values and can be used in lieu of values returned by the RGB function:

```
Result = Hex(QBColor(14))              ' &HFFFF (Light Yellow)
Result = Hex(QBColor(&HF))             ' FFFFFF (Bright White)
```

See Also

Function: RGB

Rate

Financial

Returns the interest rate per period for an annuity.

Syntax

Rate(*nper, pmt, pv, fv, due, guess*)

rate is the interest rate per period.

nper is the total number of installments (payments or deposits).

pmt is the payment made each period.

pv is the present value of the future payments.

fv is the future value (desired value after making the final payment).

due is 1 if payments are due in the beginning of the period, 0 if at the end.

guess is the value you guess the Rate function will return (usually 10% expressed as 0.1).

Usage Notes

All arguments must be numbers; passing a nonnumeric argument results in a `Type mismatch` error (trappable error #13).

pmt and *nper* must be expressed in the same time units. For example, monthly APR and number of monthly deposits, or yearly APR and number of yearly deposits.

Negative numbers represent cash paid out (such as a deposit to a savings account); positive numbers represent cash received (a dividend, for example).

If the Rate function fails, try a different value for guess.

Caution

This function is implemented in the MSAFIN.DLL library, which is installed by Access in the Windows directory, and declared in the UTILITY.MDA database. To access this function from Access version 1.0, you need to load the UTILITY.MDA by placing the following entry in the Options section of the MSACCESS.INI file (found in your Windows program directory):

```
UtilityDB=<path>UTILITY.MDA
```

Access version 1.1 loads the UTILITY.MDA automatically.

Example

To estimate the interest rate on a $14,000 car loan, with 48 $354 monthly payments due at the beginning of each month (the “guess” is 0.1 (10%)):

```
= (Rate(48, -354, 14000, 0, 1, 0.1) * 12) * 100   '10,29%
```

See Also

Functions: FV, IPmt, NPer, Pmt, PPmt, and Rate

RGB

Graphics

Returns a number representing the RGB (red, green, and blue) color value.

Syntax

RGB(*red, green, blue*)

red, *green*, and *blue* are integers representing the relative intensity of the appropriate component color.

Usage Notes

The valid range for all arguments is 0 through 255; if either argument exceeds 255, it is assumed 255. If either argument exceeds the integer range, an `Overflow` error (trappable error #6) occurs. If either argument is negative, an `Illegal function call` error (trappable error #5) is triggered.

RGB Values for standard colors are shown in the following table.

Color	*RGB Value*	*Red*	*Green*	*Blue*
Black	&H0	0	0	0
Dark Gray	&H00808080	128	128	128
Light Gray	&H00C0C0C0	192	192	192
Blue	&HFF0000	0	0	255
Green	&HFF00	0	255	0
Cyan	&HFFFF00	0	255	255
Red	&HFF	255	0	0
Magenta	&HFF00FF	255	0	255
Yellow	&HFFFF	255	255	0
White	&HFFFFFF	255	255	255

See Also

Function: QBColor

Right, Right$

Strings

Returns the specified number of the rightmost characters in a string. Right returns a Variant; Right$ returns a string.

Syntax

Right[$](*string, number*)

string must be a valid string (Variant VarType 8).

number specifies how many rightmost characters will be returned.

Usage Notes

Only Right can accept a Null value (Variant VarType 1), in which case it returns a Null value.

number must be between 0 and 65,535. A negative number triggers an `Illegal function call` error (trappable error #5). The entire string is returned when the number is equal or greater to the length of the string. An empty string is returned if the number equals zero.

Example

The following example returns the seven rightmost characters from the string "United States of America":

```
Dim s as String
s = "United States of America"
Result = Right(s, 7)                     ' America
```

See Also

Functions: InStr, Len, Left, Left$, Mid, and Mid$

Rnd — Math

Returns a random number.

Syntax

Rnd[*(number)*]

number is a "seed" for the Rnd function and can be any valid numeric expression.

Usage Notes

The empty parentheses are required only when this function is used outside Access Basic, such as in queries or when directly attached to controls in forms or reports.

number can be passed either as a decimal, hex, or octal number.

The Rnd function returns a single number in the range from 0 to 1. The behavior of this function is partially dependent on the value of *number*:

Number	*Returned Value*
< 0	Same value every time as determined by number
= 0	The most recently generated number
> 0	The next random number
(omitted)	The next random number

Examples

A sequence of "random numbers" generated by the Rnd function:

```
Result = Rnd(1)              ' 0.301948
Result = Rnd(0)              ' 0.301948
Result = Rnd(-1)             ' 0.22407
Result = Rnd                 ' 8.635235E-02
```

Caution

Numbers generated by Rnd are not truly random since the Rnd function uses the previous "random" number as a seed for the next one and generates the same sequence of "random" numbers every time unless the seed number is also random or dynamic.

For truly random numbers, use algorithms available in many general-purpose programming books.

See Also

Function: Timer

Statement: Randomize

Rtrim, Rtrim$

See the "Ltrim" function.

Second

Date and Time

Returns the seconds value of the time represented in the expression.

Syntax

Second(*expression*)

expression can be a number or an expression that evaluates to a valid time and/or date.

Usage Notes

Second returns an integer between 0 and 59.

Second accepts expressions that evaluate to a date (and/or time) between January 1, 100 through December 31, 9999.

Dates are stored internally by Access as numbers, where Jan 1, 1900 equals 2 and negative numbers represent dates prior to Dec 30, 1899. Any fractions of this number are interpreted as time by the Second function.

Example

The following example shows results of the Second function with two different arguments:

```
Result = Second("01/01/1993 12:20:12 AM")        ' 12
Result = Second(2.353)                           ' 19
```

See Also

Functions: DatePart, Hour, and Second

Chapter 10, "Understanding Access Data Types"

Seek

File I/O

Returns the current position in a file.

Syntax

Seek(*filenumber*)

filenumber can be any numeric expression that evaluates to a valid file number used in the Open statement to open the file.

Usage Notes

An invalid *filenumber* triggers a `Bad file name or number` error (trappable error #52).

For files opened in Random-access mode, Seek returns the number of the next record; for other access modes Seek returns the current byte position (1 for the beginning of the file).

Examples

Using the Seek function with files opened in sequential access modes:

```
nFile = FreeFile
Open "Test.txt" For Input As nFile
Debug.Print Seek(nFile)                    ' 1
Result = Input(20, nFile)                  ' read 20 bytes
Debug.Print Seek(nFile)                    ' 21
Close nFile
```

A simple method to position the file pointer at the end of the file using the Seek function to verify the operation performed by the Seek statement, as shown in the following example:

```
nFile = FreeFile
Open "Test.txt" For Input As nFile
fSize = LOF(nFile)                         ' file size - 5667 bytes
Seek #nFile, fSize
Debug.Print Seek(nFile)                    ' 5667
Close nFile
```

See Also

Functions: EOF, Loc, and LOF

Statements: Get, Open, Put, and Seek

Sgn

Math

Returns the sign of number.

Syntax

Sgn(*number*)

Usage Notes

number can be any decimal, octal, or hexadecimal number.

If *number* cannot be converted to a valid number a `Type mismatch` error (trappable error #13) occurs.

Sgn returns 1 for positive numbers, -1 for negative numbers, and 0 if *number* evaluates to 0. In other words, the returned value is true (non-zero) for all non-zero numbers.

Examples

The Sgn function used to return the sign of a number:

```
Result = Sgn(100)                          ' 1
Result = Sgn(-1)                           ' -1
```

The Sgn function can be used to check whether a number is zero:

```
Result = Sgn(0)                              ' 0
```

The Sgn function used to return the sign of a hexadecimal number (can also be used with octal numbers):

```
Result = Sgn(&HFFF8)                         ' -1 (decimal -8)
```

Sgn can be used to prevent division by zero, as shown in the following example:

```
nNumber = 100
If Sgn(nNumber) Then                         ' non-zero
     Result = 100/nNumber
Else
     MsgBox("Oops, attempted division by zero")
End If
```

See Also

Functions: Abs, Fix, and Int

Shell

Misc

Runs a Windows or DOS program.

Syntax

Shell(*command) [, window]*)

command is the name of the program to execute.

window is a style of the program's window.

Usage Notes

command can include any required command line parameters or switches and DOS PATH. DOS and Windows programs can be executed with the Shell function, although the *window* style defaults to full screen for DOS programs run as COM, EXE, or BAT files.

The file extension is necessary in command only DOS programs run from PIF files. If the program cannot be found in the current directory or in a directory included in DOS PATH, a `File not found` error (trappable error #53) occurs.

Other errors can also be triggered. For example, including an invalid path triggers a `Path not found` (trappable error #76), and including an invalid drive in the path triggers an `Illegal function call` (trappable error #5).

Upon success, the Shell function returns a task ID (normally not used in Access Basic); it returns 0 if for any reason the operation fails.

After starting an application, you can send keystrokes to it by using the SendKeys statement.

The following table shows the values of window.

Window	*Style*
1,5,9	Normal with focus
2	Minimized with focus
3	Maximized with focus
4,8	Normal with focus
6,7	Minimized with focus

Examples

To run minimized (as an icon) MS Write and open an existing file (TEST.WRI):

```
Result = Shell("WRITE Test", 2)
```

To run full screen dBASE IV for DOS without its opening screen and execute program TEST.PRG:

```
Result = Shell("C:\DB411\DBASE /t Test")
```

See Also

Statements: AppActivate and SendKeys

Sin

Math

Returns the sine of an angle.

Syntax

Sin(*angle*)

angle can be any valid number or expression measured in radians.

Usage Notes

Sin returns the ratio of two sides of the right triangle in the range -1 to 1.

To convert radians to degrees, multiply radians by 180 divided by the constants π. To convert degrees to radians, multiply degrees by the constants π divided by 180.

See Also

Functions: Atn, Cos, and Tan

SLN

Financial

Returns the depreciation of an asset for a single period using the straight-line method.

Syntax

SLN(*cost, salvage, life*)

cost is the initial cost of an asset.

salvage is the value of an asset at the end of its useful life.

life is the length of the useful life of an asset.

Usage Notes

The result is returned in the same unit of time (such as months or years) as the life of an asset.

A Null or a negative value of any argument triggers an `Illegal function call` error message (trappable error #5).

All arguments can be either Numeric (VarType 2, 3, 4, and 5), Currency (VarType 7), or Variant VarType 8 (String), which can be converted to a number. Different data types can be mixed.

An empty string, or a string that cannot be converted to a number, triggers a `Type mismatch` error (trappable error #13).

SLN can be used in Access Basic and directly attached to controls and properties in forms, reports, and queries.

Caution

This function is implemented in the MSAFIN.DLL library, which is installed by Access in the Windows directory, and declared in the UTILITY.MDA database. To access this function from Access version 1.0, you need to load the UTILITY.MDA by placing the following entry in the Options section of the MSACCESS.INI file (found in your Windows program directory):

```
UtilityDB=<path>UTILITY.MDA
```

Access version 1.1 loads the UTILITY.MDA automatically.

Example

The following example calculates straight-line depreciation when initial value = 1000, salvage value = 50, and lifetime is 5 years:

```
Result = SLN(1000, 50, 5)              '190.00
sCost = "1000"
Result = SLN(sCost, 50, 5)             '190.00
```

See Also

Functions: DDB and SYD

Space, Space$

String

Concatenates *n* spaces to form a string. Space returns a Variant; Space$ returns a String data type.

Syntax

Space[**$**](*number*)

number can be any expression that evaluates to a valid number.

Usage Notes

number must be in the range between 0 and 65,535; a number outside this range triggers an `Illegal function call` error (trappable error #5). The argument is converted to a Long data type.

Example

To pad the string s to the left with spaces to 20 characters total length:

```
s = "*** Twenty ***"
Result$ = Space(20 - Len(s)) + Trim$(s) '"      *** Twenty ***"
```

Caution

Some Access functions display anomalies with data conversion, especially when a literal string is passed as an argument to such a function. Note the following example:

```
aa = Space("20")          ' Error #13 (Type mismatch)

n = "20"                  ' variant that can be converted to a number
aa = Space(n)             ' This works fine
```

See Also

Functions: Spc, String, and String$

FUNCTIONS

Spc

File I/O

Skips *number* of spaces in the output line.

Syntax

Spc(*number*)

Usage Notes

The Spc function can be used only with the Print# statement or Print method.

The range of *number* is limited to 0 to 32767; values outside this range trigger an `Overflow` error (trappable error #3).

If *number* is greater than the width of the output line, the Spc skips the number of spaces represented by (number Mod line width).

If the difference between *number* and the output line width is less than *number* (or *number* Mod line width), the Spc functions skips the number of spaces represented by (*number* - (line width - current position)), starting at the beginning of the next line.

Example

Use the Spc function to space data on the output line:

```
Open "Test.txt" For Output As 1
Print #1, "Hi";Spc(10);"Boris"     '"Hi           Boris"
Close #1
```

Caution

Exercise caution when using the Spc function to align columns of text printed with a proportional font. Because of kerning, the width of the column skipped by the Spc function is calculated as the average width of all characters in a particular font set. The letter *i*, for example, occupies much less space than the letter *w*.

See Also

Functions: Space and Space$, and Tab

Statements: Print and Width

Method: Print

Sqr

Math

Calculates the square root of number.

Syntax

Sqr(*number*)

number can be any numeric expression.

Usage Notes

number must be equal to or greater than 0; a negative number triggers an `Illegal function call` error (trappable error #5).

The Sqr function returns a Double.

number can be a valid decimal, octal, or hexadecimal number.

Example

The Sqr function with arguments each of a different base:

```
Result = Sqr(16)                    '4
Result = Sqr(&H10)                  '4 (Hex 10 = Decimal 16)
```

See Also

Functions: Abs, Atn, Cos, Exp, Fix and Int, Log, Rnd, Sgn, Sin, and Tan

StDev, StDevP

SQL

Return estimates of the standard deviation represented by values from a specified field in a form, report, or a query; StDevP evaluates a population; StDev evaluates a population sample.

Syntax

StDev(*expression*)

StDevP(*expression*)

expression can be a field name containing numeric values to evaluate, the name of a control in the form, query, or report, or an expression that uses values in that field or control to perform calculations. The expression cannot contain other aggregate SQL or domain functions (such as Avg or Sum).

Usage Notes

These functions operate on sets with at least two records and return a Null when there are fewer than two records in the specified file or query.

If *expression* refers to a Memo (or OLE) data type, a `Can't have Memo or OLE object in aggregate argument <name>` error (trappable error #3115) occurs. If *expression* refers to a field containing non-numeric data, an `Illegal type in expression` error (trappable error #3169) is generated.

If *expression* refers to a nonexistent field name or control, an `Invalid reference to control <control name> in query` error (trappable error #2471) occurs.

These functions can be attached only to a query or a calculated control on a form or a report (except on a page header or footer); use the domain functions (DStDev and DStDevP) in Access Basic.

Example

Attached to a control in a form or a report, this example calculates the estimate of the standard deviation for a population for all phone charges:

```
= StDev("[Phone charges]")
```

The following example calculates the estimate of the standard deviation for all phone charges for calls made to London, England:

```
SELECT StDev("[Phone charges"]  FROM "Phone calls" WHERE [City] = "London" AND
➥[Country] = "UK"
```

See Also

Functions: Avg, Count, DStDev and DStDevP, and Var and VarP

Str, Str$ — Conversion

Return a string representation of number. String returns a Variant; Str$ returns a String

Syntax

Str[**$**]*(number)*

number can be any expression that evaluates to a valid number.

Usage Notes

If *number* cannot be converted to a valid number, a `Type mismatch` error (trappable error #13) occurs.

number can be any valid decimal, octal, or hexadecimal number.

These functions hold a placeholder for the sign of a positive number and zero (CStr doesn't).

Example

The following example shows the results of Str function conversion of different values:

```
Result = Str(123)                    ' " 123"
Result = Str(-8)                     ' "-8"
Result = Str(0)                      ' " 0"
Result = Str(&HA11)                  ' " 2577"
```

See Also

Functions: Data Conversion Functions (CStr), Format and Format$, and Val

StrComp

Strings

Compares two strings.

Syntax

StrComp(*string1, string2 [, compare]*)

string1 identifies the expression being compared.

string2 identifies the expression being compared.

compare indicates the string comparison method.

Usage Notes

The following table describes the values allowed in *compare*.

Value	*Description*
0	Case-sensitive comparison
1	Not case-sensitive comparison
2	Database method

See the Option Compare statement and ListFields method for more information about comparison methods.

If *compare* is omitted, StrComp uses the string comparison method set in the Option Compare statement, or default to the Binary method. Specifying an illegal compare method (other than 0, 1, or 2), triggers an `Illegal function call` error (trappable error #5).

StrComp converts both *string 1* and *string 2* to a Variant and returns 1 if string1 is less than *string2*, 0 if *string1* equals *string2*, and 1 if *string1* is greater than *string2*. If either string is Null, StrComp returns a Null.

Examples

The following example shows results of comparison of two strings with different comparison methods:

```
Result = StrComp("Boo","bOO",0)          ' 1
Result = StrComp("boo","Boo",0)          ' 1
Result = StrComp("Boo","bOO",1)          ' 0
Result = StrComp("Boo","bOO",2)          ' 0
```

Caution

Currently there is no Access Basic facility to obtain the setting of the Option Compare.

See Also

Function: InStr

Statement: Option Compare

Method: ListFields

String, String$ — Strings

Replicates a given character, or the first character or a given string, *number* times. String returns a Variant; String$ returns a String.

Syntax

String[**$**]*(number, charactercode)*

or

String[**$**]*(number, string)*

number can be any valid expression that evaluates to a number.

charactercode is the ANSI code for a desired character.

string is a string or a string expression.

Usage Notes

number must be between 0 and 65,535; numbers outside of this range trigger an `Illegal function call` error (trappable error #5).

Examples

The Sring function replicates the first character of a string

```
Result = String(10, "London")          ' "LLLLLLLLLL"
Result = String(2, "#")                ' "##"
```

To pad the string *s* with a character *c* to the total length of *n* characters:

```
s = "Twenty"
c = 42
n = 10
Result = String$(n - Len(s), n) + s     ' "****Twenty"
```

See Also

Functions: Space and Space$

Appendix C, "ANSI Character Set"

Sum

SQL

Returns the sum of values in a specified field in a query, form, or report.

Syntax

Sum(*expression*)

expression can be a field name containing values to count; the name of a control in the form, query, or report; or an expression that uses values in that field or control to perform calculations.

Usage Notes

Sum can be used only in queries, reports, and forms (except in a page header or footer). Use the DSum function in Access Basic code.

expression cannot contain other aggregate SQL or domain functions (such as Count).

Sum can be a part of the SQL SELECT statement.

Examples

To sum all phone charges:

```
=Sum([Phone charges])
```

To sum all phone charges for calls made to London, England:

```
= SELECT Sum([Phone charges]) FROM "Phone calls" WHERE [City] = "London" And
➥[Country] = "UK"
```

FUNCTIONS

See Also

Functions: Avg, Count, DSum, First and Last, Min and Max, StDev and StDevP, and Var and VarP

Switch

Program Flow Control

Returns a value associated with the first expression which evaluates to true.

Syntax

Switch(*varexpr1, var1 [, varexpr2, var2]...[, varexpr7, var7]*)

varexpr is an expression that evaluates to true or false (-1 or zero).

var is a value returned if the corresponding expression evaluates to true. The maximum of 7 *varexpr* are allowed.

Usage Notes

Switch returns the first (leftmost) value associated with varexpr that evaluates to true, even though there may be more than one expression that evaluates to true.

Switch returns a Null if varexpr evaluates to true, or the value associated with the first *varexpr* which evaluates to true is Null.

If there is no *var* associated with *varexpr*, a runtime `Illegal function call` error (trappable error #5) is generated.

Example

To return the name associated with cRegion = 1 (USA):

```
cRegion = 1
Result = Switch( cRegion = 1, "USA", cRegion = 2, "Canada", cRegion = 3, "Eastern
Europe", cRegion = 4, "Japan")
nVal = 2
Result = Switch(nVal = 1, "1", nVal = 2)     'Error #5
```

Caution

Even though Switch returns only one expression, it evaluates all of them. It therefore may generate various runtime errors if expressions are erroneous (such as division by zero, null variable value)—especially if expressions are based on the user input or other values unknown to the programmer.

See Also

Functions: Choose, DLookup, and IIf

Statement: Select Case

SYD

Financial

Returns the depreciation of an asset for a specified period using the sum-of-years' method.

Syntax

SYD(*cost, salvage, life, period*)

Usage Notes

cost is the initial cost of an asset.

salvage is the value of an asset at the end of its useful life.

life is the length of the useful life of an asset.

period is the period number for which asset depreciation is calculated.

life and period must be expressed in the same units (years or months, for example). If the units are different (life is expressed in years and period in months, for example) and the Period is greater than Life, an Illegal function call error (trappable error #5) is triggered; a Null or a negative value of any argument will also trigger this error.

All arguments can be either Numeric (VarType 2,3,4,5), Currency (VarType 7), or Variant VarType 8 (String) that can be converted to a number: data types can be mixed.

An empty string, or a string that cannot be converted to a number, triggers a `Type mismatch` error (trappable error #13).

SYD can be used in Access Basic and directly attached to controls and properties in forms, reports, and queries.

Caution

This function is implemented in the MSAFIN.DLL library, which is installed by Access in the Windows directory, and declared in the UTILITY.MDA database. To access this function from Access version 1.0, you need to load the UTILITY.MDA by placing the following entry in the Options section of the MSACCESS.INI file (found in your Windows program directory.)

```
UtilityDB=<path>UTILITY.MDA
```

Access version 1.1 loads the UTILITY.MDA automatically.

Example

Calculate depreciation using the sum-of-years', method when in itial value = 1000, salvage value = 50, and lifetime is 5 years. Depreciation will be calculated for the first period:

```
Result = SYD(1000, 50, 5, 1)          '316.67
Dim sCost as Variant
sCost = "1000"
Result = SYD(sCost, 50, 5,1)          '316.67
```

See Also

Functions: DDB and SLN

SysCmd

Miscellaneous

Displays a progress meter or a specified text on the Access status bar. Checks the type and version of the runtime environment. This function is documented only in the ADK (Access Distribution Kit).

Syntax

SysCmd(action[, text][, value])

action is the type of action to take (see below).

text is the string expression that will appear on the status bar.

value is the numeric value that controls the progress meter.

Usage Notes

The SysCmd function allows displaying a progress bar informing the user about progress of the current operation, if the operation has a known number of steps.

action can have the values described in the following table.

Value	*Description*
1	Initialize the progress meter to 100% based on the specified value
2	Update the progress meter with the specified value
3	Remove the progress meter
4	Set the status bar text
5	Reset the status bar text
6	Check if the full Access system or just ADK is present (version 1.1 only)
7	Return the version of Access (version 1.1 only)

text is required when *action* is equal to 1 or 4; for other values of action, *text* is prohibited. Its length can be approximately 80 characters (depending on the actual characters, since it is displayed using a proportional font). If action is equal to 1 and text is longer than the width of the status bar, text is ignored; if action is equal to 4 and text is longer than the width of the status bar, the part of text that doesn't fit on the status bar is truncated.

value is required when action is equal to 1 or 2; for other values of *action*, *value* is prohibited.

Caution

Values 6 and 7 can be used as action arguments only in version 1.1; if used in version 1.0 a trappable error #5 (Illegal function call) is generated.

Tip

You may want to replace the default Ready message on the Access status bar with something different by using the SysCmd function:

```
Result = SysCmd(4, "Whas up?...")    ' "Whas up?..." displayed
```

or

```
Result = SysCmd(4, " ")              ' no message displayed
```

And the following code resets it to the default Access message, `Ready`:

```
Result = SysCmd(5)
```

Example

To display the progress of a 10,000-iteration For...Next loop use the following code:

```
Result = SysCmd(1, "For...Next", 10000) 'initialize
For i = 1 To 10000
     Result = SysCmd(2, i)              ' update
Next i
Result = SysCmd(3)                      ' remove
```

See Also

For more examples of using the SysCmd function, see function UpdateMSAErrors in MSErrors module of the Que database supplied on the sample code disk.

Tab

File I/O

Skips *number* of columns in the output line.

Syntax

Tab*(number)*

Usage Notes

The Tab function can be used only with the Print# statement or Print method.

The range of *number* is limited to 0 to 32,767; values outside this range trigger an `Overflow` error (trappable error #3).

If *number* is greater than the width of the output line, the Tab skips (*number* Mod line width) *number* of columns; if this calculated value is less than the current column, printing begins at this position on the next line.

Example

Use the Tab function to space text on an output line:

```
Open "Test.txt" For Output As 1
Print #1, "Hi";Tab(10);"Boris"     '"Hi           Boris"
Close #1
```

Caution

Exercise caution when using the Tab function to align columns of text printed with a proportional font. Because of kerning, the width of the column skipped by the Tab function is calculated as the average width of all characters in a particular font set. The letter *i*, for example, occupies much less space than the letter *w*.

See Also

Functions: Space and Space$ and Spc

Statements: Print and Width

Method: Print

Tan — Math

Returns the tangent of an angle.

Syntax

Tan*(angle)*

angle can be any valid number or expression measured in radians.

Usage Notes

Tan returns the ratio of two sides of a right triangle as a Double number. If the returned value is greater than the largest Double number, an overflow occurs.

To convert radians to degrees, multiply radians by 180 divided by the constants Pi. To convert degrees to radians multiply degrees by the constants Pi divided by 180.

See Also

Functions: Atn, Cos, and Sin

Time, Time$

Date and Time

Returns the system time.

Syntax

Time[**$**][()]

Usage Notes

The empty parentheses are required only when these functions are used outside of Access Basic, such as in queries or when directly attached to controls in forms or reports.

The Time function returns a date data type (Variant VarType 7).

The Time$ functions returns the system time as a string, formatted as hour:minute:second, using the 24 hour (*military*) clock.

Examples

Assuming that the current system time is 8:25:21 P.M. display the current time using the Time function:

```
Result = Time                    ' 8:25:21 PM
Result = Time$                   ' 20:25:21
```

The result returned by the Time$ function is equivalent to the following:

```
Format$(Now, "hh:mm:ss")         ' 20:25:21
```

See Also

Functions: Format and Format$, Now, and Timer

Statements: Time and Time$

FUNCTIONS

Timer

Date and Time

Returns the number of seconds that have elapsed since midnight.

Syntax

Timer[( )]

Usage Notes

If Timer is used outside Access Basic, the empty parentheses must be included.

Timer returns a Single data type.

There are 86,400 seconds in 24 hours.

Example

The following empty (NOP) loop executes until midnight (when the Timer function returns zero):

```
Start! = Timer
Do
Loop Until Timer < Start!
```

See Also

Statement: Randomize

Function: Seconds

TimeSerial

Conversion

Returns the time serial for a specifed time component.

Syntax

TimeSerial(*hour, minute,. second)*

hour is a number, or an expression that evaluates to a number. For meaningful results, *hour* should fall between 0 and 23 (12 a.m. and 11 p.m.).

minute is a number, or an expression that evaluates to a number. For meaningful results, minute should fall between 0 and 59.

second is a number, or an expression that evaluates to a number. For meaningful results second should fall between 0 and 59.

Usage Notes

TimeSerial returns the time component of the date data type (Variant of VarType 7). The time is internally stored as a fractional portion of the double-precision number, in the range of 0—which expresses midnight (00:00:00)—and .99999 (11:59:59 p.m.).

The theoretical range for all arguments (hour, minute, and second) is the range of an integer (-32,768 to 32,767). Numbers outside of the range of an integer trigger an `Overflow` error message (trappable error #6).

Example

Convert three numbers, - 11, 12 and 13, to a valid time:

```
Result = TimeSerial(11, 12, 13)            '11:12:13 AM
```

Caution

If either minute or second falls outside a practical range, the DateSerial function performs the date/time arithmetic and returns a valid time, unless the conversion pushes the number of hours beyond 23. Then the TimeSerial function starts returning the correct time coupled with dates for years before the 20th century, as in the following example.

```
Result = TimeSerial(22, 100, 00)        ' 11:40:00 PM
Result = TimeSerial(23, 100, 00)        ' 12/31/1899 12:40:00 AM
```

See Also

Functions: Hour, Minute, Now, Second, Time, and TimeValue

TimeValue

Conversion

Returns the time represented by an expression.

Syntax

TimeValue(*expression*)

expression is a string representing a valid date and/or time information.

Usage Notes

TimeValue returns a date data type (Variant of VarType 7).

TimeValue recognizes all unambiguous time expressions using either a 12- or 24-hour clock (such as "12:23 PM" and "23:56").

TimeValue doesn't return the date information if a valid date is included in the expression.

If *expression* doesn't evaluate to a valid time, an `Illegal function call` error (trappable error #5) is triggered.

Example

```
TimeValue with a valid String argument:
Dim sString as String
sString = "Dec-30-1990 11:43:12 PM"
Debug.Print VarType(sString)          ' 8 (string)
Result = TimeValue(sString)           ' 11:43:12 PM
Debug.Print VarType(Result)           ' 7 (date)
```

This string doesn't evaluate to a valid time:

```
Result = TimeValue("12:88:00 PM")     ' Error #5
```

See Also

Functions: Hour, Minute, Now, Second, and TimeSerial

Trim, Trim$

See the "Ltrim" function.

UBound

Array Manipulation

Returns the largest available subscript in a given dimension of an array.

Syntax

UBound(*array [, dimension]*)

array must be the name of a declared and initialized array.

dimension indicates for which array dimension the value is returned. If omitted, 1 is assumed.

Usage Notes

UBound can only be used in Access Basic; it cannot be attached to controls and properties in Microsoft Access objects.

In Access, if an array is declared using the keyword "To," its lower bound may start from any number smaller than the upper bound of the same dimension.

Attempting to apply this function to a nonexistent dimension triggers a `Subscript out of range` error (trappable error #9). The same error is returned when an array is declared but not initialized.

Use this function in conjunction with the Lbound function to determine the actual number of available array elements for a given dimension.

Examples

To find the largest subscript in the first dimension:

```
ReDim a(0 To 10,1 To 15)
Result = UBound(a)                    ' 10
```

To find the largest subscript for a given dimension and the number of dimensions:

```
ReDim a(-3 To 5, 10 To 12)
Result = UBound(a,1)                  ' 5
Result = UBound(a,2)                  ' 12
Result = UBound(a,3)                  ' Error #9
```

See Also

Function: LBound

Statements: Dim, Global, Option Base, ReDim, and Static

UCase, UCase$

Strings

Converts letters in a string to uppercase. UCase returns a variant; UCase$ returns a string.

Syntax

UCase[**$**]*(string)*

string is any valid string expression.

Usage Notes

UCase can accept a Null value (in which case a Null is returned).

UCase$ returns a `Type mismatch` error (trappable error #13) if the argument is not a valid string.

Only lowercase letters are converted to uppercase; other characters are not changed.

Examples

```
Result = UCase("James Bond")          ' JAMES BOND
Result = UCase("jb - 007")            ' JB - 007
```

Caution

Other than checking that the ANSI value of a character falls into the range of uppercase letters, Access Basic doesn't have a built-in function to verify that a given character is uppercase. One way around this limitation is to call the Windows function IsCharUpper (which resides in the USER.EXE DLL). Before calling IsCharUpper, the function must be declared as external in the declarations section of an Access Basic module. To avoid library conflicts, use a prefix—abc_, for example—in the function name. This process is illustrated in the following example (Please see Chapter 13, "Extending Microsoft Access and Access Basic" for a general discussion and more examples on the subject of accessing the Microsoft Windows API).

In the declarations section:

```
Declare Function abc_IsCharUpper Lib "User" Alias "IsCharUpper" (ByVal CharCode as
➥Integer) as Integer
```

In Access Basic code:

```
Result = abc_IsCharUpper( Asc("m") )          ' 0 (false)
```

See Also

Functions: LCase and LCase$

User — Miscellaneous

Returns the name of the current user.

Syntax

User()

Usage Notes

Access system security must be enabled for this function to return a meaningful value. Otherwise this function returns a default string "Admin."

See Also

Chapter 2, "Working with the Access Database"

Val — Conversion

Returns the numeric value of a string.

Syntax

Val(*string*)

string is a character expression which can be interpreted as a number.

Usage Notes

Val considers decimal numbers (octal and hexadecimal only when used with the appropriate prefix), linefeeds, tabs, and blanks as parts of a numeric expression and will stop reading the *string* at the first encountered other character.

Attempts to pass a non-character expression (such as an integer) result in a `Type mismatch` error (trappable error #13).

Val returns a double data type.

If the argument is an Null, Val returns an `Invalid use of null` error (trappable error #94).

Examples

Results of the Val function with different arguments:

```
Result = Val("1234")                ' 1234
Result = Val("A1")                  ' 0
Result = Val("&HA1")                ' 161 (Hex A1)
Result = Val("1545 1 S. 17th Ave.") ' 15451
Result = Val(123)                   ' Error #13
```

Tip

If a string contains only numbers, using data conversion functions (CCur, CDbl, CInt, CLng, CSng, CVar) may be more natural.

See Also

Functions: Format and Format$, Chr and Chr$, Str and Str$, and Data Type Conversion functions

FUNCTIONS

Var, VarP

SQL

Return estimates of the variance represented by values from a specifed field in a form, report, or a query; VarP evaluates a population; Var evaluates a population sample.

Syntax

Var(*expression*)

VarP(*expression*)

expression can be a field name containing numeric values to evaluate, the name of a control in the form, query, report, or an expression that uses values in that field or control to perform calculations.

expression cannot contain other aggregate SQL or domain functions (such as Avg or Sum).

Usage Notes

Var and VarP operate on sets with at least two records and return a Null when there are fewer than two records in the specified file or query.

If *expression* refers to a Memo (or OLE) data type, a `Can't have Memo or OLE object in aggregate argument <name>` error (trappable error #3115) occurs.

If *expression* refers to a field containing nonnumeric data, an `Illegal type in expression` error (trappable error #3169) is generated.

If *expression* refers to a nonexistent field name or control, an `Invalid reference to control <control name> in query` error (trappable error #2471) occurs.

These functions can be attached only to a query or a calculated control on a form or a report (except on a page header or footer); use the domain functions (DVar and DVarP) in Access Basic.

Examples

Attached to a control in a form or a report, the following example calculates the estimate of the variance for a population for all phone:

```
= Var("[Phone charges]")
```

This example calculates the estimated variance for all calls made to London:

```
SELECT Var("[Phone charges"]  FROM "Phone calls" WHERE [City] = "London"
```

See Also

Functions: Avg, Count, DVar, DVarP, First, Last, Min, Max, StDev, StDevP, and Sum

VarType

Inspection of Variables

Returns the internal storage class of a Variant data type.

Syntax

VarType(*variant*)

variant can be any expression that evaluates to a valid MSAB data type.

Usage Notes

VarType returns values described in the following table.

Value	*Internal Storage Class*
0	Empty
1	Null
2	Integer
3	Long
4	Single
5	Double
6	Currency
7	Date
8	String

Examples

Results of the VarType function with arguments of various data types:

```
Dim a as Integer
Result = VarType(a)                 '2

a = Now
Result = VarType(a)                 '7

Dim a as Integer, b as Double
a = 100 : b = 25.6
Result = VarType(a/b)               '5

a = #01/01/92#
Result = VarType(a)                 '7
```

See Also

Functions: IsDate, IsEmpty, IsNull and IsNumeric

Statement: Dim

Chapter 10, "Understanding Access Data Types"

Weekday

Conversion

Returns the numeric day of the week for the corresponding date, starting with 1 for Sunday.

Syntax

Weekday(*number*)

number is any numeric expression that evaluates to a valid date between January 1, 100 and December 31, 9999.

Usage Notes

Dates prior to December 31, 1899 must be represented by negative numbers.

If *number* cannot be converted into a valid date, a `Type mismatch` error (trappable error #13) occurs.

If *number* is a Null, the Weekday function returns Null.

Examples

Results of the Weekday function with different date formats:

```
Result = Weekday(#01-01-92#)          '6 (Friday)
Result = Weekday("Dec 31 92")         '5 (Thursday)
```

Caution

To obtain the name of the day, use the Format( ) function, as shown in the following example:

```
Result = Format(#12-31-92#, "dddd")   ' Thursday
Result = Format(#12-31-92#, "ddd")    ' Thu
```

See Also

Functions: Date, DatePart, Day, Format, Hour, Minute, Month, Now, Second, and Year

Year

Conversion

Returns the year of the date.

Syntax

Year(*expression*)

expression can be either a date, or a number that represents a valid date.

Usage Notes

Year returns an integer representing the four digit year of the date for dates in the range January 1, 100 through December 31, 9999.

If *expression* evaluates to a Null, Year returns a Null.

Because Access stores dates internally as Double (2 equals January 1, 1900 and negative numbers represent dates before December 30, 1899) this function accepts numbers as expression.

Examples

The Year function works with any valid date, even if the date is represented by a number:

```
Result = Year(#01/01/1993#)          ' 1993
Result = Year(2)                     ' 1900
```

See Also

Functions: Date DateAdd, DateDiff, DatePart, DateSerial, DateValue, Day, Hour, Minute, Month, Now, Second, Weekday, Year, and Time

Methods

AddNew

Prepares a new record in the current table or a dynaset.

Applies to

Table and Dynaset Objects

Syntax

object.**AddNew**

object is the name of an open table or a dynaset.

Usage Notes

The values of fields in the record added to a recordset using this method are set to Null regardless of the default values specified in the underlying table's DefaultValue property.

A record added with the AddNew method doesn't become the current record, and can be reached only with the MoveLast method (if added to an unindexed table or dynaset) or the Seek method (if the record is added to an indexed table).

If the new record fits on the existing (memory) page, Access uses optimistic locking. If a new page is created, locking is pessimistic (the entire page, or more than one record, is locked).

AddNew triggers an `Object variable not set` error (trappable error #91) if the object refers to a table or dynaset that is not open.

Example

To add a record to the Test table in the current database and replace one of its fields (Due date) with a calculated value:

```
Dim CurrentDB as Database, CurrentTable as Table
Set CurrentDB = CurrentDB()
Set CurrentTable = CurrentDB.OpenTable("Test")
CurrentTable.AddNew
CurrentTable.MoveLast
CurrentTable.[Due date] = Now() + 30
CurrentTable.Update
CurrentTable.Close
```

See Also

Methods: Close, Delete, Edit, MoveFirst, MoveLast, MovePrevious, Seek, and Update

AppendChunk

Appends data from a string to a Memo or OLE field; applies to table and dynaset objects.

Applies to

Table and Dynaset Objects

Syntax

object!*field*.**AppendChunk**(*source*)

object is the name of an open table or a dynaset object.

field is the name of the Memo or OLE field.

source is the name of the object from which data is being appended.

Usage Notes

AppendChunk enables the user to get around the 64K limit of Access strings by transferring large OLE object fields in "chunks." It also enables the user to copy long strings by using smaller strings when conserving memory is important.

If you use the AppendChunk method to update a field other than a Memo or an OLE object, an `Invalid field data type` error (trappable error #3259) occurs.

If the source field contains a Null value, a `Null is invalid` error (trappable error #3162) occurs.

To clear the current field, replace it with a zero-length string.

Example

See the GetChunk method.

See Also

Methods: FieldSize and GetChunk

Circle

Draws a circle, an ellipse, or an arc.

Applies to

Report Objects

Syntax

object.**Circle** [**Step**](*x,y*), *radius[,[color]][,[start]][,[end]][, aspect]]]*

object is the name of an open report object.

Step indicates that the coordinates of the figure being drawn are relative to the object's coordinates set by the CurrentX and CurrentY properties.

x,y represents the single numbers that indicate the coordinates of the center point of the figure being drawn. The Scale... properties determine the units of measure used.

radius is a single number that indicates the radius of the figure being drawn. The Scale... properties determine the units of measure used.

color is a Long number and an RGB color of the circle outline. The default is the setting of the ForeColor property.

start, end are Single numbers that indicate the beginning and the end of the arc if a partial circle or an ellipse is drawn.

aspect is a Single number that indicates the aspect ratio of the figure; 1 yields a circle.

Usage Notes

This method can be used only on report objects in a function (or a macro) attached to a report's event properties.

You can omit the optional arguments in the middle of the syntax, but you must include the delimiting commas.

METHODS

If the figure being drawn is a closed figure (a circle, an ellipse, or a pie slice), you can fill it using the settings of the FillColor and BackStyle properties.

The width of the line used to draw a figure depends on the setting of the DrawWidth property.

Example

First draw a *very* thick circle positioned 300 pixels from the upper left corner, and then draw a solid ellipse. Reset the units to twips (by applying the Scale method with no arguments) and print a circle filled with the foreground color positioned at the upper left corner.

```
Dim Rpt As Report
Set Rpt = Reports!report2
Rpt.drawwidth = 100
Rpt.Scalemode = 3
Rpt.Circle (350, 350), 100
Rpt.Circle (650, 650), 100,,,,.1
Rpt.Scale
Rpt.Circle (350, 350), 100
```

See Also

Functions: QBColor and RGB

Properties: BackStyle, CurrentX, CurrentY, DrawMode, DrawStyle, DrawWidth, FillColor, ForeColor, ScaleHeight, ScaleWidth, ScaleLeft, ScaleTop, and ScaleMode

Clone

Creates a duplicate recordset object that refers to the same recordset.

Applies to

Recordset Object

Syntax

Set *dupset* = *origset*.**Clone()**

dupset is the name of the duplicate recordset object being created.

origset is the name of the recordset object being duplicated.

Usage Notes

Use the Clone method to create multiple dynasets when operations on multiple records from the same recordset are necessary. Using the Clone method to "multiply" existing dynasets is more efficient than creating multiple dynasets using other methods.

In dynasets created with the Clone method, the record pointer does not point to any record. To establish the current record, use one of the Move or Find methods, or use Bookmarks (which are valid across dynasets created with the Clone method).

Example

To create a dynaset from the Customers table and clone it twice:

```
Dim cDb As Database, cOrig As Dynaset, cClone1 As Dynaset, cClone2 As Dynaset
    Set cDb = CurrentDB()
    Set cOrig = cDb.CreateDynaset("Customers")
    Set cClone1 = cOrig.Clone()
    Set cClone2 = cClone1.Clone()
    (...)
```

See Also

Methods: Close, CreateDynaset, CreateSnapshot, and OpenTable

Property: Bookmark

Close

Closes the specified database object.

Applies to

Table, Dynaset, Snapshot, and QueryDef Objects

Syntax

object.**Close**

object is the name of an open table, dynaset, snapshot, or QueryDef object.

Usage Notes

The Close method closes only the specified database object; the database remains open.

Use the Update method to save any changes made to a record before using the Close method or the changes will not be saved.

Attempting to use this method on an object that is already closed results in an `Object variable not Set` error (trappable error #91).

Example

This example shows you how to use the Close method to close an object—in this case, a query defined on the fly. The defined query is visible in the query container. To delete the query, use the DeleteQueryDefinition method:

```
Dim cDb As Database, cQu As QueryDef
Set cDb = CurrentDB()
DoCmd Hourglass True
Set cQu = cDb.CreateQueryDef("November 92 calls", "SELECT * FROM [Phone calls] WHERE
Month([Call date]) = 11 And Year([Call date]) = 1992;")
DoCmd Hourglass False
'(...)
cQu.Close
```

See Also

Methods: CreateDynaset, CreateQueryDef, CreateSnapshot, OpenQueryDef, OpenTable, and Update

Function: OpenDatabase

Action: Close

CreateDynaset

Creates a dynaset object.

Applies to

Tables, Recordsets, and QueryDef Objects

Syntax

Set *dynaset* = *object*.**CreateDynaset**([*source* [, *exclusive* [, *inconsistent*]]])

dynaset is the name of the dynaset object being created.

object is the name of the existing database, recordset, QueryDef, or snapshot object.

source is the name of an existing table, query, or SQL expression. It is only used if *object* is a database object.

exclusive is True (-1) if the underlying tables are opened for exclusive use; it is False if the underlying tables are opened for shared access. If omitted, False is assumed.

inconsistent is True (-1) if the dynaset is inconsistent; it is False (0) if the dynaset is consistent. If omitted, a consistent dynaset is created.

Note

The terms *consistent* and *inconsistent* describe the update semantics of a dynaset. A consistent or *consistently updatable* dynaset permits updates only to the row that is being updated. If you create a consistent view (dynaset) as a two-table join of Orders and Customers for each order, for example, each row of the Orders data from this dynaset can be updated, because it doesn't affect other rows in the dynaset. The Customer data cannot be updated because it potentially can affect other orders for this customer, and if this data is updated, Access would have to decide whether the update to the customer's data should affect only one, a few, or all orders for this customer.

In an inconsistent dynaset, all data is updatable; updates that affect other rows in the dynaset are treated by Access as if they were made by another user. For an implicitly created dynaset (such as one created by a form), use the *AllowUpdating* property on a form to specify its update semantics. The DefaultTables setting of this property makes the underlying dynaset consistent. The AllTables setting makes the underlying dynaset inconsistent.

Usage Notes

Dynasets can be created from tables or existing select queries, or they can be directly defined by a SQL expression.

Although the CreateDynaset method can be used on existing dynasets, it is preferable to use the Clone method to duplicate existing dynasets.

Records deleted from the underlying table are displayed in a dynaset with their field values set to Null. Records added to the underlying table don't appear in the dynaset unless the dynaset is re-created.

Example

The following example demonstrates four ways to create a dynaset; all dynasets (cDy0 - cDy3) are identical:

```
Dim cDb As Database, cDy0 As Dynaset, cDy1 As Dynaset, cDy2 As    Dynaset, cDy3
➥As Dynaset
Set cDb = CurrentDB()

Set cDy0 = cDb.CreateDynaset("SELECT * FROM Customers;")
Set cDy1 = cDb.CreateDynaset("Customers")
Set cDy2 = cDy1.CreateDynaset()
Set cDy3 = cDy2.Clone()
(...)
cDy0.Close
cDy1.Close
cDy2.Close
cDy3.Close
```

Note

Although changes made to data in dynasets are reflected in underlying tables (and vice versa—changes made to data in underlying tables are reflected in dynasets based on these tables), changes made to data in other dynasets referring to the same set of data are not immediately visible across dynasets. You may need to re-create a dynaset to reflect the most current changes.

CreateQueryDef

Creates a new QueryDef object.

Applies to

QueryDef Objects

Syntax

Set *querydef* = *database*.**CreateQueryDef**(*name* [, *sqltext*])

querydef is the name of the QueryDef object.

database is the name of the database object.

name is the name of the query being created.

sqltext is the string expression that evaluates to a valid SQL statement.

Usage Notes

This method is used to programmatically define queries at runtime.

An attempt to overwrite an existing query triggers an `Object <name> already exists` error (trappable error #3012).

A query definition is saved as an "empty" query skeleton even if the sqltext definition is missing. Attempting to execute such a query results in a `Query input must contain at least one table or query` error (trappable error #3067). Such an empty query can be programmatically redefined by setting its SQL property.

Example

To create an empty query, set its SQL property, execute it, save the result as a dynaset, and then close and erase the query definition:

```
Dim cDb As Database, cQu As QueryDef, cDy as Dynaset
Set cDb = CurrentDB()
DoCmd Hourglass True
```

```
Set cQu = cDb.CreateQueryDef("November 92 calls")
cQu.SQL = "SELECT * FROM [Phone calls] WHERE  Month([Call date]) = 11 And
➥Year([Call date]) = 1992;"
Set cDy = cDb.CreateDynaset("November 92 calls"
DoCmd Hourglass False
cQu.Close
cDb.DeleteQueryDef("November 92 calls")
(...)
cDy.Close
```

See Also

Methods: Clone, Close, CreateQueryDef, CreateSnapshot, DeleteQueryDef, Execute, OpenQueryDef, and OpenTable

Properties: AllowUpdating, Filter, Sort, and SQL

CreateSnapshot

Creates a new snapshot object.

Applies to

Tables, Recordsets, and QueryDef Objects

Syntax

Set *snapshot* = *object*.**CreateSnapshot**[(*source*)]

snapshot is the name of the snapshot object being created.

object is the name of the existing database, recordset, QueryDef, or a snapshot object (except a snapshot created with any of the List... methods).

source is the name of an existing table, query, or SQL expression. It is used only if the *object* is a database object.

Usage Notes

A snapshot is an exact copy of data at the time it was created.

Data in snapshots is static; it cannot be edited and is not linked to underlying tables. Changes made to data in underlying tables, therefore, will not be reflected in the current snapshot. Attempting to edit snapshot data triggers a variety of compile and runtime errors (such as `Can't perform operation; it is illegal`, error #3219).

Use the Find... method to locate desired records in a snapshot, except in the snapshot created with ListFields, ListIndexes, ListParameters, and ListTables methods.

METHODS

Example

Snapshot cSn1 is created directly from the Customers table; snapshot cSn2 is created from a dynaset cDy created from the Customers table and sorted on the Name field; and snapshot cSn3 contains the list of fields in the Customers table that were created using the ListFields method. Consider the following example:

```
Dim cDb As Database, cTb As Table, cDy As Dynaset, cSn1 As   Snapshot, cSn2 As
  ➥Snapshot, cSn3 As Snapshot
Set cDb = CurrentDB()
Set cSn1 = cDb.CreateSnapshot("Customers")
Set cDy = cDb.CreateDynaset("Customers")
cDy.Sort = "[Name]"
Set cSn2 = cDy.CreateSnapshot()


' Now create a snapshot using ListFields in the table "Customers"

Set cTb = cDb.OpenTable("Customers")
Set cSn3 = cTb.ListFields()
(...)
cSn1.Close
cSn2.Close
cSn3.Close
cTb.Close
cDy.Close
```

See Also

Methods: CreateDynaset, CreateQueryDef, Find..., ListFields, ListIndexes, ListParameters, and ListTables

Delete

Deletes the current record in the specified recordset.

Applies to

Table and Dynaset Objects

Syntax

object.**Delete**

object is the name of an existing table or dynaset object.

Usage Notes

The deleted record remains current as long as the record pointer doesn't move to another record. Any reference to the deleted record, however, produces a `Record is deleted` error (trappable error #3167). You still can use MoveNext and MovePrevious to move to the next and previous records as if the current record wasn't deleted, but you cannot make the deleted record current again.

If you need to undelete records, enclose the deletion operation in the transaction (BeginTrans...) construct and use the Rollback statement to undelete the record if necessary.

If there is no current record in a specified recordset, a `No current record` error (trappable error #3021) occurs.

Example

Delete the last record in the Customers table and make the deletion permanent if the user so desires; otherwise, use the Rollback statement to undelete the record, as shown in the following example:

```
Dim cDb As Database, cTb As Table
Set cDb = CurrentDB()
Set cTb = cDb.OpenTable("Customers")
Const MB_YESNO = 4
Const MB_ICONQUESTION = 32
Const ID_NO = 7
cTb.MoveLast
BeginTrans
cTb.Delete
If MsgBox("Save changes?", MB_ICONQUESTION + MB_YESNO) = ID_NO Then
    Rollback
Else
    CommitTrans
End If
cTb.Close
```

See Also

Methods: AddNew, Edit, and Update

Statements: BeginTransaction and Rollback

DeleteQueryDef

Deletes an existing query definition.

Applies to

QueryDef Objects

Syntax

database.**DeleteQueryDef**(*name*)

database is the name of the database object.

name is the name of the query being deleted.

Usage Notes

Attempting to delete a nonexisting Querydef object triggers a `Couldn't find <name>` error (trappable error #3011). A reference to an open QueryDef object results in a `Can't perform operation; it is illegal` error (trappable error #3219).

See Also

Methods: Close, CreateQueryDef, and OpenQueryDef

Edit

Copies the contents of the current record into the edit buffer.

Applies to

Table and Dynaset Objects

Syntax

object.**Edit**

object is the name of an existing table or dynaset object.

Usage Notes

The Edit method copies the contents of the current record into the edit buffer for subsequent editing. All editing is done in the edit buffer and the original record is not affected until the changes are saved.

Any changes to the edited record must be saved (with the Update method) before moving from this record; merely moving the record pointer to a different record doesn't save changes.

If there is no current record in a specified recordset, a `No current record` error (trappable error #3021) occurs.

Example

To open the Customers table, move to the last record, enable editing, change the customer name, and save the change:

```
Dim cDb As Database, cTb As Table
Set cDb = CurrentDB()
Set cTb = cDb.OpenTable("Customers")
cTb.MoveLast
cTb.Edit
cTb.Name = "Little Red RoostercTb.
Update
cTb.Close
```

See Also

Methods: AddNew, Delete, and Update

Property: LockEdits

Execute

Executes an existing query.

Applies to

Queries

Syntax

querydef.**Execute**

querydef is the name of the valid QueryDef object.

Usage Notes

The Execute method can be applied only to action queries. Other query types (such as Select) trigger a `Can't execute a non-action query` error (trappable error #3065).

You can execute an existing query (opened with the OpenQueryDef method) or a query created with the CreateQueryDef method.

For parameter queries, you must supply the required parameters (with the correct data type) before the query can be executed, or a `<number> parameters were expected, but only <number> were supplied` error (trappable error #3061) occurs. You may use the ListParameters method to create a snapshot of required parameters.

Example

To execute an existing parameter query "Update Inventory" that requires the "UpdatedBy" parameters of string data type:

```
Dim cDb As Database, cQu As QueryDef
Set cDb = CurrentDB()
Set cQu = cDb.OpenQueryDef("Update Inventory")
cQu.UpdatedBy = "JB 007"        'parameter value
cQu.Execute
cQu.Close
```

See Also

Methods: Close, CreateDynaset, CreateQueryDef, CreateSnapshot, and OpenQueryDef

FieldSize

Returns the length of a Memo or an OLE object field in bytes.

Applies to

Memo Fields and OLE Objects

Syntax

object.**FieldSize()**

object is the name of an existing recordset object.

Usage Notes

The FieldSize method is used with AppendChunk and GetChunk methods to manipulate large Memo and OLE object fields.

If the FieldSize method is used to return the size of a field (other than a Memo or an OLE object), it returns zero; no error occurs.

The return value of the FieldSize method should be assigned to a variable of the Long data type (an OLE object size can exceed 64K). Because the length of a Memo field cannot exceed 32K, the return value used to store a Memo field length can be assigned to an Integer variable.

Example

See the GetChunk method.

See Also

Methods: AppendChunk, GetChunk, and ListFields

FindFirst, FindLast, FindNext, FindPrevious

Locate a specified record meeting and specified criteria in a specified dynaset or snapshot.

Applies to

Dynasets and Snapshots

Syntax

object.**FindFirst** *criteria*
object.**FindLast** *criteria*
object.**FindNext** *criteria*
object.**FindPrevious** *criteria*

object is the name of an existing dynaset or a snapshot object.

criteria is a string expression used as a condition to locate the record.

Usage Notes

The criteria consist of three parts: a field name that stores the value being searched for, the comparison operator, and the value being searched for.

Issuing FindNext(...Previous) without a FindFirst (...Last) can cause the Find... to fail without an error message even if there is one (or more) record satisfying criteria.

After an unsuccessful Find, the last current record remains current.

Note

None of the Find methods can be used with a snapshot created with ListFields, ListIndexes, ListParameters, or ListTables methods.

Example

To create a dynaset for a subset of records in the Customer table, seek the first occurrence of the customer ID TRITO, and print all subsequent occurrences in the Immediate window:

```
Dim cDb As Database, cDy As Dynaset, cTb As Table
Criteria = "ID = 'TRITO'"
Set cDb = CurrentDB()
Set cTb = cDb.OpenTable("Customers")
Set cDy = cDb.CreateDynaset("SELECT * FROM Customers WHERE   Left([Phone],3) =
➥'213';")
cDy.FindFirst Criteria
```

METHODS

```
Do Until cDy.nomatch
     Debug.Print cDy.ID, cDy.Phone
     cDy.FindNext Criteria
Loop
cTb.Close
cDy.Close
```

Note

Substituting variables for a literal expression in the criteria part of the Find... expression is a bit tricky, with different syntax for various data types.

Assuming that you are searching for the name Kennedy in the LastName field in the current dynaset referred to as cDy, the syntax is as follows for string data:

```
szFieldName = "LastName"
szValue2search = "Kennedy"
Criteria = szFieldNameN & "=" & "'" & szValue2Search & "'"
cDy.FindFirst Criteria
```

As you can see in the preceding example, the variable name needs to be delimited with single quotation marks.

The syntax is much less convoluted for data types other than string. To search for the salary of $120,000 in the Salary field, the syntax is as follows:

```
szFieldName = Salary
dwValue2Search = 120000
Criteria = szFieldName & "=" & dwValue2Search
cDy.FindFirst Criteria
```

See Also

Methods: MoveFirst, MoveLast, MoveNext, MovePrevious, and Seek

Property: NoMatch

GetChunk

Returns a specified number of bytes of a specified Memo or OLE object field.

Applies to

Recordset Objects

Syntax

recordset!*field*.**GetChunk**(*offset*, *bytes*)

recordset is the name of an open recordset object.

field is the name of the Memo or OLE field.

offset is the number of bytes to skip before copying.

bytes is the number of bytes to copy.

Usage Notes

The GetChunk method returns a string containing a specified number of bytes from a specified Memo or OLE object field.

Because the maximum length of a string variable in Access is 65535 bytes, larger OLE fields must be broken into "chunks," assigned to variables (using the GetChunk method), and then reassembled using the AppendChunk method.

If *offset* equals zero, copying starts at the first byte of the field.

If *bytes* is greater than the actual length of the field, the contents of the entire field are returned. (Use the Len function to determine the actual number of the returned string.)

Example

To divide a Memo field, Note, into 20-byte chunks using the GetChunk method and reassemble it with the AppendChunk method into the Note 1 field:

```
Dim cDb As Database, cTb As Table, c As Variant
Set cDb = CurrentDB()
Set cTb = cDb.OpenTable("Customers")
nTotalSize = cTb![Note].FieldSize()
nChunkSize = 20
NumChunks = (nTotalSize \ nChunkSize)
ReDim aChunk(1 To NumChunks)
' Divide the field into "chunks"
For i = 1 To NumChunks
    aChunk(i) = cTb!Note.GetChunk((i - 1) * nChunkSize, nChunkSize)
Next i
'(...)
' reassemble the field
cTb.Edit
For i = 1 To NumChunks
    cTb![Note 1].AppendChunk (aChunk(i))
Next i
cTb.Update
cTb.Close
```

See Also

Methods: AppendChunk and FieldSize

Function: Len

Line

Draws lines and rectangles.

Applies to

Reports Objects

Syntax

object.**Line** [[**Step1**](*x1*,*y1*)] - [**Step2**](*x2*,*y2*)[,[*color*][,**B**,[**F**]]]

object is the name of an open report object.

Step1 indicates that the starting point coordinates of the line being drawn are relative to the object's coordinates set by CurrentX and CurrentY properties.

x1,y1 represents single numbers indicating the coordinates of the starting point of the line being drawn. The Scale... properties determine the units of measure used.

Step2 indicates that the ending point of the line being drawn is relative to the starting point.

x2,y2 represents single numbers indicating the coordinates of the ending point of the line being drawn. The Scale... properties determine the units of measure used. These coordinates are required.

color is a Long number and an RGB color of the circle outline. The default is the setting of the ForeColor property.

B indicates that a box should be drawn using the coordinates specified in *x1,y1* and *x2,y2*.

F indicates that the box drawn with the B option should be filled with the same color used to draw a box (resulting in a solid box). This option cannot be used without the B option.

Usage Notes

This method can be used only on report objects in a function (or a macro) attached to report event properties such as OnFormat or OnPrint.

When you draw rectangles, start the next line precisely at the ending coordinates of the preceding line.

The width of the line depends on the DrawWidth property; the way the line or box is drawn depends on the setting of the DrawMode and DrawStyle properties.

CurrentX and CurrentY properties are set to the ending coordinates of the line being drawn.

Example

To draw three rectangles adorned by three slanted lines on a report named Report2:

```
Dim Rpt As Report
Set Rpt = reports!report2
Rpt.drawwidth = 5
Rpt.Scalemode = 3
BottX = 100
BottY = 200
For i = 1 To 3
    Rpt.Line (3, 100)-(BottX * i, BottY * i), , B
    Rpt.Line (3 * i, 100 * i)-(BottX * i, BottY * i)
Next i
```

The following example draws the peace symbol of the 1960s using the Line and Circle methods:

```
Dim Rpt As Report
Set Rpt = reports!report2
Rpt.drawwidth = 5
Rpt.Scalemode = 3
Rpt.Circle (100, 300), 100
Rpt.Line (100, 200)-(100, 400)
Rpt.Line (100, 300)-(20, 350)
Rpt.Line (100, 300)-(180, 350)
```

See Also

Functions: QBColor and RGB

Methods: Circle, Print, and PSet

Properties: BackStyle, Current X and Current Y, DrawMode, DrawStyle, DrawWidth, FillColor, ForeColor, ScaleHeight, ScaleWidth, ScaleLeft, ScaleTop, and ScaleMode

ListFields

Creates a snapshot listing of fields in the specified recordset.

Applies to

Table, Snapshot, and Dynaset Objects

Syntax

Set *snapshot* = *recordset*.**ListFields()**

snapshot is the name of the valid snapshot object.

recordset is the name of the existing recordset object.

Usage Notes

The ListFields method returns up to 255 fields in the same order as fields in the specified recordset.

You cannot use the ListFields method on snapshots created with ListFields, ListParameters, ListIndexes, or ListTables methods.

The structure of the resulting snapshot follows:

Field and Data Type	*Description*
Name (String)	Name of the field
Type (Long)	1 - Yes/No 2 - Number (byte) 3 - Number (integer) 4 - Number (long) 5 - Currency 6 - Number (single) 7 - Number (double) 8 - Date/Time 9 - (reserved) 10 - Text 11 - OLE object 12 - Memo
Size (Long)	Maximum size of the field, in bytes (exceptions are bit fields - 1, Memo and OLE objects - 0)
Attributes (Long)	1 - Fixed 16 - Autoincrement 32 - Updatable 33 - (not documented) 49 - (not documented)
SourceTable (String)	Name of the underlying table
SourceField (String)	Name of the field in the underlying table
CollatingCode (Long)	Comparison code: used to sort the resulting table to assure that the fields are in the same order as defined in the table definition. 1-256

Note

In Access version 1.0, you cannot use this method on attached tables; it triggers a `Can't perform operation; it is illegal` error (trappable error #3219).

Example

To create a snapshot of all fields in the Customers table and save it in a table named ListFields:

```
Dim cDb As Database, cTb As Table, cSn As Snapshot
Set cDb = CurrentDB()
Set cTb = cDb.OpenTable("Customers")
Set cSn = cTb.ListFields()
Set cTb = cDb.OpenTable("ListFields")
Do Until cSn.eof
    cTb.AddNew
    cTb.Name = cSn.Name
    cTb.Type = cSn.Type
    cTb.Size = cSn.Size
    cTb.Attributes = cSn.Attributes
    cTb.SourceTable = cSn.SourceTable
    cTb.SourceField = cSn.SourceField
    cTb.CollatingOrder = cSn.CollatingOrder
    cTb.Update
    cSn.MoveNext
Loop
cSn.Close
cTb.Close
```

See Also

Methods: ListIndexes, ListParameters, and ListTables

ListIndexes

Creates a snapshot listing indexes in the specified table.

Applies to

Table Objects

Syntax

Set *snapshot* = *table*.**ListIndexes()**

snapshot is the name of a valid snapshot object.

table is the name of an existing table object.

Usage Notes

If the specified table has no indexes, the resulting snapshot will have no records.

A separate record in the snapshot is created for each field in the compound index (Index1...Index5 properties).

The structure of the resulting snapshot is as shown in the following table.

METHODS

Field and Data Type	*Description*
IndexName (String)	Name of the index; the primary key is marked with the keyword "PrimaryKey"
FieldCount (Long)	Number of fields in the index
IndexAttributes (Long)	1 - Unique 4 - DisallowNull 7 - Primary key 8 - IgnoreNull
FieldName (String)	Name of the field in the table
FieldOrder (Long)	Order of the field in the compound index
FieldType (Long)	1 - Yes/No 2 - Number (byte) 3 - Number (integer) 4 - Number (long) 5 - Currency 6 - Number (single) 7 - Number (double) 8 - Date/Time 9 - (reserved) 10 - Text 11 - OLE object 12 - Memo
FieldAttributes (Long)	1 - descending
FieldCollatingOrder (Integer)	Comparison code: used to sort the resulting table to ensure that the fields are in the same order as defined in the table definition. 1-256

Note

In Access version 1.0 you cannot use this method on attached tables; it triggers a `Can't perform operation; it is illegal` error (trappable error #3219).

Example

Create a snapshot of all indexes in the Customers table. If the number of records in the snapshot is greater than 0, save it to a ListIndexes table, as shown in the following example:

```
Dim cDb As Database, cTb As Table, cSn As Snapshot
Set cDb = CurrentDB()
Set cTb = cDb.OpenTable("Customers")
Set cSn = cTb.ListIndexes()
If cSn.RecordCount > 0 Then
   Set cTb = cDb.OpenTable("ListIndexes")
   Do Until cSn.eof
       cTb.AddNew
       cTb.IndexName = cSn.IndexName
       cTb.FieldCount = cSn.FieldCount
       cTb.IndexAttributes = cSn.IndexAttributes
       cTb.FieldName = cSn.FieldName
       cTb.FieldOrder = cSn.FieldOrder
       cTb.FieldType = cSn.FieldType
       cTb.FieldAttributes = cSn.FieldAttributes
       cTb.FieldCollatingOrder = cSn.FieldCollatingOrder
       cTb.Update
       cSn.MoveNext
   Loop
Endif
cSn.Close
cTb.Close
```

See Also

Methods: ListFields, ListParameters, and ListTables

ListParameters

Creates a snapshot listing parameters of the given QueryDef object.

Applies to

QueryDef Objects

Syntax

Set *snapshot* = *querydef*.**ListParameters()**

snapshot is the name of the valid snapshot object.

querydef is the name of the existing QueryDef object.

Usage Notes

If the query has no parameters, the resulting snapshot will have no records.

The resulting snapshot has two fields: Name (String), containing a name of the parameter, and Type (Long), containing the code for the parameter's data type, as shown in the following:

0	Undefined
1	Yes/No
2	Number (byte)
3	Number (integer)
4	Number (long)
5	Currency
6	Number (single)
7	Number (double)
8	Date/Time
9	(reserved)
10	Text
11	OLE object
12	Memo

Example

To open an existing parameter query (Expenses92, based on the Exp92 table), create a snapshot of required parameters, and print the list (and the SQL statement produced by this query) to the Immediate window:

```
Dim cDb As Database, cQu As QueryDef, cSn As Snapshot
Set cDb = CurrentDB()
Set cQu = cDb.OpenQueryDef("Expenses92")
Set cSn = cQu.ListParameters()
Do Until cSn.EOF
   Debug.Print cSn.name, cSn.type    ' print parameters
   cSn.MoveNext
Loop
Debug.Print cQu.sql                  ' print SQL property
cQu.Close
cSn.Close
```

Because there is only one parameter in this query, the printout of parameters looks as follows:

```
[Enter the Expense Category]        0
```

In the next example, the parameter is buried within the WHERE clause of the SQL statement:

```
SELECT  DISTINCTROW Exp92.Type, Exp92.Date, Exp92.Amount, Exp92.Purpose,
➥Exp92.Category
FROM Exp92
WHERE ((Exp92.Category=[Enter the Expense Category]))
ORDER BY Exp92.Type, Exp92.Date
WITH OWNERACCESS OPTION;
```

See Also

Methods: ListFields, ListIndexes, and ListTables

ListTables

Creates a snapshot listing each table and QueryDef object in a specified database.

Applies to

Table and QueryDef Objects

Syntax

Set *snapshot* = *database*.**ListTables()**

snapshot is the name of the valid snapshot object.

database is the name of the existing database object.

Usage Notes

Tables and queries in the specified database are listed in alphabetical order. Access system tables are also included in the listing.

The resulting snapshot has the following structure:

Field and Data Type	*Description*
Name (String)	Name of the table or QueryDef
DateCreated (Date/Time)	Date and time the table or QueryDef was created
LastUpdated (Date/Time)	Date and time the table or QueryDef was last changed
TableType (Long)	Can be one of the following: 1 - native Access table 4 - attached ODBC table 5 - QueryDef object 6 - attached table (not via ODBC) TableType values can be accessed using explicit numbers or the following constants: DB_TABLE - native Access table DB_ATTACHEDODBC - attached ODBC table DB_QUERYDEF - QueryDef object DB_ATTACHEDTABLE - attached table (not via ODBC)

continues

Field and Data Type	*Description*
RecordCount (Long)	Number of records in the table (zero, if TableType is DB_QUERYDEF)
Attributes (Long)	File flags

Example

To create a snapshot of files in the current database and transfer it to a ListTables table with the same structure as the snapshot:

```
Dim cDb As Database, cSn As Snapshot, T As Table
Set cDb = CurrentDB()
Set cSn = cDb.ListTables()
Set T = cDb.OpenTable("ListTables")
Do Until cSn.eof

    T.AddNew
    T.Name = cSn.Name
    T.DateCreated = cSn.DateCreated
    T.LastUpdated = cSn.LastUpdated
    T.TableType = cSn.TableType
    T.RecordCount = cSn.RecordCount
    T.Attributes = cSn.Attributes
    T.Update
    cSn.MoveNext
    Loop
cSn.Close
T.Close
```

See Also

Methods: CreateSnapshot, ListIndexes, and ListFields

MoveFirst, MoveLast, MoveNext, MovePrevious

Locate the applicable record in the specified recordset and make this record current.

Applies to

Recordset Objects

Syntax

recordset.**MoveFirst**
recordset.**MoveLast**

recordset.**MoveNext**
recordset.**MovePrevious**

recordset is the name of an open recordset (table, dynaset, or snapshot) object.

Usage Notes

The Move... statement unconditionally locates the specified record and makes it the current record.

In an indexed table with an index active, movement follows the index order.

Any changes to the current record made with the Edit method must be saved with the Update method before moving from the record; merely moving the record pointer doesn't save the changes.

The following are special cases of the Move... method.

First record:

When a recordset is created (or opened), the record pointer is on the first (top) record and the BOF property is False. If the record pointer is on the first (top) record, issuing MoveFirst doesn't change the current record and the BOF property remains False.

If the record pointer is on the first record, and the BOF property is True (after a MovePrevious, for example), issuing MovePrevious again triggers a `No current record error` (trappable error #3021), the current record becomes undefined, and the BOF property stays True.

Last record:

If you issue MoveLast, the last record (logically or physically) in the table is made current and the EOF property is set to False. If the record pointer is already on the last record, issuing MoveLast doesn't change the current record and the EOF property remains False. If you issue MoveNext while the record pointer is on the last record and the EOF property is True (such as after a previous MoveNext), the current record becomes undefined, the EOF property stays True, and a `No current record` error (trappable error #3021) occurs.

Example

To open a table, move to the last record, set the Bookmark property (to be able to return to a valid record), and trigger an error by attempting to move past the last record in the table:

```
On Error Resume Next
Dim cDb As Database, cTb As Table, s1 As String
Set cDb = CurrentDB()
Set cTb = cDb.OpenTable("Customers")
cTb.MoveLast
s1 = cTb.bookmark                  ' set bookmark
cTb.MoveNext : cTbMoveNext         ' error!
If Err <> 0 Then cTb.bookmark = s1       ' return to a valid record
cTb.Close
```

See Also

Methods: Seek and Update

Properties: BOF, EOF, Index, and RecordCount

OpenQueryDef

Opens an existing QueryDef object.

Applies to

QueryDef Objects

Syntax

Set *querydef* = *database*.**OpenQueryDef**(*name*)

querydef is the name of the QueryDef object.

database is the name of the database object.

name is the name of the query being opened.

Usage Notes

For parameter queries, parameters with the correct data type must be set before the opened query can be executed or a `<number> parameters were expected, but only <number> were supplied` error (trappable error #3061) occurs. You may use the ListParameters method to create a snapshot of required parameters.

If *name* refers to a nonexisting query, a `Couldn't find input table or query <name>` error (trappable error #3078) occurs.

CreateDynaset and CreateSnapshot methods can be used on QueryDef objects opened with OpenQueryDef.

Example

To open an existing query (Expenses92) and list its SQL property and parameters in the immediate window:

```
Dim cDb As Database, cQu As QueryDef, cSn As Snapshot
Set cDb = CurrentDB()
Set cQu = cDb.OpenQueryDef("Expenses92")
Debug.Print cQu.SQL
Set cSn = cQu.ListParameters()
Debug.Print cSn.name, cSn.type
cQu.Close
cSn.Close
```

See Also

Methods: Close, CreateQueryDef, DeleteQueryDef, and ListParameters

OpenTable

Creates a table object from a specified table.

Applies to

Table Objects

Syntax

Set *table* = *database*.**OpenTable**(*name* [, *exclusive*])

table is the name of the table object to be created.

database is the name of the database object (most likely a current database).

name is the name of the table in the database specified by database.

exclusive is a Boolean value indicating whether to use the specified table in exclusive mode.

Usage Notes

Creating a table object is a necessary step before applying various methods (such as Edit, AddNew, and so on) to this table.

If exclusive is True (a nonzero value), Access attempts to lock the specified table for exclusive use. Attempting to exclusively use a table already in use triggers a `Couldn't lock table <name>; currently in use` error (trappable error #3009), or a `Table <name> is exclusively locked` error (trappable error #3008) if the table is opened in the Design view.

Shared table use mode is assumed by default unless *exclusive* has a nonzero value.

If *name* refers to a nonexistent table, a `Couldn't find object <name>` error (trappable error #3011) is generated.

For subsets of data, creating a dynaset is more useful than using the entire table. You also can use a snapshot, but because it is a static element (data in `snapshot` cannot be changed), its usefulness is limited to listings.

Note

You must always explicitly declare Database, Table, Dynaset, Snapshot, Report, and Form objects before using them, or a compile-time error `Invalid object reference` occurs.

Example

To create a table object (cTb) and use it to open a table in the current database:

```
Dim aDb As Database, aTb As Table
Set aDb = CurrentDB()
Set aTb = aDb.OpenTable("Accounts")
aTb.AddNew
(...)
aTb.Close
```

See Also

Methods: Close, CreateDynaset, CreateSnapshot, ListFields, ListIndexes, and ListTables

Print

Prints text using the current color and font.

Applies to

Debug and Reports Objects

Syntax

object.**Print** [**Spc(*n*)** | **Tab(*n*)**] [*expressionlist*] [; | ,]

object is the name of a valid Reports or Debug object.

Spc(*n*) is the Access Basic function that inserts *n* spaces into the printed output before beginning or resuming printing.

Tab(*n*) is the Access Basic function that tabs to the *n*th column before beginning or resuming printing.

expressionlist is the numeric or string expression to print. You can separate multiple expressions with a space, semicolon, comma, and **Tab** or **Spc** functions.

; | , determines the location of the next character. The semicolon means that the next character will be printed immediately after the current character. The comma forces printing of the next character in the next print zone (print zones start every 14 columns).

Usage Notes

With Reports objects, you can use only the Print method in an Access function or a macro attached to one of the report event properties such as OnFormat and OnPrint.

With the **Debug** object, the Print method is used in Access Basic to output text to the immediate window; it is the only method that you can use with the **Debug** object.

When the Print method is used with the **Debug** object, lines longer than 255 characters will wrap. Text that is too long to fit in the specified print position on the Reports object is truncated and no error occurs.

Because the number of characters that occupy a fixed-width print column vary with proportionally spaced fonts, ensure that printed columns are wide enough to accommodate a combination of wide characters or use a monospaced font (such as Courier) to ensure that printed columns align properly.

When a semicolon follows *expressionlist*, no carriage return is appended and the next character is printed immediately following the current character. If a comma follows *expressionlist*, printing will begin in the next printing zone on the same line.

The *CurrentX* and *CurrentY* properties are updated by the Print method according to the current print position.

Print with no arguments prints a blank line.

Examples

To use the Print method with the Debug object:

```
Debug.Print "This will be printed in the Immediate window"
```

To use the Print method with the Reports object (named Report2) to print a centered message in a large font:

```
Dim Rpt As Report, hMessage As String
cMessage = "This is a test"
Set Rpt = reports!report2
Rpt.drawwidth = 50
Rpt.Scalemode = 3
Rpt.Fontname = "Arial"
Rpt.fontsize = 24
nHoriz = Rpt.TextWidth(cMessage)
nVerti = Rpt.TextHeight(cMessage)
' Center the message
Rpt.currentx = (Rpt.ScaleWidth / 2 - nHoriz / 2)
Rpt.currenty = (Rpt.ScaleHeight / 2 - nVerti / 2)
Rpt.Print cMessage
```

See Also

Functions: Spc and Tab

Objects: Debug and Reports

Properties: CurrentX and CurrentY, and ScaleMode

Methods: Circle, Line, PSet, Scale, TextHeight, and TextWidth

PSet

Sets the given point on a report to a specified color.

Applies to

Reports Objects

Syntax

object.**PSet**[**Step**](*x*,*y*) [, *color*]

object is the name of an open report object.

Step indicates that the coordinates of the point to set are relative to the object's coordinates set by *CurrentX* and *CurrentY* properties.

x,*y* represents single numbers indicating the coordinates of the center point of the point to set. The *Scale...* properties determine the units of measure used.

color is an RGB color to set the point to (a Long Number). The default is the setting of the *ForeColor* property.

Usage Notes

You can use only the PSet method in an Access function or a macro attached to one of the event properties such as OnFormat and OnPrint.

The size of the area affected by the PSet method depends on the setting of the DrawWidth and ScaleMode properties. If ScaleMode is 3 (pixels) and the DrawWidth is 1, the color of a single pixel is changed. If DrawWidth is greater than 1, the affected area is centered on the specified coordinates (which provides a simple way to draw solid circles).

The way the point is drawn depends on the settings of the *DrawMode* and *DrawStyle* properties.

To clear a pixel (or an area), apply the PSet method with the background color setting as the *color* argument.

Using negative values for *x* or *y* can push the area affected by PSet beyond the printable area of the report.

Example

To print a solid circle using the PSet method:

```
Dim Rpt As Report
Set Rpt = reports!report2
Rpt.drawwidth = 100
Rpt.Scalemode = 3        ' pixels
Rpt.PSet (100, 100)
```

See Also

Functions: QBColor and RGB

Properties: CurrentX and CurrentY, DrawMode, DrawStyle, and DrawWidth.

Methods: Circle, Line, Print, and Scale

Scale

Defines the coordinate system of a Reports object.

Applies to

Reports Objects

Syntax

object.**Scale**[(*x1,y1*) - (*x2,y2*)]

object is the name of an open report object.

x1,y1 represents horizontal and vertical coordinates for the upper left corner of the object being drawn (a Single number).

x2,y2 represents horizontal and vertical coordinates for the lower right corner of the object being drawn (a Single number).

Usage Notes

Scale affects the coordinate system for the print and graphic methods.

You can use only the Scale method in an Access function or a macro attached to one of the event properties such as OnFormat and OnPrint.

Using the Scale method with no arguments resets the unit of measurement to twips.

Example

See the Circle method.

See Also

Methods: Circle, Line, Print, and PSet

Properties: ScaleHeight, ScaleMode, ScaleWidth, ScaleLeft, and ScaleTop

Seek

Locates the desired record in an indexed table.

Applies to

Table Objects Only

Syntax

table.**Seek** *comparison*, *value*

table is the name of an existing table object.

comparison is the string indicating the kind of comparison to perform.

value is the value to seek.

Usage Notes

After a successful seek, the Seek method updates the NoMatch property with False (0) and makes the located record current. If **Seek** fails, the NoMatch property equals True (-1).

In a nonunique index, Seek locates the first occurrence of a record that satisfies the seek criteria.

You must save any changes made to the record with the Update method.

comparison may be one of the following strings:

String	*Finds the First Record Which Is*
"="	Equal to *value*
">="	Greater than or equal to *value*
">"	Greater than *value*
"<="	Less than or equal to *value*
"<"	Less than *value*

If *comparison* is =, >=, or >, Seek starts at the beginning of the table. If *comparison* is <= or <, Seek starts at the end of the table and proceeds backward.

If a nonexisting index is specified, a `<name> isn't an index in this table` error (trappable error #3015) occurs. The same error occurs if no index is specified.

If the index is a multiple-field (*compound*) index, you should supply a *value* for each field in the index expression (the value for the first field in the index expression must be supplied). If the file is indexed on LastName and FirstName, for example, and you are searching for John Smith, the Seek expression may look like the following:

```
MyTable.Seek "=", "Smith", "John"
```

The data type specified in *value* must be the same as the index field data type, or Seek may erroneously fail (with or without an error message).

Tip

Batch updates of data in Access are easier and faster to perform by running an update query rather than a series of Seeks followed by programmatical edits.

Example

To locate a telephone conversation record for a particular date and display some data about the call:

```
Dim a As Database, b As Table
Set a = CurrentDB()
Set b = a.OpenTable("Phone calls")
b.index = "Call date"
b.Seek "=", #9/14/92#
If Not b.NoMatch Then                 ' success
 Debug.Print [Call charge], [Call made to]
End If
b.Close
```

See Also

Properties: BOF, EOF, Index, and NoMatch

Methods: FindFirst, FindLast, FindNext and FindPrevious, ListIndexes, MoveLast, MoveFirst, MoveNext, and MovePrevious

TextHeight

Returns the width of the text as it would be printed with the current font.

Applies to

Reports Object

Syntax

[*object.*]**TextHeight**(*expression*)

object is the reference to a valid report object.

expression is the text string for which the text height is determined.

Usage Notes

Use the **TextHeight** method to determine the amount of vertical space required to display *expression*, including the space above and below each line.

The unit of measurement of the value returned by the TextHeight method depends on the value of the ScaleMode property.

If *expression* contains embedded carriage returns, TextHeight returns the cumulative height of all lines, including the space above and below each line.

Example

See the Print method.

See Also

Methods: Print, Scale, and TextWidth

Property: ScaleMode

TextWidth

Returns the width of the text as it would be printed with the current font.

Applies to

Reports Object

Syntax

[*object.*]**TextWidth**(*expression*)

object is the reference to a valid report object.

expression is the text string for which the text width is determined.

Usage Notes

Use the TextWidth method to determine the amount of horizontal space needed to display *expression*.

The unit of measurement of the value returned by the TextWidth method depends on the value of the ScaleMode property.

If *expression* contains embedded carriage returns, TextWidth returns the length of the longest line.

Example

See the Print method.

See Also

Methods: Print, Scale, and TextHeight

Property: ScaleMode

Update

Saves changes to a record in a table or dynaset.

Applies to

Table and Dynaset Objects

Syntax

object.**Update**

object is a reference to an open table or dynaset.

Update saves any changes made to a record in a table or dynaset.

Usage Notes

The Update method overwrites the contents of the current record with the contents of the edit buffer. If there is no active edit buffer (created with the Edit method) an `Update without AddNew or Edit` error (trappable error #3020) occurs while attempting to use Update.

Note

In Access Basic, changes to a record edited with the Edit method are saved only if the Update method is invoked explicitly. Closing a table or a dynaset, or moving to a different record before using Update, will discard changes.

Example

To locate a record of the telephone conversation for a desired date, edit the phone number, and let the user decide whether to save the changes:

```
Dim cDb As Database, cTb As Table
Const MB_YESNO = 4
```

METHODS

```
Const MB_ICONQUESTION = 32
Const ID_YES = 6
Set cDb = CurrentDB()
Set cTb = cDb.OpenTable("Phone calls")
cTb.Index = "Call date"
cTb.Seek "=", #9/14/92#
If Not cTb.NoMatch Then
    cTb.Edit
    cTb![Phone number] = "1235556789"
    If MsgBox("Save changes?", MB_ICONQUESTION + MB_YESNO) = ID_YES Then
        cTb.Update
        End if
End If
cTb.Close
```

See Also

Methods: AddNew, CreateDynaset, CreateSnapshot, Edit, and OpenTable

Objects

Database, Dynasets, QueryDef, Snapshots, and Table

Are often collectively referred to as *Recordset objects*.

Usage Notes

Before referring to any of these objects in code, an object variable of the applicable type must be created.

All of these object variables can have properties and methods. Refer to Properties and Methods sections of the Reference for a full listing of properties and methods applicable to these objects.

Example

To create some recordset objects:

```
Dim a As Database, b As Table, c As Dynaset, d As Snapshot, e As QueryDef
Set a = CurrentDB()
Set b = a.OpenTable("Test")
Set c = b.CreateDynaset()
Set d = b.CreateSnapshot()
Set e = b.CreateQueryDef("Test Query", "Select * FROM Test;")
(...)
```

See Also:

Functions: CurrentDB and OpenDatabase

Methods: OpenQueryDef and OpenTable

Objects: Debug, Forms, Reports, and Screens

Statements: Clone, CreateDynaset, CreateSnapshot, Dim, and Set

Debug

Sends printed output from an Access Basic module to the Immediate window; also plays an important role in debugging Access Basic programs.

Syntax:

Debug.*Print expression*

expression is an expression (or a list of expressions) to print in the Immediate window.

Usage Notes

Only the **Print** method can be applied to Debug object; an attempt to apply other methods triggers a variety of compile-time (or *design-time* if syntax checking is enabled) errors.

Individual elements of Debug.Print... can be delimited either by commas or by semicolons. See the Print method in the reference section for more details.

Data types can be mixed and matched in *expression*.

The **Debug** object has no properties.

Example

A variety of expressions can be displayed in the Immediate window using the **Debug**.*Print* object:

```
Debug.Print Now(), Int(12.3); (8 * 14)/2
```

See Also:

Objects: Forms, Reports, and Screen

Method: Print

Forms

Refers to a particular form; you may use either the form name or number (the first active form is zero, second is one, and so on) to refer to an active form.

Syntax

Forms.**Count**

Forms!*formname*

Forms("formname")

Forms(formnumber)

formname is the name of the form to which you want to refer.

formnumber is the sequential number of the opened form.

Usage Notes

An *active form* is a form opened in either the design or open mode.

If the specified form is not active, an `Invalid form number reference` error (trappable error #2456) or `Invalid reference to form '<name>'` error (trappable error #2450) is generated.

The **Forms** object has just one property (Count) and no methods.

All Form properties listed in the form properties window can be used with the named **Forms** object (referring to a specific form).

Example

To print a form Name and Record Source properties for all active forms:

```
nCount = Forms.Count - 1
For i = 0 To nCount
     Debug.Print Forms(i).Caption, Forms(i).RecordSource
Next i
```

See Also

Objects: Debug, Reports, and Screens

Properties: ActiveControl, Count, Caption, and Dynaset

Reports

Refers to a particular report. You may use either the report name or number (first active report is zero, second is one, and so on) to refer to an active report.

Syntax

Reports.Count

Reports![*reportname***]**

Reports("*reportname***")**

Reports(*reportnumber***)**

reportname is the name of the report to which you want to refer.

reportnumber is the sequential number of the opened report.

Usage Notes

An *active report* is a report opened either in design or preview mode.

If the specified report is not active, an `Invalid report number reference` error (trappable error #2457) or `Invalid reference to report '<name>'` error (trappable error #2451) is generated.

The **Reports** object has only one property (Count) and no methods.

All Reports properties listed in the report properties window can be used with the named Reports object (referring to a specific report).

Example

Assign the number of currently open reports to a variable:

```
nCount = Reports.Count
```

See Also

Objects: Debug, Reports, and Screens

Properties: Count and ActiveReport

Screen

Can be used to refer to a form, a report, or a control in a generic fashion, without actually knowing the name of the object referred to

Syntax

Screen.*property.property....*

property can be any of the following three properties: ActiveControl, ActiveForm, and ActiveReport.

Usage Notes

No methods can be applied to the Screen object.

The following trappable errors are most likely to occur if there is no active object of the specified type:

`No control is active` (error #2474)

`No form is active` (error #2475)

`No report is active` (error #2476)

Example

Assign the caption of the active control on the current form (or report) to a variable szCurrButton:

```
szCurrButton = Screen.ActiveControl.Caption
```

See Also

Objects: Debug, Forms, and Reports

Properties: ActiveControl, ActiveForm, and ActiveReport

Operators

Concatenates two operands.

Syntax

operand1 **&** *operand2*

Usage Notes

If both operands are Null, the result is also Null. A single Null operand is converted to a zero-length string.

Unless both operands are of String data type, operands are converted to (Variant VarType 8); this can be overriden by explicitly declaring the data type for the variable holding the result of the concatenation.

Examples

The three examples below demonstrate various usages of the & operator:

```
Result = 99 & " baloons"            ' "99 baloons"
Debug.Print VarType(Result)         ' 8 (Variant VarType 8 = String)

Result = 99 & 4                     ' 994

MsgBox User() & " is currently logged in"
```

See Also

Chapter 10, "Understanding Access Data Types"

---

*

Multiplies two numeric operands.

Syntax

operand1 * *operand2*

Usage Notes

The result is converted to the type of the most precise operand; if *operands* are integers and the result of the multiplication overflows the legal range of integers, the result is converted to a Long (Variant VarType 3) data type.

If the result is greater than the largest allowed value of the particular data type, it is converted to Double.

If either, or both, values are Null, the result is also Null.

When you use the * operator to perform calculations on mixed base numbers, such as hexadecimal and decimal, the result is always returned as a decimal number.

Examples

The following examples show the results of multiplication using various Variant data types:

```
a = "500"
b = 700
Result = a * b
Debug.Print VarType(a), VarType(b), VarType(Result) '8    2    5
                                                    'String, Integer, Double
```

Multiplication of mixed base numbers (decimal and hex):

```
Result = 10 * &H10                  ' 160 decimal
```

See Also

Chapter 10, "Understanding Access Data Types"

Sums two operands.

Syntax

operand1 **+** *operand2*

Usage Notes

If either operand is a Null, the result is also a Null.

If both operands are empty, the result is also empty.

If one operand is a number, and the other is a string that cannot be converted to a number, a `Type mismatch` error (trappable error #13) occurs.

If both operands are Variants of VarType 3, 4, or 7 (Long, Single, or Date, respectively) and the result of the addition overflows the legal range for a particular data type, the result is converted to a Double (Variant VarType 5) data type.

If both operands are integers and the result of the addition overflows the legal range of integers, the result is converted to a Long (Variant VarType 3) data type.

When the + operator is used to perform calculations on mixed base numbers, such as hexadecimal and decimal, the result is always returned as a decimal number.

The following table describes the results of using the + operator on different data types (the order of operands is irrelevant):

operand1	*operand2*	*Action*	*Example*
Numeric (Integer, Long, Single, Double, Currency)	Numeric	Add	7 + 1.2 = 8.12
String	String	Concatenate	"A" + "A" = "AA"
Numeric	Variant (not Null)	Add	v = "6" 7 + v = 13
String	Variant (not Null)	Concatenate	Dim s As String s = "7" : v = 3 s + v = 73
String	Variant VarType 8 (String)	Concatenate	Dim s As String s = "7" : v = "3" s + v = "73"

continues

operand1	*operand2*	*Action*	*Example*
Any type	Variant VarType 0 (empty)	Operand is Unchanged	Dim a 7 + a = 7
Numeric	String	Error `Type mismatch`	Dim s As String Dim i As Integer s = "Z" : i = 1 s + i = error #13
Variant	Variant	Add	a = 13 : b = 3.54
VarType 2-7	VarType 2-7		13 + 3.54 = 16.54
Variant	Variant	Concatenate	a = "2" : b = "6"
VarType 8	VarType 8		a + b = "26"
Variant	Variant	Add	Dim a As Double
VarType 2-7	VarType 8		Dim s a = 43.6 : s = 9 a + s = 52.6

Example

To use the + operator with mixed base numbers:

```
Result = &H10 + &O10                    ' hexadecimal plus octal
                                        ' (16 + 8) = 24 decimal
```

See the preceding table for more examples.

See Also

Chapter 10, "Understanding Access Data Types"

–

Subtracts two numeric operands, or denotes the negative value of a number.

Syntax

operand1 - *operand2*

or

-*operand*

operand, *operand1*, and *operand2* can be any numeric expression that evaluates to a valid number.

Usage Notes

The result is converted to the type of the most precise operand (Integer, Long, Single, Double, Currency, with Integer being the least precise).

If one or both operands have a Null value, the result is also Null. An empty operand is treated as zero.

If the - operator is used to perform calculations on mixed base numbers, such as hexadecimal and decimal, the result is always returned as a decimal number.

Example

To use the - operator with various Variant data types:

```
a = 1000
Result = a - 12                           ' 988

a = "1000"
Result = a - 12                           ' 998
Debug.Print VarType(a), VarType(Result)   '8   5
                                          ' string, double
```

This example uses mixed base numbers (hex and decimal):

```
Result = &HA - 7                          ' 3 (10 - 7)
```

Subtracting zero from the hex number converts it to decimal:

```
Result =  &H25 - 0                        ' 37 (decimal)
```

See Also

Chapter 10, "Understanding Access Data Types"

/

Divides two floating-points operands.

Syntax

operand1 **/** *operand2*

Usage Notes

If *operand2* equals zero, a `Division by zero` error (trappable error #11) occurs.

The result of division is a Double number, unless both operands are Integer or Single data type (which results in a Double) or Variant VarType 2 or 4, which results in Variant VarType 4.

If either operand is a Null, the result is also a Null; an empty operand (VarType 0) is treated as 0.

If the / operator is used to perform calculations on mixed base numbers, such as hexadecimal and decimal, the result is always returned as a decimal number.

Examples

To divide two decimal numbers:

```
Result = 100.25/15                ' 4.01
```

To divide a hexadecimal number by a decimal number:

```
Result = &H10/4                 ' 4 (decimal 16/4)
```

See Also

Chapter 10, "Understanding Access Data Types"

\

Divides two integers.

Syntax

operand1 **** *operand2*

operand1 and *operand2* can be any expressions that evaluate to a valid number.

Usage Notes

Before division both operands are rounded to Integer or Long numbers, using the same rules as Int( ) and Fix( ) functions. Any fractional portion of the result is also truncated.

If any operand is Null, the result is also Null. An empty operand (Variant VarType 0) is assumed to be 0.

Using the \ operator is an equivalent to converting both operands and the result to integers as in the following example:

```
Result = Int( Int(a) / Int(b) )
```

If the / operator is used to perform calculations on mixed base numbers, such as hexadecimal and decimal, the result is always returned as a decimal number.

Examples

These two lines of code return the same result:

```
Result = 12.2 \ 3.1                      ' 4
Result = Int( Int(12.2) / Int(3.1) )     ' 4
```

To divide a hex number by an octal number:

```
Result = &H10 \ &02                      ' 8 (16\2)
```

See Also

Chapter 10, "Understanding Access Data Types"

^

Raises a number to the power of an exponent.

Syntax

operand1 ^ *operand2*

operand1 and *operand2* can be any expressions that evaluate to a valid number.

Usage Notes

The result of exponentiation is most likely to be a Double or Variant VarType 5.

operand1 can be a negative number only if *operand2* is a whole number, or an `Illegal function call` error (trappable error #5) occurs.

If you use the ^ operator to perform calculations on mixed base numbers, such as hexadecimal and decimal, the result is always returned as a decimal number.

Examples

The following examples demonstrate usage of the ^ operand:

```
Result = a ^ 3                     ' 125
a = "5"                            ' Variant VarType 8
```

OPERATORS

```
Result = a ^ 3                          ' 125
Debug.Print VarType(Result)             ' 5 (Double)
```

To raise a hex number to the power of an octal number:

```
Result = &HA ^ &O2                      ' 100 (10^2)
```

See Also

Chapter 10, "Understanding Access Data Types"

And (Logical and Bitwise)

Returns the result of the logical conjunction of two expressions.

Syntax

expr1 **And** *expr2*

expr1 and *expr2* can be any numeric or logical expressions.

Usage Notes

The And operator returns true (-1) only if both expressions evaluate to true; otherwise it returns False (0).

The following table illustrates possible results depending on the values of *expr1* and *expr2*:

expr1	*expr2*	*Result*
True	True	True
True	False	False
True	Null	Null
False	True	False
False	False	False
False	Null	False
Null	True	Null
Null	False	False
Null	Null	Null

When And is used to perform bitwise comparisons, identically positioned bits in *expr1* and *expr2* are set according to the following truth table (the value of an And-ed bit is set to 1 only if identically positioned bits in both expressions are 1).

Bit in expr1	*Bit in expr2*	*Result*
0	0	0
0	1	0
1	0	0
1	1	1

Bitwise operations can only be performed in Access Basic.

Example

The effect of the And operator is clearly visible when the And-ed values are converted to binary numbers. Consider the following examples:

```
Result = 2 And 3                            ' 2
          0000 0010  (decimal 2)
          0000 0011  (decimal 3)
          --------
Result    0000 0010  (decimal 2)

Result = -1 And 0                       [' 0]
          1111 1111  (decimal -1 (true))
          0000 0000  (decimal 0 (false))
          --------
Result    0000 0000  (decimal 0)
```

See Also

Operators: Eqv, Imp, Not, Or, and Xor.

Between...And

Determines whether an expression lies within the specified range of values.

Syntax

expression **[Not] Between** *value1* **And** *value2*

expression identifies the field that contains data.

value1, value2 is the range of values to evaluate *expression*.

Usage Notes

Between...And returns -1 (true) if *expression* is between *value1* and *value2* (inclusive); 0 (false) otherwise. If either *value1* or *value2* is a Null, the Between...And operator returns a Null.

The type of *value1* and *value2* must be the same as the type of expression; if the field identified by the expression contains numeric data, *value1* and *value2* should be numeric as well. If the field identified by *expression* contains character data (text, but not memo or OLE objects), *value1* and *value2* should be character expressions.

Between...And can be used only in forms, reports (attached to calculated controls), and queries; it cannot be used in Access Basic except in conjunction with the Eval function. The Between...And operator can also be a part of a SQL expression (such as a condition in a query).

Examples

The following is an expression attached to a control (text box) on a form. It prints the words *Small* or *Big* depending on the value of the field "Call charge," which holds numeric data:

```
=IIf([Call charge] Between 0 and 2 "Small", "Big")
```

The following expression is attached to a control (text box) on a form and prints *A-K* or *L-Z* depending on the value of the field "Call made to," which holds text data:

```
=IIf([Call made to] Between "A" and "K", "A-K", "L-Z")
```

The following example selects all records from the Calls table for phone calls made to London between 6 p.m. and 6 a.m.:

```
SELECT * FROM Calls WHERE [City] = "London" AND [Call time] Between "18:00" And
➥"6:00"
```

The last example demonstrates using the Between...And operator in Access Basic:

```
If Eval("Forms!Alpha!Age between 13 and 19") Then
     MsgBox "It's a teenager!!!"
End If
```

See Also

Function: Eval

Operators: In, Like, and Not

Comparison Operators

Syntax

expression1 **Operator** *expression2*

Operator can be one of the following:

<	Less than
<=	Less than or equal to
>	Greater than
>=	Greater than or equal to
=	Equal to
<>	Not equal to

Usage Notes

If either expression is a Null, the result is a Null.

The following tables show how the expressions are compared based on the data types of *expression1* and *expression2*. Table 21.1 refers to cases when one of the expressions is not a Variant data type. Table 21.2, both expressions are a Variant data type. The order of expressions is irrelevant.

Table 21.1. Expressions Compared When One of the Expressions Is Not a Variant Data Type

expression1	*expression2*	*Action*
Numeric	Numeric	Numeric comparison
String	String	String comparison
Numeric	Variant VarTyp 2-7 or VarTyp 8 convertible to a number	Numeric comparison
Numeric	Variant VarTyp 2-7 or VarTyp 8 not convertible to a number	Expression1 < expression2
String	Variant VarType 8 (string)	String comparison
Numeric	Empty	Numeric comparison
String	Empty	String comparison
Numeric	Variant VarType 8 (string)	Error #13 `Type mismatch`

Table 21.2. Expressions Compared When Both Expressions Are Variant Data Types

expression1	*expression2*	*Action*
Variant VarType 2-7	Variant VarType 2-7	Numeric comparison
Variant VarType 8	Variant VarType 8	String comparison
Variant VarType 8	Variant VarType 2-7	Numeric expression is less than string expression
Empty	Variant VarType 2-7	Numeric comparison
Empty	Variant VarType 8	String comparison
Empty	Empty	Expressions are equal

Example

Use a comparison operator with different Variant data types:

```
Result = 12 > 6                    ' True (-1)

Result = "12" > " [6"]             ' False (0)
```

See Also

Function: VarType

Chapter 10, "Understanding Access Data Types"

Eqv (Logical and Bitwise)

Returns the result of the logical equivalence of two expressions.

Syntax

expr1 **Eqv** *expr2*

expr1 and *expr2* can be any numeric or logical expression.

Usage Notes

If either *expression* is a Null, the result is also a Null; otherwise, the result is determined as shown in the following table.

expr1	*expr2*	*Result*
True	True	True
True	False	False
False	True	False
False	False	True

When you use Eqv to perform bitwise comparisons, identically positioned bits in *expr1* and *expr2* are set according to the following truth table (when two bits are Eqv-ed, the result is 1 only if both bits have identical values).

Bit in expr1	*Bit in expr2*	*Result*
0	0	1
0	1	0
1	0	0
1	1	1

Bitwise operations can be performed only in Access Basic.

Examples

The effect of the Eqv operator is clearly visible when the Eqv-ed values are converted to binary numbers. Consider the following examples:

```
Result = 2 Eqv 3                          ' -2
           0000 0010  (decimal 2)
           0000 0011  (decimal 3)
           ---------
Result     1111 1110  (decimal -2)

Result = -1 Eqv 0                         ' 0
           1111 1111  (decimal -1 (true))
           0000 0000  (decimal 0 (false))
           ---------
Result     0000 0000  (decimal 0)
```

See Also

Operators: And, Imp, Not, Or, and Xor

Imp (Logical and Bitwise)

Returns the result of the logical implication of two expressions.

Syntax

expr1 **Imp** *expr2*

Usage Notes

The result of a logical implication is determined as shown in the following table.

expr1	*expr2*	*Result*
True	True	True
True	False	False
True	Null	Null
False	True	True
False	False	True
False	Null	True
Null	True	True
Null	False	Null
Null	Null	Null

When the Imp operator is used to perform bitwise comparisons, identically positioned bits in *expr1* and *expr2* are set according to the following truth table (when two bits are Imp-ed, the result is 0 only if the first bit is 1 and the second is 0).

Bit in expr1	*Bit in expr2*	*Result*
0	0	1
0	1	1
1	0	0
1	1	1

Bitwise operations can be performed only in Access Basic.

Examples

The effect of the Imp operator is clearly visible when the Imp-ed values are converted to binary numbers. Consider the following examples:

```
Result = 2 Imp 3                          ' -1
          0000 0010  (decimal 2)
          0000 0011  (decimal 3)
          ---------
Result    1111 1111  (decimal -1)

Result = -1 Imp 0                         ' 0
          1111 1111  (decimal -1 (true))
          0000 0000  (decimal 0 (false))
          ---------
Result    0000 0000  (decimal 0)
```

Please note that reversing the order of expressions in the last example changes the result to -1.

See Also

Operators: And, Imp, Not, Or, and Xor

OPERATORS

In

Determines whether an expression matches any value in a given value list.

Syntax

expr **Is** [**Not**] **In** (*value1*, *value2* [,*valueN*])

expr is a name of the query expression or a control on a report or form.

value1...valueN is a list of values against which *expr* is evaluated.

Usage Notes

The In operator can be used only in queries and calculated controls in forms and reports (except in conjunction with the Eval function); use InStr, Mid, and Mid$ functions in Access Basic.

The In operator is best used in conjunction with the IIf( ) function to set the new value of a control based on a set of values from a static list.

Example

If the value of control "State" on the current report equals CA, OR, WA, or HI, the sales region should be printed as *Pacific*, as shown in the following example:

```
=IIf([State] In ('CA', 'OR', 'WA', 'HI'), "Pacific", "Other")
```

See Also

Operators: Between...And, Like, and Not

Functions: Eval, InStr, Mid, Mid$, and Switch

Is

Used only with the reserved word Null to determine whether an expression is Null.

Syntax

expr Is [Not] Null

expr is the name of a query expression or a control on a report or form.

Usage Notes

The Is operator can be used only in queries and calculated controls in forms and reports. Use the IsNull( ) function in Access Basic.

When attached to controls in reports and queries the Is operator is best used in conjunction with the IIf( ) function to set the value of a control to a value other than a Null.

Caution

The Is operator can also be used in a Select Case statament, as shown in the following example:

```
Select Case Name
Case Is = "Smith"
(...)
```

Such usage is unnecessary, however, and should be replaced with the following:

```
(...)
Case "Smith"
(...)
```

Example

To display a decimal number entered in a control called Dec on a form named Numbers as hexadecimal, check to see whether the number entered in the Dec control is a Null before performing the conversion. The following expression returns zero if the entry was a Null:

```
=IIf( Forms!Numbers.Dec Is Not Null, 0, Hex(Forms!Numbers.Dec) )
```

Caution

Checking for Null values is a very important part of manipulating controls on Access forms and reports and programming in Access Basic; many Access functions and statements generate an error if the passed argument is a Null. If in doubt, check all parameters for Null values before passing them to functions and statements or assigning them to controls in forms or reports.

See Also

Functions: IsEmpty, IsNull, and VarType

Operator: Not

Like

Returns a result of the comparison of two string expressions.

Syntax

expression **Like** *pattern*

The Like operator is a pattern matching operator that compares strings for the occurrence of any given pattern or character.

Usage Notes

Like returns a logical true (-1) if patterns match; false (0) otherwise. It returns a Null if either *expression* or *pattern* is a Null.

Unless Option Compare explicitly states the method of comparison, the Like operator uses the Binary method as a default.

You can use the following wild cards with the Like operator:

Wild Card	*Match*
?	Any single character
*	Zero or more characters
#	A single digit (0-9)
[charlist]	Any single listed character
[!charlist]	Any single unlisted charcter

All the wild-card characters in the preceding table and the left bracket ([) can be used in the pattern to match themselves only if enclosed in the square brackets. You can The right bracket (]) cannot be used within a group pattern, but only as an individual character in comparisons.

The Like operator can also match range of characters in expression.

Passing an invalid pattern results in an `Invalid pattern string` error (trappable error #93).

The rules described in the following table may be helpful in devising a pattern for matching expressions.

Pattern	*Action*
[]	None - treated as a zero-length string
[Z-A]	Error #93 ([A-Z] is a valid pattern)
[a-zA-Z0-9]	Valid multiple range pattern
[!0-9]	Valid pattern ("Not a digit")
![A-z]	Valid pattern (match the exclamation mark)
-![a-z]	Valid pattern (match the minus sign)

Examples

The following examples show different usages of the Like operator:

```
Result = "Brown" Like "B????"          ' True (-1)
Result = "Alaska" Like "*[a-l]"        ' True
Result = "Alaska" Like "#[a-z]"        ' False
Result = "Stop!" Like "????![!]"       ' True
```

Caution

The results of comparisons performed with the Like operator are affected by the setting of the Option Compare statement.

See Also

Statement: Option Compare

Function: InStr

Mod

Returns the remainder (modulus) of a division.

Syntax

operand1 **Mod** *operand2*

operand1 and *operand2* can be any expressions that evaluate to a valid number.

Usage Notes

Operands are rounded to whole numbers before performing the modulus operation.

The Mod function returns an Integer—a Long (or Variant VarType 2 or 3); if either *operand1* or *operand2* is a Null, the returned value is also a Null. An empty operand is assumed to be 0.

Example

The following example returns the modulus (remainder) of the division:

```
Result = 20 Mod 3             '2
```

It is an equivalent of the following expression:

```
Result = 20 - (3 * (20\3))    '2
```

See Also

Operators: &, /, \, *, +, and ^

Function: VarType

Not (Logical and Bitwise)

Returns the result of the negation of a numeric (arithmetic or logical) expression.

Syntax

Not *expr*

expr can be any number or an expression that evaluates to a number.

OPERATORS

Usage Notes

If *expr* is a Null, Not returns a Null.

The result of negation is determined according to the following table.

expr	*Result*
True	False
False	True
Null	Null

The range of numbers that can be used as an expression in the Not operator is -2,147,483,648 to 2,147,483,647 (the range of Long integers).

When Not is used to perform bitwise operations, identically positioned bits in *expr1* and *expr2* are reversed, as illustrated in the following truth table.

Bit in expr	*Result*
0	1
1	0

Bitwise operations can be performed only in Access Basic.

Examples

The effect of the Not operator is clearly visible when the negated values are converted to binary numbers. Consider the following examples:

```
Result = Not 0                          ' -1
          0000 0000  (decimal 0)
Result    1111 1111  (decimal -1)

Result = Not 2                          '-3
          0000 0010  (decimal 2)
Result    1111 1101  (decimal -3)
```

See Also

Operators: And, Eqv, Imp, Or, and Xor

Or (Logical and Bitwise)

Returns the result of the logical disjunction of two expressions.

Also known as the inclusive Or.

Syntax

expr1 **Or** *expr2*

expr1 and *expr2* can be any numeric or logical expression.

Usage Notes

If either *expr*ession is true, the result is always true even if the other expression evaluates to a Null.

expr1	*expr2*	*Result*
True	True	True
True	False	True
True	Null	True
False	True	True
False	False	False
False	Null	Null
Null	True	True
Null	False	Null
Null	Null	Null

When you use the Or operator to perform bitwise comparisons, identically positioned bits in *expr1* and *expr2* are set according to the following truth table (when two bits are Or-ed, the result is 0 only if both bits are 0).

Bit in expr1	*Bit in expr2*	*Result*
0	0	0
0	1	1
1	0	1
1	1	1

Bitwise operations can be performed only in Access Basic.

Examples

The effect of the Or operator is clearly visible when the Or-ed values are converted to binary numbers. Consider the following examples:

```
Result = 2 Or 3                         ' 3
          0000 0010  (decimal 2)
          0000 0011  (decimal 3)
          ---------
Result    0000 0011  (decimal 3)

Result = -1 Or 0                        ' -1
          1111 1111  (decimal -1 (true))
          0000 0000  (decimal 0 (false))
          ---------
Result    1111 1111  (decimal -1)
```

See Also

Operators: And, Eqv, Imp, Not, and Xor

Xor

Returns the result of a logical exclusion of two expressions. The Xor operator is also known as the exclusive Or operator.

Syntax

expr1 **Xor** *expr2*

expr1 and *expr2* can be any number or logical expression.

Usage Notes

When *expr1* and *expr2* are true or *expr1* and *expr2* are false, Xor returns 0 (false). When either expression is true, Xor returns -1 (true); if either expression is Null, the result is also a Null, according to the following table.

expr1	*expr2*	*Result*
True	True	False
True	False	True

expr1	*expr2*	*Result*
False	True	True
False	False	False

When Xor is used to perform bitwise comparisons, identically positioned bits in *expr1* and *expr2* are set according to the following truth table (the value of a bit Xor-ed with a 1 is inverted).

Bit in expr1	*Bit in expr2*	*Result*
0	0	0
0	1	1
1	0	1
1	1	0

Bitwise operations can be performed only in Access Basic.

OPERATORS

Examples

Consider the following example:

```
Result = (Now > Now - 1) Xor (Now = Now - 1)
```

The expression `now > now - 1` ("today's date is greater than yesterday's date") evaluates to true (-1). The second expression, `Now = Now - 1` ("today's date is equal to yesterday's date") evaluates to false. The result of the Xor operation, therefore, is true.

The effect of the Xor operator is clearly visible when the Xor-ed values are converted to binary numbers. Consider the following examples:

```
Result = 2 Xor 3                          ' 1
          0000 0010  (decimal 2)
          0000 0011  (decimal 3)
          ---------
Result    0000 0001  (decimal 1)

Result = -1 Xor 0
          1111 1111  (decimal -1 (true))
          0000 0000  (decimal 0 (false))
          ---------
Result    1111 1111  (decimal -1)
```

See Also

Operators: And, Eqv, Imp, Not, and Or

Properties

ActiveControl

Refers to the active control on a current screen object (form, report).

Applies To

Screen object

Usage

All views: Read Only

Notes

The *ActiveControl* property doesn't have settings, but you can use other properties with it to get property settings of the current control.

When all controls' properties are hidden or disabled, or there is no active control, a `No control is active` error (trappable error #2474) occurs.

Access Basic Example

Assign the name of the current control to a variable:

```
szCurrControl = Screen.ActiveControl.ControlName
```

See Also

Objects: Debug, Forms, and Reports

Properties: ActiveForm, ActiveReport, ControlName, and ControlSource

ActiveForm

Refers to the current form.

Applies To

Screen object

Usage

All views: Read Only

Note

The *ActiveForm* property doesn't have settings, but you can use other properties with it to get property settings of the current form.

Access Basic Example

A function that closes any open form (can be attached to an action property of the form or to a pushbutton, for example). *ActiveForm* uses the value returned by the *FormName* property as an argument in the **Close** action. (**On Error...** prevents an error if you make changes in Design view, switch to Form view, exit a form, and then choose Cancel from the dialog box that appears on-screen):

```
Function CloseThisForm ()
  On Error Resume Next
  DoCmd Close A_FORM, Screen.ActiveForm.FormName
End Function
```

See Also

Objects: Debug, Forms, and Reports

Properties: ActiveControl and ActiveReport

ActiveReport

Refers to the current report.

Applies To

Screen object

Usage

All views: Read Only

Note

The *ActiveReport* property doesn't have settings. You can use other properties with it, however, to get property settings of the current report.

Access Basic Example

This example uses the *Screen.ActiveReport.RecordSource* property to get the report *RecordSource* and change it:

```
szReport = "Exp92-1"
DoCmd OpenReport szReport, A_DESIGN
If InStr(Screen.ActiveReport.RecordSource, "Expenses1992") <> 0 Then
     Screen.ActiveReport.RecordSource = "Expenses1993"
End If
DoCmd SetWarnings False            ' Don't display the "Save...?" dialog box
DoCmd Close A_REPORT, szReport
DoCmd SetWarnings True
```

See Also

Objects: Debug, Forms, and Reports

Properties: ActiveControl and ActiveForm

AddColon, AutoLabel

AddColon determines whether the newly created control's labels end with a colon (settings are Yes and No—the default setting varies).

AutoLabel determines whether default labels are created for newly created controls (settings are Yes and No—the default setting varies).

Applies To

Tools on the toolbar: Text Box, Option Group, Toggle Button, Option Button, Check Box, Combo Box, List Box, Subform/Subreport, Bound Object Frame, Command Button

Usage

Not available from Access Basic

Note

This property is available only from the forms and reports design surface. You can click on the properties tool on the toolbar to display the default settings of these properties.

See Also

Properties: LabelAlign, LabelX, and LabelY

AfterUpdate

See "BeforeUpdate" property.

AllowEditing, DefaultEditing

AllowEditing enables and disables the Allow Editing option on the Records menu in Form view.

Default Editing determines the type of access to a form when the form opens: Edit, Read Only, or Data Entry.

Applies To

Forms

Usage

Design view: Read and Write

Other views: Read Only

Notes

The *AllowEditing* property has two settings:

- *Available (default).* You can edit the records.
- *Unavailable.* The editing is disabled.

The *DefaultEditing* property has three settings:

- *Allow Edits (default).* All operations are allowed.
- *Read Only.* You cannot edit, add, or delete records.
- *Data Entry.* You cannot edit existing records. You can add new records only.

In Access Basic, you can use True (-1) and False (0) intrinsic constants for settings of the *AllowEditing* property. You can use the numbers 1, 2, and 3 for the Data Entry, Allow Edits, and Read Only settings of the *DefaultEditing* property, respectively.

You can use the following combinations of these two properties:

AllowEditing	*DefaultEditing*	*Effect*
Available	Allow Edits	All records and all operations are available.
Available	Read Only	All records are available. The form opens in Read Only mode, but you can select other modes from the Records menu.
Available	Data Entry	No existing records are available. The form opens in Data Entry mode. You can edit existing records if you choose Show All Records from the Records menu and set the *AllowFilters* property to Yes.
Unavailable	Allow Edits	All records are available for all operations.
Unavailable	Read Only	All records are available for viewing only.
Unavailable	Data Entry	No records are available and no operations can be performed. You can view existing records by choosing Show All Records from the Records menu and setting the AllowFilters property to Yes.

PROPERTIES

Caution

Access is very inconsistent in defining numeric values for arguments and intrinsic constants. Some lists start with a 0 (0 - A_ADD, 1 - A_EDIT, 2 - A_READONLY, for example); other lists start with a 1 (arguments of the *DefaultEditing* property, for example). Do not assume anything!

Access Basic Example

The following code modifies the AllowEditing and Default editing properties. In Design mode, open an iconized form called Form1. Make the data in the form read only by changing the *AllowEditing* property to Unavailable (False), the *DefaultEditing* property to Read Only (3), and the *SetFilter* property to False. (SetWarnings Off suppresses the Form Close dialog box.)

```
Dim szFormName As String, fForm As Form
DoCmd OpenForm "Form1", A_DESIGN, , , , A_ICON
Set fForm = Screen.ActiveForm
szFormName = fForm.FormName
fForm.AllowEditing = True
fForm.DefaultEditing = 3
fForm.AllowFilters = False
DoCmd SetWarnings Off
DoCmd Close A_FORM, szFormName
```

See Also

Object: Screen

Action: SetWarnings

Property: SetFilter

AllowFilters

Determines whether a filter can be applied against the records on a form.

Applies To

Forms

Usage

Design view: Read and Write

Other views: Read Only

Notes

This property has two settings:

- *Yes.* Records can be filtered.
- *No.* No filters are allowed.

In Access Basic, you may use predefined constants True (for Yes) and False (for No).

If you set *AllowFilters* to No (or False in Access Basic), the following choices on the Records menu are not available in Form and Datasheet view: Edit/Filter Sort, ApplyFilter/Sort, and Show All Records.

Access Basic Example

Disable the *AllowFilters* property on the current form (you must open the form in Design view first):

```
Dim fForm As Form
(...)
Set fForm = Screen.ActiveForm
fForm.AllowFilters = False
```

See Also

Object: Screen

Properties: DefaultView and ViewsAllowed

AllowUpdating

Determines which fields and controls bound to which tables can be edited on a form.

Applies To

Forms

Usage

Design view: Read and Write

Other views: Read Only

Notes

The *AllowUpdating* property has three settings:

- *Default Tables (default).* You can edit only default tables and controls bound to their fields. (In Access Basic, you use the number 0.)
- *Any Tables.* You can edit all tables and controls bound to their fields. (In Access Basic, you can use the number 1.)
- *No Tables.* You cannot edit any tables or controls bound to their fields—the form is Read Only. (In Access Basic, you use the number 2.)

PROPERTIES

Access Basic Example

Open a form in Design view and change the *AllowUpdating* property to *No Tables* (2) if the form isn't already Read Only (its *DefaultEditing* property is not equal to 3):

```
Dim fForm As Form
DoCmd OpenForm "Alpha Form", A_DESIGN, , , ,A_ICON
Set fForm = Screen.ActiveForm
If fForm.DefaultEditing <> 3 Then
    fForm.AllowUpdating = 2
End If
```

See Also

Object: Screen

Properties: AllowEditing, DefaultEditing, and Locked

AutoLabel

See "AddColon" property.

AutoRepeat

Determines whether a macro attached to the *OnPush* property of a command button (pushbutton) on a form runs as long as the command button is pressed.

Applies To

Command button

Usage

Design view: Read and Write

Other views: Read Only

Notes

This property has two settings:

- *Yes.* Macro runs repeatedly as long as the button is pressed.
- *No* (default). Macro attached to the *OnPush* property of the control runs only once.

Setting the *AutoRepeat* property to Yes may be helpful if the attached macro performs repetitious operations, such as moving to the next or preceding record.

Referring to a control other than a command button triggers an `Invalid reference to property 'AutoRepeat'` error (trappable error #2455).

Microsoft reports an initial delay of one-half second for the first repetition and one-fourth second (or the duration of the macro—whichever is longer) for subsequent repetitions.

In Access Basic, you can use True and False constants to set the *AutoRepeat* property.

Access Basic Example

In Design mode, open the form called Test. Then check to see whether the control is a command button and whether it has a macro attached to its *OnPush* property. If it does, check the setting of the *AutoRepeat* property. If the property is set to No, change that setting to Yes:

```
DoCmd OpenForm "Test", A_DESIGN,,,, A_ICON
If TypeOf Screen.ActiveControl Is CommandButton Then
     If Screen.ActiveControl.OnPush <> "" Then
          If Screen.ActiveControl.AutoRepeat = False Then
               Screen.ActiveControl.AutoRepeat = True
          End If
     End If
End If
DoCmd Close A_FORM, "Test"
```

See Also

Object: Screen

Property: OnPush

AutoResize

Determines whether a form window opens automatically to display the complete form.

Applies To

Forms

Usage

Design view: Read and Write

Other views: Read Only

Notes

This property has two settings:

- *Yes* (default). Window sizes itself automatically to display one or more complete records (if possible), depending on the setting of the *DefaultView* property.
- *No.* Window opens with the same size when last changed and closed in Design view.

If the form is not attached to any table or query (the *RecordSource* property is blank), the window sizes itself to display a single record form.

In Access Basic, you may use True and False constants to set this property.

Access Basic Example

In Design view, open the form called Test (as an icon) and set the *AutoResize* property to Yes (True):

```
DoCmd OpenForm "Test", A_DESIGN, , , , A_ICON
Forms!Test.AutoResize = True
DoCmd Close A_FORM, "Test"
```

See Also

Objects: Form and Screen

Properties: DefaultView and RecordSource

Action: MoveSize

BackColor

Specifies the color of the interior (background) of a control.

Applies To

Form sections, report sections, tools, controls (combo box, graph, label, list box, option group, rectangle, text box, unbound object frame)

Usage

Design view: Read and Write

Other views: Read Only

Notes

In Design view, use the palette to set this property.

If *BorderStyle* and *BackStyle* properties are available, both must be set to Normal.

You use the *BackColor* property to highlight sections and controls on forms and reports—especially when printing with a color printer.

If set from Access Basic, the setting is a Long data type (such as returned by the **RGB** or **QBColor** function).

If the expression refers to a nonexisting section, an `Invalid section number reference` error (trappable error #2462) occurs. If a nonexisting field is referenced, an `Invalid reference to field "<name>"` error (trappable error #2465) is generated.

Tip

Use the following arguments of the RGB function to set the most common colors:

Light gray	RGB(192, 192, 192)	Hex value	&H00C0C0C0
Dark gray	RGB(128, 128, 128)	Hex value	&H00808080

Access Basic Example

In Design view, open the report called Report Three and change the background color of the page header section (section #3) to pitch black:

```
DoCmd OpenReport "Report Three", A_DESIGN
Reports![Report Three].Section(3).BackColor = RGB(0, 0, 0)
DoCmd Close A_REPORT, "Report Three"
```

See Also

Function: RGB

Method: PSet

Objects: Forms and Reports

Properties: BackStyle, BorderStyle, DrawMode, DrawStyle, DrawWidth, FillColor, OnFormat, OnPrint, and Section

BackStyle

Determines whether the control is transparent.

Applies To

Tools and controls: graph, label, list box, option group, rectangle, unbound object frame

Usage

Design view: Read and Write

Other views: Read Only

Notes

This property has two settings:

- *Normal* (default for all applicable properties except option group). The background color is set by the *BackColor* property. In Access Basic, you use 1 for this setting.
- *Clear* (default for option group only). The control is transparent. In Access Basic, you use 0 for this setting.

Access Basic Example

In Design view, open the form called Alpha as an icon and change the properties of the Text7 label: *SpecialEffect* to 2 (Sunken), *BackStyle* to 1 (Normal), and *BackColor* to light gray:

```
Dim cForm As Form
DoCmd SetWarnings False
DoCmd OpenForm "Alpha", A_DESIGN, , , , A_ICON
Set cForm = Forms!Alpha
cForm.Text7.SpecialEffect = 2                ' Sunken
cForm.Text7.BackStyle = 1                    ' Normal
cForm.Text7.BackColor = RGB(192, 192, 192)   ' Light Gray
DoCmd Close A_FORM, "Alpha"
```

See Also

Objects: Forms, Reports, and Screen

Properties: BackColor, BorderColor, BorderStyle, BorderWidth, and FillStyle

BeforeUpdate, AfterUpdate

Specifies an action to be performed before or after changed data in the control is updated.

Applies To

Controls on forms: combo box, list box, option group, and text box. Also apply to the following controls unless they are a part of the option group: check box, option button, toggle button

Usage

Design view: Read and Write

Other views: Read Only

Notes

You may attach macros, user-defined functions, Access Basic, or external functions to these properties. An action specified in the *BeforeUpdate* property is executed before the changed data is updated. An action attached to the *AfterUpdate* property is executed after the changed data is saved but before the control loses focus. If the data is not changed, neither action executes.

Access updates changed data in a control when the control loses focus (the cursor leaves the control, or you choose **S**ave **R**ecord from the File menu, for example).

Generally, you use actions attached to the *BeforeUpdate* property to perform data validations—usually involving complex expressions or validation based on the values of multiple controls. You may use actions attached to the *AfterUpdate* property to act conditionally depending on the data entered in the control (branch to different subforms, controls, and so on).

You cannot change the value of the current control and actions that move the focus to a different control or record in macros or functions attached to the *BeforeUpdate* property.

In Access Basic, you set these properties by using a string expression containing the name of a function or macro to execute.

Access Basic Examples

First, set the value of these properties from the control "id" on the Alpha form:

```
DoCmd OpenForm "Alpha", A_DESIGN, , , , A_ICON
Forms!Alpha.Id.AfterUpdate = "=DoAfterUpdate(Forms!Alpha.Id)"    ' function
Forms!Alpha.Id.BeforeUpdate = "DoBeforeUpdate"                   ' macro
DoCmd Close A_FORM, "Alpha"
```

The second example checks to see whether the data entered is numeric, and gives the user a chance to correct it. The **CancelEvent** action cancels saving the current record. Note that it has no effect when used in a macro (or function) attached to the *AfterUpdate* property:

```
Function DoBeforeUpdate (cCtrl As Control)
If Not IsNumeric(cCtrl) Then
      If MsgBox("This value must be a number.  Reenter?", MB_YESNO +
      ➥MB_ICONINFORMATION) = IDYES Then
        DoCmd CancelEvent
    End If
End If
End Function
```

See Also

Object: Forms

Properties: OnEnter, OnExit, and ValidationRule

PROPERTIES

BOF

Indicates whether the record pointer is positioned before the first record in the recordset.

Applies To

Recordsets

Usage

All views: Read Only

Notes

This property has no accessible settings. It returns True (-1) if the record pointer is positioned before the first record in the recordset or the recordset contains no records. Otherwise, it returns False (0).

When a recordset is created (or opened), the record pointer is on the first (top) record and the *BOF* property is False. If the record pointer is on the first (top) record, issuing MoveFirst doesn't change the current record and the *BOF* property remains False. If the record pointer is on the first record and the *BOF* property is True (after MovePrevious, for example), issuing MovePrevious again triggers a `No current record` error (trappable error #3021), the current record becomes undefined, and the *BOF* property stays True.

Access Basic Example

Move through the Customers table backwards in a **Do...Loop** that checks the *BOF* property on every iteration:

```
Dim cDb As Database, cTb As Table
Set cDb = CurrentDB()
Set cTb = cDb.OpenTable("Customers")
cTb.MoveLast                                ' Go to the last record
Do Until cTb.BOF
    (...)
    cTb.MovePrevious
Loop
Result = cTb.BOF                        ' True
cTb.MovePrevious                        ' Error 3021
cTb.Close
```

See Also

Properties: EOF and NoMatch

Bookmark

Marks the current records.

Applies To

Forms and Recordsets

Usage

All views: Read and Write

Notes

This property is usable *only* in Access Basic.

Marking the record with a bookmark is the easiest way to return later to this record. You can set as many bookmarks in the recordset (Table, Dynaset, Snapshot) as needed.

Some recordsets, such as those based on attached tables, don't support the *Bookmark* property. Check the *Bookmarkable* property before using bookmarks if you aren't sure.

Bookmarks also can work across recordsets, as in the following example, which moves the record pointer to the same record in two identical dynasets created with the **Clone** method:

```
Dim cDb As Database, cOrig As Dynaset, cClone As Dynaset
Set cDb = CurrentDB()
Set cOrig = cDb.CreateDynaset("Customers")
Set cClone = cOrig.Clone()

cMark cOrig.Bookmark           'Set bookmark
cClone.Bookmark = cMark        'Same record - different recordset
(...)
```


Access Basic Example

Seek a value in the Customers table indexed on the Id field and set a *Bookmark* to this record:

```
Dim cDb As Database, cTb As Table
Set cDb = CurrentDB()
Set cTb = cDb.OpenTable("Customers")
cTb.Index = "Id"
cTb.Seek "=", "MSOFT"

' Check for match and if the recordsets supports bookmarks
If (Not cTb.NoMatch) And cTb.Bookmarkable Then
     cMark = cTb.Bookmark       ' set bookmark
     cTb.MoveLast               ' move to the last record
     cTb.Bookmark = cMark       ' move back to the marked record
     (...)
End If

cTb.Close
```

See Also

Method: Clone

Property: Bookmarkable

Bookmarkable

Indicates whether the Bookmark property is supported by a recordset.

Applies To

Recordsets

Usage

All views: Read Only

Notes

This property returns True (-1) if the recordset supports bookmarks and False(0) otherwise.

Inspect the value of the *Bookmarkable* property before using bookmarks. Some recordsets (such as those based on attached tables without a primary index) don't support bookmarks.

Access Basic Example

See the "Bookmark" property

See Also

Property: Bookmark

BorderColor

Specifies the color of the border.

Applies To

Tools and controls: bound object frame, combo box, graph, label, line, option group, rectangle, subform, subreport, text box, unbound object frame

Usage

Design view: Read and Write

Other views: Read Only

Notes

If *BorderStyle* and *BackStyle* properties are available, both must be set to Normal; otherwise, the setting of the *BorderStyle* property becomes meaningless.

To set this property on the form design surface, use the Palette. To set the *BorderColor* property in Access Basic, use the numeric value of the desired color returned by QBColor or RGB functions.

Access Basic Example

In Design view, open the form called Alpha and set the color of the frame around the control "Id" to black (using the **QBColor** function):

```
DoCmd OpenForm "Alpha", A_DESIGN
Dim cCtrl As Control
Set cCtrl = Forms!Alpha.Id
cCtrl.SpecialEffect = 0
cCtrl.BorderStyle = 1
cCtrl.BorderColor = QBColor(0)
DoCmd Close A_FORM, "Alpha"
```

See Also

Properties: BorderStyle, BorderWidth, ForeColor, and SpecialEffect

BorderStyle

Specifies whether the control's border (frame) is visible.

Applies To

Tools and controls: bound object frame, combo box, graph, label, line, option group, rectangle, subform, subreport, text box, unbound object frame

Usage

Design view: Read and Write

Other views: Read Only

Notes

This property has two settings:

- *Clear* (default for label, graph, object frame, subreport, and text box). The border is transparent (clear). In Access Basic, use 0.
- *Normal.* The border is visible. In Access Basic, use 1.

The *SpecialEffect* property must be set to Normal (0 in Access Basic), or the setting of the *BorderStyle* property becomes meaningless.

Access Basic Example

See the "BorderColor" property

See Also

Properties: BorderColor, BackStyle, and SpecialEffect

BorderWidth

Specifies the width of the control's border (frame).

Applies To

Tools and controls: bound object frame, combo box, graph, label, line, option group, rectangle, subform, subreport, text box, unbound object frame

Usage

Design view: Read and Write

Other views: Read Only

Notes

This property has 7 settings:

- *Hairline (default).* Represents the thinnest possible border on a particular system.
- *Values 1 through 6.* Specifies the width of the border in points (the actual width is system- and printer-dependent).

Use the Palette to set the width of the border on the designer surface. In Access Basic, use 0 to set the border to the Hairline width, and integers 1 through 6 to set thicker widths.

You must set the *BorderStyle* property to Normal (1 in Access Basic) and the *SpecialEffect* property to Normal (0 in Access Basic), or the *BorderWidth* setting becomes meaningless.

Access Basic Example

Create a form using Access Basic, create 7 controls (default unbound text boxes), and set progressively thicker frames around them:

```
Dim cForm As Form, cCtrl As Control, szFormName As String
Const TEXT_BOX = 109
Set cForm = CreateForm()
szFormName = cForm.FormName
wX = 1000                        ' X coordinates of the first control
wY = 100                         ' Y coordinates of the first control
For i = 0 To 6
    Set cCtrl = CreateControl(szFormName,TEXT_BOX, 0,"","", wX, wY)
    cCtrl.BorderWidth = i
    wY = wY + 400                ' Y coordinates of the next control
Next
DoCmd Restore                    ' display the form
(...)
```

Figure 22.1 shows the effects of different settings of this property.

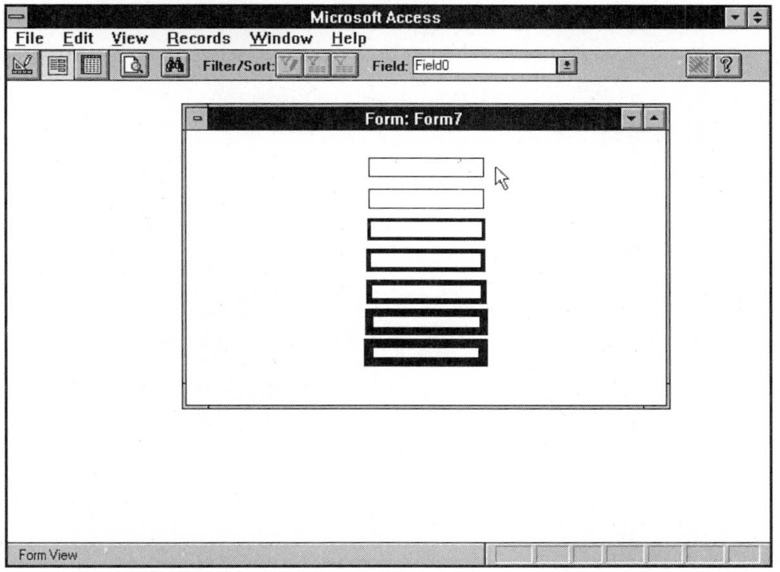

Figure 22.1. A form with borders from 0 through 6 around text boxes.

See Also

Properties: BorderColor, BackStyle, and SpecialEffect

PROPERTIES

BoundColumn

Binds a combo box or list box column to a field specified in the *ControlSource* property.

Applies To

Controls: Combo box, list box

Usage

Design view: Read and Write

Other views: Read Only

Notes

The setting of this property can be from 0 through the number of columns specified in the *ColumnCount* property. The default is 1.

The data from the column corresponding to the setting of the *BoundColumn* property in the table is stored in the current record and displayed with a combo box or a list box if the setting of this property is greater than 0. If the setting of this property equals 0, the *list index* (the row number of the selected item) is stored in the current record rather than the actual data.

Access Basic Example

Bind the second column of the second column of the table specified in the *ControlSource* property; the form must be opened in Design view.

```
Dim fForm As Form
fForm.[ComboBox1].BoundColumn = 2
```

See Also

Properties: Column, ColumnCount, ColumnHeads, ColumnWidths, ControlSource, ListRows, and ListWidths

Cancel

Determines whether a command button is designated as a Cancel button.

Applies To

Command button (pushbutton)

Usage

Design view: Read and Write

Other views: Read Only

Notes

If the command button is designated as a Cancel button, you have an option to reverse (cancel) an action (a deletion or update, for example) on the current record.

This property has two settings:

- *Yes.* The command button is a Cancel button. In Access Basic, use True (-1).
- *No* (default). The command is not the Cancel button. In Access Basic, use False (0).

Only one button on the form can be designated as a Cancel button. The *Cancel* property of all other command buttons on the form is automatically set to No.

Caution

Combining the CancelEvent action and the Cancel button can lead to unexpected results. An update action cancelled by the CancelEvent action, for example, can be undone by pressing the command button designated as the Cancel button.

Access Basic Example

Open the Alpha form and check whether the Button49 control was designated as the Cancel button. If it was, change its Caption and Default properties:

```
Dim cCtrl As Control
DoCmd OpenForm "Alpha", A_DESIGN
Set cCtrl = Forms!Alpha.Button49
If TypeOf cCtrl Is CommandButton Then
    If cCtrl.Cancel Then
        cCtrl.Caption = "Cancel Button"
        cCtrl.Default = True
    End If
End If
DoCmd Close A_FORM, "Alpha"
```

See Also

Action: CancelEvent

Property: Default

CanGrow, CanShrink

Determine whether the section or control can expand or contract vertically to accommodate the length of data being printed.

Applies To

Forms, reports sections. Subforms, subreports, text box controls.

Usage

Design view: Read and Write

Other views: Read Only

Notes

These properties work only while printing (or previewing for print) forms or reports. They have no effect when the form is displayed in the Form view.

The *CanGrow* property has two settings:

- *Yes.* The section or control can expand vertically to accommodate all data.
- *No (default).* The section or control is static and data that doesn't fit is truncated.

The *CanShrink* property also has two settings:

- *Yes.* The section or control can shrink vertically to eliminate blank lines if there isn't enough data to fill the entire section or control.
- *No (default).* The section or control remains static.

Access sets the section's *CanGrow* property to Yes if the *CanGrow* property of any control in the same section is set to Yes. (This is not true with the *CanShrink* property.)

Access Basic Example

In Design view, open the form Alpha and set the *CanGrow* property to Yes (True). Access automatically sets the detail's section *CanGrow* property to Yes:

```
Dim cForm As Form
DoCmd OpenForm "Alpha", A_DESIGN
Set cForm = Forms!Alpha
Result = cForm.Section(0).CanGrow       'False
cForm.Id.CanGrow = True
Result = cForm.Section(0).CanGrow       'True
DoCmd Close A_FORM, "Alpha"
```

See Also

Property: OnFormat

CanShrink

See "CanGrow" property.

Caption

Specifies the text that appears as the column title (for tables opened in Datasheet view), as the window caption (for forms in Form view), and in the control (for buttons and labels).

Applies To

Table fields, forms. Command button, label, toggle button.

Usage

Design view: Read and Write

Other views: Read Only

Table fields are not available.

Notes

The initial value of the *Caption* property for a form, button, or label is the control's default name given by Access. For a label of a table field dragged onto a form from the field list, the *Caption* property is set to the actual name of the created control.

The length of captions is limited to 255 characters. The maximum length of a caption in a label is 2,048 characters.

An ampersand (&) in the *Caption* property assigns the next character as a shortcut to access the control. If you want to display an ampersand in the caption, use two ampersands.

Tip

Because the *Caption* property is read-only in all views other than the Design view, consider using the Windows API functions (such as SetWindowText) to change captions at runtime. See the example in Chapter 13, "Extending Microsoft Access and Access Basic."

Access Basic Example

Open the form Alpha in Design view, and change its caption to New Alpha Form. Then change the caption of the command button to "Exit to DOS".

```
Dim cForm As Form
DoCmd OpenForm "Alpha", A_DESIGN
Set cForm = Forms!Alpha
Result = cForm.Caption                     ' "Alpha"

cForm.Caption = "New Alpha Form"           ' New window (form) caption
Result = cForm.Button40.Caption            ' "Button40"
cForm.Button40.Caption = "Exit to DOS"     ' New button caption
Result = cForm.Button40.Caption            ' "Exit to DOS"
```

See Also

Property: Description

Column

Refers to the particular column in a multi-column listing in a combo box or list box.

Applies To

Controls: Combo box, list box

Usage

All views: Read Only

Notes

This property has no user-settable settings. It refers to the contents of the particular column in the combo box or list box. Column 0 refers to the first column, 1 refers to the second column, and so on. The *Column* property returns a string or a null value when referring to a nonexisting column, or if the selection has not been made.

Caution

Some Access settings start with 0, and some start with 1. The *ColumnCount* property is 1-based, while the actual number of columns in the *Column* property is 0-based. Always check the minimum value of the setting in question before coding—don't make any assumptions!

Access Basic Example

Get the values from columns 1 and 2 of the list box and assign them to two text boxes on the same form—Column1 and Column2, respectively:

```
Dim cForm As Form
cField = "Phone owner"
Set cForm = Screen.ActiveForm
wColumnCount = cForm(cField).ColumnCount - 1
cForm.Column1 = cForm(cField).Column(0)
cForm.Column2 = cForm(cField).Column(1)
```

See Also

Object: Forms

Properties: BoundColumn and ColumnCount

ColumnCount

Specifies the number of columns displayed in a combo box or list box, or sent to an OLE object in a graph or object frame.

Applies To

Controls: Combo box, graph, list box, unbound object frame (embedded)

Usage

Design view: Read and Write

Other views: Read Only

Notes

The number of columns from the underlying table, query, or SQL expression (defined in the *RecordSource* property) specified in this setting is displayed in the combo box or list box from left to right.

The minimum setting of the *ColumnCount* property is 1. The maximum setting is the number of fields in the underlying table, query, or SQL expression.

Access Basic Example

Report the number of columns and the settings of *ColumnHeads* and *ColumnWidths* properties in the combo box:

```
Function t_ColumnCount (cCtrl As Control)
If TypeOf cCtrl Is combobox Then
     Debug.Print cCtrl.ColumnCount, cCtrl.ColumnHeads, cCtrl.ColumnWidths
End If
End Function
```

See Also

Properties: BoundColumn, Column, ColumnHeads, ColumnWidths, and ControlSource

ColumnHeads

Determines whether the field names in the underlying table or query are displayed in the combo box or list box as column headings.

Applies To

Controls: Combo box, graph, list box, unbound object frame (embedded)

Usage

Design view: Read and Write

Other views: Read Only

Notes

This property has two settings:

- *Yes.* The field names from the underlying table or query are displayed as column headings on a combo box or list box. In Access Basic, use True (-1) to set this property.
- *No (default).* No headings are displayed. In Access Basic, use False (0) to set this property.

If the setting of *ColumnHeads* is Yes, the first row of the drop-down list in a combo box or list box is occupied by the column headings.

Access Basic Example

See "ColumnCount" Property

See Also

Properties: BoundColumn, ColumnWidths, ControlSource, ListRows, ListWidth

ColumnWidths

Specifies the width of columns in a combo box or list box.

Applies To

Controls: Combo box, list box

Usage

Design view: Read and Write

Other views: Read Only

Notes

The values described in the following table may be returned for each column and are delimited with a semicolon (;). All examples assume a three-column display in a combo box with the *ListWidth* property set to 5 inches.

Value	*Meaning*
A number	Width of the column in default units of measurement (twips or inches, for example). In the example 2;2;2, the first two columns are visible. The third column must be scrolled.
0	Column is hidden. In the example 4;0;1, the first column is 4 inches wide, the second is hidden, and the third is 1 inch wide.
Blank delimited by semicolons	Column width is the default. In the example 3;;1, the first column is 3 inches wide, the second is 1 inch (the default), and the third is 1 inch.
Blank	All columns are the default, except the last one that fills the remaining horizontal space on the row. If this property is left blank, the default width of columns is 1 inch.

Note

If you specify the column width as 0 (meaning that the column is not visible in the list), you still can specify that it will be the column bound to the control by typing the number of the column in the *BoundColumn* property of the form.

In Access Basic, use a string value to set this property.

Access Basic Example

Set the value of the *BoundColumn*, *ColumnCount*, and *ColumnWidths* properties. You will have a total of four columns. The third column is bound to the control, and the first and second columns are hidden:

```
Dim cCTrl As Control
DoCmd OpenForm "Calls", A_DESIGN
Set cCTrl = Forms![Calls].[Phone owner]
cCTrl.ListWidth = 4
cCTrl.ColumnCount = 4
cCTrl.BoundColumn = 2
cCTrl.ColumnWidths = "0;0;2,2"
DoCmd Close A_FORM, "Calls"
```

See also the example in "ColumnCount."

See Also

Properties: BoundColumn, ColumnCount, ColumnHeads, ControlSource, Height, Width, ListRow, and ListWidth

ControlName

Specifies the name of a control.

Applies To

All Controls

Usage

Design view: Read and Write

Other views: Read Only

Notes

The name of a control must be unique. If you don't name the control, Access assigns it a unique name (Field65, for example).

In Access Basic, use a string expression to set the name.

Attempting to assign a duplicate name to a control results in a `You already have a control named "<name>"` error (trappable error #2104).

This property is used extensively in Access Wizards. Study the code in the WIZARDS.MDA database included with Access for more information and examples.

Access Basic Example

Change the name of the Phone Owner field to something a little longer:

```
Dim cCtrl As Control
DoCmd OpenForm "Calls", A_DESIGN
Set cCtrl = Forms![Calls].[Phone owner]
cCtrl.ControlName = "He Who Owns The Phone"
(...)
```

See Also

Property: Caption

ControlSource

Specifies the source of data for the control.

Applies To

Controls: Bound object frame, list box, option group, text box

Also applies to the following controls unless they are a part of the option group: Check box, option button, toggle button

Usage

Design view: Read and Write

Other views: Read Only

Notes

The source can be a field in a table, query, or expression. If you enter an expression, you must precede it with an equal sign.

Making a change to a control bound to a table or query field changes data in the underlying table or query. To make the control read-only, set its *Locked* property to Yes (or True in Access Basic).

In Access Basic, use a string expression to set the *ControlSource* property.

Access Basic Example

Inspect the value of the *RecordSource* property of the Call Date control on the Calls form:

```
DoCmd OpenForm "Calls"
Debug.Print Forms!Calls.[Call date].ControlSource
DoCmd Close A_FORM, "Calls"
```

See Also

Properties: RecordSource, RowSourceType, and RowSource

Count

The *Count* property, when used with forms and reports, contains the number of controls on a form or report. When used with Forms and Reports objects, it contains the number of open forms or reports.

Applies To

Forms, reports, forms objects, reports objects

Usage

All views: Read Only

Note

The *Count* property setting is an Integer zero if no forms or reports are open, or if a form or report does not have any controls.

Access Basic Example

Loop through all open forms. Display a message box with the form name and the number of controls on each form:

```
Dim cForm As Form, wFormCount As Integer
wFormCount = Forms.Count
If wFormCount > 0 Then
    For i = 0 To wFormCount - 1
        Set cForm = Forms(i)
        MsgBox "Form " & cForm.FormName & " has" & Str(cForm.Count) & " controls"
    Next
End If
```

See Also

Objects: Forms, Reports, and Screen

Properties: ActiveControl, ActiveForm, and ActiveReport

CurrentX, CurrentY

Define the horizontal and vertical coordinates for printing and drawing.

Applies To

Forms, reports

Usage

Design view: Not available

Other views: Read and Write

Notes

You can set these properties only from Access Basic. The coordinates are relative to the top left corner of a section (*CurrentX* and *CurrentY* are equal to 0 specifies the top left corner, therefore).

The value of *CurrentX* and *CurrentY* properties is a Single data type. The default units of measurement for these properties are twips.

Access sets the value of these properties when you use the following drawing methods:

- *Circle.* Both *CurrentX* and *CurrentY* are set to its center.
- *Line.* Both properties are set to the end point of a line.
- *Print.* Both properties are set to the next point position.

Access Basic Example

The following function illustrates the automatic resetting of the *CurrentX* and *CurrentY* properties when using certain drawing methods (Circle, in this case). Please note that this function can be attached only to the *OnFormat* or *OnPrint* properties of a report:

```
Function CircleAndXY (Rpt As Report)
Rpt.drawwidth = 100
Rpt.Scalemode = 3
Rpt.CurrentX = 2000
Rpt.CurrentY = 5000
Debug.Print Rpt.CurrentX; Rpt.CurrentY       ' 2000 5000
Rpt.Scale
Rpt.Circle (350, 600), 100
Debug.Print Rpt.CurrentX; Rpt.CurrentY       ' 350 600
End Function
```

See Also

Properties: DrawMode, DrawStyle, Left, Top, ScaleHeight, ScaleWidth, ScaleLeft, ScaleTop, and ScaleMode

PROPERTIES

DataType

Specifies the field data type.

Not available in Access Basic

Applies To

Table fields

Usage

Design view: Read and Write

Other views: Not Available

Notes

Access tables support the data types described in the following table.

Type	*Notes*
Counter	Long Integer. Access increments it automatically when the new record is added to the table.
Currency	Scaled Integer (occupies 8 bytes). Stores numbers from -922,337,203,685,477.5808 to 922,337,203,685,477.5807 with the precision of four decimal places. Performs fast, fixed-point arithmetic, which avoids rounding errors.
Date/Time	Stores data and time values as a double number.
Memo	Text up to 32,000 characters. Cannot be indexed.
Number	Length specified by the FieldSize property: Byte (occupies 1 byte). Stores integers from 0 to 255. *Double* (default, occupies 8 bytes). Stores numbers from -1.79769313486232E308 to 1.79769313486232E308 with 10-digit precision. Integer (occupies 2 bytes). Stores whole numbers from -32,767 through 32,767. *Long Integer* (occupies 4 bytes). Stores whole numbers from -2,147,483,648 to 2,147,483,647. *Single* (occupies 4 bytes). Stores numbers from -3,402823E38 to 3,402823E38 with six-digit precision

Type	*Notes*
OLE Object	Stores linked objects created by OLE servers. Maximum size: Version 1.0 (128M), Version 1.2 (1G). Cannot be indexed.
Text (default)	Text up to 255 characters (default is 50 characters).
Yes/No	Stores an integer(-1 or 0). This data type cannot be indexed.

Caution

Changing the data type of a field after the data has been entered in this field may produce unpredictable results if the data types are not compatible (such as changing Double to Integer).

Access Basic Example

Not available in Access Basic. To get information about the data type of a field in a table, use the field Type in a snapshot created with the **ListFields** method.

See Also

Properties: FieldSize and Format

Method: ListFields

DateCreated

Stores the date and time when the table was created.

Applies To

Tables

Usage

All views: Read Only

Notes

This property returns the date and time when a table was created as a Variant VarType 7 (Date) data type. In Access Versions 1.0 and 1.1, the date and time stamp is stored in the MSysObject table field DateCreate. Even though this property applies only to tables, *DateCreated* is stored for all Access objects in the MSysObjects table.

You can use this property only with Access Basic code.

This property is meaningless for Access system tables.

This example returns the date and time when the Cirrus table was created and the design last updated:

```
Dim cDb As Database, cTb As Table, szTableName$
szTableName = "Cirrus"
Set cDb = CurrentDB()
Set cTb = cDb.OpenTable(szTableName)
Debug.Print cTb.DateCreated            '10/12/92 5:10:42 PM
Debug.Print cTb.LastUpdated            '3/17/93 10:21:24 AM
cTb.Close
```

See Also

Property: LastUpdated

DecimalPlaces

Determines the number of decimal places used to display numbers.

Applies To

A control—text box. Table fields

Usage

Design view: Read and Write

Other views: Read Only

Notes

This property's setting is Auto (the default—numbers are displayed as specified by the Format property) or the actual number of decimal places to display. If the *Format* property is set, it controls the display of the digits to the left of the decimal point.

Access displays a maximum of 15 decimal places.

If the property *DecimalPlaces* is set for a field in the table, the setting is reflected: only in controls on forms that use that field created after the table setting was made; and only if the control was created by dragging the field onto the form from the field list.

If the *Format* property is set to General Number, the setting of the *DecimalPlaces* property is meaningless.

In Access Basic, use the actual value for the desired number of decimal places (0-15) or 255 for the Auto setting.

Access Basic Example

Inspect the value of the *DecimalPlaces* property of the current control if the control is the text box (this function may be attached to the *OnEnter* property, for example):

```
If TypeOf Screen.ActiveControl Is TextBox Then
     Debug.Print Screen.ActiveControl.DecimalPlaces
End If
```

See Also

Functions: Format and Format$

Property: Format

Default

Determines whether the command button is the default button.

Applies To

Command button (pushbutton)

Usage

Design view: Read and Write

Other views: Read Only

Notes

This property has two settings:

- *Yes.* The command button is the default button. In Access Basic, use True (-1).
- *No* (default). The command button is not the default button. In Access Basic, use False (0).

Only one button on the form can be designated as the *Default* button. The *Default* property of all other command buttons on the form is set automatically to No.

Access Basic Example

See "Cancel" property.

See Also

Property: Cancel

PROPERTIES

DefaultEditing

See the "AllowEditing" property.

DefaultValue

Specifies the default value for a table field or control.

Applies To

Table fields, controls (combo box, list box, option group, text box). Applied to the following controls if placed in an option group: check box, option button, toggle button.

Usage

Design view: Read and Write

Other views: Read Only

Notes

The value specified in this property is entered automatically when a new record is added to a table or form.

The *DefaultValue* property is a literal or an expression up to 255 characters. If you enter an expression, the default value can dynamically change at runtime, depending on the user's input, results of calculations, or the value entered in other controls or fields.

The *DefaultValue* property doesn't apply to counter and OLE fields.

If you set the *DefaultValue* for a field in the table, the setting is reflected only in controls on forms that use that field created after the table setting was made and only if the control was created by dragging the field onto the form from the field list.

Access Basic Example

In Design view, open the Customers form and set the *DefaultValue* property of the State control to CA:

```
DoCmd OpenForm "Customers", A_DESIGN
Dim cFrm as Form
Set cFrm = Forms![Customers]
cFrm.State.DefaultValue = "CA"
DoCmd SetWarnings False
DoCmd Close A_FORM, "Customers"
```

See Also

Property: ValidationRule

DefaultView, ViewsAllowed

DefaultView specifies the view in which the form opens.

ViewsAllowed specifies which views are available after the form is opened.

Applies To

Forms

Usage

Design view: Read and Write

Other views: Read Only

Notes

These properties have the following settings.

DefaultView	*Form Display Mode*
Single Form	Form displays one record at a time.
Continous Forms	Form displays as many records (detail sections of the form) as will fit in the form window. This is the default setting.
Datasheet	Fields and some controls on the form are displayed in a columnar (spreadsheet) fashion. The form is devoid of commands and toggle buttons, and many controls change their appearance.

ViewsAllowed	*Form Display Mode*
Both	You can view the form in Form view or Datasheet view. This is the default setting.
Form	Datasheet view is not available.
Datasheet	Form view is not available.

The following table shows various combinations of the settings and their effects ("Forms" in the *DefaultView* property refers to single or continous forms).

ViewsAllowed	*DefaultView*	*Effect*
Both	Any setting	Form opens in Form view. Both Form view and Datasheet view are available.
Both	Forms	Form opens in Form view. Datasheet view is not available.
Form	Datasheet	Form opens in Datasheet view. Form view is available, but after you choose it, you cannot switch back to Datasheet view.
Datasheet	Forms	Form opens in Form view. Datasheet view is available, but after you choose it, you cannot switch back to Form view.
Datasheet	Datasheet	Form opens in Datasheet view. Form view is not available.

The settings in Access Basic follow:

- *DefaultView* property
  Single Form: 0
  Continous Form: 1
  Datasheet: 2
- *ViewsAllowed* property
  Both: 0
  Form: 1
  Datasheet: 2

Caution

Because the *DefaultView* property specifies how to open the form, and the *ViewsAllowed* property specifies what to do after the form is open, it is entirely possible that the combination of these two properties will lead to illogical results. The form might be opened in Form view, for example, but the user may not be able to return to Form view after switching to Datasheet view.

Access Basic Example

Synchronize the settings of both properties to eliminate potential conflicts. If *DefaultView* is Datasheet view, set *ViewsAllowed* to Datasheet view as well. Otherwise, set *ViewsAllowed* to Both (you must open a form in Design view):

```
Function SetViews (cForm As Form)
If cForm.DefaultView = 2 Then
    cForm.ViewsAllowed = 2
Else
    cFormViewsAllowed = 0
End If
End Function
```

Description

Stores text description of the table and its fields.

Not available in Access Basic

Applies To

Table, table fields

Usage

Design view: Read and Write

Not available in Access Basic

Notes

Both tables and fields have this property.

The maximum length of Description text is 255 characters.

If this property is set for a field in the table, the setting is transferred to the *StatusBarText* property: only in controls on forms that use that field created after the table setting was made; and only if the control was created by dragging the field onto the form from the field list.

See Also

Properties: Caption and StatusBarText

DisplayWhen

Determines in which views an object is displayed.

Applies To

All controls on a form except Page Break. Also applied to Forms sections (form header, detail section, and form footer).

Usage

Design view: Read and Write

Other views: Read Only

Notes

Forms can be treated as reports. You can use the form layout to print records from the underlying recordset, for example. The *DisplayWhen* property determines whether an object is displayed when the form is viewed, when it is printed, or in both cases. It is useful to hide controls such as command buttons when printing a form.

This property has three settings:

- *Always (default).* Object is displayed in Form view and in print. In Access Basic, use 0 for this property's setting.
- *Print Only.* Object is hidden (not accessible) in Form view. In Access Basic, use 1.
- *Screen Only.* Object is not printed, but appears in Form view. In Access Basic, use 3.

Access Basic Example

Suppress buttons on a form from printing. Open a form in Design view and loop through all controls on the form. If a control is a command button or a toggle button, set its *DisplayWhen* property to Screen Only (2).

```
Dim cForm As Form, cCtrl As Control, wControls%, bChange%
bChange = False
DoCmd OpenForm "Customers", A_DESIGN, , , , A_ICON
Set cForm = Forms![Customers]
wControls = cForm.Count - 1
For i = 0 To wControls
     Set cCtrl = cForm(i)
     If TypeOf cCtrl Is CommandButton Then
          bChange = True
     ElseIf TypeOf cCtrl Is ToggleButton Then
          bChange = True
     End If
     If bChange Then
          cCtrl.DisplayWhen = 2
          bChange = False
     End If
Next
DoCmd Close A_FORM, "Customers"
```

See Also

Properties: Enabled, Locked, and OnFormat

DrawMode

Specifies how colors used in drawing reports appear when using the Line, Circle, and PSet methods.

Applies To

Reports

Usage

Design view: Not available

Other views: Read and Write

Notes

The setting of the *DrawMode* property is an Integer number.

You can access this property only from Access Basic code or macros attached to the *OnFormat* or *OnPrint* property.

Note

Setting this property produces various visual effects on the report. Test the settings for this property before using them, because the results depend on the colors used and may differ among systems.

You can use the settings described in the following table.

Setting	*Result*
1	Black pen
2	Inverse of setting 15
3	Combination of background color and inverse of pen
4	Inverse of setting 13
5	Combination of colors common to the pen and inverse of the display
6	Inverse of the display color
7	Combination of color of the pen or the display color, but not both
8	Inverse of setting 9

continues

Setting	*Result*
9	Combination of colors common to both the pen and the display
10	Inverse of setting 7
11	No change (turns off the drawing)
12	Combination of the display color and inverse of the pen color
13	Color specified in the *ForeColor* property
14	Combination of the pen color and inverse of the display color
15	Combination of the display color and pen color
16	White pen

Access Basic Example

Test all settings of the *DrawMode* property. This function should be attached to the reports' section *OnFormat* or *OnPrint* properties:

```
Function p_DrawMode ()
On Error Resume Next
Dim Rpt As Report
Set Rpt = Reports!Report2
BottX = 100: BottY = 200
For i = 1 To 16
    Rpt.DrawMode = i
    Rpt.Line (3 * i, 100 * i)-(BottX * i, BottY * i)
Next i
End Function
```

See Also

Functions: QBColor and RGB

Properties: BackColor, BackStyle, DrawStyle, DrawWidth, FillColor, ForeColor, OnFormat, and OnPrint

DrawStyle

Specifies the line style for Line and Circle methods.

Applies To

Reports

Usage

Design view: Not available

Other views: Read and Write

Notes

You can access this property only from Access Basic code or macros attached to *OnFormat* or *OnPrint* properties.

Setting	*Result*
0	Solid line (default)
1	Dash
2	Dot
3	Dash-dot
4	Dash-dot-dash
5	Invisible
6	Inside solid

The actual drawing depends also on the *DrawWidth* property setting. If *DrawWidth* is greater than 1, settings 1 through 4 of the *DrawStyle* property produce solid lines.

Access Basic Example

The following function (attached to the *OnFormat* property of a report named Report2) displays all available drawing styles:

```
Function TestDrawStyle ()
Dim Rpt As Report
Set Rpt = Reports!Report2
Rpt.DrawWidth = 1
For i = 0 To 6
    Rpt.DrawStyle = i
    Rpt.Line (100, 200 * i)-(10000, 200 * i)
Next i
End Function
```

The results of the above function are displayed in figure 22.2.

See Also

Functions: QBColor and RGB

Properties: BackColor, BackStyle, DrawMode, DrawWidth, FillColor, ForeColor, OnFormat, and OnPrint

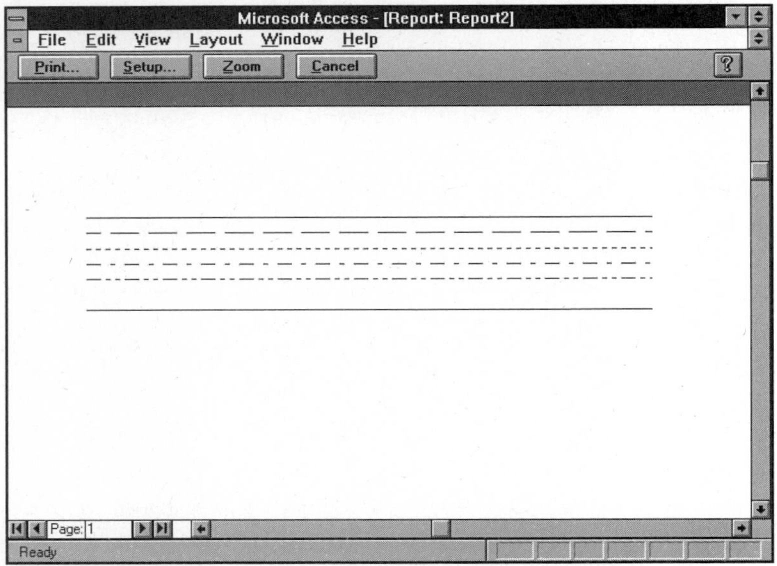

Figure 22.2. Line styles printed by the DrawStyle property.

DrawWidth

Specifies line width for the Line, Circle, and PSet methods.

Applies To

Reports

Usage

Design view: Not available

Other views: Read and Write

Notes

You can access this property only from Access Basic code or macros attached to the *OnFormat* or *OnPrint* property.

The unit of measure for this argument is *pixel*.

The value of this property must be an Integer data type in the range of 1 through 32,767.

Settings smaller than 0 trigger a `The setting you entered isn't valid for this property` error (trappable error #2101). Values from outside the range of Integer data type trigger an `Overflow` error (trappable error #6). Note that the 0 setting defaults to 1 and does not trigger an error.

The setting of this property also affects the line style specified with the *DrawStyle* property. If the setting of the *DrawWidth* property is greater than 1, the setting of the *DrawStyle* property is meaningless (for example, any visible line is drawn as a solid line, regardless of the setting of the DrawStyle property).

Access Basic Example

The following function attached to the *OnPrint* property of the header section of the report Report2 draws lines with different widths:

```
Function TestDrawWidth ()
Dim Rpt As Report
Set Rpt = Reports!Report2
For i = 1 To 50 Step 5
    Rpt.DrawWidth = i
    Rpt.Line (BottX, 200 * i / 2)-(10000, 200 * i / 2)
Next i
End Function
```

Figure 22.3 shows lines produced by this function.

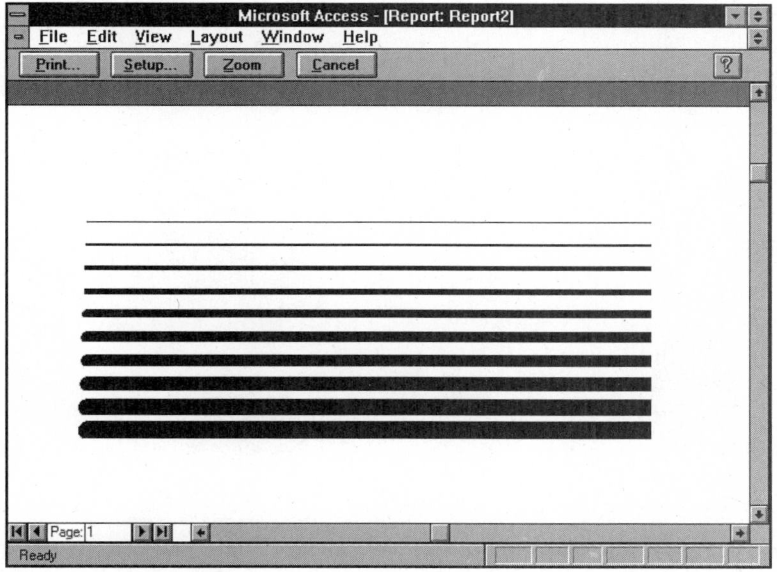

Figure 22.3. An example of line widths.

PROPERTIES

See Also

Functions: QBColor and RGB

Method: PSet

Properties: BackColor, BackStyle, DrawMode, DrawStyle, FillColor, ForeColor, OnFormat, and OnPrint

Dynaset

Returns the underlying dynaset for the specified form.

Applies To

Forms

Usage

All views: Read Only

Notes

The *Dynaset* property has no settings; it returns exactly the same recordset as the underlying recordset (table, query) of the specified form.

When a new *Dynaset* is created, it has no current record. You can use the *Bookmark* property to make the form's current record in the new dynaset, or use one of the **Move** or **Find** methods to make any record current.

The new dynaset is valid only while the form is open and the definition of the form's underlying recordset is unchanged.

Access Basic Example

This function simulates the record selector positioned on the form's horizontal scroll bar. It uses the *Dynaset* property to create a new dynaset from the form's dynaset and navigate within the new dynaset according to the value of the parameter *wOption* passed from the calling form. (The values of this parameter are selected arbitrarily here.)

The line *cDy.Bookmark = cForm.Bookmark* establishes the current record in the new dynaset. The line *cForm.Bookmark = cDy.Bookmark* establishes the new current record in the form's dynaset:

```
Function TestDynaset (wOption%)

On Error Resume Next
Dim cDy As Dynaset, cForm As Form
Set cForm = Screen.ActiveForm
Set cDy = cForm.Dynaset
```

```
cDy.Bookmark = cForm.Bookmark
Select Case wOption
Case 1: cDy.MoveLast
Case 2: cDy.MoveFirst
Case 3: cDy.MoveNext
Case 4: cDy.MovePrevious
End Select
cForm.Bookmark = cDy.Bookmark

End Function
```

You may want to expand this function to include various cases of the Find method to allow more robust navigation within a form.

The second example shows how to use the *Dynaset* property to open a form and position it on a specific record. If the value szCompanyName is found in the field Company in the dynaset underlying the form Company Setup, the form opens on this record. Otherwise it opens on the first record of the dynaset. The most logical place to attach this function is the *OnOpen* property of a form.

```
Function FindCompany(szCompanyName$)
If Not IsNull(szCompanyName) Then
     Dim cDy As Dynaset, fForm  As Form
     Set fForm = Forms![Company Setup]
     Set cDy = fForm.Dynaset
     cDy.FindFirst "[Company] = '" & szCompanyName & "'"
     If Not cDy.NoMatch Then
        fForm.Bookmark = cDy.Bookmark
     End If
End If
cDy.Close
End Function
```

See Also

Methods: FindFirst, FindLast, FindNext, FindPrevious, MoveFirst, MoveLast, MoveNext, and MovePrevious

Objects: Forms and Screen

Properties: Bookmark and RecordCount

Enabled, Locked

Enabled specifies whether a control can have focus in Form view.

Locked specifies whether the data can be changed in a control.

Applies To

Controls on a form: Bound object frame, check box, combo box, command button, list box, option button, option group, subform, text box, toggle button, unbound object frame

The locked property is not applicable to the command button and unbound object frame.

Usage

All views: Read and Write

Notes

The most frequent use for these properties is to conditionally make available certain controls on a form, depending on the underlying data or the user's action.

The settings of these properties follow:

Enabled

- *Yes.* Default for all controls except unbound object frame. Control can gain focus. In Access Basic, use the True (-1) setting.
- *No.* Default for unbound object frame only. Control cannot gain focus. If the control is an option group, no controls within this option group can gain focus. In Access Basic, use the False (0) setting.

Locked

- *Yes.* Control doesn't enable you to change its data. In Access Basic, use the True (-1) setting.
- *No.* Control enables you to change its data. This is the default setting. In Access Basic, use the False (0) setting.

Various combinations of the settings for these controls produce results described in the following table.

Enabled	*Locked*	*Result*
Yes	Yes	Control appears normally. You can copy data, but you cannot change it.
No	No	Control cannot gain focus. Data is dimmed.
Yes	Yes	Control behaves normally.
No	No	Control cannot gain focus. You cannot copy or change data.

Access Basic Example

If the user enters **Bicycle messenger** in the Deliver By field, this function disables the FAX Number control:

```
Function TestEnabledAndLocked ()
Dim cForm As Form
Set cForm = Screen.ActiveForm
If (cForm.[Deliver by] = "FAX") Then
     cForm.Fax.Enabled = True
```

```
Else
     cForm.Fax.Enabled = False
End If
End Function
```

See Also

Action: SetValue

Properties: DisplayWhen and Visible

EOF

Indicates whether the record pointer is positioned after the last record in the recordset.

Applies To

Recordsets

Usage

All views: Read Only

Notes

This property has no settings. It returns True (-1) if the current record position is past the last record in the recordset or the recordset contains no records. Otherwise, it returns False (0).

Issuing **MoveNext** while *EOF* property is True triggers a `No current record` error (trappable error #3021). The current record becomes undefined and the EOF property stays True.

Access Basic Example

Move through the Customers database and display each customer's last name in the immediate window:

```
Dim cDb As Database, cTb As Table
Set cDb = CurrentDB()
Set cTb = cDb.OpenTable("Customers")
Do Until cTb.EOF
     Debug.Print cTb.[Last name]
     cTb.MoveNext
Loop
cTb.Close
```

See Also

Property: BOF

FieldName

Specifies the name of a field in the table.

Not available in Access Basic

Applies To

Table fields

Usage

Design view: Read and Write

Other views: Not available

Note

Field names must be unique within a table.

Access Basic Example

Not available in Access Basic. Use the **ListFields** method to get information on table fields.

See Also

Method: ListFields

Property: Caption

FieldSize

Sets the maximum size of data that can be stored in the field.

Applies To

Table fields

Usage

Design view: Read and Write

Other views: Not available

Notes

Use the smallest possible value for the setting of the *FieldSize* property. Smaller fields can be processed quicker and take up less disk storage and memory during processing.

Text fields are sized explicitly by entering a number (from 1 through 255). Table fields defined as Number are sized according to the data type specified in the *FieldSize* property.

The following table specifies the length of the *FieldSize* property for various data types.

Type	*Notes and FieldSize Property Length*
Number	*Byte* (occupies 1 byte). Stores integers from 0 to 255.
	Integer (occupies 2 bytes). Stores whole numbers from -32,767 to 32,767.
	Long Integer (occupies 4 bytes). Stores whole numbers from -2,147,483,648 to 2,147,483,647.
	Single (occupies 4 bytes). Stores numbers from -3,402823E38 to 3,402823E38 with six-digit precision.
	Double (default, occupies 8 bytes). Stores numbers from -1.79769313486232E308 to 1.79769313486232E308 with 10-digit precision.
Text (default)	Text up to 255 characters (default is 50 characters).

The length of the data types described in the following table is implicit (table fields with these data types don't have the *FieldSize* property).

Type	*Length*
Counter	A Long Integer (occupies 4 bytes).
Currency	Scaled Integer (occupies 8 bytes). Stores numbers from -922,337,203,685,477.5808 to 922,337,203,685,477.5807 with the precision of four decimal places.
Date/Time	Stores data and time values as a double number (occupies 8 bytes).
Yes/No	Stores an integer (-1 or 0). Occupies 2 bytes.

OLE object fields and Memo fields don't have the *FieldSize* property. Use the **FieldSize** method to return the length of an OLE object or a Memo field.

Caution

Trying to change the *FieldSize* property after data has been entered in the field may produce unpredictable results if the data types are not compatible (such as changing Double to Integer).

Access Basic Example

Not available in Access Basic. Use the **ListFields** method to get information about table fields.

See Also

Property: DataType

Method: FieldSize

Access Data Types

FillColor

Specifies the color of the interior (Fill color) of boxes and circles drawn with Circle and Line methods.

Applies To

Reports

Usage

Design view: Not available

Other views: Read and Write

Notes

Use values returned by the **RGB** or **QBColor** function to set this property. The setting is a Long data type.

You can use this property only in Access Basic or in a macro attached to one of the event properties (*OnFormat* or *OnPrint*).

Caution

You must set the *FillStyle* property to 0, or the *FillColor* property setting is meaningless and defaults to the setting of the *BackColor* property.

Access Basic Example

Draw three circles with light gray, dark gray, and black interiors on a report section. Attach this function to the *OnPrint* (or *OnFormat*) property of the desired report section:

```
Function TestFillColor (Rpt As Report)
Rpt.DrawWidth = 12                              ' line thickness
Rpt.ScaleMode = 3                               ' pixels
Rpt.FillStyle = 0                               ' clear
Rpt.FillColor = RGB(192, 192, 192)              ' light gray
Rpt.Circle (200, 200), 100
Rpt.FillColor = RGB(128, 128, 128)              ' dark gray
Rpt.Circle (600, 200), 100
Rpt.FillColor = RGB(0, 0, 0)                    ' black
Rpt.Circle (1000, 200), 100
End Function
```

The results of the preceding function are shown in figure 22.4.

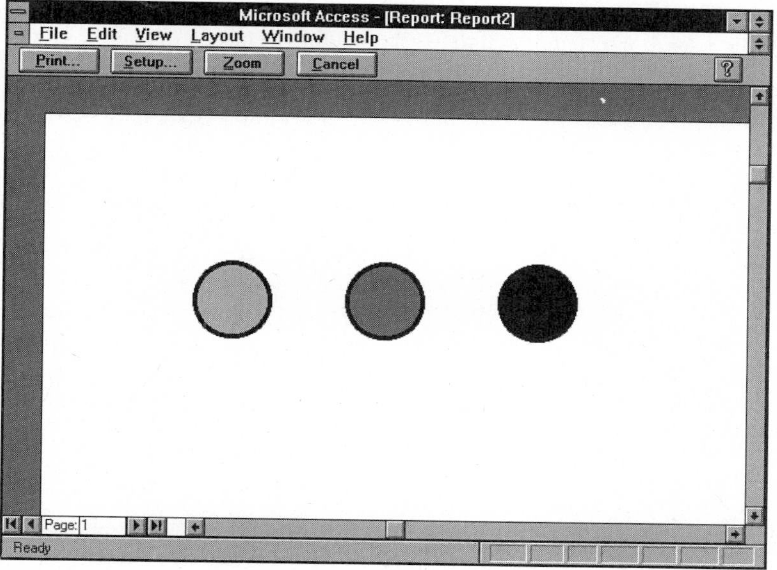

Figure 22.4. Three circles drawn by the TestFillColor() function.

See Also

Methods: Circle, Line, and PSet

Properties: DrawMode, DrawStyle, DrawWidth, FillStyle, OnFormat, and OnPrint

FillStyle

Determines whether a line drawn by the **Circle** or **Line** method is transparent.

Applies To

Reports

Usage

Design view: Not available

Other views: Read and Write

Notes

According to Microsoft documentation, the *FillStyle* property has two settings:

- *1 Normal (Default).* The line has the color set by the *ForeColor* property.
- *0 Clear.* The line is transparent (it defaults to the color behind it).

In practice, the setting of this property is meaningless in Versions 1.0 and 1.1. If you want to hide lines and circles on reports, set the *ForeColor* property to the same setting as the *BackColor* property.

You can use this property only in Access Basic or in a macro attached to one of the event properties (*OnFormat* or *OnPrint*).

Caution

Note that the entry for this property in the Microsoft documentation is incorrect.

Access Basic Example

Both settings of the *FillStyle* property print the same white circle on the Report Header section (Section 1) of a report:

```
Function TestFillStyle (Rpt As Report)
Dim dwForeColor&
Rpt.DrawWidth = 12
Rpt.ScaleMode = 3

' Set ForeColor contrasting to BackColor
If Rpt.Section(1).BackColor = 0 Then
    dwForeColor = RGB(255, 255, 255)
Else
    dwForeColor = RGB(0, 0, 0)
End If
Rpt.ForeColor = dwForeColor
```

```
Rpt.FillStyle = 1
Rpt.Circle (200, 200), 100

Rpt.FillStyle = 0
Rpt.Circle (200, 600), 100

End Function
```

See Also

Methods: Circle and Line

Properties: BorderColor, BorderStyle, BorderWidth, and FillColor

Filter

Sets a filter condition for a dynaset or snapshot.

Applies To

Dynasets, snapshots

Usage

All views: Read and Write

Notes

The setting of this property is a conditional statement—most likely, the WHERE clause of the SQL statement (the word WHERE is omitted). The filtered dynaset or snapshot then is used to create another dynaset (or snapshot) containing a subset of the records in the original dynaset or snapshot.

This property is redundant. Use the SQL SELECT statement directly in the **CreateDynaset** or **CreateSnapshot** method (*source* argument) to specify the filtering condition.

You cannot use this property with a snapshot created with the **ListFields**, **ListIndexes**, **ListParameters**, and **ListTables** methods.

Access Basic Example

The function TestFilter presents two equal methods of creating two identical dynasets. One method uses the *Filter* property. Another method uses the **CreateDynaset** method with the filtering condition (an SQL SELECT statement) entered directly as the *source* argument:

```
Function TestFilter ()
Dim cDb As Database, cDy1 As Dynaset, cDy As Dynaset
Set cDb = CurrentDB()
```

PROPERTIES

```
' Method 1. Create a dynaset from the table, filter it and create a filtered dynaset
Set cDy1 = cDb.CreateDynaset("Customers")
cDy1.Filter = "[City] ='Los Angeles'"
Set cDy = cDy1.CreateDynaset()

' Method 2. Create a filtered dynaset directly from the table
Set cDy = cDb.CreateDynaset("Select * FROM Customers WHERE [City] = 'Los Angeles'")

End Function
```

See Also

Methods: CreateDynaset and CreateSnapshot

Properties: Index and Sort

FontBold

Toggles between bold and normal fonts with the **Print** method.

Applies To

Reports

Usage

Design view: Not available

Other views: Read and Write

Notes

The *FontBold* property has two settings:

- *True (-1).* Specifies a bold font.
- *False (0).* Specifies a normal font.

This setting is valid until you reset it, or until you close the report.

You can use this property only in Access Basic or in a macro attached to one of the event properties (such as *OnFormat* or *OnPrint*).

The appearance of the bold text is display- and printer-dependent. Bold fonts may appear slightly lighter in print than on-screen.

Access Basic Example

Print bold and normal text on a report in a large Arial font:

```
Function TestFontBold (cRpt As Report)
cRpt.FontName = "Arial"
cRpt.FontSize = 30

cRpt.FontBold = True
cRpt.Print "This is bold text"

cRpt.FontBold = False
cRpt.Print "This is normal text"
End Function
```

See Also

Method: Print

Properties: BorderColor, FillColor, FontItalic, FontUnderline, FontName, FontSize, and FontWeight

FontItalic, FontUnderline

Sets the font to italic and/or underlined for the **Print** method on reports. Specifies italic and the underlined appearance of text in controls.

Applies To

Reports

Tools and controls: Combo box, command button, label, list box, text box, toggle button

Usage

Reports

Design view: Not available
Other views: Read and Write

Tools and Controls

Design view: Read and Write
Other views: Read Only

Notes

The *FontItalic* property has two settings:

- *Yes.* The font is italic. Use True (-1) to set these properties from Access Basic to Yes.
- *No* (default). The font is normal. Use False (0) to set these properties from Access Basic to No.

You may specify any combination of these settings.

For reports, you can use these properties only in Access Basic or in a macro attached to one of the event properties (such as *OnFormat* or *OnPrint*). If applied to a report, these properties' settings stay in effect for all text printed with the Print method for the entire section to which they are applied until you close the report or change the settings.

If you use these properties with controls, the settings have the effect on individual controls only.

Access Basic Example

In Design mode, open the report called Report2 and change the *FontItalic* and *FontUnderline* properties in a DOB control:

```
DoCmd OpenReport "Report2", A_DESIGN
Reports![Report2].[Dob].FontItalic = True
Reports![Report2].[Dob].FontUnderline = True
```

See Also

Method: Print

Properties: BorderColor, FontName, FontSize, and FontWeight

FontName, FontSize

FontName specifies the font name and/or size for the **Print** method in reports.

FontSize specifies the font name and size to use for text in controls.

Applies To

Reports

Tools and Controls: Combo box, command button, label, list box, text box, toggle button

Usage

Reports

Design view: Not Available
Other views: Read and Write

Tools and Controls

Design view: Read and Write
Other views: Read Only

Notes

In Windows 3.0, the default setting for the FontName is Helv.

In Windows 3.1 (and Windows for Workgroups), the default setting of the *FontName* property depends on the setting of the *LayoutForPrint* property. Use MS Sans Serif if *LayoutForPrint* is set to No; otherwise, use Arial.

You should type font names exactly as they appear in the Font menu on the Form and Report design surfaces.

If you specify a font that is not installed, or the system cannot display that font, Windows substitutes a default font.

The default setting for the FontSize property is 8 points (10 points for buttons). The *FontSize* can range from 0 to 32,767. A setting of 0 results in the 12-point font.

For reports, you can use these properties only in Access Basic or in a macro attached to one of the event properties (such as *OnFormat* or *OnPrint*). If applied to a report, these properties' settings stay in effect for all text printed with the Print method for the entire section to which they are applied until you close the report or change the settings.

Access Basic Example

Print one line in the current font, and another line of text in a different typeface and size:

```
cRpt.Print "Current font and size"
cRpt.FontName = "Times New Roman"
cRpt.FontSize = 18
cRpt.Print "Times New Roman in 18 point size"
```

See Also

Method: Print

Properties: BorderColor, FontItalic, FontUnderline, FontWeight, and LayoutForPrint

FontSize

See "FontName" property.

FontUnderline

See "FontItalic" property.

FontWeight

Specifies the width of the line used to print characters in a control (the *weight* of a font).

Applies To

Tools and Controls: Combo box, command button, label, list box, text box, toggle button

Usage

Design view: Read and Write

Other views: Read Only

Notes

The settings of this property are described in the following table.

In a Property Box	*In Access Basic*
Thin	100
Extra Light	200
Light	300
Normal	400
Medium	500
SemiBold	600
Bold	700
ExtraBold	800
Heavy	900

The appearance of fonts is display- and printer-dependent; some fonts may appear slightly lighter in print than on-screen.

If you specify a font that the system cannot display, Windows substitutes a different font weight. The acceptable range for the *FontWeight* property in Access Basic is 0 to 32,767.

Access Basic Example

Open the report called Report2, and set a large and heavy font for the Text4 control:

```
DoCmd OpenReport "Report2", A_DESIGN
Reports![Report2].Field4.FontWeight = 900
Reports![Report2].Field4.FontSize = 25
```

See Also

Properties: BorderColor, FontBold, FontItalic, FontUnderline, FontName, and FontSize

ForceNewPage

Specifies if and when a page break is inserted in a form or report section.

Applies To

Form and report sections (except page headers and page footers)

Usage

Design view: Read and Write

Other views: Read Only

Notes

You may set the applicable value for this property if you want to start printing a section of a form or a report on a new page.

The settings of the *ForceNewPage* property are described in the following table.

In a Property Box	*In Access Basic*	*Description*
No	0	Section starts printing on current page. This is the default setting.
Before Section	1	Current section is printed on a new page.
After Section	2	Next section starts printing on a new page.
Before & After	3	A page break is inserted both before and after.

Access Basic Example

Open the report called Report2 and set the value of the *ForceNewPage* property of the detail section (Section 0) to Before & After:

```
OpenReport "Report2", A_DESIGN
DoCmd Reports![Report2].Section(0).ForceNewPage = 3
```

See Also

Properties: NewRowPrCol, OnFormat, OnPrint, and Page

ForeColor

Specifies the foreground color for the **Print**, **Line**, and **Circle** methods. Specifies the color of text in controls.

Applies To

Reports

Tools and Controls: Combo box, command button, label, list box, text box, toggle button

Usage

Reports

Design view: Not available
Other views: Read and Write

Tools and Controls

Design view: Read and Write
Other views: Read Only

Notes

The value of the *ForeColor* property is a Long data type. Use the values returned by the RGB or QBColor function to set the value of this property.

Setting this property does not affect graphic elements already drawn.

For reports, you can use this property only in Access Basic or in a macro attached to one of the event properties (such as *OnFormat* or *OnPrint*).

Access Basic Example

Set the value of the *ForeColor* property to a setting other than the setting of the *BackColor* property in the report header section (Section 1):

```
If Rpt.Section(1).BackColor = 0 Then
    Rpt.ForeColor = RGB(255, 255, 255)
Else
    Rpt.ForeColor = RGB(0, 0, 0)
End If
```

See Also

Methods: Circle, Line, Print, and PSet

Properties: BackColor, BackStyle, DrawMode, DrawStyle, DrawWidth, FillStyle, OnFormat, and OnPrint

Form, Report

Refer to the current form or report.

Applies To

Forms, reports

Usage

All views: Read Only

Notes

The Form and Report properties have no settings.

You can use these properties to refer to their own controls, sections, subforms, and subreports associated with the current form or report.

Access Basic Example

The following example shows two methods of attaching an Access Basic function to any action property on a form (such as *OnFormat*). The first example uses the Forms object, the second one uses the Form property:

```
= MyFunc(Forms![MyForm].[MyControl])

= MyFunc(Form![MyControl])
```

See Also

Objects: Forms, Reports, and Screen

Format

Specifies the format for displaying and printing various types of data.

Applies To

Table fields

Controls: Text box

Usage

Design view: Read and Write

Other views: Read Only

Table fields are not available.

Notes

Access enables you to use standard (predefined) or user-defined formatting strings to format data for display or printing. The standard settings depend on the entries in the International section of the WIN.INI file. You can change these settings from the Windows Control Panel.

In Access Basic, you can use a literal formatting string to specify user-defined formats, or the numeric equivalent of the standard format.

You can use the formatting symbols described in the following table in user-defined formatting strings for any data type.

Symbol	*Description*
(Space)	Displays spaces as literal characters.
\	Displays the next character as literal. (To display a backslash, use \\.)
"ABC"	Displays a string in quotes. Use Chr(34) to indicate quotes in ABC.
[color]	Displays the string in a specified color. All basic colors (black, blue, green, cyan, red, magenta, yellow, and white) are valid.
*	Fills available space with the next character.
!	Forces left alignment instead of the standard right alignment.

For example, the string

```
"$**#0.##"
```

applied to a numeric expression equal to .23, displays

```
$*******0.23
```

The *Format* property has different settings for various data types. The following list explains acceptable formatting for various data types. Note that you cannot mix user-defined formatting strings for various types of data.

Numeric Expressions Setting	*Numeric Value*	*Effect*
General Number	0	Displays number as entered (default).
Currency	1	Displays negative numbers in red and enclosed in parentheses. DecimalPlaces property set to 2. Uses thousands separator.
Fixed	2	Displays number with at least one digit. DecimalPlaces property set to 2.
Standard	3	DecimalPlaces property set to 2. Uses thousands separator.
Percent	4	Displays the percent (%) sign. Multiply value by 100. DecimalPlaces property set to 2.
Scientific	5	Displays number in scientific notation.

The following table describes the available standard formats for numeric expressions.

Format	*Unformatted*	*Formatted*
General Number	456.87	456.87
Currency	123.562	$123.57
	-500	($500.00)
Fixed	456.891	456.89
Standard	12786	12,768.00
Percent	2	200%
	.21	21%
	.001	0.10%
Scientific	123456	1.23E+05

PROPERTIES

You can construct formatting strings for numeric expressions from the formatting symbols described in the following table.

Formatting Symbol	*Action*
Zero-length string	No formatting.
0	Displays a digit or 0. If the number being formatted has fewer digits than appear in the formatting string, the leading and trailing positions are filled with zeroes. Numbers with more digits than the formatting string are displayed without modifications.
#	Displays a digit or nothing. Numbers longer than the formatting string are truncated. If the number is shorter than the formatting string, nothing is displayed in lieu of the # character.
.	A period is a decimal separator. You set this value in the International section of the WIN.INI file.
%	The percent sign is a percentage placeholder.
	To ensure that the leading zero is always displayed for a fractional number (as in 0.17), use 0 as a digit placeholder at the position immediately preceding the decimal point.
,	The comma is a thousands separator.
E-E+e-e+	Displays a number in scientific notation.

The user-defined formatting string for the numeric data can have up to four sections:

- *Section 1.* Specifies how to display positive numbers.
- *Section 2.* Specifies how to display negative numbers.
- *Section 3.* Specifies how to display zero values.
- *Section 4.* Specifies how to display null values.

The standard format for the Currency data type is

```
"$#,##0.00;($#,##0.00)[Red]"
```

The following table describes the date and time settings that are valid in Access.

Setting	*Numeric Value*	*Displays*
General Date	6	`4/12/93 11:54 AM` (default)
Long Date	7	`Thursday, April 22, 1993` Specified in the International section of the WIN.INI file.
Medium Date	8	`12-Apr-94`

Setting	*Numeric Value*	*Displays*
Short Date	9	`4/12/94` Specified in the International section of the WIN.INI file.
Long Time	10	`11:54 AM` Specified in the International section of the WIN.INI file.
Medium Time	11	`11:54 AM`
Short Time	12	`11:54`

You can use the following formatting characters to construct a user-defined data time format. All examples are based on Friday, January 8, 1993 8:01:01 a.m.

Formatting Symbol	*Displays*
:	Time separator (set in the International section of the WIN.INI file).
/	Date separator
c	8:01:01 AM 1/8/93 (see ttttt for time, ddddd for date)
d	8 (day, no leading zero)
dd	08 (day, leading zero)
ddd	Fri (abbreviated day name)
dddd	Friday (full day name)
ddddd	1/8/93 (short date)
dddddd	Friday, January 08, 1993 (long date)
w	6 (day of the week)
ww	2 (week number)
m	1 (month, no leading zero)
mm	01 (month, leading zero)
mmm	Jan (abbreviated month)
mmmm	January (full month name)
q	1 (quarter number)
y	8 (day-of-year number)

continues

Formatting Symbol	*Displays*
yy	93 (year as two-digit number)
yyy	1993 (year as four-digit number)
h	8 (hour, no leading zeroes)
hh	08 (hour, leading zeroes)
n	1 (minute, no leading zeroes)
nn	01 (minute, leading zeroes)
s	1 (second, no leading zeroes)
ss	01 (second, the leading zeroes)
ttttt	8:01:01 AM (complete time using time separator defined in international section of WIN.INI)
AM/PM	8:01:01 AM (time, 12-hour clock)
am/pm	8:01:01 am (time, 12-hour clock)
A/P	8:01:01 A (time, 12-hour clock)
a/p	8:01:01 a (time, 12-hour clock)
AMPM	8:01:01 AM (time, 12-hour clock—depending on WIN.INI am/pm setting)

For example, the user-defined string

```
"Today is "mmmm dd","yyyy"
```

displays

```
Today is June 28, 1993
```

You can construct formatting strings for character data (text and memo) from the following formatting symbols:

Text and Memo Formatting Symbol	*Action*
@	Displays a character or space
&	Displays a character or nothing
<	Displays all characters in lowercase
>	Displays all characters in uppercase

The *Format* for character strings can have up to two sections separated by a semicolon. The first section applies to string data, and the second section applies to null and zero-length strings:

```
"@@@-@@-@@@@;Unknown"
```

The word `Unknown` is displayed if there is no data.

The following table provides examples of user-defined formatting strings.

String	*Data*	*Displays*
@@@-@@-@@@@	123456789	`123-45-6789`
(@@@) @@@-@@@@	1235554567	`(123) 555-4567`
>	sun	`SUN`
<	LaCosta	`lacosta`

The following table lists the formatting characters available for Yes/No (Boolean) data type.

Yes/No Data Setting	*Numeric Value*	*Displays*
Yes/No	13	Yes = -1; No = 0 (default)
True/False	14	True = -1; False = 0
On/Off	15	On = -1; Off = 0

User-defined formatting strings for Yes/No data types can have up to four sections separated by semicolons (only sections 2 and 3 are used):

- *Section 1.* Not used, but requires a leading semicolon.
- *Section 2.* Displays if data equals -1 (Yes, True, On).
- *Section 3.* Displays if data is equal to 0 (No, False, Off).
- *Section 4.* Not used.

The next example (entered in the *Format* property of a text box) displays `Active` in blue if the data is Yes, and `Closed` in red otherwise:

```
";Active[Blue];Closed[red]"
```

Access Basic Example

Open the Customers form in Design view and change the *Format* properties of some fields on the form:

```
Dim cForm As Form
DoCmd OpenForm "Customers", A_DESIGN
Set cForm = Forms![Customers]

cForm.AmountLastSale.Format = "$#,#.00;;New Customer"
cForm.DateLastSale.Format = 8           'Medium Date
cForm.State.Format = ">"                'Upper case
cForm.Fax.Format = "(@@@) @@@-@@@@"
```

See Also

Functions: Format and Format$

Properties: FieldSize and DataType

FormatCount

Specifies how many times the *OnFormat* property is evaluated for the current line.

Applies To

Reports

Usage

All views: Read Only

Notes

Each time a new line is formatted, the *FormatCount* property is incremented by 1. Each time the new line is formatted, the *FormatCount* property is reset to 0. Note that Access sometimes formats the same line twice. In such a case, you may use the *FormatCount* property to report formatting errors to the user.

You can use this property to increment running totals, counters, and so on, after the *FormatCount* property reaches a certain value.

The setting of this property is a Long data type.

Access Basic Example

This function, attached to the *OnFormat* property, checks for the value of the *FormatCount* property and warns the user that the same line has been formatted twice:

```
Function TestFormatCount ()
If Screen.ActiveReport.FormatCount > 1 Then
    MsgBox "One line was formatted twice..."
End If
End Function
```

See Also

Property: PrintCount

FormName

Identifies a form or report.

Applies To

Forms, reports

Usage

All views: Read Only

Notes

The value of this property is the name of the form or report as it appears in the database container.

You can set this property only from the Save (Form, Report) dialog box. When Access objects are created, they are named with the class name (Form, Query, and so on) and a unique integer number (Form2, for example).

Access Basic Example

You can include the following statement in a function called from an action property of a report. This statement prints the name of the current report to the immediate window:

```
Debug.Print Screen.ActiveReport.FormName
```

See Also

Objects: Forms, Reports, and Screen

Properties: ActiveForm, ActiveReport, and ControlName

GridX, GridY

Specify the vertical and horizontal alignment grid on the forms' and reports' design surfaces.

Applies To

Forms, reports

Affects only Design view

Usage

Design view: Read and Write

Other views: Read Only

Notes

The default settings are *GridX* - 10 and *GridY* - 12. The default unit of measurement for these properties is points. The larger the number, the more precise adjustments you can make to the placement of objects on the design surface. The range of settings for these properties is 1 through 64. A setting outside this range generates a `The setting of GridX or GridY must be from 1 to 64` error (trappable error #2130). Note that the dots signifying the grid settings are not displayed if the setting is greater than 16.

Access Basic Example

In Design view, open the Customers form and change the *GridX* and *GridY* settings to allow fine adjustments:

```
DoCmd OpenForm "Form6", A_DESIGN
Forms!Form6.Gridx = 16
Forms!Form6.GridY = 16
```

GroupInterval (documented only in ADK)

Specifies the scope (*interval*) of the values to fall into a particular group.

Applies To

Reports (group levels)

Usage

Design view: Read and Write

Other views: Read Only

Notes

The setting of this property stores the scope of values to group on in individual groups for a particular field or expression. For example, if the *GroupOn* property is set to Year, setting the *GroupInterval* property to 1 groups records for each year. Setting it to 5 groups records into 5-year groups.

The default setting of this property is 1.

If the setting of *GroupProperty* is 0 (Each Value), the *GroupInterval* property defaults to 1 (even though other values may be displayed in the property setting).

If you specify Prefix Characters for the text data, the *GroupInterval* property stores the number of leading characters in an expression to group on.

Access Basic Example

In Design view, open a report, create the group level with the data/time field, and set the *GroupOn* to Week (5) and the *GroupInterval* to 2. This process results in a biweekly grouping:

```
DoCmd OpenReport "Report1", A_DESIGN
wLevel = CreateGroupLevel("Report1", "M_DATE", False, False)
Reports!Report1.GroupLevel(wLevel).GroupOn = 5
Reports!Report1.GroupLevel(wLevel).GroupInterval = 2
```

See Also

Function: CreateGroupLevel

Properties: GroupLevel and GroupOn

GroupLevel (documented only in ADK)

Stores the entries for each level of data-grouping in a report.

Applies To

Reports

Usage

Design view: Read and Write

Other views: Read Only

Notes

The *GroupLevel* property is a dynamic array that is resized as levels of grouping data in a report are created or deleted. Access creates some groupings automatically (such as when the report is bound to a query that contains sorted fields). You can create additional groupings by using the Sorting and Grouping dialog box on the report design surface or by using the **CreateGroupLevel** function from within Access Basic code.

To use this property, you must combine it with other properties that apply to report grouping, such as *SortOrder*, *GroupOn*, or *GroupInterval*.

Referring to a nonexisting *GroupLevel* produces an `Invalid group level number reference` error (trappable error #2464).

This property is most useful when programmatically creating reports, such as in the code used in Reports Wizards.

Access Basic Example

Display *SortOrder*, *GroupOn*, and *GroupLevel* properties for the active report in the immediate window. You can attach this code to any of the action properties of a report:

```
On Error Resume Next
i = 0
Do While Err <> 2464
    Debug.Print Screen.ActiveReport.GroupLevel(i).SortOrder
    Debug.Print Screen.ActiveReport.GroupLevel(i).GroupOn
    Debug.Print Screen.ActiveReport.GroupLevel(i).GroupInterval
    i = i + 1
Loop
```

See Also

Function: CreateGroupLevel

Properties: GroupInterval, GroupOn, Section, and SortOrder

GroupOn (documented only in ADK)

Specifies how data is grouped in a report.

Applies To

Group levels in reports

Usage

Design view: Read and Write

Other views: Read Only

Notes

The setting for this property is available from the Sorting & Grouping option on the View menu in the form and report design surfaces.

The default setting of the *GroupOn* property for all data types is Each Value (0 in Access Basic). The following table describes the settings that are valid for other data types.

Data Type Setting	*Access Basic*	*Group*
Text:		
Prefix characters	1	First *n* characters of the field or expression
Date/Time:		
Year	2	Dates in the same calendar year
Qtr	3	Dates in the same calendar quarter
Month	4	Dates in the same month
Week	5	Dates in the same week
Day	6	Dates on the same date
Hour	7	Dates in the same hour
Minute	8	Dates in the same minute
Counter, Currency, Number:		
Interval	9	Values falling within the user-specified interval

In Access Basic, use the numeric settings to set the *GroupOn* property for a particular grouping level.

Access Basic Example

In Design view, open a report and change the *GroupOn* and *GroupInterval* properties of the specified GroupLevel:

```
Function TestGroupOn (szReport$, wLevel%, wInterval%)
DoCmd OpenReport szReport, A_DESIGN
Reports(szReport).GroupLevel(wLevel).GroupOn = 9
Reports(szReport).GroupLevel(wLevel).GroupInterval = wInterval
End Function
```

See Also

Function: CreateGroupLevel

Properties: GroupInterval, GroupLevel, and SortOrder

Height, Width

Specify height and width of an object.

PROPERTIES

Applies To

- *Height.* Form and report sections. All tools and controls except page break.
- *Width.* Forms and reports. All tools and controls except page break.

Usage

Design view: Read and Write

Other views: Read Only

Notes

The height and width of forms and reports are measured from the inside of their borders. Controls are measured from the center of their borders.

The setting of the Height and Width properties is expressed in twips. To enter a specified unit of measurement, use the explicit units of measurement indicator, such as twips, in, or cm. All entries are translated into default units of measurement for the country specified in the International section of the WIN.INI file (inches for the US, for example).

In Access Basic, use numeric values to set both properties (tool properties are not available).

Use the **MoveSize** action to resize forms and reports at runtime.

Access Basic Example

Inspect the values of the Height and Width properties of the Control1 control:

```
Function TestHeight (cRpt As Report)

Debug.Print cRpt.Control1.Height
Debug.Print cRpt.Control1.Width

End Function
```

See Also

Action: MoveSize

Properties: BorderWidth, Left, and Top

HelpContextID, HelpFile

The *HelpContextID* property specifies the number of the Help topic in the custom Help file specified in the *HelpFile* property.

Applies To

HelpContextID

Forms

Tools and controls: Bound object frame, check box, combo box, command button, list box, linked object frame, option group, text box, toggle button

HelpFile

Forms

Usage

Design view: Read and Write

Other views: Read Only

Notes

The *HelpFile* property stores the name of the custom Help file for a particular form (forms can have their own Help files). Access must be able to find the Help file. You can specify the full path in the setting for this property.

The value of the *HelpContextId* property is a Long data type in the range 0 (default) to 2,147,483,647. The setting 0 indicates no Help topic. If both the *HelpContextID* setting for the form and a control are 0, the custom Help file is not invoked. Instead, standard Access Help is displayed.

Access Basic Example

Inspect the settings of these properties for the current form:

```
Function TestHelpContextID (cForm As Form)
    Debug.Print cForm.HelpFile; cForm.HelpContextID
End Function
```

HelpFile

See the "HelpContextID" property.

HideDuplicates

Specifies whether the duplicate data in the particular control on a report is displayed and printed or suppressed.

PROPERTIES

Applies To

Controls on reports: Combo box, list box, option group, text box.

The following controls, unless the control is in the option group: Check box, option button, toggle button

Usage

Design view: Read and Write

Other views: Read Only

Notes

Setting the *HideDuplicates* property to Yes produces easy-to-read, uncluttered output by suppressing repetitious items in a particular control in the detail section of a report.

The *HideDuplicates* property has two settings:

- *Yes.* Does not print duplicate data. In Access Basic, use True (-1).
- *No.* Prints all data (default). In Access Basic, use False (0).

Regardless of the setting of this property, duplicate data is not suppressed on the first record in a group or the first record on a page.

Access Basic Example

Reverse the setting of the *HideDuplicates* property for the Name control on a report called Report2:

```
DoCmd OpenReport "Report2", A_DESIGN
Reports![Report2].[Name].HideDuplicates = Not Reports![Report2].[Name].HideDuplicates
```

See Also

Property: Visible

hWnd

Contains the handle to the specified window.

Applies To

Forms, reports

Usage

Design view: Not available

Other views: Read Only

Notes

The *hWnd* property returns an integer that specifies the handle to the window in which the specified form and report is displayed.

You use the *hWnd* property to communicate with Windows API procedures that require the handle to a window.

Access Basic Example

Change the caption of a form at runtime. (The Access *Caption* property is read only at runtime.) You need to declare the Windows procedure SetWindowText in the declarations section:

```
Declare Sub SetWindowText Lib "User" (ByVal hWnd%, ByVal Caption$)
```

This function assumes that the form specified in the szFormName is open (in any view):

```
Function SetNewCaption(szFormName)
    SetWindowText Forms(szFormName).hWnd, "This is a new caption"
End Function
```

See Also

Statements: Declare and DoCmd

Action: Maximize

Index

Sets the current (controlling) index in a table.

Applies To

Tables

Usage

Design view: Read and write

Available only in Access Basic code

Notes

You can apply the Index property only to tables. It generates a `Couldn't find field "<name>"` error (trappable error #3018) if applied to dynasets or snapshots. To reorder a dynaset or snapshot, use the *Sort* property.

Because Access doesn't enable you to create indexes at runtime, you must define all indexes while in Design view of a table. The setting of this property must be an existing simple index, the keyword PrimaryKey, or one of the compound (multiple-field) indexes specified in the *Index1...Index5* property. The words "Index1", "Index2", "Index3", "Index4", "Index5", and "PrimaryKey" must be enclosed in quotation marks. If you specify the name of a nonexisting index, a `"<name>" isn't an index in this table` error (trappable error #3015) is generated.

You can get the names of existing indexes by using the *ListIndexes* method.

You can use the **Seek** method on an indexed table to quickly locate specified records.

Tip

To order a table at runtime, use the CreateDynaset method. Create a dynaset based on the table by using a user-supplied parameter value in the SQL statement of the method's *Source* parameter.

Access Basic Example

Open the Customers table, set its index to "Index1" (this is a multifield index defined as "Phone;City;State"), and display the contents of these fields in the immediate window:

```
Dim cDb As Database, cTb As Table
Set cDb = CurrentDB()
Set cTb = cDb.OpenTable("Customers")
cTb.Index = "Index1"
Debug.Print cTb.Index
Do Until cTb.Eof
    Debug.Print cTb.Phone; cTb.city; cTb.state
    cTb.MoveNext
Loop
cTb.Close
```

See Also

Methods: ListIndexes and Seek

Properties: Indexed, Index1...Index5, and Sort

Index1...Index5

Sets a multiple-field (compound) index.

Applies To

Tables

Usage

Design view: Read and Write

Other views: Not available

Notes

Use this property to create a multifield index. To create simple (single-field) indexes, use the *Indexed* property of a field.

You must separate the field names in the index with semicolons.

You cannot index Memo, OLE, or Yes/No fields.

Access Basic Example

The settings of these properties are not directly available in Access Basic. Use the **ListIndexes** method to get the settings for the *Index1...Index5* properties.

See Also

Method: ListIndexes

Properties: Index, Indexed, and PrimaryKey

Indexed

Defines a single-field index.

Applies To

Table fields

Usage

Design view: Read and Write

Other views: Not available

Notes

The *Indexed* property specifies whether the index is created on a particular table field. This property has the following settings:

- *No* (default). No index.
- *Yes* (Duplicates OK). Index allows duplicate values in the indexed fields.
- *Yes* (No Duplicates). Index does not allow duplicate values in the indexed fields.

You can create as many indexes as needed (you cannot index Memo, OLE, or Yes/No fields), but keep in mind that you must update all these indexes when the data is changed, which may adversely affect the performance of the system. You may want to create filtered dynasets at runtime, rather than maintain indexes.

If the index is specified as the primary key for the table, its *Indexed* property automatically is set to Yes (No Duplicates).

Designate the index as No Duplicates if you need to enforce the uniqueness of the entries in a particular field (such as when the entry in a field is used as a foreign key in another table).

Access Basic Example

The settings of this property are not directly available in Access Basic. Use the **ListIndexes** method to obtain the settings of the *Indexed* property.

See Also

Method: ListIndexes

Property: Index1...Index5 PrimaryKey

Item

Identifies the data displayed in the linked unbound object frame.

Applies To

A control: (linked) unbound object frame

Usage

All views: Read Only

Notes

The description of data stored in this property depends on the kind of OLE object linked to the frame. For the picture, the *Item* property contains the coordinates of the picture, for example.

For OLE objects linked with the Paste Link option of the Edit menu, Access automatically updates the settings of the *SourceObject*, *OLEClass*, and *Item* properties, as in the following example:

Object	*SourceObject*	*OLEClass*	*Item*
Picture	C:\WFW\CARS.BMP	Paintbrush Picture	0 2 32 29
Worksheet	C:\EXCEL\MAY93.XLS	Microsoft Excel Worksheet	R2C2:R7C20

Applying this property to another control or object (such as an embedded OLE object) triggers an `Invalid reference to property "<name>"` error (trappable error #2455).

Object linking is different from object embedding. The linked data is stored in the application that created (and maintains) it, and is displayed only by Access. Embedded data is physically stored in the destination application. If you link an object, the source application that stores that object must be available at runtime.

Access Basic Example

Inspect the values of the *Item*, *SourceObject*, and *OLEClass* properties:

```
Dim cForm As Form
Set cForm = Forms![TestOLE]
Debug.Print cForm.Embedded14.Item
Debug.Print cForm.Embedded14.SourceObject
Debug.Print cForm.Embedded14.OLEClass
```

See Also

Properties: OLEClass and SourceObject

KeepTogether

Specifies whether Access attempts to print an entire form or report section on one page.

Applies To

Form sections, report sections (except page header and footer)

Usage

Design view: Read and Write

Other views: Read Only

Notes

The *KeepTogether* property has two settings:

- *Yes.* Section starts on next page if it doesn't fit on current page. In Access Basic, use True (-1).
- *No.* Section starts printing on current page and continues to next page as needed. This is the default setting. In Access Basic, use False (0).

If the section is longer than one page, the printing continues on the next page, regardless of the setting of this property.

Access Basic Example

Inspect the value of this property for the detail section (Section 0) of the report titled Report1:

```
Debug.Print Reports![Report1].Section(0).KeepTogether
```

See Also

Properties: CanGrow, CanShrink, ForceNewPage, and OnFormat

LabelAlign, TextAlign

Specify the text alignment in controls and tools.

Applies To

LabelAlign

Tools: Bound object frame, check box, combo box, command button, graph, list box, option button, option group, subform/subreport, text box, toggle button

TextAlign

Tools and Controls: Combo box, label, text box

Usage

Design view: Read and Write

Other views: Read Only

The *LabelAlign* property is not available in Access Basic. You cannot use the *TextAlign* property to set default settings for tools.

Notes

The *LabelAlign* and *TextAlign* properties have the following settings. (The settings for Access Basic refer to the *TextAlign* property only):

- *General.* Text is left aligned. Numbers and dates are right aligned. Labels are left aligned. This setting is the default. In Access Basic, use 0.
- *Left.* Text is left aligned. In Access Basic, use 1.
- *Center.* Text is centered. In Access Basic, use 2.
- *Right.* Text is right aligned. In Access Basic, use 3.

Tip

Instead of setting default settings for each control, create new templates for forms and reports with the settings you want.

Access Basic Example

Change the text alignment in the Field1 control to Right (3 in Access Basic). You must open the Form1 form in Design view.

```
Forms![Form1].Field1.TextAlign = 3
```

See Also

Properties: AddColon, AutoLabel, LabelX, and LabelY

PROPERTIES

LabelX, LabelY

Specify the placement of the attached label for the new control.

Applies To

Tools: Bound object frame, check box, combo box, command button, graph, list box, option button, option group, subform/subreport, text box, toggle button

Usage

Design view: Read and Write

Other views: Read Only

Notes

The *LabelX* and *LabelY* properties set the placement of a label attached to a control relative to the upper left corner of the control. The unit of measure for these properties defaults to the units of measurement for the country specified in the International section of the WIN.INI file (for example, inches in US).

To enter a specified unit of measurement, use an explicit indicator, such as twips, in, or cm. All entries are translated into default units.

The zero, positive, and negative settings of the *LabelX* and *LabelY* properties produce the following results (the *LabelAlign* property is set to General).

LabelX	*LabelY*	*Result*
0	0	Label is not attached (equal to setting the AutoLabel property to False).
Negative	0	Label is placed on same level as control, X units to left of control.
Positive	0	Label is placed on same level as the control, X units to right of control.
0	Negative	Label is placed Y units above control. Left side of control is aligned with left side of label.
0	Positive	Label is placed Y units below control. Left side of control is aligned with left side of label.
Positive	Positive	Label is placed X units below and Y units to right of control.
Negative	Negative	Label is placed X units above and Y units to left of control.

The exact placement of the label is affected by the setting of the *LabelAlign* property.

Tip

Instead of setting defaults for each tool, save time by creating new templates for forms and reports with the settings you want.

Access Basic Example

The *LabelX* and *LabelY* properties are not available in Access Basic.

See Also

Properties: AddColon, AutoLabel, LabelX, and LabelY

LastUpdated

Stores the date and time when the design of the table was last updated.

Applies To

Tables

Usage

All views: Read Only

Notes

This property returns the date and time when the design of the table was last updated as a Variant VarType 7 (Date) data type. In Access Versions 1.0 and 1.1, the date and time stamp is stored in the MSysObject table field DateUpdate. Even though this property applies to Tables only, you can obtain the date last updated for all Access objects by searching the MSysObjects table.

You can use this property only with Access Basic code.

Note that this property is meaningless for Access system tables.

Access Basic Example

See "DateCreated" property.

See Also

Property: DateCreated

LayoutForPrint

Specifies whether a form or report uses screen or printer fonts.

Applies To

Forms, reports

Usage

Design view: Read and Write

Other views: Read Only

Notes

The *LayoutForPrint* property specifies to use screen or printer fonts to design a report or form.

This property has two settings:

- *Yes.* Uses printer fonts. This is the default for reports. In Access Basic, use True (-1).
- *No.* Uses screen fonts. This is the default for forms. In Access Basic, use False (0).

With scalable fonts (such as TrueType fonts installed with Windows 3.1 and Windows for Workgroups), screen and printer fonts are identical. If you installed additional printer fonts, setting this property to Yes enables you to use these fonts for designing forms and reports.

Access displays a warning if the printer for which the report or form is designed is not available (if the printer is not installed, for example).

If you change the setting of this property after designing a form or report, some fonts used to design it may not be available to display or print it. Access substitutes a different font for any unavailable font.

Access Basic Example

Change the setting for the form called Form2 (opened in Design view):

```
Forms![Form2].LayoutForPrint = True
```

See Also

Properties: FontName and FontSize

Left, Top

Left specifies the position of the horizontal coordinate of a control.

Top specifies the position of the vertical coordinate of a control.

Applies To

All controls

Usage

Design view: Read and Write

Other views: Read Only

Notes

The location of a control is measured from the center of its left or top border to the section's left or top border.

The default unit of measurement for these properties is twips. To enter a specified unit of measurement, use the explicit indicator, such as in or cm. All entries are translated into default units for the selected country.

When you move the control on the design surfaces, Access updates its coordinates in the property sheet. These properties are most useful when programmatically creating reports, such as in the code used in Reports Wizards.

Access Basic Example

Inspect the values of the *Left* and *Top* properties of the Name control:

```
Function TestTopAndLeft (cRpt As Report)

Debug.Print cRpt.Name.Top
Debug.Print cRpt.Name.Left

End Function
```

See Also

Properties: Height and Width

LimitToList

Specifies whether the data entered in the control must match one of the items on the list of choices.

Applies To

Combo box

Usage

Design view: Read and Write

Other views: Read Only

Notes

This property has two settings:

- *Yes.* Data that doesn't match one of the items on the list of choices is rejected. In Access Basic, use True (-1).
- *No.* Any data is accepted. This is the default setting. In Access Basic, use False (0).

If the hidden column is bound to a control box (the *ColumnWidths* property is set to 0 for this column, for example), the *LimitToList* property is set to Yes. Note that the actual value of this property displayed in the property box may still be No.

Tip

If you set this property to Yes, always provide a graceful way to exit the control when the entry is erroneous. The default mode to exit the combo box with the *LimitToList* property set to Yes is to press Esc or to choose the Undo option from the Edit menu.

Access Basic Example

Go through all controls on the Calls form and set the *LimitToList* property to Yes for every combo box:

```
Function TestLimitToList ()

Dim cForm As Form, cCtrl As Control, wCount%
DoCmd OpenForm "Calls", A_DESIGN, , , , A_ICON
Set cForm = Forms!Calls
wCount = cForm.Count - 1                ' how many controls
For i = 0 To wCount
    Set cCtrl = cForm(i)                ' process a control
    If TypeOf cCtrl Is ComboBox Then    ' Combo box?
```

```
            cCtrl.LimitToList = Yes         '...set the property
        End If
    Next

    End Function
```

See Also

Properties: BoundColumn and ColumnWidths

LineSlant

Specifies whether the line slants from upper left to lower right or from upper right to lower left on the imaginary rectangle, with its corners specifying the start and end of the line.

Applies To

Line (a control on reports and forms).

Usage

Design view: Read and Write

Other views: Read Only

Notes

This property has two settings:

- \ *(backslash).* Line slants from upper left to lower right. In Access Basic, use False (0).
- / *(forward slash).* Line slants from upper right to lower left. In Access Basic, use True (-1).

Access Basic Example

Change the slant of two lines (Line2 and Line3) in the header section of the Report1 report opened in **Design view:**

```
Reports![Report1].Line2.LineSlant = False
Reports![Report1].Line3.LineSlant = True
```

Fig. 22.5 demonstrates the result of the above two settings of the *LineSlant* property. Note that both lines are drawn from the opposite corners of an imaginary rectangle, which is clearly visible in the bottom drawing.

PROPERTIES

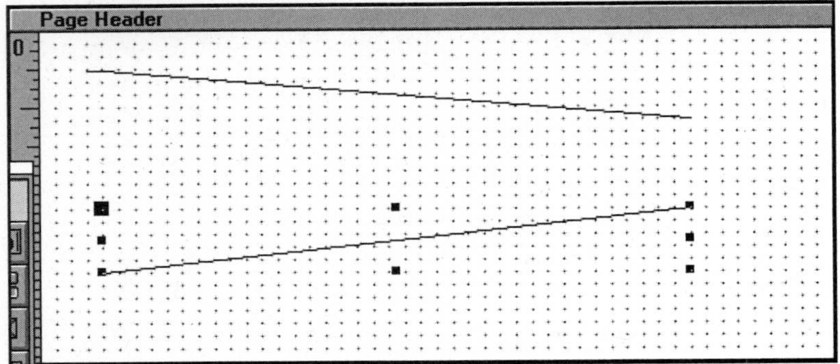

Figure 22.5. Lines drawn with different settings of the LineSlant property.

See Also

Method: Line

Properties: DrawStylr and DrawWidth

LinkChildFields, LinkMasterFields

LinkChildFields identifies fields in the child or embedded object.

LinkMasterFields identifies fields in the master form or report.

Applies To

Controls: Graph, subform/subreport, (embedded) unbound object frame

Usage

Design view: Read and Write

Other views: Read Only

Notes

The setting of these properties is a list of one or more fields that provide the link between the primary form or report and a subform/subreport or an embedded object. Each property identifies one or more fields in the primary form or report that match one or more fields in the subform/subreport or an embedded object. The data types and number of fields in both properties must match, but the names of fields don't need to be the same.

You must separate the fields in the list by semicolons.

When the subform or subreport is dragged onto the primary form or report from the database container, Access updates these properties if one of the following conditions exists:

- Both the primary form or report and the subform/subreport are based on related tables.
- Both the primary form or report and the subform/subreport contain an identical field with the same name and the same data type, which is also the primary key of the primary form's underlying table.

Access cannot establish the link if neither of these conditions exists or forms/reports are based on a query. In this case, you must enter manually the settings for both properties.

Access Basic Example

Go through all controls on the Calls form. If the control is a subform or subreport, print its *LinkChildFields* and *LinkMasterFields* properties in the immediate window:

```
Function TestLinkChildFields ()
Dim cForm As Form, cCtrl As Control, wCount%, fPrint%
DoCmd OpenForm "Calls", A_DESIGN, , , , A_ICON
Set cForm = Forms!Calls
fPrint = False
wCount = cForm.Count - 1                          ' number of controls
For i = 0 To wCount
    Set cCtrl = cForm(i)                          ' inspect a control
    If TypeOf cCtrl Is SubForm Then
        fPrint = True
    ElseIf TypeOf cCtrl Is SubReport Then
        fPrint = True
    End If
    If fPrint Then                                ' subform/report
        Debug.Print cCtrl.LinkChildFields
        Debug.Print cCtrl.LinkMasterFields
        fPrint = False
    End If
Next
End Function
```

See Also

Properties: Item, OLEClass and SourceObject

LinkMasterFields

See the "LinkChildFields" property.

PROPERTIES

ListRows

Specifies the maximum number of rows to display in the drop-down list of a combo box.

Applies To

Combo box (tool and control)

Usage

Design view: Read and Write

Other views: Read Only

Notes

This property specifies the maximum number of displayed rows of a drop-down list in a combo box in Form and Datasheet view.

The default setting for the *ListRows* property is 8. The acceptable range is 1 to 255.

If the specified setting exceeds the number of available rows on-screen, the size of the list is adjusted to the maximum that fits on-screen (the list floats on the top of other windows, possibly transcending the boundaries of the Access window).

If the number of actual rows is larger than the specified setting, the vertical scroll bar appears in the list.

Access Basic Example

Set the *ListRows* property for the Box1 combo box on the Form1 form to 21 rows:

```
Forms!Form1.Box1.ListRows = 21
```

See Also

Properties: BoundColumn, ColumnHeads, ColumnWidths, Height, Width, and ListWidth

ListWidth

Specifies the width of the drop-down list in a combo box.

Applies To

Combo box (tool and control)

Usage

Design view: Read and Write

Other views: Read Only

The Tool property is not available in Access Basic.

Notes

The settings for this property follow:

- *Auto.* The width of the combo box to which the list is attached. This is the default setting.
- The actual width expressed in the default units of measure for the country specified in the International section of the WIN.INI file (inches in the US, for example).

To enter a specified unit of measurement, use an explicit indicator, such as twips, in, or cm. Access translates all entries into the default unit.

The drop-down list can be wider than the combo box, but cannot be narrower.

In Access Basic, you can use a number or a string expression (such as 4567 twips) to set this property.

Tip

Design as narrow a drop-down list (and with as few rows) as practical. Large lists redraw slower on-screen.

Access Basic Example

Set the ListWidths property to 5 cm (approximately 2 inches) for the Box1 combo box on the Form1 form opened in **Design view:**

```
Forms![Form1].Box1.ListWidth = "5cm"
```

See Also

Properties: BoundColumn, ColumnCount, ColumnWidths, Height, Width, and ListRows

LockEdits

Sets the locking mode for editing records.

Applies To

Tables, dynasets

PROPERTIES

Usage

All views: Read and Write

Notes

This setting is available only from Access Basic.

The *LockEdits* property has two settings:

- *True (-1).* Enables the pessimistic locking scheme.
- *False (0).* Enables the optimistic locking scheme.

You use the *LockEdits* property at runtime to specify the type of locking in effect during the editing of recordsets while using the **Edit** and **Update** methods. The setting can be Optimistic or Pessimistic.

If you force Optimistic locking (the page is locked when the Update method is applied to the recordset), a `Couldn't update; currently locked by user<name> on machine <name>` error (trappable error #3260) occurs if another user already has locked the record.

If you specify Pessimistic locking (the page is locked as soon as the Edit method is applied to the recordset), other users cannot make any changes until the page is unlocked using the **Update** method.

When a page is locked, Access may report errors other than error #3260, depending on the environment (single user, network, Windows for Workgroups, and so on). It may report error #3018: `Couldn't update; currently locked.` or error #3188: `Couldn't update; currently locked by another session on this machine.`

Caution

Potential conflicts can occur if two users with different settings of this property try to edit the same record. Suppose that the same record is updated from within a form by one user with the No Locks setting of the *RecordLocks* property, and by another user using the **Update** method with optimistic locking enabled. Quite possibly, one user will face a `Data has changed...` error (trappable error #3197), and some data will be lost.

See Also

Property: RecordLocks

Methods: AddNew, Edit, and Update

Modal

Determines whether a form opens in a window that retains focus until closed.

Applies To

Forms

Usage

Design view: Read and Write

Other views: Read Only

Notes

The Modal property has two settings:

- *Yes.* Form opens in a modal window. In Access Basic, use True (-1).
- *No.* Form opens in a standard window. This setting is the default. In Access Basic, use False (0).

Access modal windows are application-modal. No part of the same session of Access can be accessed while the modal window has focus, for example. Access does not provide a built-in feature to declare a window as system-modal (no part of Windows can be accessed while the window has focus, for example); to accomplish this, you must make a call to the Windows API function **SetSysModalWindow**.

Tip

If you set the *Modal* and *PopUp* properties of a window to Yes (True), the toolbar and the Minimize and Maximize buttons are removed. You cannot resize the window, and no other part of Access can gain focus. Setting these properties to Yes may be useful when designing critical parts of an application where the user has to complete a task before proceeding.

Access Basic Example

Display the setting of this property for the Form1 form in the immediate window:

```
Debug.Print Forms![Form1].Modal
```

See Also

Property: PopUp

MoveLayout, NextRecord, PrintSection

MoveLayout specifies whether printing should start at the next printing location on the page.

NextRecord specifies whether a section should advance to the next record.

PrintSection specifies whether a record in a section should be printed on the page.

Applies To

Report sections

Usage

Design view: Not available

Other views: Read and Write

Notes

After each section and before each *OnFormat* event, all three properties are reset to True.

The settings for these properties follow:

MoveLayout:

- *True (-1).* Section's Left and Top properties are advanced to the next print location. This is the default setting.
- *False (0).* Section's Left and Top properties are unchanged.

NextRecord:

- *True (-1).* Data advances to the next record. This is the default setting.
- *False (0).* Data doesn't advance to the next record.

PrintSection:

- *True (-1).* Section is printed on the page. This is the default setting.
- *False (0).* Section is not printed on the page.

Combinations of these properties' settings have the following effects:

MoveLayout	*NextRecord*	*PrintSection*	*Effect*
True	True	True	Prints the next record at the next print location (default).
True	False	True	Prints the same record at the new print location.
False	True	False	Skips a record without leaving a blank space. If applied unconditionally to the detail section, prints only headings but no data
True	True	False	Skips a record leaving a blank space. If applied unconditionally to the detail section, prints headings and blank spaces, but no data.
True	False	False	Skips a record leaving a blank space. If applied unconditionally to the detail section, this setting can produce thousands of blank pages.
False	True	True	Prints the current record on top of the preceding record (may be used to overstrike a previous line, for example).
False	False	True	Error #2586
False	False	False	Error #2586

If the *MoveLayout* and *NextRecord* properties are both set to False (as in the two last settings in the preceding table), trappable error #2586 occurs:

```
The MoveLayout and NextRecord run-time properties can't be both set to FALSE; to
➥ensure that the report advances both have been set back to TRUE.
```

Tip

The False-True-False setting skips to the next record without leaving a blank space on the printed page. This is a good method to additionally filter records at run time. Or, you can print a different report, page or section headings, text, or notes on reports without redesigning the layout.

PROPERTIES

Attach a macro or an Access Basic function to the *OnFormat* property of the applicable section.

The syntax for these properties is different in macros than in Access Basic code. In a macro, use *Report.MoveLayout*. In the code, use *Reports!<name>.MoveLayout*.

Access Basic Example

Print only the records that don't contain the underscore character (_) in the Company Name control. Attach this function to the *OnFormat* property of the detail section of a report:

```
Function TestMoveLayout (cRpt As Report)
If InStr(cRpt.[Company Name], "_") <> 0 Then
   cRpt.MoveLayout = False
   cRpt.PrintSection = False
End If
End Function
```

See Also

Properties: NewRowOrCol and OnFormat

NewRowOrCol

Specifies whether a section in a multiple-column report starts printing at the beginning of a new row or column.

Applies To

Form sections, report sections

Usage

Design view: Read and Write

Other views: Read Only

This property is ignored for page headers and footers.

Notes

You can print the sections of a multiple-column report one after the other or in multiple columns across the page. You use the *NewRoworColumn* property to specify the placement of a section on the printed page.

This property is relevant only if the Items Across setting in the Print Setup dialog box is greater than 1. To achieve the desired results, make sure that the Width setting in the Item Size section is set so that the number of items specified in the Item Across section will fit on the page.

If the Item Layout option in the Print Setup dialog box (**More >>** section) is vertical, this property refers to a column. If the horizontal layout is selected, it refers to a row.

The *NewRowOrColumn* property has the settings described in the following table settings.

Setting	*Access Basic*	*Meaning*
None	0	Row or column breaks are determined only by the settings in the Print Setup dialog box and by available space on the page. This is the default setting.
Before Section	1	Current and next section starts printing on the same row or column.
After Section	2	Current section starts printing on current row or column. Next section starts printing on next row or column.
Before & After	3	Current and next section starts printing on next row or column.

Access Basic Example

Inspect the value of this property for the section containing the Group1 Header control:

```
Function TestNewRowOrCol (cRpt As Report)
wSectionNumber% = cRpt.[Group1 Header].Section
Debug.Print cRpt.Section(wSectionNumber%).NewRowOrCol
End Function
```

Figures 22.6 through 22.9 show the effects of different settings of this property. The records are grouped on the first letter of the name field. All examples use Print Setup settings of two items across, with a horizontal layout.

See Also

Properties: ForceNewPage, OnFormat, OnPrint, and Section

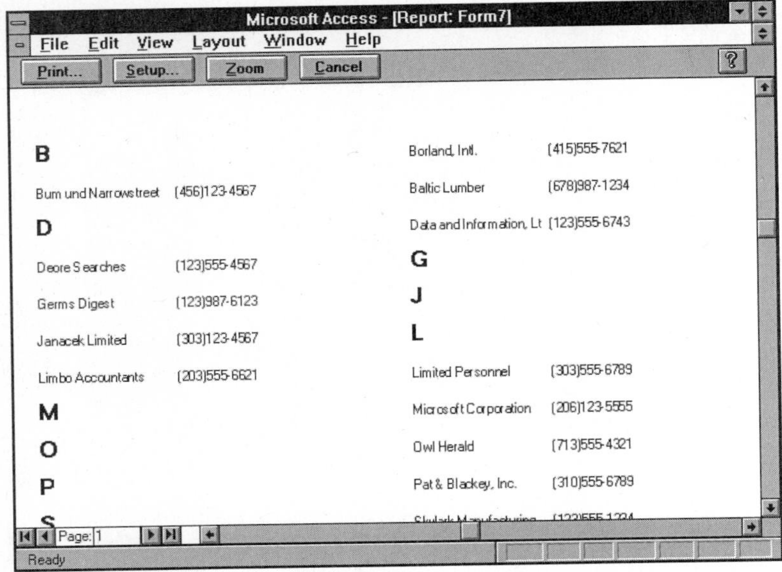

Figure 22.6. The *NewRowOrColumn* property for the group header section set to None.

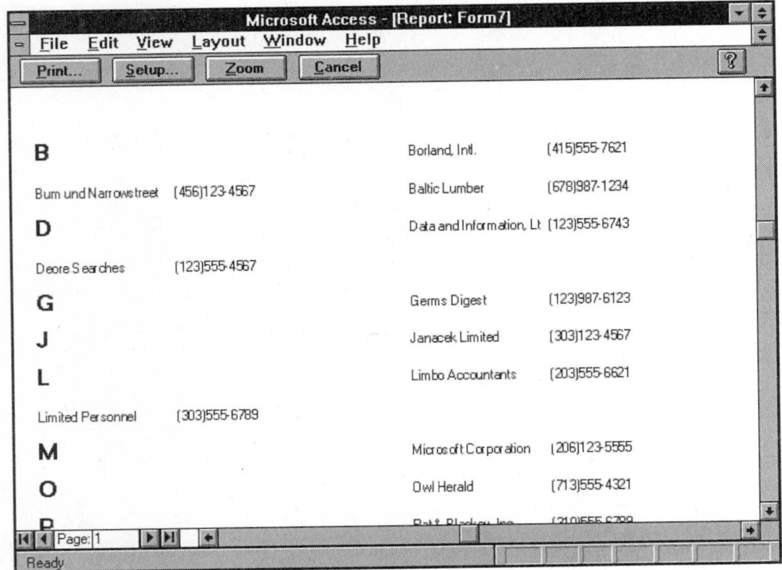

Figure 22.7. The *NewRowOrColumn* property for the group header section set to Before.

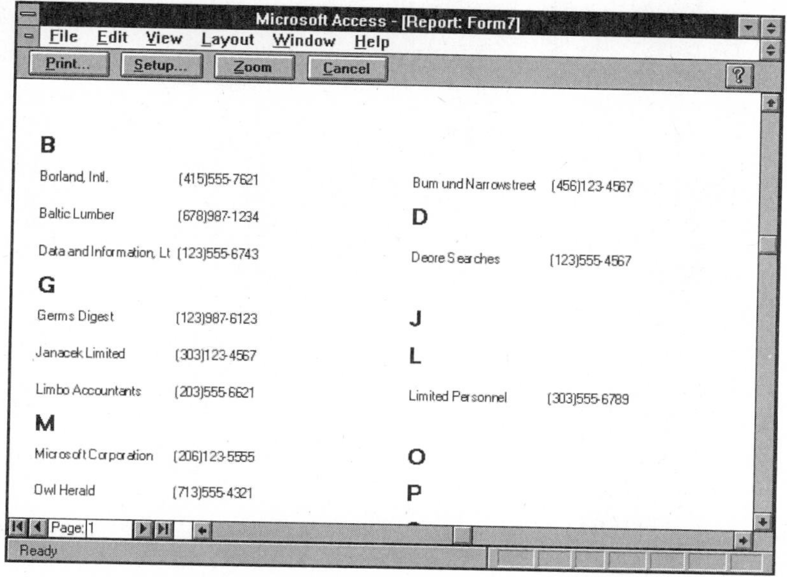

Figure 22.8. The *NewRowOrColumn* property for the group header section set to After.

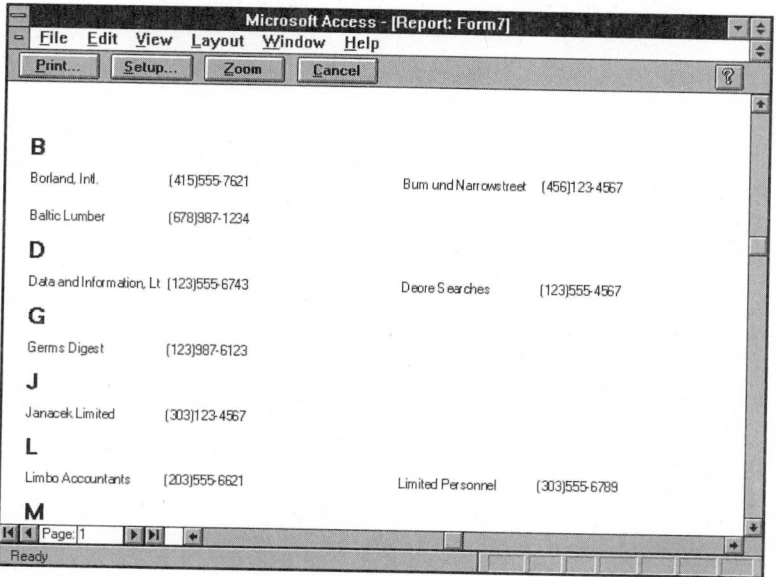

Figure 22.9. The *NewRowOrColumn* property for the group header section set to Before & After.

PROPERTIES

NextRecord

See the "MoveLayout" property.

NoMatch

Indicates whether the desired value was located in the recordset.

Applies To

Recordsets

Usage

All views: Read Only

Notes

The *NoMatch* property returns True (-1) if the desired value *wasn't* located in the recordset—for example, when a **Find...** or **Seek** method failed. It returns False (0) if the desired value *was* found.

When a recordset is opened, its *NoMatch* property is set to False.

To locate records in indexed tables, use the **Seek** method and then check the value of the *NoMatch* property. In dynasets and snapshots, use one of the **Find...** methods with this property.

When searching a recordset for many matching records, it may be more efficient to use a select (or update) query instead of many consecutive searches.

The syntax of this property often requires you to use double-negative conditions (*Not NoMatch*) to indicate a true condition (*"match" found*).

Access Basic Example

The following function demonstrates the use of the *NoMatch* property in a table and a dynaset:

```
Function TestNoMatch ()
Dim cDb As Database, cTb As Table, cDy As Dynaset
Set cDb = CurrentDB()
Set cTb = cDb.OpenTable("Customers")

' Usage in a table
cTb.Index = "Name"
cTb.Seek "=", "Owl Digest"
If Not cTb.Nomatch Then
    cTb.Edit
```

```
        cTb.Name = "Owl Review"
        cTb.Update
    End If

    ' Usage in a dynaset
    Set cDy = cTb.CreateDynaset()
    cDy.FindFirst " Name = 'Owl Review'"
    If Not cDy.Nomatch Then
        cDy.Edit
        cDy.Name = "Owl Herald"
        cDy.Update
    End If
    cTb.Close
    End Function
```

See Also

Properties: BOF and EOF

Methods: FindFirst, FindLast, FindNext, FindPrevious, and Seek

OldValue

Contains the original (previous) value of the bound control.

Applies To

Bound controls on forms

Usage

All views: Read Only

Notes

Access stores the unedited contents of the field bound to the control in the *OldValue* property. The *OldValue* property contains the same data type as the field to which the control is bound.

By attaching an Access Basic code to the *OnExit* property of a control, you can provide field-level undo capabilities by setting the value of a control to the values stored in the *Oldvalue* property.

The *OldValue* property is applicable to individual fields. Use Access's transaction processing to provide more robust Rollback (undo) capabilities applicable to whole records or sets of related records.

No error is generated if you use this property with an unbound text box. However, the *OldValue* and "new" value are equal, and therefore the action is meaningless.

Access Basic Example

The following function, attached to the *OnExit* property of a field, allows the user to cancel the changes before exiting the field:

```
Function RestoreOldValue()
vOldValue = Screen.ActiveControl.OldValue
vNewValue = Screen.ActiveControl
       If MsgBox("The value has changed from " & vOldValue & " to " & vNewValue & ".
       ➥Update field?", MB_YESNO) = IDNO Then
    Screen.ActiveControl = vOldValue
End If
End Function
```

See Also

Properties: BeforeUpdate and OnExit

Statement: Rollback

OLEClass

Stores a text description of the linked OLE object type.

Applies To

Controls: Graph, unbound object frame

Usage

All views: Read Only

Notes

The value of this property is string data, such as "Paintbrush Picture."

Access Basic Example

See the "Item" property

See Also

Properties: Item and SourceObject

OnClose

See the "OnOpen" property.

OnCurrent

Specifies the name of an event (a macro, Access Basic code, or external function) to execute when the focus moves from one record to another.

Applies To

Forms

Usage

Design view: Read and Write

Other views: Read Only

Notes

The setting for this property is a string expression that contains the name of a macro or function to execute when the focus moves to the new record. The name of an Access Basic or external function must be preceded by an equal sign and contain parentheses. A macro or function attached to the *OnCurrent* property executes before the first record is displayed.

The *CancelEvent* action has no effect when used with this property.

You can use the **GoToRecord** action called from an event specified in the *OnCurrent* property to move to a different record.

The events attached to the action properties on the form level occur in the following order:

1. OnMenu
2. OnOpen
3. OnCurrent

Access Basic Example

Set the value of the *OnCurrent* property in the Form1 form opened in **Design view:**

```
Forms!Form1.OnCurrent = "=TestOnCurrent(Forms![Form1])"
```

See Also

Properties: OnDelete and OnInsert

PROPERTIES

OnDblClick

Specifies the name of a macro, Access Basic, or external function to execute when the user double-clicks the control or its label.

Applies To

Controls: Bound object frame, combo box, command button, list box, option group, text box.

The following controls, unless the control is in the option group: Check box, option button, toggle button

Usage

Design view: Read and Write

Other views: Read Only

Notes

All selectable controls except subforms can trigger double-click events.

The setting for this property is a string expression that contains the name of a macro or function to execute when the user double-clicks a control or its label. The name of an Access Basic or external function must be preceded by an equal sign and contain parentheses. The event specified in this property (macro or code) occurs before the default double-click action occurs.

The default double-clicking action depends on the type of the control. Double-clicking a control containing an OLE object, for example, runs the application that created that object. Double-clicking the word in a text box or combo box selects the word.

If you need to disable the default double-click action, use the **CancelEvent** action in the event specified in the *OnDblClick* property. This technique also is useful when substituting a different action for the default double-click behavior.

Access Basic Example

The function TestOnDblClick( ) attached to the *OnDblClick* property of a combo box executes Word for Windows and opens a selected document. The default action is disabled with the **CancelEvent** action:

```
Function TestOnDblClick ()
szDocName = Screen.ActiveControl
If Not (IsNull(szName) And IsEmpty(szName)) Then
    aaa = Shell("I:\APPS\WINWORD\WINWORD.EXE " & szDocName, 1)
    DoCmd CancelEvent
End If
End Function
```

See Also

Properties: OnEnter and OnPush

OnDelete

See the "OnInsert" property.

OnEnter, OnExit

Specify the name of a macro, Access Basic, or external function to execute before a control gains the focus (*OnEnter*) or before a control loses the focus (*OnExit*).

Applies To

Controls: Bound object frame, combo box, command button, list box, option group, subform, text box

The following controls, unless the control is in the option group: Check box, option button, toggle button

Usage

Design view: Read and Write

Other views: Read Only

Notes

The setting for these properties is a string expression that contains the name of a macro or function to execute when the user enters or exits a control. The name of an Access Basic or external function must be preceded by an equal sign and contain parentheses. A macro or function specified in the *OnEnter* property executes after the control is selected, but before the control gains focus. The macro or function specified in the *OnExit* property executes after the control is exited, but before the control loses focus.

You can cancel the exit from the control by including the **CancelEvent** action in the macro or code triggered by an *OnExit* event. The **CancelEvent** action is meaningless in a macro or code triggered by an *OnEnter* event.

Access Basic Example

Display the settings of these properties for the control named "Last Name" on the form "Phone List" in the immediate window:

```
Debug.Print Forms![Phone List].[Last Name].OnEnter
Debug.Print Forms![Phone List].[Last Name].OnExit
```

See Also

Properties: AfterUpdate, BeforeUpate, and ValidationRule

OnExit

See the “OnEnter” property.

OnFormat

Specifies the name of a macro, Access Basic, or external function to execute before the data in a section is formatted for print preview or printing.

Applies To

Report sections

Usage

Design view: Read and Write

Other views: Read Only

Notes

The macro or function specified in the *OnFormat* property is executed for each line being formatted for printing on every section of a report for which it is defined. A macro or function specified in this property executes before the event specified in the *OnPrint* property for the same section.

You can attach code that provides calculations or runs complex tabulations based on the data in the underlying (or other) recordset, including those not printed. A macro (or code) can hide certain controls while printing a report, by setting its *Visible* property to False.

You also can change the settings of other report formatting properties that are accessible for writing at run time, such as *CanGrow*, *CanShrink*, *KeepTogether*, and so on.

If the **CancelEvent** action is included in a macro or code triggered by this property, the entire section is not formatted. If **CancelEvent** occurs in the code triggered by the *OnFormat* property in the detail section, for example, no data is printed.

Use the *FormatCount* property in a macro or function specified in the *OnFormat* property to see whether a line was formatted more than once (such a line probably will fit on the page) and take the appropriate action.

Access Basic Example

Do not print data if the Code control equals "Top Secret." Attach this function to the *OnFormat* property of a detail section:

```
Function TestOnFormat (cRpt As Report)
If cRpt.Code = "Top Secret" Then
    DoCmd CancelEvent
End If
End Function
```

See Also

Properties: FormatCount, MoveLayout, NextRecord, OnPrint, and PrintSection

OnInsert, OnDelete

Specify the name of a macro, Access Basic, or external function to execute before each new record is created (*OnInsert*) or before a record is deleted (*OnDelete*).

Applies To

Forms

Usage

Design view: Read and Write

Other views: Read Only

Notes

The setting of these properties is a string expression that contains the name of a macro or function to execute when the user inserts a new record or deletes a record. The name of an Access Basic or external function must be preceded by an equal sign and contain parentheses.

A macro or function specified in the *OnInsert* property executes after the user types the first character of a new record (into the edit buffer), but before the record actually is created. The macro or function specified in the *OnDelete* property executes after the user deletes a record (chooses the Delete command from the Edit menu), but before the record actually is deleted from the underlying recordset.

If you specify the **CancelEvent** action in a macro or function attached to the *OnInsert* property, the character typed by the user is deleted and the focus stays on the inserted record. If an analogous action is specified in a macro or function attached to the *OnDelete* property, the record is not deleted.

Access Basic Example

The following function attached to the *OnDelete* property of a form confirms the deletion of a record:

```
Function TestOnDelete ()
If MsgBox("Delete?", MB_YESNO + MB_ICONQUESTION) = IDNO Then
    DoCmd CancelEvent
End If
End Function
```

See Also

Properties: AfterUpdate and BeforeUpdate

OnMenu

Specifies the name of a menu bar macro that creates a custom menu bar for the form. Also can specify a function to execute.

Applies To

Forms

Usage

Design view: Read and Write

Other views: Read Only

Notes

The setting of these properties is a string expression that contains the name of a macro or function to execute. The name of an Access Basic or external function must be preceded by an equal sign and contain parentheses.

A macro or function specified in the *OnMenu* property probably will define a custom menu for the form. You define such a menu in a macro attached directly by the *OnMenu* property or by an Access Basic function that runs the menu bar macro. See the **AddMenuItem** action for more information on creating custom menus for forms in Access.

If a function attached to this property does not run a menu bar macro containing the custom menu definition, the display of the default Access menus is suppressed and no menu is displayed. The toolbar ribbon appears as usual.

If you use the **CancelEvent** action in a macro or function attached to this property, the form does not open.

The macro or function specified in the *OnMenu* property is triggered as soon as the form is opened.

The events attached to the action properties on the form level occur in the following order:

1. OnMenu
2. OnOpen
3. OnCurrent

Access Basic Example

The following function attached to the *OnMenu* property gives the user the choice of running a predefined custom menu or no menu at all:

```
Function TestOnMenu ()
If MsgBox("Display custom menu?", MB_YESNO) = IDYES Then
    DoCmd RunMacro "Altered Menu"
End If
End Function
```

See Also

Actions: AddMenu, DoMenuItem, and RunMacro

OnOpen, OnClose

Specify the name of a macro, Access Basic, or external function to occur before a form or report is opened (*OnOpen*) or closed (OnClose).

Applies To

Forms, reports

Usage

Design view: Read and Write

Other views: Read Only

Notes

The setting of this property is a string expression that contains the name of a macro or function to execute when the form or report is opened or closed. The name of an Access Basic or external function must be preceded by an equal sign and contain parentheses.

The macro or function attached to the *OnOpen* property on a form runs after the action specified in the *OnMenu* property, but before the first record is displayed. For a report, a macro or function runs before the report starts to print.

The macro or function specified in the *OnClose* property and a form executes after the form is closed, as the last event on the form. For a report, a macro or function runs after the report finishes printing.

If you use the **CancelEvent** action in a macro or function specified in the *OnOpen* property, you will not be able to open a form or report.

If you use the **CancelEvent** action in a macro or function attached to the *OnExit* property, you will not be able to close the form until the action is removed. **CancelEvents** has no effect on closing a report.

Events attached to the action properties on the form level occur in the following order:

1. OnMenu
2. OnOpen
3. OnCurrent

In reports, a macro or function attached to the *OnOpen* property executes first. Macros or functions attached to the *OnFormat* and *OnPrint* properties in the report sections follow.

Caution

A form or report is not considered active when a macro or function attached to the *OnOpen* property is executing. Therefore, if the function relies on *Screen.ActiveReport* or *Screen.ActiveForm* constructs, an error occurs (since there is no active form or report). Also, no control is active. You must use the **GoToControl** or **GoToRecord** action to move the focus to the control you want.

Access Basic Example

If you want to run certain reports only on certain days of the week, and the reports are named after the days of the week (Thursday, for example), you can attach the following function to the *OnOpen* property of a report:

```
Function TestOnOpen (cRpt As Report)
If Format$(Date, "dddd") <> cRpt.FormName Then
    MsgBox "Please run report: " & Format$(Date, "dddd")
    DoCmd CancelEvent
End If
End Function
```

See Also

Properties: OnFormat and OnPrint

OnPrint

Specifies the name of a macro, Access Basic, or external function to execute before the data in a section is printed or displayed in Print Preview.

Applies To

Report sections

Usage

Design view: Read and Write

Other views: Read Only

Notes

A macro or function specified in the *OnPrint* property is executed for each line being printed on every section of a report for which it is defined. A macro or function attached to the *OnPrint* property executes after a macro or function attached to the *OnFormat* property in the same section.

Use the *PrintCount* property in a macro or function attached to the *OnPrint* property to ensure that a specified action is executed only once for each printed line.

A macro or code attached to this property can run complex totals or update data in different recordsets based on the data in the report, for example.

If you use the **CancelEvent** action in a macro or function attached to the *OnPrint* property, the record is skipped and Access prints a white space in its place.

Any changes in the page or section layout should be handled in the *OnFormat* property.

PROPERTIES

Access Basic Example

Update the running total based on a control named Salary only if the *PrintCount* property equals 1 (after the first iteration of the *OnPrint* event for a printed line, for example). You must declare dwTotalSalary as a global variable:

```
Function TestOnPrint (cRpt As Report)
    If cRpt.PrintCount = 1 Then
        dwTotalSalary = dwTotalSalary + cRpt.Salary
    End If
End Function
```

See Also

Properties: MoveLayout, NextRecord, PrintSection, Page, and PrintCount

OnPush

Specifies the name of a macro, Access Basic, or external function to execute when the user chooses ("pushes") a command button.

Applies To

Controls on a form: Command button

Usage

Design view: Read and Write

Other views: Read Only

Notes

The setting of this property is a string expression that contains the name of a macro or function to execute when a command button is selected. The name of an Access Basic or external function must be preceded by an equal sign and contain parentheses.

The macro or function specified in this property runs once, unless the *AutoRepeat* property is set to Yes. If it is set to Yes, a macro or function is executed repeatedly as long as the button is pressed.

The **CancelEvent** action included in a macro or function attached to this property is ignored.

Command buttons are used mainly to trigger an action, such as switching between forms or opening or closing forms.

Access Basic Example

Display the setting of this property in the immediate window

```
Forms![MyForm].[Button1].OnPush
```

See Also

Properties: AutoRepeat, OnEnter, OnExit and OnDblClick

OptionValue

Stores the numerical value of a control in an option group.

Applies To

Controls in an option group: Check box, option button, toggle button

Usage

Design view: Read and Write

Other views: Read Only

Notes

Each control in an option group has a numeric value (a Long data type) stored in the *OptionValue* property.

Access assigns a value to controls in an option group sequentially. The first defined control is 1, the second is 2, and so on. You can overwrite the defaults.

If an option group is bound to a field in a table, the value of the field is set according to the value of this property.

The *DefaultValue* property of the option group specifies which control in the option group is selected when a new record is created.

If a check box, option button, or toggle button is not a part of an option group, referring to its *OptionValue* property triggers an `Invalid reference to property "OptionValue"` error (trappable error #245). If a check box, option button, or toggle button is not a part of an option group, the *OptionValue* property is replaced with the *ControlSource* property set to True or False.

Access Basic Example

In Design view, go through the Dances form and print the *OptionValue* property and the control name for controls that are a part of an option group:

```
On Error Resume Next
Dim cForm As Form, cCtrl As Control, wCount%
DoCmd OpenForm "Dances", A_DESIGN, , , , A_ICON
Set cForm = Forms![Dances]
wCount = cForm.Count - 1
For i = 0 To wCount
    Set cCtrl = cForm(i)
    Debug.Print cCtrl.OptionValue, cCtrl.ControlName
Next
Exit Function
```

See Also

Properties: ControlSource and DefaultValue

Page

Stores the current page number when the report is printing.

Applies To

Reports

Usage

Design view: Not available

Other views: Read and Write

Available only in an expression, macro, or Access Basic code

Notes

The most common use for this property is to print page numbers on reports in an expression

```
"Page " & Page
```

set in the *ControlSource* property of a text box and placed in the footer or header section. You also can use this property to supply alternative methods of page numbering, such as Roman numerals, words, and so on.

The data type of this property is Integer.

See Also

Properties: PageHeader, PageFooter, and SetValue

PageFooter

See the "PageHeader" property.

PageHeader, PageFooter

Specify on which pages a report header or footer prints.

Applies To

Reports

Usage

Design view: Read and Write

Other views: Read Only

Notes

You can suppress the printing of page headers or footers on certain pages in reports by using the settings of the *PageHeader* and *PageFooter* properties described the following table.

Setting	*Access Basic*	*Meaning*
All Pages	0	Page footer or header prints on all pages of the report. This is the default setting.
Not with Rpt Hdr	1	Page footer or header doesn't print on a page that contains a report header.
Not with Rpt Ftr	2	Page footer or header doesn't print on a page that contains a report footer.
Not with Rpt Hdr/Ftr	3	Page footer or header doesn't print on a page that contains a report header or footer.

The display of the page footer/header toggle is accessible from the Layout menu on the report design surface.

Access Basic Example

Open a report entitled "Report1" report in Design view and set its *PageHeader* property to 1 (the page header won't print on a page that contains a report header).

```
DoCm OpenReport "Report1", A_DESIGN
Reports!Report1.PageHeader = 1
(...)
```

See Also

Properties: OnFormat and OnPrint

Painting (documented only in ADK)

Enables or inhibits form updating.

Applies To

Forms

Usage

Design view: Read and Write

Other views: Read Only

Notes

The *Painting* property has two settings:

- *True (-1).* Repainting of a form occurs immediately. This is the default.
- *False (0).* Updating is inhibited until the property is reset to True or the form is closed.

The *Painting* property is accessible only from Access Basic.

The setting of this property is valid only until the form is closed. A newly reopened form has the default setting.

The chief use for this property is to inhibit updates while creating a form with Access Basic code (for example, using a Form Wizard).

Access Basic Example

The following function creates a form, resizes its detail section to three inches high, creates three controls (two command buttons and a text box), and restores the form. The *Painting* property is set to False in the beginning of the creation process to inhibit updates. *Painting* is set to True at the end of the creation process so the form can be displayed. If the *Painting* property remains set to False, the created form will not be visible:

```
Function TestPainting3 ()
    Dim cForm As Form, cCtrl  As Control
    Set cForm = CreateForm()
    DoCmd Hourglass True
    cForm.Painting = False
    cForm.Section(0).Height = 3 * 1440    '3 inches
    szFormName = cForm.FormName
    Set cCtrl = CreateControl(szFormName, 104, 0, "", "", 100, 200, 1000, 600)
    cCtrl.Caption = "First Button"
    Set cCtrl = CreateControl(szFormName, 104, 0, "", "", 100, 1000, 1000, 600)
    cCtrl.Caption = "Second Button"
    Set cCtrl = CreateControl(szFormName, 109, 0, "", "", 2000, 200, 2000, 600)
    DoCmd Restore
    DoCmd Hourglass False
    cForm.Painting = True
End Function
```

See Also

Actions: Echo and RepaintObject

Parent

Refers to the main form or report.

Applies To

A control: subform and subreport

Usage

All views: Read Only

Notes

This property has no settings. Use it from within a subform or subreport to refer to controls on a main (*parent*) form or report.

The *Parent* property provides a way to construct generic subforms or subreports that you can insert in a number of forms or reports. You can insert this expression in a bound text box on a subform, for example:

= *Parent.[Customer Name]*

Access Basic Example

Not available in Access Basic

See Also

Object: Forms

Property: SourceObject

Picture

Indicates whether a bitmap picture is displayed on a command button or a toggle button.

Applies To

Controls: Command button, toggle button

Usage

Design view: Read and Write

Other views: Read Only

Notes

This property has two settings:

- *None.* No bitmap picture is displayed. This is the default setting.
- *Bitmap.* Displays a bitmap picture.

To display a bitmap picture on a command button or toggle button, enter its name in the *Picture* property in the property box (include the extension BMP and a full path if necessary). If the picture is found, and is a bitmap (BMP) file, the word (picture) appears in the Picture property. The picture then is copied to the current database and *embedded* in Access. It will be displayed even if the original picture is deleted or the database is transferred to a different computer.

If both a picture and caption are specified for a control, the picture takes precedence over the caption.

Access Basic Example

Inspect the *Picture* property of a toggle button and see if it displays a bitmap picture:

```
Function TestPicture (cForm As Form)
If TypeOf cForm.Field11 Is ToggleButton Then
     Debug.Print cForm.Field11.Picture  'either (none) or (picture)
End If
End Function
```

See Also

Property: OnPush

PopUp

Specifies whether a form opens in a pop-up window.

Applies To

Forms

Usage

Design view: Read and Write

Other views: Read Only

Notes

A pop-up window has the following attributes:

- It floats on top of other windows.
- It can transcend the borders of Access's system window.
- The Maximize and Minimize buttons are removed (therefore, it cannot be minimized or maximized).
- It is not resizable.
- It has thin, single borders.
- Its system menu has only two choices: Move and Close.

The *PopUp* property has the following settings:

- *Yes.* Form opens in a pop-up window. In Access Basic, use True (-1).
- *No.* Form opens in a standard window. This is the default. In Access Basic, use False (0).

Use the *PopUp* property with the *Modal* property to define nonresizable windows that retain focus until they are closed, such as custom dialog boxes.

Caution

You still can maximize, minimize, or resize a form defined as a pop-up using the Maximize, Minimize, or MoveSize actions in a macro or function attached to any action property of a form or control. If you maximize a pop-up, you will not be able to restore it to its previous size unless the Restore (or Minimize) action is triggered by a control (such as a command button) on the form.

Access Basic Example

Display the *PopUp* property for the Form1 form:

```
If Forms![Form1].PopUp Then
     MsgBox "It's a popup!"
Endif
```

See Also

Property: Modal

PROPERTIES

PrimaryKey

Specifies the table field (or fields) that constitute the primary key for the table.

Applies To

Tables

Usage

Design view: Read and Write

Other views: Not available

Notes

The primary key in a table determines the default sort of the table. You can set the key only in Design view, and it can consist of one or more fields from the table.

An Access table must have a primary key if you plan to use it in a relationship. The primary key also speeds up sorting and searching operations.

In Access Basic, use the **ListIndexes** method to get information about indexes in a table. The primary key in the table is identified in the snapshot created by the **ListIndexes** method with the keyword PrimaryKey in the IndexName field.

You can set the *Index* property to the primary key by using the keyword PrimaryKey (enclosed in quotes). If the primary key is not defined for the table, a `"PrimaryKey" isn't an index in this table` error (trappable error #3015) is generated.

Access Basic Example

Not available in Access Basic

See Also

Method: ListIndexes

Properties: Index, Indexed, and Index1...Index5

PrintCount

Specifies how many times the *OnPrint* property is evaluated for the current line.

Applies To

Reports

Usage

All views: Read Only

Notes

Each time a new line is formatted, the *PrintCount* property is incremented by 1. Each time a new line is printed, the *PrintCount* property is reset to 0.

You can use this property to increment running totals, counters, and so on, after the *PrintCount* property reaches a certain value.

The setting of this property is a Long data type.

Access Basic Example

This function, attached to the *OnPrint* property, checks for the value of the *PrintCount* property and warns the user that the *PrintCount* property is greater than 1. Otherwise, it increments the running total:

```
Function TestPrintCount ()
If Reports![Report1].PrintCount > 1 Then
    MsgBox "The value of PrintCount is greater than one"
Else
     dwTotal = dwTotal + Reports![Report1].Salary
End If
End Function
```

See Also

Property: FormatCount

PrintSection

See “MoveLayout” property.

PrtDevMode (documented only in ADK)

Sets or returns the Print Setup and Print settings for a report.

Applies To

Reports

Usage

Design view: Read and Write

Other views: Read Only

Notes

Use this property to set the print settings for a report. These settings also are available from the PrintSetup dialog box.

The *PrtDevMode* property stores its data in the 64-byte structure (user-defined type), defined as follows:

```
Type zwtDeviceMode
    dmDeviceName As String * 32
    dmSpecVersion As Integer
    dmDriverVersion As Integer
    dmSize As Integer
    dmDriverExtra As Integer
    dmFields As Long
    dmOrientation As Integer
    dmPaperSize As Integer
    dmPaperLength As Integer
    dmPaperWidth As Integer
    dmScale As Integer
    dmCopies As Integer
    dmDefaultSource As Integer
    dmPrintQuality As Integer
    dmColor As Integer
    dmDuplex As Integer
End Type
```

The fields of this user-defined data type have the following meanings:

- *dmDeviceName.* Name of the device the driver supports (32 characters maximum), such as PCL/HP LaserJet.
- *dmSpecVersion.* Version number of the DEVMODE structure (&H000031A, 778 decimal, for Windows 3.1).
- *dmDriverVersion.* Driver version.
- *dmSize.* Size of the DEVMODE structure in bytes.
- *dmDriverExtra.* Size of the optional, driver-specific, dmDriverData field that follows the structure.
- *dmFields.* Indicates which remaining members of this structure are initialized. A combination of any number of the following constants:

DM_COLOR
DM_COPIES
DM_DEFAULTSOURCE
DM_DUPLES
DM_ORIENTATION
DM_PAPERLENGTH
DM_PAPERSIZE
DM_PAPERWIDTH
DM_PRINTQUALITY
DM_SCALE
DM_TTOPTION
DM_YRESOLUTION

- *dmOrientation.* Print orientation (portrait 1, landscape 2).
- *dmPaperSize.* Paper size. One of the following values specified, or 0 if dmPaperLength and dmPaperWidth determine the size of the paper:

```
1         ' Letter 8 1/2 x 11 in
2         ' Letter Small 8 1/2 x 11 in
3         ' Tabloid 11 x 17 in
4         ' Ledger 17 x 11 in
5         ' Legal 8 1/2 x 14 in
6         ' Statement 5 1/2 x 8 1/2 in
7         ' Executive 7 1/4 x 10 1/2 in
8         ' A3 297 x 420 mm
9         ' A4 210 x 297 mm
10        ' A4 Small 210 x 297 mm
11        ' A5 148 x 210 mm
12        ' B4 250 x 354
13        ' B5 182 x 257 mm
14        ' Folio 8 1/2 x 13 in
15        ' Quarto 215 x 275 mm
16        ' 10 x 14 in
17        ' 11 x 17 in
18        ' Note 8 1/2 x 11 in
19        ' Envelope #9 3 7/8 x 8 7/8
20        ' Envelope #10 4 1/8 x 9 1/2
21        ' Envelope #11 4 1/2 x 10 3/8
22        ' Envelope #12 4 \276 x 11
23        ' Envelope #14 5 x 11 1/2
24        ' C size sheet
25        ' D size sheet
26        ' E size sheet
27        ' Envelope DL 110 x 220 mm
28        ' Envelope C5 162 x 229 mm
29        ' Envelope C3 324 x 458 mm
30        ' Envelope C4 229 x 324 mm
31        ' Envelope C6 114 x 162 mm
32        ' Envelope C65 114 x 229 mm
33        ' Envelope B4 250 x 353 mm
34        ' Envelope B5 176 x 250 mm
35        ' Envelope B6 176 x 125 mm
36        ' Envelope 110 x 230 mm
```

```
37          ' Envelope Monarch 3.875 x 7.5 in
38          ' 6 3/4 Envelope 3 5/8 x 6 1/2 in
39          ' US Std Fanfold 14 7/8 x 11 in
40          ' German Std Fanfold 8 1/2 x 12 in
41          ' German Legal Fanfold 8 1/2 x 13 in
```

- *dmPaperLength, dmPaperWidth.* Paper length and width in millimeters. This setting overrides the setting of dmPaperSize.
- *dmScale.* Scaling factor.
- *dmCopies.* Number of copies printed.
- *dmDefaultSource.* Paper source. Use one of the following values:

```
1          ' Upper (or only) bin
2          ' Lower bin
3          ' Middle bin
4          ' Manual bin
5          ' Envelope bin
6          ' Envelope manual bin
7          ' Automatic bin
8          ' Tractor bin
9          ' Small format bin
10         ' Large format bin
11         ' Large capacity bin
14         ' Cassette bin
256        ' device specific bin
```

- *dmPrintQuality.* Specifies printer resolution:

```
-1         ' Draft resolution
-2         ' Low resolution
-3         ' Medium resolution
-4         ' High resolution
```

- *dmColor.* Specifies color printing On (1) or Off (2).
- *dmDuplex.* Specifies duplex or single-sided printing:

  1 - Single-sided

  2 - Duplex horizontal

  3 - Duplex vertical

For more information on this complex property, see the Windows SDK documentation (or any of the books on programming with Windows 3.x) under the **DeviceCapabilities** function (which provides all these settings in Windows).

Tip

If you plan to use these settings often, use constants for these settings illustrated in Appendix B.

Note that this structure is defined in the zwAllGlobals module of the WIZARD.MDA library. If your application doesn't load the WIZARD.MDA database, you must define an analogous structure in the declarations section of a module. (Make sure that you change the name of the user-defined type or you will not be able to load WIZARD.MDA with your database.) Note that Version 1.1 loads the UTILITY.MDA automatically.

Access Basic Example

In the following example, the values stored in the *PrtDevMode* property first are copied to the 64-byte string of user-defined type zwtDevModeStr, defined as follows (this structure is defined in the WIZARD.MDA database):

```
Type zwtDevModeStr
    rgb As String * 64
End Type
```

Then, using the **LSet** function, this string is copied to the target user-defined type zwtDevMode (pointed to by the variable "dV"). Then the print orientation and number of copies are specified and the new value of the *PrtDevMode* property is set. You must open a report in Design view to use this property:

```
Function TestPrtDevMode ()

Dim dm As zwtDevModeStr, dV As DeviceMode, cRpt As Report
Const DMORIENT_PORTRAIT = 1
DoCmd OpenReport "Form7", A_DESIGN
Set cRpt = Reports![Form7]

' Get current settings
dm.rgb = cRpt.PrtDevMode
LSet dV = dm

'Specify new settings
dV.dmOrientation = DMORIENT_PORTRAIT
dV.dmCopies = 2

' Copy the bytes
LSet dm = dV

'Set the new value of the PrtDevMode property
cRpt.PrtDevMode = dm.rgb
End Function
```

See Also

Property: PrtMip

PrtMip (documented only in ADK)

Sets or returns the Print settings for a report.

Applies To

Reports

Usage

Design view: Read and Write

Other views: Read Only

Notes

Use this property to set the print options for a report.

You must store the settings returned by the *PrtMip* property in the following user-defined data type:

```
Type zwtMarginInfo
    xLeftMargin As Integer
    yTopMargin As Integer
    xRightMargin As Integer
    yBotMargin As Integer
    fDataOnly As Integer
    xFormSize As Integer
    yFormSize As Integer
    fDefaultSize As Integer
    cxColumns As Integer
    xFormSpacing As Integer
    yFormSpacing As Integer
    radItemOrder As Integer
End Type
```

The following list describes the elements in the above data structure:

- *xLeftMargin*, *yTopMargin*, *xRightMargin*, *yBotMargin*. Specify the dimensions of the reports' margins (expressed in twips).
- *fDataOnly*. Specifies whether the data only is printed (no gridlines, labels, and so on). The setting is True (-1) or False (0).
- *xFormSize*, *yFormSize*. Describe the height and width of the report (expressed in twips).
- *fDefaultSize*. Represents the item size. If 1, same as detail. If 0, custom.
- *cxColumns*. Specifies number of items across page.
- *xFormSpacing*, *yFormSpacing*. Specify column and row spacing (expressed in twips).
- *radItemOrder*. Specifies item layout (1953 = horizontal, 1954 = vertical).

To perform a rough conversion of twips to inches, divide twips by 1440.

This property frequently is used with the *PrtDevMode* property to set and reset printing options for a report, especially if the report is created programmatically (using Access Basic instead of the report design surface).

Note that this structure is defined in the zwAllGlobals module of the WIZARD.MDA library. If your application doesn't load the WIZARD.MDA database, you must define an analogous structure in the declarations section of a module. (Make sure that you change the name of the user-defined type, or you will not be able to load WIZARD.MDA with your database.)

Access Basic Example

In the following example, the values stored in the *PrtMip* property first are copied to the 24-byte string of user-defined type zwfMIPSTR, defined as follows (this structure is defined in the WIZARD.MDA database):

```
Type zwfMIPSTR
    rgb As String * 24
End Type
```

Then, using the **LSet** function, the above string is copied to the target user-defined type zwtMarginInfo (pointed to by the variable "dV"). After setting the new value for top margin, the *PrtMip* property is updated:

```
Function TestPrtMip ()

Dim dV As MarginInfo, cRpt As Report, mip As zwfMIPSTR

DoCmd OpenReport "Form7", A_DESIGN
Set cRpt = Reports![Form7]

' Read the setting of the PrtMip property
mip.rgb = cRpt.PrtMip
LSet dV = mip
Debug.Print dV.yTopMargin          ' display top margin

' Set the new value for top margin (2 inches)
dV.yTopMargin = 2880

' Set the new value of the PrtMip property
LSet mip = dV
cRpt.PrtMip = mip.rgb

End Function
```

See Also

Property: PrtDevMode

RecordCount

Contains the number of records in a table or the current record in a dynaset.

Applies To

Recordsets

Usage

All views: Read Only

Notes

This property returns the total number of nondeleted records in a table or the current record in a dynaset.

To inspect the total number of records in a dynaset, use the **MoveLast** method to make the last nondeleted record in the dynaset current and inspect the *RecordCount* property. Note that the number of records in a table or dynaset can change as records are added or deleted by other users. Adding and deleting records to a table updates the *RecordCount* property if this property applied to a table, but not the *RecordCount* property of a dynaset based on this table. Therefore, inspect this property often when processing dynasets.

The number of records in a snapshot is static, even if the number of records in the underlying table has changed.

Access Basic Example

This example shows the difference between the behavior of the *RecordCount* property in tables and dynasets (and snapshots). First, it opens the State Codes table and checks its record count. Then, it creates a dynaset form, and this table checks its record number and the number of the last record (which equals the total number of records in the dynaset):

```
Dim cDb As Database, cTb As Table, cDy As Dynaset
Set cDb = CurrentDB()
Set cTb = cDb.OpenTable("State Codes")
Debug.Print cTb.RecordCount                    ' 4
Set cDy = cTb.CreateDynaset()
Debug.Print cDy.RecordCount                    ' 1
cDy.MoveLast
Debug.Print cDy.RecordCount                    ' 4
cTb.Close
```

See Also

Method: ListTable

RecordLocks

Forms specifies how the records are locked in the underlying table or query.

Reports specifies whether records in the underlying table or query are locked when the report is printed.

Applies To

Forms, reports

Usage

Design view: Read and Write

Other views: Read Only

Notes

This property has the following settings:

- *No Locks.* This is the default setting. In Access Basic, use 0.

  Reports. No records are locked while the report is previewed or printed.

  Forms. No records are locked, but Access attempts to lock the edited record before the edited data is saved. This may generate run-time errors if another user has locked the record in the multiuser environment.

- *All Records.* In Access Basic, use 1.

  All records are locked in forms and reports until the form is closed or the report finishes printing.

- *Edited Records.* In Access Basic, use 2.

  Applicable to forms only. The record is locked as soon as a user starts to edit it. The lock is released when the record is saved.

The setting of this property has no implications in the single-user environment, but can be crucial in a multiuser environment. To ensure concurrent data access, use the least restrictive setting possible for forms. If you need to ensure that the data in the reports doesn't change after the report begins to print, consider creating a Create Table query and use it as a basis for the report instead of using the All Records lock.

Access forms inherit this property from the Default Record Locking setting of the Multiuser selection from the Options menu in effect when the form is created.

The setting of Record Locking has no effect on data tables stored on the SQL Server.

Caution

Record Locking is something of a misnomer in Access because Access doesn't really lock a single record, but an entire 2K (2048 bytes) page that may contain one or more records.

Access Basic Example

Verify the setting of the *RecordLocks* property before opening a form and inform the user if the locking scheme is too restrictive. You should attach this function to the *OnOpen* property of a form:

```
Function CheckRecordLocks (cForm As Form)

If cForm.RecordLocks = 1 Then
      If MsgBox("All records in the dataset will be locked while editing.  Would you
      ➥like to change the Default Record Locks setting to less restrictive?",
      MB_YESNO +
      ➥MB_ICONINFORMATION) = IDYES Then
        DoCmd CancelEvent
      End If
End If

End Function
```

See Also

Property: LockEdits

RecordSelectors

Determines whether a form displays record selectors.

Applies To

Forms

Usage

Design view: Read and Write

Other views: Read Only

Notes

The Record selector is a vertical bar on the right side of the form that enables you to select the entire record to perform operations such as copying or deleting. Its settings follow:

- *Yes.* Each record has a record selector. This is the default setting. In Access Basic, use True (-1).

- *No.* No record selectors are displayed. In Access Basic, use False (0).

Set this property to No (False) if a form is used as a menu, dialog box, and so on, or if you provide other means to select and manipulate records.

Access Basic Example

Display the setting of this property in the immediate window:

```
Debug.Print Forms![Form3].RecordSelectors
```

See Also

Properties: PopUp and ScrollBars

RecordSource

Specifies the default recordset (table, query) on which a form or report is based.

Applies To

Forms, reports

Usage

Design view: Read and Write

Other views: Read Only

Notes

The *RecordSource* property specifies which recordset supplies data for a form or report. A form or report doesn't need to be based on any recordset. You can use a form as a menu or a dialog box, for example, and a report simply may print data generated by Access Basic code.

The *ControlSource* property binds the controls on a form or report to fields in the recordset specified in the *RecordSource* property.

Changing *RecordSource* after a form or report is designed may lead to unpredictable results—especially if some (or all) fields specified in a form or report don't exist in the new RecordSource.

Access Basic Example

Create a new report and set its *RecordSource* property to the query "Sun Spots in 1993":

```
Function TestRecordSource ()

Dim cRpt As Report
Set cRpt = CreateReport()
cRpt.RecordSource = "Sun Spots in 1993"
DoCmd Restore       'Open it in the Design view

End Function
```

See Also

Properties: ControlSource, RowSourceType, and RowSource

Report

See the "Form" property.

RowSourceType, RowSource

RowSourceType specifies the type of the object's data.

RowSource specifies the source of the data.

Applies To

Controls: Combo box, graph, list box, (embedded) unbound object frame

Usage

Design view: Read and Write

Other views: Read Only

Notes

The *RowSourceType* has the following settings:

Setting	*Access Basic*	*Source of Data*
Table/Query	"Table/Query"	A table, query, or SQL statement (default)
Value List	"Value List"	A list of items in the RowSource property
FieldList	"Field List"	A list of fields from the underlying table or query

The setting of the *RowSource* property depends on the setting of the *RowSourceType* property. For Table/Query, enter the name of a table, query, or SQL SELECT statement. For *Value List*, enter the list of acceptable choices delimited with semicolons, such as

```
Apples;Oranges;Apricots;Elephants;99 balloons;33 1/3
```

For *Field List*, enter the name of the table or a query.

Access Basic Example

Create a new form, specify its *RecordSource* property (table "Customers"), create a combo box on the detail section, specify its *RowSourceType* as a value list, enumerate a list of choices in the *RowSource* property, and set the *LimitToList* and *DefaultValue* properties for this control:

```
Function TestRecordSource ()

Dim cForm As Form, cCtrl As Control
Const COMBO_BOX = 111
Set cForm = CreateForm("","")
cForm.RecordSource = "Customers"
szFormName = cForm.FormName
Set cCtrl = CreateControl(szFormName, COMBO_BOX, 0, "", "", 1000, 1000)
cCtrl.RowSourceType = "Value List"
cCtrl.RowSource = "Apples;Oranges;Compaqs;Abacuses"
cCtrl.DefaultValue = "Oranges"
cCtrl.LimitToList = True
DoCmd Restore

End Function
```

See Also

Functions: CreateControl and CreateReportControl

Properties: BoundColumn, ColumnCount, ColumnHeads, ColumnWidths, ControlSource, LimitToList, and RecordSource

RunningSum

Specifies whether a text box displays the running total of a specified value on a report.

Applies To

A control on reports: Text box

Usage

Design view: Read and Write

Other views: Read Only

Notes

Access can calculate running totals on reports automatically.

The *ControlSource* of a *RunningSum* control specifies the operation and the field on which to perform this operation (such as Sum([Daily Sales]).

You can place the running sum control in a group footer or report footer of a report.

The *RunningTotal* property settings follow:

- *No.* Control displays current value of running total. In Access Basic, use 0.
- *Over Group.* Control displays running total until the next higher group is encountered. Then the running total is reset to 0. In Access Basic, use 1.
- *Over All.* Control displays running total for all groups on the same level until the end of the report. In Access Basic, use 2.

Access Basic Example

Set the control source and the *RunningSum* property for the Field29 control to sum the Daily Sales field over the current group. You must open a report containing this control in **Design view:**

```
Function TestRunningSum(cRpt As Report)
If TypeOf cRpt.[Field29] Is TextBox Then
     cRpt.Field29.ControlSource = "=Sum[Daily Sales]"
     cRpt.Field29.RunningSum = 1
End If
End Function
```

See Also

Property: OnFormat

ScaleHeight, ScaleWidth

Determine the vertical (*ScaleHeight*) or horizontal (*ScaleWidth*) measurements of a section on a report for use with the **Circle**, **Line**, **Print**, and **PSet** methods.

Applies To

Reports

Usage

Design view: Not available

Other views: Read Only

Available only in a macro or Access Basic code attached to the *OnFormat* or *OnPrint* property.

The settings are available only when a report is previewed or printed.

Notes

Changing the *ScaleHeight* and *ScaleWidth* properties changes the internal coordinates of a section for use with the **Circle**, **Line**, **Print**, and **PSet** methods. Setting the *ScaleHeight* to 100 specifies the section height as 100 current units, such as twips, inches, centimeters, pixels, and so on, for example. (See the *ScaleMode* property for information on settings for various units of measurement.)

Setting the *ScaleHeight* and *ScaleWidth* properties to a round number greatly facilitates designing drawings on the report.

If you set *ScaleHeight* and *ScaleWidth* to positive values, the values of coordinates increase from top to bottom and from left to right. When you set this property to a negative number, the values of coordinates increase from bottom to top and from right to left.

The default settings are the height and width of a section expressed in twips. The value of this property is a Single data type.

The *ScaleHeight* and *ScaleWidth* properties are affected by the setting of the *ScaleMode* property.

Use the **Scale** method to set *ScaleHeight*, *ScaleWidth*, *ScaleLeft*, and *ScaleTop* properties in one statement.

Access Basic Example

This function demonstrates two settings of the *ScaleHeight* and *ScaleWidth* properties.

```
Function TestScaleHeight (cRpt As Report)

cRpt.Scaleheight = 100
cRpt.ScaleWidth = 100

' Draw a large circle
cRpt.Circle (40, 40), 28

'Draw a small circle
cRpt.ScaleWidth = 600
cRpt.Circle (40, 40), 28

End Function
```

Figure 22.10 illustrates the results of these settings.

See Also

Methods: Circle, Line, Print, PSet, and Scale

Properties: DrawMode, DrawStyle, FillColor, ForeColor, ScaleLeft, ScaleTop, and ScaleMode

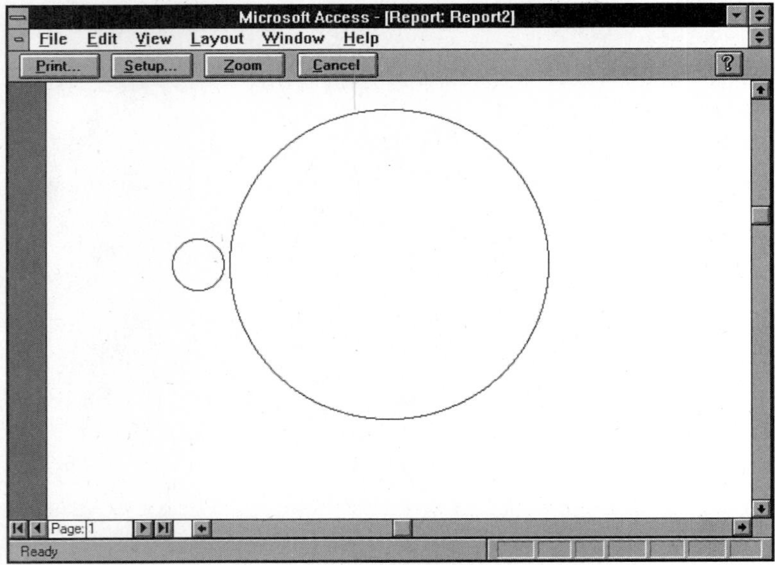

Figure 22.10. Results of the TestScaleHeight() function.

ScaleLeft, ScaleTop

Determine the vertical (*ScaleLeft*) or horizontal (*ScaleWidth*) coordinates of the left and top edges of a page for use with the **Circle**, **Line**, **Print**, and **PSet** methods.

Applies To

Reports

Usage

Design view: Not available

Other views: Read Only

Available only in a macro or Access Basic code attached to the *OnFormat* or *OnPrint* property.

The settings are available only when a report is previewed, printed to the printer, or printed to a file.

Notes

The default setting for both properties is 0. The value of this property is a Single data type.

When used with *ScaleHeight* and *ScaleWidth* properties, the *ScaleLeft* and *ScaleTop* properties establish a full coordinate system for drawing and printing on a report.

The *ScaleHeight* and *ScaleWidth* properties are affected by the setting of the *ScaleMode* property.

Use the **Scale** method to set the *ScaleHeight*, *ScaleWidth*, *ScaleLeft*, and *ScaleTop* properties in one statement.

Access Basic Example

This function demonstrates two settings of the *ScaleLeft* and *ScaleTop* properties.

```
Function TestScaleLeft (cRpt As Report)

cRpt.ScaleLeft = 100
cRpt.ScaleTop = -100

' Draw a skinny circle
cRpt.Circle (4000, 4000), 2800

cRpt.ScaleLeft = 1000
cRpt.ScaleTop = -1000

' Draw a fat circle
cRpt.DrawWidth = 20
cRpt.Circle (4000, 4000), 2800

End Function
```

Figure 22.11. illustrates the results of these settings.

See Also

Methods: Circle, Line, Print, PSet, and Scale

Properties: DrawMode, DrawStyle, FillColor, ForeColor, ScaleHeight, ScaleMode, and ScaleWidth

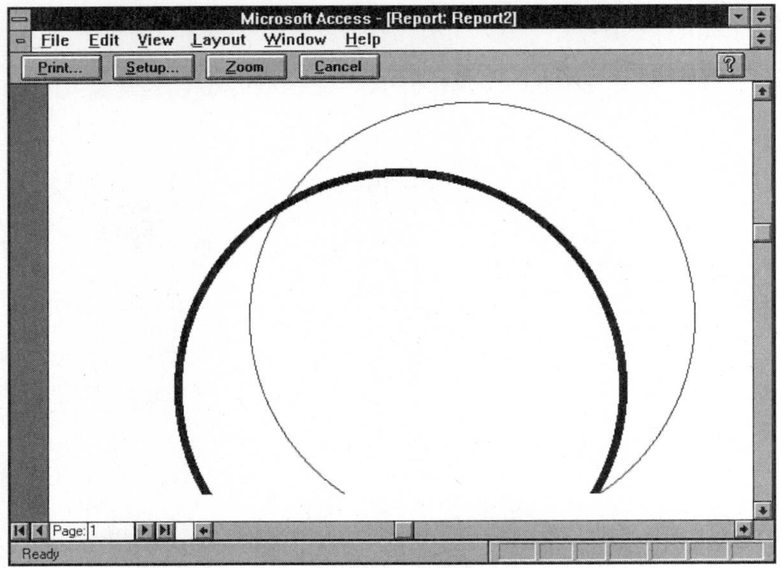

Figure 22.11. Results of the TestScaleLeft() function.

ScaleMode

Sets the units of measurements for use with the **Circle**, **Line**, **Print**, and **PSet** methods.

Applies To

Reports

Usage

Design view: Not available

Other views: Read Only

Available only in a macro or Access Basic code attached to the *OnFormat* or *OnPrint* property.

The settings are available only when a report is previewed or printed.

Notes

The *ScaleMode* property has the following settings:

Setting	*Meaning*
0	One or more *Scale...* properties are set to custom values.
1	Twips (1440 twips/inch, 567 twips/cm). This is the default setting.
2	Point (72 points/inch)
3	Pixel
4	Character (120 x 240 twips)
5	Inch
6	Millimeter
7	Centimeter

When any of the *Scale...* properties is set to a value other than its default, the *ScaleMode* property is set to 0.

When the setting of the *ScaleMode* property is changed, the coordinates specified by the *ScaleLeft* and *ScaleTop* properties are reset to 0, and the *ScaleHeight*, *ScaleWidth*, *CurrentX*, and *CurrentY* properties are reset to reflect the new unit of measurement.

The value of this property is an Integer data type.

Caution

The setting 4 (Character) triggers a `The setting you entered isn't valid for this property` error (trappable error #2101) in Access Versions 1.0 and 1.1.

Access Basic Example

Set the *ScaleMode* property to pixels (the same unit of measurement as for the DrawMode property):

```
Set cRpt = Reports![Report1]
cRpt.DrawWidth = 5
cRpt.ScaleMode = 3
cRpt.Line (100, 100)-(1000, 100)
```

See Also

Method: Scale

Properties: DrawMode, DrawStyle, FillColor, ForeColor, ScaleHeight, ScaleLeft, ScaleTop, and ScaleWidth

PROPERTIES

ScaleTop

See the "ScaleLeft" property.

ScaleWidth

See the "ScaleHeight" property.

Scaling

Determines how Access fits the contents of an object into a frame or graph.

Applies To

Controls: Bound object frame, graph, unbound object frame

Usage

Design view: Read and Write

Other views: Read Only

Notes

The *Scaling* property has three settings, as described in thhe following table.

Setting	*Access Basic*	*Meaning*
Clip	0	No size adjustments. Parts of an object that don't fit into the frame around an object are clipped off. The fastest way to display an object. This is the default setting.
Scale	1	The size is adjusted so that an object fits in the frame, causing possible distortions of the object's proportions.
Zoom	2	Either height or width of an object is adjusted to fill the height or the width of the frame. No distortion to the object's proportions.

Access Basic Example

The effects of the above three settings of the Scaling property are shown in figure 22.12.

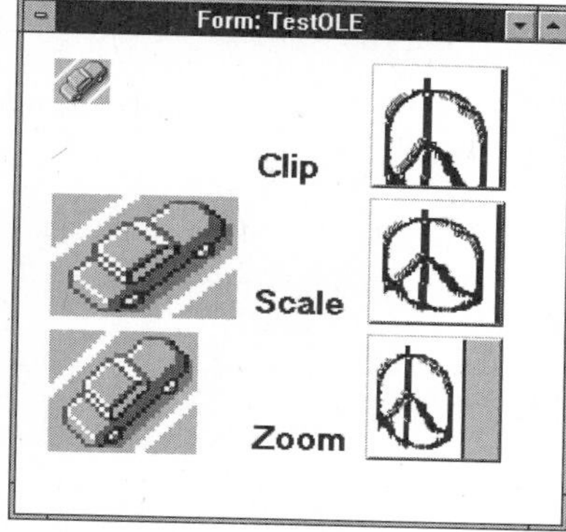

Figure 22.12. Different settings of the Scaling property.

See Also

Property: OLEClass

ScrollBars

Determines whether vertical and horizontal scroll bars appear on a form or a text box on a form.

Applies To

Forms

A control and tool on a form: Text box

Usage

Design view: Read and Write

Other views: Read Only

Notes

Vertical and horizontal scroll bars enable you to scroll a form on the screen when it is too big too fit in the form window. The horizontal scroll bar also contains the current record number and navigation buttons to move up and down in a form's recordset. These are not displayed unless the vertical bar appears on a form.

The vertical bar in a text box enables you to scroll the text in a box up and down. The scroll bar in a text box is visible only when the text box is selected.

The *ScrollBars* property has the setting, described in the following table.

Setting	*Access Basic*	*Meaning*
Neither	0	Neither the vertical nor horizontal scroll bar appears. No navigation buttons on a form. This is the text box default.
Horizontal Only	1	Not applicable to a text box. On a form, the horizontal scroll bar and navigation buttons appear.
Vertical only	2	The vertical scroll bar appears on forms and in text boxes. No navigation buttons on a form.
Both	3	Vertical and horizontal bars and navigation button appear on a form. This is the default for forms, and is not applicable to a text box.

If you often use settings different than the default for this property, create a form template with these settings and make it a default form template.

Access Basic Example

Test the ScrollBars property setting for the given form:

```
Function TestScrollBars (szForm$)
    DoCmd OpenForm szForm, A_DESIGN, , , , A_ICON
    If Forms(szForm).ScrollBars <> 1 Or Forms(szForm).ScrollBars <> 3 Then
        Debug.Print "This Form will not display navigation buttons..."
    End If
    DoCmd Close A_FORM, szForm
End Function
```

See Also

Properties: Modal, PopUp, and RecordSelectors

Section

Applies To

Forms, reports

Usage

All views: Read Only

Notes

The *Section* property has two uses:

- To determine in which section of a form or report a particular control is located. For example,

  ```
  Forms![Form1].[Field67].Section
  ```

  returns the section number on which the Field67 control is located on the Form1 form.

- To manipulate properties of a particular section on a form or report. For example,

  ```
  Reports![Report1].Section(0).CanGrow = True
  ```

  sets the *CanGrow* property of the detail section on the Report1 report to True.

Sections on forms and reports are identified as described in the following table.

Section Number	*Meaning*
0	Form or report detail section
1	Form or report header
2	Form or report footer
3	Form or report page header
4	Form or report page footer
5	Report group level 1 header
6	Report group level 1 footer
7	Report group level 2 header
8	Report group level 2 footer
9, 10,...	Additional report group level sections footer/header pairs numbered with consecutive pairs of numbers

The *Section* property is a dynamic array that is resized as you create or delete sections from a report or form. Access creates some sections automatically when you create a new form or report.

The value of this property is an Integer data type.

Referring to a nonexisting section triggers an `Invalid section number reference` error (trappable error #2462).

Access Basic Example

Change the Page Header section *OnFormat* property to execute a function called Determine Formatting, and the *Visible* property of the section that contains the Field0 control to No:

```
Function TestSection (szReport)
    DoCmd OpenReport szReport, A_DESIGN
    Reports(szReport).Section(3).OnFormat = "=DetermineFormatting()"
    Reports(szReport).Section(Reports(szReport).[Text28].Section).Visible = False
    DoCmd Close A_REPORT, szReport
End Function
```

See Also

Properties: CanGrow, CanShrink, FillColor, ForceNewPage, Height, KeepTogether, NewRowOrCol, OnFormat, OnPrint, SpecialEffect, Visible, and Width

ShowGrid

Specifies whether gridlines are visible in Datasheet view.

Applies To

Forms in Datasheet view

Usage

Design view: Read and Write

Other views: Read Only

Notes

The setting of this property is available from the Layout menu (Gridlines) in Datasheet view. This property doesn't appear in the form property box. In Access Basic, this property has the following settings:

- *True (nonzero).* Gridlines in Datasheet view are visible.
- *False (0).* Gridlines are not visible in Datasheet view.

Access Basic Example

Toggle this property on the Form1 form (you must open the form in Design view):

```
Forms![Form1].ShowGrid = Not Forms![Form1].ShowGrid
```

See Also

Properties: DefaultView and ViewsAllowed

Sort

Specifies the sort order for records.

Applies To

Dynasets, snapshots

Usage

All views: Read and Write

Notes

To set this property, specify a new sort order (a field in the recordset). You also may specify an ascending (Asc) or descending (Desc) sort order. The default sort order is ascending.

Any setting of this property overrides the sort order specified in the underlying query.

The *Sort* property doesn't have any effect on the recordset for which it is specified. Only dynasets or snapshots created from such a recordset display the sort order specified for this recordset.

You cannot use the *Sort* property with snapshots created with any of the List methods (ListFields, ListIndexes, ListParameters, and ListTables) or with tables.

You may find that it is more efficient to directly create a sorted dynaset from a table using an SQL SELECT...ORDER BY... statement in the *source* argument of the CreateDynaset method.

Access Basic Example

Create an unsorted dynaset from the Customers table and sort it on the Name field in the descending order. Then create a sorted dynaset:

```
Function TestSort ()

    Dim cDb As Database, cDy As Dynaset, cDy1 As Dynaset
    Set cDb = CurrentDB()
```

```
    Set cDy = cDb.CreateDynaset("Customers")
    cDy.Sort = "[Name] Desc"
    ' Record in the first dynaset are not sorted

    Set cDy1 = cDy.CreateDynaset()
    ' The records will be sorted by name

End Function
```

See Also

Methods: CreateDynaset and CreateSnapshot

Properties: Filter and Index

SortOrder (documented only in ADK)

Specifies the sort order of a group level.

Applies To

GroupLevel property on reports

Usage

Design view: Read and Write

Other views: Read Only

Notes

You can determine the settings for this property by choosing Sorting & Grouping from the View menu on the report design surface. You can specify this setting as Ascending (default) or Descending.

In Access Basic, the *SortOrder* property has two settings:

- *False (0).* Ascending sort order.
- *True (-1).* Descending sort order.

You cannot open the Sorting and Grouping box while setting the *SortOrder* property from within Access Basic. If you try to do this, a `Can't execute this function with the Sorting and Grouping box open` error (trappable error #2154) appears.

Access Basic Example

Create a new sort order on the M_DATE field on the report Report1 and set its *SortOrder* property to descending:

```
Function TestSortOrder ()
    DoCmd OpenReport "Report1", A_DESIGN
    wLevel = CreateGroupLevel("Report1", "M_DATE", False, False)
    Reports!Report1.GroupLevel(wLevel).GroupOn = 5
    Reports!Report1.GroupLevel(wLevel).SortOrder = True
End Function
```

See Also

Function: CreateGroupLevel

Properties: GroupInterval, GroupLevel, and GroupOn

SourceObject

Subform/subreport identifies a subform/subreport on a form or report.

Object frame identifies the file name that contains the linked data.

Applies To

Controls: Subform/subreport, (linked) unbound object frame

Usage

Subform/Subreport

Design view: Read and Write
Other views: Read Only

Object Frame

All views: Read Only

Notes

To set this property, you need to specify the name of a subform/subreport or the fully qualified name (drive, path, file name, and extension) of the file to link to the frame.

To unlink a subform/subreport from a main form or report, clear its *SourceObject* property. This action makes the subform/subreport control on the main form or report unbound. (You must remove the subform/subreport control manually.)

You can change the setting for this property for a linked frame only by choosing the Object/Change Link option from the Edit menu. Trying to change the setting of the *SourceObject* property from within Access Basic doesn't generate an error (but, of course, it has no effect on the property).

Access Basic Example

Specify a new *SourceObject* property for a subform:

```
Function TestSourceObject (szMain$, szSub$, szNewSub$)
    DoCmd OpenForm szMain, A_DESIGN, , , , A_ICON
    Forms(szMain)(szSub).SourceObject = szNewSub
End Function
```

See Also

Properties: LinkChildFields, LinkMasterFields, and Parent

SpecialEffect

Specifies a 3-D visual effect: raised, sunken, or normal (flat).

Applies To

Form sections, report sections

All tools and controls except: Command button, line, page break, and subform/subreport

Usage

Design view: Read and Write

Other views: Read Only

Notes

The settings of the *SpecialEffect* property are available from the Palette on the form and report design surfaces. In Access Basic, this property has the settings described in the following table.

Setting	*Effect*
0	Normal
1	Raised
2	Sunken

The default for all applicable objects is the Normal (flat) setting expressed in the property box for a control as "Color."

Some controls (the check box and option button, for example) appear exactly the same when raised or sunken effect is specified—especially on VGA mono and EGA displays. Setting the Button Text color (available from the Windows 3.1 Control Panel's Color selection) to a color other than gray may cure this problem.

Access Basic Example

Set the *SpecialEffect* property to 2 (Sunken) for the Label1 control on the Form1 form:

```
Forms![Form1].[Label1].SpecialEffect = 2
```

Figure 22.13 shows the effects of these settings.

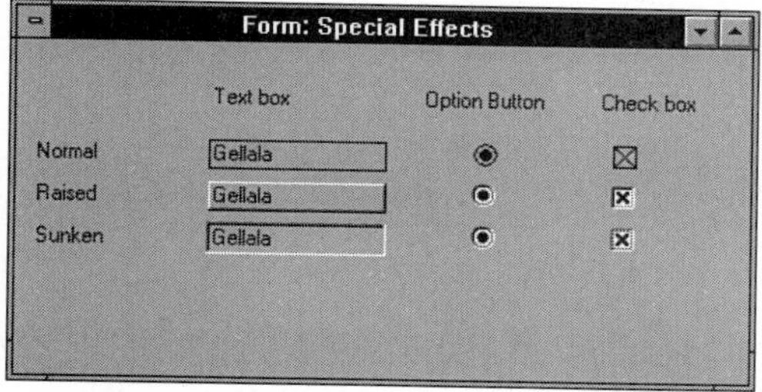

Figure 22.13. The effects of various SpecialEffect settings on VGA monitor controls (standard resolution).

See Also

Properties: BorderColor, BorderStyle, BorderWidth, and BackStyle

SQL

Sets the selection criteria for a query.

Applies To

QueryDef objects

Usage

All views: Read and Write

This property is available only in Access Basic.

Notes

The *SQL* property specifies what conditions should be applied to select, group, and order records from the underlying recordset(s).

You also may use this property to define a parameter query and to supply the value of the parameter each time before the query is executed.

Access Basic Example

Define a new query using the SQL statement stored in szSQLstring:

```
Dim cDB As Database, cQy As QueryDef, szQname$
Set cDB = CurrentDB()
szQname = "Sorted mSysObjects"

szSQLstring = "SELECT  * FROM MSysObjects ORDER BY MSysObjects.Type, MSysObjects.DateCreate;"

Set cQy = cDB.CreateQueryDef(szQname)
cQy.SQL = szSQLstring
cQy.Close
```

See Also

Object: QueryDef

Methods: CreateDynaset, CreateQueryDef, CreateSnapshot, and OpenQueryDef

Properties: Filter, Index, and Sort

StatusBarText

Specifies the text to display on the status bar when the control has focus.

Applies To

Controls: bound object frame, check box, combo box, command box, list box, option button, option group subform, text box, toggle button

Usage

Design view: Read and Write

Other views: Read Only

Notes

The maximum length of displayed text is 255 characters.

Use this property to provide information to the user: the type of data to enter, acceptable data ranges, and so on.

If you create the control by dragging a field from the fields list to a form, and the *Description* property exists for this field, the control is copied automatically to the *StatusBarText* property.

Access Basic Example

Inspect the value of the *StatusBarProperty* in the Field34 control (note that because this property can contain a Null value, the variable vText is declared as a Variant data type):

```
Dim vText
vText = Forms![Test form].[Field34].StatusBarText
MsgBox("StatusBarText is " & IIf(IsNull(vText), "None", vText))
```

See Also

Properties: Caption and Description

TextAlign

See the "LabelAlign" property.

Top

See the "Left" property.

Transactions

Specifies whether a table or dynaset supports Access transaction processing.

Applies To

Tables, dynasets

Usage

All views: Read Only

Notes

The *Transactions* property has no user-settable settings. It returns two possible values:

- *True (-1).* Table or dynaset supports Access transactions.
- *False (0).* Table or dynaset does not support transactions.

Access native tables and dynasets support transaction processing; therefore, the setting of this property is True. Mixed dynasets (those that include attached tables, such as from Paradox or other DBMS) do not support Access transaction processing, and the value returned by this property for such dynasets is False.

Use the Transactions property before issuing a **BeginTrans** statement. Using Access transactions processing on a dynaset or table that does not support transactions has no effect.

Access Basic Example

Test the *Transactions* property of two recordsets—the native Access Customers table and the dynaset based on the attached VALTABLE dBASE IV table:

```
Function TestTransactions ()
    Dim cDb As Database, cTb As Table, cDy As Dynaset
    Set cDb = CurrentDB()
    Set cTb = cDb.OpenTable("Customers")

    Debug.Print cTb.Transactions             ' True

    Set cDy = cDb.CreateDynaset("VALTABLE")
    Debug.Print cDy.Transactions             ' False
End Function
```

See Also

Statements: BeginTrans, CommitTrans, and Rollback

Transparent

Specifies whether a command button is transparent.

Applies To

Control: Command button

Usage

Design view: Read and Write

Other views: Read Only

Notes

If you set the *Transparent* property to Yes (True), the button and its label (or a picture displayed on the button) are not visible, but the button is active.

The *Transparent* property has two settings:

- *Yes.* A button is transparent. In Access Basic, use True (-1).
- *No.* A button is visible. This is the default setting. In Access Basic, use False (0).

Use this property to simulate a "touch screen" effect. You can place a transparent button on top of other controls, graphic elements, labels, and so on. After the user clicks on such an element, an action specified in an appropriate action property (*OnPush*, *OnDblClick*, and so on) of a button executes.

Access Basic Example

Set the *Transparent* property of the Button31 command button on the Form1 form (opened in Design view) to True:

```
If TypeOf Forms![Form1].Button31 Is CommandButton Then
     Forms![Form1].Button31.Transparent = True
Endif
```

See Also

Properties: DisplayWhen, Enabled, Locked, OnDblClick, OnPush, and Visible

Updatable

Indicates whether records in a table or dynaset, or their individual fields, are updatable.

Applies To

Tables, dynasets

Usage

All views: Read Only

Notes

The *Updatable* property determines whether you can edit a particular field in a table or dynaset.

If the *Updatable* property of a table returns True, you can edit all of its fields except a Counter field, which is not updatable. The *Updatable* property of a table containing a Counter field is True, however.

A dynaset can contain a mixture of updatable and nonupdatable fields. Therefore, you should test the *Updatable* property for each field before editing it. Attempting to update a nonupdatable field results in a `Couldn't update field` error (trappable error #3164).

If you use the **ListFields** method to test whether the field is updatable, you can test the Attributes field against the Access DB_UPDATABLEFIELD intrinsic constant to determine whether a particular field can be updated.

Access Basic Example

Open the TestUpdatable table, which contains a mixture of updatable and nonupdatable fields. Create a snapshot using the **ListFields** method and test its Attributes field to determine whether a field is updatable:

```
Function TestUpdatable ()
    Dim cDb As Database, cTb As Table, cSn As Snapshot
    Set cDb = CurrentDB()
    Set cTb = cDb.OpenTable("TestUpdatable")
    Set cSn = cTb.ListFields()
    Do Until cSn.EOF
    If (cSn.Attributes = DB_UPDATABLEFIELD) Then
        Debug.Print cSn.Name; " is "; "Updatable"
      End If
      cSn.MoveNext
    Loop
    cTb.Close
End Function
```

See Also

Objects: ListFields and Update

UpdateMethod

Determines whether the data in the linked frame is updated when it changes, or at predefined intervals.

Applies To

Control: (Linked) unbound object frame

Usage

Design view: Read and Write

Other views: Read Only

Notes

The *UpdateMethod* property specifies how the remote data linked to an object frame (picture, graph, sound package, and so on) is updated.

The *UpdateMode* property has two settings:

- *Automatic.* Data is updated automatically. This is the default setting. In Access Basic, use 0.
- *Manual.* Data is updated at predefined intervals. In Access Basic, use 1.

If the setting for this property is Automatic, Access refreshes the data when the remote data changes. If the setting is Manual, Access refreshes the data according to the Refresh Interval setting in the Options Multiuser dialog box, available from the View menu.

Access Basic Example

Open the TestOLE form in Design view and set the *UpdateMethod* property of the Embedded14 object frame to Manual:

```
DoCmd OpenForm "TestOLE", A_DESIGN
Forms![TestOLE].[Embedded14].UpdateMethod = 1
```

See Also

Properties: OLEClass and SourceObject

ValidationRule, ValidationText

ValidationRule is an expression that is evaluated when data in a control changes.

ValidationText is an expression to display when the expression in ValidationRule evaluates to False.

Applies To

Table fields

Controls on a form: Combo box, list box, option group, text box.

The following controls, except when a control is a part of an option group: Check box, option button, toggle button

Usage

Design view: Read and Write

Other views: Read Only

Notes

Enter a *condition* (an expression that evaluates to True or False) in the *ValidationRule* property to validate the correctness of the data entered in the control. Note that an Access Basic function attached to this property always evaluates to False, no matter what value such a function actually returns.

Enter the text in the *ValidationText* property to help users correct erroneous entries, or to instruct them on what to do next. The text specified in this property is displayed in a standard dialog box with two buttons (OK and Help). If no text is entered in this property, the default message `The value you entered is prohibited by the validation rule set for this field` appears if the condition set in the *ValidationRule* is not satisfied.

The maximum length of each property is 255 characters.

The *ValidationRule* is executed only when the data in the control is changed.

If you create a control by dragging the field from the field list to a form, its *ValidationRule* and *ValidationText* properties are copied to the analogous properties for the created control.

Use string expressions to set these properties from Access Basic.

The *ValidationRule* property provides means to perform a rudimentary validation of the entered data. To perform more robust validation involving values from other recordsets or calculations, for example, use an Access Basic function attached to the *BeforeUpdate* property.

Access Basic Example

Open the Customers form in Design view and change the settings of both *Validation...* properties for the City control:

```
Function TestValidationRule ()
    szForm = "Customers"
    szControl = "City"
    DoCmd OpenForm "Customers", A_DESIGN
    Forms(szForm)(szControl).ValidationRule = "<> 'London'"
    Forms(szForm)(szControl).ValidationText = "No Londoners, please..."
End Function
```

See Also

Properties: BeforeUpdate and OnExit

ValidationText

See the “ValidationRule” property.

ViewsAllowed

See "DefaultView" property.

Visible

Hides or shows a control.

Applies To

Forms

Form sections, report sections

Tools and controls

Usage

Forms

All views: Read and Write

Available only from Access Basic

Form and Report Sections

Design view: Read and Write

Other views: Read Only

Controls

All views: Read and Write

Notes

The *Visible* property enables you to hide and display controls on forms and report.

The *Visible* property has the following settings:

- *Yes.* The object is visible. This is the default setting. In Access Basic, use True (-1).
- *No.* The object is hidden. In Access Basic, use False (0).

Hidden objects are disabled (you cannot select them or update them).

If you set the *Visible* property of a form to True, the form "disappears" from the screen. If this happens in Design view, Access saves any changes made to the form.

Access Basic Example

Display a map of Colorado (linked to the frame “Colorado”) if the value of the state field = “CO”:

```
If Forms![Customers].State = "CO" Then
     Forms![Customers].[Colorado].Visible = True
End If
```

See Also

Properties: DisplayWhen, Enabled, Locked, OnFormat, and Transparent

Width

See “Height” property.

Statements

AppActivate

Miscellaneous

Activates an application window.

Syntax

AppActivate *title*

title is a character expression that evaluates to the name of the application to activate.

Usage Notes

title is not case-sensitive, but it must match the name of the target application character for character.

If there is more than one instance of an application specified in *title*, Windows arbitrarily chooses one.

The AppActivate statement doesn't manipulate the target application in any way; it merely switches the focus to its window (or an icon) if the target application is active.

An `Illegal function call` error (trappable error #5) is returned if the application specified in *title* is not running.

Examples

Example 1:

To switch focus to a different application with minimal error recovery:

```
On Error GoTo rorre                     ' local error routine
szAppName = "Snake in the grass"        ' application name
```

```
nErrNbr = 0                              ' error flag
AppActivate szAppName                    ' try to switch focus
If nErrNbr <> 0                          ' error occurred...
        Result = Shell(szAppName)        ' Attempt to launch it...
        AppActivate szAppName            '...and activate it again
End If
Exit Function
rorre:
nErrNbr = Err                            ' set error flag
(...)                                    ' process the error
Resume Next
```

Example 2:

The second example uses Windows API functions to first obtain the handle of the current input focus window (using the Windows GetFocus function) and uses it to go back to the same window using the Windows SetFocus function.

Declare these functions first in the declarations section of a module:

```
Declare Function GetFocus Lib "User" () As Integer
Declare Function SetFocus Lib "User" (ByVal Hwnd%) As Integer
```

Switch focus to a different application, and restore it to the current application by using Windows API functions:

```
Dim nHwnd As Integer
nHwnd = GetFocus()
AppActivate "QPW"                  ' Switch focus to Quattro Pro.
(...)                              ' manipulate QPW with SendKeys, and so on.
Result = SetFocus(nHwnd)           ' Switch focus back to Access.
```

See Also

Function: Shell

Statement: SendKeys

Beep

Miscellaneous

Sounds the computer's speaker.

Syntax

Beep

Usage Notes

The Beep statement doesn't provide any control over the duration and frequency of the sound. To achieve some degree of control, investigate the Windows API function **MessageBeep** and [sounds] section of the WIN.INI file.

Example

The Beep statement is often used with the MsgBox function or statement, as shown in the following example:

```
If Weekday(Date) = 6 Then                   ' Friday
        Beep                                ' Sound the bell and...
        MsgBox "It's Friday...!"            ' ...spread the news
End If
```

See Also

Action: Beep

BeginTrans

Database Manipulation

Starts a transaction code block.

Syntax

BeginTrans

Usage Notes

transaction is a logical block of code that manipulates data in a dataset, most commonly used to ensure that all records involved in a logically related update operation are actually updated.

Access Basic transactions can be nested up to five levels deep and must be either saved (CommitTrans) or reversed (Rollback) from the lowest nesting level up. Every transaction must be terminated with either CommitTrans or Rollback.

Transactions coded in Access Basic are performed independently of transactions performed in forms and reports.

The error most likely to occur within a transaction is an `Operation not supported in transactions` error (trappable error #3246), which can be triggered by an attempt to close the current table or database within a transaction.

Note

You can bypass a pending transaction by executing an Access action from within a transaction code block with the DoCmd statement; Actions executed with DoCmd are not affected by CommitTrans or Rollback statements.

Access transactions operate reliably only on Access native datasets; when a transaction is performed in a dynaset with mixed data sources (such as a mix of native Access and Paradox tables), only changes made to the native Access tables can be reversed with the Rollback statement. If in doubt, check the Transaction property of the dynaset in question; if the Transaction property of the dynaset is True, a Rollback can be performed on all fields in the dataset.

Example

The following constants can be defined in the declarations section:

```
Const MB_YES = 6
Const MB_YESNO = 4
Const MB_ICONQUESTION = 32

Dim cDb as Database, cTb as Table
Set cDb = CurrentDB()
Set cTb = cDb.OpenTable("Whatever")
BeginTrans
'...perform desired operations
If MsgBox("Save?",MB_YESNO + MB_ICONQUESTION,"Current transaction") = MB_YES Then
        CommitTrans
Else
        Rollback
End If
cTb.Close
```

See Also

Statements: CommitTrans, DoCmd, and Rollback

Method: Update

Property: Transactions

Call

Function and Procedure

Transfers control to a Sub procedure.

Syntax

[**Call**] *name* [(, *arglist*)]

name is a string expression that evaluates to a valid Sub procedure.

arglist is a list of expressions to pass to the Sub procedure.

Usage Notes

The Call statement is always optional and is considered obsolete.

Parentheses around the *arglist* are required only if the Call statement is used to call a Sub procedure that accepts parameters.

The Call statement can be used to call subroutines defined in Access code as well as subroutines contained in DLLs.

Please refer to Function and Sub statements for a discussion about calling conventions and parameter passing in MS Access.

Example

All three calls to the Sub procedure Sub1 from within another function or subroutine are equal, as shown in the following example:

```
Call Sub1 (1)
Sub1 1
Sub1 (1)
(...)

Sub Sub1(i As Integer)
        MsgBox("I'm in Sub1...!")
End Sub
```

See Also

Statements: Declare, Function, and Sub

ChDir

File I/O

Changes the directory on the specified drive.

Syntax

ChDir *pathexpression*

pathexpression is a string expression that evaluates to a valid path and drive formatted as follows:

[Drive:][\][directory[\directory]]

Usage Notes

pathexpression must be less than 128 characters (DOS path length), or an `Illegal function call` error (trappable error #5) is generated.

Passing an invalid path, a nonexisting directory, or the letter of a removable media drive without a disk in it, results in a `Path not found` error (trappable error #76).

If *pathexpression* is a Null, an `Invalid use of Null` error occurs.

If the drive is not specified, the current drive is assumed.

Example

To use the ChDir statement:

```
ChDir "\"                    ' change to the root directory on the current drive
ChDir "F:\"                  ' change directory to the root directory on drive F:
ChDir "F:"                   ' error 76
```

Using DOS shortcuts in pathexpression:

```
ChDir "..\DOOM"
```

See Also

Functions: CurDir and CurDir$, and Dir and Dir$

Statements: ChDrive, MkDir, and RmDir

ChDrive

File I/O

Changes the current drive.

Syntax

ChDrive *drive*

drive is a string expression that evaluates to a valid drive.

Usage Notes

If *drive* is a Null, an `Invalid use of Null` error occurs. If *drive* is a zero-length string, or points to a nonexisting drive, the current drive is assumed and the drive doesn't change. If *drive* is a multicharacter string, the ChDrive statement uses only the first character.

Example

To change drive to drive D:

```
ChDir "D"
```

Note

Passing the letter of a removable media drive without a disk in it doesn't result in the error message, but a Device unavailable error (trappable error #68) or Disk not ready error (trappable error #71) is generated when you try to access the drive.

See Also

Functions: CurDir and CurDir$, and Dir and Dir$

Statements: ChDrive, MkDir, and RmDir

Close

File I/O

Closes a file opened in Access Basic code.

Syntax

Close [[#]*filenumber*][,[#]*filenumber*]...

filenumber is a numeric expression that evaluates to a valid file number used in the Open statement.

Usage Notes

Close can close a single file, or a list of files, depending on the number of *filenumber* entries. Arguments are optional; Close without any arguments closes all open files. The Reset statement is a synonym of Close without any arguments.

When Close is executed on a file opened for output or append, Access flushes data buffers associated with this file to the operating system, which doesn't necessarily mean that data is physically written to disk at the same time; the physical disk write may be delayed by Windows or a disk cache (such as SmartDrv) with write-caching enabled.

The Close statement affects only files opened with the Open statement; it does not close open Access databases and tables.

Example

To open and close two text files:

```
nSource = FreeFile
Open "FROM.TXT" For Input as nSource
nTarget = FreeFile
Open "TO.TXT" For Output as nTarget
(...)                                   ' do something here
Close nSource, nTarget                  ' or just: Close
```

See Also

Statements: End, Open, Reset, and Stop

STATEMENTS

CommitTrans

Database Manipulation

Saves changes made in the pending transaction and ends it.

Syntax

CommitTrans

Usage Notes

transaction is a logical block of code that manipulates data in a dataset, most commonly used to ensure that all records involved in a logically related update operation are actually updated.

Access Basic transactions can be nested up to five levels deep and must be either saved (CommitTrans) or reversed (Rollback) from the lowest nesting level up. Every transaction must be terminated with either CommitTrans or Rollback. Once the transaction is committed (saved), the changes cannot be undone unless the transaction is nested within another pending transaction.

Transactions coded in Access Basic are performed independently of transactions performed in forms and reports; changes to tables made within a coded transaction are reflected in the form or report that uses this table only if the transaction is committed with CommitTrans.

The error most likely to occur within a transaction is an `Operation not supported in transactions` error (trappable error #3246) that can be triggered by an attempt to close the current table or database within a transaction.

Example

See the BeginTrans statement.

Note

You can bypass a pending transaction by executing an Access action from within a transaction code block with the DoCmd statement; changes to data made in Action executed with DoCmd will not be affected by CommitTrans.

See Also

Statements: BeginTransaction and Rollback

Method: Update

Property: Transactions

Const

Variables and Constants

Declares a symbolic constant.

Syntax

[**Global**] **Const** *name* = *expression* [, *name* = *expression*]...

name is the name of the constant being declared.

expression is a value that will be substituted for the constant.

Usage Notes

By convention, constant names are expressed in capital letters.

To increase code readability, it is a commonly accepted practice to place all declarations of constants in a single code module.

expression cannot contain basic Access Basic functions, integrated strings, variables, and references to functions or procedures.

The optional keyword Global can be used only in the declarations section of a code module; it cannot be used within a Function or Sub.

Constants are given the simplest possible data type at compile time. It is possible, however, to force a specified data type by including the proper suffix in the constant name. (The suffix doesn't become the part of the name.) The following example will have a Double data type even though the default data type for this constant would be Integer:

```
Const DW_NUMBER# = 123
```

Because the internal storage of a Variant data type is determined at runtime, and the data type is assigned to constants at compile time, a constant cannot be a Variant data type.

The scope (visibility) of a constant depends on how and where it is defined, as shown in the following table.

Where and How Defined	*Visible to*
In a Function or Sub	This Function or Sub only
In a declaration section of a module	This module only
In a declaration section of a module with the Global keyword	All modules in the database

Constants can be used in place of expressions anywhere in Access Basic code.

Example

Both constants are type integer:

```
Const DOS_PATH_LEN = 127
Const DOS_PATH_LEN% = 127
```

Define an approximation of Pi:

```
Global Const PI = 3.14
```

The following declarations are invalid:

```
Const MY_NAME = "John " & "Doe"
Const CR = CHR$(13)
Const BOO = MyFunction()
```

See Also

Statements: Def, Dim, and Global

Date, Date$

Date and Time

Sets the system date.

Date accepts string, Variant 7 (Date), and Variant 8 (String) data type; Date$ accepts only String data type.

Syntax

Date[**$**] = *dateexpression*

dateexpression can be any valid expression that evaluates to a valid date of the required formatting.

Usage Notes

Date will recognize the Short Date date format set in the international section of the WIN.INI file or any unambiguous date from January 1, 1980 through December 31, 2099. Dates outside the allowed range trigger an `Illegal function call` error (trappable error #5).

Passing an invalid date, such as "Dec 45, 1993" or any other expression that cannot be converted to a valid date, generates a `Type mismatch` error (trappable error #13) when used with the Date statement and an `Illegal function call` error (trappable error #5) when used with the Date$ statement.

The Date$ statement accepts a string formatted as mm-dd-yy, mm/dd/yy, mm-dd-yyyy, or mm/dd/yyyy. Any other formatting causes an `Illegal function call` error (trappable error #5).

If *dateexpression* in the Date statement is a Null, a `Type mismatch` error (trappable error #13) occurs. If *dateexpression* is a Null in the Date$ statement, an `Illegal use of Null` error (trappable error #94) is generated.

Examples

The following example shows Date statement valid date formats:

```
Date = "30 Dec 1992"
Date = "December 30 92"
Date = "Dec-30-1992"
Date = "12/30/92"
Date = #12-30-1992#
```

The following example shows Date$ statement valid date formats:

```
Date$ = #12/30/92#
Date$ = "12-30-92"
```

The following code generates an error because of incorrect formatting:

```
Date$ = "Dec-30-1992"              'error #5
```

A variable can be substituted for a literal date, as in this example:

```
MyDate = "01/01/1992"
Date$ = MyDate
```

Note

Some computers (most notably earlier models of PC, XT, and AT machines) may not retain the date change when the system is turned off, especially if permanently changing the date and time requires a command other than DOS Date or Time. See your computer documentation for details.

See Also

Functions: CVDate, Date and Date$, DateAdd, DateDiff, DatePart, DateSerial, DateValue, Day, Hour, Minute, Month, Now, Second, Time and Time$, Timer, Weekday, and Year.

Statements: Time and Time$

Property: DateCreated

Tip

The following entries in the WIN.INI file influence the date and time formatting:

```
[intl]
s1159=AM
s2359=PM
sDate=/
sTime=:
sShortDate=M/d/yy
sLongDate=dddd,MMMM dd,yyyy
```

DDEExecute

Dynamic Data Exchange

Sends a command to another application by way of an established channel.

Syntax

DDEExecute *channel*, *command*

channel is a DDE channel number returned by the DDEInitiate function.

command is a character expression that evaluates to a command recognized by the target application.

Usage Notes

If *command* is not recognized by the target application, a `The other application won't perform the DDE method or operation you attempted` error (trappable error #285) occurs.

If an invalid *channel* is passed to the DDEExecute statement, a `DDE conversation closed or changed` error (trappable error # 292) occurs.

Example

This example prints the current MS Word document, assuming that MS Word for Windows is already running.

```
nChannel = DDEInitiate("WinWord", "System")
DDEExecute nChannel, "[FilePrint]"
DDETerminate nChannel
```

See Also

Functions: DDEInitiate and DDERequest

Statements: DDETerminate and DDETerminateAll

Chapter 12, "OLE and DDE"

DDEPoke

Dynamic Data Exchange

Sends data to another application via an established DDE channel.

Syntax

DDEPoke *channel*, *item*, *data*

channel is a DDE channel number returned by the DDEInitiate function.

item is a string expression that evaluates to the name of a data item recognized by application.

data is a string containing data to send to an application; the string can be a literal string or an expression.

Usage Notes

data must be supplied in the plain text format.

The list of supported DDE conversation topics, items, and commands varies from application to application.

Example

Load cell A1 of the MS Excel spreadsheet with the number `1.234`.

This example assumes that MS Excel for Windows is already running.

```
Dim nChannel, cTopic, cWorksheet
nChannel = DDEInitiate("Excel", "System")
DDEExecute nChannel, "[New(1)]"
cTopic = DDERequest(nChannel, "Selection")
cWorksheet = Left(cTopic, InStr(1, cTopic, "!")-1)
DDETerminate nChannel
nChannel = DDEInitiate("Excel", cWorksheet)
DDEPoke nChannel, "A1", "1.234"
DDETerminate
```

See Also

Functions: DDE, DDEInitiate, and DDERequest

Statements: DDEExecute, DDETerminate, and DDETerminateAll

Chapter 12, "OLE and DDE"

DDETerminate

Dynamic Data Exchange

Closes the specified DDE conversation channel.

Syntax

> **DDETerminate** *channel*

channel is a DDE channel number returned by the DDEInitiate function.

Usage Notes

Quitting MS Access closes all DDE channels established by Access.

The DDETerminate statement closes only the specified link; its variation, the DDETerminateAll statement, closes all active DDE links except those links established in expressions attached to controls on forms or reports.

If an invalid *channel* is passed to the DDETerminate statement, or a subsequent call is made to an application whose DDE channel was closed with the DDETerminate statement, a `DDE conversation closed or changed` error (trappable error #292) occurs.

Example

Attempt to print a file after DDE channel closed:

```
nChannel = DDEInitite("WinWord", "System")
(...)                               'do something here
DDETerminate nChannel
DDEExecute nChannel, "[FilePrint]"      'error #292
```

See Also

Functions: DDE, DDEInitiate, and DDERequest

Statements: DDEExecute, DDEPoke, and DDETerminateAll

Chapter 12, "OLE and DDE"

DDETerminateAll

Dynamic Data Exchange

Closes all open DDE conversation channels.

Syntax

DDETerminateAll

Usage Notes

DDETerminateAll statement closes only DDE channels established in Access Basic code; it doesn't affect active DDE links attached to controls on forms or reports.

Quitting MS Access also closes all DDE channels established by Access.

If a subsequent call is made to an application whose DDE channel was closed with the DDETerminateAll or DDETerminate statements, a `DDE conversation closed or changed` error (trappable error # 292) occurs.

Example

To establish three DDE channels (links) with the "System" topic in three different Window applications (Microsoft Word, Borland Quattro Pro, and Microsoft Excel), and close all active DDE links with one statement:

```
nChannel1 = DDEInitiate("WinWord", "System")
nChannel2 = DDEInitiate("QPW", "System")
nChannel3 = DDEInitiate("Excel", "System")
(...)                              'Do something here...
DDETerminateAll                    'Close all active links
```

See Also

Functions: DDE, DDEInitiate, and DDERequest

Statements: DDEExecute, DDEPoke, and DDETerminate

Chapter 12, "OLE and DDE"

Declare

Function and Procedure

Declares an external procedure in a DLL (Dynamic Link Library).

Syntax

Declare [**Sub** | **Function**] *name* **Lib** *library* [**Alias** *alias*][(*arglist*)] [**As** *type*]

name is the name of the function to declare.

library is the name of the DLL file that contains the declared procedure.

alias is the name of the declared function as it appears in the DLL file.

arglist is a list of parameters (variables or values) required by the function.

type is the data type returned by the function.

Usage Notes

You must declare external procedures before using them; Access doesn't automatically load any DLLs except its own. All external procedures must be declared in the declarations section of any Access Basic code module and are available to all modules in the database.

Declare Sub... indicates that the declared procedure doesn't return a value. Because most DLLs are written in the C programming language or C++, a function that doesn't return a value would be declared as Void in the DLL. You may, however, declare any Void external function as a Function as well as a Sub.

Declare Function... indicates that the procedure returns a value of the type specified in the **As...** clause; you may also use standard Access Basic data type suffixes in the function name to denote the data type of the returned value. Allowed data types in the **As...** clause are Integer, Long, Single, Double, Currency, String, Variant and a user-defined type.

The optional *alias* is used only when the procedure is called by another name to avoid possible conflicts with Access reserved words and duplicate names in other libraries; the more practical reason is to shorten the usually long names of external procedures.

The exact syntax for *arglist* is as follows:

([**ByVal**] *variable* [**As** *type*] [,[**ByVal**] *variable* [**As** *type*]]...)

The keyword ByVal indicates that the argument is passed by value rather than by reference. When used with a numeric variable, the variable is converted into the data type specified in the **As...** clause. With string variables, the address of the null-terminated string is passed as the argument.

variable is a valid variable name with data of the type required by the function being called; you may use standard Access Basic data type suffixes to denote the data type and omit the **As...** clause. Any fixed-length strings passed as parameters to external procedures are converted into variable-length, null-terminated strings.

As type declares the type of the variable, the same as As type clause of the Declare statement; you may also use **Any** data type to override type checking.

Access can be vastly extended by calling functions from various dynamic-link libraries, such as those included with MS Windows, like USER.EXE. You may also want to write your own libraries that extend MS Access power, for instance, to supply serial communication capabilities. Or you can purchase any MS Windows-compatible commercial library.

Examples

The following functions are part of Windows and are included in various DLLs supplied with Microsoft Windows 3.1.

This function will exit Windows orderly unless DOS applications are active:

```
Declare Function ExitWindows Lib "User" (ByVal Nothing as Long, Msg2Dos) As Integer
```

The following function swaps left and right mouse buttons depending on the value of *i*:

```
Declare Function SwapMouseButton% Lib "User" (ByVal i%)
```

The following gets the handle of the window with input focus; this function returns an integer and doesn't accept any parameters:

```
Declare Function GetFocus% Lib "User" ()
```

See Also

Statement: Call

Chapter 13, "Extending Microsoft Access and Access Basic"

Def*Type*

Variables and Constants

Specifies the first letters of range names to which a particular data type will be set.

Syntax

Def*Int range [, range]...*
Def*Lng range [, range]...*
Def*Sng range [, range]...*
Def*Dbl range [, range]...*
Def*Cur range [, range]...*
Def*Str range [, range]...*
Def*Var range [, range]...*

range specifies the first letters of range names to which a particular data type will be set.

Usage Notes

The case of the letters in *range* is not significant.

The Def*Type* statement can be used only in the declarations section, and these definitions have a module-wide scope. Therefore, different ranges can be defined for different modules in the same database.

The Def*Type* statement must be placed before any external procedure declarations in the declarations section.

An explicit data type declaration always takes precedence over the Def*Type* declaration; Def*Type* doesn't affect user-defined data types.

If the *range* is defined as A-Z, variables with names starting with all ANSI characters default to the specified data type, and no further subranges can be included.

If you try to define *range* as, for instance, Z-A, the Access Editor reverses the order automatically and displays it as A-Z.

Example

In the next example, all variables starting with the letters A through D are defined as Integer data type; those starting with letters E through P are defined as String data type; variables starting with the letters R through Z are defined as Currency data type:

```
DefInt A-D
DefStr E-P
DefCur r-z
```

Variable *b* was defined as an Integer:

```
b = 17
Result = VarType(b)                        ' 2
```

Variable *z* was defined as a Currency:

```
z = 4.56
Result = VarType(z)                        ' 6
```

Variable *f* was defined as a String

```
f = "James Dean"
Result = VarType(f)                        ' 8
```

Variable *a* is explicitly redefined as String (originally defined as Integer with the DefInt statement above):

```
Dim a As String
a = "Mary Poppins"
Result = VarType(a)                        ' 8
```

See Also

Statements: Let and Type

Dim

Variables and Constants

Used to declare variables and allocate their storage.

Syntax

Dim *name* [([*subscripts*])] **As** *type* [, *name* [([*subscripts*])] **As** *type*]...

name is a variable name to declare.

subscripts describes the array's dimensions if an array is being declared.

type is the variable's data type.

Usage Notes

Variables in Access Basic must be declared before use only if the Option Explicit statement is included in the declarations section of a particular module; it is always wise to use Option Explicit to avoid misspelled variable names and related problems.

type may be Integer, Long, Single, Double, Currency, String (variable length string), String * n (fixed length string), Variant, a user-defined data type or an object (such as a Database, Table, Dynaset, and so on); arrays of objects are not allowed. *type* may be forced by using an appropriate Access Basic data type suffix with the variable name.

type must be defined separately for each declared variable. The following example, therefore, results in *a* and *b* being declared as a Variant, and only *c* as an Integer:

```
Dim a, b, c As Integer
```

The proper declaration is as follows:

```
Dim a As Integer, b As Integer, c As Integer
```

Declared variables are initialized at compile time as follows: numeric variables are initialized to `0`; Variant variables are initialized to Empty (`Variant VarType 0`); variable-length strings are initialized to zero; and fixed-length strings are filled with ANSI zeros (`Chr(0)`). Fields of user-defined types are initialized separately according to their data types.

Variables and arrays declared in the declarations section of a module are available to all functions and subroutines in that module; those declared inside the function or subroutine are local to that particular function or subroutine.

Arrays can be declared as *static* (with a predefined number of dimensions), or *dynamic* (declared with empty parentheses and redefined using the ReDim statement).

Arrays can have up to 60 dimensions and a range of subscripts from -32768 through 32767. An `Overflow` error occurs if this range is exceeded.

Storage requirements for a declared array can be calculated by multiplying the number of bytes required to store a particular data type by the number of array elements.

The OptionBase statement establishes the lower and upper bound for the array dimension.

If no Option Base statement is present in the declarations section of a particular module, the default lower bound for the array dimension is 0.

Examples

To declare variables with an Integer, Currency, and String (fixed length) data type:

```
Dim a As Integer, b as Currency, d As String * 20
```

To declare an Integer, Long, and Double variable:

```
Dim i%, j&, k#
```

The following three examples demonstrate various styles of defining arrays.

A single dimensional array with ten elements:

```
Dim a(10)
```

A two-dimensional array of 2500 elements (50 rows by 50 columns):

```
Dim a(50,50) As Integer
```

Another two-dimensional array:

```
Dim a(10, 10 To 20)
```

To declare a dynamic array and change its dimensions at runtime:

```
Dim aa() As String
(...)
ReDim aa(10,6 To 20)
```

See Also

Statements: Global, DefType, Erase, Option Base, Option Explicit, ReDim, Static, and Type

Access Basic Data Types

Do...Loop

Program Flow Control

Repeats a block of code as long as a condition is true or until it becomes true.

Syntax

Do [[**While** | **Until**] *condition*]
  [(...)]
  [**Exit Do**]
  [(...)]
Loop

or

Do
  [(...)]
  [**Exit Do**]
  [(...)]
Loop [[**While** | **Until**] *condition*]

condition can be any expression that evaluates to False (0) or True (nonzero).

Usage Notes

When *condition* is placed after the Do statement, the value of the condition is checked at the top of the loop. Consequently, control will be transferred to the statement following the loop from the line containing Do. If *condition* is placed after the loop, the condition will be checked at the bottom of the loop. The latter approach guarantees that the body of the loop is executed at least once.

You can negate a *condition* with the Not keyword: *Do Until condition...* is equal to **Do While Not** *condition...*

You can force an exit from a Do... loop with the Exit Do statement.

Example

This example loops as long as *i* is not more than 10; the condition is checked at the top of the loop:

```
i = 0
Do Until i > 10
        i = i + 1
Loop
```

The following code loops as long as *i* is not more than 10; the condition is checked at the bottom of the loop:

```
i = 0
Do
         i = i + 1
Loop While Not i > 10
```

The following is an example of an empty Do... loop. It doesn't do anything; it just halts execution of the program until midnight (when Timer returns 0).

```
start = Timer
Do
Loop Until Timer < start
```

Note

If you don't specify *condition*, in the form of a While or Until clause, you create an endless loop, as in the following:

```
Do
        i = i + 1
Loop
```

See Also

Statements: Exit, For...Next, and While...Wend

DoCmd

Program Flow Control

Executes an Access action.

Syntax

DoCmd *actionname* [*arguments*]

actionname is any character expression that evaluates to a valid action.

arguments is a list of parameters accepted by a particular action.

Usage Notes

The number and type of *arguments* varies from action to action; see the description of the appropriate Action for more detailed information.

The following actions cannot be directly executed from within Access Basic code, although they can be included in macros that are run with the DoCmd RunMacro statement: AddMenu, MsgBox, RunApp, RunCode, SendKeys, SetValue, StopAllMAcros, and StopMacro. Most of these actions can also be replaced with equivalent Access Basic functions or statements.

Example

You can run macros with the DoCmd statement, as shown in the following example:

```
DoCmd RunMacro "Move2End"
```

The following example uses DoCmd to execute two actions: the first one selects a table in the database window, and the second one copies it to a different database:

```
DoCmd SelectObject A_TABLE, "Phone calls", True
DoCmd CopyObject "Accounting"
```

See Also

Function: Shell

Chapter 17, "Actions Reference"

DoEvents (Statement)
DoEvents (Function)

Program Flow Control

Temporarily relinquishes control to the operating environment (Microsoft Windows).

Syntax

Statement:

DoEvents

Function:

DoEvents( )

Usage Notes

Because some programs may contain code that is CPU-intensive to the point that no other events can be processed, it is advisable to periodically yield control to Windows to process other events in the events queue. Using the DoEvents statement (a simulation of preemptive multitasking) periodically is also a sign of a well-behaved Windows program.

Microsoft recommends using the statement form of DoEvents instead of the function.

Note

Don't use DoEvents if other applications (or procedures within your application) interact with your program or data in any way during the time you have yielded control.

End

Program Flow Control

Ends an Access Basic procedure, function, or a code block.

Syntax

End [**Function** | **If** | **Select** | **Sub** | **Type**]

Usage Notes

End Function ends a function definition; it is automatically created by the Access Basic Editor for every new function.

End If ends a multiline If...Then code block; the Access Basic Editor splits Endif into End If automatically.

End Select ends a Select Case code block.

End Sub ends a subroutine definition; it is automatically created by the Access Basic Editor for every new subroutine.

End Type ends a user-defined data type definition.

End by itself ends program execution.

Example

The following function uses many forms of the End statement. This can be declared only in the declarations section of the code module:

```
Type EmployeeRec
        Name as String * 30
        Ssn as String * 9
        Salary as Long
End Type
```

The following function demonstrates many usages of the End... statement:

```
Function AllEndInOne()

        Dim Employee As EmployeeRec

        If Employee.Salary > 40000 Then
              MsgBox(Employee.Name & " makes less than $40000")
        Else
              MsgBox("Tax him more!")
        End If

        Select Case Employee.Salary
              Case 0 To 20000 : MsgBox("Raise it by 20%")
              Case 20001 To 40000 : MsgBox("Raise it by 2%")
              Case 40001 to 60000 : MsgBox("Raise it by 1%")
              Case Else : MsgBox("30% cut!")
        End Select

        'Terminate the program after a certain date
        If Date > #01/01/94# Then End


End Function
```

See Also

Statements: Exit, Function, If...Then...Else, Select Case, Stop, Sub, and Type

Erase

Array Manipulation

Reinitializes the elements of a fixed array or deallocates dynamic-array storage.

Syntax

Erase *arrayname* [, *arrayname*]

arrayname is the name of an array to be manipulated.

Usage Notes

The effect of the `Erase` statement on fixed arrays depends on the type of array elements, as shown in the following table.

Element Type	*Effect*
Numeric	Sets each element to 0
Variable-length String	Sets each element to a zero-length string ("")
Fixed-length String	Sets each element to 0
Variant (any VarType)	Sets each element to Empty (Variant VarType 0)

For fixed arrays, no memory is recovered.

Erase frees the memory used by dynamic arrays; such an array must be redeclared (with the ReDim statement) before being used again.

For arrays of user-defined types, each element is set separately as if it were a separate variable.

Example

a, *b*, and *c* are previously initialized arrays:

```
Erase a, b, c
```

See Also

Statements: Dim and ReDim

Err

Error Handling

Sets the Err function to a specific value.

Syntax

Err = *n*

n is an expression that evaluates to a valid integer between 0 and 32767.

Usage Notes

The Err statement can be used to process user-defined errors and to simulate Access runtime errors.

STATEMENTS

Note

Don't use Access internal error numbers to define your own errors. Although the highest error number documented in Access manuals is 94, the highest error number actually returned by Access Version 1.0 is 3263. For safety, use error numbers starting with the number 32,767 and work backward.

Resume..., On Error..., Exit Sub, and Exit Function statements reset the Err statement to 0.

Example

The following example shows a user-defined error and message number 30000:

```
Message30000 = "You must enter your true age"

Age% = InputBox("Enter your age","0")
If Age% <= 0 Or Age% > 200
        Err = 30000

Endif
Select Case Err
Case 30000
        MsgBox(Message30000)
       (...)                   ' Process the error
EndSelect
Err = 0
```

See Also

Functions: Err, Error and Error$

Statement: Error

Also see the MS Access Errors table in the Que database included on the sample code disk.

Error

Error Handling

Simulates the occurrence of an error.

Syntax

Error *n*

n, an error code, is an expression that evaluates to a valid integer between 0 and 32767.

Usage Notes

The Error statement can be used to process user-defined errors and to simulate Access runtime errors; the latter is very practical while testing error-handling routines.

Error sets the Err statement to a specified error code *n*.

The Error statement executed without an error-handling routine halts the program execution and displays either an appropriate Access error message or the string `User-defined error` for error codes not used by Access errors.

Note

Don't use Access internal error numbers to define your own errors. Although the highest error number documented in Access manuals is 94, the highest error number actually returned by Access Version 1.0 is 3263. For safety, use error numbers starting with the number 32,767 and work backward.

Example

The following example forces a `Subscript out of range` error:

```
Error 9
```

See Also

Functions: Err, Error and Error$

Statement: Err

MSA Errors table in the Que database included on the sample code disk.

Exit

Program Flow Control

Exits a program flow control structure or a procedure.

Syntax

Exit Do | **For** | **Function** | **Sub**

Usage Notes

All forms of Exit provide the means to terminate a control structure (most often a loop), or a procedure, at any point. Exit is most often used with various forms of If and Select Case statements.

Exit Do exits a Do...Loop loop and transfers control to the statement following the Loop statement.

Exit For exits a For...Next loop and transfers control to the statement following the Next statement.

Exit Function and Exit Sub exit a user-defined function or a subroutine and transfer control to the statement following the statement that called the function or subroutine.

Example

To force an exit from the function Boo when the parameter value equals 100:

```
Function Boo(n)

        If n = 100 Then Exit Function
        (...)
End Function
```

See Also

Statements: Do...Loop, End, For...Next, Function, Stop, and Sub

For...Next

Program Flow Control

Repeats a block of code a specified number of times.

Syntax

For counter = *start* **To** *end* [**Step** *increment*]
    (...)
    [**Exit For**]
    (...)
Next [*counter* [, *counter*]]

counter is a numeric variable used as a counter.

start is the initial value of the counter.

end is the closing value of the counter.

increment indicates the amount the counter is incremented or decremented on each iteration of the loop.

Usage Notes

counter cannot be an array element or any part of a record. You can traverse the For... loop in either direction. By specifying a negative value for increment (an *end* greater than *start*), the *end* becomes the starting point and the loop executes until *end* is less than (or equal to) *start*.

If no increment is specified, *counter* is increased (or decreased) by 1.

Note

Do not change the value of the *counter* variable inside the For... loop, or else the loop may behave in an unexpected manner.

Example

This routine prints ANSI characters in the Immediate window. The outer loop executes a total of four times, and the inner loop executes a total of 256 times. (Note the step in the outer For... loop.)

```
sChr = ""
For i = 0 To 255 Step 64
        For j = 0 To 63
                sChr = sChr & Chr$(i + j)
        Next j
        Debug.Print sChr
        sChr = ""
Next i
```

See Also

Statements: Do...Loop and While...Wend

Function

Program Flow Control

Declares a function procedure in Access Basic code.

Syntax

[Static] [Private] Function *name* ([*argumentlist*]) [**As** *type*]
(...)
End Function

The keyword Static indicates that all variables declared inside the function behave like Static variables—that is, they preserve their values between calls to the function.

The keyword Private indicates that the function is accessible only to functions and subroutines contained in the same module.

name is the function name; it must follow Access Basic naming rules.

argumentlist is a list of arguments (parameters) passed to the function.

The **As** *type* determines the type of the value returned by the function.

End Function are the required keywords that mark the end of the function (exit point from the function).

Usage Notes

Use functions if you need to return a value to the calling statement. In Access Basic, the value is returned from a function by assigning it to the function name. If no value is returned explicitly, a function returns 0 if the function type is numeric, a zero-length string if the function type is string, or Empty if the function type is a Variant. If no explicit type of the returned value is specified, the default return value type ("function type") is a Variant.

Rather than the **As** *type* clause, you can use the data type identifier (suffix) in the function name.

Valid data types returned by a function are: Integer, Long, Single, Double, Currency, String, and Variant.

argumentlist has the following syntax:

> [**ByVal**] *variablename*[*()*] [**As** *type]* [, [**ByVal**] *variablename*[*()*] [**As** *type*]...]

ByVal indicates that the variable is passed by value, not by reference.

variablename is the name of the argument (parameter); empty parentheses are used to indicate an array. *variablename* can include the data type suffix.

As *type* indicates the data type of the argument. Allowed data types are Integer, Long, Single, Double, Currency, variable-length String, and Variant. Also allowed are objects (such as controls), but not arrays of objects, and user-defined types. Omit the *As type* clause if *variablename* includes the data type suffix (identifier).

Functions can be used in expressions wherever intrinsic Access Basic functions are allowed.

Calls to functions must include the parentheses around the *argumentlist*, or empty parentheses if there are no arguments.

You cannot define another function or subroutine inside a function or subroutine.

Make sure that the *As type* in the function name clause matches the argument data type (or the internal data type conversion if possible), or else a `Type mismatch` error (trappable error #13) will occur.

Example

The following is a function that preserves the value of a and b between calls unless called with a parameter of -1; declaring a and b variables inside this function (instead of the entire function) as Static would have the same effect.

```
Static Function CountBeans(n As Currency) As Currency
        Dim a, b
        a = a + n
        b = b + 1
        If n = -1 Then a = 0
        CountBeans = a       'returned value
End Function
```

Note

Functions can call themselves recursively (in other words, from within the same function), but it may lead to stack overflow and program crashes.

See Also

Statements: Declare, Dim, Global, Option Explicit, Static, and Sub

FreeLocks

Execution

Suspends processing to allow the database engine to release locks on record pages and update local dynasets in a multiuser environment.

Syntax

FreeLocks

Usage Notes

Use the FreeLocks statement periodically in multiuser applications to ensure that data in local dynasets is updated to keep it current. Normally, Access releases locks on record pages and updates local dynasets in the background, automatically, when no other processing occurs (including mouse movements). But in a processing-intensive multiuser environment, there may not be enough idle time to allow for such normal background processing; using the FreeLocks statement ensures that data in locked dynasets gets updated to keep it current.

FreeLocks is not needed in a single-user environment unless multiple copies of an application are run simultaneously.

Example

Use FreeLocks before and after potentially lengthy operations (when traversing a table, for example):

```
(..)
FreeLocks
Do Until cTable.EOF
      (..)
Loop
FreeLocks
(...)
```

See also

Function: OpenDatabase

Method: OpenTable

Property: LockEdits

Get

File I/O

Reads data from a disk file into a variable.

Syntax

Get[**#**]*filenumber*[, *recordnumber*], *variable*

filenumber can be any numeric expression that evaluates to a valid file number used in the Open statement to open the file.

recordnumber, for files opened in the Random mode, is the record number to read; for files opened in Binary mode it represents the byte at which to start reading data.

variablename is a name of the variable that stores data.

Usage Notes

If *recordnumber* is omitted, the read occurs at the next byte position (for Binary mode) or at the beginning of the next record (for Random mode).

The largest record number is 2,147,483,647 (the maximum long integer).

You may read data into a single array element, but not the entire array.

Invalid *filenumber* triggers a `Bad file name or number` error (trappable error #52).

While performing writes to a file open in Random mode, it is important that the actual length of the record being read matches the number declared in the Len clause of the Open statement: If the record is shorter than the declared length, it will be padded to the declared length with the contents of the file buffer. If the record is longer than its declared length, a `Bad record length` error (trappable error #59) occurs.

Make sure that the Len clause of the Open statement specifies the actual length of the record plus any overhead needed to identify the data type.

Data Type	*Actual Length Read*
String, variable length	2-byte descriptor (data type and length) and the actual variable
Variant (VarType 1-7)	2-byte descriptor (identifying the variant type 0 - 7) and the actual variable according to its data type specified below: Integer 2 bytes Long 4 bytes Single 4 bytes Double 8 bytes Currency 8 bytes Date 8 bytes

Data Type	*Actual Length Read*
Variant VarType 8 (string)	4-byte descriptor (identifying the VarType and the length of the string)and the actual string
Other data types	Actual data length; no extra overhead
User-defined types	Each element written individually; no padding between elements and no extra overhead

The preceding rules are also valid for files opened in the Binary mode, with two exceptions: The Len clause of the Open statement does not apply, and records are read continuously without padding. Variable-length strings (that don't belong to a user-defined type) are read literally without the 2-byte descriptor.

Example

To read data into a three-element array from a disk file opened for random access

```
Open "TEST.TXT" For Random As #1 Len = 10
For i = 1 To 3
        Get #1,,s(i)
Next
Close #1
```

See Also

Statements: Open, Put, and Write

Global

Variables and Constants

Declares application-wide variables and constants; allocates storage for global variables.

Syntax

Global *variable*[([*subscript*])] [**As** *type*] [,*variable*[([*subscript*])]...]

or

Global Const *constant* = *expression*

variable is the name of the variable being declared.

subscript is an optional array dimension if the variable is an array.

As *type* determines the type of the variable or array.

STATEMENTS

Usage Notes

Variables and constants declared with the Global keyword become visible to all modules in the current database (therefore, they are *global* in scope).

Global variables and constants can be declared only in the declarations section of a module.

Variables are initialized at compile time; numeric variables are initialized to 0, Variant variables to Empty (Variant VarType 0), variable-length strings are initialized to zero-length strings (""), and fixed-length strings are filled with zeros. Elements of user-defined data types are each treated as a separate variable and initialized to the proper data type.

Rather than the **As** *type* clause, you may use the data type identifier (suffix) in the variable name.

Valid types are Integer, Long, Single, Double, Currency, String * (fixed length), String (variable length), Variant, user-defined types and objects (such as controls), but not arrays of objects.

See the Dim statement for more information about declaring arrays.

Examples

The following examples show various usages of the Global statement:

```
Global Const APP_NAME = "Test"            ' constant
Global a() As String                      ' dynamic array
Global a(1 To 10)                         ' static array
Global b As Long                          ' variable
Global Kounter%                           ' integer variable
```

Note

Variables, constants, and arrays declared in Access Basic are not visible to Access macros and queries, even if they are declared as global.

See Also

Statements: Global, Dim, Option Base, ReDim, Static, and Type

GoSub...Return

Program Flow Control

Branch to and return from a block of code starting at a specified line.

Syntax

GoSub *label* | *linenumber*
(...)
label:
(...)
Return

label is the name (label) of the line to which control is transferred.

linenumber is the number of the line to which control is transferred.

Usage Notes

label must end with a colon and be placed in the same procedure (either function or subroutine) from which it is called; otherwise, the compile-time error `Label not defined in this procedure` occurs. *linenumber* must be a number (40 characters or less) without the terminating colon, and each *label* and *linenumber* must be unique within the module.

You cannot call a procedure defined as Sub (or a Function, for that matter) with the GoSub statement.

Tip

GoSub...Return adds a level of unnecessary complexity to code and should be considered archaic (it originated in BASIC before the dawn of structured programming); transferring control to another Function or Sub procedure is preferable.

Example

In the following code, the Return from label2 will never execute (although the control will be transferred properly).

```
Function NaughtyCode()

        GoSub label1
        GoSub label2
        (...)
        Exit Function
label1:
        (...)
        GoSub label3
        Return
label2:
        (...)
        GoTo label1
        Return
label3:
        Return

End Function
```

See Also

Statements: Do...Loop, For...Next, GoTo, If...Then...Else, and Select Case

GoTo

Program Flow Control

Transfer control to a specified line of code.

Syntax

GoTo *label* | *linenumber*

label is the name (label) of the line to which control is transferred.

linenumber is the number of the line to which control is transferred.

Usage Notes

label must end with a colon and be placed in the procedure (either function or subroutine) from which it is called; otherwise, the compile-time error `Label not defined in this procedure` occurs.

linenumber must be a number (40 characters or less) without the terminating colon. Each *label* and *linenumber* must be unique within the module.

There is no way to return to the calling line of code other than another GoTo.

Tip

Access Basic provides many better ways of transferring control to a block of code other than GoTo, such as Do...Loop, Select Case, If...Then...Else, and For...Next. Also, good structured programming practices recommend that each function or subroutine perform just one task and call other procedures to perform other chores. GoTo should be used sparingly, if at all; many unconditional branches (*spaghetti code*) make code difficult to follow and debug.

Example

An example of spaghetti code written using the GoTo statement:

```
Function BowlONoodles()
        GoTo label3

label1:
        (...)
        Goto label2

Label2:
        Exit Function

Label3:
        (...)
        GoTo label1

End Function
```

See Also

Statements: Do...Loop, For...Next, GoSub...Return, If...Then...Else, and Select Case

If...Then...Else

Program Flow Control

Conditionally executes a block of code.

Syntax 1

If *condition* **Then** *thenaction* [**Else** *elseaction*]

condition can be any valid expression that evaluates to False (0 or Null) of True (nonzero).

thenaction is the statement to execute when the condition is True.

elseaction is the statement to execute when the condition is False.

Syntax 2

If *condition1* **Then**
    action
[**ElseIf** *conditionN* **Then**
    [*action*]]
[**Else**
    [*action*]]
End If

condition1...conditionN can be any valid expression or an Access Basic object that evaluates to False (0 or Null) of True (nonzero).

action1...actionN is the statement or group of statements to execute.

Usage Notes

Syntax 1:

condition may test for the object type with the expression If TypeOf ... Is.... Consider the following example:

```
If TypeOf Forms!MyForm!LastName Is ComboBox Then (...)
```

The following objects can be used in the expression: BoundObjectFrame, CheckBox, ComboBox, CommandButton, Graph, Label, Line, ListBox, OptionButton, OptionGroup, PageBreak, Rectangle, SubForm, TextBox, ToggleButton, and ObjectFrame for unbound OLE object frames.

If *condition* is an object being evaluated with the Is TypeOf... expression, *condition* evaluates to True if the object is of the specified type.

Tip

Use the *short* syntax of If...Then...Else to evaluate brief and uncomplicated conditions; the multiline, *long* syntax is more readable for longer conditions.

Syntax 2:

If *condition* is an object being evaluated with the Is TypeOf... expression, *condition* evaluates to True if the object is of the specified type.

The If...Then...Else statement is evaluated from the top down: If *condition* is specified in the If...Then part is False, the ElseIf...Then parts are evaluated in order, and then the Else part is evaluated.

There can be as many Else and ElseIf blocks of code as necessary, but you may want to consider the Select Case statement to evaluate expressions that may have several possible values.

The entire If...Then...Else structure can be nested as deeply as necessary within other If..., Then..., Else..., and ElseIf parts.

An If...Then...Else statement must start on a separate line; only a line number or label can precede it.

Tip

The Access Editor separates Endif into End If automatically.

There is no perceptible speed difference between the *short* and *long* syntax of the If...Then...Else statement.

Examples

Syntax 1:

One-line If...Then transfers control to a subroutine labeled "Friday", as shown in the following example:

```
        If Weekday(Date)) = 6 Then Friday
        MsgBox("Workday, get busy...")          ' pat on the back...
        Shell("WINWORD.EXE", 1)                 ' fire up MS Word
        (...)                                   ' get some work done...
        Exit Function

Friday:
MsgBox("It's Friday!")
Exit Function
```

Syntax 2:

This example demonstrates the nested If...Then...ElseIf...Else statement:

```
szName = InputBox("Enter a name of a fruit")
```

```
If szName "Orange" Then
        MsgBox("It's an orange!")
ElseIf szName = "Apple"
        szColor = InputBox("Enter the color of the apple")
        If szColor = "Blue"
               MsgBox("Really?")
        ElseIf szColor = "Red"
               MsgBox("That's more likely...")
        ElseIf szColor = "Green"
               MsgBox("Baby boomer, huh?")
        Else
               MsgBox("No such apples...")
        End If
        Else
        MsgBox("Neither Apples nor Oranges...")
End If
```

See Also

Statement: Select Case

Function: IIf

Input

File I/O

Reads data from a sequential file into a memory variable.

Syntax

Input # *filenumber*, *variablelist*

filenumber can be any numeric expression that evaluates to a valid file number used in the Open statement to open the file.

variablelist is a variable, or a list of variables, that the data from the file is read into.

Usage Notes

A variable in *variablelist* cannot be an object variable, an array, or a user-defined type, but it can be an element of an array or an item of the user-defined type.

An `Input past the end of file` error (trappable error #62) occurs when the end of the file is reached while data is being read into variable(s).

STATEMENTS

The Input# statement displays slight variations in behavior depending on the type of variables in *variablelist*.

1. Reading numeric variables (all types):

The first nonblank character (and not a comma) is considered to be the start of valid data; the input ends with a space, a comma, or the end-of-line character. If data is invalid or a line in the input file is blank, 0 (zero) is assigned to the variable.

2. Reading string variables:

String variables are filled with data starting with the first nonblank character that is also not a comma. If the data is enclosed in quotation marks, the quotation marks are ignored and all characters up to the next quotation mark are read into the variable. If the string is not delimited with "", its beginning is the first nonblank character (but not a comma) and its end is a comma, space, or the end-of-line character. A zero-length string is assigned for blank lines in the input file.

3. Reading variant variables:

The Variant data is treated as shown in the following table.

Input	*Stored as*
No data (blank line or delimiters only	VarType 0 (Empty)
A valid number	VarType 2-6 as appropriate
Literal #NULL#	VarType 1 (Null)
Date/time literal (yyyy-mm-dd hh:mm:ss#)	VarType 7 (Date)
All other data	VarType 8 (String)

Example

To read the following line of data from file "TEST.TXT" into an array "a" and variables "b" and "c":

12345,"",#NULL#,"San Antonio","1939-9-17"

Type the following:

```
ReDim a(1 To 3) As String
Dim b As Integer, c As Date
Open "TEST.TXT" For Input As 1
Input #1, b, a(1), a(2), a(3), c
Close 1
```

Note

Data items in the file must match the data type of variables in *variablelist*; otherwise, the results may be unpredictable. For example, if you declare ln as Long, but the corresponding data item in the file is formatted as "12345678" (enclosed in quotes), 0 (zero) is read in ln.

See Also

Statements: Line Input #, Open, and Write#

Functions: Input and Input$

Kill

File I/O

Deletes file(s) from disk.

Syntax

Kill *filename*

Usage Notes

filename can contain the file name, path, and drive designation; valid operating system wild cards are allowed, except *shortcut*-type wild cards, such as the following:

`Kill "C:\TMP\."` (use "C:\TMP*.*" instead)

If you attempt to delete a file with file attributes set to read-only, or a file on a server to which you don't have sufficient rights to delete, you get a `Path/File access error` error (trappable error #75). Attempting to delete all files (`Kill "*.*"`) from an empty directory, a nonexisting file, or delete files from a write-protected floppy disk results in a `File not found` error (trappable error #53). Trying to delete a file in use by Access results in a `File already open` error (trappable error #55).

Example

To delete all files in the directory \BIN\VISICALC on drive C:

```
cPath = "C:\BIN\VISICALC\"
Kill cPath & "*.*"
```

See Also

Statement: RmDir

Let (anachronism)

Variables and Constants

Assigns the value of an expression or an object reference to a variable.

Syntax

Let *variable* = *expression*

Usage Notes

Let is an anachronism that is retained for compatibility purposes with early versions of BASIC and a programming style that went out of fashion many eons ago. It is always optional and should be considered obsolete; values can be assigned to variables without the keyword Let.

Example

Both of the following assignment statements are equivalent:

```
Let s = "Las Vegas"
s = "Las Vegas"
```

Line Input

File I/O

Reads a line from a sequential file into a variable.

Syntax

Line Input # *filenumber*, *variable*

filenumber can be any numeric expression that evaluates to a valid file number used in the Open statement to open the file.

variable can be any valid Access Basic variable name.

Usage Notes

The Line Input# statement is used to read one line at a time; the entire line, without the CR/LF characters, is read into the variable.

variable can be only a String or a Variant; a compile-time error occurs if *variable* used in the Line Input# statement is of any other data type.

If you define a variable as a fixed-length string that is shorter than the actual data line in the file, only the number of characters equal to the string length is read from each line.

Example

Read a single line from the file "TEST.TXT" into a variable-length string variable "s":

```
Dim s As String
Open "TEST.TXT" For Input As 1
Line Input #1, s
Close 1
```

See Also

Statements: Input # and Open

Functions: Input and Input$

Lock, Unlock

File I/O

Lock (unlock) a file or part of a file to prevent changes to the file by other users or processes.

Syntax

Lock[**#**]*filenumber*[, *record* | *start* **To** *end*]
(...)
Unlock[**#**]*filenumber*[, *record* | *start* **To** *end*]

filenumber can be any numeric expression that evaluates to a valid file number used in the Open statement to open the file.

record is the record or byte to lock/unlock.

start is the first record or byte to lock.

end is the last record or byte to lock.

Usage Notes

The Lock/Unlock pair is used to limit access to files, or parts of files, in the networking environment. The arguments in the Lock/Unlock pair must match, or else a `Permission denied` error (trappable error #70) occurs. Attempting to lock an already locked record results in the same error message.

There are four syntactical variations of Lock/Unlock, as described in the following table.

Syntax	*Description*
Lock/Unlock ...	Locks/unlocks the entire file
Lock/Unlock ..., *recordnumber*	Locks/unlocks only the specified record
Lock/Unlock ..., *start* To *end*	Locks the specified range of records
Lock/Unlock ..., To *end*	Locks/unlocks all records from the beginning of the file to the record specified by *end*

The meaning of the record/start/end clause of the Lock/Unlock statement depends on the file access mode, as shown in the following table.

Mode	*Meaning*
Binary	Number of bytes, relative to the beginning of the file. The first byte is byte 1.
Random	Number of records relative to the beginning of the file. The first record is record 1.
Other modes	Lock/Unlock affects the entire file regardless of values specified in *start* and *end*.

The arguments in matching Lock and Unlock pairs must match exactly.

Examples

To lock only record number 1 in the file "DATA.DAT" opened for Random access:

```
Open "DATA.DAT" For Random As 1

Lock 1
(...)
Unlock 1
```

To lock only records 30 through 35:

```
Lock 30 To 35
(...)
Unlock 30 To 35
```

To lock records from number 1 through 70:

```
Lock To 70
(...)
Unlock To 70

Close 1
```

Note

Lock/Unlock requires DOS Version 3.1 or later and SHARE.EXE (unless you are using Windows for Workgroups, which loads its own version of SHARE automatically).

See Also

Statement: Open

LSet

Strings

Copies and left-aligns expressions to a variable, or copies one variable of user-defined type to another variable of a different user-defined type.

Syntax

LSet *variable*, *expression*

or

LSet variable1, variable2

variable can be any valid Access Basic variable name.

expression can be an expression, a literal, or a variable.

variable1 and *variable2* are the names of user-defined data type variables.

Usage Notes

If *expression* is shorter than *variable*, *expression* is copied to *variable* and padded with spaces to the length of *variable*. If *expression* is longer than *variable*, characters beyond the length of *variable* are truncated. The same rules apply to copying data from one user-defined type variable to another.

LSet cannot be used to copy variables of user-defined types if either variable contains a variable-length string or a Variant data type.

Example

The first part of the code uses the LSet statement to copy the contents of the string variable "a" to a fixed-length string "s" (which is shorter than string "a"). The second part of the code uses the assignment operator to perform the same operation. Note the difference in the contents of string "s" after each assignment:

```
Dim s As String * 11, a$
a = "   This is a very long, right justified string....!"

LSet s = a                     ' "This is a v"


s = a                          ' "   This is "
```

See Also

Statement: RSet

Mid, Mid$

Strings

Replace part of one string with another string. There is no difference between the Mid and Mid$ statements.

Syntax

Mid[**$**](*variable*, *start*[, *length*]) = *expression*

variable is the variable name to modify.

start is the position within variable where the replacement begins.

length is the number of characters to replace.

expression is a variable or a literal string that replaces a part of *variable*.

Usage Notes

variable must be either a String or Variant VarType 8. *start* and *length* must be between 1 and 65535. If *length* is not specified, and the *length* of *expression* is equal to or less than the total number of characters in *variable* minus *start*, the entire *expression* is used in the replacement. If *start* is greater than the *length* of *variable*, a zero, or less than zero, an `Illegal function call` error (trappable error #5) occurs.

Example

To replace a portion of string "a" with the contents of string "b" starting with the 8th character in string "a":

```
a = "Paris, France"
b = "Texas "
Mid(a,8) = b          ' "Paris, Texas "
```

See Also

Functions: Mid and Mid$, and StrComp

MkDir

File I/O

Creates a new directory.

Syntax

MkDir *pathexpression*

pathexpression is a string expression that evaluates to a valid directory name, drive, and path formatted as [Drive:][\][directory[\directory...]].

Usage Notes

pathexpression must be less than 128 characters (DOS path length), or else an `Illegal function call` error (trappable error #5) is generated.

If the specified directory already exists, a `Path/File access` error (trappable error #75) is generated. The same error message is generated when the user doesn't have rights to create a directory on the server in the multiuser environment.

Passing the letter of a removable media drive without a disk in it results in a `Path not found` error (trappable error #76).

If *pathexpression* is a Null, an `Invalid use of Null` error (trappable error #94) occurs.

If the drive is not specified, the directory is created on the current drive.

Examples

The following example uses MkDir with a fully qualified path:

```
MkDir "D:\MDB\MARCH93"
```

The following creates a directory off the root directory on the current drive:

```
MkDir "\DUCKS"
```

The following creates a directory off the current directory on the current drive:

```
MkDir "FEATHERS"
```

Note

MkDir allows embedding spaces in directory names. Consider the following example:

```
MkDir "FBI CIA"
```

This creates a directory with this name that cannot be accessed or removed with standard DOS commands (MS Access can access it). Use the Access Basic RmDir statement to remove it from the disk.

This is not the same as the old DOS trick that allows embedding spaces in DOS file/directory names by inserting ANSI character 255 (which prints as a space) in the name.

See Also

Functions: CurDir and CurDir$, and Dir and Dir$

Statements: ChDrive, ChDir, ChDrive, and RmDir

MsgBox

See "MsgBox" in the functions section of the Reference.

Name

File I/O

Changes the name of a disk file or directory.

Syntax

Name *oldname* **As** *newname*

oldname is an expression containing the name of a file or a directory to rename.

newname is an expression containing the new name for a file or a directory specified in *oldname*.

Usage Notes

The Name statement is used to rename files and directories. Optionally, it is used to move files from one directory to another.

Name moves files to a directory specified in *newname* if the path specified in *newname* is different than the path in *oldname* (and not the current directory). If both paths are the same, or there is no path, the file specified in *oldname* is renamed to the name specified in *newname*. If both paths and file names are identical, a `File already exists` error (trappable erorr #58) is generated.

You cannot rename files opened by Access (or other applications); attempting to do so triggers a `File already open` error (trappable error #55).

If the file specified in *oldname* doesn't exist, a `File not found` error (trappable error #53) occurs. If the path specified in either *oldname* or *newname* doesn't exist, a `Path not found` error (trappable error #78) is generated. Specifying a letter for a nonexisting drive triggers a `Device unavailable` error (trappable error #68).

Example

To rename a file:

```
Name "ALOHA.DAT" As "GOODBYE.TXT"
```

To move a file from one directory to another and rename it:

```
Name "C:\CURRENT\SUMMER.DAT" As "E:\ARCHIVE\SUMMER93.DAT"
```

To rename a directory:

```
Name "C:\TMP" As "C:\TEMP"
```

See Also

Statement: Kill

On Error

Error Handling

Enables or disables an error handling routine.

Syntax

On Error GoTo *line* | **Resume Next**

line can be a line number or a label name unique in the current module.

Resume Next resumes program execution of the statement immediately following the statement that triggered the error.

Usage Notes

The error handler in Access Basic is a specially labeled block of code within the same procedure where the error occurred. It is activated with the On Error GoTo... statement. You cannot execute a function or a subroutine directly from the On Error... statement.

line specifies a valid line number or a label in the current procedure that will handle runtime errors; if *line* equals 0 (as in On Error GoTo 0), the error-handling routine in the current procedure is disabled.

On Error Resume Next doesn't reset the error code returned by the Err function; it therefore enables building in-line, error-handling routines in which an error handler (usually in the form of Select Case...) is placed after critical statements in the body of the procedure rather than in a separate block of code.

The error handler is active until one of the following statements is executed: On Error GoTo 0, Exit Function, Exit Sub, or Resume.

Error trapping in Access is not recursive—in other words, if an error occurs in the error-trapping routine, it cannot be processed by the same routine. If the error routine is cascaded (for example, an error triggers the application-wide error handler), control is passed to preceding calling procedures until an inactive error handler is found and the error condition is processed. Execution of the code continues from the current procedure.

Examples

The following example illustrates a general error-handling routine:

```
Function OneBigMess()
        ' Enable the error-handling routine for this function.
        On Error GoTo rorre                ' label name
        (...)
        Exit Function

' Error handler begins here.
rorre:
' First report the nature of the error to the user.
MsgBox(Error & ". Error number " & Str(Err))
' Process the error.
Select Case Err
        Case 7                      ' Out of memory, may be fatal.
                (...)
                Exit Function
        Case 11
                (...)
        Case 292
                (...)
End Select
Resume Next
End Function
```

This next example demonstrates activating an application-wide error handler. The error handler (in the form of IntergalacticErrorHandler( ) function) does away with coding possibly redundant error handlers in each procedure.

```
Function Errorshien
        On Error GoTo ReldnahRorre
        (...)
```

```
ReldnahRorre:
Result = IntergalacticErrorHandler(Err)
If Result = 1 Then
        Exit Function
Else If...
        (...)
        Resume Next
Else
        (...)
End If

End Function
```

Note

Don't use Access internal error numbers to define your own errors. Although the highest error number documented in Access manuals is 94, the highest error number actually returned by Access version 1.0 is 3263. For safety, use error numbers starting with the number 32,767 and work backward.

See Also

Functions: Err, Erl, and Error and Error$

Statements: Err, and Error and Resume

Chapter 14, "Error Handling"

MSA Errors table and application in Que database on the disk supplied with this book.

On...GoSub, On...GoTo

Program Flow Control

Branches to a line or label in the current procedure specified by the value of an expression.

Syntax

On *expression* **GoSub** *linelist*

or

On *expression* **GoTo** *linelist*

expression can be any valid Access Basic expression that evaluates to a valid number from 0 through 255.

linelist is a list of line numbers or line labels within the current Function or Sub procedure.

Usage Notes

The number specified in *expression* determines the item number from *linelist* to which to branch.

If *expression* evaluates to 0, or to a value greater than the number of items on the list, the On...GoSub/GoTo statement is ignored.

If *expression* evaluates to a value outside the allowed range (0-255), an `Illegal function call` error (trappable error #5) occurs.

Fractional numbers in the allowed range are rounded to an integer.

There may be as many items in *linelist* as can physically fit on the single command line, but no more than 255.

Specifying a nonexisting label/line number in *linelist* triggers the compile-time error `Label not defined in this procedure`.

Example

Branch to three different labels depending on the value of the parameter n:

```
Function OneBigBranch(n as Integer)

        ' Guard against invalid values.
        If Abs(n) > 3
                Exit Function
        End If

        On Abs(n) GoSub Smurf1, Smurf2, Smurf3
        (...)
        Exit Function

Smurf1:
        (...)
        Return
Smurf2:
        (...)
        Return
Smurf3:
        (...)
        Return

End Function
```

Note

The keyword Return can be used only with the On expression GoSub... statement. When used with the GoTo variation, a `Return without GoSub` error (trappable error #3) occurs.

See Also

Statements: GoSub...Return, GoTo, On Error, and Select Case

Function: Choose

Open

File I/O

Opens a file.

Syntax

Open *file* [**For** *mode*] [**Access** *access*] [*lock*] **As**[**#**]*filenumber* [**Len =** *reclen*]

file is a file name to open; it may be qualified with a path.

mode specifies the File Open mode: Append, Binary, Input, Output, and Random.

access specifies operations allowed on the open file: Read and Write.

lock specifies operations allowed on the file by other processes: Shared, Lock Read, Lock Write, and Lock Read Write.

filenumber specifies the Access handle to the file; an integer from 1 through 255.

reclen specifies the length of a record for files opened for Random access or the number of characters buffered for sequential access files.

Usage Notes

If the file specified in *filename* doesn't exist, it is created if a file is opened in Append, Binary, Output, or Random modes. If Input mode is specified, a `File not found` error (trappable error #53) occurs.

If *mode* is omitted, the file is opened in Random mode.

For files opened for Random access, the default value for *reclen* (which specifies the length of the record) is 128 bytes, and the maximum value is 32767. For files opened for sequential access, the default value of *reclen* (which specifies the size of the Read or Write buffer) is 512 bytes.

Description of the *mode* clause:

Append opens a file in sequential output mode; the file pointer is positioned at the end of the file.

Binary opens a file in random-access for input and output; Get and Put statements can be used to read and write anywhere in the file.

Input and *Output* open a file in sequential Input or Output modes, respectively.

Random opens a file with fixed-length records for input and output.

If the *access* clause is omitted for Binary and Output modes, Access first attempts to open the file for Read and Write, then for Write only. If both previous attempts fail, Access attempts to open it for Read only.

Description of the *lock* clause:

Shared *lock* enables limitless access to the file by all processes. Lock Read and Lock Write restrict the Read or Write access, respectively, to the current process only.

A `Permission denied` error (trappable error #70) occurs when a file is already opened by another process in a conflicting lock mode.

Read and Write mode is valid only for Binary, Random, and Append modes.

Files opened in Binary, Input, and Random modes can be opened with a different *filenumber* without being closed first; files opened in Append or Output modes must be closed before being opened again.

Example

```
Open "TEST.DAT" For Random Shared As 1 Len = 256
```

See Also

Functions: FreeFile and Seek

Statements: Close, Get, Put, Write, and Seek

Option Base

Array Manipulation

Declares the default lower bound for array subscripts.

Syntax

Option Base *number*

number is a number that establishes the actual lower bound for array subscripts.

Usage Notes

number must be either 0 or 1.

The Option Base command is optional; if missing, the lower bound for array subscripts defaults to 0.

The setting specified in Option Base can be overridden in an explicit declaration of an array subscript, such as:

```
ReDim a(1 To 20)
```

or

```
ReDim a(0 To 123)
```

Example

To set default lower bound for array subscripts to 1 in the declarations section:

```
Option Base 1
```

Note

Set Option Base before declaring any array dimensions, or else an Array already dimensioned error occurs.

See Also

Statements: Dim, Global, LBound, RBound, ReDim, and Static

Option Compare

Strings

Declares the default comparison mode of character data.

Syntax

Option Compare Binary | Database | Text

Usage Notes

The Option Compare statement specifies the mode of string comparisons for the module that is specified; different modules in a database can thus use different string comparison methods (although this approach is not advisable unless it serves a specific application need).

If Option Compare is not specified for a particular module, the default comparison method for this module is Binary.

Binary comparisons compare ANSI characters directly, therefore they are case-sensitive. For example, *M* (ANSI 77) is smaller than *m* (ANSI 109).

Text comparisons are not case-sensitive, and are based on the country code setting in the international section of the WIN.INI file. For example, *M* is equal to *m*.

Database comparisons depend on the sort order specified when the database was created or compacted in the Default Database Sort Order (available from the General Options selection of the Options submenu of the View menu). There are four sort options available in the US version of Access 1.0: General, Traditional Spanish, Dutch, and Nordic.

The Option Compare Database statement is placed by default in every module. There is currently no Access Basic facility to obtain this setting.

Example

In the declarations section of a module, place this statement to change the comparison method to Text (case-independent):

```
Option Compare Text
```

See Also

Functions: IsStr and StrComp

Option Explicit

Variables and Constants

Enforces explicit declaration of variables.

Syntax

Option Explicit

Usage Notes

The Option Explicit statement can be placed only in the declarations section of a module. It forces the explicit declaration of all variables before they are used in that module.

If Option Explicit is omitted, all undeclared variables are specified as Variant, unless the default type is specified with the **Def***type* statement. In other words, using the variable implicitly declares it.

Option Explicit prevents you from using any variable before it is declared. This enables the on-line syntax checker to recognize mistyped variable names. It is advisable to follow good programming practices and enforce explicit variable declaration.

Example

To enforce explicit variable declaration in a particular module, place this statement in the declarations section:

```
Option Explicit
```

See Also

Statements: Const, Def*Type*, Dim, Function, Global, Static, and Sub

Print

File I/O

Writes data to a sequential file.

Syntax

Print #*filenumber*, *expressionlist*[; | ,]

filenumber can be any numeric expression that evaluates to a valid file number used in the Open statement to open the file.

expressionlist contains a string or numeric items to be written to the file.

Usage Notes

If an item in *expressionlist* is delimited with a comma, the next character prints in the new print zone (print zones start every 14th column); if the delimiter is a semicolon, the next character prints immediately after the last character.

The *newline* character (ANSI 13 + ANSI 10) is inserted at the end of each *expressionlist* if neither the comma or the semicolon are included at the end of *expressionlist*.

If *expressionlist* is omitted, the Print# statement writes a blank line to the file.

An invalid *filenumber* triggers a `Bad file name or number` error (trappable error #52).

For use with the Print# statement, the file must be opened in Output or Append mode.

The Print# statement writes most of the data literally; however, when Variant data is written to the file, the following exceptions apply:

Value	*Action*
VarType 1 (Null)	Literal #NULL#.
VarType 0 (Empty)	Nothing.
VarType 7 (Date)	Date format and time formatted as the short date (same as specified in the WIN.INI file), unless some components of the date are missing.

Example

To use the Print statement with various delimiters produces different output:

```
a = "Today is"
b = "years remaining in the 20th Century"
Open "TEST.TXT" For Output As 1

' delimit tems with a semicolon
Print #1, a;  Date; 2001 - Year(Date); b

'delimit items with a comma
Print #1, a,  Date, 2001 - Year(Date), b
Close #1
```

The preceding code produces following output:

```
Today is1/20/93 8 years remaining in the 20th Century
Today is      1/20/93       8           years remaining in the 20th Century
```

See Also

Statements: Open, Put, Width, and Write

Put

File I/O

Writes the contents of a variable to a disk file.

Syntax

Put[**#**]*filenumber*[, *recordnumber*], *variable*

filenumber can be any numeric expression that evaluates to a valid file number used in the Open statement to open the file.

For files opened in Random mode, *recordnumber* is the record number to write; for files opened in Binary mode, it represents a byte at which to start writing data.

variablename is the name of the variable that stores data to be written.

Usage Notes

If *recordnumber* is omitted, the write occurs at the next byte position (for Binary mode) or at the beginning of the next record (for Random mode).

The largest record number is 2,147,483,647 (the maximum long integer).

You can reference only a single array element in variable name, but not the entire array.

An invalid *filenumber* triggers a `Bad file name or number` error (trappable error #52).

While you are performing writes to a file open in Random mode, it is important that the actual length of the record being written matches the number declared in the Len clause of the Open statement. If the record is shorter than the declared length, it will be padded to the declared length with the constants of the file buffer. If the record is longer than its declared length, a `Bad record length` error (trappable error #59) occurs.

Make sure that the Len clause of the Open statement specifies the actual length of the record plus any overhead needed to identify the data type.

Data Type	*Actual Length Written*
String, variable length	2-byte descriptor (data type and length) and the actual variable
Variant VarType 0 through 7	2-byte descriptor (identifying the variable type) and the actual variable according to its data type, as specified below: Integer 2 bytes Long 4 bytes Single 4 bytes Double 8 bytes Currency 8 bytes Date 8 bytes
Variant VarType 8 (string)	4-byte descriptor (identifying the `VarType` and the length of the string) and the actual string
Other data types	Actual data length; no extra overhead
User-defined types	Each element written individually; no padding between elements and no extra overhead

The preceding rules are valid also for files opened in the Binary mode, with two exceptions: The Len clause of the Open statement does not apply, and records are written continuously without padding. Variable-length strings that don't belong to a user-defined type are written literally without the 2-byte descriptor.

Example

The following example writes three elements of an array *s* to disk:

```
Open "TEST.TXT" For Random As #1 Len = 10
For i = 1 To 3
        Put #1,,s(i)

Next
Close #1
```

See Also

Statements: Get, Open, and Write

Randomize — Math

Initializes the random number generator.

Syntax

Randomize [*number*]

number must evaluate to a valid number.

Usage Notes

If *number* is omitted, the Randomize statement uses the value returned by the Timer function.

Note

Access uses the Rnd function to generate random numbers; numbers generated by Rnd are not truly random, because the Rnd function uses the previous random number as a seed for the next one and generates the same sequence of random numbers every time unless the seed number is also random or dynamic. The Randomize statement is used to initialize the random number generator with a new seed number to ensure that a different sequence of random numbers is generated by the Rnd function each time the routine is executed. Place it (without any argument) in a procedure that executes at the beginning of the program.

See Also

Functions: Rnd and Timer

ReDim — Array Manipulation

Declares dynamic arrays and allocates (or reallocates) their storage space.

Syntax

ReDim [**Preserve**] *name*(*subscripts*) [**As** *type*] [, *array*(*subscripts*) [**As** *type*],...]

Preserve specifies if data is preserved when the array dimensions are changed.

name is an array variable name to declare.

subscripts describes the array's dimensions.

type is its data type.

Usage Notes

type may be Integer, Long, Single, Double, Currency, String (variable length string), String * n (fixed length string), Variant, a user-defined data type or an object (such as Database, Table, Dynaset, and so on); arrays of objects are not allowed. *type* may be forced by using an appropriate Access Basic data type suffix with the array name.

The keyword *Preserve* enables resizing the array without losing data, but it applies only to the last dimension of the multidimensional array. The following example preserves data in the array. Changing the first dimension from 8 to 10, for example, erases data from the entire array.

```
ReDim a(8,5)
(...)
ReDim Preserve a(8,100)
```

Arrays can be declared as static (with a predefined number of dimensions) or dynamic, declared with empty parentheses and redefined using the ReDim statement.

The ReDim statement can be used repeatedly to change the dimensions of an array, but not to change the number of dimensions (doing so triggers the compile-time error `Wrong number of dimensions`).

Attempting to change the data type of the array triggers a `Duplicate definition` compile-time error.

You cannot use Dim to declare an array inside a procedure; doing so triggers a `Use Static or ReDim to dimension arrays in this procedure` compile-time error.

Arrays can have up to 60 dimensions and a range of subscripts from -32768 through 32767. An `Overflow` error occurs if this range is exceeded.

You can calculate storage requirements for a declared array by multiplying the number of bytes required to store a particular data type by the number of array elements.

Unlike in some other languages, *type* must be defined separately for each declared array. The following example therefore results in arrays *a* and *b* being declared as a Variant, and only *c* as an Integer.

```
ReDim a(7), b(3,3), c(4,20) As Integer
```

The proper declaration would be as follows:

```
ReDim a(7) As Integer, b(3,3) As Integer, c(4,20) As Integer
```

Declared arrays are initialized at compile time as follows: numeric variables are initialized to 0; Variant variables are initialized to Empty (Variant VarType 0); variable-length strings are initialized to zero-length strings, and fixed-length strings are filled with ANSI zeroes (Chr(0)). Items of user-defined types are initialized separately according to their data types.

Arrays declared in the declarations section of a module are available to all functions and subroutines in this module; those declared inside the function or subroutine are local to this function or subroutine.

If the Option Base statement is present in the declarations section of a particular module, the default lower bound for the array's dimension is 0.

Example

The following example shows you how to declare a dynamic array and change its dimensions at runtime in the declarations section:

```
Dim aa() As String
```

This example shows you how to declare a dynamic array and change its dimensions at runtime inside a procedure:

```
ReDim aa(10,6 To 20)
```

See Also

Statements: Global, Deftype, Dim, Erase, Option Base, Option Explicit, Static, and Type

Data Type: Access Basic

Rem

Miscellaneous

Indicates a comment ("remark") in the code.

Syntax

Rem *remark*

or

'*remark*

remark is any text a programmer wants to enter to annotate the code.

Usage Notes

If Rem follows other statements on the line, it must be separated by a colon; an apostrophe doesn't need a colon separator.

Any text preceded by either form of the Rem statement is treated as a comment by Access Basic and is not executed.

The statement Rem or an apostrophe (') can be used interchangeably to denote a comment in the code.

Comments are extremely helpful in understanding program logic, especially when describing unusual programming constructs and techniques.

Example

```
Rem This is a comment.
' This is also a comment.
Dim aa(4)                           'This is a comment, too.
aa(1) = "Winter" : Rem Another comment starts here.
```

Reset

File I/O

Closes all disk files opened with the Open statement.

Syntax

Reset

Usage Notes

The Reset statement flushes the contents of all file buffers and closes all files opened with the Open statement. Files opened directly by Access (such as databases) are not affected by this statement.

Example

This is a simple routine that copies one text file into another and demonstrates usage of the Reset statement.

```
Open "File1.txt" For Input As 1
Open "File2.txt" For Output As 2
Do While Not EOF(1)
        Line Input #1, cLine
        Print #2, cLine
Loop
Reset         ' Flush file buffers and close all files.
```

See Also

Statements: Close, End, and Open

Resume

Error Handling

Resumes program execution after handling a run-time error.

Syntax

Resume 0 | **Next** | *line*

Usage Notes

The Resume statement determines where execution of the program continues after an error-handling routine terminates.

The location of the error-trapping routine, rather than the location of the error, determines where the execution of the program resumes.

The Resume statement can be used only in error-handling routines activated with the On Error statement. Either the Resume or Exit Function | Sub statement must be placed in the error-handling routine, or else a `No resume` error is generated.

Resume 0: If an error occurred in the procedure where the error handler is located, execution continues with the statement that caused the error. If an error occurred in the procedure called from the procedure that contains the error handler, execution resumes with the most recently executed statement in the procedure that contains the error handler.

Resume Next: Execution resumes at the statement immediately following the one that caused the error or the most recently executed statement in the procedure called out of the procedure that includes the error-handling routine.

Resume *line*: Execution resumes at the specified line number or a label in the same procedure as the error handler.

Example

To use the Resume Next statement in an error routine:

```
Function ErrorExample
        On Error GoTo ReldnaHRorre

        (...)
        Error 93               'Trigger error.
        Exit Function

ReldnaHRorre:
        (...)
        Resume Next            ' will execute Exit Function.

End Function
```

See Also

Statement: On Error

RmDir

File I/O

Removes an existing directory.

Syntax

RmDir *pathexpression*

pathexpression is a string expression that evaluates to a valid directory name, drive, and path formatted as [Drive:][\][directory[\directory...]].

Usage Notes

pathexpression must be less than 128 characters (DOS path length), or else an `Illegal function call` error (trappable error #5) is generated.

A `Path/File access` error (trappable error #75) is generated when the user doesn't have rights to remove a directory on the server in a multiuser environment.

If *pathexpression* refers to a nonexisting directory or includes the letter of a removable media drive without a disk in it, a `Path not found` error (trappable error #76) occurs.

If *pathexpression* is a Null, an `Invalid use of Null` error (trappable error #94) occurs.

If the drive is not specified, the directory is assumed to be on the current drive.

Examples

The following example uses RmDir with a fully qualified path:

```
RmDir "D:\MDB\MARCH93"
```

The following example removes a directory off the root directory on the current drive:

```
RmDir "\DUCKS"
```

The following line removes a directory off the current directory on the current drive:

```
RmDir "FEATHERS"
```

See Also

Functions: CurDir and CurDir$, and Dir and Dir$

Statements: ChDrive, ChDir, ChDrive, and MkDir

Note

Access statement MkDir enables you to embed spaces in directory names. Consider the following example:

```
MkDir "FBI CIA"
```

This creates a directory which cannot be accessed or removed with standard DOS commands; however, MS Access can access it. Use the Access Basic RmDir statement to remove it from disk.

```
RdDir "FBI CIA"
```

This is not the same as an old DOS trick that allows embedding spaces in DOS file/directory names by inserting ANSI character 255 (which prints as a space) in the name.

RollBack

Database Manipulation

Reverses changes made in the pending transaction and ends it.

Syntax

Rollback

Usage Notes

Transaction is a logical block of code that manipulates data in a dataset. Transactions are most commonly used to ensure that all records involved in a logically related update operation are actually updated before changes are saved.

Access Basic transactions can be nested up to five levels deep and must be either saved (`CommitTrans`) or reversed (`Rollback`) from the lowest nesting level up. Every transaction must be terminated with either `CommitTrans` or `Rollback`. After the transaction is saved with the `CommitTrans` statement, you cannot undo the changes with the `Rollback` statement unless the transaction is nested within another pending transaction.

Transactions coded in Access Basic are performed independently of transactions performed in forms and reports; changes to tables made within a coded transaction are reflected in a form or report that uses this table only if the coded transaction is reversed with `Rollback`.

The error most likely to occur within a transaction is an `Operation not supported in transactions` error (trappable error #3246). This error can be triggered by an attempt to close the current table or database within a transaction.

Example

See the BeginTrans statement.

Note

You can bypass a pending transaction by executing an Access Action from within a transaction code block with the DoCmd statement; changes to data made in an action executed with DoCmd are affected by Rollback.

See Also

Statements: BeginTransaction and CommitTrans

Method: Update

Property: Transactions

RSet

Strings

Right-aligns a string within a variable.

Syntax

RSet *variable* = *expression*

variable can be any valid Access Basic character variable name.

expression can be any valid expression, a literal, or a variable.

Usage Notes

If *expression* is shorter than *variable*, *expression* is copied to *variable* and padded with leading spaces to the length of the *variable*. If *expression* is longer than *variable*, the expression is left-justified in *variable* and excess characters beyond the length of *variable* are truncated.

RSet cannot be used to copy variables of user-defined types into another variable.

Examples

The following examples show various ways to use the RSet statement.

In this example, *expression* is longer than *variable*:

```
Dim s As String * 5, a
a = "A left justified string    "
RSet s = a                                   ' s = "A lef"
```

In this example, *expression* is shorter than *variable*:

```
Dim s As String 10, a
a = "Aloha  "

RSet s = a                                   ' s = "     Aloha"
```

STATEMENTS

See Also

Statement: LSet

Seek

File I/O

Sets the position of the file pointer within an open file.

Syntax

Seek[**#**]*filenumber*, *position*

filenumber can be any numeric expression that evaluates to a valid file number used in the Open statement to open the file.

position is an expression that evaluates to a valid number and indicates the desired position of the file pointer.

Usage Notes

position for files opened in the Random mode is the record number; for all other modes, *position* is a byte position from the beginning of the file (the position of the first byte is 1).

An explicit record number in Get and Put statements overrides the current file pointer position.

Example

To use Seek with a disk file:

```
Open "TEST.TXT" For Input As 1
Seek 1, 4000             ' find byte 4000
cVar = Input(100, 1)     ' read 100 bytes
Close 1
```

See Also

Statements: Get, Open, and Put

Function: Seek

Select Case

Program Flow Control

Conditionally executes a block of code.

Syntax

Select Case *name*
[**Case** *expressionlist*
[(...)]]
[**Case** *expressionlist*
[(...)]]
[**Case Else**
[(...)]]
End Select

name is the name of a numeric or string expression.

expressionlist is an actual value (or a list of values) to test.

Usage Notes

If any value on an *expressionlist* matches the value of *name*, the matching block of code is executed up to the next Case clause; if no *expressionlist* matches the value of *name*, the Case Else is executed (if present). Control then passes to the line following End Select. Only the first matching Case clause is executed even when more than one *expressionlist* matches the *name*.

The general syntax of *expressionlist* is as follows:

expression [, *expression*, ...]
expression **To** *expression*
Is *comparison-operator expression*

Items on *expressionlist* can be single values, or expressions using any valid comparison operator except Like. The comparison operators can be used only in conjunction with the keyword **Is**. If the keyword **To** is used to specify the range of allowed values, the smaller value of the range must precede **To**, or else this particular Case won't execute even if *name* falls within the specified range. You can mix and match operators in expressions on *expressionlist* (see the example).

The general data type of *name* and the data type of items on *expressionlist* must be identical (in other words, if *name* is any numeric data type, items on *expressionlist* must be also of any numeric type, but not, for instance, String), or else a `Type mismatch` error (trappable error #13) occurs.

Example

To select Case with a numeric value (the second Case is true):

```
b = 3 : c = 4

Select Case b
        Case 1                      ' b = 1
                (...)
        Case 2 To 6, Is > 40, 14, -5  ' b falls into various ranges.
                (...)
```

STATEMENTS

```
        Case 128/c                      ' b = 128/c
                (...)
        Case Else
                (...)
End Select
```

To select Case with a character data:

```
a = "USA", b = Canada"
Select Case a
        Case "Germany"
                (...)
        Case InStr(a ,b) > 0, Is > "Venezuela"
                (...)
        Case "USA"
                (...)
End Select
```

Note

Overlapping program flow control structures are not allowed. Consider the following example:

```
Select Case nAmountDue
        Case < 1000 : cMessage = "Small"
        Case > 10000 : cMessage = "Big"
        If Date() = #01/01/93# Then
                Case > 1000000 : cMessage = "Gross!"
        End if
End Case
```

See Also

Statements: If...Then...Else, On...GoSub, and Option Compare

Functions: Choose, IIf, and Switch

SendKeys

Miscellaneous

Sends a series of keystrokes to the active window, simulating keyboard entry.

Syntax

SendKeys *keytext* [, *wait*]

keytext is a character expression representing a sequence of keystrokes to send to the active window.

wait is a Boolean expression that is either True (nonzero) or False (0). If the expression is False, the control to the procedure is returned immediately. If it is True, the action activated with the sent keystrokes must complete before control returns to the procedure.

Usage Notes

The SendKeys statement can send keystrokes only to other Windows applications; it cannot communicate with DOS applications running under Windows.

To send a printable character, use the character itself enclosed in double quotation marks. To send the letter *A*, for example, use SendKeys "A"; to send the sequence <ABCDEF???>, use SendKeys "<ABCDEF???>".

The key codes listed in the following table are used for nonprintable characters and other special keys.

Key	*Code(s)*
Backspace	{BACKSPACE}, {BS}, {BKSP}
Break	{BREAK}
Caps Lock	{CAPSLOCK}
Clear	{CLEAR}
Del	{DELETE}, {DEL}
Down Arrow	{DOWN}
End	{END}
Enter	{ENTER}, ~
Esc	{ESCAPE}, {ESC}
Help	{HELP}
Home	{HOME}
Ins	{INSERT}
Left Arrow	{LEFT}
Num Lock	{NUMLOCK}
Page Down	{PGDN}
Page Up	{PGUP}
Print Screen	{PRTSC}
Right Arrow	{RIGHT}
Scroll Lock	{SCROLLLOCK}
Tab	{TAB}
Up Arrow	{UP}
F1 through F16	{F1} through {F16}
Ctrl	^
Shift	+
Alt	%

Because some characters have a special meaning to the SendKeys statement, you must enclose them in braces if you send them as literal characters, as shown in the following table.

Character	*How to Send It*
{, }	{{}, {}}
+	{+}
^	{^}
%	{%}
~	{~}
(,)	{(}, {)}
[,]	{[}, {]}

A single keypress character can be sent multiple times using the {*keytext number*} sequence, for example:

```
SendKeys {A 12}          ' Sends "A" twelve times.
SendKeys {TAB 5}         ' Sends the tab character five times.
```

If the Shift, Ctrl, or Alt keys need to be pressed and held down while other keystrokes are sent, enclose the codes in parentheses. For example, to specify that the Shift key is held down while the Home key and a letter *A* are entered, use SendKeys "+(HOME A)".

SendKeys "%FX" specifies that the Alt key is held down while the letter *F* is entered, followed by the letter *X*.

Tip

If you send a sequence of keystrokes that take a long time to complete, change the cursor to an hourglass to inform the user that there is an operation taking place in the background.

Example

To close a running Windows application (dBFast DBMS in this case), use the following syntax:

```
AppActivate "dBFast-Executive"
SendKeys "%FQ"
```

See Also

Statement: DoEvents

Set

Variables and Constants

Assigns an object reference to a variable.

Syntax

Set *variable* = *object*

variable is the name of the variable that holds the reference to the object.

object is an expression containing the object name, a variable holding a reference to an object of the same type, or a function or method that returns an object.

Usage Notes

The Set statement creates a reference to the object, but not its copy. Thus, any changes to the object are reflected in the variable(s) that refer to this object.

variable that holds the reference to the *object* is required when referring to methods and properties applicable to this object.

Before accepting a reference to an object, *variable* must be declared (using a Dim, Global or Static statement) as one of the following object types: Control, Database, Dynaset, QueryDef, Report, Table, or Snapshot.

Example

The following example lists all table names and their creation dates in the current database:

```
Dim d As Database, s As Snapshot
Set d = CurrentDB()
Set s = d.ListTables()
Do While Not s.EOF
        Debug.Print s.Name, s.DateCreated
        s.MoveNext
Loop
```

See Also

Statements: Dim, Global, and Static

Static

Variables and Constants

Syntax

Static *name* [([*subscripts*])] **As** *type* [, *name* [([*subscripts*])] **As** *type*]...

name is a variable name to declare.

subscripts describes an array's dimensions if an array is being declared.

type is the type of variable or array.

Usage Notes

Static variables are variables that preserve their values for the duration of the program or until explicitly reinitialized. Using the Static statement, individual variables inside a procedure can be declared as Static, or the entire procedure (Sub or Function) can be declared as Static, making all variables declared in such a procedure implicitly static.

The *type* can be Integer, Long, Single, Double, Currency, String (variable length string), String * n (fixed-length string), Variant, a user-defined data type, or an object (such as a Database, Table, Dynaset, and so on). Arrays of objects are not allowed. *type* can be forced by using an appropriate Access Basic data type suffix with the variable name.

type must be defined separately for each declared variable; therefore, the following results in *a* and *b* being declared as Variant, and only *c* as an Integer.

```
Static a, b, c As Integer
```

The proper declaration is as follows:

```
Static a As Integer, b As Integer, c As Integer
```

Declared variables are initialized at compile time as follows: numeric variables are initialized to 0; Variant variables are initialized to Empty (Variant VarType 0); variable-length strings are initialized to zero-length strings; and fixed-length strings are filled with ANSI zeroes (Chr(0)). Fields of user-defined types are initialized separately according to their data types.

The Static statement must be used to declare fixed-sized arrays in nonstatic procedures (Dim or Static can be used in static procedures to declare a static array).

Arrays can have up to 60 dimensions and a range of subscripts from -32768 through 32767. An `Overflow` error occurs if this range is exceeded.

You can calculate storage requirements for a declared array by multiplying the number of bytes required to store a particular data type by the number of array elements.

If the Option Base statement is present in the declarations section of a particular module, the default lower bound for the array dimension is 0.

You cannot declare as Static an array that has already been declared.

Example

Using the Static statement; the variable "a" in function CountEmAll preserves its value between calls.

```
Function Caller()
        Dim a%, i%
        For i = 1 to 10
                a = CountEmAll(i)
        Next i
        Debug.Print a    '55 (1+2+3+4+5+6+7+8+9+10)
End Function

Static Function CountEmAll%(n)
        Dim a%
        a = a + n
        If n = 10 Then CountEmAll = a
End Function
```

See Also

Statements: Global, Deftype, Dim, Erase, Function, Option Base, Option Explicit, ReDim, Sub, and Type

Data Type: Access Basic

Stop

Program Flow Control

Suspends execution of an Access Basic program.

Syntax

Stop

Usage Notes

The Stop statement is a debugging tool that you can place anywhere in Access Basic program code.

You can restart the suspended program by selecting Continue or Single step from the Run menu in the Module window.

Stop doesn't close files or clear variables.

See Also

Statement: End

Sub

Program Flow Control

Declares a Sub procedure in Access Basic code.

Syntax

[Static] [Private] Sub *name* ([*argumentlist*])

(...)

End Sub

The keyword Static indicates that all variables declared inside the Sub behave like Static variables—that is, they preserve their values between calls to the Sub.

The keyword Private indicates that the Sub is accessible only to functions and subroutines contained in the same module.

name is the Sub name; it must follow Access Basic naming rules.

argumentlist is a list of arguments (parameters) passed to the Sub.

End Sub are required keywords that mark the end of the Sub (the exit point from the Sub).

Usage Notes

argumentlist has the following syntax:

[**ByVal**] *variablename*[*()*] [**As** *type*] [, [**ByVal**] *variablename*[*()*] [**As** *type*]...]

ByVal indicates that the variable is passed by value rather than by reference.

variablename is the name of the argument (parameter); empty parentheses are used to indicate an array.

variablename can include the data type suffix.

As *type* indicates the data type of the argument. Allowed data types are Integer, Long, Single, Double, Currency, variable-length String, and Variant. Also allowed are objects (such as Controls), but not arrays of objects, and user-defined types. Omit the *As type* clause if *variablename* includes the data type suffix (identifier).

Calls to Subs must include the parentheses around the argumentlist, but include no empty parentheses if there are no arguments.

You cannot define another Sub or subroutine inside a Sub or subroutine.

Sub procedures, unlike functions that can return a value, cannot be used in expressions; Sub procedures can, however, make changes to Global variables.

Example

The following is a specialized subroutine that displays a message in a message box with a constant title and icon; although you can directly use the MsgBox statement for this purpose, setting the attributes of the message box in a dedicated Sub procedure saves some coding.

```
Sub SubA
      InfoMessage("Today is " & Date)    'call another Sub
End Sub

Sub InfoMessage(cMessage)
      MsgBox cMessage, 64, "Test Application"
End Sub
```

Note

Subs can call themselves recursively (that is, from within the same Sub), but doing so may lead to stack overflow and program crashes.

See Also

Statements: Declare, Dim, Function, Global, Option Explicit, and Static

Time, Time$

Date and Time

Sets the system time.

Time accepts String, Variant 7 (date), and Variant 8 (string) expressions; Time$ accepts String.

Syntax

Time[**$**] = *timeexpression*

timeexpression can be any valid expression that evaluates to a valid time with the required formatting.

Usage Notes

Both Time and Time$ statements accept time values formatted with separators defined in the [intl] section of the WIN.INI file.

The Time statement accepts any unambiguous time from 00:00:00 (midnight) through 23:59:59 in the 24-hour (military) clock, and from 00:00:00 through 11:59:59 AM/PM in the 12-hour clock.

Values outside the allowed range passed to the Time statement trigger a `Type mismatch` error (trappable error #13). The Time statement can also accept an expression that evaluates to a valid time and date, such as "Jan 3, 1993 12:12:00".

The Time$ statement accepts only valid time values. Values outside the allowed range passed to the `Time$` statement trigger an `Illegal function call` error (trappable error #5), as does passing an invalid time such as "Dec 1, 1993 23:03:20" or any other expression that cannot be converted to a valid time.

STATEMENTS

The formatting of a string passed to the Time$ statement affects the precision of the time setting:

hh sets the hour, and resets the minute and the second to 0

hh:mm sets the hour and the minute, and resets the second to zero

hh:mm:ss sets the hour, the minute, and the second.

Any other formatting is considered an invalid time and causes an `Illegal function call` error (trappable error #5). AM/PM identifiers are allowed only if all three parts (*hh:mm:ss*) are specified.

If *timeexpression* in the Time statement is a Null, a `Type mismatch` error (trappable error #13) occurs; if *timeexpression* is a Null in the Times$ statement, an `Illegal use of Null` error (trappable error #94) is generated.

Examples

The following examples show valid formatting for the Time statement:

```
Time = "12:12PM"
Time = "Jan 31, 1993 23:58:59"
```

These examples show formatting for the Time$ statement:

```
Time$ = "12 PM"
Time$ = "22:14:14"
Time$ = "10:01:00 PM"

Time$ = "Dec 23, 1992, 12:00:00"                    ' error #5
Time$ = "1 AM"                                      ' error #5
```

Note

Some computers, most notably earlier models of PC, XT, and AT machines, may not retain the time change when the system is turned off, especially if permanently changing the date and time requires a command other than DOS `Date or Time`. See your computer documentation for details.

Tip

The following entries in the international section of the WIN.INI file determine date and time formatting:

```
[intl]
s1159=AM
s2359=PM
sDate=/
sTime=:
sShortDate=M/d/yy
sLongDate=dddd,MMMM dd,yyyy
```

See Also

Functions: CVDate, Date and Date$, DateAdd, DateDiff, DatePart, DateSerial, DateValue, Day, Hour, Minute, Month, Now, Second, Time and Time$, Timer, Weekday, and Year.

Statements: Date and Date$

Property: DateCreated

Type

Variables and Constants

Creates a user-defined data type with one or more elements.

Syntax

Type *usertype*
elementname **As** *typename*
[*elementname* **As** *typename*]
...
End Type

usertype is a name of a user-defined data type.

elementname is a name of an element of the user-defined data type.

typename is a data type of elementname: Integer, Long, Single, Double, Currency, String (varable-length string), String * n (fixed-length string), Variant, or another user-defined type—but not an object data type (such as Table).

Usage Notes

User-defined data types are used most often with data records (which usually contain a number of related elements).

The Type statement can be placed only in the declarations section of a module. Before using Type, you must declare its identifier (a variable of the user-defined type) either in the declarations section of a module or inside a procedure in this module, using a Static, Dim, or Global statement.

You cannot include line numbers and labels in the Type definition block.

Examples

To declare and use a user-defined data type named "Employee":

```
'In the declarations section
Type Employee
        LName As String * 20
        FName As String * 15
```

```
        Ssn As String * 9
        DateHired As Variant
        Salary As Long
End Type

Function UpdateEmpInfo
        Dim e as Employee
        e.Ssn = "123456789"
        e.Salary = 45678.00
        (...)
End Function
```

To declare and use a static array within a user-defined type:

```
'In the declarations section:
Type Train
        Engine As String * 20
        TotalWeigth As Long
        Car(200) As String * 10
        Kaboose As String * 10
End Type

Sub A_Train
        Dim t as Train
        t.Car(100) = "GM Cars"
        (...)
End Sub
```

TypeOf...Is... — Object Manipulation

Determines the type of a control.

Syntax

|**ElseIf TypeOf** *control* **Is** *controltype* **Then**

control is the control being tested (either a control variable or an explicit argument).

controltype is a reserved word indicating the possible types of controls; it can appear only in this statement.

Usage Notes

control can be a control variable declared with the As Control type specifier, or an expresion referring explicitly to a control.

This statement can test only one control at a time and cannot be combined with any other conditions on the same line.

The following reserved words can be used as *controltype*:

BoundObjectFrame	Label	PageBreak
BoundObjectFrame	Line	Rectangle

CheckBox	ListBox	SubForm
ComboBox	ObjectFrame	SubReport
CommandButton	OptionButton	TextBox
Graph	OptionGroup	ToggleButton

These reserved words do not have user-accessible numeric values associated with them.

Example

Evaluate the type of the current control. This function can be attached to any action property (such as OnEnter). Pass the control name as the parameter ("Button1" on form "Alpha", for example):

```
=TestTypeOf(Forms![Alpha].[Button1])

Function TestTypeOf (cCtrl As Control)
If TypeOf cCtrl Is TextBox Then
-------------------------------------------------------------
   cType = "TextBox"
ElseIf TypeOf cCtrl Is CommandButton Then
    cType = "Comman
dButton"
ElseIf TypeOf cCtrl Is ToggleButton Then
    cType = "ToggleButton"
Else
    cType = "Other type"
End If
MsgBox "The type of this control is " & cType
End Function
```

See also

Statement: If...Then...Else

Unlock

See the "Lock" statement.

While...Wend

Program Flow Control

Executes a block of code as long as a condition is True.

Syntax

While *condition*
(...)
Wend

condition is an expression that evaluates to False (0 and Null) or True (nonzero).

STATEMENTS

Usage Notes

condition is checked at the top of the loop; if *condition* is no longer True, control is transferred to the expression following the Wend statement.

The While... loop can be nested to any depth.

condition can be negated with the keyword **Not**.

Avoid branching to a label inside a While... loop; doing so may make it difficult to debug run-time anomalies.

Example

This empty While loop stops program execution for 15 seconds.

```
start = Second(Time)
While Not Second(Time) = start + 15
Wend
```

See Also

Statements: Do...Loop and For...Next

Width

File I/O

Specifies the maximum number of characters on a line output to a file.

Syntax

Width # *filenumber*, *width*

filenumber can be any numeric expression that evaluates to a valid file number used in the Open statement to open the file.

width is a numeric expression that specifies how many characters may appear on an output line.

Usage Notes

width can have a value from 0 through 255; 0 indicates that there is no limit to the number of characters that can be written on one line (it will wrap around at 512 characters). Values outside the allowed range trigger an `Invalid function call` error (trappable error #5).

You can change the width of the output line in the already opened file.

An invalid *filenumber* triggers a `Bad file name or number` error (trappable error #52).

Example

To specify different widths of an output line:

```
Open "TEST.TXT" For Output As 1
' Write 1530 letters "F" (it will take almost three lines).
For i = 1 To 1530
        Print #1, "F"
Next
' Now change the width.
Width #1, 153
' Now write 1530 letters "R" (on 10 lines).
For i = 1 To 1530
        Print #1, "R"
Next
Close #1
```

Note

The width# statement has no effect on writing long strings. The following statement, for example, still wraps around the 2000-character string at 512 characters.

```
Width #1, 100

Print #1, String(2000, "P")
```

See Also

Statements: Open, Print #, and Write

Write

File I/O

Writes comma-delimited data to a sequential file.

Syntax

Write # *filenumber* [, *expressionlist*]

filenumber can be any numeric expression that evaluates to a valid file number used in the Open statement to open the file.

expressionlist contains a string or numeric items to be written to the file.

Usage Notes

An invalid *filenumber* triggers a `Bad file name or number` error (trappable error #52).

Multiple items in *expressionlist* must be delimited with a comma; if *expressionlist* is omitted, the Write# statement writes a blank line to the file.

The *newline* character (ANSI 13 + ANSI 10) is inserted at the end of each *expressionlist*.

Write# inserts commas between items, and it places quotation marks around strings.

For use with the Write# statement, the file must be opened in Output or Append mode.

When Variant data is written to the file, the following exceptions apply the values described in the following table.

Value	*Action*
VarType 1 (Null)	Literal #NULL#
VarType 0 (Empty)	Delimiting commas, if any
VarType 7 (Date)	Date format and time formatted as #yyyy-mm-dd hh:mm:ss# unless a part of the date expression is missing

Use the Write# statement to programmatically export table fields to external programs that accept delimited data as an alternative to the Export operation accessible from the File menu.

Example

To write an expression to a disk file:

```
a = "Today is"
b = "years remaining in the 20th Century"
Open "TEST.TXT" For Output As 1
Write #1, a Date, 2001 - Year(Date), b
Close #1
```

This code produces the following output line in the TEST.TXT file:

```
"Today is",#1993-01-19#,8,"years remaining in the 20th Century"
```

See Also

Statements: Open and Print #

Access Error Messages

The following listing contains all error messages returned by Microsoft Access version 1.0. (The Access manual documents only errors from 3 through 94.)

The error number is returned by the **Err** function; the error message is returned by the **Error[$]** function. The '¦' characters in the error message are replaced by an actual name of a file, object, expression, and so on, as appropriate in the context in which the error message occurs.

You can also view this listing by choosing the MSA Errors button from the main menu of the Que database included on the sample code disk. Since versions of Access later than 1.0 may return different error messages, you can update the MSA Errors table with the Update Errors application included on the sample code disk.

3	Return without GoSub
5	Illegal function call
6	Overflow
7	Out of memory
9	Subscript out of range
10	Duplicate definition
11	Division by zero
13	Type mismatch
14	Out of string space
16	String formula too complex
17	Can't continue
19	No Resume
20	Resume without error
28	Out of stack space

35	Sub or Function not defined
48	Error in loading DLL
49	Bad DLL calling convention
51	Internal error
52	Bad file name or number
53	File not found
54	Bad file mode
55	File already open
57	Device I/O error
58	File already exists
59	Bad record length
61	Disk full
62	Input past end of file
63	Bad record number
64	Bad file name
67	Too many files
68	Device unavailable
70	Permission denied
71	Disk not ready
74	Can't rename with different drive
75	Path/File access error
76	Path not found
90	Compile error
91	Object variable not Set
92	For loop not initialized
93	Invalid pattern string
94	Invalid use of Null
280	DDE channel not fully closed; awaiting response from the other application.
281	No more DDE channels are available.
282	Can't open DDE channel; Microsoft Access couldn't find the specified application and topic.
283	Can't open DDE channel; more than one application responded.
284	DDE channel is locked.
285	The other application won't perform the DDE method or operation you attempted.

286	Timeout while waiting for DDE response.
287	Operation terminated because Esc key was pressed before completion.
288	The other application is busy.
289	Data not provided when requested in DDE operation.
290	Data supplied in a DDE conversation is in the wrong format.
291	The other application quit.
292	DDE conversation closed or changed.
293	DDE method invoked with no channel open.
294	Invalid link format; can't create link to the other application.
295	Message queue filled; DDE message lost.
296	PasteLink already performed on this control.
297	Can't set LinkMode; invalid LinkTopic.
298	The DDE transaction failed. Check to ensure you have the correct version of DDEML.DLL.
2000	Not enough memory to start Cue Cards.
2001	Operation canceled.
2002	Not Yet Implemented.
2003	¦ Not Yet Implemented.
2004	Out of memory.
2005	Not enough memory to start Microsoft Access.
2006	Not a valid document name: '¦'.
2007	You already have an open document named '¦'; you must close it before you can save or rename another document under the same name.
2008	Document '¦' is open; you must close it before deleting it.
2009	Document '¦' is open; you must close it before renaming it.
2010	Document '¦' is open; you must close it before cutting it.
2011	Not a valid password.
2012	This copy of Microsoft Access has expired. Please get a new copy from your Microsoft distributor.
2013	This copy of Microsoft Access hasn't been personalized properly. Please install Microsoft Access using the provided Setup program.
2040	Incompatible version of 'WIN87EM.DLL'; Microsoft Access can't run.
2041	CE FAILED. No error was reported, though. This is a bug!!
2042	Can't start Microsoft Access. Please try again.
2043	Can't find file: '¦'. Please verify that the correct path and file name are given.

2044 Currently unable to quit Microsoft Access.

2045 An argument in the command line used to start Microsoft Access wasn't valid and was ignored.

2046 Command not available: ¦.

2047 Incompatible version of 'MSABC100.DLL'; Microsoft Access can't run.

2048 Not enough memory to open '¦'.

2049 Name '¦' contains invalid characters.

2050 OLE/DDE Timeout must be from 0 to 300 seconds.

2051 The new name, '¦', is too long. Microsoft Access object names can't exceed 64 characters.

2052 Not enough system resources to update display.

2053 Wildcard characters aren't allowed in file name.

2054 Can't change to directory; path too long.

2055 Expression not valid: '¦'.

2056 Can't supply context-sensitive Help.

2057 Not enough stack memory left.

2058 Incompatible version of '¦'; Microsoft Access can't run.

2059 The selected name is too long for Microsoft Access.

2060 Can't create a field list on an action query: '¦'.

2061 Negative numbers aren't allowed.

2062 MSACCESS.INI is missing or isn't the correct version. Import/Export isn't available.

2063 Can't create, open, or write to index file '¦'.

2064 Not a valid menu bar value: '¦'.

2065 Not a valid name for a menu bar, menu, command, or subcommand: '¦'.

2066 A display driver resolution of at least 400 x 340 pixels is required to run Microsoft Access.

2067 The AddMenu action can be used only on a menu created by an OnMenu macro.

2068 Help isn't available for this command.

2069 The key combination '¦1' in '¦2' isn't valid and will be ignored.

2070 The key combination '¦1' in '¦2' is also assigned to another macro. Only the first one will be used.

2071 Cue Cards couldn't be started because of an incomplete setup.

2072 Outdated '¦' file. Please reinstall Microsoft Access.

2073 Specification doesn't exist in this database or has no columns defined.

2074 There was an error while attempting to communicate with Cue Cards.

2075 The other application couldn't be found in any of the directories in your PATH. Please check your AUTOEXEC.BAT file.

2076 The other application couldn't be started because the .EXE file isn't valid.

2077 This database currently has no import/export specifications.

2078 Help isn't available due to lack of available memory or improper installation of Windows or Microsoft Access.

2079 Entry Required!

2080 Application is corrupted.

2081 Specification has too many columns for that table.

2082 Specification column '¦' doesn't match a table column.

2083 Database is read only — cannot create specification tables.

2084 Start and width must be greater than 0.

2085 ODBC Refresh Interval must be in the range of 1-3600 seconds.

2086 Some Add-In menu entries couldn't be loaded because too many were specified.

2087 Add-In menu expression '¦' is too long and will be ignored.

2088 Add-In menu expression is empty and will be ignored.

2100 Can't place item at this location.

2101 The setting you entered isn't valid for this property.

2102 There is no form named '¦'.

2103 There is no report named '¦'.

2104 You already have a control named '¦'.

2105 Can't go to specified record.

2106 There were ¦ errors while loading.

2107 The value you entered is prohibited by the validation rule set for this field.

2108 The GoToControl action can't be executed until the field being edited is saved.

2109 There is no control named '¦'.

2110 Can't move to control ¦.

2111 Couldn't save the changes you made. Click OK to try again, or click Cancel to undo your changes.

2112 Can't paste item.

2113 The value you entered isn't appropriate for this field.

2114 Invalid file format; can't load bitmap from file ¦.

2115 Field or record can't be saved while it's being validated.

2116	Can't restore field's previous value; choose Undo Current Record or Undo Current Field from the Edit menu.
2117	Text too long.
2118	The Requery action can't be executed until the field is saved.
2119	The Requery action can't be used on control ¦.
2120	You must select an existing table or query to use a FormWizard or ReportWizard.
2121	Data corrupted; can't open form ¦.
2122	Can't view a form as a continuous form if it contains a subform or an unbound OLE object.
2123	Not a valid control name.
2124	Not a valid form name.
2125	The setting for FontSize must be from 1 to 127.
2126	The setting for ColumnCount must be from 1 to 255.
2127	The setting for BoundColumn can't be greater than the number of columns set with the ColumnCount property.
2128	The setting for RowSourceType must be Table/Query, Value List, Field List, or the name of a valid Access Basic fill function.
2129	The setting for DefaultEditing must be Data Entry (1), Allow Edits (2), or Read Only (3).
2130	The setting for GridX or GridY must be from 1 to 64.
2131	An expression can't be longer than 2,048 characters.
2132	The setting for DecimalPlaces must be from 0 to 15. You also can enter Auto (-1) for the default.
2133	A form can't be a subform within itself.
2134	The setting for Width must be from 0 to 22 inches (55.87 cm).
2135	You can't set this property; it's read-only.
2136	This property can be set only in Design view; it's read-only otherwise.
2137	Can't use Find or Replace for one of the following reasons: There are no fields to search; fields have no data; data in fields can't be searched.
2138	Can't search field because there was an error getting its value.
2139	Can't replace current value of field.
2140	Couldn't save field. Please undo and then choose Find or Replace.
2141	No match to replace in current field.
2142	The FindRecord action requires a FindWhat argument.
2143	Search Criteria wasn't specified; use the FindRecord action or the Find command.
2144	The setting for ListRows must be from 1 to 255.

2145	ColumnWidths must be one or more values from 0 to 22 inches (55.87 cm), separated by ';' or the list separator.
2146	Couldn't save field. Please undo and then choose the Editing Allowed command.
2147	Controls can be created only in Design view.
2148	The section ID is invalid.
2149	The item type is invalid.
2150	This control can't contain other controls.
2151	This control can't contain that type of control.
2152	Group levels can be created only in reports.
2153	Maximum number of group levels exceeded.
2154	Can't execute this function with the Sorting and Grouping box open.
2155	Access Basic compile error.
2156	Access Basic compile error. Do you want to see the error in context?
2157	The page header, footer, and margins are taller than the page.
2158	Print and graphics methods and their associated properties can be used only while printing or previewing a report.
2159	Not enough memory to initialize print or graphics methods.
2160	An error occurred while initializing print or graphics methods.
2161	FindWhat argument contains an invalid expression.
2162	Can't search data using current FindRecord action arguments.
2163	Page number given as an argument for the GoToPage action is out of range.
2164	Can't disable the control that has the focus.
2165	Can't hide the control that has the focus.
2166	Can't lock the control that has the focus.
2167	The setting for this property is read-only and can't be modified.
2168	The setting for this property can be changed only with the Object/Change Link command on the Edit menu.
2169	The record being edited can't be saved. If you close the form, the changes you've made to the record will be lost. Close anyway?
2170	Can't retrieve data for the list box.
2171	Subforms can't be nested more than three deep.
2172	Can't use a form as a subform if the form is bound to a crosstab query in which the column headings can vary.
2173	Can't search in current field '¦'.
2174	Can't end browse mode from this form event.
2175	Out of memory during search.

2176	The setting for this property is too long.
2177	Reports may only be embedded in other reports, not in forms.
2178	Can't add section. Doing so would exceed maximum combined section size limit. You must shrink one of the existing sections first.
2179	Couldn't open Palette.
2180	Couldn't open toolbox.
2200	Not a valid number.
2201	An error occurred while attempting to retrieve printer information for the ¦1 on ¦2.
2202	There is no default printer. Select or install one using the Windows Control Panel.
2203	COMMDLG.DLL failed: error code '0x¦'.
2204	The 'device=¦' entry in the WIN.INI file isn't valid.
2205	The default printer driver '¦.DRV' wasn't found. Reinstall using the Windows Control Panel.
2206	Not a valid page number.
2207	Can't print macros.
2220	Couldn't open file '¦'.
2221	Text would be too long; change canceled.
2222	This control is read-only and can't be modified.
2223	The file name '¦' is too long.
2224	Name '¦' contains invalid characters.
2225	Couldn't open the Clipboard.
2226	Can't paste.
2227	Data format error; can't paste.
2228	Can't load or save object.
2229	Can't start object's source application. Use the Windows Registration Info Editor (REGEDIT.EXE) to verify that the application is properly installed.
2230	Invalid source application name.
2231	Errors encountered during OLE operation. The problem ID is '¦'.
2232	You can't edit this object because it is no longer linked or wasn't created in an application that supports OLE.
2233	Can't break link; this object is open for editing.
2234	Can't paste OLE object.
2235	There are no registered source applications. Use the Windows Registration Info Editor (REGEDIT.EXE) to view installed servers.
2236	Must finish creating OLE object before saving.

2237 The text you enter must match an entry in the list.

2238 Not a valid OLE object.

2239 '¦' is corrupted or isn't a Microsoft Access database file. To repair, open non-read only.

2240 Unexpected data exchange error.

2241 The ¦ object is corrupted and might not be displayed properly.

2242 Problem communicating with object's source application.

2243 Can't paste OLE object.

2244 An unrecoverable error occurred while reading the file '¦'.

2245 Specified icon is corrupted.

2246 Can't run query; parameter values too large.

2247 The object in this field has been corrupted and can't be loaded.

2248 An error occurred while using an OLE object. Operation failed.

2249 An error occurred while communicating with the other application.

2250 Errors encountered while communicating with the source application. Some memory couldn't be returned to the system.

2251 The OLE object is linked to a file on an unknown drive.

2252 Couldn't establish network connection needed to link object.

2253 Not a valid name for the OLE object or document.

2254 Couldn't create requested new object.

2255 The source application couldn't open the document; link may not be valid. Use the Object/Change Link command to repair the link.

2256 An error occurred while the source application was executing a command.

2257 An error occurred trying to hide or display the object's source application.

2258 Couldn't carry out requested operation on object.

2259 Couldn't rename the object.

2260 An error occurred while sending data to the object's source application.

2261 The object's source application didn't supply the requested data.

2262 This value must be a number.

2263 The number is too large.

2264 Not a recognized unit of measurement.

2265 Must specify a unit of measurement.

2266 '¦' isn't a valid setting for RowSourceType property.

2267 Not enough disk space for printing.

2268 Not enough memory to load some library databases.

2269	Some library databases couldn't be loaded because too many were specified.
2270	Couldn't compile module in utility or library databases.
2271	[Libraries] section missing from MSACCESS.INI; FormWizards and ReportWizards won't be available.
2272	The setting for the Update Retry Interval must be from 0 to 1,000 milliseconds.
2273	The setting for Insert Retries must be from 0 to 10.
2274	The database '¦' is already open as a library database.
2275	The string returned by the builder was too long. Truncating result.
2276	The current window is not the window that invoked the builder. Builder failed.
2277	Error in font initialization.
2278	Can't save changes to this object because you don't have permission to write to the record. Copy the object to the Clipboard if you want to save it, then choose Undo Field.
2320	Can't display the field in which Total cell is 'Where'. Turn off the Show option for that field.
2321	Can't set criteria unless you've specified a field.
2322	Can't sort on fields added to the QBE grid with the asterisk.
2323	Can't have a Criteria clause on fields added to the QBE grid with the asterisk.
2324	Can't show Totals on fields added to the QBE grid with the asterisk.
2325	A field name in the LinkMasterFields property is too long.
2326	Value field can't specify Group By in the Totals cell. Specify a function.
2327	Column Heading field must specify Group By in the Totals cell.
2328	Can't run update queries for fields added to the QBE grid with the asterisk.
2329	Must specify one or more Row Heading(s), one Column Heading, and one Value.
2330	Can't create join: '¦'.
2331	Must specify at least one Row Heading as Group By.
2332	Can't match fields added to the QBE grid with the asterisk to a column or expression in an append query.
2333	Must specify destination table for query.
2334	'¦' is an action query and can't be printed.
2335	LinkChildFields and LinkMasterFields property settings must have the same number of fields.

3021	No current record.
3022	Can't have duplicate key; index changes were unsuccessful.
3023	AddNew or Edit already used.
3024	Couldn't find file '¦'.
3025	Can't open any more files.
3026	Not enough space on disk.
3027	Couldn't update; database is read-only.
3028	Couldn't start Microsoft Access because file 'SYSTEM.MDA' couldn't be opened.
3029	Not a valid account name or password.
3030	'¦' isn't a valid account name.
3031	Not a valid password.
3032	Can't delete account.
3033	No permission for '¦'.
3034	Commit or Rollback without BeginTrans.
3035	Out of memory.
3036	Database has reached maximum size.
3037	Can't open any more tables or queries.
3038	Out of memory.
3039	Couldn't create index; too many indexes already defined.
3040	Disk I/O error during read.
3041	Out-of-date database format.
3042	Out of MS-DOS file handles.
3043	Disk or network error.
3044	'¦' isn't a valid path.
3045	Couldn't use '¦'; file already in use.
3046	Couldn't save; currently locked by another user.
3047	Record is too large.
3048	Can't open any more databases.
3049	'¦' is corrupted or isn't a Microsoft Access database.
3050	Couldn't lock file; SHARE.EXE hasn't been loaded.
3051	Couldn't open file '¦'.
3052	MS-DOS file sharing lock count exceeded. You need to increase the number of locks installed with SHARE.EXE.
3053	Too many client tasks.
3054	Too many Memo or OLE object fields.

3055 Not a valid file name.

3056 Couldn't repair this database.

3057 Operation not supported on attached tables.

3058 Can't have Null value in index.

3059 Operation canceled by user.

3060 Wrong data type for parameter '¦'.

3061 ¦1 parameters were expected, but only ¦2 were supplied.

3062 Duplicate output alias '¦'.

3063 Duplicate output destination '¦'.

3064 Can't open action query '¦'.

3065 Can't execute a non-action query.

3066 Query must have at least one output field.

3067 Query input must contain at least one table or query.

3068 Not a valid alias name.

3069 Can't have action query '¦' as an input.

3070 Can't bind name '¦'.

3071 Can't evaluate expression.

3073 Operation must use an updatable query.

3074 Can't repeat table name '¦' in FROM clause.

3075 ¦1 in query expression '¦2'.

3076 ¦ in criteria expression.

3077 ¦ in expression.

3078 Couldn't find input table or query '¦'.

3079 Ambiguous field reference '¦'.

3080 Joined table '¦' not listed in FROM clause.

3081 Can't join more than one table with the same name (¦).

3082 JOIN operation '¦' refers to a non-joined table.

3083 Can't use internal report query.

3084 Can't insert into action query.

3085 Undefined function '¦' in expression.

3086 Couldn't delete from specified tables.

3087 Too many expressions in GROUP BY clause.

3088 Too many expressions in ORDER BY clause.

3089 Too many expressions in DISTINCT output.

3090 Resultant table may not have more than one Counter field.

3091	HAVING clause (¦) without grouping or aggregation.
3092	Can't use HAVING clause in TRANSFORM statement.
3093	ORDER BY clause (¦) conflicts with DISTINCT.
3094	ORDER BY clause (¦) conflicts with GROUP BY clause.
3095	Can't have aggregate function in expression (¦).
3096	Can't have aggregate function in WHERE clause (¦).
3097	Can't have aggregate function in ORDER BY clause (¦).
3098	Can't have aggregate function in GROUP BY clause (¦).
3099	Can't have aggregate function in JOIN operation (¦).
3100	Can't set field '¦' in join key to Null.
3101	Join is broken by value(s) in fields '¦'.
3102	Circular reference caused by '¦'.
3103	Circular reference caused by alias '¦' in query definition's SELECT list.
3104	Can't specify Fixed Column Heading '¦' in a crosstab query more than once.
3105	Missing destination field name in SELECT INTO statement (¦).
3106	Missing destination field name in UPDATE statement (¦).
3107	Couldn't insert; no insert permission for table or query '¦'.
3108	Couldn't replace; no replace permission for table or query '¦'.
3109	Couldn't delete; no delete permission for table or query '¦'.
3110	Couldn't read definitions; no read definitions permission for table or query '¦'.
3111	Couldn't create; no create permission for table or query '¦'.
3112	Couldn't read; no read permission for table or query '¦'.
3113	Can't update '¦'; field not updatable.
3114	Can't include Memo or OLE object when you select unique values (¦).
3115	Can't have Memo or OLE object in aggregate argument (¦).
3116	Can't have Memo or OLE object in criteria (¦) for aggregate function.
3117	Can't sort on Memo or OLE object (¦).
3118	Can't join on Memo or OLE object (¦).
3119	Can't group on Memo or OLE object (¦).
3120	Can't group on fields selected with '*' (¦).
3121	Can't group on fields selected with '*'.
3122	'¦' not part of aggregate function or grouping.
3123	Can't use '*' in crosstab query.
3124	Can't input from internal report query (¦).

3125	'¦' isn't a valid name.
3126	Invalid bracketing of name '¦'.
3127	INSERT INTO statement contains unknown field name '¦'.
3128	Must specify tables to delete from.
3129	Invalid SQL statement; expected 'DELETE', 'INSERT', 'PROCEDURE', 'SELECT', or 'UPDATE'.
3130	Syntax error in DELETE statement.
3131	Syntax error in FROM clause.
3132	Syntax error in GROUP BY clause.
3133	Syntax error in HAVING clause.
3134	Syntax error in INSERT statement.
3135	Syntax error in JOIN operation.
3136	Syntax error in LEVEL clause.
3137	Missing semicolon (;) at end of SQL statement.
3138	Syntax error in ORDER BY clause.
3139	Syntax error in PARAMETER clause.
3140	Syntax error in PROCEDURE clause.
3141	Syntax error in SELECT statement.
3142	Characters found after end of SQL statement.
3143	Syntax error in TRANSFORM statement.
3144	Syntax error in UPDATE statement.
3145	Syntax error in WHERE clause.
3146	ODBC—call failed.
3147	ODBC—data buffer overflow.
3148	ODBC—connection failed.
3149	ODBC—incorrect DLL.
3150	ODBC—missing DLL.
3151	ODBC—connection to '¦' failed.
3152	ODBC—incorrect driver version '¦1'; expected version '¦2'.
3153	ODBC—incorrect server version '¦1'; expected version '¦2'.
3154	ODBC—couldn't find DLL '¦'.
3155	ODBC—insert failed.
3156	ODBC—delete failed.
3157	ODBC—update failed.
3158	Couldn't save record; currently locked by another user.

3159	Not a valid bookmark.
3160	Table isn't open.
3161	Couldn't decrypt file.
3162	Null is invalid.
3163	Couldn't insert or paste; data too long for field.
3164	Couldn't update field.
3165	Couldn't open .INF file.
3166	Missing memo file.
3167	Record is deleted.
3168	Invalid .INF file.
3169	Illegal type in expression.
3170	Couldn't find installable ISAM.
3171	Couldn't find net path or user name.
3172	Couldn't open PARADOX.NET.
3173	Couldn't open table 'MSysAccounts' in SYSTEM.MDA.
3174	Couldn't open table 'MSysGroups' in SYSTEM.MDA.
3175	Date is out of range or is in an invalid format.
3176	Couldn't open file '¦'.
3177	Not a valid table name.
3178	Out of memory.
3179	Encountered unexpected end of file.
3180	Couldn't write to file '¦'.
3181	Invalid range.
3182	Invalid file format.
3183	Not enough space on temporary disk.
3184	Couldn't execute query; couldn't find linked table.
3185	SELECT INTO remote database tried to produce too many fields.
3186	Couldn't save; currently locked by user '¦2' on machine '¦1'.
3187	Couldn't read; currently locked by user '¦2' on machine '¦1'.
3188	Couldn't update; currently locked by another session on this machine.
3189	Table '¦1' is exclusively locked by user '¦3' on machine '¦2'.
3190	Too many fields defined.
3191	Can't define field more than once.
3192	Couldn't find output table '¦'.
3193	(unknown)

3194	(unknown)
3195	(expression)
3196	Couldn't use '¦'; database already in use.
3197	Data has changed; operation stopped.
3198	Couldn't start session. Too many sessions already active.
3199	Couldn't find reference.
3200	Can't delete or change record. Since related records exist in table '¦', referential integrity rules would be violated.
3201	Can't add or change record. Referential integrity rules require a related record in table '¦'.
3202	Couldn't save; currently locked by another user.
3203	Can't specify subquery in expression (¦).
3204	Database already exists.
3205	Too many crosstab column headers (¦).
3206	Can't create a relationship between a field and itself.
3207	Operation not supported on Paradox table with no primary key.
3208	Invalid Deleted entry in [DBASE ISAM] section in MSACCESS.INI.
3209	Invalid Stats entry in [DBASE ISAM] section in MSACCESS.INI.
3210	Connect string too long.
3211	Couldn't lock table '¦1'; currently in use.
3212	Couldn't lock table '¦1'; currently in use by user '¦3' on machine '¦2'.
3213	Invalid Date entry in [DBASE ISAM] section in MSACCESS.INI.
3214	Invalid Mark entry in [dBASE ISAM] section in MSACCESS.INI.
3215	Too many Btrieve tasks.
3216	Parameter '¦' specified where a table name is required.
3217	Parameter '¦' specified where a database name is required.
3218	Couldn't update; currently locked.
3219	Can't perform operation; it is illegal.
3220	Wrong Paradox sort sequence.
3221	Invalid entries in [Btrieve ISAM] section in WIN.INI.
3222	Query can't contain a Database parameter.
3223	'¦' isn't a valid parameter name.
3224	Btrieve—data dictionary is corrupted.
3225	Encountered record locking deadlock while performing Btrieve operation.
3226	Errors encountered while using the Btrieve DLL.
3227	Invalid Century entry in [dBASE ISAM] section in MSACCESS.INI.

3228	Invalid CollatingSequence entry in [Paradox ISAM] section in MSACCESS.INI.
3229	Btrieve—can't change field.
3230	Out-of-date Paradox lock file.
3231	ODBC—field would be too long; data truncated.
3232	ODBC—couldn't create table.
3233	ODBC—incorrect driver version.
3234	ODBC—server not responding.
3235	ODBC—data type not supported on server.
3236	ODBC—encountered unexpected Null value.
3237	ODBC—unexpected type.
3238	ODBC—data out of range.
3239	Too many active users.
3240	Btrieve—missing WBTRCALL.DLL.
3241	Btrieve—out of resources.
3242	Invalid reference in SELECT statement.
3243	None of the import field names match fields in the appended table.
3244	Can't import password-protected spreadsheet.
3245	Couldn't parse field names from first row of import table.
3246	Operation not supported in transactions.
3247	ODBC—linked table definition has changed.
3248	Invalid NetworkAccess entry in MSACCESS.INI.
3249	Invalid PageTimeout entry in MSACCESS.INI.
3250	Couldn't build key.
3251	Feature not available.
3252	Illegal reentrance during query execution.
3254	ODBC—Can't lock all records.
3255	ODBC—Can't change connect string parameter.
3256	Index file not found.
3257	Syntax error in WITH OWNERACCESS OPTION declaration.
3258	Query contains ambiguous (outer) joins.
3259	Invalid field data type.
3260	Couldn't update; currently locked by user '¦2' on machine '¦1'.
3261	¦
3262	¦
3263	Invalid database object.

Access Basic Constants

Constants are symbolic representations of values, such as numbers or strings, used in computer programs. Unlike variables, constants cannot be changed at runtime because the system (compiler, interpreter) replaces every occurrence of a constant with its value before executing the program. Using constants thus improves the readibility of computer programs by replacing values repeatedly used in the code with mnemonic abbreviations. Constants also simplify making changes since the change needs to be made just in one place (where the constant is defined) and the new value will be used wherever the constant is used.

By convention, constants are represented in uppercase letters. Many constants are defined in Access (in the UTILITY.MDA database to be exact) but constants can also be defined by the programmer, as shown in the following example:

```
Global Const APP_NAME = "Very Big and Complex Computer Program"
Global Const MAX_FILES = 255
```

The following example demostrates how constants can be used effectively to display a critical error message box with two buttons (Retry and Cancel) and a custom caption:

```
Const PANIC_BOX = MB_ICONSTOP + MB_RETRYCANCEL + MB_DEFBUTTON2
Const APP_NAME = "Nerve-Wracking Application"
MsgBox "Imminent system meltdown", PANIC_BOX, APP_NAME
```

Boolean Constants

The constants described in the following table are defined directly in Access.

Constant	*Value*
True	-1
False	0
Null	#NULL# Null value ("no data")

These constants are defined in the AbcConstants module of the UTILITY.MDA database included with Access, which means that you don't have to define them with the **Const** statement in every database that uses them. The values of these constants are expressed as decimal (or hexadecimal) numbers.

> **Note:** In version 1.0 you must load the UTILITY.MDA database (with the *UtilityDB=<path>UTILITY.MDA* entry in the [Options] section of the MSACCESS.INI file) to use these constants. Version 1.1 loads the UTILITY.MDA database automatically.

Variant Constants

Applicable to:

VarType function

Constant	*Value*	*Description*
V_EMPTY	0	Empty
V_NULL	1	Null
V_INTEGER	2	Integer
V_LONG	3	Long integer
V_SINGLE	4	Single
V_DOUBLE	5	Double
V_CURRENCY	6	Currency
V_DATE	7	Date/Time
V_STRING	8	String

Updatability of a Field

Applicable to:

ListFields method *Attribute* field

Constant	*Value*	*Description*
DB_AUTOINCRFIELD	16	Counter field
DB_FIXEDFIELD	1	Fixed-length field
DB_UPDATABLEFIELD	32	Updatable (editable) field
???	33	Fixed-length field
???	49	Counter field

Note: The constants for values indicated by ??? are not defined by Microsoft.

Type of Table or Query

Applicable to:

ListFields method *TableType* field

ListTables method *TableType* field

Constant	*Value*	*Description*
DB_TABLE	1	Access native table
DB_ATTACHEDTABLE	6	Attached table (dBASE, Paradox, etc.)
DB_ATTACHEDODBC	4	Attached table (ODBC)
DB_QUERYDEF	5	QueryDef object

Data Type of a Field

Applicable to:

ListFields method *Type* field

ListIndexes method *FieldType* field

ListParameters method *Type* field

Constant	*Value*	*Description*
DB_BOOLEAN	1	Yes/No
DB_BYTE	2	Number (Byte)
DB_INTEGER	3	Number (Integer)
DB_LONG	4	Number (Long)
DB_CURRENCY	5	Currency
DB_SINGLE	6	Number (Single)
DB_DOUBLE	7	Number (Double)
DB_DATE	8	Date/time
DB_BINARY	9	Binary data
DB_TEXT	10	Text
DB_OLE	11	OLE Object
DB_MEMO	12	Memo

Type of a Query

Applicable to:

ListTables method *Attribute* field

Constant	*Value*	*Description*
DB_QACTION	240	Action query, such as:
DB_QAPPEND	64	Append query
DB_QCROSSTAB	16	Crosstab query
DB_QDELETE	32	Delete query
DB_QMAKETABLE	80	Make Table query
DB_QUPDATE	48	Update query
DB_SYSTEMOBJECT	-2147483646	System query

Type of an Index

Applicable to:

ListIndexes method *IndexAttributes* field

Constant	*Value*	*Description*
DB_NONULLS	3	Null values are not allowed in the index
DB_PRIMARY	2	Primary index (key) for the table
DB_UNIQUE	1	Only unique values are accepted

Sorting Order

Applicable to:

ListIndexes method *FieldAttributes* field

Constant	*Value*	*Description*
DB_DESCENDING	1	The field is indexed in the descending order

Constants Used with Open... Actions

Default View Constants

Applicable to:

OpenForm action *view* argument

OpenQuery action *view* argument

OpenReport action *view* argument

Constant	*Value*	*Description*
A_NORMAL	0	Form view
A_DESIGN	1	Design view
A_PREVIEW	2	Print Preview view
A_FORMDS	3	Datasheet view (Forms only)

Data Mode Constants

Applicable to:

OpenForm action *datamode* argument

OpenQuery action *datamode* argument

OpenTable action *datamode* argument

Constant	*Value*	*Description*
A_ADD	0	Can add new records but not edit existing records
A_EDIT	1	Can edit existing and add new records
A_READONLY	2	No editing allowed

Window Mode Constants

Applicable to:

OpenForm action *windowmode* argument

Constant	*Value*	*Description*
A_NORMAL	0	Standard window
A_HIDDEN	1	Form is opened but it doesn't have focus
A_ICON	2	Form is opened as an icon (minimized)
A_DIALOG	3	Form is opened in a popup window

Constants Used with the Close Action

Applicable to:

Close action *Object type* argument

TransferDatabase action *transfertype* argument

Constant	*Value*
A_TABLE	0
A_QUERY	1
A_FORM	2
A_REPORT	3
A_MACRO	4
A_MODULE	5

Other Action Constants

Constants Applicable to DoMenuItem Action

Applicable to:

DoMenuItem action *Menu bar* argument

Constant	*Value*	*Description*
A_FORMBAR	0	Menu bar in Form view

Applicable to:

DoMenuItem action *Menu name* argument

Constant	*Value*	*Description*
A_FILE	0	File menu
A_EDITMENU	1	Edit menu
A_RECORDSMENU	3	Records menu

Applicable to:

DoMenuItem action *Command* argument (the usage depends on the value of the Menu name argument)

Constant	*Value*	*Description*
A_NEW	0	New
A_SAVEFORM	2	Save Form
A_SAVEFORMAS	3	Save form as...
A_SAVERECORD	4	Save record
A_UNDO	0	Undo
A_UNDOFIELD	1	Undo current field
A_CUT	2	Cut
A_COPY	3	Copy
A_PASTE	4	Paste
A_DELETE	6	Delete
A_SELECTRECORD	7	Select record
A_SELECTALLRECORDS	8	Select all records
A_OBJECT	14	Object
A_REFRESH	2	Refresh

Applicable to:

DoMenuItem action *Subcommand* argument (the usage depends on the value of the object type)

Constant	*Value*	*Description*
A_OBJECTVERB	0	First command on the object menu
A_OBJECTUPDATE	3	Update object

Constants Applicable to FindRecord Action

Applicable to:

FindRecord action *where* argument

Constant	Value	Description
A_ANYWHERE	0	Any part of field
A_ENTIRE	1	Match whole field
A_START	2	Start of field

Applicable to:

FindRecord action *direction* argument

Constant	Value	Description
A_UP	0	Search from the current record up
A_DOWN	1	Search from the current record down

Applicable to:

FindRecord action *Search in* argument

Constant	Value	Description
A_CURRENT	0	Current field
A_ALL	1	All fields

Constants Applicable to GoToRecord Action

Applicable to:

GoToRecord action *record* argument

Constant	Value	Description
A_PREVIOUS	0	Previous record
A_NEXT	1	Next record
A_FIRST	2	First record
A_LAST	3	Last record
A_GOTO	4	Record number
A_NEWREC	5	New record (add record)

Applicable to:

Print action *printrange* argument

Constant	*Value*	*Description*
A_PRINTALL	0	The entire object
A_SELECTION	1	The selected part of an object
A_PAGES	2	Range of pages

Constants Applicable to Print Action

Applicable to:

Print action *printquality* argument

Constant	*Value*
A_HIGH	0
A_MEDIUM	1
A_LOW	2
A_DRAFT	3

Constants Applicable to Quit Action

Applicable to:

Quit action *options* argument

Constant	*Value*	*Description*
A_PROMPT	0	Ask user whether to save an object
A_SAVE	1	Save an object without asking
A_EXIT	2	Quit without saving

Constants Applicable to TransferDatabase Action

Applicable to:

TransferDatabase action *transfertype* argument

Constant	*Value*	*Description*
A_IMPORT	0	Import object
A_EXPORT	1	Export object
A_ATTACH	2	Attach table

Constants Applicable to TransferText Action

Applicable to:

TransferText action *transfertype* argument

Constant	*Value*	*Description*
A_IMPORTDELIM	0	Import delimited text
A_IMPORTFIXED	1	Import fixed width text
A_EXPORTDELIM	2	Export delimited text
A_EXPORTFIXED	3	Import fixed width text

Microsoft Windows Constants Used in Access

These constants are used in Windows by convention and are meant to make code more readable for any Windows programmer. These constants are not predefined in Access; you must define them in the declarations section of a module using the statement **Const**. You may want to declare all constants as global to make them available to all modules in the application. Numeric values are expressed as hexadecimal numbers but may be referred to by a number in any base (such as decimal).

Constants Used with Message Box (Dialog Box)

Buttons Defined in a Dialog Box

Constant	*Value*	*Description*
MB_OK	0x0000	OK
MB_OKCANCEL	0x0001	OK and Cancel
MB_ABORTRETRYIGNORE	0x0002	Abort, Retry, Ignore
MB_YESNOCANCEL	0x0003	Yes, No, Cancel
MB_YESNO	0x0004	Yes, No
MB_RETRYCANCEL	0x0005	Retry, Cancel

Icons Displayed in a Dialog Box

Constant	*Value*	*Description*
MB_ICONHAND	0x0010	The stop sign icon
MB_ICONQUESTION	0x0020	The question mark icon
MB_ICONEXCLAMATION	0x0030	The exclamation point icon
MB_ICONASTERISK	0x0040	The “i inside a circle” icon
MB_ICONINFORMATION	MB_ICONASTERISK	
MB_ICONSTOP	MB_ICONHAND	

Default Message Box Button (Selected When the Box Appears)

Constant	*Value*	*Description*
MB_DEFBUTTON1	0x0000	The defined first button
MB_DEFBUTTON2	0x0100	The second defined button
MB_DEFBUTTON3	0x0200	The third defined button

Dialog Button Return Values (IDs)

Constant	*Value*	*Description*
IDOK	1	The OK button pressed
IDCANCEL	2	The Cancel button selected
IDABORT	3	The Abort button pressed
IDRETRY	4	The Retry button pressed
IDIGNORE	5	The Ignore button pressed
IDYES	6	The Yes button pressed
IDNO	7	The No button pressed

Constants Used with *PrtDevMode* Property

Constants used with the **PrtDevMode** PROPERTY are used to test which members of the data structure have been initialized.

To check for current version of Windows, use this constant: DM_SPECVERSION, defined as 0x30A.

Constant	*Value*
DM_ORIENTATION	0x0000001L
DM_PAPERSIZE	0x0000002L
DM_PAPERLENGTH	0x0000004L
DM_PAPERWIDTH	0x0000008L
DM_SCALE	0x0000010L
DM_COPIES	0x0000100L
DM_DEFAULTSOURCE	0x0000200L
DM_PRINTQUALITY	0x0000400L
DM_COLOR	0x0000800L
DM_DUPLEX	0x0001000L
DM_YRESOLUTION	0x0002000L
DM_TTOPTION	0x0004000L

Print Orientation

Constant	*Value*	*Description*
DMORIENT_PORTRAIT	1	Portrait (vertical)
DMORIENT_LANDSCAPE	2	Landscape (horizontal)

Paper Size

Constant	*Value*	*Description*
DMPAPER_FIRST	1	Letter 8 1/2 x 11 in
DMPAPER_LETTER	1	Letter 8 1/2 x 11 in
DMPAPER_LETTERSMALL	2	Letter Small 8 1/2 x 11 in
DMPAPER_TABLOID	3	Tabloid 11 x 17 in
DMPAPER_LEDGER	4	Ledger 17 x 11 in
DMPAPER_LEGAL	5	Legal 8 1/2 x 14 in
DMPAPER_STATEMENT	6	Statement 5 1/2 x 8 1/2 in
DMPAPER_EXECUTIVE	7	Executive 7 1/4 x 10 1/2 in
DMPAPER_A3	8	A3 297 x 420 mm
DMPAPER_A4	9	A4 210 x 297 mm
DMPAPER_A4SMALL	10	A4 Small 210 x 297 mm
DMPAPER_A5	11	A5 148 x 210 mm
DMPAPER_B4	12	B4 250 x 354
DMPAPER_B5	13	B5 182 x 257 mm
DMPAPER_FOLIO	14	Folio 8 1/2 x 13 in
DMPAPER_QUARTO	15	Quarto 215 x 275 mm
DMPAPER_10X14	16	10x14 in
DMPAPER_11X17	17	11x17 in
DMPAPER_NOTE	18	Note 8 1/2 x 11 in
DMPAPER_ENV_9	19	Envelope #9 3 7/8 x 8 7/8
DMPAPER_ENV_10	20	Envelope #10 4 1/8 x 9 1/2
DMPAPER_ENV_11	21	Envelope #11 4 1/2 x 10 3/8
DMPAPER_ENV_12	22	Envelope #12 4 \276 x 11
DMPAPER_ENV_14	23	Envelope #14 5 x 11 1/2
DMPAPER_CSHEET	24	C size sheet

Constant	*Value*	*Description*
DMPAPER_DSHEET	25	D size sheet
DMPAPER_ESHEET	26	E size sheet
DMPAPER_ENV_DL	27	Envelope DL 110 x 220mm
DMPAPER_ENV_C5	28	Envelope C5 162 x 229 mm
DMPAPER_ENV_C3	29	Envelope C3 324 x 458 mm
DMPAPER_ENV_C4	30	Envelope C4 229 x 324 mm
DMPAPER_ENV_C6	31	Envelope C6 114 x 162 mm
DMPAPER_ENV_C65	32	Envelope C65 114 x 229 mm
DMPAPER_ENV_B4	33	Envelope B4 250 x 353 mm
DMPAPER_ENV_B5	34	Envelope B5 176 x 250 mm
DMPAPER_ENV_B6	35	Envelope B6 176 x 125 mm
DMPAPER_ENV_ITALY	36	Envelope 110 x 230 mm
DMPAPER_ENV_MONARCH	37	Envelope Monarch 3.875 x 7.5 in
DMPAPER_ENV_PERSONAL	38	6 3/4 Envelope 3 5/8 x 6 1/2 in
DMPAPER_FANFOLD_US	39	US Std Fanfold 14 7/8 x 11 in
DMPAPER_FANFOLD_STD_GERMAN	40	German Std Fanfold 8 1/2 x 12 in
DMPAPER_FANFOLD_LGL_GERMAN	41	German Legal Fanfold 8 1/2 x 13 in
DMPAPER_USER	256	User-defined size

Note: For user-defined sizes, don't use the range between 50 and 56 when defining new paper sizes.

Paper Source

Constant	*Value*	*Description*
DMBIN_FIRST	1	Upper (or only) bin
DMBIN_UPPER	1	Upper (or only) bin
DMBIN_ONLYONE	1	Upper (or only) bin
DMBIN_LOWER	2	Lower bin
DMBIN_MIDDLE	3	Middle bin
DMBIN_MANUAL	4	Manual bin
DMBIN_ENVELOPE	5	Envelope bin
DMBIN_ENVMANUAL	6	Envelope manual bin

continues

Constant	*Value*	*Description*
DMBIN_AUTO	7	Automatic bin
DMBIN_TRACTOR	8	Tractor bin
DMBIN_SMALLFMT	10	Large format bin
DMBIN_LARGEFMT	11	Large capacity bin
DMBIN_CASSETTE	14	Cassette bin
DMBIN_LAST	14	Cassette bin
DMBIN_USER	256	Device-specific bins start here

Print Quality

Constant	*Value*	*Description*
DMRES_DRAFT	(–1)	Draft resolution
DMRES_LOW	(–2)	Low resolution
DMRES_MEDIUM	(–3)	Medium resolution
DMRES_HIGH	(–4)	High resolution

Color Printing Toggle for Color Printers

Constant	*Value*	*Description*
DMCOLOR_MONOCHROME	1	Off
DMCOLOR_COLOR	2	On

Duplex Printing

Constant	*Value*	*Description*
DMDUP_SIMPLEX	1	Duplex off
DMDUP_VERTICAL	2	Duplex vertical on
DMDUP_HORIZONTAL	3	Duplex horizontal on

C

ANSI Character Set

Character	*Hex code*	*ANSI code*
Backspace	&H08	8
Tab	&H09	9
Line feed	&H0A	10
Carriage return	&H0D	13
Space	&H20	32
!	&H21	33
"	&H22	34

Character	*Hex code*	*ANSI code*
#	&H23	35
$	&H24	36
%	&H25	37
&	&H26	38
'	&H27	39
(	&H28	40
)	&H29	41
*	&H2A	42
+	&H2B	43
,	&H2C	44
-	&H2D	45
.	&H2E	46
/	&H2F	47
0	&H30	48
1	&H31	49
2	&H32	50
3	&H33	51
4	&H34	52
5	&H35	53
6	&H36	54
7	&H37	55
8	&H38	56
9	&H39	57
:	&H3A	58
;	&H3B	59
<	&H3C	60
=	&H3D	61
>	&H3E	62
?	&H3F	63
@	&H40	64
A	&H41	65
B	&H42	66
C	&H43	67
D	&H44	68
E	&H45	69
F	&H46	70
G	&H47	71

Character	*Hex code*	*ANSI code*
H	&H48	72
I	&H49	73
J	&H4A	74
K	&H4B	75
L	&H4C	76
M	&H4D	77
N	&H4E	78
O	&H4F	79
P	&H50	80
Q	&H51	81
R	&H52	82
S	&H53	83
T	&H54	84
U	&H55	85
V	&H56	86
W	&H57	87
X	&H58	88
Y	&H59	89
Z	&H5A	90
[	&H5B	91
\	&H5C	92
]	&H5D	93
^	&H5E	94
_	&H5F	95
`	&H60	96
a	&H61	97
b	&H62	98
c	&H63	99
d	&H64	100
e	&H65	101
f	&H66	102
g	&H67	103
h	&H68	104
i	&H69	105
j	&H6A	106
k	&H6B	107
l	&H6C	108

Character	*Hex code*	*ANSI code*
m	&H6D	109
n	&H6E	110
o	&H6F	111
p	&H70	112
q	&H71	113
r	&H72	114
s	&H73	115
t	&H74	116
u	&H75	117
v	&H76	118
w	&H77	119
x	&H78	120
y	&H79	121
z	&H7A	122
{	&H7B	123
|	&H7C	124
}	&H7D	125
~	&H7E	126
‘	&H91	145
’	&H92	146
“	&H93	147
”	&H94	148
◦	&H95	149
–	&H96	150
—	&H97	151
Space	&HA0	160
¡	&HA1	161
¢	&HA2	162
£	&HA3	163
⊗	&HA4	164
¥	&HA5	165
¦	&HA6	166
§	&HA7	167
¨	&HA8	168
©	&HA9	169
ª	&HAA	170
«	&HAB	171

Character	*Hex code*	*ANSI code*
¬	&HAC	172
-	&HAD	173
®	&HAE	174
¯	&HAF	175
°	&HB0	176
±	&HB1	177
^{2}	&HB2	178
^{3}	&HB3	179
´	&HB4	180
µ	&HB5	181
¶	&HB6	182
•	&HB7	183
^{1}	&HB8	184
	&HB9	185
º	&HBA	186
»	&HBB	187
¼	&HBC	188
½	&HBD	189
¾	&HBE	190
¿	&HBF	191
À	&HC0	192
Á	&HC1	193
Â	&HC2	194
Ã	&HC3	195
Ä	&HC4	196
Å	&HC5	197
Æ	&HC6	198
Ç	&HC7	199
È	&HC8	200
É	&HC9	201
Ê	&HCA	202
Ë	&HCB	203
Ì	&HCC	204
Í	&HCD	205
Î	&HCE	206
Ï	&HCF	207

Character	*Hex code*	*ANSI code*
Ð	&HD0	208
Ñ	&HD1	209
Ò	&HD2	210
Ó	&HD3	211
Ô	&HD4	212
Õ	&HD5	213
Ö	&HD6	214
×	&HD7	215
Ø	&HD8	216
Ù	&HD9	217
Ú	&HDA	218
Û	&HDB	219
Ü	&HDC	220
Ý	&HDD	221
Þ	&HDE	222
ß	&HDF	223
à	&HE0	224
á	&HE1	225
â	&HE2	226
ã	&HE3	227
ä	&HE4	228
å	&HE5	229
æ	&HE6	230
ç	&HE7	231
è	&HE8	232
é	&HE9	233
ê	&HEA	234
ë	&HEB	235
ì	&HEC	236
í	&HED	237
î	&HEE	238
ï	&HEF	239
ð	&HF0	240
ñ	&HF1	241
ò	&HF2	242
ó	&HF3	243

Character	*Hex code*	*ANSI code*
ô	&HF4	244
õ	&HF5	245
ö	&HF6	246
÷	&HF7	247
ø	&HF8	248
ù	&HF9	249
ú	&HFA	250
û	&HFB	251
ü	&HFC	252
ý	&HFD	253
þ	&HFE	254
ÿ	&HFF	255

D
Bibliography

Are your lights on? How to Figure What the Problem Really Is

Authors: Donald C. Gause,

Gerald M. Weinberg

Dorset House Publishing, 1990

Fourth Generation Data

Author: Dan Tasker

Prentice Hall, 1989

Intelligent Databases

Author: Kamran Parsaye

John Wiley and Sons, 1989

Object Data Management

Author: R.G.G. Cattell

Addison-Wesley, 1991

Programming in Windows 3.1

Authors: Tim Farrell

Runnoe Connally

Que Corporation, 1992

Programming Windows 3.1, Third Edition

Author: Charles Petzold

Microsoft Press, 1992

The Relational Model for Database Management, Version 2

Author: E.F. Codd

Addison-Wesley, 1990

Using Windows 3.1, Special Edition

Authors: Ron Person

Karen Rose

Que Corporation, 1993

Windows Programmer's Guide to OLE and DDE

Author: Jeffrey D. Clark

Sams, 1992

Windows 3.1 Programmer's Reference

Author: James W. McCord

Que Corporation, 1992

Using InfoDesigner/Q

Relational databases are an essential tool in the modern information-management process, but effective use of the relational structure can require a good deal of education and experience in relational theory and database management. Most current database programs assume that the average designer has such an in-depth background. But many designers don't have such experience, and therefore waste time, money, and energy in a frustrating effort to create a workable database.

InfoDesigner rescues designers from this trap by providing an integrated collection of database design tools. These tools provide a step-by-step method to create effective relational databases. Both designers and clients interact with InfoDesigner in a natural (English) language format, avoiding the use of technical terms and cryptic symbols used by third-generation computer-aided software engineering (CASE) tools. This dialogue removes a critical communication barrier between the database designer and the software package—enabling designers to make full use of the potential of the software to create well-designed, efficient information-management systems. The InfoDesigner solution provides the following advantages:

- *Use of natural language.* Communication and articulation are two processes at the heart of relational database design. InfoDesigner is based on a *natural language input format*, which removes the communication and articulation barriers that CASE tools and fourth-generation languages such as SQL impose between the database designer and client, and between the designer and the database software.
- *Automation and integration.* Many CASE design tools are designed to function independently of database packages. This arrangement forces the designer to design the database in one software package and then manually transfer that design to another program to generate a database. Unlike these tools, InfoDesigner acts as an integrated CASE tool: after the design stage is completed, InfoDesigner automatically establishes the appropriate structures for the database program being used—without further effort on the part of the designer.

- *Freedom from the need for relational theory background.* In the past, designing a well-organized relational database required education and experience in relational theory and practice. Through its use of *Formal Object Role Modeling Language* (FORML), InfoDesigner effectively bypasses this requirement. The analyst can create informationally complete and relationally correct information systems without worrying about the complexities of foreign keys and functional dependencies.
- *Formalization of design method.* The FORML design method provides a step-by-step technique, beginning with a review of the application information as it exists naturally. The process is organized and thorough, and the result is a well-designed database. And because FORML is based on natural language, even the non-technical client can verify the accuracy of the designer's application.

To walk users through the FORML design method, InfoDesigner provides a suite of user-friendly tools, including the Fact Compiler and Diagrammer window, Validator, Table Browser, Report Generator, and Native Database Generator. The following section describes the InfoDesigner tools.

InfoDesigner Process and Tools

At the start of the design process, the information exists in a coherent and easily recognizable format, such as in a report, a client invoice, or some other "real-world" piece of information. This view of the information—the *external view*—is the view from which clients see their data and from which the designer begins to formulate a conceptual view. The *conceptual view* is information about data, articulated in simple, natural concepts. It is people-oriented and implementation-independent.

InfoDesigner uses two tools to produce the conceptual view: the *Fact Compiler* and the *Diagrammer Window*. Information on the data can be entered in text form via the Fact Compiler; the Diagrammer Window then displays a graphic view of the facts derived from that information. The graphic display helps to visually identify the relationships that exist between the facts and to ensure that the design accounts for all relationships. The user can easily move back and forth between the Fact Compiler and the Diagrammer Window.

When sample data has been entered, the designer verifies the accuracy of the design with the client and then runs the *Conceptual Model Validator* to ensure that relationships have been defined correctly. From this validated conceptual view, InfoDesigner automatically generates a *logical view*, in which data is stored in abstractions called *relations*. InfoDesigner's *Table Browser* allows the designer to review the relationships between the tables. Should additional information appear necessary at this stage, the designer can add that information, and it will be integrated automatically into the design stages created earlier.

Finally, InfoDesigner automatically plots the logical schema into a *physical view*—the actual implementation on a particular database technology. With the correctly normalized schema verified, validated, and documented, the designer can proceed with the actual database generation—with the push of a button. System tables, relationships, validation rules, keys, and indexes are created automatically.

InfoDesigner/Q

InfoDesigner/Q, included in this package, is a limited version of InfoDesigner, allowing a two-page maximum for any model. It includes a tutorial to guide you through the process of using this tool. Users interested in the theoretical dimensions of *object-role modeling* can find a brief summary at the end of this appendix.

To obtain the full benefits of InfoDesigner, you can upgrade from InfoDesigner/Q to the full-featured version InfoDesigner V1.0 by filling out the upgrade coupon in this manual. It is important to note that this is a one-time offer, and that only *original* upgrade coupons will be honored for the special price of $399. Upgrading makes you a fully licensed and registered user of InfoDesigner. You then are eligible for a variety of upgrade programs and future product-release information. You also have access to an information-modeling consulting program, which provides you with a fee-based consultant to discuss implementation of your database design with FORML. Extensive training also is available in introductory and advanced database design using object-role modeling.

Hardware and Software Requirements

To set up InfoDesigner/Q on your computer, follow the directions in the text file INFOQ.TXT on the InfoDesigner/Q floppy disk. To run this software, set up your environment as indicated in the following tables.

Hardware Specification	*Minimum Value*	*Recommended Value*
CPU	386	486
Speed	20 MHz	33 MHz
RAM	8 Mb	16 Mb
Free hard disk space	10 Mb	
Monitor resolution	VGA	SVGA
Mouse	Microsoft	
Floppy drive	3 1/2-inch high density	

Software Program	*Version*
MS-DOS	5.0
Microsoft Windows	3.1

Frequently Used Tools

When using the Diagrammer window, InfoDesigner tools can be very helpful. You can perform many functions faster with the *Toolbar* than with the pull-down menus (see fig. E.1). A description of the function of each button appears in the lower left corner of the screen when you place the mouse pointer over the button. You use the *Symbols palette* frequently in constructing diagrams (see fig. E.2); when you begin adding constraints to your model, you use the *Constraints palette* (see fig. E.3).

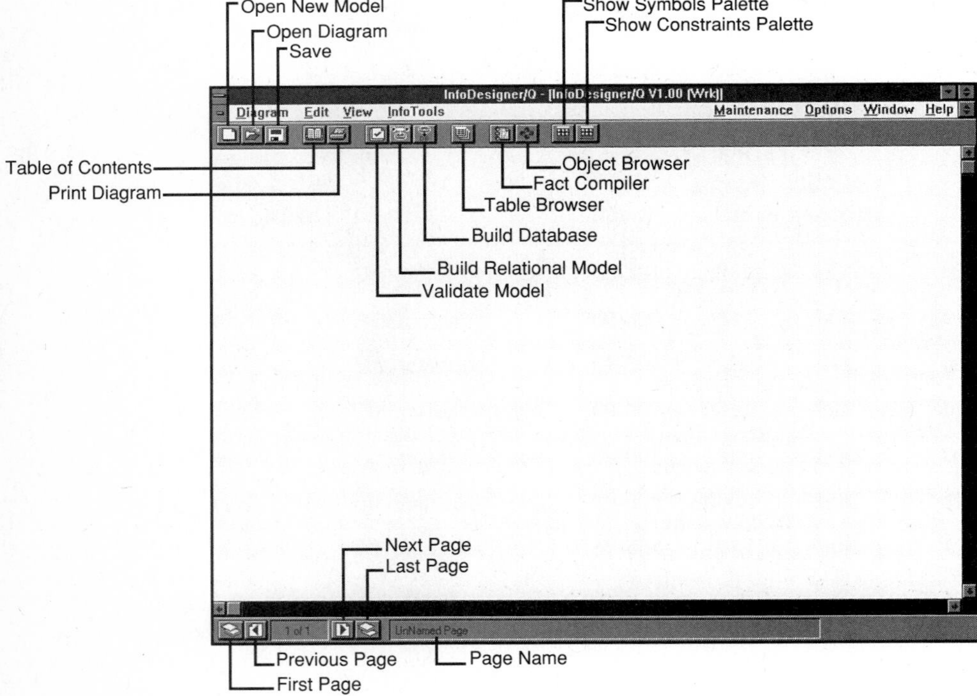

Figure E.1. The Diagrammer window.

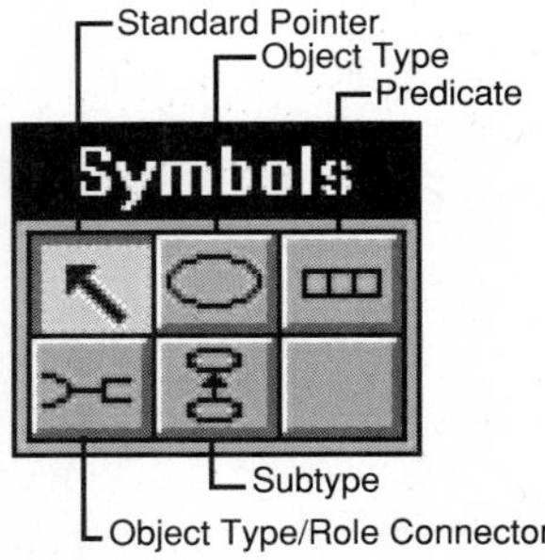

Figure E.2. The Symbols palette.

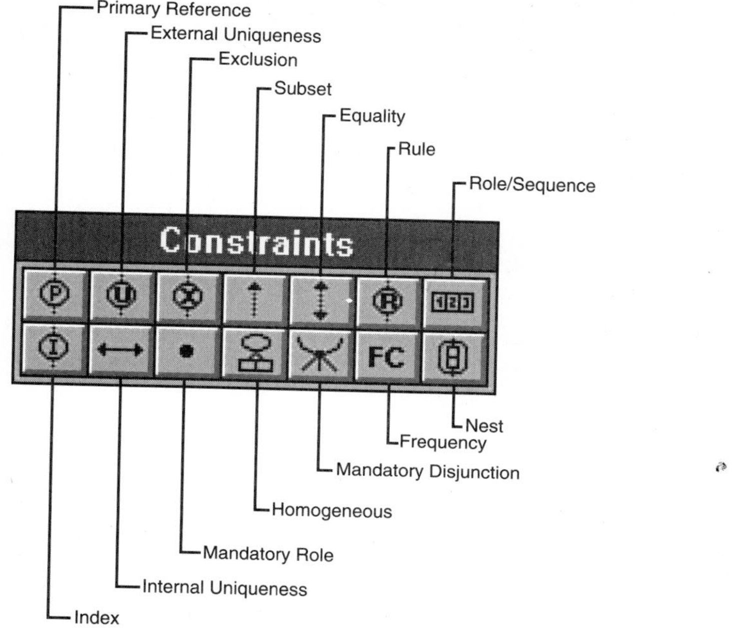

Figure E.3. The Constraints palette.

In this short tutorial in the following sections, you learn two ways of creating facts, objects, and constraints. You begin with the basics of conceptual diagramming, using the Symbols palette, the Constraints palette, and the dialog boxes associated with creating facts. Then you learn the fast way: using the Fact Compiler. The Fact Compiler allows you to type sentences and drag-and-drop them on the diagram. It provides a much more efficient way of modeling, because it reduces the total number of operations required by about 6 to 1. Your first task is to learn the fundamentals of diagramming, however, so that you can be proficient with the InfoDesigner tool set.

Managing Models

The highest level concept of InfoDesigner is that of a *repository*, which is a series of models and databases. InfoDesigner divides a model into *pages*. Each page represents a new idea, or set of facts, that forms a close conceptual grouping of the information to be modeled. This section shows you how to create, open, save, and close a model.

Creating a New Model

The first step in creating a new model is to name it. All new models begin with a single blank page to be used as a construction sheet for designing the model. The page appears in the Diagrammer window.

As your conceptual model expands, you can add pages as needed to accommodate the design. The model you are going to create in this example is for a hypothetical university administration system named Info University. It will be used to model information about instructors, departments, and course schedules.

To create a new model, follow these steps:

1. From the InfoDesigner menu, choose Diagram.
2. Select the New option (Ctrl+N). The New Model dialog box appears.
3. Type the name of the model. For this example, type **Info University1**.
4. Press Tab to move to the Description box.
5. Type the following: **A model of all facts associated with the administrative needs of Info University**.
6. Click OK to continue. The InfoDesigner Diagrammer window appears. `Info University1` appears in the InfoDesigner title bar.

Saving a Model

Use the Save button whenever you want to save changes to your model. Saving from time to time is a good practice; it protects against the accidental loss of data. To save a model, follow these steps:

1. From the InfoDesigner menu, choose Diagram.
2. Select the Save option (Ctrl+S). InfoDesigner saves the model to disk.

Closing a Model

You close a model when it is completed or when you finish a work session. Closing a model automatically saves all changes. To close a model, follow these steps:

1. From the InfoDesigner menu, choose Diagram.
2. Select the Close option (Ctrl+C). InfoDesigner removes the model from the computer's memory and clears the Diagrammer window.

Opening an Existing Model

You can use several methods to open an existing model. To open an existing model with the menu method, follow these steps:

1. From the InfoDesigner menu, choose Diagram.
2. Select the Open option (Ctrl+O). The Open Model Diagram list box appears.
3. Double-click the name of the model you want to open. For this example, double-click `Info University`. A listing for Version 1.00 of the Info University model appears.

4. Double-click the Version 1.00 entry. Listings for a working model and for draft revisions appear.
5. Double-click the Working Model listing.
6. Click OK. Page 1 of the Info University model appears. This is the model you will use for the rest of the tutorial.

In the next section, you learn how to create a fundamental component of object-role modeling: the object type.

Understanding Object Types

An *object type* is part of a *fact type*. Fact types are composed of a variety of components that help to formalize and express information correctly:

- One or more object types
- A predicate
- One or more roles
- One or more constraints
- Example data

FORML divides object types into two distinct categories: entities and values.

An *entity* is an object type that can be identified as a real object or concept in the real world, as it pertains to your application. For convenience, an entity in the real world needs some way of being uniquely referenced; in the case of an Instructor, for instance, an Instructor ID. You refer to an entity by a *reference mode*, which is a word or abbreviation that refers to a unique instance of an entity. Entities are represented in the model by solid ellipses.

A *value* is an object type that has no means of reference in your application's domain. Value object types are of two kinds: strings and numbers. *Strings* are sequences of characters or bits that can be stored in the computer; they can be compared with other strings, but not with numbers. *Numbers* represent numeric values; they may be of various storage classes, such as floating point or integers. They can be compared with other numbers, but not with strings. Values are represented in the model by dotted ellipses; the value name (its object type name) appears within its defining ellipse.

In this section, you create several object types, based on the following fact statements. In each statement, the object type is boldfaced, and the reference modes are in parentheses. Use the layout shown in figure E.4 as a guide for placing the object types on your diagram.

Fact f1	**Instructor** (ID) works fulltime.
Fact f2	Instructor (ID) is qualified to teach **Subject** (name) at SubjectLevel.
Fact f3	Instructor (ID) works for **Department** (code).

Fact f4 Instructor (ID) is qualified to teach Subject (name) at **SubjectLevel**.

Fact f5 Department (code) has **DepartmentName**.

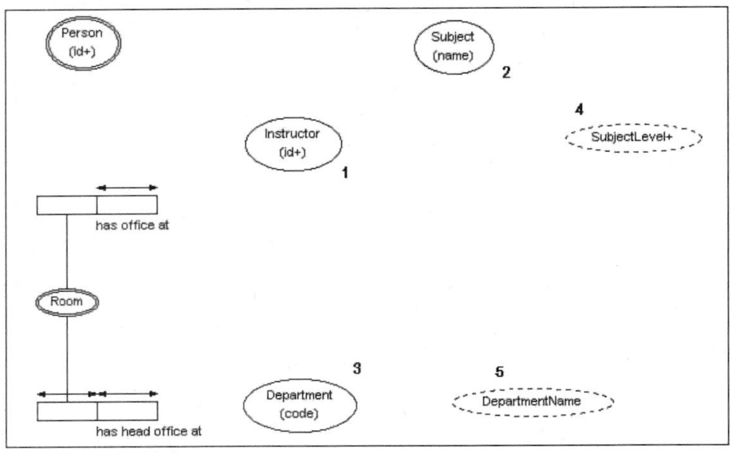

Figure E.4. The object layout guide.

> **Note:** In this section, you need to use the Symbols palette frequently (refer to fig. E.2). To display the Symbols palette, click the Show Symbols Palette button on the Toolbar (refer to fig. E.1). Then drag the Symbols palette to a convenient place on the diagram.

Creating Entity Object Types

In this section, you create the entities for the following facts:

Fact f1 **Instructor** (ID) works fulltime.

Fact f2 Instructor (ID) is qualified to teach **Subject** (name) at SubjectLevel.

Fact f3 Instructor (ID) works for **Department** (code).

Follow these steps to create the entity Instructor:

1. Click the Object Type button on the Symbols palette. The cursor changes to represent the object type.
2. Click the object type cursor on the diagram. The Object Definition dialog box appears (see fig. E.5).

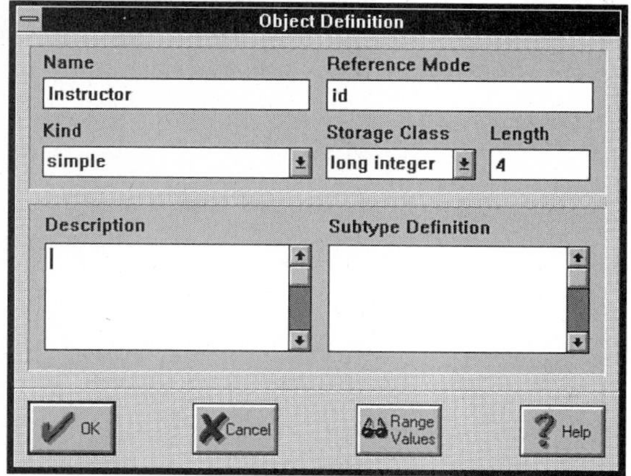

Figure E.5. The Object Definition dialog box.

3. Type **Instructor** for the object type name. Note that the first letter of object type names must be capitalized.
4. Press Tab to move to the Reference Mode box. The reference mode is a word or primary identification of an object type. It is used for object types that are simple entities.
5. Type **id** for the reference mode.
6. Click the Kind box. The program displays a list of possible kinds. For this tutorial, specify the kind as simple.
7. Click the Storage Class box to display a list box. Every object type which is a Simple entity, a String, or a Number has a data type (or storage class) associated with it. The data type you choose for an object type varies, based on the physical database you are using.
8. Select the long integer Storage Class.
9. Press Tab to move to the Length box.
10. Type **4** for the length.
11. Press Tab to move to the Description box. If you want to add free form information about this object type, type a description.

    You have completed the Instructor object type definition.
12. Click OK. The Object Definition dialog box closes, and the object type appears on the diagram in the Diagrammer window. The entity object type is represented as a solid ellipse, with the object type expressed in initial caps and its reference mode in parentheses.

Follow these steps to create the entities Subject and Department:

1. Click the object type cursor on the diagram. The Object Definition dialog box appears.
2. Specify the following settings to create an object type representing a Subject:

Name	**Subject**
Reference Mode	**name**
Kind	simple
Storage Class	text
Length	**35**
Description	(optional)

3. Click OK. The Object Definition dialog box closes, and a second simple entity object type is displayed in the Diagrammer window.
4. Click the object type cursor on the diagram. The Object Definition dialog box reappears.
5. Specify the following settings to create an object type representing a Department:

Name	**Department**
Reference Mode	**code**
Kind	simple
Storage Class	text
Length	**5**
Description	(optional)

6. Click OK. The Object Definition dialog box closes, and a third simple entity object type is displayed in the Diagrammer window.

Creating Value Object Types

In this section, you create the value object types needed for the Info University model:

Fact f4	Instructor (ID) is qualified to teach Subject (name) at **SubjectLevel**.
Fact f5	Department (code) has **DepartmentName**.

To create the SubjectLevel value object type, follow these steps:

1. Click the object type cursor on the diagram. The Object Definition dialog box appears.
2. Specify the following settings to create an object type representing the SubjectLevel:

Name	**SubjectLevel**
Kind	number
Storage Class	byte
Length	**1**
Description	(optional)

3. Click OK. The Object Definition dialog box closes, and the new object type appears on the diagram in the Diagrammer window. The value object type is represented as a dashed ellipse.

To create the DepartmentName value object type, follow these steps:

1. Click the object type cursor on the diagram. The Object Definition dialog box appears.
2. Specify the following settings to create an object type representing the DepartmentName:

Name	**DepartmentName**
Kind	string
Storage Class	text
Length	**35**
Description	(optional)

3. Click OK. The Object Definition dialog box closes, and the Diagrammer window reappears with the value object type displayed.

Creating Supertypes and Subtypes

The Info University schedule revision will include instructor information as well as student information. Students and instructors will have many facts in common; to provide for this situation in the most efficient way, a supertype (Person) represents both the Instructor and Student. However, to preserve the unique existence of each, you create subtype entities for Instructor and Student in this section.

Supertypes and subtypes are created just as any other object type, except that a subtype definition must be provided for the subtype. You provide that definition later in this tutorial as an exercise in editing object types; here, you simply show the relationship in the diagram.

To show an object subtype in the diagram, follow these steps:

1. Click the Object Subtype button on the Symbols palette. The cursor changes to represent the object subtype.
2. Click and drag from the object subtype (Instructor) to the object supertype (Person). An arrowhead appears pointing from the subtype (Instructor) to the supertype (Person). The subtype/supertype relationship is established.

Your screen should now appear as shown in figure E.6.

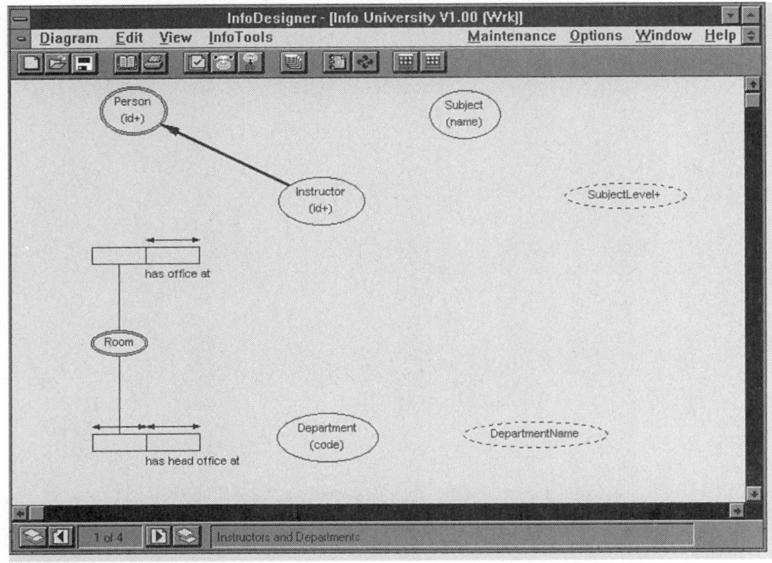

Figure E.6. Diagrammer layout at this point.

In the next section, you learn how to manage another fundamental component of object-role modeling: the predicate.

Managing Predicates

Predicates provide the meaningful context in which object types play roles within fact types. Each predicate is divided into *role positions*, which symbolically appear as boxes, called *role boxes* (see fig. E.7). Each role box in the predicate corresponds to a position in the predicate where an object plays a role. The following table describes the items shown in figure E.7.

Item	*Name*	*Definition*
1	Role positions	The grammatical positions within a predicate where object types are playing roles.
2	Role connectors	The places where object types come into contact with a predicate. Object types are said to *connect* to a role at a role position within a predicate.
3	Predicate text	The text, or verb phrase, that defines the roles being played by the object types.
4	Object holes	The places where object types come into contact with a predicate; the same idea as the role connectors, but in textual form. Each ellipsis (...) is filled by an object type.

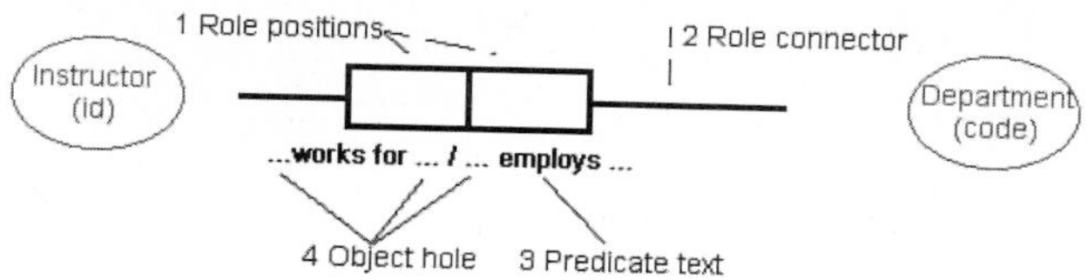

Figure E.7. Predicate boxes.

Using Inverse Predicates

Every predicate that has two or more roles can be read in reverse. In the case of the predicate in figure E.7, **works for** is only half the story. A relationship also exists between the Department and the Instructor.

In this example, you can see that the predicate can be read in reverse:

> Instructor **works for/employs** Department.

Use both forward and inverse predicate text to clarify your facts. The convention for distinguishing between them is the slash (/).

Understanding Roles

A *role* is a position in a predicate where an object type comes into context with a fact. Each role is *played by* (or *connected to*) an object type. Symbolically, a role is shown as a box with a connector to an object type. The number of roles played in a predicate is known as its *role count* or *arity*. Arity is based on the number of roles being played by object types at positions within the predicate.

Creating a Predicate

In this section, you create predicates based on the same verbalized facts you used to create the object types. Use the layout in figure E.8 as a placement guide, creating the predicates in the order shown. The fact types are as follows (the predicates are boldfaced):

Fact f1	Instructor (ID) **works fulltime**.
Fact f2	Instructor (ID) **works for/employs** Department (code).
Fact f3	Department (code) **has** DepartmentName.
Fact f4	Instructor (ID) **is qualified to teach** Subject (name) **at** SubjectLevel.

Begin by creating a *unary predicate* for Fact f1, Instructor (ID) **works fulltime**. Follow these steps:

1. Click the Predicate button on the Symbols palette . The cursor changes to represent the predicate.
2. Click the predicate cursor on the diagram. The Predicate Definition dialog box appears.

3. Type **works fulltime** in the Predicate text box. This is the predicate text. (Note that the unary fact type has no inverse predicate.)
4. In the Arity section of the dialog box, click the top symbol to indicate single arity. The completed dialog box should look like figure E.9.
5. Click OK. The Predicate Definition dialog box closes and the predicate appears on the diagram.

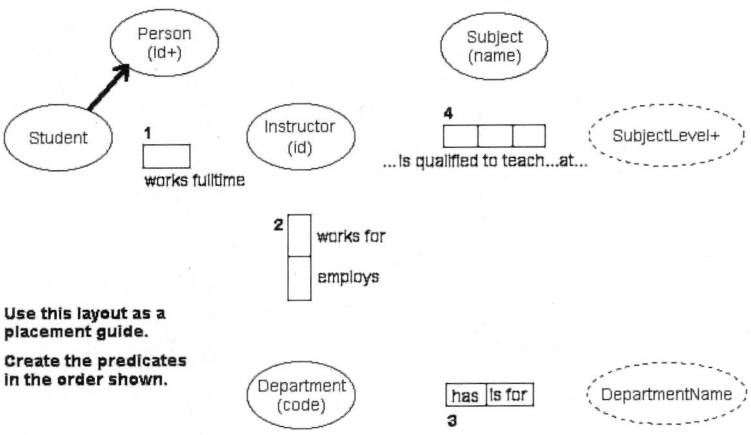

Figure E.8. The predicate placement guide

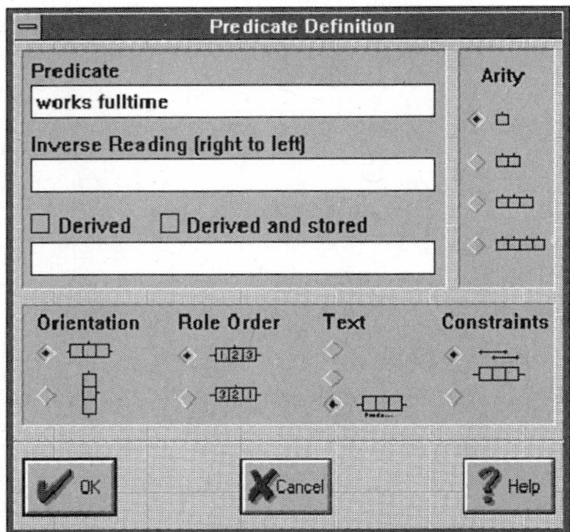

Figure E.9. The Predicate Definition dialog box.

Next, create a *binary predicate* (vertical) for Fact f2, Instructor (ID) **works for/employs** Department (code). Follow these steps:

1. Click the predicate symbol on the diagram. The Predicate Definition dialog box appears.
2. Specify the settings in the dialog box as shown in figure E.10.
3. Click OK. The Predicate Definition dialog box closes and the predicate appears on the diagram.

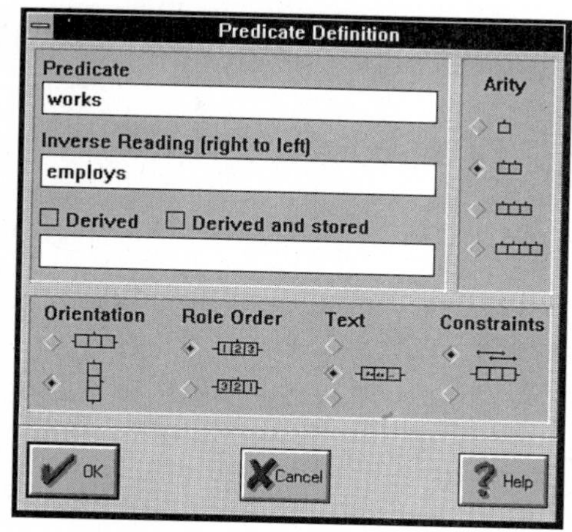

Figure E.10. A binary predicate definition with vertical display.

Now, create a binary predicate (horizontal) for Fact f3, Department (code) **has/is for** DepartmentName. Follow these steps:

1. Click the predicate symbol on the diagram. The Predicate Definition dialog box appears.
2. Specify the dialog box settings as indicated in figure E.11.
3. Click OK. The Predicate Definition dialog box closes and the predicate appears on the diagram.

Finally, create a *ternary predicate* for Fact f4, Instructor (id) **is qualified to teach** Subject (name) **at** SubjectLevel.

1. Click the predicate symbol on the diagram. The Predicate Definition dialog box appears.
2. Specify the settings as indicated in figure E.12 to create this ternary predicate.
3. Click OK. The Predicate Definition dialog box closes and the new predicate appears on the diagram.

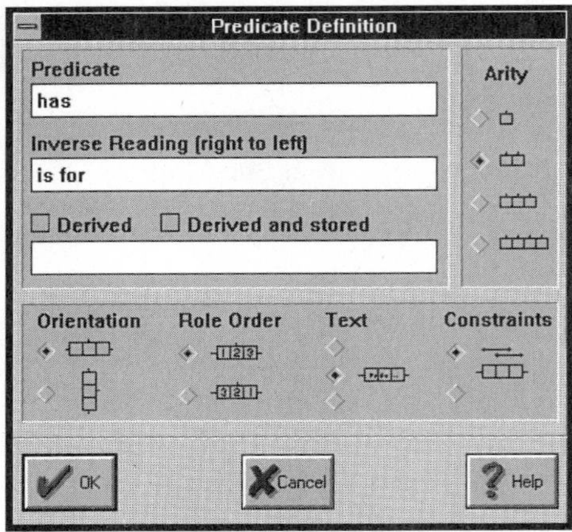

Figure E.11. A binary predicate definition with horizontal display.

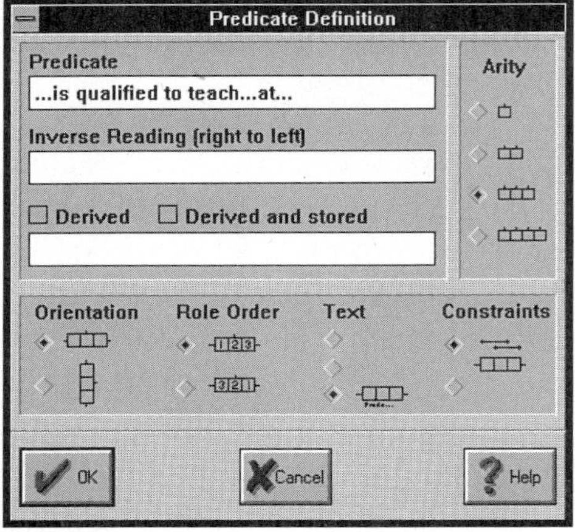

Figure E.12. A ternary predicate.

Adding an Object/Role Connection

Object/role connectors connect object types to their respective predicates. In this section, you add all the object/role connectors to page 1 of your model.

To add an object/role connector, follow these steps:

1. Click the Object Type/Role Connector button on the Symbols palette. The cursor changes to represent the object/role connector.

2. Click and drag from the predicate role **works fulltime** to the **Instructor** object type. A connecting line appears. The object is now connected to its role.
3. Add the remaining object/role connectors as shown in figure E.13.

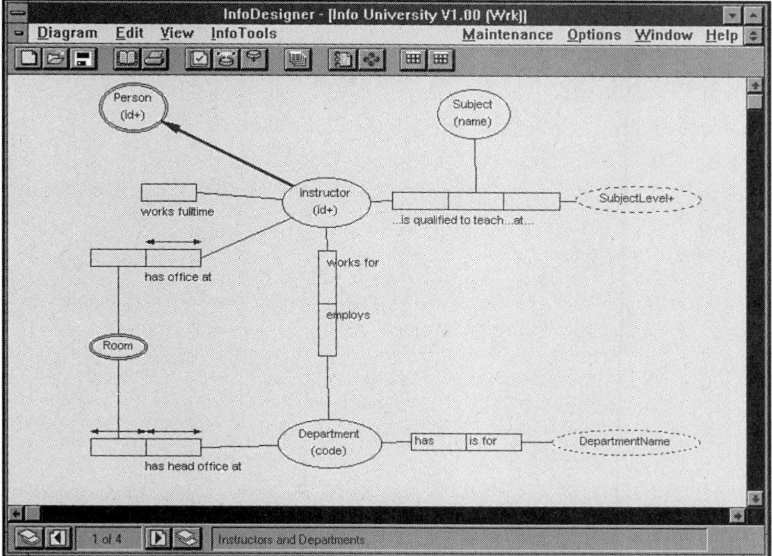

Figure E.13. The object/role connection placement guide.

> **Note:** To remove an object/role connector, click the connector, drag it away from the role, and drop it on a neutral part of the screen. The connector disappears.

In the next section, you prepare to add constraints to your model.

Selecting Roles for Adding Constraints

In this section, you learn how to select and deselect predicate roles. Role selection must be performed before constraints can be added to your predicates. The determination of when to use a single or multiple role selection depends on the fact type you are creating.

> **Note:** In this section, you need to use the Constraints palette frequently (refer to fig. E.3). To display the Constraints palette, click the Show Constraints Palette button on the Toolbar (refer to fig. E.1). Then drag the Constraints palette to a convenient place on the diagram.

Selecting and Deselecting a Role

In several situations, only a single role selection is required. If you want to add a mandatory role, for example, only one role needs to be selected. To select a predicate role in the Info University example, click the **works for** role played by the Instructor object type (see fig. E.14). The role appears shaded to indicate that it is selected. After a role is selected, you can select the applicable constraint(s) from the Constraints palette. For details, see "Adding Constraints," later in this appendix.

If you select the wrong role, hold down the Shift key and click the role. Shading is removed and the role is deselected. (Pressing the Esc key deselects all roles.)

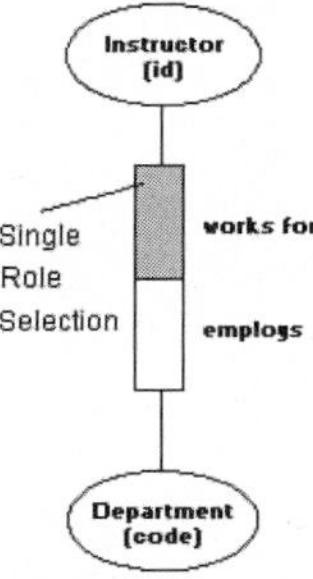

Figure E.14. Shading indicates that the single role is selected.

Selecting Multiple Roles

Multiple role selection is required in several situations. When adding an index constraint between two fact types, for example, you need to make two single role selections—one in each of the two fact types. To select multiple roles, follow these steps:

1. Click the Last Page button. The last page of the Info University model, Students/Instructors, appears.
2. Click the role played by FirstName; then hold down the Shift key and click the role played by LastName (see fig. E.15).

The roles will now appear shaded on the screen. Once the roles are selected, you can select the applicable constraint from the Constraints Palette.

3. Deselect the two roles.

You are now ready to apply constraints.

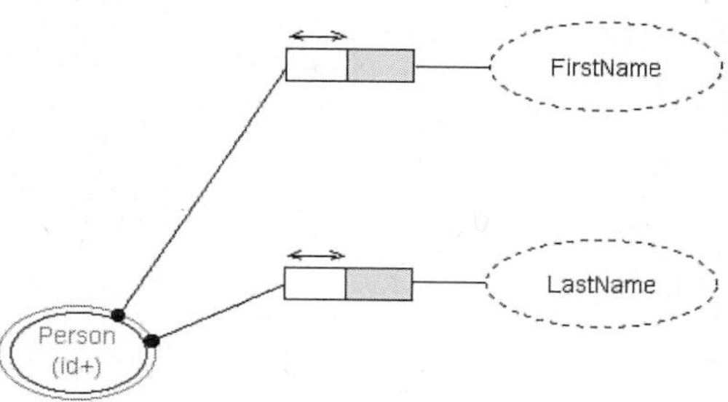

Figure E.15. Shading here indicates that multiple roles are selected.

Adding Constraints

The next step in creating your conceptual model is the application of constraints to the roles that are played. *Constraints* reflect the limitations on possible data combinations among the facts of the database. By applying constraints, you provide rules by which the various roles are bound. For instance, a room number in a building should not be the same as any other room number, and perhaps every room should have a number. These are examples of constraints.

The most common constraints are *internal uniqueness constraints* and *mandatory role constraints*. You apply these constraints and others in the steps that follow.

To express the uniqueness of data at roles, you use the FORML notation of a double-headed arrow over the role (or role sequence). Note the following uniqueness rules:

- A uniqueness constraint must span at least 2 roles for ternaries and at least 3 roles for quaternaries (role count minus one role).
- Every predicate must have at least one uniqueness constraint.

Internal Uniqueness Constraints

In this section, you add several internal uniqueness constraints to the predicates within the following fact types:

- Binary fact types (Facts f2 and f3):

  Instructor (id) **works for/employs** Department (code).

  Department (code) **has/is for** DepartmentName.

- Ternary fact type (Fact f4):

  Instructor (id) **is qualified to teach** Subject (name) **at** SubjectLevel.

To add an internal uniqueness constraint, follow these steps:

1. Return to Page 1 of your model.
2. Click the **works for** role played by the Instructor object type. The role becomes shaded, indicating that it is selected.
3. Click the Internal Uniqueness button on the Constraints palette. The internal uniqueness constraint symbol appears adjacent to the role (see fig. E.16).

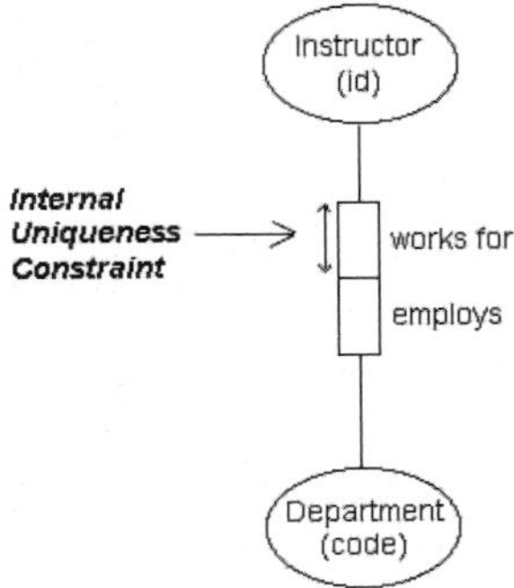

Figure E.16. The **works for** role is assigned an internal uniqueness constraint.

4. Click the **has** role played by the Department object type.
5. Click the Internal Uniqueness button on the Constraints palette. The internal uniqueness constraint symbol appears above the role **has**.
6. Click the **is for** role played by the DepartmentName object type.
7. Click the Internal Uniqueness button on the Constraints palette. The internal uniqueness constraint symbol appears above the role **is for**.
8. Click the first role position of the ternary predicate (...**is qualified to teach**...**at**...); then hold down the Shift key and click the other two roles of that predicate.
9. Click the Internal Uniqueness button on the Constraints palette. The internal uniqueness constraint symbol appears across the top of the three roles.

Mandatory Role Constraints

Whenever you have a role being played that must be recorded by all instances of an object type, the role is described as a *mandatory role*. In this section, you add several mandatory role constraints. As with internal uniqueness constraints, individual roles must be selected. The constraints will be added to the predicates of the following fact types:

Instructor (id) **works for** Department (code).

Department (code) **has** DepartmentName.

Room **has head office at** Department (code).

To express a mandatory role constraint, you use the FORML notation of a black dot. The dot appears at the intersection of the role connector and the entity. Note the following rules for mandatory role constraints:

- Only entities, not values, can play mandatory roles.
- Mandatory roles do not apply to unary fact types.

To add a mandatory role constraint, follow these steps:

1. Click the **works for** role played by the Instructor object type. The role becomes selected.
2. Click the Mandatory Role button on the Constraints palette. The mandatory role constraint symbol appears at the intersection of the role and the object type.
3. Click the **has** role played by the Department object type.
4. Click the Mandatory Role button on the Constraints palette. The mandatory role constraint symbol appears at the intersection of the role and the object type.
5. Click the **has head office at** role played by the Department object type. The role becomes selected.
6. Click the Mandatory Role button on the Constraints palette. The mandatory role constraint symbol appears at the intersection of the role and the object type (see fig. E.17).

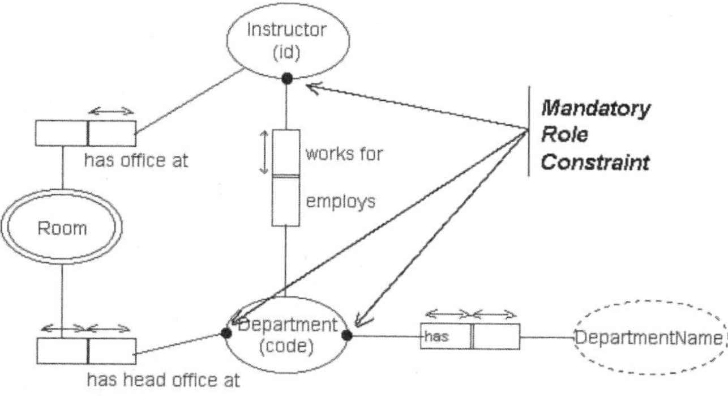

Figure E.17. Specifying mandatory role constraints.

External Uniqueness Constraints

In this section, you add an external uniqueness constraint (see fig. E.3 for the symbol). To add this constraint, you select a multiple role sequence. The constraint will be added between the following fact types:

Building (id) **is on** Campus (name).

Building (id) **has** BuildingName.

To add an external uniqueness constraint, follow these steps:

1. Click the Next Page button to move to page 2 from page 1. The Campus Location page appears.
2. Hold down the Shift key and click the right predicate roles of Building **is on** Campus (name) and Building **has** BuildingName.
3. Click the External Uniqueness button on the Constraints palette. The external uniqueness constraint symbol appears adjacent to the roles (see fig. E.18).

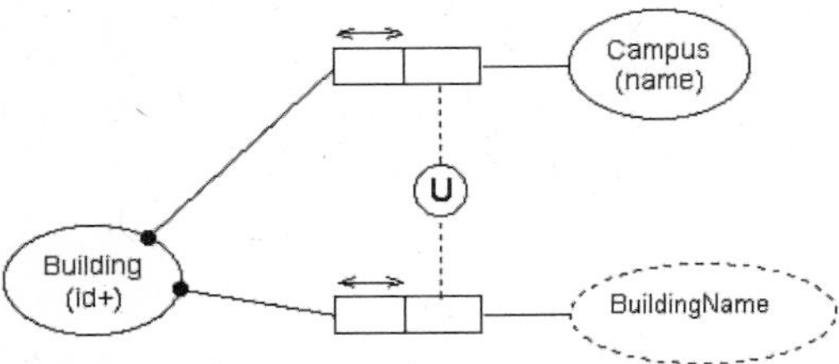

Figure E.18. An external uniqueness constraint.

Primary Reference Constraints

In this section, you add a primary reference constraint (see fig. E.3 for the symbol). To add this constraint, you select individual predicate roles. The constraint will be added to the following fact types (notice that Room is already on your diagram page):

Room **has** RoomNumber.

Room **is in** Building (id).

To add a primary reference constraint, follow these steps:

1. Click the right predicate role of Room **has** RoomNumber; then hold down the Shift key and click the right predicate of Room **is in** Building.
2. Click the Primary Reference button on the Constraints palette. The primary reference constraint symbol appears between the roles (see fig. E.19).

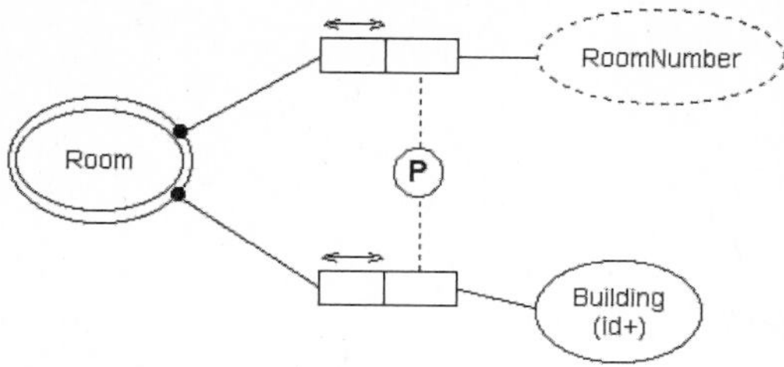

Figure E.19. A primary reference constraint.

Nesting Constraints

Whenever a fact itself must play roles, you can nest the fact's predicate. In this section, you add a nested constraint (see fig. E.3 for the symbol). To add this constraint, you select a multiple role sequence. The constraint will be added to the following fact type:

Course (id) **is assigned to** Section.

To add a nested constraint, follow these steps:

1. Click the Next Page button to move to page three of the Info University model. The Class Assignments page appears.
2. Hold down the Shift key and click both roles of the Course **is assigned to** Section fact type.
3. Click the Nest button on the Constraints palette. A nested rectangle appears around the predicate (see fig. E.20). By nesting the predicate, you end up with a new object type (CourseSection).
4. Connect the new CourseSection object type to the **is offered in** role.

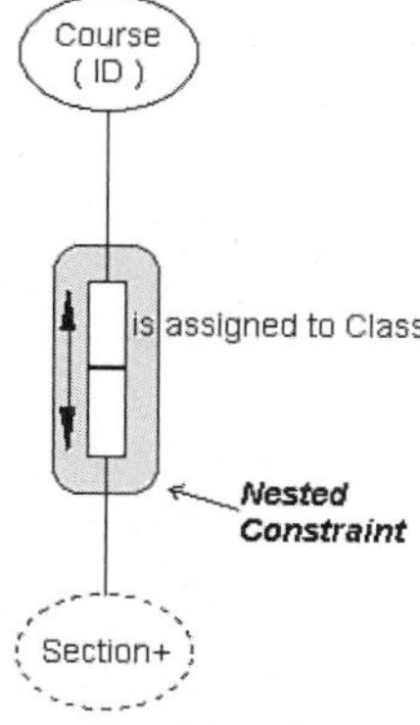

Figure E.20. A nested constraint.

By default, InfoDesigner will give you a concatenated name from the object type names involved in the predicate. In this case the default name is CourseSection. However, CourseSection is not a natural word; therefore, you may prefer to change the name. Change the cursor to the arrow pointer and double-click on the nested area; the Object Definition dialog box appears. Type in the new name **Class** and click OK.

You have now constructed your model and applied constraints; it is time to populate it.

Populating Your Model

Every fact type has a *population set* that defines it. InfoDesigner allows you to store example populations with your fact types. In this way, you can always view what kinds of data combinations are possible—very much like having a test database that defines the actual database.

Example populations are entered one row at a time. Each row contains an instance of data from the objects playing roles at role positions within a fact type. Each column represents the possible data combinations for the object type at that role.

The number of rows of data you include in your example population depends entirely on the possible combinations of data that apply. To populate a fact, you examine the example data and apply data to the roles of that fact. Look at the example data in figure E.21. Notice how the columns of example data flow into the role positions of each fact through the dotted lines. Each column of example data will be represented by a role position in a fact type.

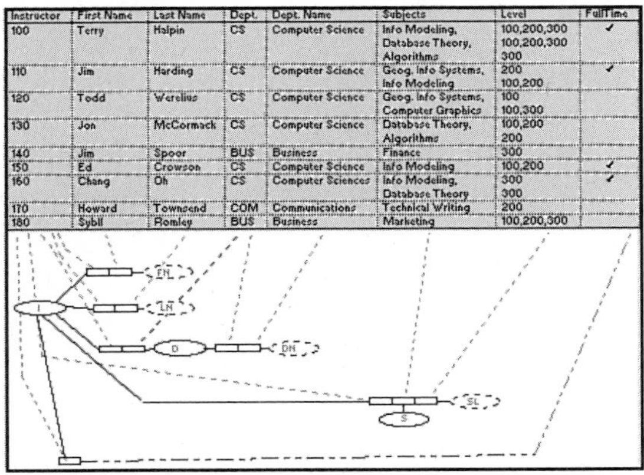

Instructor	First Name	Last Name	Dept.	Dept. Name	Subjects	Level	FullTime
100	Terry	Halpin	CS	Computer Science	Info Modeling, Database Theory, Algorithms	100,200,300 100,200,300 300	✓
110	Jim	Harding	CS	Computer Science	Geog. Info Systems, Info Modeling	200 100,200	✓
120	Todd	Werelius	CS	Computer Science	Geog. Info Systems, Computer Graphics	100 100,300	
130	Jon	McCormack	CS	Computer Science	Database Theory, Algorithms	100,200 200	
140	Jim	Spoor	BUS	Business	Finance	300	
150	Ed	Crowson	CS	Computer Science	Info Modeling	100,200	✓
160	Chang	Oh	CS	Computer Sciences	Info Modeling, Database Theory	300 300	✓
170	Howard	Townsend	COM	Communications	Technical Writing	200	
180	Sybil	Romley	BUS	Business	Marketing	100,200,300	

Figure E.21. An example of data flow.

You must follow three basic rules when defining your example populations:

- Your sample data must be significant.
- You cannot repeat a row.
- You cannot have any empty (or NULL) values.

To populate a fact type, follow these steps:

1. Return to page 1 of your model.
2. Using the *right* mouse button, click the predicate in the fact type Department (code) **has** DepartmentName. The Predicate menu appears.
3. Choose Show Examples. The Populate dialog box appears.
4. Click Edit. The Fact Examples dialog box appears.
5. Type the following example data (press Tab to move between columns):

Department	**DepartmentName**
CS	**Computer Science**
IS	**Information Science**
ENG	**English**

6. Click OK. The Fact Examples dialog box closes and the Populate dialog box reappears.
7. Click Hide. The Diagrammer window reappears.

   The example data is now a part of your model (see fig. E.22).

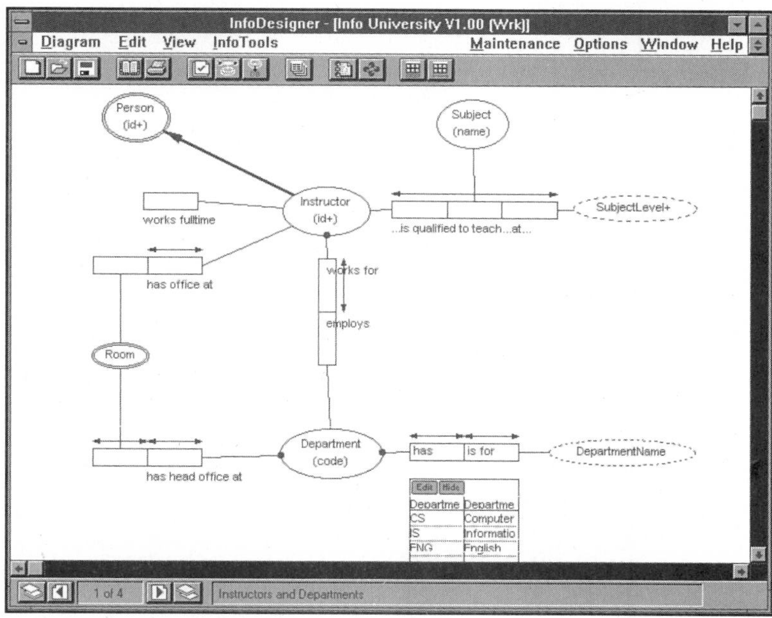

Figure E.22. How Page 1 appears with example data.

By this time, you may have decided that you need to revise some of your work. The following few sections present some tools and techniques for editing purposes.

Editing Object Types

In an earlier section of this appendix, you created a simple entity object type called Instructor. You also indicated the subtype relationship on the diagram. But you still need to supply a subtype definition for Instructor. You can do that by editing the Instructor object type definition. To start, make sure you are on Page 1 of the model.

To edit an object type, follow these steps:

1. Click the Standard Pointer button on the Symbols palette. The cursor changes to the pointer cursor.
2. Double-click the Instructor object type to be edited. The Object Type dialog box appears.
3. Press Tab to move to the Subtype Definition field, and enter the text **a Person that is of Status I**.
4. Click OK. The Diagrammer window reappears with the Instructor object subtype edited.

Reusing Object Types

Reusing object types saves time, simplifies using the same object type, and ensures accuracy.

Because the Info University schedule revision is expanding, you have added several pages to your model. To represent the expanding relationships correctly, you need to reuse several of the existing object types to other pages.

To reuse an entity object type from the current model repository, follow these steps:

1. Click the Next Page button twice. The Class Assignment page appears.
2. Click the Object Type button on the Symbols Palette. The object type cursor appears.
3. Double-click in a neutral zone in the Diagrammer window. The Object Type Selector - [model] list box appears.
4. Scroll the list and select the Subject[name] object type.
5. Click OK. The Diagrammer window reappears with the object type copied. Because the Subject object type also exists on page 1 of the Info University model, the object type appears with concentric ellipses.
6. Select the standard pointer from the Symbols Palette; then click the Subject object type and drag it to the top left corner of the diagram.

7. Click the Object Type/Role Connector button on the Symbols palette.
8. Add the object/role connector between the **Subject** and **applies to** role box.
9. Repeat steps 2 through 7, choosing the SubjectLevel object type this time. Then connect it to the **is at** role box (see fig. E.23).

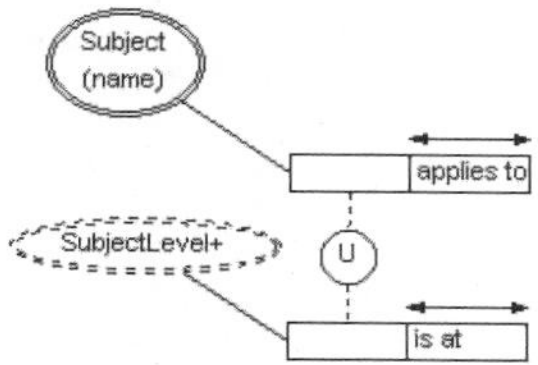

Figure E.23. How reused objects appear in the diagram.

Using the Object Browser

By using the Object Browser, you can review a list of all object types, review each predicate with which the object type is associated, and perform a goto function for the object type and predicate you select. In this section, you use the Room object type and its associated predicates.

To use the Object Browser, follow these steps:

1. From the InfoDesigner menu, choose View.
2. Select the Show Object Browser option (Ctrl+J) or click the Object Browser button on the Toolbar.

   The Object Browser dialog box appears (see fig. E.24).
3. Scroll the Model Objects list and select `Room`. The associated facts appear in the lower half of the dialog box.
4. Double-click the associated fact type `Room is in Building (id)`. InfoDesigner locates the object type within the model. The Object Browser dialog box disappears, and the Diagrammer window reappears, with the object type and the selected predicate highlighted.

Using the Fact Compiler

You can create and edit your model from within the Fact Compiler, which displays one page of your model at a time. To view the Fact Compiler, follow these steps:

1. Click the Last Page button. The Students/Instructors page appears.
2. From the InfoDesigner menu, choose View.
3. Select the Show Fact Assistant option (Ctrl+A). The Fact Compiler window appears.

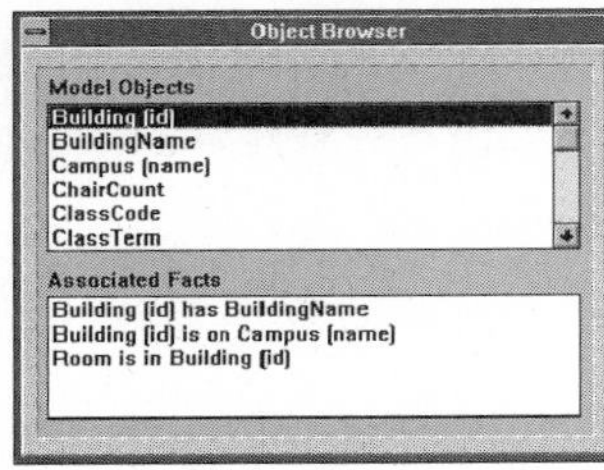

Figure E.24. The Object Browser.

The Fact Compiler is divided into four areas: menu, Toolbar, work area, and Status Bar. The following sections describe how to use the Fact Compiler.

> **Note:** The Fact Compiler stays on-screen as a dependent client of the InfoDesigner interface until you dismiss the window with its Control menu or by clicking the Fact Compiler button on the InfoDesigner toolbar.

Navigating the Work Area

The work area of the Fact Compiler is divided into individual subwindows (one for each icon). You move between subwindows and within subwindows. To move *down* between subwindows, press the Tab key; to move *up*, press Shift-Tab. To move *within* a subwindow, use the arrow keys.

To type objects and facts, click the mouse just to the right of the object type and fact type icons. The edit cursor appears; type the desired text.

To expand the subwindow to see more information, double-click the subwindow's icon. Double-click again to collapse the subwindow to a single line.

Compiling Facts

To compile a fact or object, you drag and drop it onto the diagram. For the Info University model, make sure that you have accessed the Fact Compiler as described earlier. Then follow these steps:

1. Place the cursor on the line to the right of the fact type icon; then type the following fact:

   Student has declared Major (name).

2. Move the mouse cursor over the fact type icon.
3. Hold down the left mouse button until the mouse pointer changes to a fact cursor.
4. While you continue to hold down the left mouse button, drag the fact cursor. The Fact Compiler window disappears and the diagram shows as the top window. At this point,

you can rotate the fact on the diagram (in 90-degree increments) by pressing and releasing the right mouse button repeatedly.

5. Release the left mouse button over the diagram between Student and Major.

   The fact is now compiled; if no errors occur, the fact is drawn on the diagram.

6. Dismiss the Fact Compiler by double-clicking the Control menu.
7. Using the Constraints palette, apply uniqueness and mandatory role constraints on the **has declared** role.

From here, you can use the Constraint and Symbol palettes on the fact as you would on any other fact in your diagram.

When you drop the file in the desired position, InfoDesigner compiles the fact. If no errors occur, the program writes the fact to the repository and draws it on the model. If errors occur, the fact is not drawn. If warnings occur, the program draws the fact, but notifies you of possible problems to consider. In either case, you see a dialog box that indicates the nature of the error or warning. By clicking the Descriptions check box, you can see more information about the warning message.

Decompiling a Model

To view your model in text format, you can *decompile* it page by page. Before you decompile, you can change the appearance and detail of the list. During the decompiling process, all object type, constraints, and fact types are read into a plain text list for review and editing. In the decompiled list, you also can decide whether to include item identification and verbose constraints.

To decompile a model, follow these steps:

1. Return to page 1 of your model.
2. From the Fact Compiler menu, choose Compile.
3. Select the Decompile option.

   The program lists the current model page, constraints, object types, and fact types.

4. To see additional detail, double-click the `Department (code) has DepartmentName` fact type. The fact type expands to include any subtypes, constraints, roles, and (if populated) example data.

Editing Fact Types

In this section, you learn how to insert a line in the Fact Compiler window and how to copy a fact type from another page into the new line.

To copy an object type in the Fact Compiler window, use the decompiled listing you made in the preceding section. Then perform the following steps in the Fact Compiler window:

1. Using the mouse, highlight the `Department (code) [text 5]` object type.
2. From the Fact Compiler menu, choose Edit.
3. Select the Copy option (Ctrl+Ins).

   The object type is copied to the Windows Clipboard.

Later, you will paste the copied object type into the diagram. But first you need a blank line. To insert a new line in the Fact Compiler window, follow these steps:

1. Click the Last Page button. The Students/Instructors page appears.
2. From the Fact Compiler menu, choose Compile.
3. Select the Decompile option.

   The program decompiles page 4, Students/Instructors.
4. Place the cursor on the `LastName string [text 20]` line.
5. From the Fact Compiler menu, choose Edit.
6. Select the Insert Line option (Ctrl+N).

   A new line is inserted.
7. Place the cursor on the `StreetAddress string [text 100]` line.
8. Select the Insert Line option (Ctrl+N).

   A second new line is inserted.

To paste an object type, follow these steps:

1. Place the cursor on one of the blank lines you inserted.
2. From the Fact Compiler menu, choose Edit.
3. Select the Paste option (Shift+Ins). The `Department (code) [text 5]` object type is copied to page 4 (see fig. E.25).

Validating a Model

After creating elements of your model, validation is the next step in using InfoDesigner to create your relational database model. You can validate your model at any time; however, the best time to validate is after you have created all your fact types. Validation checks all pages of a multiple page model.

To validate a model, follow these steps:

1. From the InfoDesigner menu, choose Diagram.
2. Select the Validate Model option (Ctrl+V).

The Conceptual Validation Progress information box appears. As validation of your model takes place, you see InfoDesigner checking object types, predicates, constraints, and unary semantics. As each of these passes is made, InfoDesigner displays the percentage of completeness. When validation is complete, the Diagrammer window reappears.

When you attempt to validate InfoUniversity, you will discover an error—a role (**teaches**) has not been played. To resolve the error, reuse the Instructor object type, connect it to the **teaches** role, and run the validation again.

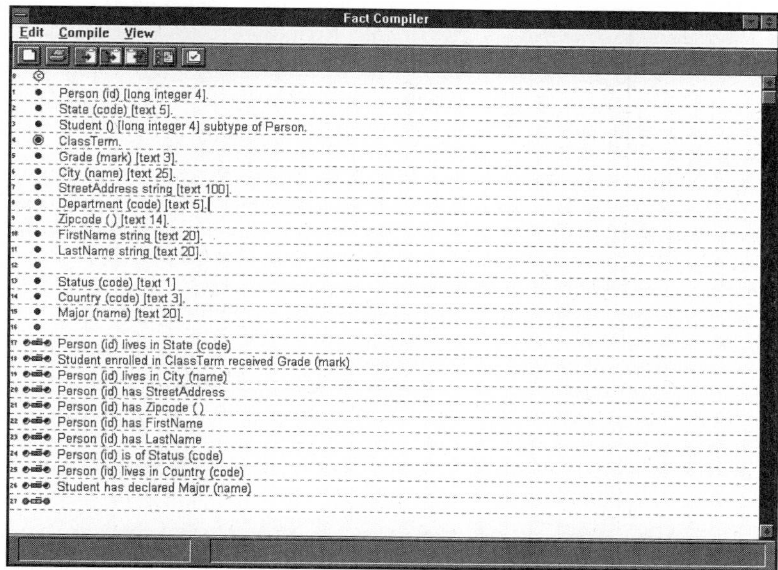

Figure E.25. The Fact Compiler contains the added object type.

Building a Relational Database Model

In this section, you learn how to build a relational model. This activity moves your model from the conceptual view to the logical view. Tables are built and their relationships (one-to-one, one-to-many, or many-to-many) are added.

To build a relational model, follow these steps:

1. From the InfoDesigner menu, choose Diagram.
2. Select the Build Relational Model option.

   The Relational Model Generation dialog box appears.
3. Click OK to start the building process.

At this point, InfoDesigner starts building the model. The program makes the following six passes of the conceptual model:

- Many-to-many Transformation Phase
- One-to-many Transformation Phase
- One-to-one Transformation Phase
- Foreign Key Analysis Pass 1
- Foreign Key Analysis Pass 2
- External Constraints Mapping

As InfoDesigner makes each of these passes, the program displays the percentage of completeness. When the relational model is built, the Diagrammer window reappears.

Using the Table Browser

In this section, you learn how to use the Table Browser to view tables. You also view table dependencies and detail. To view tables, follow these steps:

1. From the InfoDesigner menu, choose InfoTools.
2. Select the Table Browser option (Ctrl+B).

   The Table Browser window appears.
3. Click the Table list box at the top of the screen.

   The list of tables for the current model appear. The table names that appear in the list box for this example represent the tables created during the build process, earlier in this appendix.
4. Select the Instructor table for viewing.

   The table appears.

To view table dependencies, follow these steps:

1. Click the Control menu on the Instructor window.

   The Table menu appears.
2. Choose Show Dependencies. Additional tables and their dependent relationships appear superimposed on one stack.
3. Drag the tables off the stack one by one and arrange them to best view their relationships (see fig. E.26).

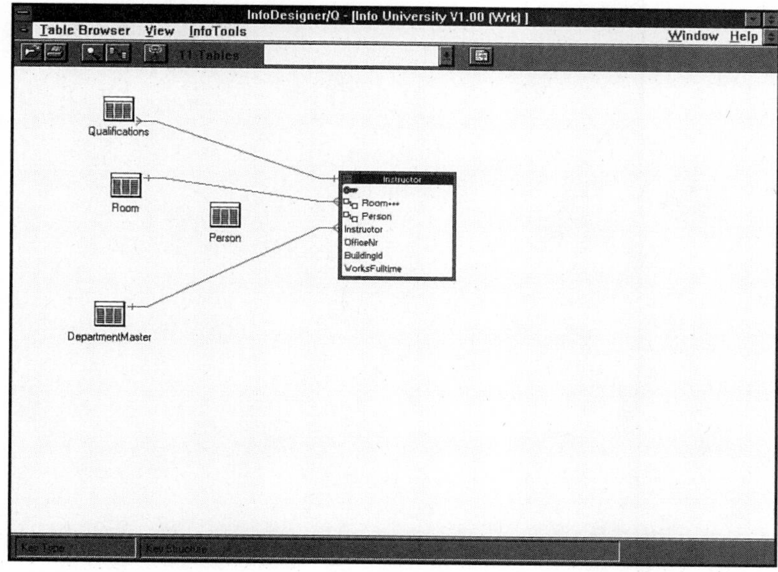

Figure E.26. Table dependencies.

Notice that the Instructor table data relates to several other tables. The other tables include InstrctrSbjctSbjctLvl, Room, Person, and DepartmentMaster. Each of these tables has a special relationship with the Instructor table. The relationships are indicated in the following table.

Table	*Left-to-Right*	*Right-to-Left*
InstrctrSbjctSbjctLvl	many-to-one	one-to-many
Room	one-to-many	many-to-one
Person	one-to-one	one-to-one
DepartmentMaster	one-to-many	many-to-one

To view table detail, click the Control menu on the Instructor window and choose Show Detail. The table detail appears. Table detail includes the following items:

- Key title
- Key composition
- Field name
- Data type (storage class)

- Length (of field)
- Required
- Page (of your model)
- Fact type

The Required, Page, and Fact Type table fields cannot be edited.

Renaming a table can assist you in referencing it later. To rename a table, follow these steps:

1. Click the InstrctrSbjctSbjctLvl Control menu and choose Table Name.

   The Table Name dialog box appears.

2. Type **Qualifications**.
3. Click OK. The table is renamed.

To close the detail view, click the Instructor Control menu and choose Show Condensed.

Building the Database

This section provides instructions for creating a physical database. Before performing these steps, you should validate your conceptual model and build your relational model. Then you can build your physical (target) database.

To build a physical database, follow these steps:

1. From the InfoDesigner menu, choose Diagram.
2. Select the Build Database option.

   The Native Database Generator dialog box appears.

3. Click the Target Database list box.

   The list box opens.

4. Select the Target Database option.

   The list box closes.

5. Press Tab to move to the File Name box.
6. Type **Infoq** for the target database file. (The Database Name box is not used in this tutorial.)
7. Click OK to start.

   The target database is generated.

This concludes the Tutorial for InfoDesigner/Q. A theoretical summary of the object-role modeling technique follows.

Object-Role Modeling: A Theoretical Overview

Editor's note: This material was supplied by T. A. Halpin, Dept. of Computer Science, University of Queensland, Australia 4072.

The quality of a database application depends critically on its design. To help ensure correctness, clarity, adaptability, and productivity, information systems are best specified first at the conceptual level, using concepts and language that people can readily understand. The conceptual design may include data, process, and behavioral perspectives; the actual database management system used to implement the design might be based on one of many logical data models, such as relational, hierarchical, network, or object-oriented models. This overview restricts attention to the data perspective, and assumes that the design is to be implemented in a relational database system.

Object-role modeling (ORM) simplifies the design process by using natural language, by using intuitive diagrams that can be populated with examples, and by examining the information in terms of simple or elementary facts. By expressing the model in terms of natural concepts like objects and roles, it provides a conceptual approach to modeling. The version discussed here is based on the formalization of the method advanced by T. A. Halpin of the University of Australia, and incorporates extensions and refinements arising from research conducted there and in the United States. The associated language FORML (Formal Object-Role Modeling Language) is supported in the InfoDesigner CASE tool.

The conceptual schema design procedure comprises seven steps:

1. Transform familiar information examples into elementary facts, and apply quality checks.
2. Draw a draft diagram of the fact types and apply a population check.
3. Check for entity types that should be combined, and note any arithmetic derivations.
4. Add uniqueness constraints and check the arity of the fact types.
5. Add mandatory role constraints, and check for logical derivations.
6. Add any value, set comparison, and subtyping constraints.
7. Add other constraints and perform final checks.

The following sections describe these steps.

Step 1

Transform familiar information examples into elementary facts, and apply quality checks.

Examples of information often are available in the form of output reports or input forms; if not, the modeler can work with the client to produce examples of output reports expected from the system. A key to ORM is the use of natural language to verbalize these examples. As an aid to this process, the speaker imagines he/she has to convey the information contained in the examples to a friend, over the telephone.

Begin a sample case study by considering a fragment of an information system used by a university to maintain details about its academic staff and academic departments. One function of the system is to print an academic staff directory, as exemplified by the report extract shown in Table E.1. Part of the modeling task is to clarify the meaning of terms used in such reports. The terms "emp#" and "ext#" abbreviate "employee number" and "extension number". A phone extension may have access to local calls only ("LOC"), national calls ("NAT"), or international calls ("INT"). International access includes national access, which includes local access. In the few cases where different rooms or staff have the same extension, the access level is the same. An academic is either tenured or on contract. Tenure guarantees employment until retirement, while contracts have an expiration date.

Table E.1. An Extract from a Directory of Academic Staff

Emp#	*Emp. name*	*Dept*	*Room*	*Phone Ext#*	*Phone Access*	*Tenured/ Contract Expiration*
715	Adams A	Computer Science	69-301	2345	LOC	01/31/95
720	Brown T	Biochemistry	62-406	9642	LOC	01/31/95
139	Cantor G	Mathematics	67-301	1221	INT	tenured
430	Codd EF	Computer Science	69-507	2911	INT	tenured
503	Hagar TA	Computer Science	69-507	2988	LOC	tenured
651	Jones E	Biochemistry	69-803	5003	LOC	12/31/96
770	Jones E	Mathematics	67-404	1946	LOC	12/31/95
112	Locke J	Philosophy	1-205	6600	INT	tenured
223	Mifune K	Elec. Engineering	50-215A	1111	LOC	tenured
951	Murphy B	Elec. Engineering	45-B19	2301	LOC	01/03/95
333	Russell B	Philosophy	1-206	6600	INT	tenured
654	Wirth N	Computer Science	69-603	4321	INT	tenured

The information contained in this table is to be stated in terms of *elementary facts*. Basically, an elementary fact asserts that a particular object has a property, or that one or more objects participate in a relationship, where that relationship cannot be expressed as a conjunction of simpler (or shorter) facts. For example, to say that Bill Clinton jogs and is the President of the United States is to assert two elementary facts.

For example, read the first row of the table. At first glance, you might read the information as the six facts f1 through f6 in the following list. Each of these facts asserts a binary relationship between two objects. For discussion purposes, the relationship type, or *logical predicate*, is shown in **bold** between the noun phrases that identify the objects. Object types are displayed in *italics*:

Fact f1 The *Academic* with emp# 715 **has** *EmpName* 'Adams A'.

Fact f2 The *Academic* with emp# 715 **works for** the *Dept* named 'Computer Science'.

Fact f3 The *Academic* with emp# 715 **occupies** the *Room* with room# '69-301'.

Fact f4 The *Academic* with emp# 715 **uses** the *Extension* with ext# '2345'.

Fact f5 The *Extension* with ext# '2345' **provides** the *AccessLevel* with code 'LOC'.

Fact f6 The *Academic* with emp# 715 **is contracted till** the *Date* with mm/dd/yy format '01/31/95'.

Row two contains different instances of these six fact types. Row three, because of its final column, provides an instance of a seventh fact type:

Fact f7 The *Academic* with emp# 139 **is tenured**.

A logical predicate may be regarded as a sentence with one or more "object holes" in it—each hole being filled by a term or noun phrase that identifies an object. The number of object holes is called the *arity* of the predicate. Each of these holes determines a different *role* played in the predicate. For example, in fact f4 the *academic* plays the role of **using**, and the *extension* plays the role of **being used**. In fact f7, the *academic* plays the role of **being tenured**. On a diagram, each role is depicted as a separate box.

Facts are assertions that objects play roles. An n-ary fact has n roles. In FORML a predicate may have any arity (1, 2, 3, and so on), but because the predicate is elementary, arities above 3 or 4 are rare. In typical applications, most predicates are binary. For these, the *inverse predicate* can be stated as well, so that the fact can be read in both directions. For example, the inverse of fact f4 is as follows:

Fact f4' The *Extension* with ext# '2345' **is used by** the *Academic* with emp# 715.

To save writing, both the normal predicate and its inverse are included in the same declaration, with the inverse predicate preceded by a slash (/). For example:

Fact f4" The *Academic* with emp# 715 **uses/is used by** the *Extension* with ext# '2345'.

As a quality check at this step, ensure that objects are well identified. Basic objects are either values or entities. *Values* are character strings or numbers, identified by constants ('Adams A', 715). *Entities* are "real world" objects, identified by a definite description (the Academic with emp# 715). In simple cases, such a description indicates the entity type (Academic), a value (715) and a *reference mode* (emp#). A reference mode is the manner in which the value refers to the entity. Entities can be tangible objects (persons, rooms) or abstract objects (access levels). Composite reference schemes are possible.

Fact f1 involves a relationship between an entity (a person) and a value (a name is just a character string). Facts f2 through f6 specify relationships between entities. Fact f7 states a property (or unary relationship) of an entity.

As a second quality check, use your familiarity with the *university of discourse* (*UoD*)—your application domain—to see if some facts should be split or recombined (a formal check on this is applied later). For example, suppose facts f1 and f2 were verbalized as the single fact f8:

Fact f8 The *Academic* with emp# 715 and EmpName 'Adams A' **works for** the *Dept* named 'Computer Science'.

The presence of the word "and" suggests that fact f8 can be split without information loss. The repetition of "Jones E" on different rows of Table E.1 shows that academics cannot be identified by just their name. However, the uniqueness of emp# in the sample population suggests that this suffices for reference. Because the "and test" is only a means of discovery, and because sometimes a composite naming scheme is required for identification, the UoD expert is consulted to verify that emp# by itself is sufficient for identification. With this assurance obtained, fact f8 is now split into f1 and f2.

As an alternative to specifying complete facts one at a time, the reference schemes can be declared initially and then assumed in later facts. Simple reference schemes are declared by enclosing the reference mode in parentheses. For example, the entity types and their identification schemes can be declared as Academic (emp#), Dept (name), Room (room#), etc.

Then facts f1 through f7 may be stated more briefly as follows (note that the names of object types must begin with a capital letter):

Fact f1 Academic 715 has EmpName 'Adams A'.

Fact f2 Academic 715 works for Dept 'Computer Science'.

Fact f3 Academic 715 occupies Room '69-301'.

Fact f4 Academic 715 uses Extension '2345'.

Fact f5 Extension '2345' provides AccessLevel 'LOC'.

Fact f6 Academic 715 is contracted till Date '01/31/95'.

Fact f7 Academic 139 is tenured.

These facts are instances of the following fact types:

F1 Academic has EmpName

F2 Academic works for Dept

F3 Academic occupies Room

F4 Academic uses Extension

F5 Extension provides AccessLevel

F6 Academic is contracted till Date

F7 Academic is tenured

Step 2

Draw a draft diagram of the fact types and apply a population check.

Entity types are depicted as named ellipses (see fig. E.27). Predicates are shown as named sequences of one or more role boxes, with the predicate name starting in or beside the first role box. Each predicate is ordered, from its first role box to the other end. An n-ary predicate has n role boxes. (Note that the inverse predicate names have been omitted in fig. E.27.) Value types are displayed as named, broken ellipses. Lines connect object types to the roles they play. Reference modes are written in parentheses.

In this example there are seven fact types. As a check, each has been populated with at least one fact, shown as a row of entries in the associated fact table, using the data from rows 1 and 3 of Table E.1. The English sentences listed earlier as facts f1 through f7, as well as other facts from row 3, can be read directly from this figure.

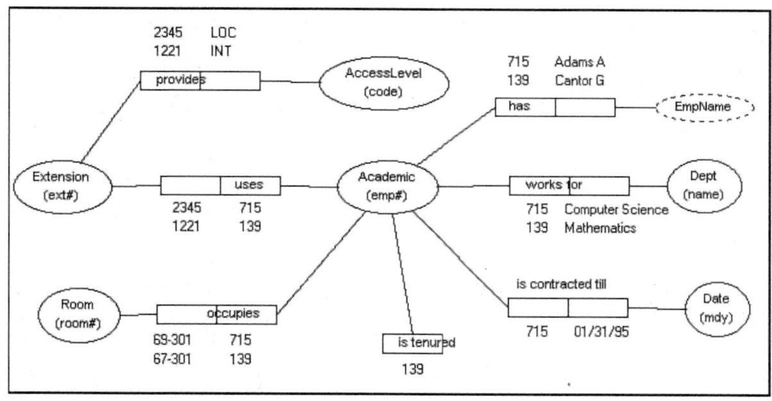

Figure E.27. A draft diagram of fact types with sample population.

The sample population is not part of the conceptual schema. Though useful for validating the model with the client and for understanding constraints, the population is excluded from the conceptual schema diagram itself.

Now widen the example. Suppose that the information system also is required to assist in the production of departmental handbooks. Perhaps the task of schema design has been divided, and another modeler works on the subschema relevant to department handbooks. The following text shows an extract from a page of one such handbook. In this university, academic staff are classified as professors, senior lecturers, or lecturers, and each professor holds a "chair" in a research area. Details are shown here for 4 of the 22 academics in that department. The data is, of course, fictitious.

```
Department:     Computer Science

         Home phone of Dept head: 9765432

Chairs          Professors (5)

Databases    Codd EF   BSc (UQ); PhD (UCLA) (Head of Dept)
Algorithms   Wirth N   BSc (UQ); MSc (ANU); DSc (MIT)

—

Senior Lecturers (9)

Hagar TA        BInfTech (UQ); PhD (UQ)

—

Lecturers (8)

Adams A         MSc (OXON)

—
```

In verbalizing a report, at least one instance of each fact type should be stated. Suppose that the designer for this part of the application suggests the following fact set, after first declaring the following reference schemes: Dept (name); Professor (name); SeniorLecturer (name); Lecturer (name); Quantity (nr)+; Chair (name); Degree (code); University (code); HomePhone (phone#). The "+" in "Quantity (nr)+" indicates that Quantity is referenced by a number, not a character string, and hence can be operated on by numeric operators such as "+". For discussion purposes, the predicates are shown here in bold:

Fact f9 Dept 'Computer Science' **has professors in** Quantity 5.

Fact f10 Professor 'Codd EF' **holds** Chair 'Databases'.

Fact f11 Professor 'Codd EF' **obtained** Degree 'BSc' **from** University 'UQ'.

Fact f12 Professor 'Codd EF' **heads** Dept 'Computer Science'.

Fact f13 Professor 'Codd EF' **has** HomePhone '9765432'.

Fact f14 Dept 'Computer Science' **has senior lecturers in** Quantity 9.

Fact f15 SeniorLecturer 'Hagar TA' **obtained** Degree 'BInfTech' **from** University 'UQ'.

Fact f16 Department 'Computer Science' **has lecturers in** Quantity 8.

Fact f17 Lecturer 'Adams A' **obtained** Degree 'MSc' **from** University 'OXON'.

As a quality check for Step 1, again consider whether entities are well identified. It appears from the handbook example that, within a single department, academics may be identified by their name. However, the complete application requires handling all departments in the same information system, and integrating this subschema with the directory subschema considered earlier. Therefore, you must replace the academic naming convention used for the handbook example with the global scheme used earlier (that is, emp#).

Step 3

Check for entity types that should be combined, and note any arithmetic derivations.

The first part of this step requires looking carefully at the fact types for facts f11, f15 and f17. Currently these are handled as three ternary fact types: Professor obtained Degree from University, SeniorLecturer obtained Degree from University, and Lecturer obtained Degree from University. The common predicate suggests that the entity types Professor, SeniorLecturer, and Lecturer should be collapsed to the single entity type Academic, with this predicate now shown only once. To preserve the original information about who is a professor, senior lecturer, or lecturer, introduce the fact type Academic has Rank. Use the codes "P", "SL", and "L" for the ranks of professor, senior lecturer, and lecturer. For example, instead of fact f10 you now have the following:

Fact f18 Academic 430 has EmpName 'Codd EF'.

Fact f19 Academic 430 has Rank 'P'.

Fact f20 Academic 430 holds Chair 'Databases'.

Facts of the kind expressed in f9, f14, and f16 now can be expressed in terms of the ternary fact type Dept employs academics of Rank in Quantity. For example, 'f9 can be replaced by the following:

Fact f9' Dept 'Computer Science' **employs academics of** Rank 'P' **in** Quantity 5.

However, this does not indicate *which* professors work for the Computer Science department. Indeed, given that many departments exist, the verbalization in facts f9 through f17 failed to capture the information about who worked for that department. This information is implicit in the listing of the academics in the Computer Science handbook. To capture this information in the application model, introduce the fact type Academic works for Dept. For example, one fact of this kind is as follows:

Fact f21 Academic 430 **works for** Dept 'Computer Science'.

The second aspect of Step 3 is to see if some fact types can be derived from others by the use of arithmetic. Because you now record the rank of academics as well as their departments, you can compute the number in each rank in each department simply by counting; so facts like f9' are *derivable*. If desired, derived fact types can be included on a schema diagram, as long as they are marked with an asterisk (*) to indicate their derivability.

Step 4

Add uniqueness constraints and check the arity of the fact types.

Uniqueness constraints are used to assert that entries in one or more roles are associated occur there *at most once*. A bar across n roles indicates that each corresponding n-tuple in the associated fact table is unique (no duplicates are allowed for that column combination). Arrow tips at the ends of the bar are needed if the roles are noncontiguous (otherwise arrow tips are optional). A uniqueness constraint spanning roles of different predicates is indicated by a circled "u": this specifies that in the natural join of the predicates, the combination of connected roles is unique (refer to fig. E.18).

After uniqueness constraints have been added, an arity check is performed. A sufficient but not necessary condition for splittability of an n-ary fact type is that it has a uniqueness constraint that misses two roles. For example, suppose that you tried to use the ternary shown in figure E.28. Because each academic has only one rank and works for only one department, the uniqueness constraint spans just the first role. Because this example misses two roles of the ternary, the fact type must be split on the source of the uniqueness constraint into the two binaries: Academic has Rank, and Academic works for Dept.

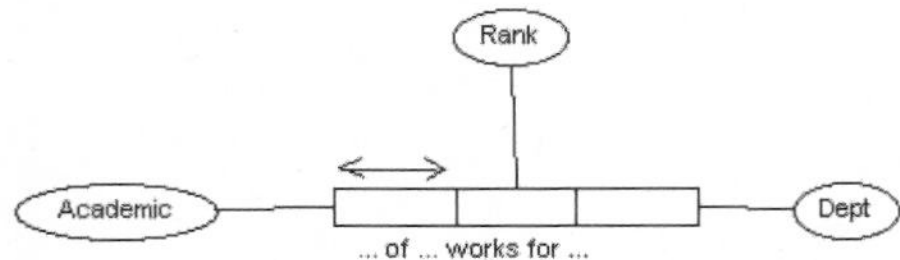

Figure E.28. This fact type splits because 2 roles are missed by the uniqueness constraint.

If a fact type is elementary, all its functional dependencies (FDs) are implied by uniqueness constraints. For example, each academic has only one rank; hence in the fact table Academic has Rank. Entries in the rank column are a function of entries in the academic column.

Step 5

Add mandatory role constraints, and check for logical derivations.

A role is mandatory (or total) for an object type if and only if every object of that type which is referenced in the database must be known to play that role. This is explicitly shown by means of a *mandatory role dot* where the role connects with object type (refer to fig. E.17). If two or more roles are connected to the same mandatory role dot, the *disjunction* of the roles is mandatory (that is, each object in the population of the object type must play at least one of these roles).

Roles that are not mandatory are *optional*. The role of having a chair is optional. The roles of being contracted or being tenured are optional also, but their disjunction is mandatory. If an object type plays only one fact role in the global schema, by default this is mandatory, but a dot is not shown (for example, the role played by Rank is mandatory by implication).

Now that uniqueness and mandatory role constraints have been discussed, reference schemes can be better understood. Simple reference schemes involve a mandatory 1:1 mapping from entity type to value type. For example, the notation "Rank (code)" abbreviates the binary reference type: Rank has Rankcode. If shown explicitly, both roles of this binary have a simple uniqueness constraint, and the reference role played by Rank has a mandatory role dot.

The second stage of Step 5 is to check for logical derivations (that is, can some fact type be derived from others without the use of arithmetic?). One strategy here is to ask whether there are any relationships (especially functional relationships) which are of interest but which have been omitted so far. Another strategy is to look for transitive patterns of functional dependencies. For example, if an academic has only one phone extension and an extension is in only one room, you can use these facts to determine the room of the academic. However, for this application the same extension may be used in many rooms, so you must discard this idea. Suppose, however, that the client confirms that the rank of an academic determines the access level of his/her extension. For example, suppose that the current business rule is that professors get international access while lecturers and senior lecturers get local access. This rule might change in time (for example, senior lecturers might be arguing for national access). To minimize later changes to the schema, store the rule as data in a table (see the following example). The rule then can be updated as required by an authorized user, without having to recompile the schema. The access level of an extension can now be logically derived from this rule and the rank of the academic using the extension.

Rank	*Access*
P	SL
L	INT
LOC	LOC

Step 6

Add any value, set comparison and subtyping constraints.

Value constraints specify a list of possible values for a value type. These usually take the form of an enumeration or range, and are displayed in braces beside the value type or its associated entity type. For example, Rankcode is restricted to {'P','SL','L'} and AccessLevelcode to {'INT','NAT','LOC'}.

Set comparison constraints specify subset, equality, or exclusion constraints between compatible roles or between sequences of compatible roles. Roles are compatible if they are played by the same object type (or by object types with a common supertype). For example, the roles of being tenured and having a contract expiration date are exclusive.

Subtyping is determined by inspecting each optional role; if the role is played solely by some well-defined subtype, a subtype node is introduced with this role attached. Subtype definitions are written below the diagram and subtype links are shown as directed line segments from subtypes to supertypes. For example, Professor is a subtype of Academic.

Step 7

Add other constraints and perform final checks.

This is the time to add any additional constraints (see the InfoDesigner/Q tutorial earlier in this appendix for more examples). It is also time to determine that the schema is consistent with the original examples, that it avoids redundancy, and that it is complete.

Once the global schema is drafted and the target DBMS is decided, various optimizations can usually be performed to improve the efficiency of the logical schema.

Entity-Relationship Modeling

Another conceptual approach is provided by *entity-relationship* (*ER*) *modeling*. Although ER models can be of use when the design process is finished, they are less suitable for formulating, transforming, or evolving a design for a number of reasons. ER diagrams are further removed from natural language, cannot be populated with fact instances, require complex design choices about attributes, lack the expressibility and simplicity of a role-based notation for constraints, hide information about the semantic domains that glue the model together, and lack adequate support for formal transformations. For such reasons, ORM works better for conceptual modeling.

Index

Symbols

A

B

D

F

G

H

I

M

N

O

P

Q

R

S

U

V

Find It Fast with Que's Quick References!

Que's Quick References are the compact, easy-to-use guides to essential application information. Written for all users, Quick References include vital command information under easy-to-find alphabetical listings. Quick References are a must for anyone who needs command information fast!

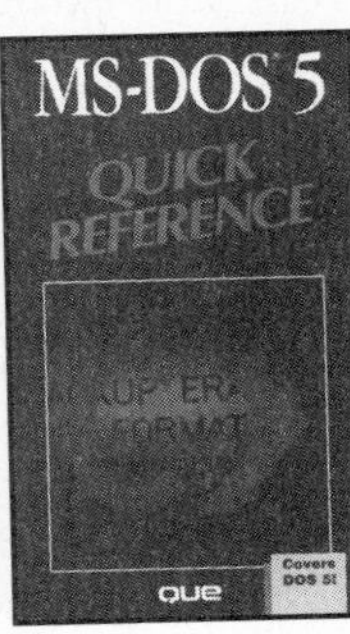

1-2-3 Release 2.4 Quick Reference
Release 2.4
$9.95 USA
0-88022-987-X, 160 pp., $4^{3}/_{4}$ x 8

1-2-3 for DOS Release 3.4 Quick Reference
Releases 3.4
$9.95 USA
1-56529-010-0, 160 pp., $4^{3}/_{4}$ x 8

1-2-3 for Windows Quick Reference
1-2-3 for Windows
$9.95 USA
0-88022-783-4, 160 pp., $4^{3}/_{4}$ x 8

AutoCAD Release 12 Quick Reference
Releases 12
$9.95 USA
1-56529-024-0, 160 pp., $4^{3}/_{4}$ x 8

Batch File and Macros Quick Reference
Through DOS 5
$9.95 USA
0-88022-699-4, 160 pp., $4^{3}/_{4}$ x 8

dBASE IV 1.5 Quick Reference
Through Version 1.5
$9.95 USA
0-88022-905-5, 160 pp., $4^{3}/_{4}$ x 8

DR DOS 6 Quick Reference
Version 6
$9.95 USA
0-88022-827-X, 160 pp., $4^{3}/_{4}$ x 8

Excel 4 for Windows Quick Reference
Version 4
$9.95 USA
0-88022-958-6, 160 pp., $4^{3}/_{4}$ x 8

Hard Disk Quick Reference, 1992 Edition
Major hard disks & MS-DOS 5
$9.95 USA
0-88022-826-1, 160 pp., $4^{3}/_{4}$ x 8

Harvard Graphics 3 Quick Reference
Version 3
$9.95 USA
0-88022-887-3, 160 pp., $4^{3}/_{4}$ x 8

Harvard Graphics Quick Reference
Version 2.3
$8.95 USA
0-88022-538-6, 160 pp., $4^{3}/_{4}$ x 8

Microsoft Word Quick Reference
Through Version 5.5
$9.95 USA
0-88022-720-6, 160 pp., $4^{3}/_{4}$ x8

MS-DOS 6 Quick Reference
Version 6
$9.95 USA
1-56529-137-9, 160 pp., $4^{3}/_{4}$ x 8

Norton Utilites 6 Quick Reference
Version 6
$9.95 USA
0-88022-858-X, 160 pp., $4^{3}/_{4}$ x 8

Paradox Quick Reference, 2nd Edition
Version 4
$9.95 USA
0-88022-891-1, 160 pp., $4^{3}/_{4}$ x 8

Paradox 3.5 Quick Reference
Version 3.5
$9.95 USA
0-88022-824-5, 160 pp., $4^{3}/_{4}$ x 8

PC Tools 8 Quick Reference
Through Version 8
$9.95 USA
1-56529-148-4, 160 pp., $4^{3}/_{4}$ x 8

Q&A 4 Quick Reference
Versions 2, 3, & 4
$9.95 USA
0-88022-828-8, 160 pp., $4^{3}/_{4}$ x 8

Quattro Pro Quick Reference
Through Version 3
$8.95 USA
0-88022-692-7, 160 pp., $4^{3}/_{4}$ x 8

Quicken 5 Quick Reference
Versions 4 & 5.0
$9.95 USA
0-88022-900-4, 160 pp., $4^{3}/_{4}$ x 8

Windows 3.1 Quick Reference
Through Version 3.1
$9.95 USA
0-88022-740-0, 160 pp., $4^{3}/_{4}$ x 8

WordPerfect 5.1 Quick Reference
WordPerfect 5.1
$9.95 USA
0-88022-576-9, 160 pp., $4^{3}/_{4}$ x 8

WordPerfect for Windows Quick Reference
WordPerfect 5.1 for Windows
$9.95 USA
0-88022-785-0, 160 pp., $4^{3}/_{4}$ x 8

To Order, Call: (800) 428-5331
OR (317) 573-2500

Count on Que for the Most Up-to-Date Information on Integrated Packages

Using Microsoft Works for Windows, Special Edition
Douglas Wolf

This book provides plenty of timesaving tips and hints on sharing information between Works' modules. A comprehensive reference and tutorial, this book will give you everything you need to know about Microsoft Works.

Version 1

$24.95 USA
0-88022-757-5, 550 pp., 7 3/8 x 9 1/4

Using Microsoft Works: IBM Version
Douglas Wolf

Through Version 2

$22.95 USA
0-88022-467-3, 444 pp., 7 3/8 x 9 1/4

Using Q&A 4
David Ewing & Bill Langenes

Version 4

$27.95 USA
0-88022-643-9, 550 pp., 7 3/8 x 9 1/4

Q&A 4 Quick Reference
Que Development Group

Latest Version

$9.95 USA
0-88022-828-8, 160 pp., 4 3/4 x 8

Q&A 4 QuickStart
Que Development Group

Version 4

$19.95 USA
0-88022-653-6, 400 pp., 7 3/8 x 9 1/4

Que's Using Enable
Walter Bruce

All Versions Through Enable/OA4

$29.95 USA
0-88022-701-X, 700 pp., 7 3/8 x 9 1/4

Using Lotus Works 3.0
J. D. Watson

Release 3.0

$24.95 USA
0-88022-771-0, 500 pp., 7 3/8 x 9 1/4

Using PFS: First Choice 4.0
Katherine Murray

Through Version 4.0

$27.95 USA
0-88022-969-1, 600 pp., 7 3/8 x 9 1/4

Using PFS: WindowsWorks 2
Deanna Bebb

Through Version 2

$29.95 USA
1-56529-073-9, 500 pp., 7 3/8 x 9 1/4

To Order, Call: (800) 428-5331
OR (317) 573-2500

READ THE TERMS AND CONDITIONS OF THIS LICENSE AGREEMENT CAREFULLY BEFORE OPENING THE ENVELOPE CONTAINING THE DISKETTES.

THE DISKETTES, THE COMPUTER SOFTWARE THEREIN, AND THE ACCOMPANYING USER DOCUMENTATION CONSTITUTE THE "PROGRAM." THE PROGRAM IS COPYRIGHTED AND LICENSED (NOT SOLD). BY OPENING THE PACKAGE CONTAINING THE DISKETTES, YOU (EITHER AN INDIVIDUAL OR AN ENTITY) ARE ACCEPTING AND AGREEING TO THE TERMS OF THIS AGREEMENT. IF YOU ARE NOT WILLING TO BE BOUND BY THE TERMS OF THIS AGREEMENT, PROMPTLY RETURN THE UNOPENED ENVELOPE AND THE REMAINDER OF THE PACKAGE TO ASYMETRIX CORPORATION ("ASYMETRIX") AND YOU WILL RECEIVE A FULL REFUND. THIS AGREEMENT REPRESENTS THE ENTIRE AGREEMENT CONCERNING THE PROGRAM BETWEEN YOU AND ASYMETRIX AND IT SUPERSEDES ANY PRIOR PROPOSAL, CONTRACT, OR UNDERSTANDING BETWEEN THE PARTIES.

1. **License Grant.** Asymetrix hereby grants to you, and you accept, a non-exclusive license to use the Program Diskettes and the computer programs contained therein in machine-readable, object code form (collectively referred to as the "Software") and the accompanying User Documentation, only as authorized in this Agreement. The Software may be used only on a single computer which is owned, leased, or otherwise controlled by you; or in the event of the inoperability of that computer, on a backup computer selected by you. Neither concurrent use on two or more computers nor use by more than one person at a time in a local area network or other network is permitted without separate authorization and the payment of additional license fees. You agree that you will not assign, sublicense, transfer, pledge, lease, rent, or share your rights under this Agreement. You agree that you may not reverse assemble, reverse compile, or otherwise translate the Software.

   Upon loading the Software into your computer, you may retain the Program Diskettes for backup purposes. In addition, you may make one copy of the Software on a second set of diskettes for the purpose of backup in the event the Program Diskettes are damaged or destroyed. You may not copy the User Documentation. Any copies of the Software shall include Asymetrix's copyright and other proprietary notices. Except as authorized under this paragraph, no copies of the Program or any portions thereof may be made by you or any person under your authority or control.

2. **Asymetrix's Rights.** You acknowledge and agree that the Software and the User Documentation are proprietary products of Asymetrix which are protected under U.S. copyright laws and international treaty provisions. You further acknowledge and agree that all right, title, and interest in and to the Program, including associated intellectual property rights, are and shall remain with Asymetrix. This License does not convey to you an interest in or to the Program, but only a limited right of use revocable in accordance with the terms of this License.

3. **License Fees.** The license fees paid by you are paid in consideration of the licenses granted under this License. The terms and conditions of your purchase order(s), if any, shall not be binding between the parties.

4. **Term.** This Agreement is effective upon your opening of the diskette envelope and shall continue until terminated. You may terminate this Agreement at any time by returning the Program and all copies thereof and extracts therefrom to Asymetrix. Asymetrix may terminate this Agreement upon the breach by you of any material term hereof. Upon such termination by Asymetrix, you agree to return to Asymetrix the Program and all copies and portions thereof.

5. **Limited Warranty.** Asymetrix warrants, for your benefit alone, for a period of 90 days from the date of commencement of this License (referred to as the "Warranty Period") that the Program Diskettes in which the Software is contained are free from defects in material and workmanship. Asymetrix further warrants, for your benefit alone, that during the Warranty Period the Program shall operate substantially in accordance with the functional specifications in the User Documentation. If during the Warranty Period, a defect in the Program appears, you may return the Program to Asymetrix for either replacement or, if so elected by Asymetrix, refund of amounts paid by you under this Agreement. You agree that the foregoing constitutes your sole and exclusive remedy for breach by Asymetrix of any warranties made under this Agreement. EXCEPT FOR THE WARRANTIES SET FORTH ABOVE, THE PROGRAM AND THE SOFTWARE CONTAINED THEREIN ARE LICENSED "AS IS," AND ASYMETRIX DISCLAIMS ANY AND ALL OTHER WARRANTIES, WHETHER EXPRESS OR IMPLIED, INCLUDING, WITHOUT LIMITATION, ANY IMPLIED WARRANTIES OF MERCHANTABILITY OR FITNESS FOR A PARTICULAR PURPOSE.

6. **Limitation of Liability.** ASYMETRIX's CUMULATIVE LIABILITY TO YOU OR ANY OTHER PARTY FOR ANY LOSS OR DAMAGES RESULTING FROM ANY CLAIMS, DEMANDS, OR ACTIONS ARISING OUT OF OR RELATING TO THIS AGREEMENT SHALL NOT EXCEED THE LICENSE FEES PAID TO ASYMETRIX FOR THE USE OF THE PROGRAM. IN NO EVENT SHALL ASYMETRIX BE LIABLE FOR ANY INDIRECT, INCIDENTAL, CONSEQUENTIAL, SPECIAL, OR EXEMPLARY DAMAGES OR LOST PROFITS, EVEN IF ASYMETRIX HAS BEEN ADVISED OF THE POSSIBILITY OF SUCH DAMAGES.

7. **Trademark.** You must reproduce all copyright and other proprietary notices on any partial or full copy of the Program. No licenses or other rights are granted under any trademarks, logos, or other proprietary rights except as specifically granted under this license.

8. **Governing Law.** This License shall be construed and governed in accordance with the laws of the State of Washington.

9. **Costs of Litigation.** If any action is brought by either party to this License against the other party regarding the subject matter hereof, the prevailing party shall be entitled to recover, in addition to any other relief granted, reasonable attorney fees and expenses of litigation.

10. **Severability.** Should any term of this License be declared void or unenforceable by any court of competent jurisdiction, such declaration shall have no effect on the remaining terms hereof.

11. **No Waiver.** The failure of either party to enforce any rights granted hereunder or to take action against the other party in the event of any breach hereunder shall not be deemed a waiver by that party as to subsequent enforcement of rights or subsequent actions in the event of future breaches.

12. **U.S. GOVERNMENT RESTRICTED RIGHTS.** The Program is provided with RESTRICTED RIGHTS. U.S.Government Restricted Rights, Use, duplication, or disclosure by the Government is subject to restrictions as set forth in subparagraph (c)(1)(ii) of the Rights in Technical Data and Computer software clause at DFARS 252.227-7013 (Oct. 1988) and FAR 52.227-19 (June 1987). Contractor is:

Asymetrix Corporation, 110-110th Ave. NE, Suite 700, Bellevue, Washington 98004-5840

QUE

LEADING COMPUTER KNOWLEDGE

By opening this package, you are agreeing to be bound by the following agreement.

To use the files on the disk, open the Que database in the ACCPP directory from Access version 1.1.

Asymetrix InfoDesigner Version 1.0 Update Offer

☐ YES! Please send me InfoDesigner for Desktop Database Systems full product Version 1.0 update for $399.00*.

Name____________________

Title____________________

Company____________________

Address____________________

____

City__________State_____Zip_______

Country____________________

Phone (   )__________Fax (   )__________

☐ Check enclosed
☐ Visa/MasterCard
☐ American Express

____
Card No.

____
Expiration Date

____
Signature

***Original coupons only!** No copies or reproductions of any kind will be accepted.
*Canada add $25 for shipping and handling and ***GS Tax*** and any applicable state tax. Payment in US dollars only. Check payment must be on US bank or clearing house. Countries outside the USA and Canada will be shipped freight collect.
* This offer expires 12/31/94.

Asymetrix InfoDesigner Documentation/Training Offer

☐ YES! Please send me the InfoDesigner Documentation set for $60.00.
☐ YES! Please send information on how I can receive a 10% discount on your InfoDesigner information Modeling Training Workshop.

Name____________________

Title____________________

Company____________________

Address____________________

____

City__________State_____Zip_______

Country____________________

Phone (   )__________Fax(   )__________

☐ Check enclosed
☐ Visa/MasterCard
☐ American Express

____
Card No.

____
Expiration Date

____
Signature

***Original coupons only!** No copies or reproductions of any kind will be accepted.
*Canada add $25 for shipping and handling and ***GS Tax*** and any applicable state tax. Payment in US dollars only. Check payment must be on US bank or clearing house. Countries outside the USA and Canada will be shipped freight collect.
* This offer expires 12/31/94.

NO POSTAGE
NECESSARY
IF MAILED
IN THE
UNITED STATES

BUSINESS REPLY MAIL

FIRST CLASS MAIL PERMIT NO 1039 BELLEVUE, WASHINGTON

POSTAGE WILL BE PAID BY ADDRESSEE

ATTN: CUSTOMER SERVICE
ASYMETRIX CORPORATION
110 110TH AVE NE STE 700
BELLEVUE WA 98004-9959